D1789476

RESEARCH HANDBOOK ON THE SOCIOLOGY OF GLOBALIZATION

RESEARCH HANDBOOKS IN SOCIOLOGY

Series Editor: Hans-Peter Blossfeld, *Professor of Sociology, University of Bamberg, Germany*

The Research Handbooks in Sociology series provides an up-to-date overview on the frontier developments in current sociological research fields. The series takes a theoretical, methodological and comparative perspective to the study of social phenomena. This includes different analytical approaches, competing theoretical views and methodological innovations leading to new insights in relevant sociological research areas. Each *Research Handbook* in this series provides timely, influential works of lasting significance. These volumes will be edited by one or more outstanding academics with a high international reputation in the respective research field, under the overall guidance of series editor Hans-Peter Blossfeld, Professor of Sociology at the University of Bamberg. The *Research Handbooks* feature a wide range of original contributions by well-known authors, carefully selected to ensure a thorough coverage of current research. The *Research Handbooks* will serve as vital reference guides for undergraduate students, doctoral students, postdoctorate students and research practitioners in sociology, aiming to expand current debates, and to discern the likely research agendas of the future.

For a full list of Edward Elgar published titles, including the titles in this series, visit our website at www.e-elgar.com.

Research Handbook on the Sociology of Globalization

Edited by

Christian Karner

Professor of Sociology, School of Social and Political Sciences, University of Lincoln, UK

Dirk Hofäcker

Professor of Quantitative Research Methods, Institute for Social Work and Social Policy, University of Duisburg-Essen, Germany

RESEARCH HANDBOOKS IN SOCIOLOGY

Edward Elgar
PUBLISHING

Cheltenham, UK • Northampton, MA, USA

© Christian Karner and Dirk Hofäcker 2023

Cover image: Yoav Aziz on Unsplash

All rights reserved. No part of this publication may be reproduced, stored in a retrieval system or transmitted in any form or by any means, electronic, mechanical or photocopying, recording, or otherwise without the prior permission of the publisher.

Published by
Edward Elgar Publishing Limited
The Lypiatts
15 Lansdown Road
Cheltenham
Glos GL50 2JA
UK

Edward Elgar Publishing, Inc.
William Pratt House
9 Dewey Court
Northampton
Massachusetts 01060
USA

A catalogue record for this book
is available from the British Library

Library of Congress Control Number: 2023936954

This book is available electronically in the **Elgar**online
Sociology, Social Policy and Education subject collection
http://dx.doi.org/10.4337/9781839101571

ISBN 978 1 83910 156 4 (cased)
ISBN 978 1 83910 157 1 (eBook)

Printed and bound by CPI Group (UK) Ltd, Croydon, CR0 4YY

Contents

List of figures		viii
List of tables		ix
List of contributors		x

The sociology of globalization   1
Christian Karner and Dirk Hofäcker

PART I   HISTORY/SOCIOLOGY

1   When did globalization start?   16
    Zinovia Lialiouti

2   Methodological dilemmas or promises? The sociological imagination
    and globalization   25
    Magali Peyrefitte

PART II   (INFRA)STRUCTURAL PARAMETERS

3   Work and employment in a globalizing age   34
    David Pick

4   Global commodity circuits   45
    Craig Martin and Giovanni Marmont

5   Global networks and hybrid cities   60
    Kristian Kloeckl

6   Global risks   72
    Jean-Christophe Le Coze

7   Global waste   83
    Zsuzsa Gille

PART III   FLOWS AND FRICTIONS

8   Globalization and forced migration   97
    Inka Stock

9   Global tourism   108
    Esther Bott

10   Globalization as an extension of the triple movement: care workers'
     struggles for emancipation   117
     Bernhard Weicht

11   Human rights as ends or means of a global moral horizon   127
     José Julián López

12   Memory for the global age   142
     Marcin Napiórkowski

13   The globalization of religion as a complex phenomenon   151
     Ugo Dessì

14   The gendered dynamics of migration deterrence and anti-trafficking
     interventions: the case of Nigerian sex workers in Kumasi, Ghana   164
     Sam Okyere

15   Glocalized subjectivities: Egyptian female identities   174
     Amal Treacher Kabesh

16   The American guitar in the global market: worldwide flows of people,
     commodities and symbols   186
     Frédéric Moulène

PART IV   POLITICS

17   Globalization: opportunity or threat to the European Union?   196
     Robert Kissack

18   Cosmopolitans versus communitarians? Or something altogether more
     nuanced?   206
     Christian Karner

19   Alternative globalization   217
     Luke Martell

20   The rise of racism and antisemitism in the age of globalization   225
     Gerald J. Steinacher

21   The globalization of extremism: an odd paradox   238
     Joshua Skoczylis and Matthew Leavesley

22   From multiculturalism to superdiversity and (in)hospitality? Shifting
     policy responses to global migratory flows in the UK   248
     Sureyya Sonmez Efe

PART V   GLOBALIZATION AND THE LIFE COURSE

23   Globalization, uncertainty and changing life courses in modern societies 264
     Hans-Peter Blossfeld and Gwendolin Josephine Blossfeld

24   Does a higher minimum salary protect youth from in-work poverty?
      Cross-national evidence from the EU   275
      Kadri Täht, Marge Unt and Thomas Biegert

25   Globalization and the transition from education to employment in the
      MENA region   288
      Michael Gebel

26   Reimagining globalization through a gender lens   298
      Esuna Dugarova

27   Pension governance in a globalizing world   308
      Bernhard Ebbinghaus

28   Globalization and the transition from work to retirement   319
      Dirk Hofäcker, Stefanie König and Moritz Heß

PART VI   METHODOLOGICAL AND CONCEPTUAL LESSONS,
           EMERGING QUESTIONS

29   Global – and local – commodity circuits   329
      Dawn Lyon

30   Travelling methods   339
      Caroline Knowles

Epilogue   348
Christian Karner and Dirk Hofäcker

Index   360

Figures

23.1 How globalization creates increasing uncertainty and impacts
life-course transitions   265

23.2 Description of the globalization process based on the KOF
Globalisation Index, 1970–2018   267

24.1 Relative poverty of young adults in EU countries, 2005–2019   279

24.2 Subjectively perceived poverty of young adults in EU countries, 2005–2019 280

24.3 Employment trajectories of young adults in Europe   281

28.1 Employment rate age 60–64   323

Tables

10.1   Four ideal-typical care arrangements   121

24.1   Multilevel regression model for in-work poverty   283

27.1   Social expenditure and assets for public and private pensions, OECD, 2017/2018   309

Contributors

Thomas Biegert is Assistant Professor in Social Policy at the London School of Economics and Political Science, UK.

Gwendolin Josephine Blossfeld is Postdoc in the Twinning Project 'Youthlife' at the University of Bamberg, Germany.

Hans-Peter Blossfeld is Emeritus of Excellence at the University of Bamberg, Germany. He is the founder of the National Educational Panel Study and held a Chair of Sociology at the University of Bamberg from 2002 until 2020.

Esther Bott is Associate Professor in the School of Sociology and Social Policy at the University of Nottingham, UK.

Ugo Dessì is FWF Professorial Fellow in the Department of Religious Studies at the University of Vienna, Austria.

Esuna Dugarova is Policy Expert in Gender Equality at the United Nations Development Programme and Research Fellow at Columbia University, USA.

Bernhard Ebbinghaus is Professor of Sociology at the University of Mannheim, previously he was Professor of Social Policy at the University of Oxford.

Michael Gebel is Professor of Methods of Empirical Social Research at the Institute of Sociology at the University of Bamberg, Germany.

Zsuzsa Gille is Professor of Sociology at the University of Illinois at Urbana-Champaign, USA.

Moritz Heß is Professor of Gerontology at the Hochschule Niederrhein – University of Applied Sciences, Germany.

Dirk Hofäcker is Professor in Quantitative Research Methods at the Institute for Social Work and Social Policy at the University of Essen, Germany.

Christian Karner is Professor of Sociology at the University of Lincoln, UK.

Robert Kissack is Associate Professor and Head of Studies at the Institut Barcelona d'Estudis Internacionals, Spain.

Kristian Kloeckl is Associate Professor in the Department of Art and Design and the School of Architecture at Northeastern University, USA.

Caroline Knowles is a Global Professorial Fellow at Queen Mary, University of London, UK and Director of the British Academy's Programme on Urban Infrastructures of Well-Being.

Stefanie König is Researcher in the Department of Psychology at the University of Gothenburg and for the Swedish Social Insurance Inspectorate, Sweden.

Jean-Christophe Le Coze is Head of Research at the Institut National de l'Environnement Industriel et des Risques, France.

Matthew Leavesley is completing a PhD in Criminology at the University of Lincoln, UK.

Zinovia Lialiouti is Assistant Professor of Modern and Contemporary European History in the Department of Political Science and Public Administration at the National and Kapodistrian University of Athens, Greece.

José Julián López is Professor in the School of Sociological and Anthropological Studies at the University of Ottawa, Canada.

Dawn Lyon is Reader in Sociology at the University of Kent, UK.

Giovanni Marmont has taught and tutored at the University of Edinburgh, at London College of Communication, and at the University of Brighton, UK.

Luke Martell is Professor of Sociology and Teaching Fellow at the University of Sussex, UK.

Craig Martin is Reader in Design Cultures at the University of Edinburgh, UK.

Frédéric Moulène is a Teaching Fellow at the Université of Reims and Associate Researcher at the Université of Bourgogne-Franche-Comté, France.

Marcin Napiórkowski is Associate Professor at the University of Warsaw, Poland.

Sam Okyere is Senior Lecturer in Sociology at the University of Bristol, UK.

Magali Peyrefitte is Senior Lecturer in Criminology in the School of Politics and Social Sciences at Brunel University, UK.

David Pick is an Adjunct Research Fellow at Curtin University, Australia.

Joshua Skoczylis is Senior Lecturer in Criminology and Counterterrorism at the University of Lincoln, UK.

Sureyya Sonmez Efe is Senior Lecturer in the School of Social and Political Sciences at the University of Lincoln, UK.

Gerald J. Steinacher is the James A. Rawley Professor of History at the University of Nebraska-Lincoln, USA.

Inka Stock is a Research Fellow at the Interdisciplinary Centre for Gender Studies at Bielefeld University, Germany.

Kadri Täht is Associate Professor of Sociology of Work and Education in the School of Governance, Law and Society and the Institute of International Social Studies of Tallinn University, Estonia.

Amal Treacher Kabesh was Associate Professor in the School of Sociology and Social Policy at the University of Nottingham, UK.

Marge Unt is Professor of Comparative Sociology and Head of the Institute of International Social Studies at Tallinn University, Estonia.

Bernhard Weicht is Assistant Professor at the University of Innsbruck, Austria.

The sociology of globalization

Christian Karner and Dirk Hofäcker

Much of our individual and collective work on this research handbook coincided with what has, arguably, been among the most global of crises since the end of the Second World War. The contributors to this research handbook have found themselves reflecting on their research on *global flows and interconnections* at a time when many of our transnational interdependencies have suddenly seemed fragile, precarious and in a state of possible disintegration. The context we are alluding to is of course the Covid-19 pandemic. In addition to the enormous loss of life and global, human suffering this has entailed, Covid-19 has also transformed all of our everyday lives. So deeply engrained had sociological – and much more general narratives of our era's fluidity, mobility and *liquid-likeness* (e.g. see Bauman 2000) – become, that we have found ourselves utterly unprepared – socially, economically and psychologically – for what has unfolded since early 2020. Generations socialized into easy travel, assuming a certain level of affluence, were suddenly house-bound. International supply chains appeared – or rather *were* – in danger of failing. Mass unemployment has loomed, no longer because of multinational corporations choosing to move their operations to low(er)-wage economies but because entire industries were suddenly faced with vanishing demands and hence bankruptcy. For all the self-congratulatory talk about how the pandemic has also reinvigorated "communities," a trope of which many sociologists are rightly rather suspicious, we have also witnessed a remarkable retrenchment of boundaries and a disconcerting recalibration of many people's primary frame of reference and interpretation in terms that are defined in unapologetically and exclusively national terms. Put more simply, the pandemic appears to be fanning the flames of a neo-nationalism that had already been rampant long before Covid-19 struck (see e.g. Gingrich and Banks 2006). There are currently no shortage of political actors declaring, in some cases in an unapologetically celebratory tone, the "end of globalization," or that at least far-reaching changes are now called for (see Karner 2020). Tellingly, few such declarations take the time or care to define what exactly is meant by the term "globalization."

From the micro- to the macro-scale, then, all our lives are currently undergoing far-reaching changes. Notwithstanding our digital era's technological-cum-communicative capacities to negate and cross geographical distances at will, many of us have recently experienced the pain of distance and longing. Some of us living transnational lives have not seen families and friends in other parts of the world for a long time, with no certainty at all that this will change or return to our previous "normality" any time soon. Many others, generally those much less privileged, have long known that national boundaries can constitute real barriers. Seen from the vantage point of many of the world's millions of forced migrants, talk about our world in the twenty-first century as a "global village" must have long seemed hugely selective at best, or profoundly cynical at worst. For those wanting to migrate but prevented from doing so by our era's fortifications and newly erected walls, their world was often one of "forced *im*mobility" (Stock 2019, italics added) already, long before Covid-19. Now, however, for many more of us, including those who were previously fortunate and privileged enough to be not only consumers of globally traded commodities but also regular travelers enjoying certain freedoms of movement, the world has suddenly appeared to be shrinking and to develop "blockages" (Karner 2022) alongside and in counter-reaction to the *flows* (Appadurai 1990) with which globalization had long been associated. Yet others barely attempt to hide their glee at such blockages, as they revel in a purported restoration of a past – allegedly "pre-globalization" – that never was, at least not in the way their nostalgic accounts misportray it (see Karner and Weicht 2016).

These explorations demonstrate that, while the Covid-19 pandemic may have promoted a re-emergence of national boundaries, the phenomenon of globalization still remains an elementary characteristic, or at least a relevant point of reference, in individuals' everyday lives as well as in the political action of governments and various economic actors. Reflecting on this issue in scientific terms thus continues to be a worthwhile endeavor. Considering the challenges that globalization entails both at the individual micro-level as well as at the societal macro-level, a sociological, rather than a merely economic perspective, appears to be well justified. This handbook contributes to the sociological discourse on globalization by bringing together scientists from various sociological fields and methodological strands to share their views on the eminent challenges generated through globalization.

Against this backdrop of a world that is simultaneously facing truly global crises *and* politically contracting, a sociology of globalization acquires further topicality and yet greater urgency. In this introductory chapter, we set the scene – conceptually and thematically – for the ensuing contributions to this handbook in the sociology of globalization. We do so by providing an initial "detour" through select strands of classical and contemporary sociology before turning to thematic clusters in the established, distinctly interdisciplinary study of globalization. This, in turn, prepares the ground for an anticipation of the thematic foci of our chapter contributions.

HOW TO THINK SOCIOLOGICALLY ABOUT GLOBALIZATION

The necessary starting point for what follows must be provided by sound definitional work. This involves, first, a clarification of what – in general terms – a sociological approach to, or conceptualization of, a given phenomenon entails; and, second, a delineation of our shared objectives of discussion and analysis. Put differently, our aims in this introductory chapter are to establish a framework for sociological thought and to then delineate the particular social, political, economic, cultural and technological phenomena that are constitutive of what is commonly, and more often than not vaguely, referred to as "globalization." Both definitional moves, with regard to sociology's disciplinary orientation as well as in relation to our shared thematic foci in this handbook, call for a brief discussion of seminal contributions to the associated bodies of scholarly literature.

Thinking and writing about globalization are, as we shall discover, profoundly interdisciplinary endeavors. Interdisciplinarity will therefore constitute a defining characteristic in the discussions that follow, in reflection of the diversity of the intellectual backgrounds our contributors bring to their discussions as well as of the methodological and conceptual breadth their research agendas demand. We therefore want to underscore from the outset that a subject matter as enormous and complex as globalization does not allow for any one disciplinary monopoly being exercised in its study and analysis. At the same time, and while this handbook thus endorses and actively embraces interdisciplinary scholarship throughout, part of our task also consists of specifying what a distinctly sociological view of globalization looks like.

For the purposes of delineating such a distinctly sociological vantage point, few discussions in the history of the discipline have been as enduring and productive as Georg Simmel's *Soziologie: Untersuchungen über die Formen der Vergesellschaftung* (Sociology: Inquiries into the Construction of Social Forms). In thematically or conceptually specific terms, there is much in Simmel's magnum opus that either anticipates later themes in the study of globalization or yields itself to being reappropriated in light of our era's globalizing tendencies. Simmel's influential concept of "social circles" and the category of "the stranger" are cases in point. With regard to the former, Simmel conceptualizes individuals' (multiple) social ties through the metaphor of social "circles" that, together, constitute a "coordinate system"; what is more, the intersection of a person's multiple social circles in a very specific point then describes their very idiosyncratic (subject) position in the world (Simmel 1992 [1908]: 54, 466f.). Projected onto the subject matter of the present handbook, this enables us to ask how the structural, long-distance, cross-border interdependencies that are defining features of our globalizing world have altered, or are in the process of altering, people's social circles of (cultural) belonging and (structural) interconnectedness. As we shall discover, this indeed constitutes a viable way of assessing the impact of global forces on an individual's or group's lived realities. The category of "the stranger," meanwhile, refers to people who "come today and stay tomorrow" and thereby personify a "unity of proximity and distance" (Simmel 1992 [1908]: 764f., our translation). This has long been recognized as providing a heuristic lens crucial for social scientific assessments of political responses – ranging from societal segregation or exclusion to enforced assimilation – to migrants (e.g. Lévi-Strauss 1974 [1955]; Bauman 1993). As several of the later chapters illustrate (see the contributions by Efe, Karner, Okyere and Stock), questions pertaining to migration, pluralism and the political "management" of diversity are indeed among the core concerns in contemporary scholarship on globalization. As such, Simmel's category of "the stranger" possesses an enduring relevance to some of the arguably defining features commonly associated with globalization.

However, there is a much wider, more general sense, in which Simmel offers a most pertinent point of departure for our discussions. This is due to his attempts to distil a distinctly sociological perspective from within a wider set of domains and concerns that sociologists typically share with other social sciences. In other words, the question as to what is peculiarly sociological about a sociology of globalization can be answered perhaps most concisely through Simmel. The reason for this can be found in Simmel's famous dictum that hunger, love, greed, work, technology and religion are not intrinsically social phenomena but acquire social dimensions when they establish – "as causes or purposes – interactions between individuals" (Simmel 1992 [1908]: 899, our translation). Simmel's central term, the German *Wechselwirkungen*, has no fully adequate English equivalent: the German original includes the domain of intersubjective interactions yet it extends considerably beyond it. *Wechselwirkungen* also describe enduring structural arrangements and hence institutional connections and mutual impacts between individuals and their respective subject positions. In other words, sociology – viewed from Simmel's perspective – attains its disciplinary coherence through a focus on the structured relationships, interactions and interdependencies *between* people. In Simmel's very own elaboration, the objects of research and analysis for a science of society are therefore to be found in "those forms of mutual relationships" that include – among many others – structural configurations of hierarchy, "competition and cooperation," group formation, closure and exclusion, as well as alliance-building (Simmel 1992 [1908]: 900, our translation). Projected onto our present concerns, we thus begin to discern the contours of a possible sociology of globalization. It is commonly assumed and argued that globalization is defined by a technologically enabled "compression" of geographical and temporal distances (e.g. Harvey 1989) as well as by growing, systemic-structural connections and various *flows* cutting across national boundaries (see below). Building on Simmel, we may then conclude that a distinctly sociological perspective will examine globalization, thus defined, for its constitutive and emerging *Wechselwirkungen*: for the interactions and structural-cum-social forms between people that both enable, and are enabled by, our era's globalization.

This latter formulation begins to acknowledge that a sociology of globalization has a historical dimension or, put differently, that it must also ask questions concerning the historical novelty (or otherwise) of its object of discussion. In other words, the much debated question (e.g. see Martell 2017: 32–55) as to when globalization started matters more than merely for the purposes of dating the origins of the phenomena at stake here. It seems clear to us that dominant political, media and everyday discourses assume globalization to be a (relatively) recent phenomenon, one widely associated with the rise of neo-liberalism, its generally assumed "link to the globalization of capital" (Hanafi 2020: 9) and the post-Cold War context. This is strongly challenged by much of the scholarly and historical literature: while the origins of globalization continue to be the subject of scholarly debate, a more convincing historiographical delineation located its "big bang" in the 1820s (O'Rourke and Williamson 2002). While other scholarly arguments go considerably further back in time, there is at least compelling evidence testifying to a "first globalization of finance and trade" by the period between 1870 and 1914 (Piketty 2014: 28); and, on the level of everyday life-worlds, to an "internationalism of almost everything" (including science, technology, intellectual life and political ideologies) by the early decades of the twentieth century (Luft 2021: 52). It is in light of the importance of such historical dimensions and the associated debates that our list of chapters, following this introduction, begins with Zinovia Lialiouti's revisiting of the question as to when globalization started.

In addition to such valuable historiographical angles, what follows can be framed through prominent strands of social theorizing. It is, of course, no secret that the history of sociology is commonly – and arguably somewhat limitingly – retold as a history of Western-centric ideas and interpretative frameworks that are applied to the still relatively recent but societally transformative experiences of modernity and industrialization (e.g. see Parker 1997; Bhambra 2007). Arguably, much of what is commonly subsumed – in everyday and political discourse as well as in parts of the academic literature – under the label "globalization" can be read as the continuation of those very historical experiences. In other words, one may indeed postulate that a basic conceptualization of globalization needs to revolve around the following, mutually interconnected historical parameters: first, what German sociologist Hartmut Rosa (2019: 44ff.; 376, our translation) describes as the "nucleus of the modern relationship to the world," namely one premised on notions of growth, acceleration, innovation, self-determination and geographically "far-reaching chains of interaction"; and second, technological developments that have led to the successive shrinkage, or "compression" (Harvey 1989), of geographical distances and a communicative simultaneity across (transnational) space that have facilitated ever growing, structural (i.e. economic and institutional) and cultural interconnections between different parts of the globe. In other words, such a basic conceptualization recognizes globalization as comprising ideational, technological and systemic dimensions, each of which is in turn seen in its wider historical contexts. While this goes some way towards establishing a shared definitional base, on which our later contributions will build, more conceptual groundwork is needed.

A sociological focus on globalization can, however, not confine itself to looking at inter-individual relationships alone. The lives and actions of individuals are embedded into contextual constellations that define the opportunities and restrictions of individual action and behavior. Such contextual conditions may, for example, be societal institutions (e.g. welfare states, legal or regulatory systems) but also cultural frameworks (e.g. societal values and norms) that may both set reference points for socially acceptable behavior. These macro-societal phenomena often act as "filters" that mediate the impact of globalization on individuals (Buchholz et al. 2009). In the past such filters were often located at the nation-state level. More recently, both the additional relevance of sub-national contexts as well as the influence of supranational institutions or actors have been discussed. All these factors are themselves dynamic and have changed over time as globalization has further progressed. A sociology of globalization thus is met with the challenge to adequately consider these changing macro-conditions, both *per se* but also in their interplay with individual life courses and living conditions. This handbook thus combines the focus on both micro- and macro-sociological phenomena and their mutual interplay.

FURTHER CONCEPTUAL CONTEXTS

We will leave actual reviews of the wider bodies of academic literature that are relevant to specific chapters for our individual authors to develop as part of their thematically focused discussions. However, there is a need for a "pre-weaving" of some recurring, conceptual strands that run through some or all of our contributions. As we have already hinted, the most general of working definitions regards globalization as comprising (widening and deepening) *interdependencies and connections, both structural and cultural, that span long distances and cut across national and other, narrowly defined political boundaries and institutions*. Like most working definitions, this arguably raises more questions than it can answer. In a next step, we therefore push beyond it to review, as concisely as possible, some of the wider conceptual debates in the interdisciplinary scholarship on globalization.

By way of a more extensive conceptual grounding for what follows, we propose to build on a recent overview (Karner 2020) of seminal contributions that offer understandings of globalization more nuanced than those contained in discussions about its historical origins or about the required geographical and systemic reach of transnational interconnections and global interdependencies (for a summary of those discussions see Martell 2017). Charles Lemert has been among those to develop a more nuanced corrective. Building on insights into our epoch's technologically enabled and economically exploited "time-space compressions" (e.g. Harvey 1989), Lemert (2015: 95) offers an understanding of globalization as both a "process and [emerging] structures." This, in turn, raises questions about the particular *kinds of* processes and structures that define globalization today; and it poses the question as to how to disentangle political claims about such processes and structures from their social scientific analysis. Just how blurry the line between political claim-making and sociological commentary on globalization can be is illustrated by the often repeated assertion that globalization is, at least in the cultural domains, purportedly tantamount to growing standardization.

Advocates of the "homogenization thesis" who seek academic backing have often invoked George Ritzer's work on *The McDonaldization of Society* (1993). However, as the very first paragraph in this introduction and the most cursory of glances at our contents page and chapter headings demonstrate, the homogenization thesis receives little, if any, backing in the present handbook. Instead, we have taken our cue from Arjun Appadurai's influential counterargument. According to Appadurai (1990), globalization comprises several "global flows": those of people (*ethnoscapes*), capital (*financescapes*), technologies (*technoscapes*), ideas and ideologies (*ideoscapes*) and mediated information (*mediascapes*). What is more, Appadurai correctly insists that the multiple "scapes and flows" (also see Urry 2000: 208) spanning national boundaries can spur antagonisms, instead of homogenizing localities, practices and identifications around the world. Appadurai's formulation (1990: 295f.) of the "forces of sameness and difference cannibalizing" one another encapsulates an understanding of globalization that is processual and sensitive to its asymmetries, local appropriations and conflicts.

Thirty years after Appadurai's initial formulation, it is stating the obvious to point out that in our now fully blown, digital *information age* (e.g. Castells 1996), the internet and social media have not only accelerated and multiplied the global flows of technologies and ideas but that ideological polarizations and fragmentations, which Appadurai also acknowledged as part of our globalizing age, are being exacerbated, too. In other words, the last three decades have seen a widening and speeding up of the processes of globalization, a further crystallizing of its structures, but also an undeniable entrenchment of powerful counter-reactions and resulting conflicts. There are numerous other "global flows" – including those of natural resources, commodities and other material objects, signs (e.g. Benzecry 2008) and entire sign systems, waste (e.g. Gille 2013) and environmental hazards (e.g. Le Coze 2017) – to be considered. Furthermore, important recent scholarship has examined the infrastructural means and transformations implicated in our current age of globalization, including the "containerization" of the global economy (Martin 2016) as well as its widely overlooked "backroads" (Knowles 2014). Common to other pertinent literature (e.g. Levitt and Glick Schiller 2004; Lyon and Back 2012) is a recognition that globalization is best viewed from the vantage points of localities and through the lenses of those experiencing the global locally. This echoes Roland Robertson's accounts of *glocalization* as "the reconstruction [of] home, community and locality" (Robertson 1995: 30) under new conditions. Similarly relevant in this context are Thomas Hylland Eriksen's anthropological reflections on "the relationship between the global and the local." The latter, Eriksen argues, implicates not always easily co-existing phenomena: capital's growing "disembed[ding] from territory" in an era of multinational corporations, transnational value chains and global financial markets and, concurrently, our epoch is defined by far-reaching, systemic "interconnectedness" across geographical distances. Finally, and most directly relevant to some of our later discussion, Eriksen reports "local appropriations of global processes," or *localizing strategies*, such as attempted "reembeddings" through identity politics that claim "cultural 'authenticity' and rooted identities." Taking stock of globalization's uneven political consequences, Eriksen reflects on the fact that "some walls are torn down and others appear. The idea of an unbounded world has not been realized" (Eriksen 2015: 371–384).

Adding to this thematic strand, Ulrich Beck (2000: 46) has formulated the concept of the "local–global nexus": this directs our attention to multiple and multidirectional flows, it recognizes local actors as active participants in – rather than passive recipients of – transnational flows and it acknowledges that elements of cultural homogenization and a local reassertion of particularism and concurrent re-entrenchment of contextually meaningful boundaries can sit alongside one another, however uneasily, in any one "local–global nexus." Beck's posthumously published *The Metamorphosis of the World* (2017) adds yet further insights, including Beck's disentangling of political beliefs from "frames of action": thereby, Beck is able to show that nationalist retrenchment, for instance, while advocating a return to a narrowly delineated and ethnically exclusive life-world, often also relies (e.g. in terms of its political networks, information and communication technologies) on unmistakably global frames and conditions of possibility.

Findings from empirical life-course sociology has also challenged the notion of globalization as promoting "coercive convergence," or at least mimetic imitation through increasing pressure on national welfares states due to rising pressure from supranational organizations (Mills et al. 2009: 564). Instead, institutional or cultural characteristics at the nation-state level – such as reflected in welfare regimes, education systems or industrial relations – continue to exert an influence on the way in which globalization "trickles down" to the level of individual life courses. The adaptation process of modern societies to globalization thus continues to be strongly path-dependent. Mills et al. (2009: 565f.) describe this development as one of "converging divergences" in which some common responses in relation to globalization can be observed at the nation-state level across the globe; yet the way in which these responses are being implemented as well as the way in which they impact on the lives of individuals still display strongly national features. This hypothesis on the continuing significance of national filters can be corroborated in various analyses of specific life-course phases, including youth (Blossfeld et al. 2005, 2008), mid-career (Blossfeld and Hofmeister 2006; Blossfeld et al. 2006b) and late career and retirement (Blossfeld et al. 2006a; Hofäcker et al. 2016). These research results further demonstrated that institutions also mold the way in which globalization changes nation-specific structures of social inequalities. All in all, there is a tendency that risk and uncertainty generated through globalization often is passed along to those with lower educational degrees, lower occupational status and/or women (Breen 1997). Globalization thus tends to extend if not even exacerbate existing social inequalities. Yet, while this effect pertains to individuals almost unfiltered in the residual welfare systems of liberal countries (such as the United Kingdom or the United States), it is mediated in the protective welfare regimes of Scandinavian countries or channeled towards specific groups of "outsiders" in the conservative welfare states of Central Europe (Buchholz et al. 2009).

The emerging picture of globalization, at least up to the present point in our introductory overview, thus depicts multiple, transnational flows and political contests in terms of the local or national reception and appropriation of such flows. Usefully, this marks another point of departure for our ensuing discussions. In many ways, what follows is best described as a series of thematically more narrowly delineated explorations, written by experts in their respective areas of research, of different aspects and manifestations of the multidimensionalities and complexities of today's globalization. This leads us to a more precise anticipation of the contributions to follow.

SETTING THE SCENE FOR GLOBAL, PUBLIC (AND INTERDISCIPLINARY) SOCIOLOGIES

As shown elsewhere (e.g. Karner 2022: chapter 1), the following account is paradigmatic of some of the most common associations triggered by the term globalization:

> For every job lost to deindustrialization in Ohio, workers in the Pearl River Delta are drawn to Shenzen, built on ... once fertile soil. In time, the Pearl River having been depleted, what work there is will move to Vietnam or Bangladesh, and then ... will reappear in the American rust belt where labor once again is cheap. Workers and their families, productive lands, nature's resource wealth, and much more are mined into bits and fed to the machine of capitalist production – from which surplus values are extracted out of the wreckage of human lives. Capitalism ... is about the endless accumulation of capital ... destructive of the very economic (and social) order from which it extracts its profits. (Lemert 2015: 148)

Let us be clear: this account undeniably depicts disconcerting features of globalization today, including the social, economic and environmental consequences of a global capitalist system that drives the much debated "race to the bottom" in terms of the deregulation of taxation, environmental laws and workers' rights. As this introduction has already stressed, such developments have far-reaching, if frequently or at least partly unintended, consequences, and they spur often powerful counter-reactions. In her case for a neo-Polanyian conceptualization of contemporary crises, Nancy Fraser (2014), one of the most prominent and critical commentators on global capitalism, thus views twenty-first-century social realities through her notion of a *triple movement*: between the forces of "marketization" (or the commodification of ever widening resources and social domains); various "social protectionisms" that reassert or demand entitlements and privileges, often in exclusivist and divisive fashion, against marketization; and emancipation against the inequalities perpetuated either through market forces or through exclusionary politics. A sociology of globalization worth its salt must certainly deal with each of these aspects of our globalizing world; parts of this handbook will do precisely that.

At the same time, the sociology of globalization depicted across the following chapters will do more. In fact, it is our conviction that we must resist the all-too-common reduction of "globalization" to neo-liberalism, marketization, privatization and flexible, global production. While these phenomena are all part of our era's version of globalization, they do not fully cover it. Globalization today entails deindustrialization in formerly affluent parts of the world and often exploitative, environmentally destructive production among the (even more) unprotected. Yet, as we shall discover, this is certainly not all that globalization entails. Our fundamental challenge, then, will be to capture and do analytical justice both to what Lemert's account above and many others like it depict, and to what they exclude. In more concrete terms, this handbook sets itself a complex and two-fold goal: first, to include and capture experiences of privatization, competitive individualism, transnational "outsourcing," the commodification of formerly public goods and other facets of neo-liberal, global capitalism and its consequences for individual lives; and second, at the same time, we aim to avoid a one-sided, often ideologically motivated conflation of globalization with neo-liberalism and, instead, to think of globalization in considerably bigger and more nuanced terms. To therefore cast our empirical and conceptual net more widely, we ask ourselves which transnational flows, social forms and interactive as well as institutional *Wechselwirkungen* – in Simmel's broad conceptualization of the term – are constitutive of globalization today. Which types of political responses, appropriations and contests do our era's global flows and connections give rise to? On the level of social actors' life-worlds, how do global forces impact on biographies and localities?

The most obvious way of approaching what follows is in a linear fashion. Following this introductory outline, our handbook proceeds through a series of thematic clusters. Part I prepares more conceptual ground by re-examining the historicity of contemporary globalization (Lialiouti) and through a revisiting, by Magali Peyrefitte (Chapter 2), of C. Wright Mills' notion of the *sociological imagination* in light of present circumstances. This is followed by a thematic cluster focused on some of the broad, (infra)structural parameters underpinning globalization today. More accurately, Part II comprises chapters that variously examine issues of work and employment, of global commodity circuits, of the interplay of global-digital networks and urban spaces, of risks and of global waste, while Part III includes a series of examinations of the flows (Appadurai 1990) and frictions (Knowles 2014: 13) that define our transnational entanglements and interconnections in the early twenty-first century. Individual chapters within the section in question focus on forced migration, tourism, care work, human rights, transnational memories, religion, sex-trafficking, "glocalized subjectivities" and particular forms of musical practice (and its associated industries). Part IV then turns in an unmistakably political direction. There, chapters variously examine the impact of globalization on specific political institutions, most notably the European Union as the quintessential "network state" (Castells 2000: 3); alternative forms of globalization; the global dimensions of racism and anti-Semitism today; the globalization of extremism; dimensions of multiculturalism and "superdiversity" (Vertovec 2007) in the specific context of the United Kingdom's recent responses to global migratory flows; and the conflicting politics of belonging that are articulated by forms of cosmopolitanism on one hand and by communitarian (i.e. local or nationalist) exclusions on the other. Part V builds on this by subjecting the nation-specific responses to globalization through specific policies and their impacts on individual life courses to careful scrutiny. To this end, the chapters in Part V follow a chronological pattern, investigating the nation-specific effects of globalization on pivotal life-course transitions, from labor market entry and family formation to older age and the transition to retirement. Chapters particularly highlight the role of policies in mitigating the influence of globalization at the national level. Part VI includes two chapters and an epilogue that reflect on some of the broader disciplinary, methodological and conceptual lessons drawn and on wider questions arising from them.

There are, however, also other, non-linear ways of reading this handbook. We began this project with a broad plan, namely to extend Appudurai's original understanding of globalization as comprising the five transnational "flows and scapes" (Appadurai 1990; see also Urry 2000: 35f.) summarized above. Our handbook can indeed also be approached through Appadurai's lens: some contributions can therefore be regarded as thematically updated, in-depth explorations of various *ethnoscapes* (e.g. see chapters by Efe, Stock, Okyere), *technoscapes* (e.g. as in Kloeckl's chapter) or *ideoscapes* (e.g. the respective chapters by Karner, Kissack, Skoczylis and Leavesley, and Steinacher). At the same time, other contributions extend Appadurai's framework very considerably by drawing attention to other transnational flows: for instance, those of religion (as explored by Dessì), work (Pick), global commodity circuits (Martin and Marmont), waste (Gille), risks (Le Coze), cultural memories (Napiórkowski) or music (Moulène). As our collective work progressed, however, it became increasingly clear that a single, overarching analytical frame – namely the "flows and scapes paradigm" – would not suffice. This is reflected in the fact that some of our other contributions illuminate crucial dimensions of contemporary globalization that could only partly, if at all, be accommodated under Appadurai's conceptual "umbrella." Amal Treacher Kabesh's discussion of glocalized, gendered subjectivities (see below) is a case in point, as are Esther Bott's critical engagement with the global tourist industry, Luke Martell's discussion of alternative globalization and Bernhard Weicht's exploration of aspects of transnational care work. Yet other contributions, particularly the chapters by José López and Sam Okyere, extend our overall discussions yet further and in axiological directions, by encouraging us to think about the global relevance, reach and possible limitations (or negative, if unintended consequences) of specific values and rights or discourses about such rights. As attentive readers will soon discover, our shared conceptualization of globalization is one that approaches the phenomena under consideration from specific, highly localized and hence context-specific angles. This enables our contributing authors to build on their empirical expertise, and it echoes long-established approaches that do not conceptualize the local and the global as abstract, diametrical opposites but as mutually implicated and mutually constitutive components of our twenty-first-century lived realities (e.g. see Rhys-Taylor 2013).

There are further ways of approaching this handbook. In addition to the empirically focused explorations just mentioned, there are other, thematic and analytical strands that also structure our collection of chapters. We start our handbook with Zinovia Lialiouti's revisiting of historiographical discussions concerning the origins and precise dating of globalization. Questions of historical context and diachronic (dis)continuities subsequently recur across a number of other chapters. Within Part V, contributions focus on how social policy impacts the individual life courses under conditions of globalization. Hans-Peter and Gwendolin Blossfeld demonstrate how globalization generally has triggered increasing life-course uncertainty. Relying on results from the pertinent project "Globalife – Life Courses in the Globalization Process," they outline how differently this life-course uncertainty has trickled down to the life courses of individuals under different contextual conditions at the national level. While Blossfeld and Blossfeld provide an overall picture of globalization-related transformations across the life course, specific chapters in this section focus on single life-course phases. Two chapters focus particularly on young people and their often insecure transition from education to employment (see the chapter by Gebel) and their risk of poverty in early career (see the chapter by Täht et al.). Esuna Dugarova focuses on the effects of globalization through a gender lens, outlining how globalization has changed, yet not eradicated, gender-based inequalities in multiple fields. Contributions by Bernhard Ebbinghaus (on the changes in the governance of pension systems) and Dirk Hofäcker et al. (on the related changes in late employment and retirement) conclude the life-course perspective with a focus on the older generation. A further, similarly important strand running through different parts of our handbook revisits and explores some of the "deeper," methodological and conceptual challenges that globalization poses for the social sciences at large. While the significance of nation-specific institutions and their remarkable resilience to globally unifying forces remains valid, other contributions to the existing literature have called for a "sociology beyond societies" (Urry 2000), for alternatives to the "methodological nationalism" (e.g. Wimmer and Glick Schiller 2002) or for a global social science "of connections" that is perhaps most "properly thought of as a series of local social sciences in dialogue with each other and open to transformation in the light of other perspectives and locations of knowledge" (Holmwood 2007: 79). In the present handbook, these wider, conceptual and methodological questions are developed further, as well as in different and distinctive ways, in the respective chapters by Dawn Lyon and Magali Peyrefitte. In a similar vein, the late

Amal Treacher Kabesh interweaves the theoretical with the methodological in her exploration of Egyptian women's "glocalized subjectivities": to capture those, Treacher Kabesh combines feminist, postcolonial and psychoanalytical perspectives with autoethnographic insights and thereby delineates further important, though hitherto often overlooked, dimensions required for a comprehensive sociology of globalization. Subsequently, Caroline Knowles' chapter, which offers further reflections on the "travelling methods" she has pioneered elsewhere (Knowles 2014), brings this methodological thread to a productive and thought-provoking conclusion. This, in turn, is followed by the editors' epilogue reflecting on the handbook in its entirety and taking stock of what may be described as our current moment of multiple and undeniably global crises.

Finally, this handbook can also be understood as a productive way of responding to Sari Hanafi's (2020: 3) recent call for a *global sociology* that "supplement[s] the postcolonial approach with an anti-authoritarian one" and theorizes "post-secular society." Different parts of this handbook deliver on each of those levels, while also meeting further challenges that Hanafi outlines for a global sociology today: the establishment of transnational "dialogue" between different "national sociologies"; the reassertion of the "universality of certain concepts" (e.g. social class, democracy) and "values (human rights, gender equality)"; as well as a form of "knowledge production" across geographical scales, from the local to the international, in the service of an unmistakably "public sociology" (Hanafi 2020: 14–15). In other words, the intellectual spirit informing this handbook meets Michael Burawoy's seminal definition of public sociologies as involving a "double conversation," whereby sociology is brought "into conversation with publics, understood as people who are themselves involved in conversation" (Burawoy 2005: 7). We begin to see how such public sociologies become global public sociologies through an argument recently formulated by Anna Amelina, Manuela Boatcă, Gregor Bongaerts and Anja Weiß: our understanding of "society across borders," they argue, requires us to take "globalization, transnationalization and postcolonial entanglements" seriously, in contrast to much previous work in the social sciences. According to Amelina et al., then, what is at stake is nothing less than the question as to "how we want to do sociology." Their response, like ours, is that for an understanding of globalization we must, by definition, transcend the continuing trappings of the methodologically nationalist equation of "the analytical categories of 'society' and of 'the nation-state,'" particularly where such a logic manifests in globalization being reduced to an overly schematic "comparison between nation-states" (Amelina et al. 2021: 304, 311). In what follows, we argue for approaches to researching globalization that considers but at the same time cuts across national and other boundaries, that are methodologically innovative, unmistakably interdisciplinary in their conceptual borrowings and dedicated to the critical and wider conversations that define public sociologies.

The very term "globalization" has, as is well known, triggered contrasting reactions among social scientists. To some (e.g. see Pries 2005: 168) the term has too often lacked definitional clarity or agreement to result in anything more productive than inflationary usage and semantic confusion. It will not come as a surprise to our readers that our own position is much closer to a point previously made by one of our contributors, Jean-Christophe Le Coze, who has argued that globalization – while there are different ways of "fram[ing], approach[ing], challeng[ing] and theoriz[ing] it" – is also "one of the most important concepts of the beginning of the twenty-first century [and] at the heart of a renewal of the intellectual background of the social sciences" (Le Coze 2017: 60). Not dissimilarly, Ulrich Beck and Manuel Le Grande have postulated that the conflicting vectors of "global entanglement and interconnectedness" on one hand and "powerful counter-movements" (e.g. neo-nationalism) on the other define "the coming 'world society' of the Second Modernity" (Beck and Grande 2010: 419). The chapters in this handbook testify to the importance and breadth of the questions, issues and challenges under the concept of globalization. In some ways, the situation we find ourselves in is comparable to how Stuart Hall once assessed the term "identity": following a detour through various relevant theoretical discussions, Hall concluded – contrary to critics who would rather have disbanded the term *identity* altogether – that while careful definition and conceptualization were certainly required, a range of core concerns in the social sciences and the world they are dedicated to making sense of could not be talked about at all without recourse to the concept of identity (Hall 1996). A similar point holds with regard to globalization. The term requires considerably more careful definitional work and conceptual discussion than it often receives, most certainly in political discourse, and at times in academic settings also. Parts of our handbook aim to provide precisely the kind of conceptual work that has, admittedly, often been absent from debates about globalization. Without us investing in the hard work required both for theoretical reflection and for empirical exploration concerning different facets of globalization, some of the most pressing contemporary issues cannot be thought about at all. What is more, at a point in time when much public discourse across the world seems only too content (dangerously content, some of us would warn) to retreat to nationalist echo chambers, the case for a sociology of global flows, connections and interdependencies could hardly be more obvious. This handbook constitutes our collective contribution to the theoretical reflections, methodological innovations and empirical explorations such a sociology requires.

REFERENCES

Amelina, Anna, Boatcă, Manuela, Bongaerts, Gregor and Weiß, Anja (2021) "Theorizing societalization across borders: globality, transnationality, postcoloniality," *Current Sociology* 69 (3), 303–314.
Appadurai, Arjun (1990) "Disjuncture and difference in the global cultural economy," in Mike Featherstone (ed.) *Global Culture: Nationalism, Globalization and Modernity*, London: Sage, 295–310.
Bauman, Zygmunt (1993) *Postmodern Ethics*, Oxford: Blackwell.
Bauman, Zygmunt (2000) *Liquid Modernity*, Cambridge: Polity.
Beck, Ulrich (2000) *What Is Globalization?*, Cambridge: Polity.
Beck, Ulrich (2017) *Die Metamorphose der Welt*, Berlin: Suhrkamp.
Beck, Ulrich and Grande, Edgar (2010) "Varieties of second modernity: the cosmopolitan turn in social and political theory and research," *British Journal of Sociology* 61 (3), 409–443.
Benzecry, Claudio E. (2008) "Azul y Oro: the many social lives of a football jersey," *Theory, Culture & Society* 25 (1), 49–76.
Bhambra, Gurminder K. (2007) *Rethinking Modernity: Postcolonialism and the Sociological Imagination*, Basingstoke: Palgrave Macmillan.
Blossfeld, Hans-Peter and Hofmeister, Heather (eds) (2006) *Globalization, Uncertainty and Women's Careers in International Comparison*, Cheltenham, UK and Northampton, MA, USA: Edward Elgar Publishing.
Blossfeld, Hans-Peter, Mills, Melinda, Klijzing, Erik and Kurz, Karin (eds) (2005) *Globalization, Uncertainty and Youth in Society*, London: Routledge.
Blossfeld, Hans-Peter, Buchholz, Sandra and Hofäcker, Dirk (2006a) *Globalization, Uncertainty and Late Careers in Society*, London: Routledge.
Blossfeld, H.-P., Mills, M. and Bernardi, F. (2006b) *Globalization, Uncertainty and Men's Careers in International Comparison*, Cheltenham, UK and Northampton, MA, USA: Edward Elgar Publishing.

Blossfeld, Hans-Peter, Hofäcker, Dirk and Bertolini, Sonia (eds) (2008) *Youth on Globalised Labour Markets: Rising Uncertainty and Its Effects on Early Employment and Family Lives in Europe*, Opladen: Barbara Budrich.

Buchholz, Sandra, Hofäcker, Dirk, Mills, Melinda, Blossfeld, Hans-Peter, Kurz, Karin and Hofmeister, Heather (2009) "Life courses in the globalization process: the development of social inequalities in modern societies," *European Sociological Review* 25 (1), 53–71.

Breen, Richard (1997) "Risk, recommodification and stratification," *Sociology* 31 (3), 473–489.

Burawoy, Michael (2005) "For public sociology," *American Sociological Review* 70 (1), 4–28.

Castells, Manuel (1996) *The Rise of the Network Society*, Oxford: Blackwell.

Castells, Manuel (2000) *End of Millennium*, Oxford: Blackwell.

Eriksen, Thomas Hylland (2015) *Small Places, Large Issues*, London: Pluto.

Fraser, Nancy (2014) "Can society be commodities all the way down? Post-Polanyian reflections on capitalist crisis," *Economy and Society* 43 (3), 541–558.

Gille, Zsuzsa (2013) "From risk to waste: global food waste regimes," *The Sociological Review* 60 (2), 27–46.

Gingrich, André and Banks, Marcus (eds) (2006) *Neo-Nationalism in Europe and Beyond*, New York: Berghahn.

Hall, Stuart (1996) "Introduction: who needs identity?," in Stuart Hall and Paul du Gay (eds) *Questions of Cultural Identity*, London: Sage, 1–17.

Hanafi, Sari (2020) "Global sociology revisited: toward new directions," *Current Sociology* 68 (1), 3–21.

Harvey, David (1989) *The Condition of Postmodernity*, Oxford: Blackwell.

Hofäcker, Dirk, Hess, Moritz and König, Stefanie (eds) (2016) *Delaying Retirement: Progress and Challenges of Active Ageing in Europe, the United States and Japan*, London: Palgrave Macmillan.

Holmwood, John (2007) "'Only connect': the challenge of globalization for the social sciences," *Twenty-First Century Society* 2 (1), 79–94.

Karner, Christian (2020) "The competing politics of Austrian glocalization: Covid-19, crime and (anti-) racism," *Glocalism: Journal of Culture, Politics and Innovation* 3 (2), 1–33.

Karner, Christian (2022) *Sociology in Times of Glocalization*, London: Anthem Press.

Karner, Christian and Weicht, Bernhard (eds) (2016) *The Commonalities of Global Crises*, London: Palgrave Macmillan.

Knowles, Caroline (2014) *Flip-Flop: A Journey through Globalisation's Backroads*, London: Pluto.

Le Coze, Jean-Christophe (2017) "Globalization and high-risk systems," *Policy and Practice in Health and Safety* 15 (1), 57–81.

Lemert, Charles (2015) *Globalization: An Introduction to the End of the Known World*, London: Routledge.

Lévi-Strauss, Claude (1974 [1955]) *Tristes Tropiques*, New York: Atheneum.

Levitt, Peggy and Glick Schiller, Nina (2004) "Conceptualizing simultaneity: a transnational social field perspective on society," *International Migration Review* 38 (3), 1002–1039.

Luft, David (2021) *The Austrian Dimension in German Intellectual History*, London: Bloomsbury.

Lyon, Dawn and Back, Les (2012) "Fishmongers in a global economy: craft and social relations on a London market," *Sociological Research Online* 17 (2), www.socresonline.org.uk/17/2/23.html.

Martell, Luke (2017) *The Sociology of Globalization* (second edition), Cambridge: Polity.

Martin, Craig (2016) *Shipping Container*, New York: Bloomsbury.

Mills Melinda, Blossfeld, Hans-Peter, Buchholz, Sandra, Hofäcker, Dirk, Bernardi, Fabrizio and Hofmeister, Heather (2009) "Converging divergences? An international comparison of the impact of globalization on industrial relations and employment careers," *International Sociology* 23 (4), 561–595.

O'Rourke, Kevin and Williamson, Jeffrey (2002) "When did globalisation begin?," *European Review of Economic History* 6, 23–50.

Parker, David (1997) "Why bother with Durkheim? Teaching sociology in the 1990s," *The Sociological Review* 45 (1), 122–146.

Piketty, Thomas (2014) *Capital in the Twenty-First Century*, Cambridge, MA: Belknap Press.

Pries, Ludger (2005) "Configurations of geographic and societal spaces: a sociological proposal between 'methodological nationalism' and the 'spaces of flows,'" *Global Networks* 5 (2), 167–190.

Rhys-Taylor, Alex (2013) "The essences of multiculture: a sensory exploration of an inner-city street market," *Identities; Global Studies in Culture and Power* 20 (4), 393–406.

Ritzer, George (1993) *The McDonaldization of Society*, London: Sage.

Robertson, Roland (1995) "Glocalization: time-space and homogeneity-heterogeneity," in Mike Featherstone, Scott Lash and Roland Robertson (eds) *Global Modernities*, London: Sage, 25–44.

Rosa, Hartmut (2019) *Resonanz: Eine Soziologie der Weltbeziehungen*, Berlin: Suhrkamp.

Simmel, Georg (1992 [1908]) *Soziologie: Untersuchungen über die Formen der Vergesellschaftung*, Frankfurt a.M.: Suhrkamp.

Stock, Inka (2019) *Time, Migration and Forced Immobility: Sub-Saharan African Migrants in Morocco*, Bristol: Bristol University Press.

Urry, John (2000) *Sociology beyond Societies*, London: Routledge.

Vertovec, Steven (2007) "Super-diversity and its implications," *Ethnic and Racial Studies* 30 (6), 1024–1054.

Wimmer, Andreas and Glick-Schiller, Nina (2002) "Methodological nationalism and beyond," *Global Networks* 2 (4), 301–334.

PART I

HISTORY/SOCIOLOGY

1. When did globalization start?

Zinovia Lialiouti

INTRODUCTION

When attending my sociology class as an undergraduate student in the late 1990s globalization seemed to be a rather recent phenomenon, with scholars tracing its emergence roughly
in the late 1960s and definitely in the post-Second World War period. Academic handbooks
would inform students that the essence of globalization consisted in the interdependence of
national economies, the weakening of nation state-level institutions and the developments in
transportation and communication technologies leading to a new experience in human history.
Twenty years later, I find myself teaching the same subject which now seems to be considerably older in its origins, for many scholars, going as far back as the Agrarian Revolution
(fourth millennium BC). The question how old globalization is is currently much debated
and researched from an interdisciplinary perspective. But for that question to be answered,
historians and sociologists have first to conclude what globalization actually is. An attempt by
Al-Rodhan and Stoudmann in 2006 to collect definitions of globalization from academic and
non-academic sources resulted in a grouping of 114 definitions dating from 1974, over half of
which (67) revolve around the economic and market component (Al-Rodhan & Stoudmann
2006). Nevertheless, the authors felt that globalization could not be 'defined clearly with
a beginning and an end' (3) and concluded that it should be addressed as a 'process ... that has
been impacting communities, cultures, and economies for hundreds of years' (5). Any attempt
to provide a historical account of globalization revolves around questions of definition. One
has to reflect what the essential component of globalization is in order to trace its starting
point. This chapter attempts to summarize the various perspectives on the historical evolution
of globalization in order to address the question of its origins. It shares the view that globalization is a process, and its ending cannot be determined, but will try to provide an estimation on
its beginning. Among the many, and insightful, proposed definitions, the chapter is structured
upon the perception of globalization as 'an historical process which engenders a significant
shift in the spatial reach of networks and systems of social relations to transcontinental or
interregional patterns of human organization, activity and the exercise of power' (McGrew
1998: 327). Moreover, the approach taken here is in accordance with the crucial remark made
by Roland Robertson that globalization should be understood as both 'the compression of the
world and the intensification of consciousness of the world as a whole' (Robertson 1992: 8).

'ANCIENT' VERSUS 'CONTEMPORARY' GLOBALIZATION?

Globalization studies have benefited greatly from the development of the global history
paradigm in the late twentieth century which brought to the epicentre of historical research
a multiplicity of connections, links and flows that cut across time and space. As far as the
perception of globalization is concerned, the influence of global history was decisive in chal-

lenging Eurocentric approaches as well as shifting the attention from the economy to other spheres of human activity that are also essential in the experience of globalization. Starting from the assumption that 'globalization is something that has been with us as long as there have been people who are both interdependent and aware of that fact' (Gills & Thompson 2006: i), contributions in the field have traced the origins of globalization: 'Maximally ... since Homo sapiens began migrating from the African continent ... Minimally ... since the sixteenth-century's connection of the Americas to Afro-Eurasia' (Gills & Thompson 2006: 1; Sheffield et al. 2013).

In this line of reasoning, the concept of World-System (Wallerstein 2011 [1974]) has often been employed to describe the historical evolution of globalization from the Neolithic Age to the twentieth century as 'the story of this distinctively human type of linking up. Community by community, humans shared ideas, information, technologies, stories, and goods. And as they did so, networks of exchange increased in size and became more diverse, despite periods of breakdown and retrogression' (Zinkina et al. 2019: 6). Zinkina et al. combine a series of criteria to determine the content of globalization as involving the establishment of networks for the diffusion of information, innovation and ideas, trade networks both for mass consumption goods and luxury goods, as well as political and military networks. They summarize existing literature on the age of globalization as involving the following four phases: (1) 'archaic' globalization starting 5–10.000 years ago; (2) 'pre-modern'/'proto-modern' globalization going back to the sixteenth century and to the Age of Discovery; (3) modern globalization dating from the eighteenth century to the early twentieth century; and (4) the latest phase of globalization originating roughly in the mid-twentieth century (2019: 10–13).

Focusing on the approaches that address globalization within the course of modernity, the question arises whether its beginnings should be placed in the 'long' nineteenth century or in the 'short' twentieth century. The scholar production that prioritizes twentieth-century developments in the formulation of globalization has provided valuable conceptual tools for the understanding of the nexus of ties and relations that derive from the use of the Internet, new forms of global capitalism, the rise of transnational forms of governance and policy making. Manuel Castells' reference work has contributed to the study of globalization focusing on new forms of networks and connectivity shaped by the technological advances in the fields of information and communication. The 'information age' and 'network society' became among the most powerful interpretive prisms for social experience in the late twentieth century (Castells 2010 [1996]).

In parallel, Saskia Sassen's contribution on the spatial and economic dimensions of globalization traced the origins of a novel phase in world history defined by transnational forms of production and, at the same time, of transnational forms of labour migration to the 1960s (Sassen 1988). Sassen argues that these developments have been generated by a set of economic, social, cultural and ideological factors, thus sustaining the argument of profound and complex interdependence between societies across the globe. The rise of 'global cities' (London, New York, Tokyo) and later of a 'transnational urban system' has been described as the product of the mobility of capital and labour in the context of networked economies with finance, media and specialized services playing a key role (Sassen 2001 [1991]).

Nevertheless, scholars have challenged the notion that the rise of global economic and urban systems that are not confined to state-formulated territorial boundaries represents a truly novel phenomenon in human history. The broadening of the historical and geographical perspective is valuable in this respect. Focusing on the development of a world-trade system Abu-Lughod shifts the attention to the emergence of a 'world-economy' in the thirteenth century linking the Middle East area, India, China, as well as parts of Europe at the time being at the periphery of the system (Abu-Lughod 1989). According to her compelling argument, the years 1250–1350 represent a 'critical "turning point"' in world history. Moreover, she examines the emergence of a so-called 'archipelago' of cities across the world system where contact between merchants and producers would take place in a milieu of multiple cultural, linguistic and monetary norms and symbols (1989: 12–14). Scholarship on the pre-modern and extra-European origins of globalization thus challenges the view of a 'contemporary' globalization starting in the twentieth century.

However meaningful a macro-historical perspective, the overextension of the concept of globalization leads to misleading abstractions which obscure the novel dimensions involved in the phenomenon. Thus, this chapter will not discuss further the conceptualizations of 'archaic' or 'proto-globalization'. It is here argued that globalization cannot be understood separately from the transformations that define the rise of modernity. In this attempt to trace the starting point of globalization we should consider the many layers of interdependence and spheres of action involved as well as the element of awareness. Thus, globalization is inextricably linked to a new form of consciousness which affects individual and collective identities. As far as the latter aspect is concerned, our argumentation is inscribed in the tradition of hermeneutics which addresses human history within the process of producing and sharing meanings. Thus, the ideological and cultural realms are integral parts in reconstructing the historical outline of globalization. In this respect, it is argued that a history of globalization should also revolve around ideas and belief systems that sought to address a global audience on the assumption that their relevance and applicability was and should be ecumenical.

GLOBALIZATION AND MODERNITY

This chapter takes the view that globalization should be contextualized within the 'long' nineteenth century as conceptualized by Eric Hobsbawm, starting in the 1780s and coming to an end with the outburst of the First World War in 1914. Thus, it is inextricably linked to the dual-revolution scheme taking also into account its subsequent revisions by various scholars. The most influential historian of the twentieth century provided an impressive, in its breadth and detailed processing of primary sources, account of two interacting currents, the Industrial and the French Revolutions. His trilogy *The Age of Revolution (1789–1848)*, *The Age of Capital (1848–1875)* and the *Age of Empire (1875–1914)* (Hobsbawm 1996a [1962], 1996b [1975], 1989 [1987]) sought to reconstruct this far-reaching process of social transformation, the 'greatest' the world had witnessed since ancient times in Hobsbawm's phrasing (Hobsbawm 1996a [1962]: 1).

At the core of his argument lies the perception that the French Revolution and the Industrial Revolution – with Great Britain as the birthplace of the latter – represent the two sides of the same coin, that is the rise of the bourgeoisie and the consolidation of capitalism mainly identified with industrial capitalism. Since the 1780s onwards this dual-revolutionary process integrated gradually most of the world on the basis of similar – but certainly not uniform – modes of producing and exchanging goods, consumption patterns, power structures, family relations and bodily practices, ideas on state formation and social relations (Bayly 2004).

Subsequent approaches have incorporated early modernity in their accounts of globalization. Among the most prominent, historians Osterhammel and Peterson proposed a historical account of globalization stretching from the sixteenth century and involving four phases: (1) from the sixteenth to the eighteenth century; (2) from 1750 to 1850; (3) from 1880 to 1945; and (4) from 1945 to the present with the 1970s as an internal milestone (Osterhammel & Peterson 2005). A similar approach to the subject is provided by the sociologist Roland Robertson. Robertson designates a 'germinal' phase in globalization from the fifteenth to the mid-eighteenth century followed by an 'incipient' phase from the mid-eighteenth century to the 1870s (Robertson 1992: 59). Nevertheless, the 'long' nineteenth century, despite its many revisions and contestations, remains a coherent and persuasive argument in what is inevitably a conventional chronology attempt.

Criticism of Hobsbawm's conception focuses mainly on the centrality of Europe as the birthplace of the twin revolutions, on the historical accuracy of the coincidence of the rise of the bourgeoisie and the Industrial Revolution, as well as on various aspects of the Industrial Revolution scheme (e.g. Goldstone 1991; Mann 1993). Thus, Bayly has sought to demonstrate that the origins of globalization during the early phase of modernity should be traced across the globe, in political and economic developments in India, Iran, etc. and not solely in Europe. He stresses that a series of conflicts taking place in the American and Asian continents between Europeans and non-Europeans during the years 1756–1763 should be held accountable for the weakening of European anciens régimes both in terms of their fiscal resilience and the legitimization associated with their perceived efficiency. He has also maintained that this 'polycentric' globalization survived even during the period of European hegemony in the nineteenth century. In Bayly's account the 'long' nineteenth century consists of a gradual process of deconstruction of 'anciens régimes' in a variety of geographical settings which involved the consolidation of uniform patterns in government and religious structures and economic relations. The outcome of this process was a dynamic relationship between the external uniformity of societies and their growing internal differentiation. Thus, Bayly moves from the twin-revolution scheme to a nexus of converging revolutions (2004: 86–120, 553–556). In this reading, the rise of modernity is intertwined with the rise of globalization. In a similar vein, Osterhammel has emphasized that the European revolutions were 'only a part of a general crisis' and argued that the nineteenth century should be perceived more as a period of erosion of traditional elites and power structures than as a period where the prominence of the bourgeoisie was already an established social reality (Osterhammel 2014: 60).

Moreover, a corpus of literature has focused on reformulating the Industrial Revolution hypothesis. Among the various inputs in the debate, it is worth citing the commercial 'consumer revolution' thesis. In this argumentation, a significant increase in supply of consumer goods in Great Britain combined with an unprecedented rise of the consumption of luxury and semi-luxury commodities beyond the aristocracy preceded the Industrial Revolution and was decisive in its emergence (McKendrick et al. 1982; Berg 2007; Allen 2009). Coining the term 'industrious revolution', De Vries focuses on the household as a unit of analysis and expands the geographical focus from England to Northwestern Europe and the American colonies to argue that the household was the decisive factor both in the increase of supply of labour and in the increase of demand for commodities (De Vries 1994: 249–270). In parallel, the contribution of non-Europeans in this evolution is emphasized; it was the import of Asian (namely Chinese) luxury goods that triggered innovation in British ways of production as the latter sought to imitate Asian artifacts (Berg 2004, 2007). Asian, African and American resources and outlets in the context of the Imperial setting were instrumental in bringing about the transformation of British production and trade. The conclusion drawn is that global markets and 'global commodities' not only preceded but were preconditions for the Industrial Revolution.

Before contemplating on the impact of the Age of Revolutions in terms of concrete political and social revolutionary endeavours, one would have to consider the conceptual rupture that the word revolution has entailed since 1789. From that point onwards the concept of revolution was radically transformed and was no longer associated with a circular understanding of the changes of political regimes and social conditions. Revolution became associated with 'a new horizon of expectations' and involved a novel perception of time and space. As has been eloquently argued by Reinhart Koselleck, acceleration of time and global range are inherent implications of modern revolution. In his view, 'all modern expressions of "Revolution" spatially imply a world revolution and temporally imply that they be permanent until their objective is reached' (Koselleck 2004: 52). These features relate to current experiences of time and space which have been at the core of the globalization debate as can be easily detected in some of the most popular definitions. Thus, a history of globalization cannot but consider the conceptual legacy of the American (1776), French (1789) and Russian Revolutions (1917).

The pursuit of the ideas of nationalism and liberalism that emerged as a result of the French Revolution, as well as the reaction triggered by the claims raised by those ideas, shaped domestic and international political affairs until the aftermath of the First World War. In this respect, the Paris Treaties (1919–1920) that sealed the collapse of empires (German, Austro-Hungarian, Russian and Ottoman) and sought to implement the principle of nationalities in the successor states were the final chapter in the revolutionary process that developed from 1789 to 1848 (Berstein & Milza 1996: 99–105).

The following historical detail drawn from pre-revolutionary Greece is revealing for the global implications of revolutionary ideas in a geographic region where empires clashed and bordered. The most prominent military figure in the Greek War of Independence (1821–1828), Theodoros Kolokotronis, a former warrior-bandit who would only learn to write in the last years of his life, tried to explain the causes and meaning of the Greek Revolution by arguing: 'According to my judgement, the French Revolution and the doings of Napoleon opened the eyes of the world' (Stavrianos 1958: 212). Forced to leave his birthplace, the region of Peloponese, which was under Ottoman rule, Kolokotronis joined the Russian Navy in 1805 and then moved to the Heptanese, under British rule at the time, and served in the British military. Shortly afterwards, the Heptanese became a French protectorate (1807–1814). Thus, Kolokotronis became acquainted with European military practices, revolutionary ideas and even fashion style, adopting the red helmet of the British military uniform.

In a similar vein, Slavoj Žižek describes a scene drawn from the Haitian Revolution on the battlefield where the army of Napoleon approaches the Haitian army of self-liberated slaves. At first, the French soldiers thought the enemy was singing a tribal war chant, but then it became clear that the Haitians were actually singing the Marseillaise. Žižek's interpretation of the scene emphasizes the contradictions of European modernity but also highlights the multiple and non-linear nature of modern globalization. According to Žižek:

> [T]he message of the Haitian soldiers' Marseillaise was not 'You see, even we, the primitive blacks, are able to assimilate ourselves to your high culture and politics, to imitate it as a model!' but a much more precise one: 'in this battle, we are more French than you, the Frenchmen, are – we stand for the innermost consequences of your revolutionary ideology, the very consequences you were not able to assume'. (Žižek 2009: 113)

In parallel, the emergence of the idea of an international order and the creation of institutions serving that order is also an important novelty of the nineteenth century with apparent continuities with twentieth-century British and American hegemonic endeavours (Mazower 2012; Rosenboim 2017). Conceptions of the world as an entity based on political or religious foundations had certainly existed throughout history (Roman Empire, Christiandom, Islam, etc.); since the Napoleonic Wars, however, the 'international' emerged as a distinct political space along with debate on its optimal form of governance (Mazower 2012: 1–34). The constitution of the Concert of Europe (1815), regardless of its reactionary orientation, marked the beginning of 'the new art of international government' (25). Nevertheless, the 'international' was also the point of reference for the various movements opposing the Concert; thus, it rose as a terrain both for the restoration of order and for radical transformation mainly through its articulation with nationalism (25–34).

Valuable insights provided by conceptual approaches can also be detected in relation to a key concept in most accounts of the globalization process: the concept of capitalism. Capitalism as a noun referring to a distinct social experience emerged only in the second half of the nineteenth century in Europe and the United States. As Kocka has argued, capitalism involves an inherent connotation of difference as it is used in contrast either to a previous state of affairs, thus understood as a rupture in the social and economic realm, or to a future vision of radical social transformation (Kocka 2016a: 1–3). Even though Marx rarely employed the word 'capitalism' as such, his conception of the capitalist system introduced the idea that capitalism had the tendency and the power to transform existing structures across the world, and that this transformational impact was not limited to the economic sphere (Kocka 2016b: 9). This view was eventually shared in both critical and positive accounts of capitalism. Moreover, capitalism in its employment by historians as an analytical concept has been perceived as a 'world-historical development' (Kocka 2016a: 3). Thus, the concept has been closely associated with the processes of modernity and globalization. In the emblematic phrasing of Immanuel Wallerstein, the structure of the current historical system is that of a 'capitalist world-economy' (2016: 188). Even though it was not the sole component of capitalism, industrialization has nonetheless been acknowledged as the main driving force behind the rise of global trends in terms of technological advances, organizational structures and labour relations since its emergence in late eighteenth-century England and through its expansion to continental Europe and the United States in the nineteenth century (Kocka 2016a: 97–103).

The assumption that the transformation of the horizon of expectations, individual and collective beliefs, cognitive schemes and conceptual tools cannot be excluded from a historical account of globalization that sustains the argument that agency should be acknowledged as an important factor in the evolution of the phenomenon. Recent historical scholarship has shifted the focus to the concept of the middle class and its crucial role both as a 'product' of the revolutionary transformations that shaped the long nineteenth century and as an active agent in the changes in economics, politics, society and culture across the globe. Christian Bayly has coined the term 'third global revolution' to capture the significance of the development of a global middle class (2004: 114–120). According to his argument, the rise of a commercial middle class preceded the Industrial Revolution and was the outcome of significant advancement in craftmanship but also of the prevailing of global consumption patterns. Defined roughly as the social group standing between the aristocracy and peasants and workers, the middle class has been acknowledged as the 'most effective proponent' of globalization (Dejung et al. 2019: 1). Dejung et al. have thoroughly explored the manifestations of the rise of the middle classes in various national and local contexts, as well as the connections developed between the different middle classes, convincingly making the case that middle class is not a Western phenomenon and thus revising a previous bias in the literature. The authors highlight the inherently hybrid nature of the global middle classes which is shaped by a process of constant interaction between Western influences and local conditions. 'Merchants in Shanghai, lawyers in Delhi, bankers in New York, doctors in Cairo, professors in Vienna, and schoolteachers on the Gold Coast', alongside housewives across the American and European continents (Dejung et al. 2019: 2) introduced and consolidated new institutional practices involving state, society, science and religion, and a range of 'bodily practices' that changed family relations, eating habits, hygiene norms and dress codes (Bayly 2004: 1).

The following quote by John Maynard Keynes describing a typical scene from the life of a Londoner in the early twentieth century most eloquently summarizes aspects of globalization that stem from the interplay of capitalism and European imperialism, but also revolve around a distinct horizon of expectations which reflects consciousness about the global condition:

> The inhabitant of London could order by telephone, sipping his morning tea in bed, the various products of the whole earth, in such quantity as he might see fit, and reasonably expect their early delivery upon his doorstep; he could at the same moment and by the same means adventure his wealth in the natural resources and new enterprises of any quarter of the world, and share, without exertion or even trouble, in their prospective fruits and advantages … But most important of all, he regarded this state of affairs as normal, certain, and permanent, and any deviation from it as aberrant, scandalous, and avoidable. (Keynes 2012 [1919]: 11)

This is also a description that echoes the 'middle class, consuming society' as an important feature of globalization (Bayly 2004: 116).

Globalized consumption patterns emerged in the late nineteenth century promoted by branding and marketing techniques originating from the United States. One of the most emblematic products in the twentieth-century debate on the supposedly homogenizing effects of globalization, Coca-Cola (the coining of the term 'coca-colonization' is revealing for the perception of globalization as a version of American cultural imperialism) originated in the 1880s American food industry and its production and distribution expanded rapidly. Nevertheless, the shaping of global mass consumption should not be understood as a reflection of power relations on the world map. The example of dietary trends tells a different story as the Chinese remained rather indifferent to Western culinary habits while Chinese cuisine had a profound influence on Western cities (Osterhammel 2014: 227–233).

Even though the widening of the geographical perspective is indispensable in addressing the rise of globalization, one should not neglect the decisive role of European great powers in promoting and expanding the reach of globalization processes. The power struggle between them and the resulting 'new imperialism' which involved direct and indirect forms of colonialism is a crucial component in understanding the particular shape and content of nineteenth-century globalization (Evans 2016). The intensification of intra-state competition after 1870 brought European empires to the fore as power agents controlling, to a significant extent, the global 'flows of goods, people and ideals' (Bayly 2004: 472; Osterhammel 2014: 64–66).

Despite different approaches to the role of Europe as regards the origins of globalization, most scholars agree that the period 1880/1890–1914 represents a culmination point in the economic, social and cultural transformation of the world. Those are the years of the 'great acceleration' (Bayly 2004: 451–487) – the 'take-off phase of globalization' in Robertson's scheme lasting from 1870 to 1920 (Robertson 1992: 59) – when the growth of international trade and migration flows, alongside the spread of the Second Industrial Revolution and the rise of multinational corporations, shaped a new social and economic order (Osterhammel 2014: 64, 711). In Osterhammel's analysis this is a milestone in the history of globalization which 'for the first time linked all continents into economic and communication networks' (64). The development of various networks – from railways to cable networks and urban planning – was followed by a conceptual development: societies began to imagine themselves as networks either in positive or negative terms (711). Thus, apart from constituting economic and social change, this is a milestone in the history of ideas as the 'consciousness of the world as an interconnected whole' was consolidated (Mazower 2012: 36). The 'shrinkage of time and space' as a growing perception both among the elites and the masses nurtured a variety of collective and individual behaviours ranging from late nineteenth-century colonialism to transcontinental migration and the development of geography as a scientific discipline (Mazower 2012).

CONCLUSION

Acknowledging that the history of globalization has grown with the broadening of the concept, we argue that globalization started with the rise of modernity perceived as a set of transformations in the economic, social, political and cultural realms. Thus, the present approach rejects both views of an 'ancient' globalization and views of a 'contemporary' globalization roughly starting after 1945. The former fails to grasp the novel aspects of the phenomenon while the latter does not acknowledge properly the historical grounding of current trends. Globalization is considered to be inextricably linked to the consolidation of industrial and commercial capitalism, the spread of revolutionary ideas, the rise of the middle classes in their various manifestations and the growing consciousness of a global order and global links. Under this prism, it is assumed that the long nineteenth century is the essential starting point of globalization. Especially, the period from 1880 to the First World War represents a peak in the historical evolution of the phenomenon. Finally, in this approach, globalization is also addressed in the context of ideas that either claimed global relevance or involved the conception of the world as a whole.

REFERENCES

Abu-Lughod, Janet (1989), *Before European Hegemony: The World System A.D. 1250–1350*, Oxford: Oxford University Press.

Al-Rodhan, N.R.F. & G. Stoudmann (2006), 'Definitions of Globalization: A Comprehensive Overview and a Proposed Definition', *Geneva Centre for Security Policy*, 1–21.

Allen, Robert (2009), *The British Industrial Revolution in Global Perspective*, Cambridge: Cambridge University Press.

Bayly, Christopher Alan (2004), *The Birth of the Modern World, 1780–1914*, Malden, MA: Blackwell.

Berg, Maxine (2004), 'In Pursuit of Luxury: Global History and British Consumer Goods in the Eighteenth Century', *Past & Present*, 182, 85–142.

Berg, Maxine (2007), *Luxury and Pleasure in Eighteenth-Century Britain*, Oxford: Oxford University Press.

Berstein, Serge & Pierre Milza (1996), *Histoire du XXe siècle. Tome 1: 1900–1945: La fin du monde europeén*, Paris: Hatier.

Castells, Manuel (2010 [1996]), *The Rise of the Network Society*, Chichester: Wiley-Blackwell.
De Vries, Jan (1994), 'The Industrial Revolution and the Industrious Revolution', *Journal of Economic History*, 54(2), 249–270.
Dejung, Christof, David Motadel & Jürgen Osterhammel (2019), 'Worlds of the Bourgeoisie', in Christof Dejung, David Motadel & Jürgen Osterhammel (eds), *The Global Bourgeoisie: The Rise of the Middle Classes in the Age of Empire*, Princeton, NJ: Princeton University Press, pp. 1–39.
Evans, R. J. (2016), *The Pursuit of Power: Europe 1815–1914*, London: Penguin.
Gills, Barry K. & William R. Thompson (eds) (2006), *Globalization and Global History*, London: Routledge.
Goldstone, Jack (1991), *Revolution and Rebellion in the Early Modern World*, Berkeley, CA: University of California Press.
Hobsbawm, Eric (1989 [1987]), *The Age of Empire, 1985–1914*, New York: Vintage Books.
Hobsbawm, Eric (1996a [1962]), *The Age of Revolution, 1789–1848*, New York: Vintage Books.
Hobsbawm, Eric (1996b [1975]), *The Age of Capital, 1848–1875*, New York: Vintage Books.
Keynes, John Maynard (2012 [1919]), *The Economic Consequences of the Peace*, London: Independent Publishing Platform.
Kocka, Jürgen (2016a), 'Introduction', in Jürgen Kocka & Marcel van der Linden (eds), *Capitalism: The Reemergence of a Historical Concept*, London: Bloomsbury, pp. 1–10.
Kocka, Jürgen (2016b), *Capitalism. A Shorth History*, translated by Jeremiah Riemer, Princeton, NJ: Princeton University Press.
Koselleck, Reinhart (2004), *Futures Past: On the Semantics of Historical Time*, translated by Keith Tribe, New York: Columbia University Press.
Mann, Michael (1993), *The Sources of Social Power, Volume 2: The Rise of Classes and Nation-States, 1760–1914*, Cambridge: Cambridge University Press.
Mazower, Mark (2012), *Governing the World: The History of an Idea*, New York: Penguin Press.
McGrew, Anthony G. (1998), 'Global Legal Interaction and Present-Day Patterns of Globalization', in V. Gessner & A.C. Budak (eds), *Emerging Legal Certainty: Empirical Studies on the Globalization of Law*, Ashgate: Dartmouth Publishing, pp. 325–346.
McKendrick, Neil, John Brewer & J.H. Plumb (1982), *The Birth of a Consumer Society: The Commercialization of Eighteenth-Century England*, Bloomington, IN: Indiana University Press.
Osterhammel, Jürgen (2014), *The Transformation of the World: A Global History of the Nineteenth Century*, translated by Patrick Camiller, Princeton, NJ: Princeton University Press.
Osterhammel, Jürgen & Niels P. Peterson (2005), *Globalization: A Short History*, translated by Dona Geyer, Princeton, NJ: Princeton University Press.
Robertson, Roland (1992), *Globalization: Social Theory and Global Culture*, London: Sage.
Rosenboim, Or (2017), *The Emergence of Globalism: Visions of World Order in Britain and the United States, 1939–1950*, Princeton, NJ: Princeton University Press.
Sassen, Saskia (1988), *The Mobility of Capital and Labor: A Study in International Investment and Labor Flow*, Cambridge: Cambridge University Press.
Sassen, Saskia (2001 [1991]), *The Global City: New York, London, Tokyo*, Princeton NJ: Princeton University Press.
Sheffield, Jim, Andrey Korotayev & Leonid Grinin (eds) (2013), *Globalization. Yesterday, Today, and Tomorrow*, Litchfield Park: Emergent Publications.
Stavrianos, L.S. (1958), *The Balkans since 1453*, New York: Rinehart & Co.
Wallerstein, Immanuel (2011 [1974]), *The Modern World-System I: Capitalist Agriculture and the Origins of the European World-Economy in the Sixteenth Century*, Berkeley, CA: University of California Press.
Wallerstein, Immanuel (2016), 'Capitalism as an Essential Concept to Understand Modernity', in Jürgen Kocka & Marcel van der Linden (eds), *Capitalism: The Reemergence of a Historical Concept*, London: Bloomsbury, pp. 187–204.
Zinkina, Julia, David Christian, Leonid Grinin, Ilya Ilyin, Alexey Andreev, Ivan Aleshkovski et al. (2019), *A Big History of Globalization: The Emergence of a Global World System*, London: Springer.
Žižek, Slavoj (2009), *First as Tragedy, Then as Farce*, London: Verso.

2. Methodological dilemmas or promises? The sociological imagination and globalization

Magali Peyrefitte

INTRODUCTION

The different chapters in this volume demonstrate the complex and multi-faceted nature of globalization. Globalization is indeed marked by mechanisms, networks and flows of supra-territoriality and interconnectivity as well as tensions and oppositions, but also frictions at the juncture between the local and the global. Processes of cultural imperialism and homogenization contrast for instance with evidences of socio-cultural and economic hybridization or indigenization (Appadurai, 1990). These considerations are to be reflected in the methodological choices that are to be made in addressing research questions relating to globalization.

Discussions regarding methodological approaches in globalization studies have looked at the differences between quantitative and qualitative approaches and at times their complementarity (Sullivan and Brockington, 2004). Macro-level perspectives through quantitative research have tended to dominate the study of globalization, but it has increasingly appeared necessary to turn to qualitative research to capture processes of 'glocalization', the intersubjective transformations that take place at the interface between the global and the local (Brown and Labonté, 2011: 2–4). This has notably been led by the work of anthropologists. Unlike Burawoy (2000), I do not think that a distinction must necessarily be made between anthropology and sociology in the way the study of globalization is approached from an ethnographic perspective. Appadurai developed his 'model of global cultural flow' (Appadurai, 1990: 301) drawing on his anthropological work. In this, he paid a great deal of attention to the actors of a global cultural economy in making sense of the way disjuncture between the different scapes (ethnoscapes, mediascapes, technoscapes, financescapes and ideoscapes) occurs in a 'fluid and uncertain interplay' (306): 'Indeed, the individual actor is the last locus of this perspectival set of landscapes, for these landscapes are eventually navigated by agents who both experience and constitute larger formations, in part by their own sense of what these landscapes offer' (296).

Reviewing emerging ethnographies in anthropology that have adapted 'long-standing modes of ethnographic practices to more complex objects of study', Marcus argued for a continued move away from the conventions of ethnographies in single-site locations and henceforth advocated for a multi-sited ethnography (Marcus, 1995: 95). In particular, he identified the global as: 'an emergent dimension of arguing about the connection among sites in a multi-sited ethnography' (99).

According to Marcus a multi-sited ethnography can indeed be attentive to different modes of construction of increasingly complex objects of study, notably as a result of globalization problematizing the negotiation of identity and culture in time and space. These modes are premised on the following: follow the people; follow the thing; follow the metaphor; follow the plot, story or allegory; follow the life or biography; follow the conflict; the strategically situated (single-site) ethnography. Two of these aspects – following the plot, story or allegory and following the life or biography – for me expand beyond the anthropological parameters of a multi-sited ethnography and more generally respond to the sociological imagination's imperatives to link individual biographies to social structures. The plot, story or allegory and the life or biography have been at the core of my methodological approach, especially when considering diasporic and migrant identities.

In this chapter, I first discuss the connection between sociological imagination, storytelling and globalization. The operationalization and activation of a sociological imagination is methodologically translated in the endeavour to work with individual stories as a way to explore and disentangle the collective impacts and effects of globalization and the way it is lived and experienced. This approach offers the possibility to explore individual biographies that can be connected to global economic, political and socio-cultural structures. Drawing on my empirical interest in working with stories, I present some methodological examples of ways of working with stories to explore meaning-making processes, especially in questions of identity, migration and diaspora. These stories can offer a counter-narrative and even a 'counter-memory, for the future' (Gordon, 2008: 22). I expand this discussion to include considerations of what role storytelling – the emergence, analysis and writing of stories – plays in the communication of a sociological imagination in a global and late capitalist era more broadly, as this could have the potential to be a political and pedagogical tool in contesting the power inequalities and forms of injustice that are exacerbated or created by the forces of globalization.

THE SOCIOLOGICAL IMAGINATION, STORYTELLING AND GLOBALIZATION

In focusing his analysis of globalization around social changes and transformations, Schuerkens (2017: 5) argues:

> An analysis of social changes must take into account social relations among the concerned populations, the impact of globalized social structures on the local populations, and the phenomenon of change that results from the interaction of different social systems. The analysis of the transformation of a society is characterized by extreme diversity. Only an investigation that takes into account these three aspects can show the complex character of these social relations and the specific nature of these transformations.

Schuerkens' theorization raises the importance of linking globalized social structures to local culture and populations and possible friction in this interaction with a particular attention on structural changes and transformations incurred by globalization in different areas. But how are these changes and transformations lived and experienced? This is where the sociological imagination becomes a useful tool.

The foundation of our sociological labour, trade or craft is the sociological imagination: the optical lens through which we ought to look at the social world – a globalized social world in this case. Sarah Burton (2016) describes the sociological imagination as the home that connects sociologists in all their diversity. C. Wright Mills (1959) encourages a 'quality of mind' that engages with the social world thanks to a sociological imagination which envisages the relationship between individual experiences and social structures, individual biographies and history, personal troubles and public issues (3–24). For Mills, this quality of mind and sociological imagination should not be limited to sociologists, and it is interesting to also take into account his advocacy to creatively write for different 'reading publics' (Back, 2007: 164). The craft of the sociologists is to conjure up the social world by connecting individual stories to the structures, but in doing so, it is also essential to look at the intersection of different social categories and resulting hierarchies and power relations in this process. The principles of intersectionality (Crenshaw, 2017), in this respect, come to complement the examination of individual stories in relation to social structures. Bauman and May (2001) further establish the principles and particularities of thinking sociologically beyond common sense. This is more relevant than ever as so much of what the discipline is concerned with is directly or indirectly linked to the complex workings of globalization and its effects on the everyday.

A sociological imagination applied to globalization considers the complexity and entanglement of the different structures and actors that are constituted by and constitutive of the flows of goods, money, people, information and ideas. In line with Urry, Knowles (2010) prefers to talk of mobilities rather than flows to translate the problematic and diversified processes and ways in which people and objects journey through space and time in a globalized world. In all cases, I argue that we should be reminded of this key tool, that the sociological imagination is, in the way we approach the study of globalization and define the methodological scope with which we ought to research it. This grounding presents the potential to pay particular attention to the mechanisms and effects of globalization in its everyday lived experiences and quotidian materiality. This is particularly possible by taking into account the importance of stories and storytelling as activating the principles of a sociological imagination as stories are useful in connecting everyday lived experiences with structures, especially as we try to make sense of these structures within the complexity of a globalized world. Globalization is not a new phenomenon but its acceleration means it has become a ubiquitously major driver of social change, and qualitative research has much to teach on its everyday lived reality.

In qualitative research, sociologists work with the stories of others through analysis, interpretation and representation. They write about data from 'real-life encounters' that 'could tell many different stories' (Smart, 2010: 3). Storytelling is therefore, as Carol Smart argues, a central part of our role as sociologists and encourages us to explore different forms of writing in conjuring up social life while remaining reflexive of our role in the production of knowledge (6). Simultaneously, Smart (5) reminds us that sociologists are not writers of fiction and instead must still work within 'ethical and analytical codes' in sensitively telling the stories of the social world they are entrusted with. The analytical codes established by Mills' sociological imagination offer a cornerstone that is expanded upon by Gordon (2008) and Smart (2010, 2014).

In envisaging sociologists as storytellers, Smart was influenced by the inspiring work of Avery Gordon (Smart, 2010: 4). Gordon (2008) invites sociologists to adopt a sociological imagination that is unconventional in aiming to make the invisible visible. Gordon's 'invitation' to acknowledge and work with 'ghostly matters' forces us to think beyond immediacy and what is to be explored beyond empirical evidence. Connecting with the ghosts and their haunting to more effectively address the working of power relations and subjugation is especially relevant when working on issues related to globalization, of which many of the effects are pervasive but not necessarily easily discernible in everyday life and thus to be unearthed through this kind of sociological imagination. Both Gordon (2008) and Smart (2010, 2014) have raised key questions and made major contributions regarding the work of representation in writing sociologically through storytelling, and I shall return to these challenges in the concluding remarks.

Storytelling takes place at different levels other than at the stage of the writing: in the dialectical moment of knowledge production between interviewer and interviewee; in the way the audience will receive, read and in turn interpret the story. At the stage of data collection, it is essential to think about the ways in which stories are first brought to life in the research process. The semi-structure or better the life-story interview can provide glimpses into the biography of the participants but it is still a relatively formatted structure that can limit the process of storytelling. More creative subject-centred methods have the potential to provide a more definite emphasis on the biographical in aiming to connect biographies with structural changes incurred by globalization.

CREATIVE METHODS FOR STORYTELLING AND THE ROLE OF OBJECTS AND ARTEFACTS: EXAMPLES IN PRACTICE

In this section, I more particularly focus on my own research practice as a way to discuss forms of data collection that can encourage storytelling through a creative process. For instance, I approached my doctoral investigation of South Asian suburbanization in Nottingham through a range of methods designed to explore diasporic trajectories of migration in relation to socio-economic and geographic mobilities in the city. The methodology, a combination of life-story interviews, visual tours (in the home and/or in the streets of the city) and photo-elicitation interviews in some cases, as well as some archival research, helped convey narratives that were individual as well as collective. The analysis of personal stories highlighted collective connections as individual biographies were inscribed in the historical matrices of the diaspora. Looking at the construction and negotiation of identities in diaspora space, Avtar Brah brings to light the importance of stories and the role of intersubjectivity as individual narratives are constructed in dialogue with the 'collective experience' (Brah, 1996: 11). She argues that: 'the diasporic imagined community is far from fixed and pre-given. It is constituted within the crucible of the materiality of everyday life; in the everyday stories we tell ourselves individually and collectively' (183).

Identities in the diaspora are shaped in the intersubjective dynamic of storytelling about the self and the self in relation to the other: the group(s) one feels they belong to and the one(s) they do not. The combination of traditional and more creative methods in my PhD study facilitated a diverse range of stories, especially as participants in home interviews and in visual tours were confronted by the physicality and materiality of their home or of the city in constructing these stories (Peyrefitte, 2012). Individual stories of social and geographical mobility in the city revealed that processes of suburbanization were to be understood as part of collective diasporic narratives of social advancement.

Similarly, in using digital storytelling (DS) in a project looking at migrant women working in the voluntary sector in London from a feminist perspective (Vachelli and Peyrefitte, 2018), we uncovered intersubjectivity in the construction of their narratives. The process of DS is premised on the use of digital technology as well as participatory approaches, and the co-production of personal stories. This unique approach, which results in the creation of a 2–5 minute audio-visual clip, supported, in our case, the voices and the stories of women whose roles too often remain invisible. Despite diverse experiences of migration and then of work in the voluntary sector with migrant organizations, their stories all expressed the gendered challenges of structural inequalities and their impact on work trajectories in a migratory context.

In both of these projects, individual biographies unveiled the intersubjectivity of narratives that are formed at the crossroad between the individual and the collective experience of migration. In both these research projects, objects and artefacts also played a part in coaxing stories. In DS, participants are asked to bring an object to initiate the formulation of their individual biography in the first stage of the process, called the 'story circle' (Hartley and McWilliam, 2009). In the study we conducted using DS, participants were asked to bring an object that had particular significance in relation to their experience of migration and work in the United Kingdom (UK). In facilitating storytelling, objects and artefacts can be used in semi-structured and life-story interviews as well as in other creative methods such as home tours, photo-elicitation interviews, DS and body-mapping. In all cases, objects provide a point of reflection, a mnemonic connection in creating a space for the story to unfold. It can be particularly useful to include in the research process the objects and artefacts people travel with, acquire during their journey or obtain as they make a home in the country they settle in.

In doing so, it is important to consider the quotidian materiality of home and belonging in what Brah calls 'homing desire' in 'diaspora space'. This 'includes the entanglement of genealogies of dispersion with those of 'staying put' (Brah, 1996: 181). McMillan's (2009) archival study and installations exemplify this by powerfully recreating the idiosyncrasies of front rooms as decorated by migrants from the West Indies. The material and visual culture of the front room is for him an example of the ways in which British working-class and migrant aesthetics intersect in the vernacular domesticity of the home. The home and its materiality is the everyday expression of the connections that constitute homing desire in the diaspora (Brah, 1996). Tolia-Kelly (2004a, 2004b, 2004c) exemplifies these scales of connection and belonging in her investigation of visual and material cultures within South Asian women's homes in London. She is particularly attentive to the multi-sensorial connections of lived landscapes in colonial territories as they are integrated into the home through various artefacts 'materialising post-colonial geographies' (Tolia-Kelly, 2004a). Conducting 'biographical mapping', Tolia-Kelly (2004b) further interrogates the connections to different landscapes that have meaning in the South Asian diaspora and how these play a role in 'shaping diasporic geographies of belonging and being within the UK' (2004b: 277). She considers domestic materiality as 'precipates of re-memory as they figure as social heritage' (Tolia-Kelly, 2004c: 326).

Diasporic narratives are constituted at the temporal and spatial interstice of individual, familial and collective memory and re-memory. In this discussion it is important to consider memory and memory work in the way they can be connected to the more invisible aspects of identity formation. They should be uncovered by a more creative approach in the research design in engaging in sociological attentiveness and exercising sociological imagination as we have discussed so far in light of Smart (2014) in conversation with Gordon (2008). In this exercise, objects help probe, explore and conjure up different forms of knowledge at the stage of data collection. The 'exploratory analysis' (Smart, 2014: 147) of the stories connected to the objects must then pay attention to the haunting experience of migration over the experience of home-making and identity formation. In my doctoral study, it was evident that memories of migration were for instance shared across generations. This was most notably revealed in a home tour followed by a photo-elicitation interview with a second-generation Sikh participant. The most cherished objects in the house were a clock that had travelled with the family since the Partition, a family portrait and a photograph of his grandfather, both taken in India before they migrated to the UK. These objects and the stories associated with them were meaningful in the construction of his biography and to his sense of identity, home and belonging, and were analysed as a material and symbolic expression of intersubjective and intergenerational diasporic connection.

Objects are, however, not simply there to coax, as they are an integral part of the story and hold a value in themselves – an agency. For those who wish to pursue that method of enquiry, I want to point out a more recent contribution made by Holmes (Holmes and Hall, 2020), who argues for object-focused research that pays equal attention to the subject and the object and advocates an approach in object interviewing that covers materiality, practice and biography. More broadly, objects can be seen as the material signifiers of journeys and flows in the different 'scapes' of globalization (Appadurai, 1990). Applying an attentive sociological imagination to the analysis of stories connected to objects then works to reveal important aspects of the everyday lived experiences of global processes. In light of my research, I concentrated on individual and collectively shared experiences of migration and diaspora. More generally, I tried and demonstrated the potential of 'following the story' and storytelling in bringing to light intersubjectivity and ultimately the way stories are to be situated within the workings of global structures, flows, mobilities and connections.

FINAL REMARKS AND FURTHER REFLECTIONS

It would be presumptuous to give solutions on the methodological dilemmas of researching globalization, as it is pervasive, multifarious and thus the source of a wide range of research questions that must find methodological rationales that are specifically tailored to them. In all cases, it is essential to adapt to the context of the research and the research question(s) – in increments perhaps – responding gradually to the field, the participants and sometimes adapting to emerging issues. Quoting Mills (1959: 121), whose sociological imagination forms the foundations of the meta-argument of this chapter:

> every working social scientist must be his own methodologist and his own theorist, which means only that he must be an intellectual craftsman. Every craftsman can of course learn something from over-all attempts to codify methods, but it is often not much more than a general kind of awareness. That is why 'crash programs' in methodology are not likely to help social science to develop. Really useful accounts of methods cannot be forced in that way, if they are very firmly related to the actual working of social study, a sense of significant problem and the passion to solve it – nowadays so often lost – cannot be allowed full play in the mind of the working social scientist.

At the centre of a commitment to carefully adapt methods to the research question(s) and context, the sociological imagination offers a compass that I argue should be orientated towards the importance of working with stories and storytelling in line with Smart (2010, 2014) and Gordon (2008). Qualitative sociologists can continue to make a key contribution to a sociology of globalization by telling and connecting stories using a sociological imagination that is attentive and sensitive to intersubjectivity and the way stories are to be situated within the (visible or invisible, spoken or unspoken) workings of global structures, flows, mobilities and connections. This contribution will be sustained by a continued effort to question and reflect upon the ways in which, through storytelling, research representations express the complexity of identity and culture in relation to the social structures of a globalized world – finding new and creative ways to write and represent the stories while thinking about knowledge production in ways that contest forms of marginalization, stigmatization or injustice which are either exacerbated or created by globalization. These considerations can also be attentive to long-standing postcolonial and poststructuralist reflections on the role of the ethnographer or qualitative researcher and their relationship to the researched/observed (Clifford, 1988). The 'politics of knowledge production' from a postcolonial perspective (Bhambra, 2007) are to be contended with, considering subaltern or marginalized stories and how they are to be acknowledged by a sociology truly reflective of its power in its Eurocentric tendencies and in some of its methodological canons.

The recognition of different ways of knowing may also imply that sociologists consider stories that already exist in the public domain independent of an academic framework and a 'systematic academic enquiry' (Appadurai, 2000: 13). We can look at fictions, various texts of popular culture and artistic outputs as storytelling translating global and diasporic connections found through different channels and media. Artists and writers contribute to incorporate more marginalized points of view and their voices often play a key role in putting the subject at the centre of the debate as opposed to being an object of research. The sociological approach can work in dialogue with other disciplines, especially as sociological storytelling entails a constant reflection on the representation of different voices.

The digital connectivity offered by globalization is another horizon to be explored qualitatively with the emergence of a range of new media and technologies where groups and individuals write their own narratives. Greater connectivity and networking opportunities through information technologies also present advantages in global forms of activism and protest. The Arab Spring is a good example of a social movement that spread across different nation-states and needed both social media and the physical space of streets, parks and squares to exist. In recent years, a globalization of protests can more generally be observed with, for instance, the 2018 Women's March, the climate change strikes during the 'Global Week for the Future' in September 2019 and the 'Black Lives Matter' movement in 2020. The streets of cities across the world have been global in their revindication and dissent.

Sassen (2001b: 588) points out a 'growth of networked cross-border dynamics among global cities' that can notably facilitate activism. In parallel, the global city (Sassen, 2001a) is constantly shaped and reshaped by the social inequalities engendered by the global flows of neoliberal capitalism. The 2007–2009 financial crisis intensified levels of global inequality (see Schuerkens, 2017: 72, 111) ensuing a wave of protests that were 'nationally driven but globally conscious movements' (Burawoy, 2015: 16). In a late capitalist era defined by a global search for profit, these levels of inequality have persisted as a new crisis is emerging as a result of the COVID-19 global pandemic. Beyond the more visible protests and social movements, a sociology of globalization must address local expressions of globalization and its everyday lived reality through a methodology that pays attention to the stories of those who are most directly affected by it at the intersection of different social factors.

REFERENCES

Appadurai, A. (1990). 'Disjuncture and Differences in the Global Cultural Economy', *Theory, Culture and Society*, 7: 295–310.
Appadurai, A. (2000). 'Grassroots Globalisation and the Research Imagination', *Public Culture*, 12(1): 1–19.

Back, L. (2007). *The Art of Listening*, Oxford: Berg.

Bauman, Z. and May, T. (2001). *Thinking Sociologically*, Oxford: Blackwell.

Bhambra, G. (2007). *Rethinking Modernity: Postcolonialism and the Sociological Imagination*, Basingstoke: Palgrave Macmillan.

Brah, A. (1996). *Cartographies of Diaspora: Contesting Identities*, London: Routledge.

Brown, G.W. and Labonté, R. (2011). 'Globalization and Its Methodological Discontents: Contextualizing Globalization through the Study of HIV/AIDS, *Globalization and Health*, 7(29): 2–12.

Burawoy, M. (2000). 'Introduction: Reaching for the Global', in M. Burawoy, J.A. Blum, S. George, Z. Gille, T. Gowan, L. Haney et al. (eds), *Global Ethnography: Forces, Connections and Imaginations in a Postmodern World*, London: University of California Press, pp. 1–40.

Burawoy, M. (2015). 'Facing an Unequal World', *Current Sociology*, 63(1): 5–34.

Burton, S. (2016). Becoming Sociological: Disciplinarity and Sense of Home, *Sociology*, 50(5): 984–992.

Clifford, J. (1988). *The Predicament of Culture: Twentieth Century Ethnography, Literature and Art*, *Cambridge*, MA: Harvard University Press.

Crenshaw, K. (2017). *On Intersectionality: Essential Writings*, New York: The New Press.

Gordon, A. (2008). *Ghostly Matters: Haunting and the Sociological Imagination*, London: University of Minnesota Press.

Hartley, J. and McWilliam, K. (eds) (2009). *Story Circle: Digital Storytelling around the World*, Hoboken, NJ: John Wiley and Sons.

Holmes, H. and Hall, S.M. (2020). *Mundane Methods: Innovative Ways to Research the Everyday*, Manchester: Manchester University Press.

Knowles, C. (2010). 'Mobile Sociology: Commentary on John Urry's Work', *British Journal of Sociology*, 61: 373–379.

Marcus, G.E. (1995). 'Ethnography in/of World System: The Emergence of Multi-Sited Ethnography', *Annual Review of Anthropology*, 24: 95–117.

McMillan, M. (2009). *The Front Room: Migrant Aesthetics in the Home*, London: Blackdog Publishing.

Mills, C. Wright (1959). *The Sociological Imagination*, Oxford: Oxford University Press.

Peyrefitte, M. (2012). 'Ways of Seeing, Ways of Being and Ways of Knowing in the Inner-City: Exploring Sense of Place through Visual Tours', *Sociological Research Online*, 17(4).

Sassen, S. (2001a). *The Global City*, Oxford: Princeton University Press.

Sassen, S. (2001b). 'Cities: Capital, Global and World', in *International Encyclopedia of the Social and Behavioral Sciences*, 2nd edition, Volume 3, pp. 1808–1816.

Schuerkens, U. (2017). *Social Changes in a Global World*, London: Sage.

Smart, C. (2010). *Disciplined Writing: On the Problem of Writing Sociologically*, Southampton: ESRC National Centre for Research Methods.

Smart, C. (2014). 'Fragments: Living with Other People's Lives as Analytical Practice', in C. Smart, J. Hockey and A. James (eds), *The Craft of Knowledge: Experiences of Living with Data*, Basingstoke: Palgrave Macmillan, pp. 131–148.

Sullivan, S. and Brockington, D. (2004). 'Qualitative Methods in Globalisation Studies; or Saying Something about the World without Counting or Inventing It', Working Paper No. 139/04, Centre for the Study of Globalisation and Regionalisation.

Tolia-Kelly, D.P. (2004a). 'Materializing Post-Colonial Geographies: Examining the Textural Landscapes of Migration in the South Asian Home', in *Geoforum*, 35, 675–688.

Tolia-Kelly, D.P. (2004b). 'Landscape, Race and Memory: Biographical Mapping of the Routes of British Asian Landscape Values', *Landscape Research*, 29(3), 277–292.

Tolia-Kelly, D.P. (2004c). 'Locating Processes of Identification: Studying the Precipitates of Re-memory through Artefacts in the British Asian Home', *Transactions of the Institute of British Geographers*, 29, 314–329.

Vacchelli, E. and Peyrefitte, M. (2018). 'Telling Digital Stories as Feminist Research and Practice: A Two-Day Workshop with Migrant Women in London', *Methodological Innovations*, 11(1), 1–11.

PART II

(INFRA)STRUCTURAL PARAMETERS

3. Work and employment in a globalizing age
David Pick

INTRODUCTION

Six decades of intensifying globalization has transformed social, economic and cultural relations at every scale. One of the most affected areas of social and economic relations is work and employment. Initially, globalization promised much. With expanding markets, the global spread of contemporary Western European norms about improving working conditions and wages promised rising socio-economic standards that would lift millions of people out of penury. It was assumed that while the rich might get richer, the poor would also receive a share of the economic spoils of global growth. The research evidence of the past two decades, however, points to a failure of this globalization project. Early this century, Stiglitz (2002, p. 214) argued that 'Globalization is not working for many of the world's poor'. On revisiting the topic, Stiglitz (2018) contends that not only has globalization failed the poor, but its negative effects have spread to the prosperous industrialized nations of Europe, North America and the western Pacific that had previously been its main beneficiaries. This spread of negative effects is reflected in a widening and deepening of inequalities within and between nations (Bieler & Lindberg, 2010) that accelerated after the Global Financial Crisis of 2008. This trend has been accompanied by political upheaval over the last five years not seen since the 1930s. The rise of populist and authoritarian governments around the world and the pursuit of nationalist, isolationist political agendas (e.g., Brexit and Trumpism) has disturbed the stability of global relations. In 2020, the world entered uncharted territory as the COVID-19 epidemic cut a swathe through economies and disrupted global trade. This has left workers in many nations without the means to make a living and without a social security safety net. In light of these trends, the aim of this chapter is to map out research that identifies the drivers, processes, consequences and possible futures of globalization for work and employment relations since the Global Financial Crisis up to the present.

DRIVERS

Neoliberalism

Over the past three decades, neoliberal-inspired policies have been applied broadly and deeply in a wide array of policy areas by international, national, state and local governments. Neoliberal policies are essentially about shrinking the size and role of the state. They are characterized by the adoption of tight fiscal discipline (sometimes dubbed 'austerity') that limits the provision of welfare and public health services, privatization and contracting out government-run organizations that provide goods and services (e.g., transport, health, prisons, education, housing) and the deregulation of markets (e.g., finance, banking, labour, trade, retail). While the deregulation of labour markets has had the most directs effect on employment, reductions in welfare provision and the privatization of government services have intensified the effects of deregulation by diminishing social safety nets (e.g., income support, social services) and employment protections (e.g., unfair dismissal laws, trade union rights) that go well beyond the workplace to impact on family life (Harvey, 2005; Kalleberg & Hewison, 2013; Stiglitz, 2002, 2018).

Globalized Production

The globalization of production has continued at pace over the past decade to the extent that now over two-thirds of world trade crosses at least one national border before final assembly and delivery to market (Dollar, 2019). Understanding this phenomenon is therefore important when considering the effects of globalization on work and employment. Examining globalized production patterns has been of interest to scholars but there are a number of different terms that are used in relation to this. They are sometime used interchangeably and it is useful to provide definitions of the most used terms before proceeding further.

The first is global commodity chain (GCC). This refers to coordinated and internationally dispersed production activities dedicated to specific commodities (e.g., coffee, chocolate, minerals) or manufactured goods (e.g., computers, clothing, furniture) (Raikes et al., 2000). The second is global supply chain (GSC). This refers to a globally dispersed, linear chain of design, planning, production, distribution and consumption of goods and services. The difference between a GSC and a GCC is that in a supply chain there is communication of information between the echelons (stages) of production (Beaman, 1999). In a contemporary GSC model (GSC 4.0) there is widespread application of information communications technology (e.g., internet of things, big data analysis, autonomous robotics) forming a non-linear, networked integrated supply chain in which information can pass up and down the supply chain while centralized information collection nodes are employed to monitor the whole GSC in real time (Dollar, 2019). The third term often used is global value chain (GVC). This refers to the ways in which the global activities are dispersed with the aim of creating, adding and capturing value at each stage of the production process (Henderson et al., 2002). This is different again from a GCC and a GSC in that the focus goes beyond how production is organized (GCC) and how it is organized, managed, monitored and controlled (GSC). A GVC draws attention to the seeking of efficiencies in production and lowering costs as much as possible. This means splitting the chain of production into different specialized parts depending on the technology required, the skilled labour needed, the ability of management to deploy just-in-time organization and where labour is appropriately flexible (Islam, 2015).

While GCCs, GSCs and GVCs have received much attention, their analytical power has been brought into question. Henderson et al. (2002) argue that it would be better to use the term 'network' rather than 'chain' because the latter implies a vertical and linear characteristic. They contend that global production is more than links between firms in various places and that we must also include the differing national social and institutional contexts within which firms in production chains are embedded. Instead, Henderson et al. (2002) suggest that the term global production network (GPN) should be used as a more accurate representation of the multi-scalar spatial dimensions and relational scope of globalized production. The GPN idea has been significantly developed and accepted since it was first introduced in the early 2000s, especially by Yeung and Coe (2015) and Coe and Yeung (2019). The notion of GPN 2.0 (Coe & Yeung, 2019) has gained traction recently. This develops the original GPN heuristic to focus on exploring causative relationships, especially in relation to social connectedness, social relations and the embeddedness of GPNs in social relationships beyond the commercial sphere (e.g., gendered labour, CSR, codes of conduct) (Reinecke et al., 2018). The influence of GPN 2.0 on research is evidenced by the inclusion of network concepts in the development of GSC 4.0 discussed earlier.

Research into GCCs, GSCs, GVCs and GPNs strongly suggests that the globalization of production is an important driver of change to work and employment internationally. In recent times, the global dispersion of production has continued as global businesses seek out the lowest cost locations for each stage of the production process that in turn are connected to a global division of labour that has profound and often negative impacts on labour market processes and outcomes (Dollar, 2019; Islam, 2015).

PROCESSES

While the processes of economic globalization associated with work and employment have been of major interest to researchers, this volume is concerned with social processes. In light of the drivers discussed in the previous section, the focus of this section is necessarily on examining the major processes affecting social relations at work and beyond. Current research evidence points to five processes that have been identified to occur at a range of scales from the international to the individual level.

The Global Spread of Advanced Footloose Capital

The application of information and communication technology and the widespread liberalization of foreign investment rules around the globe have allowed capital to become highly mobile (Cumbers et al., 2016), leading to a constant disruption of organizations in GSCs. This means that firms competing for business in GSCs are squeezing their costs to ward off being undercut by a rival. This increasingly competitive environment (Ayaz et al., 2019) is exerting continuous downward pressure on conditions of employment worldwide because an important element in the search for cost reduction is labour. Actions by businesses include downsizing (automation), outsourcing (contracting out), importing foreign (cheaper) labour and offshoring work (such as call centres) (Reinecke et al., 2018). These have the effect of putting pressure on existing workers to accept reduced standards of pay and conditions to gain employment if they are out of work or avoid redundancy if they are in work.

Local Embedding of GSCs

This process might better be described as 're-embedding' after an initial process of disembedding GSCs through economic globalization. This first disembedding process is a 'lifting out' (Giddens, 1994) of domestic supply chains from their existing local, spatial and temporal contexts as they reorganize themselves to serve the demands of global capitalism. This breaks local attachments of businesses leaving them untethered from their location. The second process is re-embedding of GSCs in particular locations as businesses establish strategic alliances and partnerships with governments, suppliers, labour agencies, etc. (Seal et al., 2004). As this economic re-embedding takes place, there is also a wider process of re-embedding

GSCs as they become part of the local ecosystem of social relations and institutional norms and expectations (e.g., female labour hiring practices, corporate social responsibility, local politics) (Reinecke et al., 2018). This has the effect of quilting GSCs into their production locations where they can influence their local social conditions (e.g., labour law) but they can also be influenced by their local social conditions (e.g., regulation, social action).

Destabilization of National Employment Regulation

This phenomenon has been recognized as a growing problem worldwide. It was originally found mainly in developing nations but has now spread globally. Pressures arising from the need to remain internationally competitive in GPNs and GSCs have led nations to establish free trade agreements in goods and services that often include the loosening of restrictions on the movement of labour across international boundaries. These free trade agreements have often required nations to deregulate their employment laws. This, when coupled with migration, has increased competition within national labour markets and has forced people to accept more flexible, insecure employment and lower pay and conditions (Maerdi & Marginson, 2014). The fragmentation and specialization of production and an intensification of competition within GPNs and GSCs exacerbate this process of destabilization. This is in turn paralleled by a fragmentation and specialization of a demand for labour. The environment is then a fragmented and localized patchwork of casualized and informalized labour markets that disempower labour in favour of capital (Bieler & Lindberg, 2010; Todd et al., 2020).

The Establishment of Global Labour Networks

The fragmentation of production within GSCs and GPNs has presented significant problems for organized labour. This is problematic because the exploitation of labour is central to value creation, capture and transfer (Cumbers et al., 2008) and has been an abiding feature of the architecture of GSCs and GPNs, particularly those businesses located in developing nations (see, e.g., Alamgir & Banerjee, 2019). The response to exploitative labour practices has been the establishment of transnational labour networks, for example the global framework agreements devised by trade unions that specify minimum agreed labour standards in a GPN (Cumbers et al., 2008). These have developed more recently into agreements forged by Global Union Federations that are more responsive to the fluid nature of GPN and GSC structures, especially in the area of embedding local practices within agreements (Helfen & Fichter, 2013). These global labour networks are now morphing into organizational forms that mirror more closely the fluid nature of GPNs and GSCs, particularly in terms of engaging in multi-scalar coordination activities such as forming cross-organizational networks and alliances within GPNs and GSCs, international strategy formation in GVCs and working beyond established institutions such as trade unions, non-governmental organizations (NGOs), etc. and instead focusing on grassroots organizations (Zajak et al., 2017).

Labour Becoming an Actor within GPNs and GSCs

The status of labour as the main source of value creation in GSCs and GPNs means that workers have a high-level scope for agency. It is interesting to note here that so far, this agency potential has been largely constrained by the actions of GPNs in concert with international,

national and local institutions and structures that act as subordinates to global pressures in supply chains (Todd et al., 2020). It remains the case though that there are leverage points in GSCs where labour agency can be most effective, particularly at choke points (e.g., supply chain logistics arteries and hubs) (Alford et al., 2017) or where there might be labour shortages in particular occupations (e.g., train drivers) (Cumbers et al., 2016). It is at these types of juncture where the logic of global capital intersects with local social, cultural and economic contexts and in which labour agency can arise (Ayaz et al., 2019), especially when it is connected to wider supportive campaigns (Cumbers et al., 2010). Labour agency in GPNs and GSCs seems to occur where there exists networked translocal action across spatial and organizational boundaries that support grassroots interventions (Cumbers et al., 2016). The development of this type of agency can be seen where individuals and groups of workers take collective action to create new products, services and networks that assist them in shaping how they are incorporated into GSCs and GPNs (Alford et al., 2019). How and to what extent labour agency develops, however, depends on variations in worker age, education, gender, locality, migration history, skills and expertise (Pun et al., 2020).

OUTCOMES

Outcomes for Individuals

One of the major outcomes of globalization in work and employment for individuals is the growth of precarious work. Precarious work emerged as a response by businesses to intensifying competition in supply chains that forced down market prices and to government policies that severely limited welfare provisions (Sifaki, 2019). It replaces the 'standard employment relationship' with a range of employment conditions including sub-contracting, labour hire agencies, casual work, temporary migrant work and limited-term contracts. These are characterized by uncertainty, instability and insecurity as employees bear the risks of work and receive limited entitlements (e.g., sick pay, holiday pay, superannuation, etc.) and social welfare support (Kalleberg & Hewison, 2013). While precarious work was previously common in developing nations, it has spread to wealthier nations over the past two decades. In Australia, 25 per cent of workers are employed on a casual basis (OECD, 2019). This growth of precarious work has been associated with tensions between different groups of workers, for example migrant workers being accused of undercutting local labour by accepting reduced pay and conditions (Alford et al., 2017). It has also been seen to be associated with a more disciplined workforce willing to accept slow wage growth and limits on the ability to form collective organizations at work (Kalleberg & Hewison, 2013).

Societal Outcomes

The broader social outcomes of the globalization of work and employment are associated with the spread of precarious work. This can be seen as a way of defining certain workers as 'disposable', consigning them to economic subordination, and it disproportionally affects vulnerable and minority groups such as women (e.g., Ayaz et al., 2019; Sifaki, 2019) and migrant workers (e.g., Alford et al., 2017). This can then accentuate existing inequality and social precarity and, as such, it can be argued that precarious work is a social bad (Siegmann

& Schiphorst, 2016) that has many social dimensions including unfree labour, repression of organized labour, capture of the state by GPNs and increasing social inequality within and between regions.

Unfree labour is essentially when a person is coerced or tricked into becoming trapped in an exploitative relationship with an employer that they cannot escape from (Barrientos, 2013). It can be seen in a range of employment modes from involuntary exploitation (e.g., modern slavery), through debt bondage, to exploitative employment contracts that preclude entry to other forms of employment (e.g., zero-hour contracts). In the Global North, unfree labour is concentrated among migrants engaged in work that is often harsh, degrading and in dangerous conditions that violate labour and human rights in industries such as construction, cleaning, care, agriculture, food production, hospitality, domestic service and sex work (Lewis et al., 2015; Strauss, 2017). It is these people who are the most vulnerable, especially if they are undocumented. It is often the case that unfree labour is sourced through labour contractors and third-party agents who deal in debt bondage and transnational trafficking. Migrant workers can find themselves in debt through very high interest rates on loans, placement fees, high charges for rent, travel, training, documentation and so on (Barrientos, 2013). The person then becomes trapped through threats or acts of violence (sometimes sexual) and penalties including withholding identity documents or threats of reporting them to the authorities (Lewis et al., 2015). The situation in the Global South is similar but often more extreme and it is more common to find instances in GSCs in which women are more vulnerable than men because of their unequal position within society (Le Baron & Gore, 2020). Overall, globally, the prevalence of unfree labour tends to be associated with the intersection of migrant status and gender where undocumented migrants and women are most at risk.

The spread of precarious work has been accompanied by an intensification of socio-economic inequality that is underpinned by asymmetries in market power, social power and political power to the extent that inequality and asymmetries of power are foundational to the functioning of GPNs and GVCs (Phillips, 2017). This is especially evident in the Global South where widely unequal power relationships between large corporations and those involved in production are common. Vicol and colleagues (2019) report disparities of land ownership, income, social status and educational opportunities between poor landless people and smallholders reliant on agricultural production and those who own larger areas of land and have diversified economic means. Alamgir and Bannerjee (2019) present similar evidence in the garment manufacturing sector in Bangladesh where power is exercised to ensure that most of the value created in the supply chain is captured by Western brands and retailers. Here, it is found that power is exercised through three regimes: a state regime established by a combination of the ruling political party working closely with peak industry associations to create supply chains that suit large multinational corporations; regimes of representation that exclude organizations that work in the best interests of employees; and regimes of compliance that ensure any efforts to improve working conditions through regulation have only limited effect. What we see is a continuing draining of life from those government and non-government institutions that are charged with addressing socio-economic inequality through the provision of social welfare, protecting and enhancing working conditions and protecting vulnerable people (Kalleberg & Hewison, 2013).

FUTURE PROSPECTS FOR REFORM AND IMPROVEMENT

The previous sections are reflective of the large body of research evidence which suggests that the future globalization of work and employment will produce a broadening and further intensification of exploitative labour practices that will most likely be associated with deepening socio-economic inequalities. The COVID-19 pandemic has disrupted global production and value chains, putting in jeopardy the future prospects of vulnerable and marginalized workers and the communities in which they live. These vulnerable people are seeing efforts to improve their employment conditions threatened as businesses focus on surviving the convulsions rippling through GSCs (Frenkel & Schuessler, 2021; Majumdar et al., 2020). It also seems that COVID-19 heralded the beginning of a rearrangement of GSCs driven by an accelerated application of robotics and artificial intelligence. This increasing use of advanced automation is progressively normalizing machine-dominated business supply chain operations and has the potential to transform the nature of work and employment in ways that could further disadvantage workers (Lin, 2021). How this plays out will only be fully understood in hindsight. One ray of optimism can however be found in a small but growing area of research that points to hopes of a renaissance of labour agency and an increasing willingness and capacity of NGOs, unions and governments to intervene in GPNs and GVCs to improve working conditions.

As global production became more fragmented but at the same time networked, the agency of workers became weaker. In response, those institutions representing workers' interests were forced to take on new forms. In the first two decades of the twenty-first century trade unions formed global union federations and transnational union networks in an attempt to mirror the fluid, cross-border structures of GPNs and GVCs. This led to the establishment of global framework agreements that addressed workers' rights and conditions of employment (Helfen & Fichter, 2013). While this helped trade unions coordinate across national borders, they have not been able to keep up with the rapid changes that can occur in GPNs and GVCs. More recently, labour agency has moved beyond traditional trade union structures and become more fluid. Where trade unions have organized into new spatial forms, in different places and across social divides (e.g., class, race and gender) by deploying social media and other electronic communication strategies, they have also become more successful (Cumbers et al., 2016). These emerging forms of labour agency seem to be most successful when founded on community-based action that is then scaled up in conjunction with trade unions, NGOs, etc. and focused on leverage (or choke) points in a GVC where interventions have the most effect (Alford et al., 2017). These can be called networks of labour activism and include various types of organization from the grassroots level of individual workers, community organizations, NGOs and transnational trade unions (Zajak et al., 2017). These transnational networking capabilities of labour hold most hope for workers' efforts to improve regulation of their wages and conditions, although more research needs to be conducted in this area (Hastings, 2019).

One other area of hope for future improvements for workers is in the emergence of global labour governance. This idea has gained more traction over the past five years in response to the need for more concerted action to address exploitative labour practices in GPNs/GSCs. Maerdi and Marginson (2014) argue that the idea of global labour governance is underpinned by three assumptions: (1) that globalized production necessarily creates problems for labour; (2) that it assumes that existing national and international forms of governance are not sufficient to tackle these problems; and (3) that there is a need for international coordination and new governance structures that will help establish internationally shared understandings about what fair labour standards are. The imperative of implementing good governance practices by lead firms in GPNs relates to maintaining good customer and supplier relationships (Gereffi & Lee, 2016). The reputational risk to these lead firms is such that it can be used as leverage by stakeholders, such as trade unions, in the quest to secure improved wages and working conditions (Wright, 2016).

Recent research has explored the ideas advanced by Maerdi and Marginson (2014). Helfen et al. (2018) describe how employment relations could contribute to enhancing labour standards and social responsibility practices in GSCs through multi-stakeholder initiatives that include external, non-firm actors. They cite the example of IKEA, a large multinational retail chain that uses its considerable buying power to leverage improvements to labour standards among businesses in its supply chain. Helfen et al. (2018) argue that networked configurations of labour governance and practice need to mirror the networks of global production to be most effective. This is reflected in the work of Thomas and Turnbull (2018), who contend that this networked governance works well when it has a vertical structure along the supply chain (e.g., Maritime Labour Convention and Global Supply Chain Standards). These efforts can be reinforced through combining buyer codes with supplier voluntary commitments, such as voluntary labour codes/certification backed up by independent verification (Jayasinghe & Hunter, 2020).

One important element of global labour governance is the role of the brokers who span and facilitate business between firms in a GPN/GSC. These include supply chain managers, labour supply brokers, sourcing agents, NGOs and national governments that establish and maintain trust, coordination and social connections between businesses (Reinecke et al., 2018). Soundrarajan et al. (2018) contend that labour-sourcing agents can and do ensure the implementation of policies and practices that improve working conditions because they understand local conditions and, because they are trusted, they can establish common understandings about fair working conditions and wages. However, as Munir et al. (2018) argue, these intermediaries, as they call them, could also work against workers' interests by promulgating an agenda that favours the economic interests of the social elite. Therefore, those acting as brokers in GPNs/GSCs must have legitimacy (i.e., act in the interest of good labour governance) to create trust and a capacity to engage in effective boundary spanning (Reinecke et al., 2018; Soundrarajan et al., 2018).

CONCLUSION

The story so far in the globalization of work and employment in the twenty-first century is (with the exception of mobile, highly qualified professionals) mainly one of exploitation. This exploitation can be seen as an inevitable and, perhaps, necessary consequence of the governance arrangements and organizational practices in GPNs and GSCs. The priority has been, and remains, the maximizing of profit margins that benefit a wealthy elite over the implementation of fair work practices. This is because of the relational, networked character of GPNs and GSCs in which powerful social, economic and political interests work together to position workers as having little or no agency to influence their terms and conditions of employment. While the outlook seems bleak, there are glimmers of hope. It is this networked, relational nature of global production that provides a space for working people to bring about change for the better. Research suggests that labour agency might be effectively exerted at 'choke points' in GSCs, through networked international action and through establishing new forms of global labour governance. It is interesting to note here that most of the research discussed in this chapter might be termed 'pre-COVID-19'. As more studies emerge, a fuller picture of the work and employment landscape in GPNs and GSCs post-COVID-19 should emerge. While there is much to be concerned about, there is also some room for optimism that the turmoil caused by the pandemic might provide an impetus for global action to improve the conditions for vulnerable people employed in precarious work.

REFERENCES

Alamgir, F., & Banerjee, S. B. (2019). 'Contested compliance in global production networks: Insights from the Bangladesh garment industry'. *Human Relations*, *72* (2), 272–297.

Alford, M., Barrientos, S., & Visser, M. (2017). 'Multi-scaler labour agency in global production networks: Contestation and crisis in the South African fruit sector'. *Development and Change*, *48* (4), 721–745.

Alford, M., Kothari, U., & Pottinger, L. (2019). 'Re-articulating labour in global production networks: The case of street traders in Barcelona'. *Society and Space*, *37* (6), 1081–1099.

Ayaz, M., Ashraf, M. J., & Hopper, T. (2019). 'Precariousness, gender, resistance and consent in the face of global production network's "reforms" of Pakistan's garment manufacturing industry'. *Work, Employment and Society*, *33* (6), 895–912.

Beaman, B. M. (1999). 'Designing the green supply chain'. *Logistics Information Management*, *12* (4), 332–342.

Barrientos, S. W. (2013). '"Labour chains": Analysing the role of labour contractors in global production networks'. *Journal of Development Studies*, *49* (8), 1058–1071.

Bieler, A., & Lindberg, I. (2010). 'Globalisation and the new challenges for transnational solidarity'. In A. Bieler & I. Lindberg (Eds), *Global Restructuring, Labour and the Challenges for Transnational Solidarity* (pp. 3–15). London: Routledge.

Coe, N., & Yeung, H. W. (2019). 'Global production networks: Mapping recent conceptual developments'. *Journal of Economic Geography*, *19* (4), 775–801.

Cumbers, A., Nativel, C., & Routledge, P. (2008). 'Labour agency and union positionalities in global production networks'. *Journal of Economic Geography*, *8* (3), 369–387.

Cumbers, A., Mackinnon, D., & Shaw, J. (2010). 'Labour, organisational rescaling and the politics of production: Union renewal in the privatised rail industry'. *Work, Employment and Society*, *24* (1), 127–144.

Cumbers, A., Featherstone, D., Mackinnon, D., Ince, A., & Strauss, K. (2016). 'Intervening in globalization: The spatial possibilities and institutional barriers to labour's collective agency'. *Journal of Economic Geography*, *16* (1), 93–108.

Dollar, D. (2019). 'Executive summary'. In D. Dollar, E. Ganne, V. Stolzenburg & Z. Wang (Eds), *Technological Innovation, Supply Chain Trade and Workers in a Globalized World* (pp. 1–7). Geneva: World Trade Organization.

Frenkel, S. J., & Schuessler, E. S. (2021). 'From Rana Plaza to COVID-19: Deficiencies and opportunities for a new labour governance system in garment global supply chains'. *International Labour Review*, *160* (4), 591–609.

Gereffi, G., & Lee, J. (2016). 'Economic and social upgrading in global value chains and industrial clusters: Why governance matters'. *Journal of Business Ethics*, *133* (1), 25–38.

Giddens, A. (1994). 'Living in a post-traditionalist society'. In U. Beck, A. Giddens & S. Lash (Eds), *Reflexive Modernization: Politics, Tradition and Aesthetics in the Modern Social Order* (pp. 56–109). Cambridge: Polity Press.

Harvey, D. (2005). *A Brief History of Neoliberalism*. Oxford: Oxford University Press.

Hastings, T. (2019). 'Leveraging Nordic links: South African labour's role in regulating labour standards in wine global production networks'. *Journal of Economic Geography*, *19* (4), 921–942.

Helfen, M., & Fichter, M. (2013). 'Building transnational union networks across global production networks: Conceptualising a new arena of labour-management relations'. *British Journal of Employment Relations*, *51* (3), 553–576.

Helfen, M., Schussler, E., & Sydow, J. (2018). 'How can employment relations in global value networks be managed towards social responsibility?'. *Human Relations*, *71* (12), 1640–1665.

Henderson, J., Dicken, P., Hess, M., Coe, N., & Yeung, H. W. (2002). 'Global production networks and the analysis of economic development'. *Review of International Political Economy*, *9* (3), 436464.

Islam, R. (2015). *Globalization of Production, Work and Human Development: Is a Race to the Bottom Inevitable?* New York: UNDP.

Jayasinghe, M., & Hunter, L. W. (2020). 'The impact of suppliers' adoption of voluntary labour codes/certifications on job quality in global supply chains: The Sri Lankan case of Garments without Guilt'. *British Journal of Industrial Relations*, *58* (4), 844–873.

Kalleberg, A. L., & Hewison, K. (2013). 'Precarious work and the challenge for Asia'. *American Behavioral Scientist*, *57* (3), 271–288.

Le Baron, G., & Gore, E. (2020). 'Gender and forced labour: Understanding the links in global cocoa supply chains'. *Journal of Development Studies*, *26* (6), 1095–1117.

Lewis, H., Dwyer, P., Hodkinson, S., & Wiate, L. (2015). 'Hyper-precarious lives: Migrants and forced labour in the Global North'. *Progress in Human Geography*, *39* (5), 580–600.

Lin, W. (2021). 'Automated infrastructure: COVID-19 and the shifting geographies of supply chain capitalism'. *Progress in Human Geography*, *46* (2).

Maerdi, G., & Marginson, P. (2014). 'Global labour governance: Potential and limits of an emerging perspective'. *Work, Employment and Society*, *28* (4), 651–662.

Majumdar, A., Shaw, M. & Sinha, S. K. (2020). 'COVID-19 debunks the myth of socially sustainable supply chain: A case of the clothing industry in South Asian countries'. *Sustainable Production and Consumption*, *24*, 150–155.

Munir, K., Ayaz, M., Levy, D. L., & Willmott, H. (2018). 'The role of intermediaries in governance of global production networks: Restructuring work relations in Pakistan's apparel industry'. *Human Relations*, *71* (4), 560–583.

OECD (2019). *Employment Outlook 2019: The Future of Work*. Paris: OECD Publishing.

Phillips, N. (2017). 'Power and inequality in the global political economy'. *International Affairs*, *93* (2), 429–444.

Pun, N., Tse, T., Shin, V., & Fan, L. (2020). 'Conceptualising socio-economic formations of labour and workers' power in global production networks'. *Sociology*, *54* (4).

Raikes, P., Friis Jensen, M., & Ponte, S. (2000). 'Global commodity chain analysis and the French filière approach: Comparison and critique'. *Economy and Society*, *29* (3), 390–417.

Reinecke, J., Donaghey, J., Wilkinson, A., & Wood, G. (2018). 'Global supply chains and social relations at work: Brokering across boundaries'. *Human Relations*, *71* (4), 459–480.

Seal, W., Berry, A., & Cullen, J. (2004). 'Disembedding the supply chain: Institutional reflexivity and inter-firm accounting'. *Accounting, Organization and Society*, *29* (1), 73–92.

Siegmann, K. A., & Schiphorst, F. (2016). 'Understanding the globalizing precariat: From informal sector to precarious work'. *Progress in Development Studies*, *16* (2), 111–123.

Sifaki, E. (2019). 'Women's work and agency in GPNs during economic crises: The case of the Greek table grapes export sector'. *Feminist Economics*, *25* (3), 70–95.

Soundararajan, V., Khan, Z., & Tarba, S. Y. (2018). 'Beyond brokering: Sourcing agents, boundary work and working conditions in global supply chains'. *Human Relations*, *71* (4), 481–509.

Stiglitz, J. (2002). *Globalization and Its Discontents*. Camberwell: Penguin Allen Lane.

Stiglitz, J. (2018). *Globalization and Its Discontents Revisited: Anti-Globalization in the Era of Trump*. Melbourne, Victoria: Penguin.

Strauss, K. (2017). 'Sorting victims from workers: Forced labour trafficking, and the process of jurisdiction'. *Progress in Human Geography*, *41* (2), 140–158.

Thomas, H., & Turnbull, P. (2018). 'From horizontal to vertical labour governance: The International Labour Organization (ILO) and decent work in global supply chains'. *Human Relations*, *71* (4), 536 559.

Todd, P., Ellem, B., Goods, C., Rainnie, A., & Smith, L. (2020). 'Labour in global production networks: Workers and unions in mining engineering work'. *Economic and Industrial Democracy, 41* (1), 98–120.

Vicol, M., Fold, N., Pritchard, B., & Neilson, J. (2019). 'Global production networks, regional development trajectories and smallholder livelihoods in the Global South'. *Journal of Economic Geography, 19* (4), 973–993.

Wright, C. F. (2016). 'Leveraging reputational risk: Sustainable sourcing campaigns for improving labour standards in production networks'. *Journal of Business Ethics, 137* (1), 195–210.

Yeung, H. W. C., & Coe, N. (2015). 'Toward a dynamic theory of global production networks'. *Economic Geography, 91* (1), 29–58.

Zajak, S., Egels-Zanden, N., & Piper, N. (2017). 'Networks of labour activism – collective action across Asia and beyond: An introduction to the debate'. *Development and Change, 48* (5), 899–921.

4. Global commodity circuits

Craig Martin and Giovanni Marmont

INTRODUCTION

The global COVID-19 pandemic has affected so many aspects of the social, cultural, economic, environmental and political fabric of our lives. Where previous epidemics spread at much slower rates due to limited transnational transport networks, the spread of the SARS-CoV-2 virus exemplifies the interconnectedness of the global mobilities of people and goods. Freedom of movement – so central to the ideologies of global capital – has become an emblem of threat, of the uncontrolled distribution of the virus through the infrastructures of circulation. As Tim Cresswell noted, viruses themselves cannot travel, they require a host of sorts, be that from body to body or across larger-scale infrastructures at local, regional and global scales: 'today's highly mobile and interconnected world is the best kind of assemblage for viral mobilities' (Cresswell, 2020).

The virus highlights the tensions central to the operation of global mobility flows. On the one hand global trade relies on the efficiency of the supposed infrastructures of 'seamlessness' associated with global supply chain logistics. However, the virus, earlier epidemics (Ali and Keil, 2010) and other forms of risk such as geopolitical turmoil or natural disasters (Adey and Anderson, 2011) demonstrate the formidable vulnerability of global mobility systems. In the wake of the pandemic borders were closed to international travellers and travel bans enacted to curtail viral spread. Concomitant risk factors were perceivable in the movement of goods and commodities where the demand and supply side of global trade was severely impacted in 2020. According to the United Nations Conference on Trade and Development (UNCTAD), the flows in foreign direct investment as a marker of global trade were projected to decrease by 40 per cent in 2020 (UNCTAD, 2020: x). Global container trade volumes – another barometer of economic activity – saw a reduction in services between the Far East and Europe of up to 30 per cent (International Transport Forum, 2020: 2; also see Goodman et al., 2021). The UNCTAD report goes on to identify other structural factors which have the potential to disrupt global trade, including economic nationalism and protectionism. At a more situated level, fears over food supply and food security led to stockpiling of products by countries such as Vietnam, whilst export controls were introduced on medical products such as ventilators and personal protective equipment (PPE) (Gruszczynski, 2020: 339). The control of PPE procurement and distribution alerts us to the geopolitics of circulation. For instance, Angela Mitropoulos (2020: 99) describes how the United States (US) federal government's emergency supply chain unit facilitated the expansion of PPE, ventilator and test-kit markets through the use of favoured companies. As a result of the US dollar's relative value the US government intervened in the global sales of PPE, thus reshaping 'both supply-chains and markets' (Mitropoulos, 2020: 104). The geopolitics of commodity supply also played out in the uneven distribution of the COVID-19 vaccines, where national and supranational bodies such as the European Union (EU) were engaged in disputes over the production and distribution of vaccines (see Boffey, 2021).

Using the COVID-19 pandemic as a backdrop, this chapter addresses the spatialities of global commodity circuits, specifically the geographical reach of these global production networks and distribution infrastructures. Although the pandemic has profoundly illustrated the underlying risk factors affecting such tightly coupled spatial configurations, the chapter aims to provide an overview of the competing forces of global commodity circuits, both in terms of the logic of organization, control and securitization, but equally through envisioning this as a space of complexity, contestation and immanent fallibility.

We begin with a discussion of the origins of global commodity chains, whilst contrasting the metaphor of the 'chain' with that of commodity circuits and networks. Using these in a somewhat interchangeable manner, the opening section unpacks the key shifts in the rise of global trade, including the centrality of transnational corporations. Through their adaptability and flexibility these corporations affected a shift in the constitution of manufacturing bases from traditional 'core' territories to 'peripheral' economies. As such, we demonstrate how globalization might be described as the articulation of commodity production and consumption through practices of circulation.

Where these opening debates on the spatial configuration of global commodity circulation attempt to posit the 'shape' of globalization, the following section deals with the concrete practices of logistics and supply chain management. In doing so we argue – in straightforward terms – that logistics is concerned with the preparation, administration and implementation of physical and informational movement. Echoing this, Bruce Allen describes logistics as 'a multidisciplinary approach concerned with how to coordinate all purchasing, selling, and producing activities together in order to assemble and distribute the right products in the right amounts to the right locations in the right condition so as to maximize profits for the firm' (Allen, 1997: 116). However, given commercial logistics' origins in military logistics, such a definition fails to underscore how logistics embodies the strategic projection of power across geographical territory, by envisioning time and space as legible, manageable and calculable. Briefly summarizing the main arguments and intellectual strands animating critical scholarship on the subject, we go on to show how the quest for profit maximization operated through logistics is entirely reliant upon, and conductive to, various practices of extraction, exploitation and neocolonial dispossession as absolutely core to the globalizing flows of capital (e.g., Harney and Moten, 2013; Cowen, 2014; Chua et al., 2018; Mezzadra and Neilson, 2019; Archer, 2020). We build on such discussions in the third section by articulating the tensions at the heart of global commodity circulation and logistics through the *differential* nature of such practices.

In our concluding thoughts we will highlight two lines of inquiry that – particularly in the midst of the unfolding global pandemic – may serve to advance 'a critical engagement with logistics in its manifold forms' (Chua et al., 2018: 618): first, in the context of the COVID-19 pandemic we ask what the possible resurgence of inventory stockpiling may mean for a global system ostensibly reliant on continuous flows; and second, we shift our attention onto logistics as a terrain of political struggle, in order to consider how micro and macro forms of insurgency may hinge on interrupting or redirecting the circulation of commodities. Ultimately, it is our hope that this chapter will function as an introductory overview, rounding up a rich and rapidly growing set of debates that, albeit from a variety of perspectives, share a common awareness of commodity circuits' tremendous socio-political import.

SPATIO-TEMPORALITIES OF GLOBAL COMMODITY CIRCUITS

As the implications of PPE supply and fears over food security testify to, the interrelationship between production, distribution and consumption is dependent on the transnational circulation of goods and services. When these are disrupted the fallibility of this tightly bound interconnectivity becomes ever more apparent. In large part this is a result of the interrelated and integrated aspects of globalization and its attendant economic, cultural and political processes.

Writing of the geographical connectivity enacted through globalization, Sack describes how this 'set in motion a series of connections among extraction, production, and distribution, which occurs from one place to another, and each place is transformed by these connections' (Sack, 1997: 242). The spatio-temporalities of globalization are clearly evident in this description and speak to the broader shifts in the changing constitution of commodity mobilities under the auspice of globalization. Significant structural changes at the political, economic and spatial level need to be briefly posited. In particular there is a move away from a world economy operating across national borders towards integrated global circuits. Very much parallel to this is the profound dominance of globalized systems of production and financial services. As Dicken argues, a geographical outsourcing of production shifts manufacturing bases in the Global North to the so-called 'peripheries' of the Global South (Dicken, 2011: 14; see also Hardt and Negri, 2000: 294). Aligned to this are flexible approaches to manufacturing where changes in production tooling for example can be expedited in relatively quick time. New forms of worker domination, insecurity and inequality are central to the flexibility of labour itself with a loss of unionized and organized representation, leading inevitably to forms of precarity (Virno, 2004; Joseph, 2005).

Central to many of these profound changes has been the rise of transnational corporations that wield the economic power to influence nation states and macro-economic policy. For Dicken (2011), the power of transnational corporations is a result of two key factors: first, their adaptability in procuring access to a range of natural resources and raw materials, capital, labour markets and state subsidies; and second, their geographical flexibility (i.e., active in multiple territories) affords the opportunity to move resources according to demand. Leanness and flexibility are two critical factors in the context of the post-Fordist production processes which delineate many of the fundamental characteristics of globalization. In particular, advancements in transportation and communication technologies provide companies with the opportunity to extend their territorial reach to a global level. Key to this has been the importance of *circulation*: with the rise of the geographical extensivity of company functions comes a concomitant role for interconnectivity between sites of production, distribution of raw materials, spare parts, etc.

A productive way of conceiving these forms of circulation is to envisage a kind of diagrammatic spatiality where the movement of commodities on a global level is imagined in metaphorical terms.[1] Echoing John Urry's (2003) identification of distinct metaphors of global complexity (such as regions, networks and fluids), the literature on the movement of commodities at a global level has deployed a range of metaphorical constructs – from chains and circuits to networks – but equally a broad array of intellectual agendas.

Emanating out of the historical sociology of Immanuel Wallerstein's work and his trademark 'world-systems theory' approach, research into the genealogy of capitalism posited the importance of identifying 'market and production networks that eventually brought all peoples around the world into its logic and into a single worldwide structure' (Robinson, 2011: 728).

Hopkins and Wallerstein's work from the late 1970s and 1980s is perhaps one of the key milestones in the delineation of the manifold processes involved in commodity production (Hopkins and Wallerstein, 1977, 1986). They describe a 'commodity chain' as 'a network of labor and production processes whose end result is a finished commodity' (Hopkins and Wallerstein, 1986: 159). Whilst acknowledging Bair's (2008: 1) assertion that work falling under the guise of 'global chains studies' has a distinct intellectual history, Gereffi and Korzeniewicz (1994) developed this early phase by placing emphasis on the feedback between geographical cores and peripheries, positing the inherent distributedness of commodity chains themselves, as they clearly stretched across sites of production to consumption. The mobility of individual (often industrial) commodities is a central facet of the commodity chains approach (Leslie and Reimer, 1999: 402; Raikes et al., 2000), and the conceptualization of the 'chain' itself helps to situate specific sites of linkage *along* the chain of commodity movements. The value of the commodity chains approach is that it posits the distributed nature of commodities, rather than the singularity of the commodity itself. However, at the same time, the method has been critiqued on the grounds that it conforms to 'a simplified set of industrial rationalities' (Murdoch and Miele, 2004: 106) without due regard for the complexities underpinning the production and circulation of commodities. Indeed, the metaphorical constitution of the 'chain' has been critiqued for being overtly linear (Leslie and Reimer, 1999), thus neglecting the complexity of global processes (Urry, 2003).

Addressing the limitations of the linearity of global commodity chains is the literature on commodity circuits. Hughes and Reimer (2004: 3) note that work in this field offers an alternative reading of commodities, where the image of a circuit as opposed to a chain speaks to the process of how commodities circulate in a complex manner, encountering a range of contexts with traditional production settings. The likes of Jackson (1999) and Crang (1996) have suggested that shifting perspectives away from the realm of production, taking in the importance of the different phases of circulation (including distribution and consumption) affords a greater understanding of the social lives of commodities. Indeed, distinct from the sociological origins of global commodity chains, the literature associated with the 'circuits' approach is indebted to anthropology and particularly material culture studies (see Kopytoff, 1986; McCracken, 1990). Hughes and Reimer (2004: 4) further highlight an ethnographic thickness to the work of global commodity circuits, with emphasis placed on how the cultural hermeneutics of commodities shift according to the distinct phases of circulation (see du Gay et al., 1997).

Aligned with work on commodity circuits is a body of literature focused on a further spatial form: the 'network' (Dicken et al., 2001). A network configuration is a valuable conceptual apparatus for further appreciating the nuances of how commodities circulate. According to Murdoch and Miele (2004: 107), 'instead of the simplified world of capitalist ordering, we here encounter complex arrangements that comprise multiple rationalities, ordered in a variety of ways according to mixtures of entities assembled within networks'. Whilst this echoes the commodity circuits approach in recognizing that flows of commodities are localized at specific sites, the work of commodity networks scholars employs a horizontal approach to understanding commodity dynamics. For Barrett et al. (2004: 21), a vertical reading of commodity interrelationships promotes a hierarchically determined, ordered flow of goods, whilst a flattened horizontality foregrounds distributed forms of interdependency amongst a much wider array of actors that are emergent orderings, in the sense that the work required to move commodities is highly complex. Hughes and Reimer (2004: 4) note the intellectual legacy of actor network theory to commodity networks work, articulating both the now widely appreciated importance of human and more-than-human actors in the configuration of these networks. Noting the work of Whatmore and Thorne (1997), Hughes and Reimer (2004: 5) outline how the distributed connectivity of networks challenges the linearity of the core–periphery approach seen with global commodity chains.

The distinct nuances between global commodity chains, circuits and networks provide us with a helpful underpinning to our understanding of the configuration of commodity movements. These include the interlinkages between production, distribution and consumption, but with the recent work under 'circuits' and 'networks' an even richer appreciation of the multitude of different actors responsible for these processes, as well as the power dynamics involved. Now we have briefly outlined the wider spatio-temporal conceptualization of commodity processes, it is vital to understand the infrastructural mechanisms which are effectively the tools and concrete practices for *mobilizing* the movement of commodities, be that in the form of chains, circuits or networks. We turn now to the 'enabling technologies' of logistics and supply chain management (Beaverstock, 2008: 119).

THE LOGISTICS OF CIRCULATION

If the multifaceted processes that have come to be loosely defined as 'globalization' are at once a spatial, temporal and epistemological phenomenon (e.g., see respectively Sassen, 2006; Mitchell, 2000; Mignolo, 2011) inextricably linked to and propelled by the expansion of capitalist economies, a key vector driving this is the infrastructures of circulation. If there is one discipline more than any other invested in the production of circulation, performing the role of '*ars combinatoria*' (Benvegnù et al., 2019: 12), that is the field of logistics and supply chain management.

Popularly indicating all sorts of humdrum preliminary planning activities, at its most basic level the term 'logistics' names a particular approach to the management of circulatory and distributive processes underpinned by a logic of quantitative optimization. This approach has steadily expanded in scope and asserted its influence over global trade and beyond, currently driving a gargantuan '\$4.7 trillion industry' that is 'said to be the world's largest employer' (Hildyard, 2020: 5). Yet, mainly due to a combination of its contested historical trajectory, and the multifaceted nature of its operations, this is no easy discipline to define.

For a start, whilst primarily associated with commerce and business management (see Drucker, 1962), many agree that logistics has its genesis in warfare (Virilio, 2006). Indeed, logistics was originally a 'military art of moving soldiers and supplies to the front' (Cowen, 2014: 6) that allowed 'provisioning armies with the means of living and the means of waging war' (Chua et al., 2018: 618), so that campaigns would not have to rely on 'the tyranny of plunder' (van Creveld, 1977) or be excessively burdened in their operations. It is in the wake of the Second World War that this practice, aimed at enhancing military effectiveness, explicitly and officially entered the realm of commercial trade – a moment that, as Deborah Cowen (2014: 6) warned us, marks a deeper entanglement of war and trade rather than a mere shift towards the civilianization of warfare or a militarization of commerce.[2] The pairing of rapid technological developments – the intermodal shipping container being perhaps the most significant example – and a structural reorganization of capitalist economies led, in the 1950s and 1960s, to what commentators have described as the 'revolution in logistics', or 'logistics revolution' (e.g., Allen, 1997; Bonacich and Wilson, 2008; Cowen, 2014; Danyluk, 2018; Mezzadra and Neilson, 2019),[3] and the birth of supply chain management as a distinct field.

This occurrence saw a fundamental and progressive alteration in focus within global trade operations. By adopting increasingly rationalized 'systems approaches' as a way of 'integrating circulation into the time of production' (Benvegnù et al., 2019: 10), and indeed by fully subordinating the latter to the logic of the former (Bernes, 2013), the logistics revolution turns circulatory practices into the key paradigm of capitalist economies. Transportation and distribution thus cease to be the object of a mere 'exercise in cost minimisation' to become instead a – if not *the* – central avenue of profit maximization (Mezzadra and Neilson, 2019: 148); a transformation of the logic of value extraction that anthropologist Anna Tsing (2009) has famously christened 'supply chain capitalism'.

With this in mind, Cowen has offered a broad description of the field: logistics, she writes, is the '"science" of the efficient organization of movement within spatial systems that entails the design and management of supply chains' (Cowen, 2010: 601). This initial characterization can allow us to grapple with some of the discipline's key aspects. First, Cowen's definition emphasizes logistics' purported scientific approach to movement: this is an important point, because it has largely enabled the sector to present itself – and be treated – as a purely technical, objective and thus ostensibly *apolitical* profession. Yet, given its origins in the mobilization of military hardware and troop movements, Chua et al. have convincingly noted how this self-asserted neutrality should be squarely rejected because it naturalizes 'the expansion and reorganisation of material flows as desirable goals' (2018: 619), thus concealing logistics' highly political role in driving economic architectures of accumulation and domination that are, in fact, all but uncontested.

This aspect leads us to a second, crucial feature of logistical operations: its focus on efficiency. Both spatial and temporal, the drive towards efficiency associated with logistics and post-Fordist production and supply circuits has most readily been ascribed to the 'just-in-time' (JIT) ethos. In contrast with Fordist approaches to inventory stockpiling, JIT thinking is driven by systemic leanness and efficiency based on current rather than forecasted demand, so that supply resources are mobilized as quickly as possible (see Schoenberger, 2000). With the already mentioned application of so-called systems thinking to the sphere of commodity manufacturing and distribution, assisted by the calculative capabilities afforded by the advent of computer technologies, business logisticians developed a 'total cost' approach to corporate strategy. As the name suggests, total cost analysis entails extending the assessment and management of circulatory practices to include all auxiliary, previously unaccounted-for activities such as 'inventory carrying and obsolescence, warehousing, transportation, production alternatives, communications and data processing, customer service, alternative facilities use, channels of distribution, and cost concessions' (Cowen, 2014: 36). This results in a principle of total calculability, or a 'calculative rationality' (Chua et al., 2018: 621), whereby efficiency is at once logistics' horizon and its very *modus operandi*. In other words, logistics is not so much concerned with a set optimal (a means-to-end relationship), as with a perpetual practice of total *optimization* through which supply chains are configured as a 'giant wall-less global factory' (Benvegnù et al., 2019: 10) so as to allow capital that 'squeezes labour at every stage in the production process' (Hildyard, 2020: 6). Still, as we shall discuss in the following section, precisely because logistics is ultimately interested in the profitability of supply chains *in their totality* – rather than in this or that discrete phase – it is only apparently paradoxical for 'logistical systems [to] produce as well as eliminate frictions and inefficiencies' (Mezzadra and Neilson, 2019: 149) along the line.

Which takes us to a third consideration prompted by Cowen's definition. Logistics, far from being limited to the management of circulation, is thoroughly invested in the *design* of the spatial systems enabling the orchestration of global commodity circuits. Indeed, a pivotal factor in the rise of the industry has been the proliferation of ever more sophisticated 'spatial products' (Easterling, 2014) such as standardized infrastructures of containerization (Martin, 2016). Whilst the histories and practices of standardization are too detailed to unpack here,[4] in the context of the logistics of global commodity circulation a fundamental characteristic is that of infrastructural interchangeability. If the image of globalization is perpetuated by seamless mobility across geographical jurisdictions this is a highly complex assemblage of integrated infrastructures, both in technical as well as regulatory terms.[5] Where we might think of the material apparatus of containerization there is the concomitant standardization of regulatory procedures to facilitate the global distribution of commodities. To be sure, the socio-technical dimensions of standardization are governed by coordination, organization and systemic completeness (Barry, 2001). Whilst we should of course be acutely aware of the huge amount of infrastructural maintenance and upkeep (Graham and Thrift, 2007) required to mobilize commodities, at the global level the operative logic of standardization is that social, economic, political and technical domains are made knowable and governable (Higgins and Larner, 2010). Indeed, the notion of 'fit' in relation to standards – as described by Star (1991) – is determined by the stabilization of interconnection across various infrastructural forms associated with global commodity circuits. Although we perhaps associate such 'spatial products' with a technical apparatus, Easterling's work in particular highlights how the mantra of standardization permeates a vast amount of other such 'products', including larger-scale logistics hubs[6] as well as the creation of trade corridors and geopolitical products such as Special Economic Zones (SEZs). Yet at the same time, as Easterling notes, these ballooning[7] spatio-economic innovations boost the profitability of distributive practices by allowing business to opportunistically 'circulate products between jurisdictions, trading exemptions and filling quotas within the complex engineering of supply chains' (Easterling, 2014: 39) – i.e., by exploiting not only standardization but also heterogeneity and discontinuities.

As the proliferation of new zones of economic activity associated with commodity circulation testifies to, the increasing dexterity of logistics innovations has seen its increasing presence in many other spheres of life (Tsing, 2009; Neilson, 2012; Cowen, 2014; Cuppini et al., 2015). Which is to say, logistics has contributed to the production of new identities, whether as a precondition for, or a reaction against, the dramatic reorganization and fragmentation of global labour forces precipitated by the rise of this industry and related transnational companies. Indeed, Cuppini et al. write, 'logistics flattens out spaces, models bodies, and produces subjectivities as flexible as adaptation to the conditions of circulation requires', but also provokes the emergence of 'antagonistic' subjectivities and struggles along the supply chain (Cuppini et al., 2015: 122).[8]

It is by taking stock of the complexities described up to this point that we can adopt something like a 'logistical gaze' and begin to grapple with 'the global and variegated dimensions of contemporary transnational value chains' (Benvegnù et al., 2019: 12). Adopting such a gaze ultimately allows us to see logistics as a field not exclusively concerned with managing flow but, more radically, with flow as itself a mode of total management (also see Martin, 2012:

148). We now briefly address some of the crucial tensions at the heart of global commodity circuits and the totalizing gaze of logistics.

DIFFERENTIAL MOBILITIES

Now, one aspect of logistical approaches to circulation that must be emphasized is the particular way in which the logistics mindset exploits and indeed thrives on tensions and apparent contradictions. We have already noted how standardization goes hand in hand with increasing heterogeneity in the arrangement, maintenance and upkeep of supply chains. Furthermore, Mezzadra and Neilson (2019: 150–151) draw our attention to the fact that logistics, despite the sector's public self-image, should not be mistaken for a mere 'fetishization of speed' but rather appreciated as a '*making elastic* of time and temporality' through the coordinated acceleration and deceleration of flows 'that [are] characteristic of current capitalist development and crisis'. Crucially, this reliance on structural tensions connects commodity circulation and globalization in spatial terms, too, by troubling the image of the latter as an inexorable shift beyond the boundedness of nation states and towards a frictionless, unified whole, by way of the supply chain technologies described above. This 'illusion' of seamlessness (Mezzadra and Neilson, 2019: 154), of progressive dissolution of old demarcations and hurdles, goes hand in hand with a pervasive yet equally flawed understanding of the political economy that has arguably fuelled globalization: neoliberalism. While the neoliberal project is commonly associated with tropes of 'unchecked' and 'self-regulating' markets, Slobodian instead argues that wholesale reliance on these mantras ignores that many of neoliberalism's most influential proponents actually sought 'not to *liberate* the markets but to *encase* them' (2018: 2, our emphasis), so as to *protect* them from the volatility of democracy. In order to achieve such an encasement, Slobodian notes, self-described neoliberals advocated 'neither the disappearance of the state nor the disappearance of borders', but rather the design of supranational institutions,[9] infrastructures and regulatory frameworks that could safeguard the flows of capital at the global scale *through* its monitoring and ordering.

Both states and borders thus 'fulfil a necessary function' (Slobodian, 2018: 2) in ensuring such ordering. Indeed, as Mezzadra and Neilson (2013: 165) show us, borders are not superseded as such by globalizing tendencies, but rather 'reformatted' and, in fact, diffused and extended well beyond geographically defined boundaries, through a proliferation of other bordering techniques of both inclusion *and* exclusion.[10] On the one hand, states and borders are jointly instrumental in facilitating certain distributive processes, for instance through the already-mentioned establishment of SEZs, trade corridors and other circulatory business practices, such as the so-called Flag of Convenience,[11] that benefit from specific countries' trade regulations and legal frameworks. But equally, they serve to produce the systematic confinement of vast swathes of the world's population, locked in place by immigration restrictions within areas with little to no labour protections, hence furnishing pools of highly exploitable workforces for multinational corporations aiming to cut costs by outsourcing production.

So, to put it differently: if it is partly true that the logistics sector cultivates a 'fantasy' of smooth, seamless mobilization for goods and capital (Neilson, 2012: 331), this same commitment is utterly dependent upon the simultaneous 'immobilization' of one very particular commodity: people, as labour power – or, more precisely, the 'global poor' (Jones, 2016: 73–74). A regime of *differential mobility* through the managed porosity of bordering techniques of various kinds, which Angela Mitropoulos (2020: 4) has described as 'the arbitrage which makes exploitation possible', is thus integral to the globalizing project of commodity circulation and logistics (also see Yuval-Davis et al., 2019).

CONCLUDING THOUGHTS: MOVING FORWARD, MOVING SIDEWAYS

As outlined in the previous section the spatio-temporal practices of commodity mobilities are differential, driven by the tensions inherent in the competing factors of circulation and control. To bring the chapter to a conclusion – and to point to new directions for research in this area – we briefly deal with the idea of *disruption* as a mechanism underpinning the forces of globalization. We take two disruptive instances in the logic of circulation: first, by returning to the discussion of the COVID-19 pandemic in the introduction, specifically the aporias of JIT manufacturing and distribution; and second, by examining alternative logistical forms, through the counterlogistics of looting.

Supply Chain Shifts

If the pandemic has exemplified the entanglement of spatial scales – the global spread affecting individuated bodies (Jensen, 2021) – it has also changed many of the taken-for-granted configurations of mobility (Adey et al., 2021), but most importantly for our discussion the distribution of goods. At the start of the global pandemic in 2020, media accounts of panic buying and stockpiling of everyday consumer items abounded. Whilst the underlying psychological conditions affecting individuals' stockpiling of consumer goods has been identified (Micalizzi et al., 2021; Taylor, 2021), a similar structural recalibration is evident in the spatialities of commodity circulation, notably with critiques of JIT systems.

Fickling (2020) notes how 'global supply chains allow companies to benefit from lower labor costs in emerging economies, but leave them exposed if trade tensions or pandemics tighten border controls'. The exposure to such vulnerabilities are inherent characteristics of JIT.[12] Such structural weaknesses have led critical logistics scholars (Hesse, 2020) and industry professionals (Fickling, 2020) to reconsider the continued dominance of the JIT system and the globalization of production more generally. Given the ongoing nature of the fallout of the pandemic, Fickling speculates how the efficiencies of JIT manufacture and distribution leave companies open to shortages in supply due to the loss of the 'just-in-case' safety net of traditional forms of inventory stockpiling. Where the automotive manufacturer Toyota pioneered JIT manufacturing (Womack et al., 2007), Fickling (2020) provides telling data on the company's inventory holdings in recent years: in December 2019 Toyota was holding 36 days' worth of inventory compared with one week less in 2010.[13]

One further condition of the pandemic, as well as the geopolitical tensions of US–China trade disputes, is the potential diversification of supply chains themselves, where US companies for example are moving outsourced manufacturing to countries such as Mexico, away from China (Oxford Business Group, 2020). This is a twofold perspective for both private companies and governments: with the former, shortening supply chains may prove more efficient and less prone to shortages; with the latter, this would limit the reliance on other countries where pandemics, natural disasters or geopolitical disputes threaten supply chain securities (Gruszczynski, 2020: 341).[14] Although there is little to suggest an immediate rewriting of the spatialities of global commodity circuits, the potential implications of increased inventory stockpiling or the shortening of supply chains speak to the manifold ways in which circulation has many wider geopolitical ramifications.

The Counterlogistics of Looting

Another trajectory worth underscoring here concerns understanding logistics as a terrain of political conflict. Within this far from untapped line of inquiry, the focus has so far been on interruptions of commodity circuits at the nexus between production and distribution (e.g., Neilson, 2012; Bernes, 2013; Cuppini et al., 2015; Alimahomed-Wilson and Ness, 2018; Khalili, 2020). However, a complementary aspect could be further illuminated, particularly by way of Joshua Clover's (2016) theorization of riots and Vicky Osterweil's (2020) historiography of looting: namely, looting's central role in 'circulation struggles' (Clover, 2016: 28) when reframed as itself a legitimate form of counterlogistics – albeit a use/consumption-based[15] one – alongside labour-related modes of insurgency.[16] This shift allows us to emphasize 'how counterlogistical contestation is being waged not only in the sectors we might immediately associate with goods circulation but so too in the broader social relations of logistical society' (Chua et al., 2018: 623).[17] Furthermore, if 'capital's power rests not only in speeding up circulation but also in the capacity to slow it down', then there certainly is 'a danger in fetishizing the tactics of material interruption per se' (Chua et al., 2018: 624).

   Without rehearsing Osterweil's argument, we propose that looting enacts a mode of counterlogistics in at least three important ways. First, it interjects the established flows of capital with the intent of diverting its distribution, rather than interrupting it, opening up alternative logistical circuits. This is the case when looters seize luxury goods and electronic products for their rewarding exchange value, which can be efficiently converted by reselling these items on more or less licit markets (Clover, 2016: 29; Osterweil, 2020: 11). Second, looters intercept products of subsistence, such as food and drink, with the explicit aim of directly redistributing these goods among those participating in an uprising (Osterweil, 2020: 4). What we see in this instance exemplifies 'the possible repurposing of logistical models as sources of care and social reproduction' (Chua et al., 2018: 623; see also Dyer-Witheford et al., 2020). Third, and most important, when looting serves immediate use, whether personal or collective, it extracts goods from a circuit of profit realization, thus fundamentally destroying their very nature as commodities by the 'setting of prices at zero' (Clover, 2016: 123).

   By positioning these two trajectories – forwards and sideways – within the larger framework of commodity circulation we highlight its determinedly political dimensions. This chapter has provided an overview of the core debates on global commodity circuits and attendant practices of logistics and supply chain management. As we hope is now apparent, the spatio-temporal ordering practices required to mobilize the vast array of commodities around the globe are ever operative: that is, they are never fixed and never fully stabilized, even though this is partly the dream of seamless flows. Where the 'spatial products' associated with the global circulation of commodities might appear as embedded norms in our everyday lives, we have strived to show how the ideological apparatus of logistics and supply chain management attempts to render them thus. Our effort to address the multiple ways in which commodity circuits shape and reshape the globe will hopefully give new impetus to scholarship on the topic, helping it move forward, and sideways.

NOTES

1. Angela Mitropoulos adds to this diagrammatic conception by stating that supply chains are economic formations made up of a 'complex bundle of contracts', adding that such contracts are 'at once fragile and entrepreneurial, facilitating the assembly and movements of a commodity to its final destination' (2020: 98).
2. A prime example of this entanglement is represented by logistics behemoth Amazon's subsidiary Amazon Web Services, whose cloud infrastructure hosts data and algorithms gathered by data-mining firm Palantine on behalf of the US Immigration and Customs Enforcement agency and Department of Homeland Security (see Mijente et al., 2018).
3. In more recent studies, Megan Archer (2020) and the collective Into the Black Box (2019) have both renamed this moment the '*counter*-revolution in logistics', in order to draw our attention to the counterinsurgent character and colonial matrix of the extractive initiatives and development projects implemented through and as logistical rationality.
4. For an historical genealogy of standardization, particularly in relation to design, mechanization and manufacturing, see Giedion (1948).
5. Once again, the historical interdependency between the military and industrial complexes is apparent in the standardization of machine parts for manufacture (see Higgins and Hallström, 2007: 691) and that of the manufacture of firearms (DeLanda, 1991: 31).
6. Logistics hubs (or clusters) are 'broadly defined as areas specialising in the processing, warehousing and onward transportation of goods in a supply chain [that] now dot the globe' (Hildyard, 2020: 3). In his recent report, Nicholas Hildyard provides several examples of logistics hubs – including Shanghai's massive container port and Dubai's Logistic City, to name just two – and notes that many such areas are strategically located in SEZs where they can benefit from both fiscal and regulatory incentives.
7. According to the latest United Nations *World Investment Report*, 'There are now more than 5,400 SEZs across nearly 150 economies, up from 4,000 in 2015, and hundreds more are in the planning stage' (UNCTAD, 2020: 148).
8. Furthermore, logistical rationality is internalized beyond the workplace, through everyday incitements to behave efficiently, adapt flexibly and ceaselessly invest in forms of self-improvement, thus embracing what Julian Reid (2006) has termed a 'logistical life'.
9. Such as the EU and its Border and Coast Guard Agency (Frontex), the United Nations, the World Trade Organization and the International Monetary Fund.
10. In the case of global container transportation a case in point is the US Customs and Border Protection Agency's Container Security Initiative (Office of Policy and Planning and Office of International Affairs, Container Security Division, 2006). Launched in 2002 this initiative effectively extends the US border to regions where shipping containers originate from by pre-screening them in the port of origin, thus securing the flow of containers into US sovereign territory.
11. As explained by Laleh Khalili (2020: 272), 'flags of convenience' – also known as 'open registries' – are 'a maritime registration mechanism in which a given country allows ships from other countries to register under its rules', usually in order to take advantage of 'laxer tax, labour, and environmental laws'.
12. Moody (2020) asserts that the interconnectedness of JIT global supply chains increased the transmission of the virus, noting how it is far from coincidental that concentrations of the virus in the US map onto concentrations of manufacturing, transportation and warehousing sites.
13. Although data for the increase in Toyota inventory holdings is from December 2019 this reflects other disruptions, such as the Japanese earthquake in 2011.
14. Cresswell (2020) writes of the potential rise in 'localism' as a result of the pandemic. This can be read from a variety of perspectives, positively and negatively. For example, the growth in local food production may have a marked impact on carbon emissions related to transport, whereas right-wing nationalist sentiments call for the reassertion of traditional manufacturing bases in the Global North.
15. We want to insist that these two terms – use and consumption – are not synonyms describing the same sphere of activity, although this is clearly not the place to elaborate on their distinction.
16. As a side note, already by considering that the term 'loot' 'is taken up from the Hindi *lút* – similar to "plunder"' (Osterweil, 2020: 3), we can glimpse a link between this practice and the history of

logistics described earlier on in the chapter. Equally, however, this connection should compel us not to treat looting uncritically, particularly at a moment when important calls are increasingly being issued for the repatriation of objects looted by colonial empires.

17. Of course, it is important to acknowledge that the rapid rise of 'e-commerce' business models is drastically transforming and securitizing the geographies of retail and consumption through 'last mile' innovations and a general 'Amazonification of logistics' (Alimahomed-Wilson, 2020: 69).

REFERENCES

Adey, Peter and Ben Anderson (2011). 'Anticipation, Materiality, Event: The Icelandic Ash Cloud Disruption and the Security of Mobility'. *Mobilities* 6(1): 11–20.

Adey, Peter, Kevin Hannam Kevin, Mimi Sheller and David Tyfield (2021). 'Pandemic (Im)mobilities'. *Mobilities* 16(1): 1–19.

Ali, S. Harris and Roger Keil (2010). 'Securitizing Networked Flows: Infectious Diseases and Airports'. In: Stephen Graham (Ed.). *Disrupted Cities: When Infrastructure Fails*. Abingdon: Routledge, 97–110.

Alimahomed-Wilson, Jake (2020). 'The Amazonification of Logistics: E-Commerce, Labor, and Exploitation in the Last Mile'. In: Jake Alimahomed-Wilson and Ellen Reese (Eds). *The Cost of Free Shipping: Amazon in the Global Economy*. London: Pluto Press, 69–84.

Alimahomed-Wilson, Jake and Immanuel Ness (Eds) (2018). *Choke Points: Logistics Workers Disrupting the Global Supply Chain*. London: Pluto Press.

Allen, Bruce W. (1997). 'The Logistics Revolution and Transportation'. *Annals of the American Academy of Political Science* 553: 106–116.

Archer, Megan (2020). 'Logistics as Rationality: Excavating the Coloniality of Contemporary Logistical Formations'. PhD thesis, University of Brighton.

Bair, Jennifer (2008). 'Global Commodity Chains: Genealogy and Review'. In: Jennifer Bair (Ed.). *Frontiers of Commodity Chain Research*. Stanford: Stanford University Press, 1–34.

Barrett, Hazel R., Angela W. Browne and Brian W. Ilbery (2004). 'From Farm to Supermarket: The Trade in Fresh Horticultural Produce from Sub-Saharan Africa to the United Kingdom'. In: Alex Hughes and Suzanne Reimer (Eds). *Geographies of Commodity Chains*. London: Routledge, 19–38.

Barry, Andrew (2001). *Political Machines: Governing a Technological Society*. London: Continuum.

Beaverstock, Jonathan V. (2008). 'Global Shift (1986): Peter Dicken'. In: Phil Hubbard, Rob Kitchin and Gill Valentine (Eds). *Key Texts in Human Geography*. London: Sage, 117–123.

Benvegnù, Carlotta, Niccolò Cuppini, Mattia Frapporti, Floriano Milesi and Maurilio Pirone (2019). 'Logistical Gazes'. *Work Organisation, Labour & Globalisation* 13(1): 9–14.

Bernes, Jasper (2013). 'Logistics, Counterlogistics and the Communist Prospect'. *Endnotes* 3: 172–201.

Boffey, Daniel (2021). 'COVID Vaccine Row: EU Has Exported 34m Doses – Including 9m to UK'. Available: www.theguardian.com/world/2021/mar/10/britain-has-no-ban-on-covid-vaccine-exports-eu-concedes

Bonacich, Edna and Jake B. Wilson (2008). *Getting the Goods: Ports, Labour, and the Logistics Revolution*. Ithaca: Cornell University Press.

Chua, Charmaine, Martin Danyluk, Deborah Cowen and Laleh Khalili (2018). 'Introduction: Turbulent Circulation: Building a Critical Engagement with Logistics'. *Environment and Planning D: Society and Space* 36(4): 617–629.

Clover, Joshua (2016). *Riot. Strike. Riot: The New Era of Uprising*. London: Verso.

Cowen, Deborah (2010). 'A Geography of Logistics: Market Authority and the Security of Supply Chains'. *Annals of the Association of American Geographers* 100(3): 600–620.

Cowen, Deborah (2014). *The Deadly Life of Logistics*. Minneapolis: University of Minnesota Press.

Crang, Philip (1996). 'Displacement, Consumption and Identity'. *Environment and Planning A* 28(1): 47–67.

Cresswell, Tim (2020). 'Valuing Mobility in a Post COVID-19 World'. *Mobilities* 16(1): 51–65.

Cuppini, Niccolò, Mattia Frapporti and Maurilio Pirone (2015). 'Logistics Struggles in the Po Valley Region: Territorial Transformations and Processes of Antagonistic Subjectivation'. *South Atlantic Quarterly* 114(1): 119–134.

Danyluk, Martin (2018). 'Capital's Logistical Fix: Accumulation, Globalization, and the Survival of Capitalism'. *Environment and Planning D: Society and Space* 36(4): 630–647.

DeLanda, Manuel (1991). *War in the Age of Intelligent Machines*. New York: Zone Books.

Dicken, Peter (2011). *Global Shift: Mapping the Changing Contours of the World Economy*. London: Sage.

Dicken, Peter, Philp F. Kelly, Kris Olds and Henry Wai-Chung Yeung (2001). 'Chains and Networks, Territories and Scales: Towards a Relational Framework for Analysing the Global Economy'. *Global Networks* 1(2): 89–112.

Drucker, Peter (1962). 'The Economy's Dark Continent'. *Fortune* April: 103–104.

du Gay, Paul, Stuart Hall, Linda Janes, Anders Koed Madsen, Hugh Mackay and Keith Negus (1997). *Doing Cultural Studies: The Story of the Sony Walkman*. London: Sage.

Dyer-Witheford, Nick, Jaime Brenes Reyes and Michelle Liu (2020). 'Riot Logistics'. *Into the Black Box*. www.intotheblackbox.com/articoli/riot-logistics/

Easterling, Keller (2014). *Extrastatecraft: The Power of Infrastructure Space*. London: Verso.

Fickling, David (2020). 'Coronavirus Will Stretch, Not Break, Global Supply Chains'. www.bloomberg .com/opinion/articles/2020-05-16/coronavirus-won-t-break-global-supply-chains

Gereffi, Gary and Miguel Korzeniewicz (Eds) (1994). *Commodity Chains and Global Capitalism*. Westport: Praeger.

Giedion, Sigfried (1948). *Mechanization Takes Command: A Contribution to Anonymous History*. New York: W.W. Norton and Co.

Goodman, Peter, Alexandra Stevenson, Niraj Chokshi and Michael Corkery (2021). '"I've Never Seen Anything Like This": Chaos Strikes Global Shipping'. www.nytimes.com/2021/03/06/business/ global-shipping.html

Graham, Stephen and Nigel Thrift (2007). 'Out of Order: Understanding Repair and Maintenance'. *Theory, Culture & Society* 24(3): 1–25.

Gruszczynski, Lukasz (2020). 'The COVID-19 Pandemic and International Trade: Temporary Turbulence or Paradigm Shift?'. *European Journal of Risk Regulation* 11: 337–342.

Hardt, Michael and Antonio Negri (2000). *Empire*. Cambridge, MA: Harvard University Press.

Harney, Stefano and Fred Moten (2013). *The Undercommons: Fugitive Planning and Black Study*. Wivenhoe: Minor Compositions.

Hesse, Markus (2020). 'Logistics after COVID-19: Just Repair the Chains, or Is It Time for a Reset?'. https://blog.geographydirections.com/2020/06/16/logistics-after-covid-19-just-repair-the-chains-or -is-it-time-for-reset/

Higgins, Vaughan and Wendy Larner (2010). 'Standards and Standardization as a Social Scientific Problem'. In: Vaughan Higgins and Wendy Larner (Eds). *Calculating the Social: Standards and the Reconfiguration of Governing*. Basingstoke: Palgrave MacMillan, 1–17.

Higgins, Winton and Kristina Tamm Hallström (2007). 'Standardization, Globalization and Rationalities of Government'. *Organization* 14(5): 685–704.

Hildyard, Nicholas (2020). *Corridors as Factories: Supply Chains, Logistics and Labour*. Report for Counter Balance. https://counter-balance.org/publications/corridors-as-factories-supply-chains -logistics-and-labour

Hopkins, Terence K. and Immanuel Wallerstein (1977). 'Patterns of Development of the Modern World-System'. *Review* 1(2): 111–145.

Hopkins, Terence K. and Immanuel Wallerstein (1986). 'Commodity Chains in the World Economy Prior to 1800'. *Review* 10(1): 157–170.

Hughes, Alex and Suzanne Reimer (2004). 'Introduction'. In: Alex Hughes and Suzanne Reimer (Eds). *Geographies of Commodity Chains*. London: Routledge, 1–16.

International Transport Forum (2020). *COVID-19 Transport Brief: Global Container Shipping and the Coronavirus Crisis*. Paris: International Transport Forum.

Into the Black Box (2019). 'Critical Logistics: A Manifesto'. www.intotheblackbox.com/manifesto/ critical-logistics-a-manifesto/

Jackson, Peter (1999). 'Commodity Culture: The Traffic in Things'. *Transactions of the Institute of British Geographers* 24: 95–108.

Jensen, O.B. (2021). 'Pandemic Disruption, Extended Bodies, and Elastic Situations: Reflections on COVID-19 and Mobilities'. *Mobilities* 16(1): 66–80.

Jones, Reece (2016). *Violent Borders: Refugees and the Right to Move*. London: Verso.

Joseph, Branden W. (2005). 'Interview with Paolo Virno'. *Grey Room* 21: 26–37.

Khalili, Laleh (2020). *Sinews of War and Trade: Shipping and Capitalism in the Arabian Peninsula*. London: Verso.

Kopytoff, Igor (1986). 'The Cultural Biography of Things: Commoditization as Process'. In: Arjun Appadurai (Ed.). *The Social Life of Things: Commodities in Cultural Perspective*. Cambridge: Cambridge University Press, 64–91.

Leslie, Deborah and Suzanne Reimer (1999). 'Spatializing Commodity Chains'. *Progress in Human Geography* 23(3): 401–420.

Martin, Craig (2012). 'Controlling Flow: On the Logistics of Distributive Space'. In: Andrew Ballantyne and Chris L. Smith (Eds). *Architecture in the Space of Flows*. London: Routledge, 147–159.

Martin, Craig (2016). *Shipping Container*. New York: Bloomsbury Academic.

McCracken, Grant (1990). *Culture and Consumption: New Approaches to the Symbolic Character of Consumer Goods and Activities*. Bloomington: Indiana University Press.

Mezzadra, Sandro and Brett Neilson (2013). *Border as Method, or, the Multiplication of Labor*. Durham: Duke University Press.

Mezzadra, Sandro and Brett Neilson (2019). *The Politics of Operations: Excavating Contemporary Capitalism*. Durham: Duke University Press.

Micalizzi, L., Zambrotta, N.S. and Bernstein, M.H. (2021). 'Stockpiling in the Time of COVID-19'. *British Journal of Health Psychology* 26(2): 535–543.

Mignolo, Walter (2011). *The Darker Side of Western Modernity: Global Futures, Decolonial Options*. Durham: Duke University Press.

Mijente, Immigrant Defense Project and National Immigration Project (2018). *Who's Behind ICE? The Tech and Data Companies Fuelling Deportations*. Report. www.immigrationresearch.org/node/2370

Mitchell, Timothy (Ed.) (2000). *Questions of Modernity*. Minneapolis: University of Minnesota Press.

Mitropoulos, Angela (2020). *Pandemonium: Proliferating Borders of Capital and the Pandemic Swerve*. London: Pluto Press.

Moody, Kim (2020). 'How "Just-in-Time" Capitalism Spread COVID-19: Trade Routes, Transmission, and International Solidarity'. https://spectrejournal.com/how-just-in-time-capitalism-spread-covid -19/

Murdoch, Jonathan and Mara Miele (2004). 'Culinary Networks and Cultural Connections: A Conventions Perspective'. In: Alex Hughes and Suzanne Reimer (Eds). *Geographies of Commodity Chains*. London: Routledge, 102–119.

Neilson, Brett (2012). 'Five Theses on Understanding Logistics as Power'. *Distinktion: Journal of Social Theory* 13(3): 322–339.

Office of Policy and Planning and Office of International Affairs, Container Security Division (2006). *Container Security Initiative: 2006–2011 Strategic Plan*. Washington: US Customs and Border Protection.

Osterweil, Vicky (2020). *In Defence of Looting: A Riotous History of Uncivil Action*. New York: Bold Type Books.

Oxford Business Group (2020). 'The Impact of COVID-19 on Global Supply Chains'. https://oxfordbusinessgroup.com/news/impact-covid-19-global-supply-chains

Raikes, Philip, Michael Friis Jensen and Stefano Ponte (2000). 'Global Commodity Chain Analysis and the French *Filière* Approach: Comparison and Critique'. *Economy and Society* 29(3): 390–417.

Reid, Julian (2006). *The Biopolitics of the War on Terror: Life Struggles, Liberal Modernity, and the Defence of Logistical Societies*. Manchester: Manchester University Press.

Robinson, William I. (2011). 'Globalization and the Sociology of Immanuel Wallerstein: A Critical Appraisal'. *International Sociology* 26(6): 723–745.

Sack, Robert (1997). *Homo Geographicus: A Framework for Action, Awareness and Moral Concern*. Baltimore: Johns Hopkins University.

Sassen, Saskia (2006). *Territory, Authority, Rights: From Medieval to Global Assemblages*. Princeton: Princeton University Press.

Schoenberger, Erica (2000). 'The Management of Time and Space'. In: Gordon L. Clark, Maryann P. Feldman and Meric S. Gertler (Eds). *The Oxford Handbook of Economic Geography*. Oxford: Oxford University Press, 317–332.

Slobodian, Quinn (2018). *Globalists: The End of Empire and the Birth of Neoliberalism*. Cambridge, MA: Harvard University Press.

Star, Susan Leigh (1991). 'Power, Technology and the Phenomenology of Conventions: On Being Allergic to Onions'. In: John Law (Ed.). *A Sociology of Monsters: Essays on Power, Technology and Domination*. London: Routledge, 26–56.

Taylor, S. (2021). 'Understanding and Managing Pandemic-Related Panic Buying'. *Journal of Anxiety Disorders* 78: 1–8.

Tsing, Anna (2009). 'Supply Chains and the Human Condition'. *Rethinking Marxism* 21(2): 148–176.

UNCTAD (2020). *World Investment Report 2020: International Production beyond the Pandemic*. Report. New York: United Nations Publications.

Urry, John (2003). *Global Complexity*. Cambridge: Polity.

van Creveld, Martin (1977). *Supplying War: Logistics from Wallenstein to Patton*. Cambridge: Cambridge University Press.

Virilio, Paul (2006). *Speed and Politics*. New York: Semiotext(e).

Virno, Paulo (2004). *A Grammar of the Multitude*. New York: Semiotext(e).

Whatmore, Sarah and Lorraine Thorne (1997). 'Nourishing Networks: Alternative Geographies of Food'. In: David Goodman and Michael Watts (Eds). *Globalising Food: Agrarian Questions and Global Restructuring*. London: Routledge, 211–224.

Womack, James, Daniel Jones and Daniel Roos (2007). *The Machine That Changed the World: How Lean Production Revolutionized the Global Car Wars*. London: Simon & Schuster.

Yuval-Davis, Nira, Georgie Wemyss and Kathryn Cassidy (2019). *Bordering*. London: Polity Press.

5. Global networks and hybrid cities
Kristian Kloeckl

WHEN TWO NETWORKS MEET

When, in 1969, the first digital message was sent on the precursor of today's internet, ARPANET, little did those involved know about the massive impact their nascent digital network would have on our physical environment. Today, networked digital technologies that blanket our cities and that connect them globally influence at a fundamental level how we move in and between them, the way we understand them, the way we operate and transform them, as well as the way we act in and experience them.

> The archetypical structure of the network, with its accumulation and habitation sites, links, dynamic flow patterns, interdependencies, and control points, is now repeated at every scale from that of neural networks (neurons, axons, synapses) and digital circuitry (registers, electron pathways, switches) to that of global transportation networks (warehouses, shipping and air routes, ports of entry). (Mitchell, 2003: 9)

These networks connect people, objects, and places. Electricity is supplied via the grid to housing, vehicles, and mobile devices; phone calls are routed to cellphones on the go; and the location of every package is monitored by tags and readers connected to central servers that blanket the globe. People, objects, and places are connected unlike ever before.

The increasing intertwining of digital networked technologies and cities has given rise to various names and conceptualizations that range from "wired cities" (Dutton et al., 1987), the "city of bits" (Mitchell, 1995), "cyber cities" (Graham and Marvin, 2001), "computable cities" (Batty, 1997), "digital cities" (Ishida and Ibister, 2000), "real-time cities" (Calabrese et al., 2007), as well as concepts summarized as the Internet of Things. Research and practice related to these has brought about domains such as urban informatics (Foth, 2008) and urban computing (Greenfield and Shepard, 2007).

Before looking at information networks and cities more specifically, it is worthwhile to consider that cities have always been networks – long before the dawn of the information age. From the early settlements, people constructed connections between their dwellings and settlements for the transfer of people, goods, and information. The Viae Romanae, the public road network of the Roman state comprised of the Via Aurelia, Via Cassia, Via Tiburtina, and others, connected cities throughout the Roman state's territory. It was a vital network for the development of the Roman Republic and Empire, providing for movement of people and goods as well as for the transmission of information by way of human messengers. Within the Roman city, the Decumanus Maximus crosses the perpendicular Cardo Maximus, typically at the location of the Forum – the center of Rome's daily life and venue for public speeches, processions, and elections. Around these, other roads would form the network to connect the entire city. Today's fiberglass networks that connect the buildings within and between cities are the Viae Romanae of our age. It is the cellphone antennae, satellite, and cable infrastructure that blanket large parts of the globe, enabling communication between people, things, and places.

Today's cities are entangled with a growing number of digital information networks, an array of systems that connect diverse sets of entities in many different ways: cable-based high-speed networks provide fast transmission of information; the wireless cellphone network is based on a vast array of antennae disseminated throughout the territory; and mobile phones dynamically negotiate the most efficient tower to connect to in terms of signal strength and available capacity. Wi-Fi, Bluetooth, and RFID network technologies are other types of wireless networks that connect devices, each offering different traits in terms of signal strength, reach, transmission speed, and energy consumption. Wireless protocols enable networks to be formed ad hoc, enabling devices to connect and disconnect dynamically to networks in automated or user-triggered ways. Different types of these networks are used to offer different functionalities through devices and systems connected to them.

Sociologist Manuel Castells was among the first to develop a comprehensive framework to comprehend the seismic impact of information technologies on our cities and our lives. His spatial logic related to a space of flows is in direct opposition to space as place (Castells, 2010: 408). It is based on a new economy that, in Castells' terms, is informational, global, and networked. It is a coming together of "the knowledge-information base of the economy, its global reach, its network-based organizational form, and the information technology revolution that has given birth to a new, distinctive economic system" (Castells, 2010: 77). The advanced services that Castells describes and that are enabled by globally networked technologies are "pervasive, and they are located throughout the geography of the planet, excepting the 'black holes' of marginality." Yet, while global, they create different concentrations in different tiers of urban centers, Saskia Sassen emphasizes in her seminal study of the joint dominance in global finance and business of New York, Tokyo, and London (Sassen, 1991).

The focus has shifted onto these urban poles and on the connections between these poles rather than the spaces between cities, their territory, or hinterlands. "As the global economy expands and incorporates new markets it also organizes the production of advanced services required to manage the new units joining the system, and the conditions of their ever-changing linkages" (Castells, 2010: 408). The networked economy, while being global and networked, organizes and structures the conditions of the sites in which it manifests itself and which are directly experienced by people. It is not only the connections that the network economy enables, it is also the different work and leisure practices that it enables at the local level that are significant. It is in this way that the networked economy shapes people's practice and experience in concrete ways.

Today's network technologies have become *mobile* and *embedded*. For once, they are tightly integrated with the built urban fabric, and ever more of its elements are becoming programmable and uniquely addressable through any one or multiple networks (Jackson and Kyriakou, 2015). For example, the most advanced lighting grids of a city today can address and control each and every lamppost individually and in distinct ways. This results in a city-wide network that can be controlled down to its individual units and, combined with sensors at these individual units, also provides a continuous data flow that describes the network's operation at that level of granularity. Connected devices are the nodes of these networks, cables or wireless signals are the links between these nodes.

People become connected to these networks via cellphones, smart watches, electronic transportation tickets, and similar items that are worn or carried along. Places become connected to these networks when devices are location-aware; when a lamppost in a city square contains information about its specific location and orientation; or when devices in a room "know" that they are in that room, in that car, on that road, or at that specific latitude and longitude.

The connections are not point to point but are based largely on the widespread availability of networks of many connections between many points along which paths are routed and packages of information or matter are sent. When I order a cup of coffee on my smartphone standing outside a Starbucks cafe, the order passes from my device to the cellphone network and then to Starbucks' central server systems, where the information is processed and sent through a landline or cellular telecommunication network to the cafe which I am about to enter. As it comes to the attention of the barista in the cafe I will already have entered the cafe, ready to receive my coffee. In ways like these the networked city redefines space and time, it redefines the here and now. It also complicates notions of presence and absence as I may not have engaged at all with any of the staff throughout this entire process. And, it also brings into play notions of privacy as the information about my presence, actions, choices, and preferences are broadcast beyond my immediate awareness and beyond my apparent control.

Embedded sensors can monitor a situation in one place, convey data to another location where data are processed and analyzed, and can then connect back to the original location, conditioning the original situation that gave rise to the data being generated in the first place. In the same way, a person acting in a city contributes herself to dynamics of which others are not aware when making their decisions. Looked upon in this way, a city resembles what philosophers Jacques Deleuze and Félix Guattari describe as a rhizome, a philosophical network structure where every part is necessarily connected with every other part of the system. Every connection in a rhizome alters the overall network structure for which there are no preferential connections and, as a consequence, the rhizome cannot be plotted since the plotting action itself is part of the rhizome, and thus in the very moment of plotting its structure, the structure changes. Understood in this way, it is a paradox that today's cities entangled with global digital networks have become the most mapped and charted, while these acts of mapping and charting alter the very connections that are being mapped given the real-time information flows inherent in the charting process.

In the following two sections I will look at the impact that global information technologies have had on the mapping and understanding of cities as well as the operations before, offering a critique of this still young terrain of research and practice.

MAPPING HYBRID CITIES FOR NEW FORMS OF UNDERSTANDING

With the advent of pervasive digital networks embedded in our everyday environment, it has become second nature to consider today's cities as entities that "talk," that can be part of something akin to a conversation. That may even improvise an ad hoc dialogue in real time (Kloeckl, 2020). It is a significant departure from a centuries' old consideration of cities as stable entities in terms of their constructed environments, far from the immediacy and quickness of talk.

Before cities were viewed as talking entities, however, they could be read. This was a slower, more reflective act of reading, applied to the city viewed as an urban fabric made up of streets, squares, buildings, gardens, and waterways – a texture and a text.

For a long time, urbanites read their cities through various forms of maps – abstract representations of its physical and social structures seen from above. In the mid-eighteenth century Italian architect Giambattista Nolli created the *Pianta Grande di Roma*, today commonly known as the Nolli Map. It was the most accurate map of the City of Rome when created and was used by the City until as late as the late twentieth century. The map is a figure-ground representation that depicts the city's buildings on the backdrop of the spaces that surround them. It reveals the relations between public and private spaces in the city. Private buildings are shown in gray, carved into public spaces both covered and uncovered. Interiors of churches read the same way as piazzas and courtyards of palaces. Nolli's map is a representation of the results of the complex processes that are involved in planning and building a city's physical structure. It provides a snapshot in time of this process that knows no end and offers an exclusive focus on the physicality of the constructed environment. William Mitchell (1995: 131) had ample foresight when pondering, "Perhaps some electronic cartographer of the future will produce an appropriately nuanced Nolli map of the Net." Not only would electronic cartographers map the Internet but electronic mapping would be folded back onto the city that Nolli once drew in ink.

As networked digital technologies began to pervade spaces and practices of human activity, these technologies not only opened up a new era of increased computational potential for all kinds of operations. Pervasive digital technology networks also began to generate data as a consequence of the operation of these technologies. For example, while an urban public transport system based on paper tickets registers how many tickets are sold and when and where they are sold as a historic account, e-ticket systems such as London's Oyster Card or Singapore's EZ-Link Card generate a slew of data about every single trip of a card holder, and it does so for thousands or even millions of trips every single day.

This new abundance of data is also digital and as such enables easy data exchange across systems, organizations, and contexts of inquiry in a way unheard of before. This seems trivial today, but consider paper surveys that can only be used in one location and for their originally intended purpose as long as they are not digitized. Digital data logs can be used and reused with different software tools, in radically different contexts, and in distant locations.

Increased computing power and software capability was necessary to effectively work with this large unprecedented dimension of datasets. *Big data* is a term that became as much a hype as *smart city* in this relation. It is no technical term and escapes a clear definition. In trying, nevertheless, it can be described as a dataset that is too large to be processed and worked with using commonly available tools. Or, as someone once put it more colloquially, a dataset too large to open in Excel. As such, big data always describes a transitory condition, valid only until tool development catches up to the "new normal" of data size.

Since the early 2000s we have witnessed an explosive growth in urban data generated continuously by digital devices that are incidental to human activity, and this has opened up a fascinating new terrain for research about human activity in cities. This is a radical departure from previous modes of data collection that required deliberate effort to obtain limited samples collected over a limited period of time. Once-every-ten-year surveys were the norm in a city's transportation planning. Today, data inform this process that is generated every second and at much finer granularity, covering the entirety of instances rather than a limited sample. The map that Nolli drew with ink on paper and that remained static for centuries could now come alive and be constantly drawn and redrawn by data generated by digital networks ever more entangled with human activity itself.

These amounts of data are not easily interpreted and of limited use if not represented in a meaningful way. This novel condition has given rise to significant development in the field of data visualization. Related to the domain of information design, the human tradition of visually representing data goes back centuries, but today's availability of massive amounts of data in digital formats poses new challenges and opportunities when generating new digital maps of cities to be readily understood by wider audiences. To name but a few examples, we can look at the Mobile Landscape Graz data visualization of cellphone activity, developed by Senseable City Lab in 2005 and exhibited at the M-City exhibition at the Kunsthaus Graz, curated by Marco De Michelis (Ratti et al., 2007). The digital maps show the cellphone network activity of an entire city over time. It is an illustration of connectivity between technology devices, but these devices become proxies for human movements and interactions once carried in our pockets. Travel Times on Commuter Rail, developed by Amanda Cox and Matthew Ericson in 2007, maps rail lines by the actual time of travel between stations as observed by the rail's internal logging infrastructure, rather than by geographic location or planned schedule, turning the map into a representation of the actual movements of trains with all the incidental delays, stops, and interruptions, rather than a planned schedule. CityMurmur, developed in 2008 by a team at the Politecnico di Milano (2008), generates maps of cities that do not represent geographic relationships and physical infrastructures and constructions. Rather, these digital maps are generated by online media discourses about parts of a city, giving more prominence to elements that appear more frequently in these online chatters and less to others. The project represents an early combination of media and geography of cities. As part of the 2008 Design and the Elastic Mind exhibition at MoMA in New York, the author together with his team at MIT developed the New York Talk Exchange project that consisted in a real-time visualization of telephone network connectivities between New York City and the rest of the world (Rojas et al., 2008). The digital maps generated provided a glimpse into how a global city connected with cities around the world and how those cities connected to different New York City neighborhoods in different ways and at different times. The work the author led with the WikiCity and the Live Singapore! projects did in 2007 and 2010 respectively point towards the topic of the next section, closing the feedback loop. Both projects consisted in real-time data systems that brought together urban data streams from different urban operators such as public transport, electricity, taxi, cellphone, etc. and provided insights into directly or indirectly related urban dynamics through constantly updating visual maps.

As Mitchell predicted, electronic maps did get generated from the Internet, but even more so, the tight integration of networked technologies in our physical urban environment has enabled such maps to be generated that reflect continuously evolving urban dynamics in real time.

CLOSING THE FEEDBACK LOOP

The global expansion and pervasiveness of ubiquitous digital networked information technologies does more than generate the often acclaimed data deluge (*The Economist*, 2010) to be mined for new forms of understanding. The same technologies that generate the massive amounts of data as part of their operations are also responsible for another key condition of hybrid cities: *real-time* data transmission. Data generated by sensors or other digital devices are broadcast instantly to computational units for processing and analysis. Real-world dynamics are instantly converted into digital maps that continuously update the view of the world itself. The world, it seems, has in this way become a map itself – not unlike Jorge Luis Borges's fictional quote in his short story *On Exactitude in Science*:

> in that Empire, the Art of Cartography attained such Perfection that the map of a single Province occupied the entirety of a City, and the map of the Empire, the entirety of a Province. In time, those Unconscionable Maps no longer satisfied, and the Cartographers Guilds struck a Map of the Empire whose size was that of the Empire, and which coincided point for point with it. (Presented as a fictional quote in Borges, 1946)

Data collected from millions of mobile and embedded devices can be collected, processed, analyzed, and then be broadcast back to the very same people that were involved in its generation in the first place. Information provided to people in such a way becomes a formidable support for decision making. Real-time data provide a basis for people to make decisions and act in a way that is more in sync with the actual context and situation they find themselves in. It allows people and systems to adapt to the ever changing condition of their environment in a way that wouldn't be possible without access to such information (Kloeckl, 2020).

Most early examples of data visualization that used urban real-time data streams were ad hoc developments for a specific research or application. With the increasing awareness of the power of the novel medium, so-called urban dashboards became adopted in more and more cities (Kitchin et al., 2015b; Mattern, 2015). Urban dashboards have become a specific type of visual representation of data. They are visualization frameworks to work with continuously updating data streams from different sources of interest to urban administrations, decision makers, and the general public. Dashboards allow for organizing and interacting with data in visual ways; they enable filtering data as well as viewing relationships between different elements and overlaying multiple datasets (Few, 2006; Rivard and Cogswell, 2004).

While real-time data visualizations and dashboards have made data from global and local technology networks consultable, it is the modern smartphone that has become a formidable device for dissemination and access to real-time information in a way that is time- and location-specific. The confluence of global information technologies, pervasive real-time sensing, analytics, and data visualization, together with a mobile and personal device created the conditions for today's hybrid cities to emerge around the world.

In Boston, public transport agency MBTA limited itself to publicly releasing the real-time data stream online. The agency did not itself provide any end user frontend for this data stream but sparked a fertile dynamic among developers that led to the creation of numerous smartphone apps informing riders of bus arrival times. Bus schedules were frequently off schedule but being able to have access to actual arrival times enabled a new use of the system. In Kenya, the Digital Matatus project led by MIT's Civic Data Design Lab was developed and deployed mobile phone apps to more efficiently collect location data of Nairobi's Matatus – the city's decentralized bus system – making it available to the public to make the service more accessible, safe, and transparent (Williams et al., 2015).

In these examples data are generated by technology systems and made accessible to citizens. Inversely, the pervasiveness of smartphones has also fostered setups by which these devices become input devices for citizens themselves to contribute data actively and deliberately in a crowd-sourced modality.

Prominent examples of this way of sourcing citizen participation have been various implementations of 311 civic services in different cities. 311 used to be a telephone service in many cities in the United States for non-emergency services. The development of Open 311 in 2010 paved the way for the implementation of smartphone application services specific to cities (for example Boston 311, NYC 311). Open 311 services enable citizens to inform their city administration of complaints, suggestions, and things that need fixing, in this way crowd sourcing at a large scale scouting activity by city officials (O'Brien, 2015). Similar to 311, SeeClickFix is a service that is somewhat a mix between 311 and a social network, allowing citizens to share information with other local residents as well as with the city.

Smartphones have also come to be tools to directly interact with physical elements in cities, connecting the ephemeral nature of digital data streams with the physicality of urban space. A good example is the latest evolution of public bike-share schemes. While previous iterations of these schemes required fixed docking stations and payment by credit card at interactive kiosks, the latest iteration of dockless bike-share schemes cleverly leverages a combination of pervasive information technologies for bikes to be left anywhere in a city's territory. GPS technology tracks the bikes' location and people's personal smartphones are used to scan a visual code, enable Bluetooth communication between the phone and the lock to unlock the bike, and register the phone's owner as the rider for the trip.

Information technologies have enabled the built urban environment to be conceived as a dynamic entity that adjusts and adapts directly in response to environmental conditions or human activity. Some of the most advanced urban lighting systems employ sensor technology that allow streetlamps not only to be triggered by ambient light conditions but also by human presence. In this way, lights are dimmed in the absence of people and brighten up when people are detected nearby, with an overall result of reducing energy consumption and light pollution (Cardwell, 2014). Networked traffic lights that dynamically respond to traffic dynamics and dynamic road pricing are further examples.

The above examples illustrate how pervasive digital technology systems not only provide their primary functions and generate data that can provide massive datasets for research, they also create a new condition in which citizens can access dynamic information in real time that depicts the current state of their environment and thus support decision making.

This has shifted people's use of urban information from a static format to information that is dynamic, time- and location-specific, and that reflects ever changing contexts. In many ways we can say that this kind of real-time information enables people to respond dynamically to context, not following pre-made plans but constructively engaging with real-world disruptions that are part of the messiness and unpredictability of urban life – to improvise (Suchman, 1987; Kloeckl, 2020).

CRITIQUE AND OUTLOOK

The instances described above have come to be frequently associated with one term – *smart city*. The term reveals itself as a blessing and a curse. Heralded by some – foremost the technology industry supplying the infrastructure – and passionately debated and critiqued by others. It is a term and also a concept and both have come under scrutiny.

Before the smarts were declared for cities we had smart technologies and smart materials. Developed in the 1980s, smart materials have qualities that change in response to environmental conditions such as light, pressure, or temperature. For example, shape-memory alloys can be bent and returned to their original shape when exposed to heat. In a similar way, smart technologies describe technology systems that display a response that is context-dependent and leverage constellations based on sensors, computational devices, and actuators. The smart label works when attributed to engineering systems that overcome rigid plans of operation but runs into trouble when applied to a complex and multi-faceted entity that has more than only material and technology components, but includes social, institutional, economic, historical, cultural, and other aspects.

There is a plethora of different smart city definitions, but a common element in all is the widespread deployment of mobile and embedded networked information and communication technologies that are integrated into the physical fabric of the city (Mitchell, 1995; Batty, 1997; Townsend, 2001). The declared objective of this ideal of interconnectivity is to support urban operations and planning for an increase in efficiency of services to improve the social, economic, and environmental wellbeing of citizens (Kitchin, 2015). What the terms of such efficiency are is indeed one of the controversies in the critical debate about the smart city.

Confident – perhaps too confident – claims associated with this position point towards efficiency in terms of zero energy wastage, no traffic jams, no air and water pollution, and zero crime threatening inhabitants. IBM, in one of its "Smarter Planet" ads in 2008, suggested systems would "reduce traffic by 20%," "preventing crime before it happens," and promised "[s]marter public safety for a smarter planet." Living PlanIT claims that "a complete picture of building state, usage, and operations is continually maintained, allowing constant optimization of energy, resources, environment and occupant support and convenience systems." Germany-based Siemens instead looks ahead, claiming that "several decades from now, cities will have countless autonomous, intelligently functioning IT systems that will have perfect knowledge of users' habits and energy consumption, and provide optimum service" (Greenfield, 2013: loc. 185 of 2470).

The smart city model has evolved into an idea of a city as being akin to a computer (Batty, 1997). The model represents a perspective on cities in which all kinds of issues can be addressed with software solutions and that solutions developed once can then be replicated and applied in other cities as well. The alluring elements of this conception are the assumption of bringing the scalability of computer codes from the context of a computer to that of a city. As promoted by the Silicon Valley tech startup culture, the argument is that there is only a need to write code once and have it work the same way whether it serves 100 or 1 million users. One direct consequence of this perspective has been the idea of developing operating systems for cities as well as the installation of urban control centers.

However, the smart city concept has its critics. It is criticized for a techno-centric mindset that sympathizes with notions of "total control" and that undermines views of cities as complex social and territorial entities where structures emerge based on citizens' collective activity (Greenfield, 2013; Hollands, 2015a). The installation of city control centers such as the Rio de Janeiro Operations Center installed by IBM is one example. It brings together data streams from a range of urban systems that become visible to operators of technology systems and city administrations but remain invisible to citizens (Kitchin, 2014). Smart city interventions are prone to disrupt established processes of democratic decision making and accountability under the pretense of an algorithmically based drive for efficiency of which the terms are often not fully known and have not been agreed upon democratically. Inhabitants that are subjected to the "smartness" of such urban systems often have little ability to understand the processes and have little agency in the operations, resulting in new forms of as well as the reinforcement of old forms of disenfranchisement.

Another critique is that the smart city ignores the diversity of socio-cultural contexts and outsources governance to corporations. The critique also regards a one-solution-fits-all approach based on information technologies and a predominant reference to formats of Western industrialized cities. This conflicts with the real diversity of urban conditions that exist in different parts of the world as well as even within any one city itself (Nnaemeka, 2013; Datta, 2015; Odendaal, 2015). True to its technology-based origin, the smart city concept has come to view the deployment of technology in cities as progressive per se and is critiqued for the application of predictive profiling and a depiction of the use of algorithms and analytics as objective and void of ideology (Hollands, 2015b; Kitchin et al., 2015a).

The smart city concept in this way shares traits with the early twentieth-century modernist movement that declared traditional forms of practice obsolete and unfit for the new socio-economic context of the industrialized world. To make things new became the imperative then; to make them smart would seem to be its equivalent today.

As a response to this techno-centric mindset of the smart city concept, a more substantial consideration of human and social aspects in the consideration of urban technologies has recently moved the focus from smart city to smart citizen (Townsend, 2013: 284; Roche et al., 2012; Cardullo and Kitchin, 2017). Social dynamics and the human component have here moved to center stage in working with urban information technologies and aspire to respond more directly to the needs, dreams, and aspirations of citizens (Goldsmith and Crawford, 2014).

As part of this changed perspective, participatory forms of design in the context of networked technologies in urban environments have taken ground that go beyond a simplistic problem–solution coupling that has its origin in an underlying human-centered design approach. Calls for an integration of perspectives of participatory and speculative design approaches point to notions of non-anthropocentric design. This perspective is based on a conceptual decentering of the human as well as new forms of citizenship and cohabitation to address socio-technical complexity such as economic and ecological crisis in more responsible, accountable, and ethical ways when working with emerging technologies (DiSalvo and Lukens, 2011; Forlano, 2016; de Waal and Dignum, 2017; Foth, 2017).

Citizen participation is seen as key to a more critical way of working with networked urban technologies, yet forms of participation vary considerably. In some instances, the focus is on compliance to expected behaviors that are identified as desirable, including strategies of nudging or incentive-based systems (Liu et al., 2011; Kim et al., 2013). Another form of participation regards citizens as a source of information provided through smartphone apps or other digital interfaces. Citizen participation in the form of direct involvement in the planning and management processes, instead, involves residents more comprehensively and taps into informal networks of knowledge, creating a sense of ownership (Hollands, 2008).

Different modes of designing interventions that integrate networked information technologies directly impact constitutional practices of city making. They change the experience citizens have of their cities but, even more, they change the nature of the subject, of what it means to be a citizen and what it means to have agency. They condition the modes of urban politics and reshape the foundations of the democratic way we live together in cities (Gabrys, 2016).

A reference that is notably absent from smart city literature is Horst Rittel's notion of the *wicked problem*. Wicked problems are those that are ill-defined and that involve a considerable social component – where different people affected by an issue may have differing views of what the actual problem is and what could be considered a solution. Rittel suggests that such problems can never be solved as such but rather they are re-solved over and over again. As they are highly entangled with every aspect of their specific context "there is no immediate and no ultimate test of a solution to a wicked problem … any solution, after being implemented, will generate waves of consequences" (Rittel and Webber, 1973). Most if not all issues that smart city initiatives claim to solve are such wicked problems, issues to which straightforward approaches of problem solving do not apply. Moving forward, it is of importance to start with this consideration in order to leverage data-driven technologies in cities in a way that respects and fully valorizes the rich and complex entities that are our cities.

REFERENCES

Batty, Michael (1997), "The computable city." *International Planning Studies*, 2, 155–173.

Borges, Jorge Luis (1946), *On exactitude in science*, trans. A. Hurley. Viking Penguin.

Calabrese, Francesco, Kristian Kloeckl, and Carlo Ratti (2007), "WikiCity: Real-time location-sensitive tools for the city." *IEEE Pervasive Computing, Mobile and Ubiquitous Systems*, 6 (3), 52–53.

Cardullo, Paolo and Rob Kitchin (2017), "Being a 'citizen' in the smart city: Up and down the scaffold of smart citizen participation." The Programmable City, Working Paper 30. http://progcity .maynoothuniversity.ie/

Cardwell, Diane (2014), "Copenhagen lighting the way to greener, more efficient cities." *The New York Times*, December 8. www.nytimes.com/2014/12/09/business/energy

Castells, Manuel (2010), *The rise of the network society* (2nd ed.). Wiley-Blackwell.

CityMurmur (2008), Writing academic English. www.citymurmur.org

Cox, A. and M. Ericson (2007), "Travel times on commuter rail." *New York Times*, December 18. https://archive.nytimes.com/www.nytimes.com/imagepages/2007/03/17/nyregion/nyregionspecial2/ 20070318_TRAIN_GRAPHIC.html

Datta, Ayona (2015), "The smart entrepreneurial city: Dholera and 100 other utopias in India," in Simon Marvin, Andrés Luque-Ayala, and Colin McFarlane (eds), *Smart urbanism: Utopian vision or false dawn*. Abingdon: Routledge, 52–70.

de Waal, Martijn and Marloes Dignum (2017), "The citizen in the smart city: How the smart city could transform citizenship," *it-Information Technology*, 59 (6), 263–73.

DiSalvo, Carl and Jonathan Lukens (2011), "Ropocentrism and the nonhuman in design: Possibilities for designing new forms of engagement with and through technology," in Marcus Foth, Laura Forlano, Christine Satchell, and Martin Gibbs (eds), *From social butterfly to engaged citizen: Urban informatics, social media, ubiquitous computing, and mobile technology to support citizen engagement*. MIT Press.

Dutton, William H., Jay G. Blumler, and Kenneth L. Kraemer (1987), *Wired cities: Shaping the future of communications*. G.K. Hall & Co.

Few, Stephen (2006), *Information dashboard design: The effective visual communication of data*. O'Reilly Media.

Forlano, Laura (2016), "Decentering the human in the design of collaborative cities." *Design Issues*, 32 (3), 42–54.

Foth, Marcus (2008), *Handbook of research on urban informatics: The practice and promise of the real-time city*. IGI Global.

Foth, Marcus (2017), "The next urban paradigm: Cohabitation in the smart city." *it-Information Technology*, 59 (6), 259–262.

Gabrys, Jennifer (2016), *Program Earth: Environmental sensing technology and the making of a computational planet (electronic mediations)*. University of Minnesota Press.

Goldsmith, Stephen and Susan Crawford (2014), *The responsive city: Engaging communities through data-smart governance*. John Wiley & Sons.

Graham, Stephen and Simon Marvin (2001), *Splintering urbanism: Networked infrastructures, technological mobilities and the urban condition*. Psychology Press.

Greenfield, Adam (2013), *Against the smart city*. Do Projects.

Greenfield, Adam and Mark Shepard (2007), *Urban computing and its discontents*. Architectural League of New York.

Hollands, Robert G. (2008), "Will the real smart city please stand up? Intelligent, progressive or entrepreneurial." *City*, 12 (3), 303–320.

Hollands, Robert G. (2015a), "Critical interventions into the corporate smart city." *Cambridge Journal of Regions, Economy and Society*, 8 (1), 61–77.

Hollands, Robert G. (2015b), "Beyond the corporate smart city? Glimpses of other possibilities of smartness." *Smart Urbanism*, 184–200.

Ishida, Toru and Katherine Isbister (eds) (2000), *Digital cities: Technologies, experiences, and future perspectives*. Springer Science & Business Media.

Jackson, Davina and Mary-Anne Kyriakou (2015), *SuperLux: Smart light art, design and architecture for cities*. Thames & Hudson.

Kim, Sunyoung, Jennifer Mankoff, and Eric Paulos (2013), "Sense: Evaluating a flexible framework for authoring mobile data-collection tools for citizen science." *Proceedings of the 2013 Conference on Computer Supported Cooperative Work*, 1453–1462.

Kitchin, Rob (2014), "The real-time city? Big data and smart urbanism." *GeoJournal*, 79 (1), 1–14.

Kitchin, Rob (2015), "Making sense of smart cities: Addressing present shortcomings." *Cambridge Journal of Regions, Economy and Society*, 8 (1), 131–136.

Kitchin, Rob, Tracey P. Lauriault, and Gavin McArdle (2015a), "Smart cities and the politics of urban data." *Smart Urbanism: Utopian Vision or False Dawn*, 16–33.

Kitchin, Rob, Tracey P. Lauriault, and Gavin McArdle (2015b), "Knowing and governing cities through urban indicators, city benchmarking and real-time dashboards." *Regional Studies, Regional Science*, 2 (1), 6–28.

Kloeckl, Kristian (2020), *The urban improvise: Improvisation-based design for hybrid cities*. Yale University Press.

Liu, Yong, Pratch Piyawongwisal, Sahil Handa, Liang Yu, Yan Xu, and Arjmand Samuel (2011), "Going beyond citizen data collection with Mapster: A mobile+ cloud real-time citizen science experiment." *e-Science Workshops*, 1–6.

Mattern, Shannon (2015), "Mission control: A history of the urban dashboard," *Places Journal*. https://doi.org/10.22269/150309

Mitchell, William (1995), *City of bits: Space, place, and the Infobahn*. MIT Press.

Mitchell, William (2003), *ME++: The cyborg self and the network city*. MIT Press.

Nnaemeka, C.Z. (2013), "The unexotic underclass." *MIT Entrepreneurship Review*. https://miter.mit.edu/the-unexotic-underclass/

O'Brien, Daniel Tumminelli (2015), "Custodians and custodianship in urban neighborhoods: A methodology using reports of public issues received by a city's 311 hotline." *Environment and Behavior*, 47 (3), 304–327.

Odendaal, Nancy (2015), "Getting smart about smart cities in Cape Town: Beyond the rhetoric," in Simon Marvin, Andrés Luque-Ayala, and Colin McFarlane (eds), *Smart Urbanism: Utopian vision or false dawn*. Routledge, 71–87.

Ratti, Carlo, Andres Sevtsuk, Sonya Huang, and Rudolf Pailer (2007), "Mobile landscapes: Graz in real time," in Georg Gartner, William Cartwright, and Michael P. Peterson (eds), *Location-Based Services and Telecartography*. Springer, 433–444.

Rittel, H. and M. Webber (1973), "Dilemmas in a general theory of planning." *Policy Sciences*, 4, 155–169.

Rivard, Kurt and Doug Cogswell (2004), "Are you drowning in BI reports? Using analytical dashboards to cut through the clutter." *DM Review*, 14 (4), 26.

Roche, Stéphane, N. Nabian, K. Kloeckl, and C. Ratti (2012), "Are 'smart cities' smart enough?," in Abbas Rajabifard and David Coleman (eds), *Spatially enabling government, industry and citizens: Research and development perspectives*. GSDI Association Press, 215–235.

Rojas, Francisca and Kristian Kloeckl et al. (2008), *New York Talk Exchange*. SA+P Press.

Sassen, Saskia (1991), *The global city: New York, London, Tokyo*. Princeton University Press.

Suchman, Lucy A. (1987), *Plans and situated actions: The problem of human–machine communication* (2nd ed.). Cambridge University Press.

The Economist (2010), "The data deluge." Special supplement, February 25.

Townsend, Anthony M. (2001), "The Internet and the rise of the new network cities, 1969–1999." *Environment and Planning B: Planning and Design*, 28 (1), 39–58.

Townsend, Anthony M. (2013), *Smart cities: Big data, civic hackers, and the quest for a new utopia.* W.W. Norton & Company.

Williams, Sarah, Adam White, Peter Waiganjo Wagacha, and Dan Orwa Ochieng (2015), "The digital matatu project: Using cell phones to create an open source data for Nairobi's semi-formal bus system." *Journal of Transport Geography*, 49, 39–51.

6.   Global risks
Jean-Christophe Le Coze

INTRODUCTION

Global risks are both recent and old phenomena. They are recent because the success of the formulation 'global risks' across audiences is fairly new (two to three decades). They translate mounting concerns of societies over their short- or long-term well-being, security and safety. Yet, global risks are also old because humanity has always been facing and experiencing many types of threat. Indeed, if by global risks one refers to the possibility of events with large-scale immediate or long-term consequences across geographies, global risks are nothing new (Testot, 2017). Some are very ancient, predating humanity, like an asteroid impact on Earth or a supervolcanic eruption. Some are more recent and come with our technological developments such as the possibility of a nuclear 'doomsday' war. Some have older histories, such as pandemics, financial crises or climate changes. Thus, differences between epochs and global risks are of scope or range, scale, likelihood, intensity, speed and/or control. They also come with different stages of technological, social and political developments, degree and type of interconnectedness between continents, ecosystems, cultures and civilisations throughout world history (McNeill & McNeill, 2003).

In this chapter I follow the emergence of several discourses that one can associate with global risks in the past two to three decades. I argue that these recent formulations of categories of global risk have translated different phases of reflexivity by scholars (and beyond) about some of the profound changes faced by contemporary societies. From technological risks in the 1970s and 1980s (associated with the description of large technical systems (LTS)), to systemic risks in the 1990s and 2000s (linked to discourses on globalisation) then existential risks in the 2000s and 2010s (connected to the narratives of the Anthropocene and technoscience), global risks can be interpreted as translations of successive and cumulative contemporary trends and related threats. The interest of proceeding in this way is that LTS can serve as links between these different categorisations. One core issue of global risks is indeed our ability to assess, (re)design, manage and regulate LTS, which is a cultural, managerial, social, political and geopolitical challenge.

REFLEXIVITY OR COMPLEXITY?

One standard view of risks from a sociological perspective is Beck's thesis of 'risk society' developed in the 1980s (Beck, 1992 [1986]). For Beck, some risks were global in the sense, first, that they did not stop at one nation's borders (e.g. the nuclear accident at Chernobyl in 1986), second, that they could affect all social classes, not only poor ones (but Beck added that poor classes were nevertheless more exposed than wealthier classes, and he also wrote that Third World countries were more exposed to risks than rich countries) and, third, that they were manufactured, directly connected to industrial activities and technoscience, human-made risks, and were not external to societies. In Beck's thesis, the notion of risks was also linked to a broad range of issues together which translated and diagnosed profound changes in European societies in the 1970s and 1980s.

Risk was associated with many different uncertainties expressed from a sociological perspective. These included for Beck the development of science and technology and its unintended consequences which eroded societies' trust in progress. In his terminology, the 'goods' of modernity were challenged by the 'bads' but included the crumbling of what had been, for a few decades after the Second World War in Western countries, stable institutions such as social classes, work, families and welfare states. Throughout 30 years of research, these ideas have been discussed in relation to globalisation and analysed through a process of cosmopolitanisation of a 'world risk society' (Beck, 2002), which was to become the study of 'metamorphosis' (Beck, 2017).

Although an influential sociological contribution (Bourg et al., 2013; see also Giddens on risk, globalisation and social theory, 1990, 2000), the starting point of the view developed in this chapter is different than this standard approach of risk through Beck. It also builds an argument for the need of global risks as a sociological category but starts from a different analytical and descriptive point of departure: high-risk systems and technological risks within their political-institutional contexts as defined and studied by another sociologist, Perrow (1984, 2002, 2011). Indeed, in this chapter, some of the analytical ideas of Perrow (coupling, complexity, society of organisations, negative externalities, 'error-prone' and 'error-avoiding' systems) are used to frame some of the issues associated with global risks. While Beck was guided by the hope of the advent of a reflexive modernity turned into a process of cosmopolitanisation in the current global era, this chapter builds on a reflection from Perrow's idea of coupling, complexity and regulation of LTS in relation to global risks (Le Coze, 2020).

SOCIOTECHNOLOGICAL RISKS

In the 1980s, Perrow was concerned with risks in the United States (US) in a different way than Beck was concerned with risks during the same period in Europe. Following the incident at the nuclear power plant of Three Miles Island in 1979 in the US, Perrow developed an analysis of high-risk systems. Nuclear power plants, nuclear weapons, aircraft, dams, maritime transport or mines were typical examples of sociotechnical systems which could produce negative externalities (explosions, crashes, pollution) when those in charge and societies lost their control, which was, considering their size, reach and ubiquitous presence in developed countries, a first categorisation of global risks in the sense of a greater feeling of dependency and exposure to these systems (Perrow, 1984).

Perrow sees in the features of some of these systems, namely their coupling and degree of interaction, a potential for catastrophic surprises. 'Coupling' is defined by buffering characteristics such as the substitution of supplies, slack and redundancy. A tightly coupled system has less buffer than a loosely coupled system. A tightly coupled system cannot absorb shocks as well as a loosely coupled one can. It has no way of substituting one process with another, of diverting a production phase to replace a dysfunctioning one, of relying on extra resources (slack) to compensate for a loss of resources, namely a redundant system to cover for the loss of another. The notion of 'interaction' introduces features such as the presence of unexpected feedback loops, of specialisation of personnel or of information sources. The continuum in terms of 'interaction' is between a linear mode of interactions and a complex one. In the complex one, the likelihood of non-linear feedback loops is higher with less ability to fully understand their dynamic when they occur because of obscure causal mechanisms which cannot be traced in real time to ensure a proper response.

It is the combination of these features which provides an interesting analytical tool for Perrow. A loosely coupled and linear system is defined by available slack, direct information sources and little unexpected feedback loops between subsystems. In other words, it is intrinsically safer. Conversely, a tightly coupled and complex system has, among other things, less slack, indirect access to information sources and multiple unexpected feedback loops between subsystems. In tightly coupled and complex systems, such as nuclear power plants, accidents are likely to occur without being able to anticipate them. They are, in Perrow's terminology, likely to generate 'normal accidents', unexpected products of fully unknowable systems created by humans. Perrow then classified systems according to these criteria.

His proposition was to decouple and make some of these systems simpler, to avoid problems and bad surprises, and had particularly in mind the nuclear industry, described as tightly coupled and interactively complex. But Perrow also understood high-risk systems not only from their technological or structural features (coupling, interaction) but went beyond this type of technological determinism. He analysed them from a wider perspective which includes their social, political and institutional contexts. When regulations and multiple interests align (i.e. insurers, strong unions, active civil society 'watchdogs', powerful regulators), systems reach higher levels of safe performance. He contrasts in this respect what he describes as 'error-prone' systems (such as the maritime industry) and 'error-avoiding' ones (such as aviation). Aviation is in this respect configured to reach a higher level of safety than the maritime industry. From a sociological point of view, he explains why some of these systems are safer than others by describing the balance of power which underpin their operations (Perrow, 1999). In other words, if features of coupling and complexity greatly matter, this is not the whole story, and how high-risk systems are managed, regulated and governed is key to the attainment of safe performance.

Perrow was a sociologist who had indeed an interest in organisations in relation to societies, businesses and states, and analysed them as very influential entities through their ability to shape societies, for their own interests, in multiple ways. For Perrow, who considered that we lived in a society of organisations (1991, 2002), strong states were needed to curb, through regulations, the intrinsic tendency of private organisations to favour profits (and other purposes, such as prestige or hubris of their leaders) over societies' interests. This critical view need not be fully embraced to understand that, retrospectively, the heuristic value of looking through such systems is quite strong from a risk point of view. Our lives have long been indeed depending (and more so since the Industrial Revolution of the nineteenth century; Otter, 2016) on organisations' technological and scientific developments based on the ingenuity of innovators which managed, through research and developments funded by private and public initiatives, to design the artificial world in which we live, and its associated risks. Perrow was not entirely deterministic as his main thesis, normal accident, might have made us think; he was critical and believed in the need for the regulation of organisations' negative externalities by states (Perrow, 2015).

Perrow was not the only writer interested in technological innovations and organisations in the 1970s and 1980s, and what has become known as large technical systems (e.g. electricity, transport and information networks) were also a growing concern for many at the time (La

Porte, 1975; Winner, 1978, 1986; Hughes, 1989). These LTS were indeed becoming more and more prominent in the functioning of our societies and their failures, too, as illustrated by Bhopal (1984), Chernobyl (1986) and Challenger (1986), when Perrow published his book in the 1980s. The proposition in this chapter is to see the notion of LTS as a very broad category embracing diverse systems and their acute long-term risks (negative externalities), including the agro-food to medical through finance and digital industries on which a very large part of many countries' contemporary lifestyles, and associated risks, depend. A question becomes one of managing, anticipating and regulating risks as they develop from the spread and greater reach of LTS. Their dual dimension of positive and negative dimensions of LTS is one core contemporary issue. If one takes the medical domain, corporations can be a source of harm when not properly regulated (e.g. the opioid crisis in the US) but also a source of resilience (e.g. the production of vaccines in the case of Covid-19).

Global risks can therefore be further defined in relation to these LTS broadly described, in Perrow's terms, by their complexity and degree of coupling but also their management, regulation and governance, by their potential acute (explosions, loss of containment of hazardous chemicals) or long-term consequences (pollution, degradation) on Earth (e.g. geology, ecosystems, climate), humanity and societies (e.g. health, safety, inclusion, prosperity, freedom) but also their ability to withstand internal and external stresses or events (e.g. resilience). Therefore, to understand how such LTS grow, develop, are managed and regulated and the part they play in shaping the landscape of increasing global risks constitutes an interesting angle of analysis. If they are global because of their size, reach and ubiquitous presence they are also global because they have been at the heart of a new category of risks: systemic risks.

SYSTEMIC RISKS

If history shows that global risks are far from new, as introduced in this chapter, the extent, reach and contribution of our current LTS in comparison with other epochs make them indeed a good way to pursue an analysis of this topic. Global risks materialise through, within and across core LTS of our man-made world, as studied from the 1970s onwards. Thirty to forty years after the publication of Perrow, in 2020, these systems have indeed become the core sociotechnical infrastructures of our current globalised era. Flows of people, energy, capital, images, goods, data but also viruses (e.g. SARS, Covid-19) travel across the world at great speed throughout such infrastructures, which encompass both private and public organisations (from multinational enterprises to national and international organisations and administrations). Transnational commerce, financial transactions, geological extraction and transportation, digital coordination and tourist travel rely on maritime, rail, aviation and informational infrastructures to concretely make globalisation a reality.

The myriad of links created by these flows across continents, allowed by the information and communication technology (ICT) revolution, combined with the politics of liberalisation of trade and finance (and privatisation and deregulation) by powerful states in the 1980s and 1990s, started to shape a new context for societies. This context was defined as a new era, an era of globalisation, which was associated with risks of global scale (Giddens, 1990, 2000; Beck, 1992 [1986], 1999). These risks were then defined as 'systemic', embracing events such as terrorism, pandemics, financial crises and natural catastrophes (OECD, 2003). In the early 2000s, the 9/11 terrorist attacks, the internet financial bubble and the SARS virus episode were clear examples of this category. Of course, such risks (financial crisis, terrorism, pandemic) were far from new and had existed for a long time, but, because of the increase of speed, intensity and range of flows connecting many nations and continents, it created new potentialities. For this reason, financial risks, supply chain risks, infrastructure risks (transportation, energy, and internet[1]), pandemics and health risks, ecological risks, inequality and social risks are now prime examples of the systemic risks addressed in the literature (Goldin & Mariasathan, 2015; Goldin & Muggah, 2020).

In other words, the disruption of flows (goods, capital, people, information), the amplification of the circulation of unwanted flows (viruses) and an imbalanced distribution of capital and wealth flows across (and within) continents (inequalities) create new contexts for global systemic risks. Such global risks thrive on the increasingly complex architecture of interactions throughout the development and mode of operating in their social, political and institutional contexts of these LTS across the world. Perrow saw the importance of these systemic risks (natural catastrophes, terrorism, cybersecurity) and commented on what he expected to be the next catastrophes in relation to them (Perrow, 2007) but he also commented explicitly how, in return, the mode of operating these LTS have been deeply affected by the ICT revolution, and neoliberal policies propelling globalisation such as the liberalisation of trade and finance but also the politics of deregulation and privatisation of the past decades (Perrow, 2009).

Importantly, what used to be the more national, vertical and internalised modes of operating have become transnational, horizontal and externalised towards networked configurations (Castells, 2001; Veltz, 2008). The financial capitalism of the late twentieth and early twenty-first century has indeed strongly influenced companies' strategies to re-engineer their organisations through outsourcing, subcontracting or offshoring activities beyond their core competences, while favouring shareholders' return on investment driving short-term investments (Weil, 2014). But public administrations, industries or services have also been reshaped by principles of deregulation and privatisation, transforming their modes of operating through neoliberal ideologies of extending markets to many areas, with, for instance, principles of new public management.

The same globalised capitalism created opportunities to extend activities across continents within global value chains (Baldwin, 2016), with several transformations including new regulatory tools beyond traditional state tools, such as standards and self-regulatory philosophies (Ponte et al., 2019). The notion of hybrid governance in which civil societies, states, non-governmental organisations and private organisations interact across geographic areas captures this problem of dealing with the market, environment, social, health and safety aspects of these activities (Graz, 2012). Whether in finance, oil and gas, healthcare, food or aviation, the complex LTS of our epoch exhibit now such strong network properties under the influence of two to three decades of globalisation (Dicken, 2015). One consequence, during the Covid-19 crisis, is the difficulty, in some countries, to access ventilators or masks when needed for medical staff because of supply chains of certain material from far-away countries unable to respond to global demand (see the analysis for the US in Gereffi, 2020).

Other examples of events, beyond Covid-19, which help translate concretely these transformations can be mentioned, from the Rana Plaza collapse in Bangladesh in 2013 in the garment industry, to the BP/Transocean Deepwater Horizon offshore platform explosion in the Gulf of Mexico in 2010 through the subprime financial crisis of 2008. In all three cases, their global dimension is unmistakable. Rana Plaza exemplifies poorly regulated global value chains which are driven by lead firms looking for the cheapest ways to compete on the markets (Blair et al., 2013), Deepwater Horizon illustrates a failed merger and acquisition of a networked and financialised United Kingdom corporation which put profits first while being poorly regulated in the US (Bergin, 2011; Hopkins, 2012) and the financial crisis illustrates a lack of control over the use of sophisticated products despite their obvious weaknesses, which consisted of selling houses to poor people who could not afford to pay their mortgage as rates increased (Stiglitz, 2010; Kay, 2015).

Many other examples of events could be used to connect the materialisation of these globalised flows and what it reveals of the current state of the world from the micro to the macro dimension of global flow and governance, as done for instance in the context of Covid-19 (Schwab & Malleret, 2020). Although sketched in this chapter, LTS developments of course are to be understood as the product of forces exerted by powerful actors, regions and institutions at the world stage through many complex mechanisms of governance. And there is not much need to remind us that the benefits of globalisation are hardly unambiguous and highly heterogeneous but are instead unequally distributed. Despite real improvement in terms of extreme world poverty and other markers of well-being and emancipation, globalisation remains defined by asymmetries and contrasts in terms of wealth, safety, health, life expectancy, learning, freedom, prosperity and environmental degradation across but also now within nations and geographies (Badie & Vidal, 2016). Such sustained and increasing inequalities strongly contribute to the dynamics of systemic risks, as is particularly well illustrated in the case of Covid-19 and the diversity of responses within and across nations (Boyer, 2020). Perrow's categories of complexity and coupling developed in the 1980s have been in this respect converted at a macro level of analysis to discuss the properties of such complex interactions and their ways of failing (Guillén, 2015).

Guillén scales up the analytical framework of Perrow from the coupling and complexity of high-risk systems (such as a nuclear power plant) to the coupling and complexity of global flows, networks and nodes of the globalised landscape, in a context of mega trends and potential turning points (e.g. emerging countries, population ageing, urbanisation, deepening inequalities; Guillén, 2012). For Guillén, with certain simplification for this chapter, at this macro level of analysis, networks are characterised by intensity of flows (e.g. trade, goods, currency, people) across nodes (e.g. states, geographical regions). Complexity of networks (intensity but also asymmetries or imbalances of flows between nodes) must then be considered in relation to the node characteristics also described, in Guillén's definition, in terms of their complexity (e.g. democracy, state capacity, industry diversification) and coupling (e.g. ageing of population, cities, income and wealth inequalities).

Systemic risks materialise in specific contexts of networks and node properties and dynamics of coupling and complexity are extrapolated here at the global level. For Guillén, the current economic state of the world is one of tight coupling and interactive complexity, creating an 'architecture of collapse' (Guillén, 2015). He applies these ideas to explain some of the intertwined backlashes of early twenty-first-century globalisation including financial crisis, failed states, terrorism and populism (Guillén, 2018). One important point to extract from his analysis is that nodes (nations, regions) are not equally endowed when it comes to anticipate, mitigate or compensate systemic risks when they materialise, something that Covid-19 illustrates vividly when studying the various strategic responses and handling of the crisis by different states and regions (Boyer, 2020).

One consequence is that, to prevent and respond to crises, a high degree of coupling and interactive complexity requires a strong level of management, regulation and governance at the global level which in turn depends on a geopolitical context favourable to cooperation and coordination. This issue is illustrated with Covid-19 by the difficulties of the World Health Organization and its global response (e.g. to trigger virus/pandemic alert; to make sure that all countries can access vaccines) in the context of geopolitical tensions between the US and China, and Europe in the middle trying to promote a more multilateral response (Boniface, 2020). To use Perrow's terminology, this architecture of collapse described by Guillén exhibits the features of an 'error-prone' system. All global risks are indeed not equally managed, regulated and governed at the same level of expectation but a global world requires global coordination (Beck, 2017).

EXISTENTIAL RISKS

This search for analytical lenses to explore global risks does not stop with systemic ones. Another recent characterisation of global risks is now available with the prospect of 'existential' risks formulated in the late 2000s (Bostrom & Ćirković, 2008; Smil, 2008; Bostrom, 2014, 2019; Baum & Barrett, 2015). This new category encompasses scale, scope and timeframe of events which threaten the survival of societies, and humanity. Existential risks introduce possibilities of extreme consequences. They include, among others, the incidence of a nearby collapsing star, the consequences of an asteroid's impact on earth or of a supervolcano eruption, the impacts of a climate catastrophe, of a doomsday war or a deadly pandemic (there are more aggressive viruses than Covid-19, although this could also mutate) but also the rise of machine superintelligence threatening the digital infrastructure of the future on which we more and more depend (Bostrom & Ćirković, 2008; Bostrom, 2014, 2019).

Again, the existential risk category refers to many of our current and future LTS, their regulation and governance but also their ability to counteract some of the most fearsome and dystopic of these threats, from the need of the ability to divert an asteroid's trajectory, to identify deadly viruses early and develop programs to fight them or to programme superintelligence in order to remain within the control of humans, preferably under democratic values (Bostrom, 2014). One form of existential risk derived from the latter from the point of view of freedom is the advent of totalitarian regimes backed up by extended technological reach through digital and artificial intelligence capabilities. Behind the promoters of these notions, existential risks are strongly connected to our increasing level of technological development, understood as both a source of potential harm (e.g. a doomsday nuclear war) but also of salvation when for instance finding solutions to prevent an asteroid collision.

This faith in technology fuels a transhumanist ideology which prophesises the advent of a posthuman, and the possibility of shaping a brighter, future, in a discourse of progress through technoscience, and particularly so when confronted with existential threats. This again is about the development, design, management and governance of LTS. Let's illustrate this view with the notion of the Anthropocene, one of the four existential risks along with a (deadly) pandemic, doomsday nuclear war or terrorism which, according to Smil (2008), is the most likely to threaten humanity in the next 50 years. The Anthropocene as a concept addresses the growing concern over the impact of human activities on the planet and considers humanity acting as the equivalent of a geological force (Hamilton et al., 2015; Bonneuil & Fressoz, 2016). It is a historical, social and political interrogation of the human origins of these transformations with competing analyses about the major contributors (e.g. agriculture, industrial revolution, war, consumption society) and the solutions available to limit its consequences. Coupling and complexity can easily be accommodated to the Anthropocene discourse because of the threshold effects, tipping points and circular causalities of positive and negative feedback loops across and between the tight coupling of core variables characterising the dynamics of the geological, ecological, industrial, technological and social networks involved.

From an analytical point of view, the Anthropocene indeed regroups a number of highly interdependent dimensions, themes and measured variables associated with diverse types of impact including global warming (i.e. carbon dioxide emissions, rising water levels, ice melting, average temperature increases, acidification of oceans, health-related effects), biodiversity loss (i.e. eutrophication of oceans, forest devastation, invasive species, agriculture extensions and fish depletions) and pollution (i.e. plastics, wastes, pesticides, endocrine disruptors) (Gemene & Rankovic, 2019). The reasoning behind the notion of the Anthropocene is highly systemic because of the explanation of global interactions between these multiple dimensions while they apply to different, and even bigger, planetary objects. In this context, Covid-19 can be understood as the manifestation of the increase of the likelihood of virus transmission from animals to humans (zoonose) as the coupling between humans and wildlife intensifies through demographic increases and deforestation (Mackenzie, 2020).

But one of the most visible and felt consequences of the Anthropocene, despite diversity and heterogeneity across the world, is a higher frequency of extreme natural events (e.g. fire, drought, floods, hurricanes). Many LTS, which were the primary concern of Perrow and others for the risks they created to societies through their negative externalities then their systemic properties because of their contributions to global flows, are now part of the much wider problem of the Anthropocene. Many of these LTS have indeed had an impact on the climate, ecosystems and several ecological milieus (e.g. ocean, air, ground), including human health through the use of fossil fuels in their current stage of technological development (e.g. aviation, cargo, cruise ships, cars) or through their active role as extractor and provider of fossil fuels (i.e. offshore platforms, refineries, pipelines, mining) or through their potential of long-term pollution on ecosystems and humanity (e.g. chemical products, nuclear waste). However, other LTS which were not initially associated with the Anthropocene need now to be included, such as the material infrastructures of the digital world (data centres) which raise questions about their environmental imprint in terms of energy consumption. Sociotechnical, systemic and existential risks are indeed strongly connected through incredibly complex loops which are difficult to fully embrace.

In this respect, solutions to limit deleterious trends which drastically threaten the conditions of living of societies and humanity include on the one hand the redesign of our current lifestyles based on smaller-scale technologies with less potential to damage ecosystems, nature and humans or, on the other hand, a full-blown, grand-scale technological ambition which further artificialises nature. The philosophy of the former consists in downsizing the human imprint of the planet by abandoning what is interpreted as a sort of technological hubris of the past decades which relied on the development of extractivist, polluting or dangerous LTS (an example of which is the nuclear industry). In this option, the decentralised, local and low tech are favoured, leading to degrowth, deglobalisation, a sort of general decoupling and lower level of complexity (Arnsperger & Bourg, 2017). The philosophy of the latter is to consider the artificialisation of nature not to be a problem and to keep relying instead on the expansion of LTS to limit global warming, including the possibility of geoengineering the Earth to cool down what they believe to be an unavoidable increase of temperatures (Keith, 2013). This view is based on an 'ecomodernist' discourse to maintain the ability of sustaining the living of a growing population, in a context of very asymmetric situations in terms of current lifestyle across the planet (Symons, 2019). Less coupling or less complexity is not necessarily part of the agenda in this latter option.

CONCLUSION

Global risks are not new but they are recent in their current formulation and dynamics. Pandemics, supervolcano eruptions, nuclear reactor meltdowns, a doomsday war, financial crisis, global warming or an asteroid impact are examples of global risks with sometimes long histories. To provide a way of organising this topic in relation to our contemporary epoch, in the 2020s, three categories of global risk have been introduced. They correspond to their historical emergence in academic discourses over the past three decades: sociotechnical, systemic and existential risks. These three categories refer to different stages of development and awareness of what is described in this chapter as LTS (sociotechnical risks), globalisation (systemic risks) and technoscience and the Anthropocene (existential risks). It is argued that an analysis of these three different categories can be explored through LTS and their management, regulation and governance. Global risks can indeed be defined in relation first to their potential (technological disasters), second to their long-term consequences (pollution, degradation) on Earth (e.g. geology, ecosystems, climate) and on humanity and societies (e.g. health, safety, inclusion, equality, prosperity, freedom) but also, third, to their ability to withstand internal and external stresses or events (e.g. resilience). Therefore, to understand how such LTS grow, develop, are managed and regulated and the part they play in shaping the landscape of increasing global risks constitutes a highly relevant angle of analysis. To analyse, anticipate, prevent and respond to global risks consists in, quite fundamentally, assessing, (re)designing, managing, regulating and governing LTS at a global scale. In this respect, the global risk landscape is one of tight coupling and complexity at several scales which requires a strong level of management, regulation and governance at the global level which in turn depends on a geopolitical context, as illustrated by the Covid-19 crisis.

NOTE

1.   The expansion of the internet infrastructure has created new 'digitalised risks' which include cyber attacks (Lupton, 2016).

REFERENCES

Arnsperger, C., & Bourg, D. 2017. *Ecologie Intégrale. Pour une société permacirculaire.* Paris: Presses Universitaires de France.
Badie, B., & Vidal, D. 2016. *L'état du monde 2016. Un monde d'inégalités.* Paris: La Découverte.
Baldwin, R. 2016. *The great convergence: Information technology and the new globalization.* Cambridge, MA: Belknap Press of Harvard University Press.
Baum, S.D., & Barrett, A.M. 2015. *The most extreme risks – global catastrophes: The Gower handbook of extreme risks.* Aldershot: Gower.

Beck, U. 1992 [1986]. *Risikogesellschaft. Auf dem Weg in eine andere Moderne* [Risk society: Towards a new modernity]. Frankfurt am Main: Suhrkamp.

Beck, U. 1999. *World risk society*. Cambridge: Polity Press.

Beck, U. 2002. *Pouvoir et contre-pouvoir à l'ère de la globalisation*. Paris: Flammarion.

Beck, U. 2017 *Metamorphosis of the world: How climate change is transforming our concept of the world*. Cambridge: Polity Press.

Bergin, T. 2011. *Spin and spill: The inside story of BP*. London: Random House Business.

Blair, J., Anner, M., & Blasi, J. 2013. Towards joint liability in global supply chains: Addressing the root causes of labor violations in international subcontracting networks. *Comparative Labour Law and Policy Journal*, 35(1), 1–43.

Boniface, P. 2020. *Géopolitique du Covid-19. Ce que nous révèle la crise du coronavirus*. Paris: Eyrolles.

Bonneuil, C., & Fressoz, J.-B. 2016. *L'événement anthropocène. L'histoire, la terre et nous*. Paris: Le Seuil.

Bostrom, N. 2014. *Superintelligence. Path. Danger. Strategy*. Oxford: Oxford University Press.

Bostrom, N. 2019. The vulnerable world hypothesis. *Global Policy*, 10(4), 455–476.

Bostrom, N., & Ćirković, M.M. (eds). 2008. *Global catastrophic risks*. Oxford: Oxford University Press.

Bourg, D., Joly, P.-B., & Kaufmann, A. (eds). 2013. *Du risque à la menace. Penser la catastrophe*. Paris: Presses Universitaires de France.

Boyer, R. 2020. *Les capitalismes à l'épreuve de la pandémie*. Paris: La Découverte.

Castells, M. 2001. *The rise of the network society*, Second Edition. Oxford: Blackwell.

Dicken, P. 2015. *Global Shifts: Mapping the changing contours of the world economy*, Seventh Edition. Los Angeles, CA: Sage.

Gemene, F., & Rankovic, A. 2019. *Atlas de l'anthropocène*. Paris: Presses de Science Po.

Gereffi, G. 2020. What does the COVID-19 pandemic teach us about global value chains? The case of medical supplies. *Journal of International Business Policy*, 3, 287–301.

Giddens, A. 1990. *The consequences of modernity*. Stanford, CA: Stanford University Press.

Giddens, A. 2000. *Runaway world: How globalization is reshaping our lives*. New York: Profile Books.

Graz, J.C. 2012. *La gouvernance de la mondialisation*. Paris: La Découverte.

Guillén, M. 2012. *Global turning points: The challenges for business and society in the 21st century*. Cambridge: Cambridge University Press.

Guillén, M. 2015. *The architecture of collapse: The global system in the 21st century*. Oxford: Oxford University Press.

Guillén, M. 2018. *Rude awakening: Threats to the global liberal order*. Philadelphia, PA: University of Pennsylvania Press.

Goldin, I., & Mariathasan, M. 2015. *The butterfly defect: How globalization creates systemic risks, and what to do about it*. Princeton, NJ: Princeton University Press.

Goldin, I., & Muggah, R. 2020. Terra incognita: *100 maps to survive the next 100 years*. London: Penguin.

Hamilton, C., Bonneuil, C., & Gemene, F. (eds). 2015. *The Anthropocene and the global environmental crisis: Rethinking modernity in a new epoch*. London: Routledge.

Hopkins, A. 2012. *Disastrous decisions: The human and organisational causes of the Gulf of Mexico blowout*. Washington, DC: CCH.

Hughes, T. 1989. *American genesis: A century of invention and technological enthusiasm, 1870–1970*. New York: Viking.

Kay, J. 2015. *Other people's money: Master of the universe or servants of the people?* London: Profile Books.

Keith, D. 2013. *A case for climate engineering*. Cambridge, MA: MIT Press.

La Porte, T.R. (ed.). 1975. *Organized social complexity: Challenge to politics and policy*. Princeton, NJ: Princeton University Press.

Le Coze, J.C. 2020. *Post normal accident: Revisiting Perrow's classic*. Boca Raton, FL: CRC Press.

Lupton, D. 2016. Digital risk society. In A. Burgess, A. Alemmano, & O. Zin (eds), *Routledge handbook of risk studies*. London: Routledge.

Mackenzie, D. 2020. *The pandemic that never should have happened, and how to stop the next one*. Wicklow Town: Bridge Street Press.

McNeill, J.R., & McNeill, W.H. 2003. *The human web: A bird's-eye view of world history*. New York: W.W. Norton.

OECD. 2003. *Emerging systemic risks: Final report to the OECD future project*. Paris: OECD.

Otter, C. 2016. Artificial Britain: Risk, systems and synthetics since 1800. In T. Crook & Mike Esbester (eds), *Governing risks in modern Britain: Danger, safety and accidents c. 1800–2000*. London: Palgrave Macmillan.

Perrow, C. 1984. *Normal accidents, living with high-risk technology*. Princeton, NJ: Princeton University Press.

Perrow, C. 1991. A society of organizations. *Theory and Society*, 20, 725–762.

Perrow, C. 1999. *Normal accidents, living with high risk technologies*, Second Edition. New York: Basic Books.

Perrow, C. 2002. *Organising America: Wealth, power and the origins of corporate capitalism*. Princeton, NJ: Princeton University Press.

Perrow, C. 2007. *The next catastrophe: Reducing our vulnerabilities to natural, industrial and terrorist disasters*. Princeton, NJ: Princeton University Press.

Perrow, C. 2009. Modeling firms in the global economy. *Theory and Society*, 38(3), 217–243.

Perrow, C. 2011. *The next catastrophe: Reducing our vulnerabilities to natural, industrial and terrorist disasters*. Princeton, NJ: Princeton University Press.

Perrow, C. 2015. Cracks in the 'regulatory state'. *Social Currents*, 2(3), 203–212.

Ponte, S., Gereffi, G., & Gale, R.-R. 2019. *Handbook of global value chains*. Cheltenham, UK and Northampton, MA, USA: Edward Elgar Publishing.

Schwab, K., & Malleret, T. 2020. *Covid-19: The great reset*. Geneva: Agentur Schweiz.

Smil, V. 2008. Global *catastrophes and trends: The next fifty years*. Cambridge, MA: MIT Press.

Stiglitz, J.E. 2010. *Freefall: America, free markets, and the sinking of the world economy*. New York: W.W. Norton & Company.

Symons, J. 2019. *Ecomodernism: Technology, politics and the climate crisis*. Cambridge: Polity Press.

Testot, L. 2017. *Cataclysmes. Une histoire environnementale de l'humanité*. Paris: Payot.

Veltz, P. 2008. *Le nouveau monde industriel. Edition revue et augmentée*. Paris: Le débat, Gallimard.

Weil, D. 2014. *The fissured workplace: Why work became so bad for so many and what can be done to improve it*. Cambridge, MA: Harvard University Press.

Winner, L. 1978. *Autonomous technology: Technics-out-of-control as a theme in political* thought. Cambridge, MA: MIT Press.

Winner, L. 1986. *The whale and the reactor, a search for limits in an age of high technology*. Chicago, IL: University of Chicago Press.

7. Global waste

Zsuzsa Gille

INTRODUCTION

Global waste. What image do you associate with this term? Plastic islands floating in the ocean? Waste-infested places visible from space, such as a burning tire dump in Kuwait in 2012, or the mounds of the New York Fresh Kills landfill? Or would you zoom in on spaces representing the global? Ports where ships carrying plastic or toxic wastes are stranded for weeks or months on end because their dubious cargo isn't allowed to enter the country? Other waterways, like Beirut's river of trash? Indeed, waste *is* global in the sense of size: it is present in unprecedented physical magnitudes and in ever increasing spatial expansion.

But in another commonly used meaning of the word, as universal, the world's waste problems aren't global. Nor are they *only* global in the sense of manifesting at the global scale. Wastes are produced and distributed in uneven ways, in specific social settings, and in particular materialities. To get at this unevenness and diversity, social scientists have subjected waste to several different types of analysis, each with different implications for theory, method, and policy priorities and design. This chapter analyzes the scholarship from the perspective of global and transnational sociology by describing and evaluating the ways in which it refers to or incorporates the global scale, and translocal and transnational social relations. Prior to that overview, however, I will provide a brief introduction to waste as a subject matter for sociology and for the social sciences more broadly. As a proviso, in the interest of cohesion and space, a few areas of scholarship, such as nuclear waste, sewage, necro-waste, and the concept of humans as waste, have to remain outside the scope of this chapter.

WASTE IN SOCIOLOGY

Waste is a relatively new subject for sociology. In the United States (US) it was new social activism that demanded sociological treatment. From the late 1980s there had been increasing opposition to waste treatment facilities, such as landfills and incinerators. High-temperature incineration emerged at that time as newly available technology that could "disappear" hazardous wastes previously much less amenable to treatment. Since many of these highly toxic facilities were (and still are) sited in or near communities of color, scholars took their inspiration from the social movement scholarship in laying down the foundations of what is now known as the environmental racism/environmental justice field (Bullard 1990; Szasz and Meuser 1997; Brook 1998; Weinberg et al. 2000; Pellow and Brulle 2005). In a few years this scholarship extended its attention to global inequalities, primarily by demonstrating outsourcing and waste export in the Global South; I will review that part of the literature below.

In the European context, waste received a different type of attention, mostly from scholars studying consumption, food waste, and second-hand and thrift shopping (Gregson and Crewe 2003; Hetherington 2004; Gregson 2007; Evans 2012), and as a result this scholarship built primarily on the sociology of consumption, a subdiscipline that had had stronger traditions in Western Europe to begin with. Another branch of European waste scholarship dissected governance issues in waste collection and recycling (Fagan 2003; Davies 2008; Bulkeley and Gregson 2009). The ecological modernization scholarship, which had a distinctly Western European (and to a lesser extent Japanese) origin and focus, included waste only somewhat tangentially. By describing increasing corporate efforts at waste reuse and recycling and, to a lesser extent, at waste minimization, it placed much faith in an environmentally sensitive capitalism taking root globally. US sociologists, especially those informed by a political economy approach, tended to be more skeptical. They pointed to evidence of Western European greening in good part facilitated by outsourcing and global dumping, as well as to the continued addiction of market economies to growth, which, according to the dominant US environmental sociology paradigm, the treadmill of production—first developed by Allan Schnaiberg (1980) and then tweaked by other scholars (Pellow et al. 2000)—is inherent in the logic of capitalism, with the implication that gains in ecological efficiency and other technological innovations will never result in the reduction of environmental harms in absolute terms. Recent European scholarship on circular economy policies and zero waste projects have tended to confirm this skepticism (O'Brien 2013; Alexander and Reno 2014; Gregson et al. 2015).

In the Global South, where most waste collection and treatment are not regulated, or even collectively organized, most scholars focused on the public health and environmental consequences of waste disposal and on informal waste workers, for whom municipal waste collection, sorting, and disassembly provided their only source of livelihood. Scholars of the Global South (Post et al. 2003; Nzeadibe and Adama 2015; Ogando et al. 2017; Shankar and Sahni 2017) received much less attention or even mention in this scholarship than those of the Global North and, admittedly, my knowledge of their contributions is also rather limited. The most widely cited works on informal waste labor are by Rosalind Fredericks (2009, 2018), Jutta Gutberlet (2008), Martin Medina (2007), Kathleen Millar (2008, 2018), and Faranak Miraftab (2004). I will review this scholarship below.

This division of labor meant that scholars in these traditions concentrated on two different types of waste streams: in the US on hazardous waste that was primarily of industrial origin; and in Europe on municipal, that is household, waste and in the Global South on electronic and plastic waste, most of which was also of household origin. While these are not isolated streams, studying them from a social science perspective will have rather different theoretical and methodological requirements and implications. Research on household—that is, municipal—waste implies that the key actors studied will be consumers and waste collectors. In contrast, focusing on hazardous waste of manufacturing origin, which constitutes the minority of waste studies scholarship, shifts attention to those living near incinerators and landfills, and to only a small extent to producers, such as chemical companies. This tendency to "study down" and the lack of focus on production waste and the many ways producers limit consumer choice in how much and what kinds of waste they produce—let alone what they are able to recycle—have been a major shortcoming of the literature. This is all the more striking when we consider that in the most developed countries only about 3–10 percent of all wastes are of household origin; the rest is generated by construction, mining, and manufacturing (ADEME 2009; Liboiron 2010; Eurostat 2014). This thematic focus is, in great part, fueled by the lack of access to data and research subjects in the private sphere. While there are case studies focusing on individual firms, most of these works are about corporate sustainability efforts, such as zero waste or other circular economy-type approaches, so they tend to strike a celebratory tone and give the impression that these positive cases are more common or easier to emulate than they really are. While the described greening of private manufacturing is welcome, only a few studies focus on the global structures that facilitate a certain amount and kind of greening, at the expense of environmental quality and even of increasing waste elsewhere. This limitation of the scholarship is based on and reinforces a shortsighted definition of waste, as I explain below.

While there are quite a few texts that engage with the definitional conundrum (Moore 2012; O'Brien 2007; Furniss 2017), most social scientists that study waste issues do not offer an explicit definition of waste. Their implied conceptualization often reflects extant policy and legal definitions (Gourlay 1992; O'Brien 2013), namely, that waste is a material that is discarded. While obviously the social aspect of waste problems isn't neglected, that waste is a material, whether a potentially useful resource or something that is inherently risky, is usually not questioned. But how and what kinds of material are rendered into waste, and who decides—and how—that they are ripe for disposal, is much less studied. This means that in all of the scholarly traditions mentioned above the bulk of the analytical focus falls on what happens to materials once they are deemed useless or harmful. This lends a particularly end-of-pipe focus to the waste scholarship; that is, most social scientists focus on waste distribution and much less so on waste production (for an example of how the latter could be done, see Vermeulen and Ras 2006). This is all the more troubling from a sociological perspective, because taken-for-granted ways of distributing and treating waste facilitate and arguably maintain particular waste production practices and technologies (Gregson and Foreman 2021). For example, if manufacturers and consumers couldn't rely on cheap disposal and recycling, wherever those may take place, they would have to reconsider and change the quantity and quality (chemical composition) of the materials they buy, use, and discard. We may start seeing this effect after China's ban of plastic waste import (Huang et al. 2020). This is an obvious example of environmental externalities as well as of Jason Moore's concept of "cheap nature." In his definition, food, labor, energy, and raw materials are cheap "to the degree that their reproduction costs can be largely kept 'off the books' or—in the case of mineral deposits—extracted at well below prevailing extraction costs" (Moore 2017: 606). Such cheapness in return is made possible by global structures such as colonialism, development, and globalization. This means that we must shift our focus not only upstream—that is, to the generation of waste—and examine the social relations that constitute waste generation, including its quantity and material quality, but we also need to transcend what in global and transnational sociology has been termed the fallacy of methodological nationalism. Methodological nationalism stems from the assumption of classic social science research that the social is co-extensive with the national. It is not that the social sciences ignored interstate, meaning international, social relations but that, first, such links tended to form among well-bounded nations, as a whole, and second, the national tended to ontologically precede the international. So the social was not only co-extensive with the national, but this nationally bounded social was also the origin and the cause of the international. This framework becomes a built-in obstacle to the discovery that the international may in fact precede and shape the social space of the nation.

In contrast I suggest, following Gourlay, that we define waste as material that we failed to use (for whatever reason). This immediately shifts focus to the practice of disuse and disposal, and their socio-material determinants. Questions that arise from such a perspectival shift include: What values and mentalities inform the determination that an object is no longer useful or safe? What economic interests are involved in selecting input materials in production whose life-cycle characteristics cause environmental and social problems? What economic interests and cultural norms shape how much waste we produce? What global social relations facilitate the use of such materials and the distancing of the resulting residues (removal from their place of generation for treatment or recycling)? How do global social inequalities inform national waste policies?

To reflect this definition, I will divide the review of existing scholarship on global waste into two main sections: the transnational production and the transnational distribution of waste. I will focus on the effects of globalization and the expansion of transnational social relations on waste production and distribution, as that has been the most relevant intersection between global and transnational sociology on the one hand and waste studies on the other. In my conclusions, however, I will point to an emergent field that reverses the arrow and shows some of the ways that particular modes and practices of wasting facilitate or otherwise shape global spaces, globalization and transnational social relations, and society itself.

TRANSNATIONAL WASTE PRODUCTION

Most studies that interrogate the transnational movement of waste, primarily hazardous waste, focus on the export of already-generated waste. However, just as commodities are increasingly manufactured and assembled in multiple countries according to relations of domination and comparative advantages—which include not just available resources or know-how, but also wage levels and the regulatory environment—so are wastes produced transnationally. Empirical evidence suggests that multinational corporations often delegate the most toxic or most waste-intensive parts of the production process to the Global South or other countries with low-level regulation or lax enforcement (Adeola 2000; Frey 2003; White 2008; Brownell 2011); and Michael Baram (1994) as well as Peter Little and Cristina Lucier (2017) have documented how waste-related codes of conduct and other voluntary environmental standards corporations implemented in the Global North do not translate into higher environmental performance further down the supply chain, especially if subcontractors are from developing countries. In fact, corporations' lobbying efforts against environmental regulation exacerbate this situation (Orsini 2011).

Another way in which waste is produced transnationally or in which globalization affects waste generation is through rising household consumption all over the globe, albeit in an uneven fashion. This is particularly the case for goods that have a cache of Westernness or modernity, or are markers of a middle-class status, such as cars, electronic devices, and high-turnover apparel fashion (Princen et al. 2002; Dauvergne 2010; Tong and Wang 2012). While increased consumption does not necessarily lead to higher discards, and we have come a long way from the moralizing tone of earlier scholarship that blamed the consumer (O'Brien 2007; Evans 2012), due to our current modes of consumption, the built-in obsolescence of most products, and various retail practices, among several other factors, this correlation currently can neither be avoided nor is it denied by the scholarship. There is ample literature on different forms of consumer activism that have tried to counter this tendency, though these have mostly struck roots in the Global North, and where they exist in the Global South they are often initiated by Northern non-governmental organizations or certificate schemes. Specifically in the area of waste this means household recycling, buying used or upcycled commodities or goods with higher recycled content, and buying in bulk or using reusable shopping bags. Increasingly, corporations also offer buybacks, deposits, or other tools that fall under what has come to be called extended producer responsibility. Apparel manufacturers, especially high-end global brands, now also ask consumers to return their used clothing to them, which then is presumably recycled. The right-to-repair movement, though not without its pitfalls, is expected to bring some much-needed progress in this area (Graziano and Trogal 2017).

The literature has pointed to a number of problems with such waste-reduction and waste-reuse efforts in the realm of consumer goods. One is wish-cycling: individuals do place their discards in recycling bins but their level of contamination, from food or from mixing in other non-recyclable materials, often means that these will ultimately not be recycled but dumped or incinerated (O'Neill 2018). To date, MacBride (2013) has the most encompassing overview of how current institutions charged with collecting, separating, and recycling municipal wastes fail for deeply structural reasons. There is also the phenomenon Catherine Alexander and Joshua Reno (2012) call "feel-good reuse," donating or purchasing reused goods, which turn out to be so low quality that they soon also end up discarded, textiles being a prime example (Norris 2012). Finally, scholars have identified a rebound effect, or what in a different context has been called Jevons Paradox: consumers feel encouraged to buy (and potentially waste) more if they feel that their purchases are ecologically conscious, or if they have more discretionary income due to savings from buying recycled or reusable products or using energy-efficient appliances (Clark and York 2005; Takase et al. 2005). A good case study is on the paperless office by York (2006).

Finally, another key global driver of waste is food production. The above drivers associated with middle-class and Western modes of consumption are relevant here as well, but there are some important factors unique to this sector. The increasing liberalization of cross-national trade—that is, the importing and exporting of agricultural products without previously customary custom duties or other protectionist measures—exerts novel pressures for food waste generation. As much of food trade is unevenly liberalized, allowing governments of the Global North, primarily the European Union and the US, to retain farm subsidies while Global South countries are compelled to eliminate them, farmers from those most developed parts of the world can undersell farmers in the less developed parts. This not only threatens food security and sovereignty in the latter, but also renders any infrastructural development that would connect local farmers to local customers more likely uneconomical. Investments in roads, warehouses, refrigeration, and sanitation make less and less sense, leading to the key manifestation of food waste in developing countries: postharvest loss. I have analyzed how current forms of food aid, primarily because they are in kind rather than in cash, contribute to the same dynamic, whereby produce from the Global North make local production and storage capacities uneconomical (Gille 2013).

In contrast, in the Global North, in absolute terms, food waste is primarily generated in households and restaurants. However, as Max Liboiron (2014) points out, in terms of per capita food waste generation, the losses in the pre-consumer stage outweigh those in the postconsumer phase here, too. Indeed, as a few scholars have pointed out, the causes of waste generated by households are not necessarily to be found at this scale. Several aspects of globalization drive structures in food production and retail that make it more likely that consumers will discard food—according to estimates, as much as 30–50 percent of what they buy. Since food travels greater and greater distances, most food is pre-packaged. This doesn't just translate into huge amounts of packaging waste, most of which is plastic, but also results in portion sizes that don't necessarily conform to a variety of household sizes and tastes. The compulsion to buy more than what one needs is not simply driven by advertising but by producers' and supermarkets' portioning and packaging practices (Hawkins 2001; Stuart 2009). Food safety standards have the same effect, not only through increased packaging but also through appending confusing labels to expiration dates, such as "sell by," "best before," "use by," etc. Erring on the side of caution, consumers discard much still-edible food (Gille 2013; Milne 2013; Watson and Meah 2013; O'Neill 2018).

These food safety standards in turn represent another facet of globalization, namely, protection from adverse effects of the increasingly free market. Again, it is only countries in the Global North that are able to implement and enforce quality and safety standards and provide protections for their own farmers by making it illegal for competitors outside designated geographical regions to market food items, primarily wine, cheese, and meat, wearing labels that indicate a certain set of qualities, know-how, and origin. Examples of this include Parma ham and Bourdeaux wine. Such geographical-origin protections are usually bundled with safety and quality standards, meaning that produce with certain aesthetic qualities are routinely discarded or never even harvested, and thus contribute to the above-mentioned drivers of food waste.

Another type of postharvest loss in the Global North is driven by retail power. Many have identified the precipitous decline in the prices that retailers and integrators pay to farmers as the cause of the phenomenon of walk-bys (Bloom 2011). Retailers and integrators increasingly are multinational corporations that, thanks to trade liberalization, are able to pressure primary producers to sell at prices that barely cover their costs, so they routinely find it more economical to not even harvest perfectly edible produce.

TRANSNATIONAL WASTE DISTRIBUTION AND TREATMENT

As mentioned, a key area where waste studies intersects with global studies is international waste trade. Much of the scholarly focus has been on particular waste streams: e-waste, plastic (mostly packaging) waste, hazardous waste, and used apparel. Early studies on electronic waste assumed that the primary direction of this stream was from the Global North to the Global South. Today however, a new consensus is emerging that suggests a more complex set of relations between waste producers, collectors, distributors, disassemblers, and resellers (Crang et al. 2013; Lepawsky 2018).

Plastic wastes however do conform to this expectation of North-to-South directionality. Until recently, China and several other East Asian countries served as the main destinations for plastic waste, mostly of municipal origin in the US and Europe. Scholars understood China's initial willingness to take plastic as the result of its developed sorting and recycling sector, cheap labor, and hunger for the kinds of resources needed for its rapid industrialization and urbanization (Duraiappah et al. 2002; Goldstein 2020), as well as the relatively high price of plastic recyclates (Alexander and Reno 2012). These factors are still present for e-waste although, as argued above, China isn't nearly as dominant a destination as previously assumed. In 2018 China decided not so much to ban plastic waste imports as to enforce its standards about the purity of wastes accepted. Since exporter countries couldn't ensure such low contamination levels for plastics, they found themselves without willing takers, especially after Malaysia, Thailand, Taiwan, and Vietnam also followed suit, albeit some only temporarily.

An accompaniment to studies of waste exports, studies of international treaties, and legal devices regulating such exports have also dominated the literature. Some sociologists focused on the institutional diffusion effect of globalization. The Basel Convention understandably received the most attention, as it is the most important international treaty with the largest number of signatories that regulates the export and import of wastes. Studies on the Basel Convention all conclude that it provides insufficient protection for developing countries, in part because of the letter of these laws, and in part because of the ease with which powerful interests both in the sending and receiving countries can avoid detection and enforcement (Lucier and Gareau 2015; Lepawsky 2018). What Dana Fisher and William Freudenburg (2004) call "environmental institutionalization without actual environmental protection action" not only explains this common finding but also calls into question the scholarly and policy merit of diffusionist studies.

THE ROLE OF INFORMALITY AND CIVIL SOCIETY IN TRANSNATIONAL WASTE DISTRIBUTION

No other issue has received as much attention in the global and transnational waste scholarship as the struggles of informal waste pickers in the Global South. These are precarious laborers whose livelihood depends entirely on municipal waste collection and the sale of valuable materials to a variety of sellers. Many books and articles share the findings about their living and working conditions: that they are unhealthy, uncertain, and skirting illegality (Shankar and Sahni 2017; Nyathi et al. 2018). These in turn are produced by structural causes that are also shared across a great many countries, cities, and villages. Most important among these are the simultaneous rise in household waste and in unemployment, or what globalization and labor scholars described as the emergence of a global precariat. At the same time, state incomes, whether at the local or national scale, have dwindled, in part due to structural adjustment policies imposed as loan conditions from the International Monetary Fund and the World Bank, leaving governments unable to pay for collective waste collection and treatment along with other public goods (Miraftab 2004; Millar 2008). Informal workers have seen an opportunity in ridding neighborhoods of their garbage piles and salvaging still valuable materials. (Millar 2008; Fredericks 2009; Knowles 2017). As has been documented, however, the value from salvaging materials tends not to accrue to the community that expends its labor. The inclusion of women in waste collection and salvaging has been uneven. In some sites their work is decidedly gendered (Miraftab 2004; Fredericks 2009; Nzeadibe and Adama 2015), with all the attendant social consequences documented by globalization and labor scholars writing on the feminization of labor and the informal economy; while in other places, they are excluded or prevented from accessing the most valuable materials (Ogando et al. 2017).

In many countries the sight of these workers or the mess they occasionally leave behind (especially if they scavenge without much training or without sufficient organization), along with probably exaggerated public safety concerns, has placed pressure on municipal governments to "professionalize" waste collection; however, due to lack of funds, these mostly had to take the form of public–private partnerships (Post et al. 2003; Miraftab 2004; Dinler 2016). Waste management firms, often branches of multinational corporations headquartered in the Global North, struck deals with these governments, a legal consequence of which was that collecting wastes informally was now considered theft. The scholarship, however, also documents how in some countries waste pickers organized themselves, demonstrated their expertise and superior waste selection skills, carved out contracts with regular wages, health and legal protections, and now even advise the government on waste-related policies (van Horen 2004; Gutberlet 2009, 2022).

CONCLUSION

This chapter reviews the scholarship on global waste as a field where globalization studies intersects with waste studies. So far, I have presented this intersection as thematic; that is, I have focused on key problem areas where the two fields addressed shared concerns or where achievement in one informed the other. To be sure, the direction of this influence has so far been from the former to the latter: globalization studies providing a context for waste studies.

While this is understandable given the size and influence of the former, there is certainly room for future scholarship to reverse the arrow and investigate how waste practices shape globalization, the industries that drive it, the forms of urbanizations we witness, and, not least, the nature of global social inequalities. For such an inquiry to be successful scholars would need to dive much deeper into neglected areas of the literature: production waste and the materiality of waste. One example is Caroline Knowles's (2017) and Ingrid Behrsin and Salvatore Paulo De Rosa's (2020) studies of how waste materials that are mobilized in urban mining are literally and metaphorically what global cities are built from. The phenomenon of what we might call waste-dependent development is also increasingly documented (Millar 2008; Fredericks 2009; Brownell 2011; Knowles 2017; Behrsin and de Rosa 2020; Krones 2020). Such studies can also learn from Martin O'Brien's (2007) more foundational argument that waste is generative of society, or Kevin Hetherington's (2004) argument that all consumption necessitates some amount and certain kinds of wasting. Recently scholars have also redefined the Anthropocene, which increasingly functions as a synonym of "the global," as the apotheosis of waste (Hecht 2018), as Wasteocene (Armiero and De Angelis 2017), and even, extending Jason Moore's (2017) concept of the Capitalocene, as hinging on a transnational waste regime that includes the former Second World (Gille 2022).

By treating waste as only a by-product of production and consumption, it has been necessarily delegated to the margins of social science scholarship, which is all the more a pity because such studies could inform policies and directions for technological innovation. Presently, scholars have followed the flashlight wielded by corporations and a distinctly neoliberal economic discourse, focusing almost exclusively on individual household recycling, conscious consumerism, and voluntary standards—that is, self-regulation of industry (Little and Lucier 2017). It is time for us to use our own flashlights and light up areas that have conveniently stayed in the dark: production waste and structural drivers waste. Because data on the latter are admittedly harder to find than on recycling rates and consumer-driven waste reduction and reuse, we have found ourselves in a situation whereby the data-tail wags the theory-dog, rather than the other way around (MacBride 2013; Liboiron 2014, 2010).

In addition to the thematic intersections of the two bodies of scholarship, however, there are methodological ones as well. Here sociological innovations could inform waste studies much more. I will mention three. The sociology of globalization and transnational social relations have identified a number of limitations of traditional social science epistemology and methodology. The first is that of methodological nationalism, as mentioned above. For waste studies this has meant that waste policies have been assumed to be driven only by domestic factors. While the nation state is certainly not dead, as early globalization studies claimed or predicted, the ever thicker inter, trans, and supranational relations sociologists have identified exert novel (not just more) pressures on national policies and waste practices. As a corollary, the validity of quantitative or qualitative cross-national comparisons is much reduced, since we can no longer take for granted the independence of the units compared. Second, comparing nations and correlating their records in environmental policies or their waste data, for example with gross domestic product per capita, will necessarily yield skewed results since wastes, as the literature I analyzed above demonstrates, are unevenly mobile, as are the producers who generate wastes, and the policies affecting those data are also driven and informed by trans and supranational actors, such as the European Union or multinational corporations. Third, we can no longer take for granted the classical scalar hierarchy of the local, the national, and the global or supranational. These scales are no longer fully nested within each other, as Russian dolls, rather, as Saskia Sassen (2006) has shown, functions of the national shift both the supra and the subnational. Local actors can also increasingly directly access certain supranational actors without the mediation of their respective national governments. This is perhaps most evident in transnational social movements (Keck and Sikkink 1998) and has been relevant for environmental and waste-related activism, as well. The importance of analyzing waste issues at multiple scales and their relationships has been increasingly recognized by waste scholars. Samantha MacBride (2013) demonstrates how by limiting the scales at which the selections of waste for recycling occurs, household and municipal scale, leaves untouched the greatest waste stream which, as I discussed above, is generated by industry whether at the scale of national or transnational. Joshua Lepawsky (2018) is similarly critical of the scalar assumptions of the e-waste scholarship that has focused too much on postconsumer e-waste, rather than the wastes, not less toxic and much larger, than what the manufacturing of electronics generates, including raw material extraction. As a result, the spatial distribution of those wastes in the world is misrepresented, depriving policymakers as well as activists of crucial information needed to combat contamination resulting from the full life cycle of electronics. In a most fascinating and sobering analysis he shows how a single smelter generated more waste than the total annual tonnage of postconsumer e-waste arising in the US. To combat these problematic assumptions, he suggests the worlding of e-waste. Worlding in his vocabulary might be best compared to what we sociologists refer to as social construction of a social problem, perhaps with more spatial and scalar implications. It is about re-representing the connections, human and non-human, and the practices across multiples scales that make wastes.

Global and transnational sociology has a lot to contribute to waste studies, however, the latter has also come a long way, and has much to contribute to our understanding of globalization and transnational social relations.

REFERENCES

ADEME (Agence de l'Environnement et de la Maîtrise de l'Energie) [Environment and Energy Management Agency] (2009). *Waste Figures for France: Data and Figures*. Angers: ADEME. www .ademe.fr/sites/default/files/assets/documents/69417_6768_waste_figures_for_france_interactif_def .pdf

Adeola, Francis O. (2000). Cross-National Environmental Injustice and Human Rights Issues: A Review of Evidence in the Developing World. *American Behavioral Scientist* 43 (4): 686–706.

Alexander, Catherine and Joshua Reno, eds (2012). *Economies of Recycling: The Global Transformation of Materials, Values and Social Relations*. London: Zed Books.

Alexander, Catherine and Joshua Reno (2014). From Biopower to Energopolitics in England's Modern Waste Technology. *Anthropological Quarterly* 87 (2): 335–358.

Armiero, Marco and Massimo De Angelis (2017). Anthropocene: Victims, Narrators, and Revolutionaries. *South Atlantic Quarterly* 116 (2): 345–362.

Baram, Michael S. (1994). Multinational Corporations, Private Codes, and Technology Transfer for Sustainable Development. *Environmental Law* 24 (1): 33–66.

Behrsin, Ingrid and Salvatore Paolo De Rosa (2020). Contaminant, Commodity and Fuel: A Multi-Sited Study of Waste's Roles in Urban Transformations from Italy to Austria. *International Journal of Urban and Regional Research* 44 (1): 90–107.

Bloom, Jonathan (2011). *American Wasteland: How America Throws Away Nearly Half of Its Food (and What We Can Do about It)*. Cambridge, MA: De Capo Press.

Brook, Daniel (1998). Environmental Genocide: Native Americans and Toxic Waste. *American Journal of Economics and Sociology* 57 (1): 105–113.

Brownell, Emily (2011). Negotiating the New Economic Order of Waste. *Environmental History* 16 (2): 262–289.

Bulkeley, Harriet and Nicky Gregson (2009). Crossing the Threshold: Municipal Waste Policy and Household Waste Generation. *Environment and Planning A* 41 (4): 929–945.

Bullard, Robert (1990). *Dumping in Dixie: Race, Class, and Environmental Quality*. Boulder, CO: Westview.

Clark, Brett and Richard York (2005). Carbon Metabolism: Global Capitalism, Climate Change, and the Biospheric Rift. *Theory and Society* 34: 391–428.

Crang, Mike, Alex Hughes, Nicky Gregson, Lucy Norris, and Farid Ahamed (2013). Rethinking Governance and Value in Commodity Chains through Global Recycling Networks. *Transactions of the Institute of British Geographers* 38 (1): 12–24.

Dauvergne, Peter (2010). *The Shadows of Consumption: Consequences for the Global Environment*. Cambridge, MA: MIT Press.

Davies, Anna (2008). *The Geographies of Garbage Governance: Interventions, Interactions and Outcomes*. Aldershot: Ashgate.

Dinler, Demet Ş. (2016). New Forms of Wage Labour and Struggle in the Informal Sector: The Case of Waste Pickers in Turkey. *Third World Quarterly* 37 (10): 1834–1854.

Duraiappah, Anantha Kumar, Zhao Xin, and Pieter J. H. Van Beukering (2002). Issues in Production, Recycling and International Trade: Analysing the Chinese Plastic Sector Using an Optimal Life Cycle (OLC) Model. *Environment and Development Economics* 7 (1): 47–74.

Eurostat (2014). *Statistics Explained*. http://epp.eurostat.ec.europa.eu/statistics_explained/index.php/Waste_statistics

Evans, David (2012). Beyond the Throwaway Society: Ordinary Domestic Practice and a Sociological Approach to Household Food Waste. *Sociology* 46 (1): 41–56.

Fagan, G. Honor (2003). Sociological Reflections on Governing Waste. *Irish Journal of Sociology* 12 (1): 67–84.

Fisher, Dana R. and William R. Freudenburg (2004). Postindustrialization and Environmental Quality: An Empirical Analysis of the Environmental State. *Social Forces* 83 (1): 157–188.

Fredericks, Rosalind (2009). Wearing the Pants: The Gendered Politics of Trashwork in Senegal's Capital City. *HAGAR: Studies in Culture, Polity and Identities* 9 (1): 119–146.

Fredericks, Rosalind (2018). *Garbage Citizenship: Vital Infrastructures of Labor in Dakar, Senegal*. Durham, NC: Duke University Press.

Frey, R. Scott (2003). The Transfer of Core-Based Hazardous Production Processes to the Export Processing Zones of the Periphery: The Maquiladora Centers of Northern Mexico. *Journal of World-Systems Research* 9 (2): 317–354.

Furniss, Jamie (2017). What Type of Problem Is Waste in Egypt? *Social Anthropology/Anthropologie Sociale* 25 (3): 301–317.

Gille, Zsuzsa (2013). From Risk to Waste: Global Food Waste Regimes. *Sociological Review Monograph Series* 60 (S2): 27–46.

Gille, Zsuzsa (2022). Was There a Socialocene? From Capitalocene to Transnational Waste Regimes. *Antipode.*

Goldstein, Joshua (2020). *Remains of the Everyday: A Century of Recycling in Beijing.* Berkely, CA: University of California Press.

Gourlay, Ken A. (1992). *World of Waste: Dilemmas of Industrial Development.* London: Zed Books.

Graziano, Valeria and Kim Trogal (2017). The Politics of Collective Repair: Examining Object-Relations in a Postwork Society. *Cultural Studies* 31 (5): 634–658.

Gregson, Nicky (2007). *Living with Things: Ridding, Accommodation, Dwelling.* Wantage: Sean Kingston.

Gregson, Nicky and Louise Crewe (2003). *Second-Hand Cultures.* Oxford: Berg.

Gregson, Nicky and Peter J. Foreman (2021). England's Municipal Waste Regime: Challenges and Prospects. *The Geographical Journal.* https://doi.org/10.1111/geoj.12386.

Gregson, Nicky, Mike Crang, Sara Fuller, and Helen Holmes (2015). Interrogating the Circular Economy: The Moral Economy of Resource Recovery in the EU. *Economy and Society* 44 (2): 218–243.

Gutberlet, Jutta (2008). *Recovering Resources—Recycling Citizenship: Urban Poverty Reduction in Latin America.* London: Routledge.

Gutberlet, Jutta (2009). Solidarity Economy and Recycling Co-Ops in São Paulo: Micro-Credit to Alleviate Poverty. *Development in Practice* 19 (6): 737–751.

Gutberlet, Jutta (2022). Waste Picker Organizations and Urban Sustainability. In Zsuzsa Gille and Joshua Lepawsky, eds. *Routledge Handbook of Waste Studies.* London: Routledge.

Hawkins, Gay (2001). Plastic Bags: Living with Rubbish. *International Journal of Cultural Studies* 4 (1): 5–23.

Hecht, Gabrielle (2018). Interscalar Vehicles for an African Anthropocene: On Waste, Temporality, and Violence. *Cultural Anthropology* 33 (1): 109–141.

Hetherington, Kevin (2004). Secondhandedness: Consumption, Disposal, and Absent Presence. *Environment and Planning D: Society and Space* 22 (1): 157–173.

Huang, Qiao, Guangwu Chen, Yafei Wang, Shaoquing Chen, Lixiao Xu, and Rui Wang (2020). Modelling the Global Impact of China's Ban on Plastic Waste Imports. *Resources, Conservation and Recycling* 154.

Keck, Margaret E. and Kathryn Sikkink (1998). *Activists beyond Borders: Advocacy Networks in International Politics.* Ithaca, NY: Cornell University Press.

Knowles, Caroline (2017). Untangling Translocal Urban Textures of Trash: Plastics and Plasticity in Addis Ababa. *Social Anthropology* 25 (3): 288–300.

Krones, Jonathan Seth (2020). The Emergence of a Food-Waste-Based Commodity Frontier in the United States. *Capitalism Nature Socialism* 31 (4): 91–105.

Lepawsky, Joshua (2018). *Reassembling Rubbish: Worlding Electronic Waste.* Cambridge, MA: MIT Press.

Liboiron, Max (2010). Recycling as a Crisis of Meaning. *eTOPIA: Canadian Journal of Cultural Studies* 4: 1–9.

Liboiron, Max (2014). Against Awareness, for Scale: Garbage Is Infrastructure, Not Behavior. *Discard Studies* (January 23). https://discardstudies.com/2014/01/23/against-awareness-for-scale-garbage-is-infrastructure-not-behavior/

Little, Peter C. and Cristina Lucier (2017). Global Electronic Waste, Third Party Certification Standards, and Resisting the Undoing of Environmental Justice Politics. *Human Organization* 76 (3): 204–214.

Lucier, Cristina and Brian Gareau (2015). From Waste to Resources? Interrogating "Race to the Bottom" in the Global Environmental Governance of the Hazardous Waste Trade. *Journal of World-Systems Research* 21 (2): 495–520.

MacBride, Samantha (2013). *Recycling Reconsidered: The Present Failure and Future Promise of Environmental Action in the United States.* Cambridge, MA: MIT Press.

Medina, Martin (2007). *The World's Scavengers: Salvaging for Sustainable Consumption and Production.* Plymouth: Altamira Press.

Millar, Kathleen (2008). Making Trash into Treasure: Struggles for Autonomy on a Brazilian Garbage Dump. *Anthropology of Work Review* 29 (2): 25–34.

Millar, Kathleen (2018). *Reclaiming the Discarded: Life and Labor on Rio's Garbage Dump.* Durham, NC: Duke University Press.

Milne, Richard (2013). Arbiters of Waste: Date Labels, the Consumer and Knowing Good, Safe Food. *The Sociological Review* 60 (S2): 84–101.

Miraftab, Faranak (2004). Neoliberalism and Casualization of Public Sector Services: The Case of Waste Collection Services in Cape Town, South Africa. *International Journal of Urban & Regional Research* 28 (4): 874–892.

Moore, Jason W. (2017). The Capitalocene, Part I: On the Nature and Origins of Our Ecological Crisis. *Journal of Peasant Studies* 44 (3): 594–630.

Moore, Sarah A. (2012). Garbage Matters: Concepts in New Geographies of Waste. *Progress in Human Geography* 36 (6): 780–799.

Norris, Lucy (2012). Shoddy Rags and Relief Blankets: Perceptions of Textile Recycling in North India. In Catherine Alexander and Joshua Reno, eds. *Economies of Recycling: The Global Transformation of Materials, Values and Social Relations*. London: Zed Books, 35–58.

Nyathi, Senzeni, Joshua O. Olowoyo, and Agboola Oludare (2018). Perception of Scavengers and Occupational Health Hazards Associated with Scavenging from a Waste Dumpsite in Pretoria, South Africa. *Journal of Environmental and Public Health*. doi:10.1155/2018/9458156

Nzeadibe, Thaddeus Chidi and Onyanta Adama (2015). Ingrained Inequalities? Deconstructing Gendered Spaces in the Informal Waste Economy of Nigerian Cities. *Urban Forum* 26 (2): 113–130.

O'Brien, Martin (2007). *A Crisis of Waste? Understanding the Rubbish Society*. London: Routledge.

O'Brien, Martin (2013). A "Lasting Transformation" of Capitalist Surplus: From Food Stocks to Feedstocks. *Sociologicial Review* 60 (2): 192–211.

O'Neill, Kate (2018). *Waste*. Hoboken, NJ: Wiley.

Ogando, Ana Carolina, Sally Roever, and Michael Rogan (2017). Gender and Informal Livelihoods: Coping Strategies and Perceptions of Waste Pickers in Sub-Saharan Africa and Latin America. *International Journal of Sociology and Social Policy* 37 (7–8): 435–451.

Orsini, Amandine (2011). Thinking Transnationally, Acting Individually: Business Lobby Coalitions in International Environmental Negotiations. *Global Society* 25 (3): 311–329.

Pellow, David N. and Robert J. Brulle, eds (2005). *Power, Justice, and the Environment: A Critical Appraisal of the Environmental Justice Movement*. Cambridge, MA: MIT Press.

Pellow, David N., Allan Schnaiberg, and Adam S. Weinberg (2000). Putting the Ecological Modernisation Thesis to the Test: The Promises and Performances of Urban Recycling. *Environmental Politics* 9 (1): 109–137.

Post, Johan, Jaap Broekema and Nelson Obirih-Opareh (2003). Trial and Error in Privatisation: Experiences in Urban Solid Waste Collection in Accra (Ghana) and Hyderabad (India). *Urban Studies* 40 (4): 835–852.

Princen, Thomas, Michael Maniates, and Ken Conca, eds (2002). *Confronting Consumption*. Cambridge, MA: MIT Press.

Sassen, Saskia (2006). *Territory, Authority, Rights: From Medieval to Global Assemblages*. Princeton, NJ: Princeton University Press.

Schnaiberg, Allan (1980). *The Environment: From Surplus to Scarcity*. New York: Oxford University Press.

Shankar, V. Kalyan and Rohini Sahni (2017). The Inheritance of Precarious Labor: Three Generations in Waste Picking in an Indian City. *WSQ: Women's Studies Quarterly* 45 (3–4): 245–262.

Stuart, Tristram (2009). *Waste: Uncovering the Global Food Scandal*. London: Penguin.

Szasz, Andrew and Michael Meuser (1997). Environmental Inequalities: Literature Review and Proposals for New Directions in Research and Theory. *Current Sociology* 45 (3): 99–120.

Takase, Koji, Yasushi Kondo, and Ayu Washizu (2005). An Analysis of Sustainable Consumption by the Waste Input–Output Model. *Journal of Industrial Ecology* 9 (1–2): 201–219.

Tong, Xin and Jici Wang (2012). The Shadow of the Global Network: E-waste Flows to China. In Catherine Alexander and Joshua Reno, eds. *Economies of Recycling: The Global Transformation of Materials, Values and Social Relations*. London: Zed Books, 98–118.

van Horen, Basil (2004). Fragmented Coherence: Solid Waste Management in Colombo. *International Journal of Urban and Regional Research* 28 (4): 757–773.

Vermeulen, Walter J. V. and P. J. Ras (2006). The Challenge of Greening Global Product Chains: Meeting Both Ends. *Sustainable Development* 14 (4): 245–256.

Watson, Matt and Angela Meah (2013). Food, Waste and Safety: Negotiating Conflicting Social Anxieties into the Practices of Domestic Provisioning. *Sociological Review* 60 (2): 102–120.

Weinberg, Adam, David N. Pellow, and Allan Schnaiberg (2000). *Urban Recycling and the Search for Sustainable Community Development*. Princeton, NJ: Princeton University Press.

White, Rob (2008). Toxic Cities: Globalizing the Problem of Waste. *Social Justice* 35 (3): 107–119.

York, Richard (2006). Ecological Paradoxes: William Stanley Jevons and the Paperless Office. *Human Ecology Review* 13 (2): 143–147.

PART III

FLOWS AND FRICTIONS

8. Globalization and forced migration

Inka Stock

INTRODUCTION

It is a longstanding premise in migration research that processes of forced and voluntary migration are intrinsically tangled up with processes of economic development, social transformation and political events in both origin and destination countries (Castles 2003). Most scholars agree that these factors need to be considered in a holistic manner when investigating the causes for forced displacement and that this therefore constitutes a rather complex task. This chapter contributes to these debates by analysing if and how globalization processes impact on peoples' choices how and where to move across borders.

Broadly speaking, globalization refers here to the widening, deepening and speeding up of worldwide interconnectedness in all aspects of contemporary social, economic and political life across different nations (Held et al. 1999, 2). This creates a global system of interconnected communication and transportation networks, markets, organizations and people, covering the entire planet (Silbey 2006, 245). A key dimension of globalization is thus a rapid increase in cross-border flows of all sorts, including finance and trade, but also encompassing, ideas, ideologies, knowledge and people (Castles and Miller 2009). However, these cross-border flows have not always been equally distributed, and while some ideas, ideologies or people can move more easily and freely, others are increasingly 'stuck' and 'forcibly immobilized' (Stock et al. 2019) through globalization.

On an economic level, for example, market liberalization, technological innovation, privatization and deregularization have been a driving element in many globalization processes (Gore 2000; Stiglitz 2002). Even though this global move towards the expansion of deregulated forms of global capitalist structures has brought about economic wealth and political cooperation across certain nations, it has also contributed to increased international and domestic economic inequalities, leading to a persistent demand for low-skilled migrant labour in the segmented labour markets of wealthy societies and to a lack of opportunities, along with oppression and violent conflicts in other countries (Castles 2003; Milanovich 2007; Sassen 2007). In particular, globalization has sharply increased North–South inequalities (Munck 2008) and thereby contributed to increased inequality of access to economic resources and political participation across the globe (Delgado Wise and Covarrubias 2008). This in turn has created new forms of migratory flows and altered their directions (Czaika and de Haas 2015; Sassen 2007).

Globalization processes also involve political change in normative and ideological terms. Above all, globalization has implied an ideological shift towards a universalism of western liberal democratic values (Fukuyama 1992). This has created a new world order with its own internationally working institutions and power structures that replaces those associated with the nation state (Petras and Veltmayer 2000). These structures are also increasingly visible as characteristics of international forms of governance in the realm of refugee and migration policies. The Global Compact on Refugees, established by the United Nations High Commissioner for Refugees (UNHCR) in 2018 (2020c), is a poignant example of the international community's efforts to develop a framework in which the responsibility for refugees and their access to human rights is shared globally. At the same time, it appears that these institutional changes have not been accompanied by a diminishing power of nation states to control their borders in order to police unauthorized movements and flows, often by sourcing out control mechanisms to private entities (Gammeltoft-Hansen 2011), so as to make it impossible for many people to travel, migrate or escape violence across borders.

In light of this contradictory evidence on the effects of globalization on mobility and settlement, this chapter seeks to establish how the current dynamics of forced migration can be meaningfully related to globalization processes. In order to do so, the focus will be on the ways in which globalization has changed the importance and the meaning of movement and settlement. The first part of the chapter focuses on what we actually understand by 'forced' migration. By focusing on forced aspects of movement and settlement, we are connecting globalization processes to the range of choices people have to adapt to changing economic, political or social circumstances. The second part of the chapter looks more concretely at the changing nature of forced migratory flows by describing their growing diversity and concentration in particular places. The third part of the chapter looks at globalized forms of governance of forced migration and describes how the control of forced mobility is becoming an increasing area of international cooperation, while the facilitation of cross-border mobility rarely features high on the agenda of policy makers. The conclusion summarizes how a view on forced migration enables us to recognize an inherent feature of globalization mechanisms, namely, that mobility as well as settlement becomes a highly priced resource whose attainment is dependent on one's location within the powers that condition movement and stay (Massey 1993). The chapter shows that the changing values attributed to both mobility and settlement have had contradictory effects on both the dynamics and flows of forced migration, which affects not only the labelling practices of states around who counts as forced migrants and who does not, but also affects the analytical importance of the concept as an object of knowledge.

WHAT IS FORCED MIGRATION?

I start from the premise that the effects of globalization processes on forced and voluntary migration movements can be differentiated. In order to show that, it is first necessary to analytically describe what we understand by the term 'forced migration'. Conceptualizing something is necessary in order to make common understanding and collective action possible, but it is always contingent on the conceptual maps we can already draw upon, and these are conditioned culturally and socially by our experience. In this sense, forced migration is not something to be discovered, but something that we make: we are converting it into an object of knowledge (Turton 2003, 3). This is not to say that it is not really existing, but that the way we think and understand it is shaped by political realities, economic context, culture and history. Understanding concepts like forced migration in this way helps us to stay alert to the fact that its meanings may be varied, and furthermore imbued with contradictory expectations and images. Thus, when we are not careful, a concept like forced migration can easily become a label, particularly when we are not describing it as an analytical category in order to think with, but instead are constructing it in convenient images so that it can be instrumentalized for political or economic purposes (Zetter 2007, 173).

When we choose to analytically distinguish between forced and voluntary migrants, we actually consider the degree of choice people have over their migratory movement as being the determining factor of distinction between different mobility experiences (Faist 2007). This means that, contrary to the administrative labels given to different mobility experiences which separate international movers into refugees, asylum seekers, international students or guest workers, the term 'forced' or 'voluntary' migrant does not distinguish between the purpose of the migrants' stay, but chooses instead to focus on the factors that conditioned their movement when they left their origin country (Castles 2006). When looking at the impact of globalization on forced migration, we are therefore primarily concerned with understanding the ways in which globalization processes have limited or enhanced people's choices related to their aspirations to move across borders or – on the contrary – to stay put somewhere. One advantage of such a conceptualization is that we move away from policy-driven images that come with some of the labels that forced migrants are usually given by states, such as 'refugees', 'asylum seekers', 'people under temporary protection' or 'irregular migrants' (Zetter 2007). When doing the latter, we run the danger of thinking about forced movements and those who are forcibly moved from states' points of view and not from the perspective of the people concerned.

One analytical problem in this endeavour is of course that it is not always possible or desirable to determine exactly where coercion starts and free will ends because mobility choices are also intrinsically tied up with the possibilities for settlement that mobile people can draw on in both origin and destination. This means that the final decision to migrate and where to is often not only determined by an individual's aspirations, but also by political, economic or social factors that are operating both in origin and destination countries. Migrants will weigh their decision to move by pondering the costs and benefits of leaving or staying. They will consider threats to physical violence, their financial situation, but also existing family networks abroad or the possibilities to access the job market and settlement permits when choosing their preferred country of destination – always depending on the information they have access to. In that sense, there is *always* a limit to the range of choices people have when choosing their migration destination or the time of migration, independent of the fact that one is forced to move or not, and this limit is not only dependent on individual free will but influenced by structural factors, such as class, gender and also 'race' or ethnic origin (van Hear 2014).

We should also not forget that there are a number of people who start their migratory project as voluntary migrants but become forcibly displaced later on, such as those who attempt to migrate for economic reasons into neighbouring countries and are then driven out due to political instability or persecution. Likewise, there may be forced migrants who decide to leave safe destinations to take up study or work in a third country. This interdependency is captured by the term 'migration–asylum nexus' (Castles 2007), which demonstrates that often, both forced and voluntary migrants use the same migratory routes, face the same acts of violence or economic hardship and similar administrative treatment. They also often shift administrative migration categories frequently before, during and after ending their migratory project, making it difficult to analytically distinguish between the forced and voluntary aspects of movement so clearly (Schuster 2005).

This last point is connected to a third analytical problem when looking at the connection between globalization and forced migration which is related to the relation between forced migration, the state and the market, because it has made it difficult to establish each actor's responsibilities in terms of the protection of migrants' rights – both nationally and internationally. Most contemporary national and international migration policies are based on the premise that forcibly displaced individuals deserve state protection, because they are considered vulnerable population groups. By contrast, those moving voluntarily in search of work or education are often subject to state control in the form of visa or work permit restrictions, limited access to social services and other forms of state support. In this sense, the term forced/ voluntary often implicitly contains a certain dichotomy in terms of the migrants' rights and position in relation to the receiving and the sending state.

At this stage, however, it is important to note that not all forced migrants are beneficiaries of specific protection from a receiving state because this often depends on the administrative categories and labels they are allocated (Zetter 2007). The status of refugees, for example, is only conferred to those forced migrants that fall under the regulations of the so-called Geneva Convention, which grants refugee status in the international communities of states since the 1950s (UNHCR 2020b). According to the Convention, only migrants who have left their country due to political persecution are considered refugees. The legal status 'refugee' thus implies that the person in question has lost their legal standing, citizenship rights and protection from a nation state they belong to. They are therefore under the protection of the international community of states (Kleist 2015). Many other forced migrants, who were obliged to leave their origin country because of economic hardship or environmental disaster, are excluded from this specific status. Internally displaced people, or other so-called people of concern to the UNHCR, who are nevertheless forced migrants, even though they do not cross state borders, are also excluded from this definition.

In the past decades, the diversity of forced displacements which are not due to political persecution have increased. Today, the group of forced migrants includes those who have been affected by displacement due to natural disaster or environmental degradation caused by private companies (like large infrastructure projects such as the building of dams or deforestation) as well as people that have been coerced to move abroad against their will (Bloch and Dona 2019). These groups of people cannot claim refugee status and state protection in the same ways as recognized asylum seekers can because there are simply no internationally binding agreements between nation states that would regulate this in a satisfactory manner. Market actors, such as big companies, rarely accept financial or political responsibilities for the forcible displacement that their activities may cause either.

Despite these ambiguities, the analytical distinction of forced and voluntary migration is important, because it moves our attention away from the policy-driven labelling processes of different types of movement and rather focuses on distinguishing the structural causes of movement and settlement and how these impact on moving people's relationship with states and markets. This is exactly what we are interested in when analysing the impact of globalization processes on changes in the causes of movement and settlement.

DYNAMICS OF MIGRATION AND FORCED MIGRATION BEFORE AND AFTER GLOBALIZATION

It is certainly a well-established fact that the globalization of labour markets has resulted in increasing numbers of countries being incorporated into global migration systems (Sassen 2007), which in turn has resulted in an increased demand for labour migration. However, there is also evidence to suggest that the move towards democratization after the Cold War era has brought about a number of 'failing states' in different parts of the world, whose subsequent demise was built on violent forms of ethnic nationalism and sometimes ethnic cleansing, thus contributing to the rise in conflict and forced displacement worldwide (Castles 2003; Duffield 2001). However, Czaika and de Haas (2015) are right to point out that in order to understand the real impact of globalization processes on migratory movements, it is necessary to go beyond the usually established link between global markets, increased conflict and an increased volume of migration and to also analyse the ways in which globalization processes may have contributed to changes in the geographical scope, diversity and directionality of migratory movements.

This can be proven by looking at UNHCR statistics on the increase of forced displacements. The number of people who have had to leave their country because of persecution, conflict or generalized violence has more than doubled in the past decade (UNHCR 2019). According to UNHCR figures, 70.8 million people had been forcibly displaced by the end of 2018. Among them were 25.9 million refugees, 41.3 million internally displaced and 3.5 million asylum seekers. This is the highest number since the Second World War. Such statistics show that it is important to keep in mind that forcibly displaced persons are not only comprised of refugees and asylum seekers who seek protection in other countries, but also, and indeed mainly, of individuals who have been displaced within the borders of their own countries. At the end of 2019, the number of people displaced internally by conflict, violence and disaster had reached 50.8 million. Of these, 45.7 million people in 61 countries were internally displaced by conflict and violence and 5.1 million people in 95 countries were internally displaced due to natural disasters (Internal Displacement Monitoring Centre 2020).

Faist (2007) alerts us to the fact that these dynamics are not necessarily pointing at changes in mobility rates in real terms, because while forced migration may have increased in absolute numbers, it has not done so in relation to the overall increase of the world population. In fact, the total percentage of mobile people in the world has stayed remarkably stable in the past decades at around 3.5 per cent of the world population (Czaika and de Haas 2015; Faist 2007). Instead, there is evidence to suggest that globalization has contributed to an unequal distribution of forced migration flows in the world. For example, 6.7 of the 20 million refugees under direct protection of the UNHCR come from Syria, and of these, 3.6 million are registered in the neighbouring Turkey, and not in Sweden or Germany (UNHCR 2019). In general, refugee flows are mostly concentrated in the Global South, and differ therefore from other migratory movements which mostly go in the direction from South to North (Munck 2008). This means that most refugees originate from the Global South and move within the region. Only a small minority of forced migrants actually migrates to the Northern Hemisphere.

This is a significant change from the situation in the 20th century, when the majority of refugees and forced migrants came from Europe, particularly after the displacements caused by the Second World War. By 1945, there were well over 40 million refugees in Europe, mostly due to ethnic and nationalistic ideas which developed in the aftermath of the war in the different nation states that had participated in it (Bundy 2016). This situation contributed also to the establishment of the first international conventions for the protection of refugees in 1951 by the United Nations, which was later adapted to include an amendment in the form of an additional protocol in 1967, integrating a geographical and temporal restriction on nations' responsibilities to accept refugees. Because of this, the states of Madagascar, Democratic Republic of the Congo and Turkey are still today exempt from accepting refugees that come from countries outside of Europe (UNHCR 2020a). This historical development of the international system of protection of refugees is illustrative of the western-centric view on forced migration that was very dominant at the time. It is possible that in subsequent decades, the concomitant effect of increasing inequality and conflict in regions other than Europe, as well as technological developments that made travel easier and cheaper, have contributed to a shifting of the regions in which people become refugees and forced migrants and those where they can actually move to protect themselves from violence.

Within the regions of high outflow of forced displacement, there are also high concentrations of forced migrants who come from particular countries. The drastic increase of forced displacement that occurred between 2009 and 2018 was mainly due to the Syrian conflict, other conflicts in the region, conflicts in Sub-Saharan Africa and the inflow of Rohingya refugees to Bangladesh. More than two-thirds (67 per cent) of refugees in 2018 came from five countries: the Syrian Arab Republic (6.7 million), Afghanistan (2.7 million), South Sudan (2.3 million), Myanmar (1.1 million) and Somalia (0.9 million) (UNHCR 2019). The five countries with the highest number of new internal displacements due to conflict and violence were the Syrian Arab Republic (1.8 million), Democratic Republic of Congo (1.7 million), Ethiopia (1.1 million), Burkina Faso (513,000) and Afghanistan (461,00). The five countries with the highest number of new internal displacements due to disasters were India (5 million), the Philippines (4.1 million), Bangladesh (4.1 million), China (4 million) and the United States (916,000) (Internal Displacement Monitoring Centre 2020).

While forced migrants appear to come from increasingly fewer origin countries, they are settling in a growing number of destinations, a trend that is also visible in the case of voluntary migrants (Czaika and de Haas 2015). Vertovec (2007) coined the term 'super-diversity' to denominate the growing diversity of origin countries from which migrants to Britain and other immigrant-receiving countries were coming from. In contrast to earlier decades, we were now witnessing 'new, small and scattered, multiple origin, transnationally connected, socio-economically differentiated and legally stratified immigrants' (Vertovec 2007, 1024). This is partly due to the economic and political globalization processes, which have bound political, economic and cultural systems of exchange of a growing number of countries together across the globe. This has facilitated the flow of both forced and voluntary migrants between a growing number of different countries and accelerated the emergence of international migration systems in different regions (Skelton 1997).

This shows that globalization has increased the absolute numbers of refugees and forced migrants and has contributed to a diversification of refugee as well as migration flows by changing distances, destinations and volume. At the same time, it appears to have contributed to concentrate destination and origin countries to a small number. However, at the same time, globalization has *not* increased the relative flow of forced migrants. The fact that forced migratory movements have become more regionalized and at the same time more diversified points to the fact that there is more limited choice of destinations than ever before, and that movement itself – even if involuntary – has not increased significantly.

IMPACTS OF GLOBALIZATION ON MIGRATION GOVERNANCE AND THE RESPONSIBILITIES OF STATES AND MARKETS

One reason for the increasing diversification of destinations that forced (and voluntary) migrants move to, even though they stem from fewer origin countries which are mostly located in the Global South, is an inherent contradictory mechanism of globalization in what concerns the selective rights to mobility and settlement that nation states grant their citizens. It seems to be that while goods, services and capital are increasingly free to cross borders, the movement of people has not been subject to the same liberalizing trend. On the contrary, it could even be argued that the current system of global economic governance serves to control, direct and selectively manage the potential movement of the global labour force across borders. This is because globalized trade regimes call for the further integration of national and regional labour markets into an emerging global labour market by selectively promoting specific forms of labour mobility (Leon and Overbeek 2015, 38). This means that for economic purposes, migrant labour has to comply with certain characteristics in order to be efficiently used. As a consequence, regional and even global migration policies often promote possibilities for the international mobility of highly educated individuals who work in certain economic sectors (such as information technology professionals, nurses or financial experts) while making it increasingly difficult for others to move (such as family members of migrants or unaccompanied minors).

This has not only led to overall fewer legal possibilities for labour migrants and their families or students to move and settle in different countries, but has also impacted the possibilities that forced migrants have to legally move across borders in order to claim asylum in a different country. Paradoxically, it also means that, for many people, the only secure way of being able to settle in a different country in the Global North (and increasingly also in the Global South) is by entering through irregular means (Ghosh 2005). Claiming asylum, then, becomes one of the few legal avenues in order to apply for residency permits which would allow one to access work and study. Increasing border controls and limited possibilities for legal migration across the globe have thus converted a refugee status into one of the few legally sanctioned means to claim settlement rights and governmental protection in destination countries.

This state of affairs is partly due to the fact that international law only recognizes the right of persons to leave a country and return to his/her own country, but does not simultaneously grant non-nationals the right to enter a foreign state. In other words, while the right to leave is conceded, there is no corresponding obligation for states to receive non-nationals on their territory, except for the right to seek asylum and the corresponding duties of states not to prevent the claiming of this right by returning the individual to a country where he/she faces persecution.

As a result, there is still not any unified, international system of migration governance, which would be comparable to trade regimes, in that there are international guidelines for facilitating the mobility of people across borders as well as their settlement (Likic-Brboric 2018). Instead, we are seeing a tendency for a globalization of migration control (Gammeltoft-Hansen 2011), in which exterritorial and privatized means are used as 'political strategies by nation states to bypass human rights and reclaim discretional power over mobility and settlement, especially with regards to the obligation to protect vulnerable individuals'. This is done in a variety of ways, for example by engaging airlines in the visa controls of their passengers, the enforcement of border control mechanisms through police forces or through regulations to maximize visa restrictions.

So while there is an increased consensus about the fact that forced migrants should receive protection from the international communities of states, as well as access to human rights, these efforts have not dismantled the power of nation states to deny forced migrants access to their territory or to social, economic or cultural opportunities in their countries. On the contrary, the power of nation states to deny this access has been strengthened through a growing number of international cooperation and agreements.

One example for this contradictory nature of international cooperation in the field of forced migration is visible in the European Union's (EU) efforts to respond to refugee movements that have been caused by the Syrian conflict. When growing numbers of Syrians fled the war and moved to Turkey, Jordan and Lebanon, the EU became the leading donor in the international response to the Syria crisis, granting 1.135 billion euros to Jordan and Lebanon, which is almost 50 per cent of the total support of the European Commission. Much of the funds are managed through an EU regional trust fund in response to the Syrian crisis, composed of funds from 16 EU member states. It is channelled through the United Nations, international organizations and international non-governmental organizations, thus demonstrating the capacity of regional and global institutional networks to distribute and mobilize humanitarian aid for forced migrants in remote areas and over great distances (European Commission n.d.).

At the same time, however, the EU has received a lot of attention for the EU–Turkey deal which was signed in 2016 and composed of measures to address irregular border crossings from Syrian refugees in Turkey into the EU via Greece. It effectively allowed EU governments to minimize their international commitments to refugee protections as signatories to the 1951 Geneva Convention by introducing a kind of 'population swap' as part of the agreement (Rygiel et al. 2016): Turkey admits and returns irregular migrants from the Greek islands and in exchange will send Syrian refugees in Turkey to Europe for resettlement. Critically, in this is the fact that refugees in Turkey are only able to count on limited protection and rights as well as a temporary status as refugees, whereas in Europe, they are eligible to full refugee status. This has contributed to a situation in which many Syrian refugees in Turkey could effectively be considered 'stuck' in a situation of forced immobility because they are unable to build a sustainable future in the country for themselves and their children while simultaneously being hindered to either move onwards to another country or back to their origin country.

The example above illustrates how globalization processes have particularly worked well to increase international cooperation between states in order to control and limit forced migratory movements across borders, particularly if these are directed from the Global South towards the Global North (Stock et al. 2019). This has led to increased irregular migration flows and a diversification of routes and destinations to which migrants are travelling. At the same time, this move towards the externalization of border controls from the North towards the South has also entailed increased forced immobility for a number of migrants who are stuck in countries they did not intend to migrate and without the possibility of either moving further onwards or returning to where they came from.

CONCLUSION

As a process of selective inclusion and exclusion of specific areas and groups into capitalist systems of production, globalization has maintained and exacerbated inequality. This has had a direct impact on the dynamics of both voluntary and forced migratory movements. While increasing mobility of people, goods and values between distant and not so distant places have contributed to the expansion of liberal, democratic values and prosperity in todays globalized world, economic liberalism and privatization have also led to increasing inequality, poverty, involuntary displacement (Sassen 2007) and increasing immobility.

This chapter has focused on the connections between these kinds of globalization processes and forced migration, drawing out particularly two points. First, by focusing on the dynamics of forced migration movements, we are able to show that the negative effects of globalization on mobility are not found everywhere to the same extent. While globalization processes have produced and/or intensified violent conflicts, poverty and increasing inequality in certain parts of the world, leading to forced displacements and/or forced immobility, this has not been the case in every country and to the same extent. Rather, there is evidence to suggest that globalization has diversified flows of forced migration and intensified those flows coming from the Global South towards the Global South and into the Global North (Castles 2003). Second, focusing on the efforts of both the international communities of states and individual nation states to protect and control the movement of forced migrants further helps us to understand that globalization processes not only promote internationally shared values of governance and increased cooperation between states but also lead to increased nationalism and localized policy initiatives with regards to refugee management.

This shows that the meaning we give to forced and voluntary migration and what the distinction between the two concepts actually means today also affects the ways in which we understand globalization processes. The analysis of the ways in which labels are applied to different types of forced and voluntary migrants helps us to better understand how patterns of mobile life worlds are mediated and ultimately controlled and reformulated by states and markets (Zetter 2007). There is evidence to suggest that while the definitions of what counts as forced migrant has changed over the course of history, there is a remarkable resilience in adapting our understanding of different types of mobility and their benefits or dangers for world society. This is visible in both contemporary policies directed at forced migrants and in academic research agendas. This state of affairs is intrinsically tangled up with the specific understandings of globalization that inform both policy making and academic quests for knowledge. The dominant paradigm is based on the premise that mobility is a selective resource, which should primarily be used to further economic interests, rather than the human rights quest of individuals. Given these conceptual entanglements, it is important for both policy makers and academics alike to use the concept of 'forced migration' as an analytical lens through which to investigate the importance of the politics of movement and settlement in the study of globalization processes, and not primarily as a policy issue to be 'solved'.

REFERENCES

Bloch, A. and G. Dona (eds) (2019), *Forced Migration: Current Issues and Debates*, Abingdon: Routledge.

Bundy, C. (2016), 'Migrants, refugees, history and precedents', *Forced Migration Review* 51, 5–6.

Castles, S. (2003), 'Towards a sociology of forced migration and social transformation', *Sociology*, 37 (1), 13–34.

Castles, S. (2006), 'Global perspectives on forced migration', *Asian and Pacific Migration Journal*, 15 (1), 7–28.

Castles, S. (2007), 'The migration–asylum nexus and regional approaches', in S. Kneebone and F. Rawlings-Sanaei (eds), *New regionalism and asylum seekers: challenges ahead*, New York: Berghahn Books, pp. 25–42.

Castles, S. and M.J. Miller (2009), *The Age of Migration: International Population Movements in the Modern World*, Basingstoke: Palgrave Macmillan.

Czaika, M. and H. de Haas (2015), 'The globalization of migration: Has the world become more migratory?', *International Migration Review*, 48 (2), 283–323.

Delgado Wise, R. and H.M. Covarrubias (2008), 'Capitalist restructuring, development and labour migration: The Mexico–US case', *Third World Quarterly*, 29 (7), 1359–1374.

Duffield, M. (2001), *Global Governance and the New Wars, the Merging of Development and Security*, London: Zed Books.

European Commission (n.d.), 'Managing the refugee crisis: EU support to Lebanon and Jordan since the onset of the Syria Crisis'. www.ec.europa.eu/home-affairs/sites/homeaffairs/files/what-we-do/policies/european-agenda-migration/background-information/docs/eu_support_to_lebanon_and _jordan_since_the_onset_of_syria_crisis_en.pdf

Faist, T. (2007), 'Transnationale Migration als relative Immobilität in einer globalisierten Welt', *Berliner Journal für Soziologie*, 17 (3), 415–437.

Fukuyama, F. (1992), *The End of History and the Last Man*, New York: New Press.

Gammeltoft-Hansen, T. (2011), *Access to Asylum: International Refugee Law and the Globalization of Migration Control*, Cambridge: Cambridge University Press.

Ghosh, B. (2005), 'Managing migration: Wither the missing regime?'. www.unesco.unesco.org/ark:/48223/pf0000

Gore, C. (2000), 'The rise and fall of the Washington Consensus as a paradigm for developing countries', *World Development*, 28 (5), 789–804.

Held, D., A. McGrew, D. Goldblatt and J. Perraton (1999), *Global Transformation: Politics, Economics, and Culture*, Cambridge: Policy Press.

Internal Displacement Monitoring Centre (2020), 'Global report on internal displacement 2020'. www .internal-displacement.org/global-report/grid2020/

Kleist, O. (2015), 'Über Flucht forschen. Herausforderungen der Flüchtlingsforschung', *Peripherie*, 35 (2), 150–169.

Leon, A.I. and H. Overbeek (2015), 'Neoliberal globalisation, transnational migration and global governance', in L.S. Talani and S. McMahon (eds), *Handbook of the International Political Economy of Migration*, Cheltenham, UK and Northampton, MA, USA: Edward Elgar Publishing, pp. 37–53.

Likic-Brboric, B. (2018), 'Global migration governance, civil society and the paradoxes of sustainability', *Globalizations*, 15 (6), 762–778.

Massey, D. (1993), 'Power geometry and a progressive sense of place', in J. Bird, B. Curtis, T. Putman and I. Tickner (eds), *Mapping the Futures: Local Cultures, Global change*, Basingstoke: Macmillan.

Milanovich, B. (2007), 'Globalization and Inequality', in D. Held and A. Kaya (eds), *Global Inequality: Patterns and Explanations*, Cambridge: Polity Press, pp. 26–49.

Munck, R. (2008), 'Globalisation, governance and migration: An introduction', *Third World Quarterly*, 29 (7), 1227–1246.

Petras, J. and H. Veltmayer (2000), 'Globalisation or imperialism', *Cambridge Review of International Affairs*, 14 (1), 1–15.

Rygiel, K., T. Baban and S. Ilcan (2016), 'The Syrian refugee crisis: The EU–Turkey deal and temporary protection', *Global Policy Review*, 16 (3), 315–320.

Sassen, S. (2007), 'The making of international migrants', in J.C. Alexander (ed.), *Contemporary Societies*, New York: W.W. Norton, pp. 129–163.

Schuster, L. (2005), 'The continuing mobility of migrants in Italy: Shifting between places and statuses', *Journal of Ethnic and Migration Studies*, 31 (4), 757–774.

Silbey, S. (2006), 'Globalisation', in B.S. Turner (ed.), *The Cambridge Dictionary of Sociology*, Cambridge: Cambridge University Press, pp. 245–248.

Skelton, R. (1997), *Migration and Development: A Global Interpretation*, London: Longman.

Stiglitz, J. (2002), *Globalization and Its Discontents*, London: Penguin Press.

Stock, I., A. Üstübici and S.U. Schultz (2019), 'Externalization at work: Responses to migration policies from the Global South', *Comparative Migration Studies*, 7 (1), 1–9.

Turton, D. (2003), 'Conceptualizing forced migration'. www.rsc.ox.ac.uk/files/files-1/wp12 -conceptualising-forced-migration-2003.pdf

UNHCR (United Nations High Commissioner for Refugees) (2019), 'Global trends: Forced displacement in 2018'. www.unhcr.org/globaltrends2018/

UNHCR (United Nations High Commissioner for Refugees) (2020a), 'States parties to the 1951 Convention and its 1967 Protocol'. www.unhcr.org/protect/PROTECTION/3b73b0d63.pdf

UNHCR (United Nations High Commissioner for Refugees) (2020b), 'The 1951 Convention relating to the status of refugees and its 1967 Protocol'. www.unhcr.org/uk/about-us/background/4ec262df9/1951-convention-relating-status-refugees-its-1967-protocol.html

UNHCR (United Nations High Commissioner for Refugees) (2020c), 'The global compact on refugees'. www.unhcr.org/the-global-compact-on-refugees.html

van Hear, N. (2014), 'Reconsidering migration and class', *International Migration Review*, 48 (1), 100–121.

Vertovec, S. (2007), 'Super-diversity and its implications', *Ethnics and Racial Studies*, 30 (6), 1024–1054.

Zetter, R. (2007), 'More labels, fewer refugees: Remaking the refugee label in an era of globalization', *Refugee Studies*, 20 (2), 172–192.

9.   Global tourism

Esther Bott

INTRODUCTION

The growing interconnectedness and interdependence of world economies, cultures and populations that characterise globalisation are also key features of global tourism, and the two realms are intricately linked. Indeed, the explosive growth of tourism in the past several decades has provided a significant portion of the transport and communications networks that have facilitated hugely accelerated physical mobility in the era of globalisation. Tourism is implicated not only in the expansion of global transport networks but also in the worldwide ubiquity of hotel chains, corporate advertising, iconography and 'destination branding', whose interconnectedness represents the 'swirling vortex of global tourism' (Urry 2001, p. 3). Technological advancements of the globalised, 'shrinking world' have also increased the ease and speed with which holidays are sought and booked and, with an annual growth rate of 4 per cent, tourism is one of the world's fastest growing industries (Lenzen et al. 2018), generating approximately 5.8 trillion United States dollars (Statista 2021).

The key dimensions of globalisation – namely, economic, political, cultural and ecological (Held 1999; Steger 2009) – are also central to global tourism and how it is understood. Debates on tourism across a range of disciplines are perennially concerned with the economic, political, social/cultural and environmental drivers and consequences of global tourism. Specifically, scholars working on tourism studies and its related disciplines are increasingly recognising the great structural divisions that underpin global tourism and sustain patterns of inequality.

As one of global capitalism's fastest growing businesses, tourism is an increasingly important source of employment and income. Yet tourism jobs are often low status, poorly paid and insecure. Further, concentrating on tourism can detract from investment in more long-term enterprises, and while many economies are almost entirely dependent on tourism, this is not without significant risk. As we saw in 2020, unforeseen events such as a global health emergency can ground flights and halt tourism trade overnight, with devastating consequences for the many whose livelihoods depend on it. International tourism arrivals declined by 70 per cent in January to August 2020, and recovery is expected to be slow (UNWTO 2020). This has meant massive job losses across the globe. In areas with few labour alternatives because of an over-reliance on tourism, and especially where no state welfare support is offered, the consequences of sudden emergencies, including terrorist attacks, natural disasters, conflict or even the more gradual falling out of fashion in the fickle world of tourism trends, can be devastating. In many developing countries, which are ever popular with Western tourists, the type of wealth that can provide enough security to withstand catastrophe is generally held by a small number of business owners and professionals; unskilled casual workers who make up the vast majority of tourism's workforce exist in more precarious conditions.

A common critique of globalisation is that it concentrates power and wealth with global elites at the expense of the masses (McMichael 2007; Seabrook 1988; Stiglitz 2002). Phillip McMichael argues that globalisation is a deliberately stratifying form of global economic organisation, bringing prosperity to a minority of elites and hardships for the masses. McMichael argues:

> The globalization project has two faces: the face of unprecedented prosperity for a minority of the world's investors and consumers; and the face of poverty, displacement, job and food insecurity, health crises (AIDS), and a widening band of informal activity (over 1 billion slum-dwellers) as people make do in lieu of stable jobs, government supports, and sustainable habitats. (McMichael 2007, p. 192)

These problems apply to global tourism, where power and wealth are overwhelmingly concentrated in Western circles, with multinational corporations and local elites. Also, the many drawbacks of tourism, including overcrowding, pollution, environmental degradation and inflated property and commodity prices, disproportionately affect the poorest inhabitants, many or most of whom, aside from daily subsistence, are excluded from the gratifying and sustaining elements of tourism. Unequal positioning in the structures of global tourism therefore affect one's capacity for mobility and prosperity, since informal work rarely leads to accumulation of capital. Some of the proposed solutions to these issues, including sustainable tourism development, 'pro-poor' initiatives, ecotourism and so on, have yielded varied results, and are themselves the subject of much critical debate.

GLOBAL MOBILITY AND THE COSMOPOLITAN TOURIST

The physical movement of people around the world is a central theme of late capitalist life, whose 'accelerated culture' both demands and celebrates hyper-mobility (Brinkmann 2017); as such, holidays are key to consumer status, marking not simply material wealth but also class distinctions and 'cultural capital' (Munt 1994). Such positive evaluations of physical mobility have gained unprecedented exposure with the explosion of social media usage in the twenty-first century, whose *zeitgeist* also encourages metaphorical and allegorical journeys of self-transformation.

The desire to 'broaden horizons' by travelling abroad involves the cosmopolitan notion of what John Urry calls an 'entitlement to travel'. Urry notes that 'cultures become so mobile that contemporary citizens ... are thought to possess the rights to pass over and into other places and other cultures' (Urry 2001, p. 6). Tourism is a growing part of the global flow of products and images from other cultural forms and ideas offered consumers a 'cosmopolitan culinary eclecticism' (Beck 2002, p. 28). Tourists who seek out degrees and particular types of 'foreignness' from the glut of contemporary travel opportunities might be labelled 'cultural omnivores' (Bennett 2009) whose 'cosmopolitan capital' distinguishes them from more provincial 'others' (Skey 2013). This increasingly involves a rejection of the seductions of mass tourism (Meethan 2001), and the desire for 'authentic' experiences in 'underdeveloped' settings; hence, the growing appetite among Westerners for holidays in the global South.

New markets such as slum tours in Indian and South American cities, especially in the *favelas* of Brazil, exemplify a tourist encounter in which social and economic deprivation (and often crime and violence) are commodified. As such, experiences grow in popularity and commercial mediators are quick to reproduce an aesthetic of underdevelopment and poverty. Such 'spatialisation' of poverty means that there are certain places where poverty is experienced and 'enjoyed' as a cosmopolitan encounter (Steinbrink 2012).

Yet these entitlements are contingent on relative structural privileges that give access to the prerequisites of tourism: valid travel documents and identification, the financial means to buy tickets and take time off work and so on: resources that delineate difference in such unequal tourist encounters. Cosmopolitan capital embodied in international tourism will, therefore, always exclude those outside its economic and social advantages. In 2019 almost 1.5 billion people out of a world population of 7.7 billion went on holiday, meaning that only approximately 20 per cent of the world population travels for leisure. Despite the potential 'democratisation' of travel by budget airfares and new technologies, and the concomitant expectation that air travel has, for many, become 'a norm or even a right' (Shaw & Thomas 2006, p. 209), tourism remains a comparatively elite undertaking and an exemplar of vast global disparities in access to wealth, leisure time and other resources. This imbalance in mobility between those with/without the means to travel broadly speaking maps onto rich and poor countries of the world, respectively. Whilst parts of Europe and the United States consistently receive the most visitors, they also are major sending countries. 'Periphery' countries, on the other hand, are overwhelmingly tourist receivers.

GLOBALISED VALUE REGIMES IN TOURISM

Globalisation involves the interconnectedness, or 'flow' (Appadurai 1990) of things: of social relations, ideologies, goods, technologies, culture and people across national boundaries via a globally networked society. These interactions involve the exchange of cultures across various 'scapes' in increasingly rapid and influential ways. Appadurai argues that through culture flows, commodities have not only an economic worth but political and social values, too. Such value is constructed through cultural and economic processes in what he terms 'regimes of value', which create a logic of varied and context-dependent exchange and worth. Appadurai argues that commodity exchange does not necessarily presuppose 'a complete cultural sharing of assumptions, but rather that the degree of value coherence may be highly variable from situation to situation' (Appardurai 1986, p. 15).

In terms of the global 'flow' of tourism commodities, Appadurai's value theorising led Crossley and Picard to conceive of value as 'socially constructed within particular regimes, yet potentially transcendent of cultural boundaries, as demonstrated in tourism by transactions that take place between actors from different cultures' (2014, p. 202). Crossley and Prichard argue that whether in terms of its economic, cultural or personal manifestations, tourism 'not only feeds off existing conceptions of value but is also instrumental in reproducing and reinforcing regimes of value' (2014, p. 203).

The value regimes of the global North are reinforced through the diverse cultural meanings that are articulated through tourism trade. Such cultural values and meanings are produced and consumed across a 'complex web of sociocultural relations within the highly distorted power structures of the global politico-cultural economy' (Atelijevic & Doorne 2003, p. 124). These power structures privilege Western tourists and the hegemonic Western tourism discourses on which they draw. Such articulations of value are often profoundly racialised, relying on the presence of 'Othered' locals. The arguably Orientalist desires of tourists are accommodated through the structural (dis)position of Othered locals, whose poverty leads them into markets that satisfy the whims of foreign tourists. Indeed, there are longstanding concerns about the potentially negative implications of the power discrepancy between locals and tourists in marketised settings that usually favours tourists in their powerful role as consumers (Bruner 1991; MacCannell 1992) and it is argued that 'host' communities are often required to adjust to tourist worldviews and lifestyles (Hall & Tucker 2004; Hollinshead 2004; Sin & Minca 2014).

Value is also problematically expressed and reproduced in tourism marketing, which, as Echtner and Prasad note, is predominantly produced in the 'First World', and that target audiences are fed deliberately constructed fantasy versions of their chosen destination:

> The primary targets of these marketing efforts are also located in the First World, as the developed countries are the main generators of tourists. As a result, the vast majority of Third World destination marketing is created and distributed by First World promoters who are economically motivated to sell a particular brand of fantasy to a First World market. (Echtner & Prasad 2003, p. 661)

Tourism advertising is thus a powerful disseminator of essentialised descriptions that appeal to would-be tourists (Cohen 1993; Morgan & Pritchard 1998) which can engender problematic and unrealistic expectations amongst visitors (Bott 2018). These expectations manifest in tourists' behaviour; in their consumption habits, attitudes, activities, interactions and so on, all of which express and reflect their dominant position as consumers in the tourism service industry.

TOURISM AND POSTCOLONIAL ENCOUNTERS

The fastest growth area in tourism is in global South countries, many of which are former colonies. The close relationship between tourism and postcolonialism has grown in prominence in tourism debates (Caton & Santos 2008; Hall & Tucker 2004; Hollinshead 2004; Ryan & Aicken 2005). The neocolonial dimensions of tourism have also been discussed (see Bandyopadhyay & Nascimento 2010; Craik 1994; Echtner & Prasad 2003), with particular focus on Western dominance of tourism development and the everyday power relationships that manifest as a result. Mowforth and Munt hold that countries remain fixed as neocolonialist economies despite having gained independence because their economic stability and prosperity rely on tourism from Western countries (2009). This has a significant impact on the physical and aesthetic environment, and it also imposes the social dynamics of the service industry on interactions between locals and tourists (Crick 1994). This can erode local social and cultural traditions and re-entrench colonial racial inequalities between the tourists who are 'served' and the locals who 'serve' them.

As noted above, cross-cultural encounters can be pivotal to cosmopolitanism, including, according to Salazar, the 'capacity to interact across cultural lines ... flexible intellectual and aesthetic openness towards divergent cultural experiences ... and towards the allure of elsewhere and Otherness' (Salazar 2010, p. 78). And yet, encounters and interactions are underpinned by myths that circulate marketing material to the developing world. These myths suggest that tourism destinations in the global South should be unchanged, unrestrained and uncivilised (Echtner & Prasad 2003) and are therefore reminiscent of the colonial 'first encounter'. Tucker and Akama contend that the cultural representations, exploitative relationships and economic structures inherited by colonised countries are alive and well in global tourism (2009, p. 504).

As Spivak argues, neocolonialism need not necessarily include the physical act of colonising a territory; it also refers to economic processes that create new forms of domination and acquisition of resources (1999). Tourism routinely encourages and legitimises land and property acquisition and the formation of elite enclaves, and reinforces spatial and socioeconomic inequalities (Brohman 1996). As such, tourism plays a major role in shaping postcolonial and neocolonial states, not only in terms of embodied tourist encounters but also, as Carrigan states, as 'a powerful agent of social, cultural and environmental transformation', whose power is 'at the heart of many development agendas' (2015, p. 236).

TOURISM DEVELOPMENT AND 'GLOBALISATION FROM ABOVE'

Tourism has long been regarded as an important tool for alleviating poverty and stimulating socioeconomic development in the Global South. Interventions, from neoliberal structural adjustment programmes of earlier decades to more recent national and international projects that fall under the umbrella term 'sustainable development', recognise the potential for tourism development to benefit local people and fuel growth. The United Nations identifies the development of tourism as a way for the world's least economically developed countries to meet the Millennium Development Goals (MDGs). With the potential for tourism to provide jobs and generate income for communities that, in some cases, lack viable alternative means of employment, and its capacity to encourage flexible labour markets that offer diverse working opportunities, tourism can help realise several MDGs, including alleviating poverty and promoting gender equality, environmental sustainability and global partnerships (Ajake & Amalu 2012).

Other global agencies including the World Bank and many local development agencies, ministries, charities and non-governmental organisations adopt the position that tourism is key to poverty alleviation. There is a widespread assumption that tourism development benefits the poor through the 'trickle-down' effect, eventually reaching those occupying the lowest paying service work jobs that are so essential to tourism. However, research shows that the relationship between low earners – especially in the least economically developed countries – and the tourism market is complex and unpredictable. There is a growing body of evidence to suggest that tourism chiefly benefits local elites and foreign companies, generating mostly low-paying, precarious and low-status employment. In addition, tourism that is poorly planned and badly managed as is the case in many laissez-faire developing contexts can disrupt social and cultural lifestyles, destroy ecological systems and raise the cost of living for local people (Holden 2013; Jamieson et al. 2004).

There is much critique of the dominance of global development policy, which can be viewed as a form of 'globalisation from above'. This is the use of globalisation to dominate and exploit the poor, which in turn empowers and enriches the wealthy and inhibits democracy. Corporate globalisation generally has a negative effect on poorer rural communities, as control of resources is assumed by large transnational companies, corporations and trade bodies. This largely disempowers and disenfranchises rural communities, and contributes to mass rural–urban migration. Corporate globalisation mostly benefits those already in a structural position to access the opportunities it creates, and uncontrolled international business development does not alleviate poverty for most (Reid 2003).

The links between 'globalisation from above' and the direction of capitalist tourism markets and trends are clear. Tourism is characterised by large-scale global commodification, which is mostly mediated and controlled by those who have the economic and ideological power to 'shape institutions and consciousness to suit their ends' (Llewellyn Watson & Kopachevsky

1994, p. 651). This occurs at both the private corporate level and in formal regulatory systems. An example of this is the control of tourist provision and development by international trade associations, which impose standards (building, safety and so on) on a global scale. Regulations that are conceived in rich Western contexts are imposed on local developers and businesses, often meaning that only local/expatriated elites and international investors are able to afford the considerable expense required. Local entrepreneurs are frequently edged out of the market by richer investors, which feeds the cycle of impoverishment and displacement characteristic of tourism in the Global South.

Whilst research has shown that tourism is potentially a viable tool for local community development in poor countries (Ajake & Amalu 2012; Alrawadieh et al. 2019; Pappas & Papatheodorou 2017; Sharpley 2009), lack of coordination between community residents and government has been identified as a barrier (Ajake & Amalu 2012). Failure to adequately consult and include 'grassroots' beneficiaries of development projects is a symptom of Western hegemony in development, and is an urgent area for participatory empirical research.

ECOLOGY OF GLOBAL TOURISM

Changing tourism trends are leading tourists to seek out ever more 'authentic' and remote experiences in pristine, natural environments and 'traditional' cultural settings. Greater numbers are visiting mountain ranges, rainforests, lakes, rivers and marine environments, as well as remote rural communities. Whilst this potentiates increased local participation and a sense of environmental 'stewardship' (Moghimehfar & Halpenny 2016), many delicate environments are damaged by tourists' presence.

Moreover, global developmentalism encourages poorer countries to prosper from tourism through a combination of incentives and pressure, with the overall aim of bringing weak economies in line with the strongest. Since the economies of rich countries are also aiming for a state of perpetual growth, the goal seems at best unattainable. And given the fact that overconsumption in rich countries already constitutes a 60 per cent overshoot in the Earth's ecological capacity (Wackernagel & Beyers 2019), the goal is entirely unsustainable. There are also tensions and problems contained in global development programmes designed in the West for implementation in the South, such as the United Nations Sustainable Development Goals, which, since they rely on the logic of perpetual expansion and prioritise economic growth over environmental protection, are viewed by some as a neoliberal and unsustainable form of green capitalism (see Adelman 2018; Ponte 2019).

CONCLUSIONS

The key research concerns of critical tourism scholars increasingly centre on the discrepancies in power and resources that manifest in tourist encounters as part of the broader political economy of globalised capitalism, which generally fails to significantly improve the lives of the world's poor. Although tourism is certainly a significant source of revenue in countries spanning most parts of the world and is frequently cited as an important industry for growth and development (Brida & Risso 2009; Tang & Tan 2013), there are many drawbacks and dilemmas to be considered.

The industry's main growth areas are in global South countries, and the concomitant tourism promotional discourses are problematic. Further, tourism growth in poor countries generates and exacerbates exclusionary practices and inequities by creating tourist-only enclaves and raising property, land and commodity prices. Tourism revenue 'leakage' is widespread (Lejárraga & Walkenhorst 2010; Stabler et al. 2010), which not only favours foreign investors and local elites but can also siphon off state expenditure on infrastructure and vital services. Although well-managed 'pro-poor' tourism development can be beneficial for local communities, the opposite is often the case. Tourism growth under conditions of neoliberal globalisation has contributed to the impoverishment of many rural communities in the 'periphery' whilst encouraging urban growth and migration. Moreover, the development of a corporatised tourism sector under the conditions of capitalism and neoliberalism has done little to fund development and improvement beyond the main urban and tourist hubs (Higgins-Desbiolles 2006).

REFERENCES

Adelman, S. (2018). The Sustainable Development Goals, anthropocentrism and neoliberalism. In D. French & L. Kotzé (eds), *Sustainable Development Goals* (pp. 15–40). Cheltenham, UK and Northampton, MA, USA: Edward Elgar Publishing.

Ajake, A.O. & Amalu, T.E. (2012). The relevance of tourism on the economic development of Cross River State, Nigeria. *Journal of Geography and Regional Planning*, 5(1): 14–20.

Alrawadieh, Z., Karayilan, E. & Cetin, G. (2019). Understanding the challenges of refugee entrepreneurship in tourism and hospitality. *The Service Industries Journal*, 39(9–10): 717–740.

Appadurai, A. (1986). *The Social Life of Things: Commodities in Cultural Perspective*. Cambridge: Cambridge University Press.

Appadurai, A. (1990). Disjuncture and difference in the global cultural economy. *Theory, Culture & Society*, 7(2–3): 295–310.

Atelijevic, I. & Doorne, S. (2003). Culture, economy and tourism commodities: Social relations of production and consumption. *Tourist Studies*, 3(2): 123–141.

Bandyopadhyay, R. & Nascimento, K. (2010). 'Where fantasy becomes reality': How tourism forces made Brazil a sexual playground. *Journal of Sustainable Tourism*, 18(8): 933–949.

Beck, U. (2002). The cosmopolitan society and its enemies. *Theory, Culture & Society*, 19(1–2): 17–44.

Bennett, T. (2009). *Culture, Class, Distinction*. London: Routledge.

Bott, E. (2018). Among the piranhas: The troubling lifespan of ethnic tropes in 'tribal' tourism to Vietnam. *Journal of Sustainable Tourism*, 26(8): 1291–1307.

Brida, J.G. & Risso, W.A. (2009). Tourism as a factor of long-run economic growth: An empirical analysis for Chile. *European Journal of Tourism Research*, 2(2): 178–185.

Brinkmann, S. (2017). *Stand Firm: Resisting the Self-Improvement Craze*. Cambridge: Polity Press.

Brohman, J. (1996). New directions in tourism for Third World development. *Annals of Tourism Research*, 23(1): 48–70.

Bruner, E. (1991). Transformation of self in tourism. *Annals of Tourism Research*.

Carrigan, A. (2015). Dark tourism and postcolonial studies: Critical intersections. *Postcolonial Studies*, 17(3): 236–250.

Caton, K. & Santos, C.A. (2008). Closing the hermeneutic circle? Photographic encounters with the other. *Annals of Tourism Research*, 35(1): 7–26.

Cohen, E. (1993). The study of touristic images of native people: Mitigating the stereotype of a stereotype. In D. Pearce & R. Butler (eds), *Tourism Research* (pp. 36–69). London: Routledge.

Craik, J. (1994). Peripheral pleasures: The peculiarities of post-colonial tourism. *Culture and Policy*, 6: 1.

Crick, M. (1994). *Resplendent Sites, Discordant Voices: Sri Lankans and International Tourism*. Langhorne, PA: Harwood Academic Publishers.

Crossley, É. & Picard, D. (2014). Regimes of value in tourism. *Journal of Tourism and Cultural Change*, 12(3): 201–205.

Echtner, C.M. & Prasad, P. (2003). The context of third world tourism marketing. *Annals of Tourism Research*, 30: 660–682.

Hall, C.M. & Tucker, H. (2004). *Tourism and Postcolonialism: Contested Discourses, Identities and Representations*. London: Routledge.

Held, D. (1999). *Global Transformations: Politics, Economics and Culture*. Cambridge: Polity Press.

Higgins-Desbiolles, B.F. (2006). *Another World Is Possible: Tourism, Globalization and the Responsible Alternative*. Adelaide: Flinders University of South Australia. Unpublished PhD thesis.

Holden A. (2013). *Tourism, Poverty and Development*. London: Routledge.

Hollinshead, K. (2004). A primer in ontological craft. In J. Phillimore & L. Goodson (eds), *Qualitative Research in Tourism* (pp. 63–82). London: Routledge.

Jamieson, W., Goodwin, H. & Edmunds, C. (2004). Contribution of tourism to poverty alleviation: Pro-poor tourism and the challenge of measuring impacts. Transport Policy and Tourism Section Transport and Tourism Division, UN ESCAP. www.haroldgoodwin.info/resources/povertyalleviation.pdf

Lejárraga, I. & Walkenhorst, P. (2010). On linkages and leakages: Measuring the secondary effects of tourism. *Applied Economics Letters*, 17(5): 417–421.

Lenzen, M., Sun, Y., Faturay, F., Ting, Y., Geschke, A. & Malik, A. (2018). The carbon footprint of global tourism. *Nature Climate Change*, 8(6): 522–528.

Llewellyn Watson, G. & Kopachevsky, J.P. (1994). Interpretations of tourism as commodity. *Annals of Tourism Research*, 21(3): 643–660.

MacCannell, D. (1992). *Empty Meeting Grounds: The Tourist Papers*. London: Routledge.

McMichael, P. (2007). *Development and Social Change: A Global Perspective*. Thousand Oaks, CA: Pine Forge Press.

Meethan, K. (2001). T*ourism in Global Society: Place, Culture, Consumption*. London: Palgrave Macmillan.

Moghimehfar, F. & Halpenny, E.A. (2016). How do people negotiate through their constraints to engage in pro-environmental behavior? A study of front-country campers in Alberta, Canada. *Tourism Management*, 57: 362–372.

Morgan, N. & Pritchard, A. (1998). *Tourism Promotion and Power: Creating Images, Creating Identities*. Chichester: Wiley.

Mowforth, M. & Munt, I. (2009). *Tourism and Sustainability: Development, Globalization and New Tourism in the Third World*, Third Edition. London: Routledge.

Munt, I. (1994). The 'other' postmodern tourist: Culture, travel and new middle classes. *Theory, Culture and Society*, 11: 101–124.

Pappas, N. & Papatheodorou, A. (2017). Tourism and the refugee crisis in Greece: Perceptions and decision-making of accommodation providers. *Tourism Management*, 63: 31–41.

Ponte, S. (2019). Green capitalism and unjust sustainabilities. *Samfundsøkonomen*, 4: 102–108.

Reid, D. (2003). *Tourism, Globalization and Development: Responsible Tourism Planning*. London: Pluto Press.

Ryan, C. & Aicken, M. (eds) (2005). *Indigenous Tourism: The Commodification and Management of Culture*. Oxford: Elsevier.

Salazar, N.B. (2010). *Envisioning Eden: Mobilizing Imaginaries in Tourism and Beyond*. Oxford: Berghahn.

Seabrook, J. (1988). *The Race for Riches: The Human Cost of Wealth*. Basingstoke: Marshall Pickering.

Sharpley, R. (2009). *Tourism, Development and the Environment: Beyond Sustainability?* London: Earthscan.

Shaw, S. & Thomas, C. (2006). Discussion note: Social and cultural dimensions of air travel demand – hyper-mobility in the UK? *Journal of Sustainable Tourism*, 14(2): 209–215.

Sin, H.L. & Minca, C. (2014). Touring responsibly. *Geoforum*, 52: 96–106.

Skey, M. (2013). What does it mean to be cosmopolitan? An examination of the varying meaningfulness and commensurability of everyday 'cosmopolitan' practices. *Identities*, 20(3): 235 252.

Spivak, G.C. (1999). *A Critique of Postcolonial Reason: Towards a History of the Vanishing Present*. Cambridge, MA: Harvard University Press.

Stabler, M.J., Papatheodorou, A. & Sinclair, M.T. (2010). *The Economics of Tourism,* Second Edition. Abingdon: Routledge.

Statista (2021). Travel and tourism: Share of global GDP 2021. www.statista.com/statistics/1099933/travel-and-tourism-share-of-gdp

Steger, M. (2009). *Globalization: A Very Short Introduction.* New York: Oxford University Press.

Steinbrink, M. (2012). 'We did the slum!': Urban poverty tourism in historical perspective. *Tourism Geographies: An International Journal of Tourism Space, Place and Environment,* 14(2): 213–234.

Stiglitz, J. (2002). *Globalization and Its Discontents.* London: Allen Lane/Penguin Press.

Tang, C.F. & Tan, E.C. (2013). How stable is the tourism-led growth hypothesis in Malaysia? Evidence from disaggregated tourism markets. *Tourism Management,* 37: 52–57.

Tucker, H. & Akama, J. (2009). Tourism as postcolonialism. In T. Jamal & M. Robinson (eds), *The SAGE Handbook of Tourism Studies* (pp. 505–521). London: SAGE .

UNWTO (2020). Impact assessment of the Covid-19 outbreak on international tourism. www.unwto.org/impact-assessment-of-the-covid-19-outbreak-on-international-tourism

Urry, J. (2001). Globalizing the tourist gaze. www.comp.lancs.ac.uk/sociology/papers/Urry-Globalizing-the-Tourist-Gaze.pdf

Wackernagel, M. & Beyers, B. (2019). *Ecological Footprint: Managing Our Biocapacity Budget.* Vancouver: New Society Publishers.

10. Globalization as an extension of the triple movement: care workers' struggles for emancipation

Bernhard Weicht

INTRODUCTION

Over the last decades public and political debates on globalization have strongly focused on the increasing entanglement of local markets on the one hand and the rise of global market-places and players on the other. At the same time, social movements with global perspectives and politics have emerged which directly address global challenges arising from markets and other forms of domination. One important critique of globalizing marketization has been that social protection measures can, due to their national embeddedness, only inadequately cover risks arising from the very processes (Fraser 2014). Moreover, many social movements do not address resistance to marketization processes specifically and exclusively, but rather focus on other forms of emancipation from domination (Fraser 2013).

In the light of these developments, the last years have seen a resurgence of interest in the work of Karl Polanyi. His main contribution, *The Great Transformation* (2001), has informed many investigations into the double movement of marketization and social protectionism (Karner and Weicht 2016; Atzmüller et al. 2019). Several scholars have attempted to transfer Polanyi's analysis from the 1940s onto global developments of the early twenty-first century (Brie 2015; Dale et al. 2019; Kirby 2021). On a conceptual and theoretical level, Nancy Fraser's (2013) work has been particularly influential. Capturing movements and developments of the late twentieth and early twenty-first centuries, Fraser adds another layer and perspective to Polanyi's double movement. Societal development, she argues, needs to be understood as a triple movement in which emancipation perspectives align themselves with either marketization or social protectionism.

Drawing on Nancy Fraser's (2013) interpretation and development of Karl Polanyi's analysis, I seek to conceptualize globalization as an extension of the triple movement beyond national borders. Utilizing the example of care workers' struggles for emancipation, I argue that the ambivalent conjunctions Fraser describes need to be extended by a local/global perspective. This means that emancipation movements cannot only align themselves with market forces or protectionism; rather, the alliances can additionally be distinguished by their focus on the local or the global. Globalization understood in this way requires social movements to reflect on their own positioning, in defining their closeness/distance to capitalist developments and their spatial perspectives.

UNDERSTANDING GLOBALIZATION AS A GLOBAL TRIPLE MOVEMENT

As indicated above, globalization can be understood as the process of a permanent extension of marketization beyond borders and regions. This means that, globally, communities and societal structures are affected by the dynamics of markets. Karl Polanyi (2001) famously identified the shifts between the economy vis-à-vis society as the crucial attribute of the 'great transformation' in which marketization refers to a subordination of the 'substance of society itself to the laws of the market' (Polanyi 2001, p. 75). However, as Polanyi observed, the trend of increasing commodification is met by resistance, advocating a move toward stronger social protection, finally resulting in what Polanyi termed the 'double movement'.

Two aspects of Polanyi's work, which Wood et al. (2019) oddly term the soft and the hard Polanyi, are particularly important for an understanding of globalization processes. First, in modern capitalism, markets are always embedded within (state) structures and disputes over states' control and influence over the functioning and results of markets emerge. Polanyi (2001) not only emphasizes the essential embeddedness of markets but, consequently, the parallel evolution of markets and regulation. Second, Polanyi understands the process of commodification as a goal shift from the creation of use value to the production of exchange value. To guarantee a continuous, flexible mode of production, the commodification process extends to labour, land and money and, consequentially, creates markets for those means of production: 'This makes clear what the employers' demand for mobility of labor and flexibility of wages really means: precisely that which we circumscribed above as a market in which human labor is a commodity' (Polanyi 2001, p. 185).

However, due to their constitutive role for the fabric of social life itself, labour, land and money can only be commodified unsatisfactorily and, hence, Polanyi (2001) terms them 'fictitious commodities'. Polanyi's analysis of fictitious commodities then demonstrates the inevitable resistance to an unrestricted marketization. Extension of the organizing principle of the market, 'aiming at the establishment of a self-regulating market' therefore clashes with 'the principle of social protection aiming at the conservation of man and nature as well as productive organization' (Polanyi 2001, pp. 138–9). Polanyi's first insight (that markets are always embedded) thus needs to be nuanced in a way that the structures in which the embeddedness takes place allow for freedom and protection of individuals and communities (López 2016).

Nancy Fraser (2014) has picked up both of those aspects of Polanyi's work but argues for an extension of the double movement on two levels. First, instead of Polanyi's ontological conception of 'fictitious commodities', Fraser (2014) proposes a structural reading which emphasizes that marketization of labour necessarily undermines and destroys its own conditions of possibility, for example in the realm of reproductive labour. Second, and related to Fraser's structural understanding of fictitious commodities, Polanyi's solely negative account of commodification, Fraser argues, is uncritically romanticizing the realm of society, and employs a 'communitarian bias', which leads to an ignorance of 'forms of domination that are not grounded in market mechanisms' (Fraser 2014, p. 548). In other words, Polanyi misses (or ignores) the communal or family context: 'Preoccupied exclusively with the corrosive effects of commodification upon communities, it neglects injustices within communities, including injustices, such as slavery, serfdom and patriarchy, that depend on social constructions of labour, land and money precisely as non-commodities' (Fraser 2014, p. 544).

Fraser thus seeks to extend the concept of the double movement and introduces a third pole – emancipation. Historically, Fraser (2013) argues, emancipation has not only been reached by the help of public provisions but has often been secured through alignment with marketization processes. Social struggles are thus sometimes directed against processes of commodification and the increasing exploitation of labour and at other instances against injustices and domination stemming from the realms of social protection and communal embeddedness. Hence, Fraser identifies 'three-sided struggles, encompassing not only neoliberals and social protectionists, but also proponents of emancipation' (Fraser 2014, p. 551). Emancipation in this triple movement can then align itself with social protection against markets or with markets against structures of the state and community. The ambivalent nature of emancipation leads to parallel struggles for liberalization, protection and emancipation.

MISFRAMING THE TRIPLE MOVEMENT

Fraser's insightful rereading of Polanyi provides a useful perspective on an understanding of globalization processes in terms of the triple movement of liberalization, social protectionism and emancipation struggles. However, while potentially of global range, both Polanyi's and Fraser's analyses focus on nation state-defined structures of embedding and disembedding. Likewise, struggles for emancipation and/or social protection are, either explicitly or implicitly, directed at traditional political structures and actors, situated within national borders.

Ironically, Nancy Fraser's earlier work provides the necessary tools to extend the limited focus of the triple movement. In *Scales of Justice: Reimagining Political Space in a Globalizing World* (2008), Fraser acknowledges that, empirically, the sole direction towards nation states has never fully been true but that significant changes have occurred. Two developments require theoretical attention: first, the increasing heterogeneity of justice discourses, which can alternate between claims for redistribution and recognition (see Fraser 2003) and, second, the increasing plurality of competing frames for how justice claims are expressed and directed (Fraser 2008). For the latter, Fraser (2013) argues, the nation state still functions as a political imaginary, characterized by a sharp distinction between the domestic and international space and the state's function as addressee of claims for recognition and redistribution: 'Long hegemonic, that metric represented political communities as geographically bounded units, demarcated by sharply drawn borders and arrayed side by side' (Fraser 2008, p. 4).

Fraser thus extends her original model that recognizes justice claims for economic redistribution and cultural recognition by a third perspective, political representation and participation (Fraser 2008). Struggles over and negotiations about the 'what' of justice are thus met by the 'who' and 'how' of justice. The 'who' of justice refers to those members of a society or community to whom regulations, policies and political actions refer. National borders and boundaries demarcate this group, purposefully creating insiders and outsiders: 'Constituting both members and non-members in a single stroke, this decision effectively excludes the latter from the universe of those entitled to consideration within the community in matters of distribution, recognition, and ordinary-political representation' (Fraser 2008, p. 19).

The 'who' and 'how' of justice thus refer to the frame within which first-order questions of justice are debated and decided (Fraser 2008, p. 15). Since 'the idea that state-territoriality can serve as a proxy for social effectivity is no longer plausible' (Fraser 2008, p. 24), Fraser speaks of a politics of framing in a globalizing world in which questions of meta-justice need to be considered alongside claims for redistribution and/or recognition. Social movements struggling for emancipation and/or protection cannot ignore the political level of framing since political participation is ineffective or impossible if injustices occur on a global stage (Fraser 2013). While transnational social movements explicitly 'contest the national frame within which justice conflicts have historically been situated and seek to re-map the bounds of justice on a broader scale' (Fraser 2008, p. 1), the evaluation of framing needs to be applied for all actors of the triple movement throughout.

Thus, introducing a fourth category (referring to the framing of local/global) to analytically extend Fraser's perspective fosters our understanding of the differences of the various emancipation struggles. Fraser's notion of the 'ambivalences of feminism' (since emancipation struggles align themselves with both liberalization and protection; see Fraser 2016) can thus be extended by the notion of 'ambivalences of globalization'. Emancipation in this extended model can associate itself with markets or social protectionism while both alignments could be framed locally or globally. In the following section this model will be illustrated by focusing on various emancipation movements of care workers.

THE EXAMPLE OF CARE WORKERS: LOCAL AND GLOBAL EMANCIPATION STRUGGLES

The care crisis, Fraser (2016) argues, is an inherent feature stemming from the social-reproductive contradictions of financialized capitalism. Care giving and social reproductive labour are essential to 'produce and maintain social bonds' (Fraser 2016, p. 101) and thus to allow the continuation and extension of global capitalism. While care can be (and historically has been) provided by (women within) families, recent decades have seen first state provision and later an upsurge of markets in the field. Indeed, in times of retrenching welfare states, a global commodification of care (Lutz 2018) has emerged in which different forms of marketization have become a near global response to ensure support for vulnerable people (Fine and Davidson 2018). While the particularities of design differ, states commonly transfer direct responsibility for service provision to some forms of markets or quasi markets (Fine and Davidson 2018). Both in terms of policies and practices, the economic shift in the field of care work (Aulenbacher et al. 2018) is directly linked to the role of government policy in offloading services to the market (Aronson and Neysmith 2006).

From the perspective of the triple movement, a process has taken shape in which the care sector – traditionally not belonging to the market sphere – is increasingly commodified. While for many women emancipation from family-based care responsibilities allows some form of liberation (Fraser 2013; Weicht 2019), the marketization of care also challenges the public provision of services (Fraser and Bedford 2008). The result, Fraser (2016, p. 104) demonstrates, 'is a new, dualized organization of social reproduction, commodified for those who can pay for it and privatized for those who cannot'. Like the original example of labour, however, care functions as a fictitious commodity since care needs must be addressed not least to allow capitalist production to continue. Emancipation struggles of care workers (i.e., struggles for redistribution, recognition and representation) align themselves with state structures and provisions on the one hand and marketization dynamics on the other. Importantly, however, in a global care labour market (see Lutz 2018) these alignments can take local or global perspectives.

In line with the model sketched above, care workers must negotiate their emancipation struggles between the market and the welfare state, and between the local and the global context. In an ideal-type analysis, four possible alignments emerge. Care workers can, for example, draw on:

1. global care chains as individual emancipation possibilities;
2. local struggles for better working conditions in care settings;
3. global care workers' initiatives advocating for domestic workers; and/or
4. the emancipation through self-organized market arrangements.

In the following sections I will briefly explore these four angles of the extended triple movement, in which the possibilities of marketization or social protectionism are intersected with local or global perspectives. Table 10.1 illustrates the four examples.

Table 10.1   Four ideal-typical care arrangements

	Global	Local
Marketization	Care migration	Buurtzorg
Social protectionism	International Labour Organization Convention	Local labour disputes

Care Migration as Emancipation

A lack of satisfying employment opportunities and promising financial possibilities to provide for one's families lead many women to enter the global and transnational labour markets in the field of care (Clark and Bettini 2017). Global care chains (Lutz 2018) or gendered care labour supply chains (Saraswati 2017) have established a worldwide market for care workers. Fostered by loosened migration policies for care workers (Chau 2019), migration to work in care forms an important opportunity for many to find emancipation possibilities through global markets. In the example of Austria, a system was established in which various agencies arrange the engagement of formally self-employed migrant care workers, financed to a large extent by a generous cash-for-care scheme and additional government subsidies (Da Roit and Weicht 2013; Weicht and Österle 2016). Predominantly women from Eastern European countries seek employment opportunities (Österle and Bauer 2016) and can escape struggles within their local labour markets. The promise of employment, higher income and a better future for one's family are the main determents of care migration (Bahna 2016; Safuta et al. 2016). Care markets in that sense, with their aim to deliver empowerment to those in need (Brennan et al. 2012), can thus also offer new opportunities and emancipation for disadvantaged women.

Importantly, Larsen et al. (2005) demonstrate how migrant care workers must not be reduced to economic migrants. Rather, migrant workers adopt a transnational perspective on life, heavily influenced by an international orientation. Emancipation aligned with marketization here utilizes global opportunities and perspectives.

Labour Disputes

At the other end of the local/global triple movement matrix we find the alignment with social protectionism in the local context. Illustrative examples for these kinds of emancipation struggles can be found in local labour disputes. Over the last years, many different countries have seen an upsurge of strikes, industrial action or demonstrations of care workers. Countermovements against a shift towards economization in the field of care either draw on existing social protectionism structures or create new ones (Aulenbacher et al. 2018). Becker et al. (2018) provide interesting examples for countermovements with transformative potential, moving beyond classical wage conflicts and rather addressing the capitalist expansion into care itself.

The type of organization varies with trade unions only representing one of the major organizing forms (Hellgren 2015). Additional to professionally trained and institutionally organized nurses (Granberg and Nygren 2017), globally recruited migrant care workers have started to address the local political arena. This 'migrant precariat' (Hellgren 2015) has identified their own positioning in society as a lever for activism and protest (Elias 2010).

Two challenges arise in the context of traditional labour rights struggles. First, due to the nature of the work and the relational basis of it, strikes and industrial action in the (health-)care sector are particularly challenging (Dhai and Mahomed 2018). Second, Elias (2010) points out the difficulties arising from the fact that dominant labour regulations are often state centred. Nevertheless, an increasing interest of traditional actors in industrial action is noticeable. Swiss trade unions, for example, have taken to support Central and Eastern European migrant workers with the aim of not only improving the latter's negotiation position but to strengthen care workers' rights in general (Rogalewski 2018).

International Labour Organization Convention

While this social protectionist approach, aligning emancipation with the improvement of social rights, is largely focusing on local political structures, the third angle of the matrix extends its perspective onto the global sphere. A landmark policy in this context has been the implementation of the International Labour Organization (ILO) Convention in 2011 on migrant domestic workers (Pape 2016). Being the result of extraordinary global political struggles, the Convention on Domestic Workers is an explicit attempt to address domestic workers' rights as 'global rights' (Cherubini et al. 2018).

Recognizing that the employment of domestic workers has become an issue of global governance (Marchetti 2018), domestic workers themselves start emphasizing their global interlinkages as a new political subject. Blofield and Jokela (2018) specifically point to the links between local and transnational organizations of domestic workers with national governments leading to the ratification of the ILO Convention. Moreover, as Gottfried and Chun (2018) argue, the worldwide commodification of care has been the starting point for collective agency, claiming rights as workers and citizens. The ILO Convention itself now provides the basis for many local labour disputes, in which migrant workers do not stick to the side-lines but are recognized as the main group of care workers in many countries. The recognition of their identity as migrant workers also brings to the foreground the complex intersections of labour, employment and migrants' rights (Gottfried and Chun 2018). Being able to address struggles for emancipation through the route of social protectionism for those migrant workers is only possible through a global outlook and practice.

Buurtzorg

The final example sketches the angle of emancipation struggles through marketization on a local level. Many countries with formerly well-established public provisions have been heavily influenced by neoliberal politics with an emphasis on economic efficiency and cost reduction through competition (Andersson and Kvist 2014; Weicht 2016). As seen above, these commodification attempts have often been met by resistance of care workers, both in local and global frames. One particularly interesting example in which emancipation struggles have manifested themselves is the Dutch organization of Buurtzorg. Being a response to both commodification processes linked to profit interests and large institutionalized arrangements of care, the idea of small-scale, localized and self-managed care teams (Alders 2015) provides an innovative approach in the matrix sketched above.

The idea that nurses and care workers organize and manage their own work (Johansen and van den Bosch 2017) compellingly exemplifies Fraser's account of emancipation through marketization. Initiated by a local entrepreneur, the explicit aim is to provide a more humane and humanistic approach to care management (Johansen and van den Bosch 2017). Being an attack on both market-driven private companies and large, state-run institutions, Buurtzorg has meanwhile become a role model for other countries who seek a radically localized approach to care beyond the family, the state and traditional for-profit organizations (Leask et al. 2020). In that sense, Buurtzorg is slowly developing into a phenomenon of glocalization (Robertson 1995), in which a global market idea accomplishes localized struggles.

CONCLUSIONS

In this chapter, I have offered a reading of globalization as a triple movement beyond nation-state borders. Traditionally, globalization is understood as increasing and fostering marketization. Likewise, struggles of resistance are progressively turning towards global perspectives. If we complement Fraser's triple movement by her earlier analysis of justice struggles for (political) representation and participation, we see that emancipation struggles do not only align themselves with the poles of marketization or social protectionism; additionally, they can be framed locally and globally. Ambivalence in emancipation struggles thus stems from both the perspective of alignment and the local/global focus.

Economic globalization alters the space for manoeuvre for emancipation struggles, 'influencing who are the social actors, on what scales they organise, how issues and identities are framed, who are the targets (employers or states), and what communities are imagined' (Gottfried and Chun 2018, p. 1006). Table 10.1 can illustrate these different perspectives and possibilities. For care workers' struggles the various angles need to be reflected and negotiated. Emancipation of care workers sometimes aligns itself with market structures and sometimes with state institutions. They can be local or global in focus. Whether an extension of the model presented above, seeking emancipation beyond markets and beyond state institutions, bridging the local and global levels, such as the search for new forms of commons (Federici 2012; Brie 2015), can formulate new frames for justice claims is open for further research. The values and goals represented in Polanyi's and Fraser's original double or triple movement, namely liberalization, social protection and emancipation, will remain central. The limitations of nation states to those claims, however, will make new lines of thinking inevitable. Exemplified by Joan Tronto's (2013) proposal for an extension of (citizenship) rights along the lines of transnational care relations, globalization requires an understanding of the necessity of framings of emancipation movements aligning themselves with different poles (markets/social protection) and levels (local/global).

REFERENCES

Alders, P. (2015), 'Self-managed care teams to improve community care for frail older adults in the Netherlands', *International Journal of Care Coordination*, 18(2–3), 57–61.

Andersson, K. and E. Kvist (2014), 'The neoliberal turn and the marketization of care: The transformation of eldercare in Sweden', *European Journal of Women's Studies*, 22(3), 274–287.

Aronson, J. and S.M. Neysmith (2006), 'Obscuring the costs of home care: Restructuring at work', *Work, Employment and Society*, 20(1), 27–45.

Atzmüller, R., B. Aulenbacher, U. Brand, F. Décieux, K. Fischer and B. Sauer (eds) (2019), *Capitalism in Transformation: Movements and Countermovements in the 21st Century*, Cheltenham, UK and Northampton, MA, USA: Edward Elgar Publishing.

Aulenbacher, B., F. Décieux and B. Riegraf (2018), 'Capitalism goes care: Elder and child care between market, state, profession, and family and questions of justice and inequality', *Equality, Diversity and Inclusion: An International Journal*, 37(4), 347–360.

Bahna, M. (2016), 'Slowakische 24-Stunden-BetreuerInnen in Österreich: Nur ein weiterer Migrationsstrom aus der Slowakei?', in B. Weicht and A. Österle (eds), *Im Ausland zu Hause pflegen: Die Beschäftigung von MigrantInnen in der 24-Stunden-Betreuung*, Vienna: LIT Verlag, pp. 199–220.

Becker, K., K. Dörre and Y. Kutlu (2018), 'Counter-Landnahme ? Labour disputes in the care-work field', *Equality, Diversity and Inclusion: An International Journal*, 37(4), 361–375.

Blofield, M. and M. Jokela (2018), 'Paid domestic work and the struggles of care workers in Latin America', *Current Sociology*, 66(4), 531–546.

Brennan, D., B. Cass, S. Himmelweit and M. Szebehely (2012), 'The marketization of care: Rationales and consequences in Nordic and liberal care regimes', *Journal of European Social Policy*, 22(4), 377–391.

Brie, M. (2015), *Polanyi neu entdecken: Das hellblaue Bändchen zu einem möglichen Dialog von Nancy Fraser und Karl Polanyi*, Hamburg: VSA Verlag.

Chau, H.S. (2019), 'Producing (im)mobilities in home care for the elderly: The role of home care agencies in Switzerland', *International Journal of Ageing and Later Life*, 13(2), 23–50.

Cherubini, D., G. Garofalo Geymonat and S. Marchetti (2018), 'Global rights and local struggles: The case of the ILO Convention n. 189 on domestic work'. *Partecipazione & Conflitto*, 11(3).

Clark, N. and G. Bettini (2017), '"Floods" of migrants, flows of care: Between climate displacement and global care chains', *The Sociological Review*, 65(2), 36–54.

Da Roit, B. and B. Weicht (2013), 'Migrant care work and care, migration and employment regimes: A fuzzy-set analysis', *Journal of European Social Policy*, 23(5), 469–486.

Dale, G., C. Holmes and M. Markantonatou (eds) (2019), *Karl Polanyi's Political and Economic Thought: A Critical Guide*, Newcastle upon Tyne: Agenda Publishing.

Dhai, A. and S. Mahomed (2018), 'The National Education, Health and Allied Workers' Union (NEHAWU) strikes: South Africa's healthcare battlefield', *South African Medical Journal*, 108(8), 632–633.

Elias, J. (2010), 'Gendered political economy and the politics of migrant worker rights: The view from South-East Asia', *Australian Journal of International Affairs*, 64(1), 70–85.

Federici, S. (2012), *Recolution at Point Zero: Housework, Reproduction, and Feminist Struggle*, Oakland, CA: PM Press.

Fine, M. and B. Davidson (2018), 'The marketization of care: Global challenges and national responses in Australia', *Current Sociology*, 66(4), 503–516.

Fraser, N. (2003), 'Social justice in the age of identity politics: Redistribution, recognition, and participation', in N. Fraser and A. Honneth (eds), *Redistribution or Recognition: A Political-Philosophical Exchange*, London: Verso, pp. 7–109.

Fraser, N. (2008), *Scales of Justice: Reimagining Political Space in a Globalizing World*, Cambridge: Polity Press.

Fraser, N. (2013), *Fortunes of Feminism: From State-Managed Capitalism to Neoliberal Crisis*, London: Verso.

Fraser, N. (2014), 'Can society be commodities all the way down: Post-Polanyian reflections on capitalist crisis', *Economy and Society*, 43(4), 541–558.

Fraser, N. (2016), 'Contradictions of capital and care', *New Left Review*, 100(July–August), 99–117.

Fraser, N. and K. Bedford (2008), 'Social rights and gender justice in the neoliberal moment: A conversation about welfare and transnational politics', *Feminist Theory*, 9(2), 225–245.

Gottfried, H. and J.J. Chun (2018), 'Care work in transition: Transnational circuits of gender, migration, and care', *Critical Sociology*, 44(7–8), 997–1012.

Granberg, M. and K.G. Nygren (2017), 'Paradoxes of anti-austerity protest: Matters of neoliberalism, gender, and subjectivity in a case of collective resignation', *Gender, Work and Organization*, 24(1), 56–68.

Hellgren, Z. (2015), 'Markets, regimes, and the role of stakeholders: Explaining precariousness of migrant domestic/care workers in different institutional frameworks', *Social Politics*, 22(2), 220–241.

Johansen, F. and S. van den Bosch (2017), 'The scaling-up of neighbourhood care: From experiment towards a transformative movement in healthcare', *Futures*, 89, 60–73.

Karner, C. and B. Weicht (eds) (2016), *The Commonalities of Global Crises: Markets, Communities and Nostalgia*, London: Palgrave Macmillan.

Kirby, P. (2021), *Karl Polanyi and the Contemporary Political Crisis: Transforming Market Society in the Era of Climate Change*, London: Bloomsbury Academic.

Larsen, J.A., H.T. Allan, K. Bryan and P. Smith (2005), 'Overseas nurses' motivations for working in the UK: Globalization and life politics', *Work, Employment and Society*, 19(2), 349–368.

Leask, C.F., J. Bell and F. Murray (2020), 'Acceptability of delivering an adapted Buurtzorg model in the Scottish care context', *Public Health*, 179, 111–117.

López, J.J. (2016), 'Disembedding the embedded/disembedded opposition', in C. Karner and B. Weicht (eds), *The Commonalities of Global Crises: Markets, Communities and Nostalgia*, London: Palgrave Macmillan, pp. 223–247.

Lutz, H. (2018), 'Care migration: The connectivity between care chains, care circulation and transnational social inequality', *Current Sociology*, 66(4), 577–589.

Marchetti, S. (2018), 'The global governance of paid domestic work: Comparing the impact of ILO Convention no. 189 in Ecuador and India', *Critical Sociology*, 44(7–8), 1191–1205.

Österle, A. and G. Bauer (2016), 'The legalization of rotational 24-hours care work in Austria: Implications for migrant care workers', *Social Politics*, 23(2), 192–213.

Pape, K. (2016), 'ILO Convention C189 – a good start for the protection of domestic workers: An insider's view', *Progress in Development Studies*, 16(2), 189–202.

Polanyi, K. (2001 [1944]), *The Great Transformation: The Political and Economic Origins of Our Time*, Boston, MA: Beacon Press.

Robertson, R. (1995), 'Glocalization: Time-space and homogeneity-heterogeneity', in M. Featherstone, S. Lash and R. Robertson (eds), *Global Modernities*, London: Sage, pp. 25–44.

Rogalewski, A. (2018), 'Organising and mobilising Central and Eastern European migrant women working in care: A case study of a successful care workers' strike in Switzerland in 2014', *Transfer: European Review of Labour and Research*, 24(4), 421–436.

Safuta, A., A. Kordasiewicz and S. Urbańska (2016), 'Verpasste Kreuzung: Polen als Herkunfts- und Zielland für migrantische Pflege- und Haushaltskräfte', in B. Weicht and A. Österle (eds), *Im Ausland zu Hause pflegen: Die Beschäftigung von MigrantInnen in der 24-Stunden-Betreuung*, Vienna: LIT Verlag, pp. 221–244.

Saraswati, L.A. (2017), 'The gender politics of human waste and human-as-waste: Indonesian migrant workers and elderly care in Japan', *Gender, Work & Organization*, 24(6), 594–609.

Tronto, J.C. (2013), *Caring Democracy: Markets, Equality, and Justice*, New York: New York University Press.

Weicht, B. (2016), 'State, market, or back to the family? Nostalgic struggles for proper elder care', in C. Karner and B. Weicht (eds), *The Commonalities of Global Crises: Markets, Communities and Nostalgia*, London: Palgrave Macmillan, pp. 115–141.

Weicht, B. (2019), 'The commodification of informal care: Joining and resisting marketization processes', in R. Atzmüller, B. Aulenbacher, U. Brand, F. Décieux, K. Fischer and B. Sauer (eds), *Capitalism in Transformation: Movements and Countermovements in the 21st Century*, Cheltenham, UK and Northampton, MA, USA: Edward Elgar Publishing, pp. 261–273.

Weicht, B. and A. Österle (eds) (2016), *Im Ausland zu Hause pflegen: Die Beschäftigung von MigrantInnen in der 24-Stunden-Betreuung*, Vienna: LIT Verlag.

Wood, A.J., M. Graham, V. Lehdonvirta and I. Hjorth (2019), 'Networked but commodified: The (dis) embeddedness of digital labour in the gig economy', *Sociology*, 53(5), 931–950.

11. Human rights as ends or means of a global moral horizon

José Julián López

INTRODUCTION

The reality of the global spread of human rights, their globalization(s), is hard to deny. A number of scholars argue that some type of commitment to human rights, even if only perfunctory in nature, is a prerequisite for nation states to legitimately exercise their sovereignty (Hafner-Burton and Tsutsui, 2005; Levy and Sznaider, 2010; Meyer et al., 1997; Soysal, 1994). Some scholars speak about the diffusion of human rights as a sweeping world historical cultural wave whose high tide has lifted individual autonomy onto a secure global footing (Elliott, 2007; Meyer, 2009; Meyer and Jepperson, 2000; Soysal, 1994). Others draw attention to the spectacular rise of transnational assemblages of human rights institutional actors and processes. These have contributed to the dissemination, though not always the successful enactment, of human rights norms (Beitz, 2011; Donnelly, 2007; Power and Allison, 2016; Risse et al., 1999, 2013; Sikkink, 2011; Simmons, 2009).

More tentatively, some scholars argue that the global field of human rights is constituted by ongoing struggles to secure and advance these vital rights, sometimes in the face of formidable resistance (Armaline et al., 2015; Blau and Frezzo, 2012; Blau and Moncada, 2005; Goodale, 2009; Kurasawa, 2007; Roberts, 2015; Somers and Roberts, 2008; Stammers, 2009). Of course, some oppose human rights for ideological reasons, typically but not always casting them as neoliberalism or imperialism's inadvertent or, as the case may be, compliant accomplice (Arendt, 1973, ch. 9; Bricmont, 2006; Brown, 2004; Douzinas, 2007; Englund, 2006; Samson, 2020; Teeple, 2005; Whyte, 2019; Žižek, 2005). Yet others resist some particular instantiation of human rights on cultural grounds (Akbarzadeh and MacQueen, 2008; An-Na'im, 2010; Bauer and Bell, 1999; Baxi, 2002; Bell, 2000; De Sousa Santos, 2008; Ibhawoh, 2008, 2018; Mauzy, 1997; Mayer, 2018, 2002; Nault, 2021). It is worth noting, however, that the struggle to change or broaden their current form, or even their outright rejection, point to human rights' contemporary global centrality no less than their vociferous support. Today, human rights appear to be an unavoidable dimension of the global moral and ethical landscape.

Registering their contemporary global prevalence, however, reveals little about how human rights have been globalized and the ethical or moral consequences that follow from their globalization. The cultural sociologist Roland Robertson (1992), an early contributor to the debates on the intersection of human rights and globalization, underscored the importance of paying attention to the forms of consciousness through which the world was, indeed is, being made into a diverse yet nonetheless single place. In the context of human rights, we can take this to mean the following: what are the forms of ethically and morally representing, understanding, and acting in what is increasingly becoming imagined as a single world, an imagined ethico-political community, or a political imaginary (López, 2018)? In this chapter, drawing on Robertson's insight, two interrelated but distinct forms of understanding how human rights are contributing to making the world into one place are presented.

The first, *human rights as an indisputable global moral horizon*, traces the origin and definition to the 1948 United Nations Universal Declaration of Human Rights (UDHR). This manner of understanding the globalization of human rights focuses on the national and trans-national political efforts and institutional mechanisms through which human rights norms and principles – purportedly enshrined in the UDHR, and subsequently in other legal instruments – have been, and are being, disseminated. In this form, human rights are taken as self-evident ends, constituting an indisputable global moral horizon that no reasonable ethical person or community would reject. Human rights norms are construed as the product of a moral evolution enabled by a singular consensus in the aftermath of the barbarism of the Second World War. This vision endows all individuals with civil, political, social, cultural, and economic rights in virtue of their common humanity. The ethical and moral task is to ensure the global scope of their political, legal, and ethical efficacy.

The second, *human rights as an evolving global moral horizon*, understands the UDHR as prefiguring rather than definitively establishing a global moral horizon. In this case, unlike the preceding form, the UDHR is not understood as the defining moment for human rights, whose self-evidence propels their global adoption. Instead, human rights are understood as the pursuit of an evolving global moral horizon. Diverse communities, of different scales, and identity groups appropriate them and, in doing so, inject them with substantive meaning. Naturally, this necessarily eventuates in their alteration. This form of globalizing human rights is under-stood as the product of efforts to bend the arc of the global normative power of human rights to different worldviews, experiences, and interests. Consequently, rather than unassailable self-evident *ends*, human rights are the ever-evolving *means* towards a global moral horizon that is being defined in the process. Their global circulation necessarily presupposes their ongoing transformation. At their best, then, human rights represent the possibility of a global moral community unified in its ethical, and contradictory, diversity.

Looking at the globalization of human rights through the prism of these two forms draws attention to two different processes for representing the globalization of human rights: (1) the spread of norms, principles, and legal instruments, preferably consensually but sometimes by force if necessary, and (2) the ongoing redefinition of a plural global moral horizon. Equally, exploring the globalization of human rights in this way makes it possible to identify the gaps between the world that human rights purport to make, and the world that they are in fact making. The next section expands on Robertson's contribution to explore the role of con-sciousness in the forging of an imagined global community. This is followed by an elaboration of two forms of consciousness associated with the globalization of human rights. Finally, the chapter concludes by briefly exploring the ethical, moral, and political consequences that follow from these two forms, and draws on recent historiographical and socio-legal work to query the centrality of human rights both as an end and a means for a global moral horizon.

IMAGINING A GLOBAL MORAL COMMUNITY

In a thoughtful effort to wrestle with the meaning of the meteoric rise of the concept, and the idea, of globalization in the early 1990s, Robertson suggested that we understand the concept as referring to 'both the compression of the world and the intensification of consciousness of the world as a whole' (1992, p. 8). This, of course, did not mean seeing the world as a homogeneous and non-contradictory space. Robertson's goal was to draw attention to '*the form*[s] in terms of which the world becomes "united"' (Robertson, 1990, p. 18, emphasis in original), rather than to globalization as some predetermined *fait accompli* driven by a singular logic such as imperialism, Americanization, or neoliberalism.

Robertson not only drew attention to the significance of focusing on the *forms* of globalization, he distinguished between two modes of thinking about them: 'compression' – connectivity in his subsequent work – and 'consciousness' (Robertson, 2011). Although both are vital for grasping the ongoing dynamics of globalization, the former, connectivity or 'rapidly increasing interconnectedness' (Robertson, 2011, p. 1337), has been dominant in accounts of globalization. This has been particularly the case in the fields of politics, international relations, and economics. While the latter, i.e., consciousness, defined as 'a shared sense of the world as a whole', has received considerably less attention, and has been the purview of anthropologists, sociologists, area studies, and postcolonial studies (Robertson and White, 2007, p. 64). As it happens, it is the latter that is crucial for understanding the intersection between human rights and globalization. This is because a decisive component of this 'shared sense of the world as a whole' has been modulated by an emerging common 'conception of humanity' to which the idea(s) (Robertson, 1992, p. 133) and, more crucially, the practices of human rights have contributed substantially (López, 2018).

This is visible in the way human rights, as a mode of seeing the world, enjoin us to stretch or 'imagine' our sense of community beyond the nation (Anderson, 2004) to a world community. A community where rights (should) derive from 'individual personhood', rather than 'national belonging' (Soysal, 1994). Indeed, human rights are intricately tied up with contemporary efforts to realize a postnational form of citizenship, a global citizenship (Bosniak, 2000; Brysk, 2002; Brysk and Shafir, 2004; Frezzo, 2014; Jacobson, 1996; Levy and Sznaider, 2006, 2010; Sassen, 2009; Shafir and Brysk, 2006; Soysal, 1994, 2012). A related worldview, conjugating human commonality with a deep reverence for the uniqueness of individuals and their cultures, is found in cosmopolitanism. Cosmopolitanism, an imagined global community, envisages a 'global order in which the idea of human rights is an operative principle of justice, with mechanisms of global governance established specifically for their protection' (Fine, 2009, p. 8). The cosmopolitan worldview is also conjoined with a particular stance towards the diversity of the world, viewing 'otherness and cultural difference as something desirable ... a cultural mode of seeing and valuing difference' (Kendall et al., 2009, p. 105).

Through variably weighting and differentially weaving political and cultural threads, a variety of scholars of cosmopolitanism, or indeed cosmopolitan scholars, are chronicling, and/or contributing to the diffusion of a consciousness of diversity rooted in a global commonality driven by human rights (Appiah, 1997; Beck, 2006; Benhabib, 2004, 2013; Braidotti et al., 2012; Breckenridge et al., 2002; Carens, 2013; Delanty, 2006, 2009; Held, 1995, 2010; Kendall et al., 2009; Kurasawa, 2007; Nussbaum, 1996, 1998; Pogge, 2008; Turner, 2006). The political philosopher Michael Ignatieff would appear to speak for many when he claims that human rights have become 'the lingua franca of global moral thought' (Ignatieff, 2001, p. 53).

The legal scholar Costas Douzinas goes further, suggesting that contemporary human rights 'do not belong to humans ... they construct humans', contributing to humans' very sense of self (2007, p. 45). In a similar vein, the historian Lynn Hunt argues that human rights have had a hand in constituting a global community of feeling that reacts powerfully to human rights violations (2007). For those whose ethical and political sensibilities have been tutored by the moral horizon of human rights – the 'global moral lingua franca' – it is not difficult to authenticate Hunt's claim with the imprimatur of personal experience. Human rights' tutees cannot avoid feeling moral revulsion, when not outrage, as well as an indomitable need to act when provided with documented graphic evidence of a person, be they near or far, broken by unspeakable brutality. Such a reaction captures human rights as a form of global consciousness at its most elemental state. It captures the emotional dimension of the desire to make the world a singular place. A better place, one dares to hope.

But what kind of a single place is human rights consciousness making possible? What are the particular forms of action that have the capacity to make the world one place? What is the strength of the global communities that are thus being imagined?

A number of years ago, the political scientist and historian Benedict Anderson brilliantly argued that communities are not to be distinguished by 'falsity/genuineness, but by the style in which they are imagined' (2004, p. 6). He then asserted that the nation was one such imagined community 'because regardless of the actual inequality and exploitation that may prevail in each, the nation is always conceived as a deep, horizontal comradeship' (2004, p. 7). As seen thus far, a number of scholars detect, or argue in support of, a new style of belonging, a global one in which human rights are, or are in the process of, contributing to the consciousness of what we can call, paraphrasing Anderson, a horizonal global community. A fellowship based on shared humanity. Exploring the forms that are generating this consciousness, to which we turn in the next two sections, can help us to gauge the depth and consequently the strength of this imagined global community, as well as its possible scope and limits.

HUMAN RIGHTS AS AN INDISPUTABLE GLOBAL MORAL HORIZON

This first form of consciousness is intimately tied to an origin story. Human rights are imagined as a series of inherently persuasive and binding norms, principles, and legal obligations, revealed through the UDHR. They are envisioned as a moral and ethical global response to the devastation sown by the Second World War and its genocidal savagery, in particular in the case of the Shoah (Cohen, 2012). The presumed product of an unprecedented global consensus, in the words of the historian Paul Lauren, the declaration 'struck a chord among the peoples of the world and rapidly began to take on a life of its own' (1998, p. 232). The UDHR, it is claimed, equally added ferment to the emerging postcolonial imagination that would shortly contribute to dramatically redrawing the political map of the world (Burke, 2011; Moses et al., 2020).

Despite an auspicious global birth, the sudden onset of the Cold War geopolitical confrontation would almost immediately break their stride. Subsequently, human rights would gingerly tread back on the global stage in the late 1960s and 1970s, guided by the flickering flame of the fledgling human rights organization Amnesty International (Hopgood, 2006). The focus of Amnesty International, however, unlike the grander visions of the immediate postwar, which were underwritten by the equalizing potential of the developing welfare state (López, 2018; Moyn, 2010, 2018; see also Borgwardt, 2007), was minimalist. It zeroed in on the worst excesses of political state violence of authoritarian regimes of the left and the right –

i.e., torture, disappearings, and prisoners of conscience – particularly in the Soviet Union and South America.

This emerging form of activism, some scholars and activists argued, was predicated on the formation of transnational 'advocacy networks' capable of producing a 'boomerang effect' to activate the soft power of the international human rights system. Local activists learnt to overcome domestic inattention to political violence, or even mitigate it, by fostering international networks to 'curve' around, or bypass, unresponsive local state actors. In turn, international policy elites would apply external international pressure in the hope of contributing to resolving the local human rights grievances (Keck and Sikkink, 1998; Khagram et al., 2002; Murdie and Polizzi, 2017). The success, real or perceived, of this form of enacting human rights attracted other non-governmental organizations and institutional actors. Human rights were a centre piece of the Helsinki Final Act, signed in 1975 by European countries, the Soviet Union and the United States (US) and Canada (Snyder, 2011). Human rights were equally woven into US (Keys, 2012, 2014) and European foreign policy objectives (Madsen, 2011). All this, and more that can be related here, engendered a collective effervescence that not only led to the institutionalization of the human rights movement (Cmiel, 2004; Neier, 2012; Snyder, 2011), it also encouraged the extension of human rights to new domains, i.e., economic, cultural, and social rights (López, 2015; Nelson and Dorsey, 2008; Roth, 2004; Rubenstein, 2004). Human rights became a broad political project for global transformation (Hafner-Burton, 2013; Moyn, 2010).

However, it was the end of the Cold War in the 1990s that would finally provide human rights with the global reach that had earlier been denied them. In that decade, as the historian Samuel Moyn wrote, 'it became common to assume that, ever since their birth in a moment of postgenocidal revulsion and wisdom [in 1948], human rights had become embedded slowly but steadily in human consciousness in what amounted to a revolution of moral life' (2014, p. 72). This kindled the curiosity of historians who began, and continue, to develop 'backstories' (Moyn, 2014, p. 1) capable of accounting for what appeared to be the stunning consolidation of a unique and, for many indisputable, global moral horizon as the twentieth century neared its end.

Some historians focused on the visionary heroes, the likes of Eleanor Roosevelt, Raphael Lemkin, and Réné Cassin, at the United Nations who lit the flame, and on the handful of individuals – international lawyers and philosophers for the most part – that sheltered it from the unforgiving licks of Cold War winds (Glendon, 2002; Lauren, 1998; Morsink, 1999; Normand and Zaidi, 2008). While others, judging that such a striking and wide-reaching agreement must have deep historical roots, have searched for precursors in the writings of 'Greeks or Jews, Medieval Christians or early modern philosophers, democratic revolutionaries or abolitionist heroes, American internationalists or antiracist visionaries' (Moyn, 2010, p. 20; see also Alston, 2012; Blackburn, 2013; Borgwardt, 2007; Burke, 2011; Cmiel, 2004; Hunt, 2007; Ishay, 2004; Lauren, 1998; Sunstein, 2009).

Social scientists, legal theorists, philosophers, and activists have turned their attention to tracking the circulation and exegesis of human rights principles in international treaties and agreements. They have queried which normative arguments might be more persuasive and which legal forms and standards more efficacious (Alston and Mégret, 2013; Beitz, 2011; Donnelly, 2007; Falk, 2000, 2009; Held, 2009, 2010; Power and Allison, 2016; Steiner et al., 2008). More empirically minded human rights scholars have tried to gauge, and measure (Hafner-Burton and Tsutsui, 2005; Landman, 2005; Landman and Carvahlho, 2010), the strength of the association between the espousal of human rights norms and the behaviour of states. The objective has been to tease out how international advocacy and political and diplomatic pressure is best leveraged to enforce human rights laws and norms (Risse et al., 1999, 2013; Simmons, 2009). Other scholars have endeavoured to determine the extent to which international human rights trials, and the assemblages of advocacy that make them possible, have unleashed a global 'justice cascade' (Sikkink, 2011), or the impact of democratic transitions underwritten by human rights norms (Wiebelhaus-Brahm, 2010; Skaar et al., 2015, 2016). Finally, a sociological school has become defined around the development of a purported world culture powered by the secular sacralization of the autonomous individual on which human rights are purported to rest (Boli and Thomas, 1999; Elliott, 2007; Krücken and Drori, 2009; Soysal, 2012).

What brings together the inevitably brief historical sketch of the trajectory of human rights, with which this section begins, and the subsequent snapshot of the human rights scholarship is a particular conception of human rights. Human rights norms and principles are assumed to have the capacity to project a transcendent global moral horizon; one that no decent individual or community could contest. They also are assumed to have the capacity, when properly calibrated, to bring humanity closer to that global moral horizon, preferably by consensus but sometimes by force if necessary. It is the norms and the principles, embodied and carried in the consciousness of people, and the moral persuasiveness, if not coercion, of legal instruments, that are contributing to making the world into one place.

To the extent that these norms and principles become densely woven into domestic and international institutions, binding laws and agreements, and consequently the everyday moral and ethical consciousness of individuals around the globe, the global community, the fellowship, will continue to expand. It nurtures the hope that one day, in a not too distant future, this global community will encompass every single individual human. The shortcomings or failures that might be encountered along the way, and of course it is fully acknowledged that there will be many, reaffirm, rather than gainsay, the centrality of human rights norms and laws. They point to the necessity of continuing to work towards human rights as an indisputable global moral horizon.

HUMAN RIGHTS AS AN EVOLVING GLOBAL MORAL HORIZON

The second form of human rights consciousness, while recognizing human rights as a powerful global moral horizon, refuses their reduction to their legal forms in domestic legislation, international agreements, or taken-for-granted norms. What is more, it is founded on profound scepticism regarding the putative 'consensus' underpinning the birth of the UDHR; not least due to its domination by imperial hegemons, excluding breathtaking swathes of peoples subjected to colonialism (Afshari, 2007; Mazower, 2004, 2009; Simpson, 2001). As the historian Mark Mazower has shown, the United Nations 'was the product of empire and indeed, at least at the outset, regarded by those with colonies to keep as a more than adequate mechanism for its defence' (Mazower, 2009, p. 17; see also Christoffersen and Madsen, 2011; Madsen, 2010, 2012; Sellars, 2002; Simpson, 2001; Woodiwiss, 2005). Thus, the narrative of the consensual global expansion on which the first form of consciousness relies is, from the perspective of this second form of consciousness, untenable.

There is not one history but plural histories of human rights to be told, rooted in dissension and the struggle to bend them towards liberatory forms for which human rights were not necessarily intended (Anderson, 2003; Anghie, 2007; Baxi, 1998, 2002; Burke, 2011; De Sousa Santos, 2008; Goodhart, 2013; Ibhawoh, 2008; Iriye et al., 2012; Moor and Simpson, 2005; Moses et al., 2020; Roberts, 2015; Samson, 2020; Stammers, 2009; Suárez-Krabbe, 2015; Woodiwiss, 2003). As the Indian legal scholar, Upendra Baxi asserts, there is not a single but many 'conflicting worlds of human rights' (2002, p. 5). Thus, for the cultural sociologist Fuyuki Kurasawa, the globalization of human rights is an arduous global ethico-political labour – i.e., forms of structured and structuring practices (2007, p. 17). Moreover, neither their success nor their continuity can be assumed, as the labour of human rights is constantly stalked by their global nemeses (Kurasawa, 2007, p. 33), not to mention manifold forms of social denial (Cohen, 2001).

Human rights, or their global diffusion, cannot be reduced to a unified set of norms, principles, or set of legal instruments. Conceiving them thus 'reifies' human rights 'by reducing them to things legally and institutionally allocated to subjects according to processes that seemingly operate above their heads' (Kurasawa, 2007, p. 195). Instead, as the anthropologist Mark Goodale writes, 'human rights remain fluid and essentially plural and depend not on a hypothetical set of principles articulated by a small sliver of the global community but on the social actors for whom human rights come to form part of their contextualized legal, moral and political practices' (Goodale, 2009, p. 106; see also Goodale, 2013; Goodale and Merry, 2007; Hynes et al., 2011; López, 2015; Nash, 2012, 2015). Therefore, to the extent that human rights take root in new localities, they do so through a process the legal anthropologist Sally Engle Merry has coined as 'vernacularization': that is to say the social, cultural, and political processes whereby 'ideas from transnational sources' are 'adapted to local institutions and meanings' primarily through the agency of 'intermediaries or translators' (2006, p. 39). These interpreters 'translate the discourses and practices from the arena of international law and legal institutions to specific situations of suffering and violation' (Merry, 2006, p. 39).

Consequently, in this second form of human rights consciousness, the globalization of human rights is uneven in form and its results. Nor can it be presumed that human rights are always efficacious or desirable! Indeed, many scholars and activists focus not only on their contextualization in differing locales but also on the (mis)alignment between human rights and particular issues or communities, e.g., gender (Kapur, 2018; Lahai and Moyo, 2018; Merry, 2009), indigenous rights (Kulchyski, 2013; Samson, 2020; Short and Lennox, 2016), sexual orientation (Nicol et al., 2018; Thoreson, 2014), and disability (Heyer, 2015; Iriarte et al., 2015; Katsui and Chalklen, 2020).

The representative image of the globalization of human rights provided by this second form of consciousness is not the unified rollout of norms, principles, and legal instruments stretched around the surface of the globe. Instead, a notion suggested by Goodale is that of a *grapevine*: 'networks of human rights actors' stringing together 'disparate groups of communities beyond both the nation-state and the international human rights system that had been created in the postwar settlement' (2009, p. 91). Conceived thus, human rights are not taken as ends but as potential means whose vernacularization or 'provincialization' (Woodiwiss, 2012, p. 966) enables the pursuit of a heteroglossic global moral horizon. The imagined global community is not merely horizontal, i.e., the set of the arithmetic sum of all human beings, but, to paraphrase Boaventura de Sousa Santos, also a global community that is perpetually being reconstructed interculturally in the pursuit of a global horizon in constant evolution (De Sousa Santos, 2008).

CONCLUSION

This chapter has explored two different forms of conceptualizing human rights consciousness and how each is contributing to imagining a global community. The first is spurred by the conviction, in thought and deed, that human rights constitute an indisputable global moral horizon that no reasonable person or community of conscience would reject. The second frames human rights as an evolving and pliable idea, spreading unevenly, but capable of linking humanity together in its inexorable diversity. The first requires the tireless extension of human rights norms and laws through persuasion, and sometimes coercion. The second requires the careful stitching together of a diverse global moral quilt, whose final form and content remains to be determined. This said, both forms are conjoined by the moral and ethical certitude that human rights laws and norms, be they as end or means, are crucial in the pursuit of a global community founded on solidarity and justice.

We live in a world where human rights consciousness, inscribed in things and people, contributes to a powerful awareness of a common humanity. This is human rights' most impressive achievement (López, 2018, p. 414; see also Ron et al., 2017). However, the contemporary reality of violence and exploitation that are the daily existence of large swathes of humanity are a rude reminder of the limits of human rights. It is difficult, even for those most committed, to deny that human rights fail the people who need them the most (Fassin, 2012; Hafner-Burton, 2013; Hafner-Burton and Tsutsui, 2005; Kennedy, 2005; Moyn, 2012a, 2018; Mueller, 2014; Pogge, 2008; Posner, 2014; Snyder and Vinjamuri, 2006). Indeed, as the legal theorist Eric Posner argues, the most one can currently say about the power of human rights is that they 'may have improved a small number of human rights outcomes in a small number of countries by a small, possibly trivial amount' (2014, p. 78).

This has led some scholars to draw attention to the surprising 'law naïveté' that is presupposed by human rights' elevation to a global moral horizon (López, 2018, pp. 319–402; see also Deflem and Chicoine, 2011; Dezalay and Garth, 2002; Hafner-Burton, 2013; Posner, 2014; Woodiwiss, 2003, 2005). Law naïveté, 'rule naïveté' (Posner, 2014), 'global legalism' (Hafner-Burton, 2013), or 'Kryptolegalism' (Deflem and Chicoine, 2011) all attribute a social power to legal norms and instruments that socio-legal scholars have long demonstrated they lack. This might have less to do with any deficiency of human rights norms or law, per se, than with the power(lessness) of rights as such. As Anthony Woodiwiss has persuasively argued, the efficacy of human rights, like all rights, depends on their resonating with the broader social relations in which they are immersed. Although they can protect individuals, in some instances from abuse, rights alone cannot dismantle socially and relationally inscribed forms of inequality (Woodiwiss, 2012, p. 967; see also Scheingold, 2004).

A related issue is the nature of the political imaginary that hoisted human rights as a global moral horizon. Historians and social science scholars have been exploring the ramifications of the fact that the proximal take-off period for human rights was in the 1970s rather than the postwar period (Eckel and Moyn, 2014; Fassin, 2012; Hoffmann, 2010; Hopgood, 2006, 2013; Iriye et al., 2012; Keys, 2012, 2014; López, 2015, 2018; Moyn, 2010, 2012a, 2012b, 2014, 2015, 2018; Woodiwiss, 2005). Fuelled by the highly moralistic and minimalist politics of Amnesty International and focused on combatting the most extreme forms of political violence meant that the human rights political imaginary was founded on the incontrovertible distinction between the perpetrator and the innocent victim. Therein lay its persuasive moral and ethical power (López, 2018, p. 280). Human rights arose as a form of political minimalism, indeed as a rejection of the grand postwar projects that eventuated in so much human suffering and misery – i.e., capitalism, socialism, and postcolonialism (Moyn, 2010). Are human rights sufficiently capacious to bring about the maximalist visions associated with the two dominant forms of contemporary human rights consciousness? And what about the figure of the innocent victim that is so crucial to the moral persuasiveness of human rights? Can human rights abandon the centrality of victimhood and remain morally persuasive?

The naïve global ascendancy of human rights law or the minimalist politics that made them so compelling open up new vistas on the two dominant forms of understanding human rights consciousness explored in this chapter. The contemporary prominence of human rights can be grasped, as many of the authors cited in this conclusion contend, as a consequential accident of history rather than a moment of human moral transcendence. Seen thus, human rights are neither the privileged ends in a morally evolved global horizon nor particularly efficacious means for the global pursuit of a substantive moral horizon oriented towards justice. Instead, they can be understood as a set of ethico-political practices, a 'political imaginary' (López, 2018) that has achieved global traction as a result of the contingent alignment of concrete socio-historical configurations.

While not stripping human rights entirely of their moral and ethical valence, this form of grasping human rights' globalization, as political imaginary, yields a sobering verdict. Human rights, as currently conceived and globalized, are likely to disappoint both as ends and means in the pursuit of a moral global horizon, self-evident or otherwise. However, in this disappointment is sown the seed of new, and we dare hope more effective, forms of imagining but also and, crucially, constructing ethical global communities.

REFERENCES

Afshari, R. (2007) 'On Historiography of Human Rights Reflections on Paul Gordon Lauren's *The Evolution of International Human Rights: Visions Seen*', *Human Rights Quarterly*, 29(1), pp. 1–67.

Akbarzadeh, S. and MacQueen, B. (2008) *Islam and Human Rights in Practice: Perspectives across the Ummah*. London: Routledge.

Alston, P. (2012) 'Does the Past Matter: On the Origins of Human Rights Book Review', *Harvard Law Review*, 126(7), pp. 2043–2082.

Alston, P. and Mégret, F. (eds) (2013) *The United Nations and Human Rights: A Critical Appraisal*. Oxford: Oxford University Press.

An-Na'im, A. A. (ed.) (2010) *Human Rights in Cross-Cultural Perspectives: A Quest for Consensus*. Philadelphia, PA: University of Pennsylvania Press.

Anderson, B. (2004) *Imagined Communities: Reflections on the Origin and Spread of Nationalism*. London: Verso.

Anderson, C. E. (2003) *Eyes off the Prize: The United Nations and the African American Struggle for Human Rights, 1944–1955*. Cambridge: Cambridge University Press.

Anghie, A. (2007) *Imperialism, Sovereignty and the Making of International Law*. Cambridge: Cambridge University Press.

Appiah, K. A. (1997) 'Cosmopolitan Patriots', *Critical Inquiry*, 23(3), pp. 617–639.

Arendt, H. (1973) *The Origins of Totalitarianism*. San Diego: Harcourt.

Armaline, W. T., Glasberg, D. S., and Purkayastha, B. (2015) *The Human Rights Enterprise: Political Sociology, State Power, and Social Movements*. Cambridge: Polity.

Bauer, J. R. and Bell, D. A. (eds) (1999) *The East Asian Challenge for Human Rights*. Cambridge: Cambridge University Press.

Baxi, U. (1998) 'Voices of Suffering and the Future of Human Rights', *Transnational Life & Contemporary Problems*, 8, pp. 125–169.

Baxi, U. (2002) *The Future of Human Rights*. Oxford: Oxford University Press.

Beck, U. (2006) *Cosmopolitan Vision*. Cambridge: Polity.

Beitz, C. R. (2011) *The Idea of Human Rights*. Oxford: Oxford University Press.

Bell, D. A. (2000) *East Meets West: Human Rights and Democracy in East Asia*. Princeton, NJ: Princeton University Press.

Benhabib, S. (2004) *The Rights of Others: Aliens, Residents, and Citizens*. Cambridge: Cambridge University Press.

Benhabib, S. (2013) *Dignity in Adversity: Human Rights in Troubled Times*. Chichester: John Wiley & Sons.

Blackburn, R. (2013) *The American Crucible: Slavery, Emancipation and Human Rights*. London: Verso.

Blau, J. R. and Frezzo, M. (eds) (2012) *Sociology and Human Rights: A Bill of Rights for the Twenty-First Century*. London: SAGE.

Blau, J. R. and Moncada, A. (2005) *Human Rights: Beyond the Liberal Vision*. Lanham, MD: Rowman & Littlefield.

Boli, J. and Thomas, G. M. (1999) *Constructing World Culture: International Nongovernmental Organizations since 1875*. Stanford, CA: Stanford University Press.

Borgwardt, E. (2007) *A New Deal for the World*. Cambridge, MA: Harvard University Press.

Bosniak, L. (2000) 'Citizenship Denationalized', *Indiana Journal of Global Legal Studies*, 7(2), pp. 447–509.

Braidotti, R., Hanafin, P., and Blaagaard, B. (eds) (2012) *After Cosmopolitanism*. Abingdon: Routledge.

Breckenridge, C. A., Pollock, S., Bhabha, H. K., and Chakrabarty, D. (eds) (2002) *Cosmopolitanism*. Durham, NC: Duke University Press.

Bricmont, J. (2006) *Humanitarian Imperialism: Using Human Rights to Sell War*. New York: New York University Press.

Brown, W. (2004) '"The Most We Can Hope For …": Human Rights and the Politics of Fatalism', *South Atlantic Quarterly*, 103(2), pp. 451–463.

Brysk, A. (2002) *Globalization and Human Rights*. Berkeley, CA: University of California Press.

Brysk, A. and Shafir, G. (2004) *People Out of Place: Globalization, Human Rights and the Citizenship Gap*. London: Routledge.

Burke, R. (2011) *Decolonization and the Evolution of International Human Rights*. Philadelphia, PA: University of Pennsylvania Press.

Carens, J. (2013) *The Ethics of Immigration*. Oxford: Oxford University Press.

Christoffersen, J. and Madsen, M. R. (eds) (2011) *The European Court of Human Rights between Law and Politics*. Oxford: Oxford University Press.

Cmiel, K. (2004) 'The Recent History of Human Rights', *American Historical Review*, 109(1), pp. 117–135.

Cohen, G. D. (2012) 'The Holocaust and the "Human Rights Revolution": A Reassessment', in A. Iriye, P. Goedde, W. I. and Hitchcock (eds), *The Human Rights Revolution: An International History*. Oxford: Oxford University Press, pp. 53–72.

Cohen, S. (2001) *States of Denial: Knowing about Atrocities and Suffering*. Cambridge: Polity Press.

De Sousa Santos, B. (2008) 'Human Rights as an Emancipatory Script: Cultural and Political Conditions', in B. De Sousa Santos (ed.), *Another Knowledge Is Possible*. London: Verso, pp. 3–40.

Deflem, M. and Chicoine, S. (2011) 'The Sociological Discourse on Human Rights: Lessons from the Sociology of Law', *Development and Society*, 40(1), pp. 101–115.

Delanty, G. (2006) 'The Cosmopolitan Imagination: Critical Cosmopolitanism and Social Theory', *British Journal of Sociology*, 57(1), pp. 25–47.

Delanty, G. (2009) *The Cosmopolitan Imagination: The Renewal of Critical Social Theory*. Cambridge: Cambridge University Press.

Dezalay, Y. and Garth, B. G. (2002) *The Internationalization of Palace Wars: Lawyers, Economists, and the Contest to Transform Latin American States*. Chicago, IL: University of Chicago Press.

Donnelly, J. (2007) *International Human Rights*. Boulder, CO: Westview Press.

Douzinas, C. (2007) *Human Rights and Empire: The Political Philosophy of Cosmopolitanism*. London: Routledge.

Eckel, J. and Moyn, S. (eds) (2014) *The Breakthrough: Human Rights in the 1970s*. Philadelphia, PA: University of Pennsylvania Press.

Elliott, M. (2007) 'Human Rights and the Triumph of the Individual in World Culture', *Cultural Sociology*, 1(3), pp. 343–363.

Englund, H. (2006) *Prisoners of Freedom: Human Rights and the African Poor*. Cambridge: Cambridge University Press.

Falk, R. (2000) *Human Rights Horizons: The Pursuit of Justice in a Globalizing World*. New York: Routledge.

Falk, R. (2009) *Achieving Human Rights*. New York: Routledge.

Fassin, D. (2012) *Humanitarian Reason: A Moral History of the Present*. Berkeley, CA: University of California Press.

Fine, R. (2009) 'Cosmopolitanism and Human Rights: Radicalism in a Global Age', *Metaphilosophy*, 40(1), pp. 8–23.

Frezzo, M. (2014) *The Sociology of Human Rights*. Chichester: John Wiley & Sons.

Glendon, M. A. (2002) *A World Made New: Eleanor Roosevelt and the Universal Declaration of Human Rights*. New York: Random House.

Goodale, M. (2009) *Surrendering to Utopia: An Anthropology of Human Rights*. Stanford, CA: Stanford University Press.

Goodale, M. (ed.) (2013) *Human Rights at the Crossroads*. Oxford: Oxford University Press.

Goodale, M. and Merry, S. E. (2007) *The Practice of Human Rights: Tracking Law between the Global and the Local*. Cambridge: Cambridge University Press.

Goodhart, M. (2013) 'Human Rights and the Politics of Contestation', in M. Goodale (ed.), *Human Rights at the Crossroads*. Oxford: Oxford University Press, pp. 31–44.

Hafner-Burton, E. M. (2013) *Making Human Rights a Reality*. Princeton, NJ: Princeton University Press.

Hafner-Burton, E. M. and Tsutsui, K. (2005) 'Human Rights in a Globalizing World: The Paradox of Empty Promises', *American Journal of Sociology*, 110(5), pp. 1373–1411.

Held, D. (1995) *Democracy and the Global Order: From the Modern State to Cosmopolitan Governance*. Stanford, CA: Stanford University Press.

Held, D. (2009) 'Restructuring Global Governance: Cosmopolitanism, Democracy and the Global Order', *Millennium – Journal of International Studies*, 37(3), pp. 535–547.

Held, D. (2010) *Cosmopolitanism: Ideals and Realities*. Cambridge: Polity Press.

Heyer, K. (2015) *Rights Enabled: The Disability Revolution, from the US, to Germany and Japan, to the United Nations*. Ann Arbor, MI: University of Michigan Press.

Hoffmann, S.-L. (2010) *Human Rights in the Twentieth Century*. Cambridge: Cambridge University Press.

Hopgood, S. (2006) *Keepers of the Flame: Understanding Amnesty International*. New York: Cornell University Press.

Hopgood, S. (2013) *The Endtimes of Human Rights*. New York: Cornell University Press.

Hunt, L. A. (2007) *Inventing Human Rights: A History*. New York: W. W. Norton & Company.

Hynes, P., Lamb, M., Short, D., and Waites, M. (2011) *Sociology and Human Rights: New Engagements*. London: Routledge.

Ibhawoh, B. (2008) *Imperialism and Human Rights: Colonial Discourses of Rights and Liberties in African History*. New York: SUNY Press.

Ibhawoh, B. (2018) *Human Rights in Africa*. Cambridge: Cambridge University Press.

Ignatieff, M. (2001) *Human Rights as Politics and Human Rights as Idolatry*. Princeton, NJ: Princeton University Press.

Iriarte, E. G., McConkey, R., and Gilligan, R. (eds) (2015) *Disability and Human Rights: Global Perspectives*. London: Palgrave Macmillan.

Iriye, A., Goedde, P., and Hitchcock, W. I. (eds) (2012) *The Human Rights Revolution: An International History*. Oxford: Oxford University Press.

Ishay, M. R. (2004) *The History of Human Rights*. Berkeley, CA: University of California Press.

Jacobson, D. (1996) *Rights across Borders: Immigration and the Decline of Citizenship*. Leiden: Brill.

Kapur, R. (2018) *Gender, Alterity and Human Rights: Freedom in a Fishbowl*. Cheltenham, UK and Northampton, MA, USA: Edward Elgar Publishing.

Katsui, H. and Chalklen, S. (eds) (2020) *Disability, Globalization and Human Rights*. London: Taylor Francis.

Keck, M. E. and Sikkink, K. (1998) *Activists beyond Borders: Advocacy Networks in International Politics*. Ithaca, NY: Cornell University Press.

Kendall, G., Woodward, I., and Skrbis, Z. (2009) *The Sociology of Cosmopolitanism: Globalization, Identity, Culture and Government*. New York: Palgrave Macmillan.

Kennedy, D. (2005) *The Dark Sides of Virtue: Reassessing International Humanitarianism*. Princeton, NJ: Princeton University Press.

Keys, B. J. (2012) 'Anti-Torture Politics: Amnesty International, the Greek Junta, and the Origins of the Human Rights "Boom in the United States"', in A. Iriye, P. Goedde, and W. I. Hitchcock (eds), *The Human Rights Revolution: An International History*. Oxford: Oxford University Press, pp. 201–222.

Keys, B. J. (2014) *Reclaiming American Virtue*. Cambridge, MA: Harvard University Press.

Khagram, S., Riker, J. V., and Sikkink, K. (2002) *Restructuring World Politics: Transnational Social Movements, Networks, and Norms*. Minneapolis, MN: University of Minnesota Press.

Krücken, G. and Drori, G. S. (2009) *World Society: The Writings of John W. Meyer*. Oxford: Oxford University Press.

Kulchyski, P. K. (2013) *Aboriginal Rights Are Not Human Rights: In Defence of Indigenous Struggles*. Winnipeg: ARP Books.

Kurasawa, F. (2007) *The Work of Global Justice: Human Rights as Practices*. Cambridge: Cambridge University Press.

Lahai, J. I. and Moyo, K. (eds) (2018) *Gender in Human Rights and Transitional Justice*. New York: Palgrave Macmillan.

Landman, T. (2005) *Protecting Human Rights: A Comparative Study*. Washington, DC: Georgetown University Press.

Landman, T. and Carvahlho, E. (2010) *Measuring Human Rights*. London: Routledge.

Lauren, P. G. (1998) *The Evolution of International Human Rights: Visions Seen*. Philadelphia, PA: University of Pennsylvania Press.

Levy, D. and Sznaider, N. (2006) 'Sovereignty Transformed: A Sociology of Human Rights', *British Journal of Sociology*, 57(4), pp. 657–676.

Levy, D. and Sznaider, N. (2010) *Human Rights and Memory*. University Park, PA: Penn State Press.

López, J. J. (2015) 'The Human Right to Food as Political Imaginary', *Journal of Historical Sociology*, 30(2), pp. 239–261.

López, J. J. (2018) *Human Rights as Political Imaginary*. London: Palgrave Macmillan.

Madsen, M. R. (2010) *La genèse de l'Europe des droits de l'homme: Enjeux juridiques et stratégies d'Etat (1945–1970)*. Strasbourg: Presses Universitaires de Strasbourg.

Madsen, M. R. (2011) 'The Protracted Institutionalization of the Strasbourg Court: From Legal Diplomacy to Integrationist Jurisprudence', in J. Christoffersen and M. R. Madsen (eds), *The European Court of Human Rights between Law and Politics*. Oxford: Oxford University Press, pp. 43–59.

Madsen, M. R. (2012) 'Human Rights and the Hegemony of Ideology: European Lawyers and the Cold War Battle over International Human Rights', in Y. Dezalay and B. Garth (eds), *Lawyers and the Construction of Transnational Justice*. Abingdon: Routledge, pp. 258–276.

Mauzy, D. K. (1997) 'The Human Rights and "Asian Values" Debate in Southeast Asia: Trying to Clarify the Key Issues', *The Pacific Review*, 10(2), pp. 210–236.

Mayer, A. E. (2002) 'The Universality of Human Rights: Lessons from the Islamic Republic', *Social Research*, 67(2), pp. 519–536.

Mayer, A. E. (2018) *Islam and Human Rights: Tradition and Politics*. London: Routledge.

Mazower, M. (2004) 'The Strange Triumph of Human Rights, 1933–1950', *The Historical Journal*, 47(2), pp. 379–398.

Mazower, M. (2009) *No Enchanted Palace: The End of Empire and the Ideological Origins of the United Nations*. Princeton, NJ: Princeton University Press.

Merry, S. E. (2006) 'Transnational Human Rights and Local Activism: Mapping the Middle', *American Anthropologist*, 108(1), pp. 38–51.

Merry, S. E. (2009) *Human Rights and Gender Violence: Translating International Law into Local Justice*. Chicago, IL: University of Chicago Press.

Meyer, J. W. (2009) 'World Society, the Welfare State, and the Life Course: An Institutionalist Perspective', in G. Krücken and G. S. Drori (eds), *World Society: the Writings of John W. Meyer*. Oxford: Oxford University Press, pp. 280–295.

Meyer, J. W. and Jepperson, R. L. (2000) 'The "Actors" of Modern Society: The Cultural Construction of Social Agency', *Sociological Theory*, 18(1), pp. 100–120.

Meyer, J. W., Boli, J., Thomas, G. M., and Ramirez, F. O. (1997) 'World Society and the Nation-State', *American Journal of Sociology*, 103(1), pp. 144–181.

Moor, L. and Simpson, A. B. (2005) 'Ghosts of Colonialism in the European Convention on Human Rights', *British Year Book of International Law*, 76(1), pp. 121–194.

Morsink, J. (1999) *The Universal Declaration of Human Rights: Origins, Drafting, and Intent*. Philadelphia, PA: University of Pennsylvania Press.

Moses, A. D., Duranti, M., and Burke, R. (2020) *Decolonization, Self-Determination, and the Rise of Global Human Rights Politics*. Cambridge: Cambridge University Press.

Moyn, S. (2010) *The Last Utopia*. Cambridge, MA: Harvard University Press.

Moyn, S. (2012a) 'Do Human Rights Treaties Make Enough of a Difference?', in C. Gearty and C. Douzinas (eds), *Cambridge Companion to Human Rights Law*. Cambridge: Cambridge University Press, pp. 329–347.

Moyn, S. (2012b) 'Imperialism, Self-Determination, and the Rise of Human Rights', in A. Iriye, P. Goedde, and W. I. Hitchcock (eds), *The Human Rights Revolution: An International History*. Oxford: Oxford University Press, pp. 159–178.

Moyn, S. (2014) *Human Rights and the Uses of History*. London: Verso.

Moyn, S. (2015) *Christian Human Rights*. Philadelphia, PA: University of Pennsylvania Press.

Moyn, S. (2018) *Not Enough: Human Rights in an Unequal World*. Cambridge, MA: Harvard University Press.

Mueller, S. D. (2014) 'Kenya and the International Criminal Court (ICC): Politics, the Election and the Law', *Journal of Eastern African Studies*, 8(1), pp. 25–42.

Murdie, A. and Polizzi, M. (2017) 'Human Rights and Transnational Advocacy Networks', in J. N. Victor, A. H. Montgomery, and M. Lubell (eds), *The Oxford Handbook of Political Networks*. Oxford: Oxford University Press, pp. 715–732.

Nash, K. (2012) 'Towards a Political Sociology of Human Rights', in E. Amenta, K. Nash, and A. Scott (eds), *The Wiley-Blackwell Companion to Political Sociology*. Malden, MA: Wiley Blackwell, pp. 444–454.

Nash, K. (2015) *The Political Sociology of Human Rights*. Cambridge: Cambridge University Press.

Nault, D. M. (2021) *Africa and the Shaping of International Human Rights*. Oxford: Oxford University Press.

Neier, A. (2012) *The International Human Rights Movement: A History*. Princeton, NJ: Princeton University Press.

Nelson, P. J. and Dorsey, E. (2008) *New Rights Advocacy: Changing Strategies of Development and Human Rights NGOs*. Washington, DC: Georgetown University Press.

Nicol, N., Jjuuko, A., Lusimbo, R., Mulé, N., Ursel, S., Wahab, A., and Waugh, P. (eds) (2018) *Envisioning Global LGBT Human Rights: (Neo)colonialism, Neoliberalism, Resistance and Hope*. London: University of London Press.

Normand, R. and Zaidi, S. (2008) *Human Rights at the UN: The Political History of Universal Justice*. Bloomington, IN: Indiana University Press.

Nussbaum, M. C. (1996) 'Patriotism and Cosmopolitanism', in J. Cohen (ed.), *For Love of Country?* Boston, MA: Beacon Press, pp. 2–20.

Nussbaum, M. C. (1998) *Cultivating Humanity*. Cambridge, MA: Harvard University Press.

Pogge, T. W. (2008) *World Poverty and Human Rights: Cosmopolitan Responsibilities and Reforms*. Cambridge: Polity Press.

Posner, E. A. (2014) *The Twilight of Human Rights Law*. Oxford: Oxford University Press.

Power, S. and Allison, G. (eds) (2016) *Realizing Human Rights: Moving from Inspiration to Impact*. New York: St Martin's Press.

Risse, T., Ropp, S. C., and Sikkink, K. (1999) *The Power of Human Rights: International Norms and Domestic Change*. Cambridge: Cambridge University Press.

Risse, T., Ropp, S. C., and Sikkink, K. (2013) *The Persistent Power of Human Rights: From Commitment to Compliance*. Cambridge University Press.

Roberts, C. N. J. (2015) *The Contentious History of the International Bill of Human Rights*. New York: Cambridge University Press.

Robertson, R. (1990) 'Mapping the Global Condition: Globalization as the Central Concept', *Theory, Culture & Society*, 7(2–3), pp. 15–30.

Robertson, R. (1992) *Globalization: Social Theory and Global Culture*. London: SAGE.

Robertson, R. (2011) 'Global Connectivity and Global Consciousness', *American Behavioral Scientist*, 55(10), pp. 1336–1345.

Robertson, R. and White, K. E. (2007) 'What Is Globalization', in G. Ritzer (ed.), *The Blackwell Companion to Globalization*. Malden, MA: Blackwell, pp. 54–66.

Ron, J., Golden, S., Crow, D., and Pandya, A. (2017) *Taking Root: Human Rights and Public Opinion in the Global South*. Oxford: Oxford University Press.

Roth, K. (2004) 'Defending Economic Social and Cultural Rights: Practical Issues Faced by an International Human Rights Organization', *Human Rights Quarterly*, 26, pp. 63–73.

Rubenstein, L. S. (2004) 'How International Human Rights Organizations Can Advance Economic, Social, and Cultural Rights: A Response to Kenneth Roth', *Human Rights Quarterly*, pp. 845–865.

Samson, C. (2020) *The Colonialism of Human Rights: Ongoing Hypocrisies of Western Liberalism*. Cambridge: Polity Press.

Sassen, S. (2009) 'Incompleteness and the Possibility of Making: Towards Denationalized Citizenship?', in D. E. Davis and J. Go (eds), *Political Power and Social Theory*. Bingley: Emerald Group Publishing, pp. 229–258.

Scheingold, S. A. (2004) *The Politics of Rights: Lawyers, Public Policy, and Political Change*. Ann Arbor, MI: University of Michigan Press.

Sellars, K. (2002) *The Rise and Rise of Human Rights*. Stroud: Sutton.

Shafir, G. and Brysk, A. (2006) 'The globalization of rights: From citizenship to human rights', *Citizenship Studies*, 10(3), pp. 275–287.

Short, D. and Lennox, C. (eds) (2016) *Handbook of Indigenous Peoples' Rights*. London: Routledge.

Sikkink, K. (2011) *The Justice Cascade: How Human Rights Are Changing World Politics*. New York: W. W. Norton & Company.

Simmons, B. A. (2009) *Mobilizing for Human Rights: International Law in Domestic Politics*. Cambridge: Cambridge University Press.

Simpson, A. W. B. (2001) *Human Rights and the End of Empire: Britain and the Genesis of the European Convention*. Oxford: Oxford University Press.

Skaar, E., Malca, C. G., and Eide, T. (2015) *After Violence: Transitional Justice, Peace, and Democracy*. London: Routledge.

Skaar, E., Garcia-Godos, J., and Collins, C. (2016) *Transitional Justice in Latin America: The Uneven Road from Impunity towards Accountability*. London: Routledge.

Snyder, J. and Vinjamuri, L. (2006) 'Trials and Errors: Principle and Pragmatism in Strategies of International Justice', *International Security*, 28(3), pp. 5–44.

Snyder, S. B. (2011) *Human Rights Activism and the End of the Cold War: A Transnational History of the Helsinki Network*. Cambridge: Cambridge University Press.

Somers, M. R. and Roberts, C. N. (2008) 'Toward a New Sociology of Rights: A Genealogy of "Buried Bodies" of Citizenship and Human Rights', *Annual Review of Law and Social Science*, 4, pp. 385–425.

Soysal, Y. N. (1994) *Limits of Citizenship: Migrants and Postnational Membership in Europe*. Chicago, IL: University of Chicago Press.

Soysal, Y. N. (2012) 'Citizenship, Immigration, and the European Social Project: Rights and Obligations of Individuality', *British Journal of Sociology*, 63(1), pp. 1–21.

Stammers, N. (2009) *Human Rights and Social Movements*. London: Pluto Press.

Steiner, H. J., Alston, P., and Goodman, R. (2008) *International Human Rights in Context: Law, Politics, Morals: Text and Materials*. Oxford: Oxford University Press.

Suárez-Krabbe, J. (2015) 'Race, Social Struggles and "Human" Rights: Contributions from the Global South', in E. A. Andersen and E. M. Lassen (eds), *Europe and the Americas: Transatlantic Approaches to Human Rights*. Leiden: Brill Nijhoff, pp. 41–72.

Sunstein, C. (2009) *The Second Bill of Rights: FDR's Unfinished Revolution – and Why We Need It More Than Ever*. New York: Basic Books.

Teeple, G. (2005) *The Riddle of Human Rights*. Toronto: University of Toronto Press.

Thoreson, R. R. (2014) *Transnational LGBT Activism: Working for Sexual Rights Worldwide*. Minneapolis, MN: University of Minnesota Press.

Turner (2006) *Vulnerability and Human Rights*. Philadelphia, PA: Penn State Press.

Whyte, J. (2019) *The Morals of the Market: Human Rights and the Rise of Neoliberalism*. London: Verso.

Wiebelhaus-Brahm, E. (2010) *Truth Commissions and Transitional Societies: The Impact on Human Rights and Democracy*. London: Routledge.

Woodiwiss, A. (2003) *Making Human Rights Work Globally*. London: Glass House Press.

Woodiwiss, A. (2005) *Human Rights*. London: Routledge, 2005.

Woodiwiss, A. (2012) 'Asia, Enforceable Benevolence and the Future of Human Rights', *Sociology*, 46(5), pp. 966–981.

Žižek, S. (2005) 'Against Human Rights', *New Left Review*, 34(July–August), pp. 115–131.

12. Memory for the global age

Marcin Napiórkowski

Suddenly the past has become one of the most compelling languages for reimagining the future. The recent years have seen a global confluence of social justice and commemorative justice. In the United States, toppling monuments, giving the voice to the voiceless and revising the cultural canon has become a key part of protests against police brutality. The Spanish *Indignados* referred to the Spanish Civil War and anti-Francoist guerrillas. In Greece, the juxtaposition of European creditors with the Nazi occupation was an important motif in both political rhetoric and street folklore, as evidenced by the widely circulated images of Angela Merkel depicted as Adolf Hitler. Many protesters on Maidan Square in Kyiv waved the red-and-black flags of the Ukrainian Insurgent Army, commemorating a nationalist paramilitary group from the Second World War whose leaders believed that some form of collaboration with the Third Reich was the only way to defeat the Soviets and Poles and build a sovereign Ukrainian state. In turn, young people more or less spontaneously setting out to fight for "independent republics" in eastern Ukraine in a Russia-sponsored hybrid war felt that, like their grandfathers 70 years before, they were resisting the fascist invasion. Memory dominates politics also in my native Poland, where protesters refer to the anti-Nazi resistance no matter what issue they are protesting against. Symbols of the Warsaw Uprising of 1944 are easily spotted on rallies against internet regulations, worker exploitation and restrictions on reproductive rights.

When Antonio Negri and Michael Hardt (2000) described the mass protest movements of the end of the last century, they argued that they did not develop into a single global uprising mostly because they lacked a universal language. At the dawn of the twenty-first century, diverse forms of protest and public mobilization quite unexpectedly found a common repertoire of symbols in the vocabulary of historical analogies. "The future has been cancelled," "There is no alternative" – in the world of late capitalism, collective imagination seems very reluctant to engage in inventing utopias (Srnicek and Williams, 2016). Instead of simply imagining a better future, contemporary protesters increasingly look for meaning in history, as if these new revolutions were marching through the streets of the revolted cities backwards, always gazing into the past – not unlike the famous Angel of History described by Walter Benjamin (1969, p. 249).

Of course, the demonstrators in Cairo, Madrid, New York and Warsaw were never referring to the same history. Even among protesters in one place, there was not always agreement on how to interpret the past. Protesters in Turkey argued about Atatürk's legacy and Ukrainians are still divided over the view on the Second World War. But the very fact that different factions use the language of memory make their discourses compatible. We may disagree about a particular vision of the past, but increasingly we are united by the belief that the past is a key to the future. Collective memory brings us together to divide us. It makes the world more connected and develops a network of interdependencies. However, just like globalization, it does not necessarily bridge differences and inequalities.

A GLOBAL MEMORY BOOM

While one global memory may not be an obvious concept, the global memory *boom* is an undeniable fact. Departments and faculties of memory studies are being opened at the universities around the world, international associations are founded, specialized academic journals and publishing series are started. National governments, local non-governmental organizations and international institutions inspire each other to build commemorative museums and organize more or less spontaneous public events. Remembrance becomes a universal recipe for the restoration of tourism and product branding, as well as a tool of political propaganda.

There is a common denominator of these extremely diverse phenomena. It is a transition from history to memory – from a past that simply happened and remains an object of study for historians to a past as a constantly changing, malleable element of the present, susceptible to the actions of various agents (Olick and Robbins, 1998, pp. 122–130).

While the concept of collective memory is simple enough, the identity of memory studies as a discipline is an extremely complicated issue. Already in 1997 Alon Confino claimed that memory had taken its place, "the leading term, in cultural history," replacing, as Kerwin Lee Klein (2000, p. 128) notes ironically, "old favorites nature, culture, language." After a "linguistic turn," a "performative turn" or a "pictorial turn" the list of "turns" in contemporary humanities and social sciences – already long enough – may be, thus, supplemented with a "mnemonic turn" or, as many scholars like to call it, a "memory boom" (Berliner, 2005).

"The study of memory has virtually erased interdisciplinary boundaries" – writes Barbie Zelizer (1995, p. 216). May this diverse, transnational and transdisciplinary interest in past and various forms of its cultural reinterpretation be understood as an emerging new discipline? Has it already constituted or is it, as some authors claim, still "awaiting its birth" (Roediger and Wertsch, 2008)? Jeffrey Olick and Joyce Robbins (1998, p. 106) describe memory studies as a "nonparadigmatic, transdisciplinary, centerless enterprise." Astrid Erll (2011a, p. 7) proposes to treat memory more as "an umbrella term for all those processes of a biological, medial, or social nature which relate past and present (and future) in sociocultural contexts." From the point of view of the relationship between memory and globalization two issues seem to be crucial.

First, the current interest in the past was born out of a sense of acceleration fueled by progress and technology. In 1948 Daniel Halévy wrote about the "acceleration of history" that changes the role of memory radically. In the contemporary world, claims Halévy, everything we know is moving quickly to the past, replaced with the new and unfamiliar in a mnemonic version of "all that is solid melts into air." Four decades later his insight was developed by Pierre Nora – the author of the famous "Lieux de Memoire," usually named among the founding fathers of the modern memory boom. "We speak so much of memory because there is so little of it left," writes Nora (1989, p. 7). Viewed in this perspective, memory boom and globalization are closely related. Globalization is the context for memory even when we are not interested in global memory per se. This is evident especially when we focus on rituals, practices or even tastes and smells that are becoming a thing of the past precisely because of globalization (Seremetakis, 1996).

Second, despite all the focus on circulation, transnationality and diverse communities, memory studies started as a movement closely associated with the nation-state. The aforementioned work of Nora provides an excellent example. Its purpose was essentially to codify and stabilize the French identity in an accelerating world. Nora reimagines France as a republic of memory. As Jeffrey Olick (1998, p. 376) summarizes it, "Memory and the nation have a peculiar synergy. Even when other identities compete with or supplant the national in postmodernity, they draw on the expanded role for memory generated in the crucible of the nation-state."

Acceleration against persistence and the national against the cosmopolitan – these lines of tension will be crucial for understanding the global memory at the beginning of the twenty-first century.

GLOBAL MEMORY AND GLOBAL EMPATHY

Memory studies seems to follow the generalizing path from the individual through a community (primarily a nation) to humanity. Such a vision of progressing abstraction can be associated with the ideas of the European Enlightenment embodied in Immanuel Kant's project of perpetual peace or Nicolas de Condorcet's idea of progress. However, the key to successive degrees of abstraction turned out not to be development itself, but the universal nature of suffering.

A Memory of Solferino published by Henry Dunant in 1862 provides a good example of such a new vision of memory. This cornerstone for the modern humanitarian movement proposes an entirely new way of looking at the battlefield, where the suffering of an individual is put before the interest of a monarch or a nation-state. "Stripped of its heroism and splendor, war became a series of brutal set pieces in which soldiers were sacrificed and then abandoned to suffer until they died" (Barnett, 2011). Victory or defeat may have tribal, ethnic or national dimensions, but suffering is universal. As a result, a new view on guilt and responsibility emerged. It was no longer only the executioners who were to blame for the suffering of the victims. Passive witnesses also bore responsibility.

With time, the same model was projected more and more onto the past, changing our understanding of history. Geographical "discoveries" were rediscovered as "encounters" and then outright "conquests." Judged against these new criteria, past heroes became more nuanced as they turned out to be not only great strategists and charismatic leaders but also tyrants, racists or slave owners. Global memory offered a new reading of old books, a new look at old paintings and a new reception of old films. Empathy shattered the pleasant vision of a heroic past, but it also provided a new moral code and a path to reconciliation with a difficult history. "Humanitarianism helps the living come to terms with their ghosts. It is a form of theodicy, providing a means by which survivors can reconcile their belief in the possibility of a more perfect world with cruelty, suffering, and evil" (Barnett, 2011, p. 226). Such an equalizing vision of the human individual as a suffering subject lies at the heart of transitional justice or commissions for truth and reconciliation (Bell, 2006, p. 16).

COMMEMORATIVE BACKLASH AGAINST GLOBALIZATION

Who does the globalization of memory serve? Whose interests does it actually represent? At least since the times of Maurice Halbwachs (1992) we have been defining collective memory as belonging to a certain group. Would not extending this group to the whole of humanity invalidate the very concept of remembering together? If there are no "others" to whom we can contrast "our" memory, does such a concept of memory still retain any anthropological or sociological reality?

This kind of objection to the concept of global memory is raised by many scholars who explicitly claim that, unlike national cultures, global culture (if such a term can be used at all) is by definition memoryless and does not respond to the fundamental human need for identity building (Smith, 1990, p. 180). The naive vision of "global culture" of memory may in fact turn out to be yet another projection of the Western Enlightenment values onto the whole world. As Anthony Smith (1995) puts it, globalization itself is "memoryless" and incapable of creating strong cultural bonds. Cosmopolitan culture is, thus, "flat" in contrast with "deep" national and local cultures saturated with memory.

> Presumably a global culture would be equally hybrid in character with a number of ambivalent, even contradictory, components: a pastiche of traditional local, folk and national motifs and styles; a modern scientific, quantitative and technical discourse; a culture of mass consumerism consisting of standardized mass commodities, images, practices and slogans; and an interdependence of all these elements across the globe, based upon the unifying pressures of global telecommunications and computerized information systems. (Smith, 1995, p. 24)

According to Smith, these characteristics render global culture essentially rootless: trapped in presentism, fluid, ubiquitous and historically shallow. Similar doubts towards the idea of global memory were expressed by many other political and cultural scholars, including Michael Walzer (1994, p. 7), who proposed an inspiring dichotomy between thick and thin morality:

> Societies are necessarily particular because they have members and memories, members with memories not only of their own but also of their common life. Humanity, by contrast, has members but no memory, and so it has no history and no culture, no customary practices, no familiar life-ways, no festivals, no shared understanding of social goods.

It is worth noting that while this vision of a universal but timeless global future is disturbingly close to Francis Fukuyama's vision of the end of history, the contrast between "thick" bonds linking members of a certain nation and "thin," artificial bonds unifying humanity lies at the heart of the recent renaissance of strong nationalisms. This explains the crucial role memory plays in the current wave of a paradoxical global backlash against globalization.

As Krastev and Holmes (2019) put it, globalization "has always signified modernization by imitation and integration by assimilation." After 1989 there was only one path towards the future and the best thing countries like Turkey, Russia or Poland could do was to imitate the West. Many prominent political leaders such as Recep Tayyip Erdoğan, Vladimir Putin and Jarosław Kaczyński built their enormous popularity on rejecting the politics of imitation, rediscovering the past of their homelands and stoking the pride associated with it.

If global culture is indeed imagined as a memoryless community stripped of its history, collective remembering seems a reasonable way to put down roots and build a sense of security in a liquid world of global complexity. When the humanitarian vision of unifying suffering is equated with the obliteration of identity, national egoism becomes a form of opposition to an ever accelerating reality. This is how modern "retrotopias" are born (Bauman, 2019). They preach the superiority of the "circular time" (the "politics of eternity") over the vision of progress that was expressed by the "politics of inevitability" guiding globalization. As Timothy Snyder (2018, p. 7) puts it, "Eternity places one nation at the center of a cyclical story of victimhood. Time is no longer a line into the future, but a circle that endlessly returns the same threats from the past." As Duncan Bell (2006, p. 26) summarizes it: "As people become increasingly worried about their 'obsolescence' in a world defined by rapid change, so they seek an anchorage in some 'authentic' past, in memory. The latest mnemonic turn is a function of technological transformation and the discipline imposed by the global neo-liberal economic regime."

GLOBAL ETHICS OF MEMORY

The birth of the global memory and the past-oriented moral imperative can be interpreted as the result of the collapse of the Enlightenment faith in progress after the world wars. The crisis of one master narrative created space for another, in which progress was replaced by empathy. Thus, the trauma of the Holocaust became the cornerstone of the new global ethics of memory. This principle is best known in the formulation of Theodor W. Adorno, who writes that the new ethical imperative is to act so that the Holocaust is never repeated (Adorno, 2003). Adorno thus created a framework for describing the Holocaust not as a crime committed by specific perpetrators against specific victims, but as a tragedy of universal moral significance whose most important message becomes the principle of "never again" and the "duty of memory" (Margalit, 2002). This universal dimension of the Holocaust was emphasized by the most important initiators of the practice of its commemoration, including Elie Wiesel, who repeatedly said that in the Holocaust it was not the Jews who were killed but people, or even the very "idea of humanity" (Mate, 2003, pp. 9–32).

As Andreas Huyssen (2003, p. 13) summarizes:

> On the one hand, the Holocaust has become a cipher for the twentieth century as a whole and for the failure of the project of enlightenment. It serves as proof of Western civilization's failure to practice anamnesis, to reflect on its constitutive inability to live in peace with difference and otherness, and to draw the consequences from the insidious relationship among enlightened modernity, racial oppression, and organized violence. On the other hand, this totalizing dimension of Holocaust discourse so prevalent in much postmodern thought is accompanied by a dimension that particularizes and localizes ... Holocaust loses its quality as index from the specific historical event and begins to function as a metaphor for other traumatic histories and memories.

Yet the Holocaust did not become the new ethical norm of global memory immediately after the Second World War. Numerous authors have pointed out the crucial role that the pacifist movement, particularly the protests against the Vietnam War, played in establishing this new paradigm (Molden, 2010). The protest movement of the late 1960s prepared the collective consciousness for the experience of the trauma of the Holocaust by creating a new, universal and ahistorical figure of the genocide victim. The establishment of the Vietnam War Crimes Tribunal on the initiative of Bertrand Russell was a pivotal moment. The commission was chaired by Jean-Paul Sartre and its members included some of the most important intellectuals of the time, including Claude Lanzmann.

This universal model of a new ethics collides with the entanglement of collective memory in the category of the nation. The combination of memory as the "new moral imperative" and national identity gives rise to a "victimhood nationalism" (Lim, 2010), which encourages underprivileged nations to "over-contextualize the past, which provides them with a morally comfortable position as historical victims."

Thus, it seems that the suffering-driven global memory may fuel the mechanism of victim competition (Chaumont, 2000). Within this framework, various traumatic events compete in the collective imagination for the title of the "greatest crime" that would ensure their immortalization as the moral universal. In this way, memory becomes a tool for building soft power and internal and external propaganda. The memory of past wrongs becomes a powerful political resource and inexhaustible fuel for nationalism, separatism and terrorism (Rieff, 2011).

GLOBAL ESTHETICS OF MEMORY

The creation of global memory is not only an ethical challenge but also an esthetic one. Echoing Marshall McLuhan's famous words, one can say that the content of memory is interdependent with its form. The story of building a global community of empathy is also the story of the development of the press, television, cinema and now social media (Barnett, 2011).

According to Jeffrey Alexander (2002), the Holocaust became a source of the new global memory in a complex process of universalization that required a psychological identification with the victims that would enable the worldwide audience to co-experience the trauma of the event. Alexander's theory of "cultural trauma" aims to explain how the Holocaust, as a moral universe, is the result of a complex process of mediation.

Daniel Levy and Natan Sznaider (2001) show how Adorno's moral postulates were put into practice not by philosophers or politicians, but rather the mass media through which memory was dressed in images and universalized. They point to the role of Hollywood in the creation of the founding myth for the new, post-national community of the "Western world." This process of making the Holocaust an icon of the new global memory is analyzed in detail by Aleida Assmann (2010, p. 106). "After memory has left the national containers and become deterritorialized with the help of mass media, the cosmopolitan memory of the Holocaust can guarantee human rights and offer a moral foundation for future humanity." According to Assmann the basic characteristics of global Holocaust memory include iconicity, decontextualization, symbolic extension to all of humanity, emotional identification and the principle of analogy. The development of television and new electronic media has allowed for the instantaneous circulation of various types of messages (especially images) creating a global audience. However, this audience is more a product of forms of mediation than of the remembered content itself (Hoskins, 2001).

Critics of the term "global memory" often point out that the alleged global character may turn out to be only a projection of the dominant American culture that has been extended to the majority of the world (Beck et al., 2003), and that the globalized memory is subject to processes of commercialization and homogenization. From this point of view the publication of Norman Finkelstein's *The Holocaust Industry* (2000) was an important milestone in the criticism of the concept of global memory. Finkelstein writes about the appropriation of the Holocaust by a relatively small network of institutions and its transformation into a memory enterprise. An interesting answer to this kind of criticism may be found in concepts such as "multidirectional memory" (Rothberg, 2011) or "traveling memory" (Erll, 2011b), that redefine global memory through the prism of the interaction of many different subjects, showing that the alleged Western domination is rather a complex interplay between various hegemonic and counter-hegemonic visions of the past.

PAST MISTAKES, FUTURE CHALLENGES

Duncan Bell starts his introduction to the inspiring collective volume *Memory Trauma and World Politics* with a quotation from Lewis Carroll: "Alice remarked, 'I can't remember things before they happen.' 'It's a poor sort of memory that only works backwards,' the Queen remarked." According to Bell (2006, p. 22), this is a suggestive reminder that "historical memory is as much about the present and the future as it is about the past." Memory may obviously provide a valuable lesson, as captured in the famous dictum "*historia magistra vitae.*" However, it may also easily trap us in a sort of "eternal return" – a vision of the universe doomed to repeat old mistakes and atrocities over and over again (Rieff, 2011; Snyder, 2018). This renders memory a rather unstable foundation for a new world peace dreamed up by Kant and his followers. Turning to the past may easily cost us a loss of faith in the future.

As Andreas Huyssen (2003, p. 11) puts it:

> One of the most surprising cultural and political phenomena of recent years has been the emergence of memory as a key cultural and political concern in Western societies, a turning toward the past that stands in stark contrast to the privileging of the future so characteristic of earlier decades of twentieth-century modernity.

Some scholars and commentators, like Charles Maier (1993) and David Rieff (2011), go even further, suggesting that this "surfeit of memory" or "memory fever" leads to an unhealthy, neurasthenic fixation on the past. In stark contrast to the dreams of the founding fathers of the "humanitarian paradigm" horrified by the tragedy at Solferino, no positive scenario for a better future will be credible in a world where only eternal repetition of the past lies ahead. As a result, memory boom fuels apocalyptic imagination, as it becomes "another variation of the millennial obsession with endings" (Bell, 2006, p. 26).

Memory organizes the collective imagination. The domination of "retrotopia" and the "politics of eternity" extends not only to the speeches of politicians and programs of their parties. Through the links analyzed by Alexander, Levy and Sznaider it also extends to popular culture as a whole, where apocalyptic narratives dominate over inspiring utopias or visions of collective mobilization. Scenarios such as "Mad Max" or countless zombie apocalypse movies suggest no hope for a humanitarian eternal peace, but rather a vision of the world trapped in a Hobbesian war of all against all. The naive vision of the "end of history" and a world liberated from its own past has been replaced by an equally simplistic vision of a constant return of the worst. Unadjusted accounts of wrongs too often cause us to dwell on past misfortunes instead of working together toward a better future.

Climate catastrophe, global social inequality, the rise of multinational corporations that no longer can be controlled by nation-states with their traditional prerogatives and geographical distribution of responsibility – there is no doubt that in the face of these challenges we need the lessons of solidarity and empathy drawn from a global ethic of memory. However, we also need new definitions of community and new frameworks for action and we need them fast. We need a memory that is a lesson and a starting point, not a final destination. We need memory as a challenge, not an obligation, a burden or a trauma.

Because without new challenging and inspiring memories for a global age, there will be no better future.

REFERENCES

Adorno, T. (2003) *Negative Dialectics*. London: Routledge.

Alexander, J. H. (2002) "On the social construction of moral universals. The 'Holocaust' from war crime to trauma drama," *European Journal of Social Theory*, 5(1), pp. 5–85.

Assmann, A. (2010) "The Holocaust – a global memory? Extensions and limits of a new memory community," in A. Assmann and S. Conrad (eds), *Memory in a Global Age: Discourses, Practices and Trajectories*. New York: Palgrave MacMillan, pp. 97–117.

Barnett, M. (2011) *Empire of Humanity: History of Humanitarianism*. Ithaca, NY: Cornell University Press.

Bauman Z. (2019) *Retrotopia*. Hoboken, NJ: John Wiley & Sons.

Beck, U., Sznaider, N. and Winter, R. (eds) (2003) *Global America? The Cultural Consequences of Globalization*. Liverpool: Liverpool University Press.

Bell, D. (2006) "Introduction," in D. Bell (ed.), *Memory, Trauma and World Politics: Reflections on the Relationship between Past and Present*. London: Springer.

Benjamin, W. (1969) *Illuminations*, trans. Harry Zohn. New York: Schocken Books.

Berliner, D. C. (2005) "The Abuses of Memory: Reflections on the Memory Boom in Anthropology," *Anthropological Quarterly*, 78(1), pp. 197–211.

Chaumont, J.-M. (2000) "Du culte des héros à la concurrence des victimes," *Criminologie*, 33(1), pp. 167–183.

Confino, A. (1997) "Collective Memory and Cultural History: Problems of Method," *American Historical Review*, 102(5), pp. 1386–1403.

Dunant, H. (1959) *A Memory of Solferino*. Geneva: International Committee of the Red Cross.

Erll, A. (2011a) *Memory in Culture.* London: Palgrave Macmillan.

Erll, A. (2011b) "Travelling Memory," *Parallax*, 17(4), pp. 4–18.

Finkelstein, N. G. (2000) *The Holocaust Industry*. London: Verso.

Halbwachs, M. (1992) *On Collective Memory*. Chicago, IL: University of Chicago Press.

Halévy, D. (1948) *Essai sur l'accélération de l'histoire*. Paris: Fallois.

Hoskins, A. (2001) "New memory: Mediating history," *Historical Journal of Film, Radio and Television*, 21(4), 333–346.

Huyssen, A. (2003) *Present Pasts: Urban Palimpsests and the Politics of Memory*. Stanford, CA: Stanford University Press.

Klein, K. L. (2000) "On the emergence of memory in historical discourse," *Representations*, 69, pp. 127–150.

Krastev, I. and Holmes, S. (2019) *The Light That Failed*. London: Penguin.

Levy, D. and Sznaider, N. (2001) *Erinnerung im globalen Zeitalter: Der Holocaust*. Frankfurt am Main: Suhrkamp.

Lim, J. H. (2010) "Victimhood nationalism in contested memories: National mourning and global accountability," in A. Assman and S. Conrad (eds), *Memory in a Global Age*. London: Palgrave Macmillan, pp. 138–162.

Maier, C. S. (1993) "A surfeit of memory? Reflections on history, melancholy and denial," *History and Memory*, 5(2), pp. 136–152.

Margalit, A. (2002) *The Ethics of Memory*. Cambridge, MA: Harvard University Press.

Mate, R. (2003) *Memoria de Auschwitz. Actualidad moral y política*. Madrid: Trotta.

Molden, B. (2010) "Vietnam, the New Left and the Holocaust: How the Cold War Changed Discourse on Genocide," in A. Assman and S. Conrad (eds), *Memory in a Global Age*. London: Palgrave Macmillan, pp. 79–96.

Negri, A. and Hardt, M. (2000) *Empire*. Cambridge, MA: Harvard University Press.

Nora, P. (1989) "Between memory and history: Les lieux de mémoire," *Representations*, 26, pp. 7–24.

Olick, J. K. (1998) "Introduction: Memory and the nation – continuities, conflicts, and transformations," *Social Science History*, 22(4), pp. 377–387.

Olick, J. K. and Robbins, J. (1998) "Social memory studies: From 'collective memory' to the historical sociology of mnemonic practices," *Annual Review of Sociology*, 24(1), pp. 105–140.

Rieff, D. (2011) *Against Remembrance*. Melbourne: Melbourne Univ. Publishing.

Roediger, H. L. and Wertsch, J. (2008) "Creating a new discipline of memory studies," *Memory Studies*, 1(1), pp. 9–22.

Rothberg, M. (2011) "From Gaza to Warsaw: Mapping multidirectional memory," *Criticism*, 53(4), pp. 523–548.

Seremetakis, N., ed. (1996) *The Senses Still*. Chicago, IL: University of Chicago Press.

Smith, A. D. (1990) "Towards a global culture," in M. Featherstone (ed.), *Global Culture: Nationalism, Globalization and Modernity*. New York: SAGE, pp. 171–192.

Smith, A. D. (1995) *Nations and Nationalism in a Global Era*. Cambridge: Polity.

Snyder, T. (2018) *The Road to Unfreedom: Russia, Europe, America*. New York: Tim Duggan Books.

Srnicek, N. and Williams, A. (2016) *Inventing the Future: Postcapitalism and a World without Work*. London: Verso Books.

Walzer, M. (1994) *Thick and Thin: Moral Argument at Home and Abroad*. Notre Dame, IN: University of Notre Dame Press.

Zelizer, B. (1995) "Reading the past against the grain: The shape of memory studies," *Critical Studies in Mass Communication*, 12(2), pp. 213–239.

13. The globalization of religion as a complex phenomenon

Ugo Dessì

INTRODUCTION

Consistent with the globalization turn in cultural studies and the development of the study of globalization and culture (e.g. Robertson 1992, 1995; Appadurai 1996; Hannerz 1996; Tomlinson 1999; Nederveen Pieterse 2009), since the 1990s the interplay of religion and globalization has attracted the interest of scholars at the crossroads of sociology, social anthropology, religious studies, and international politics. This trend gained momentum especially with the publication of Peter Beyer's work inspired by Niklas Luhmann's theory (Beyer 1994), the rediscovery of transnationalism (e.g. Rudolph and Piscatori 1997), and the realization of the increasingly global impact of Pentecostalism and Charismatic Christianity (e.g. Dempster et al. 1999). Resulting studies have contributed to shape a field of research covering many religious cultures, within which there is an increasing consensus on the idea that religion, rather than being a force external to globalization, operates *within* globalization in various and frequently ambivalent ways. One of the possible approaches to this field, as I will illustrate in the following, is to distinguish four broad and often overlapping areas of enquiry in the debate on religion and globalization: (1) the diffusion and transnational flow of religion brought about by globalization; (2) the interactions between religion and powerful global systems such as politics and the economy; (3) the interactions between different religious traditions and groups operating in the international arena; and (4) the interactions between religion and specific aspects of global culture, which are related to the issues of glocalization and hybridization. Approaching the interplay of religion and global dynamics from this perspective requires a working definition of globalization flexible enough to account for the augmented connections and interactions enabled by the development of new media and civil transportation, especially since the second half of the twentieth century, some continuities with processes started in premodern history, and the underlying power relations and psychological effects of this interplay. Thus, throughout this chapter I will refer to globalization as the worldwide, multicentric process of cross-cultural interactions and hybridizations beginning in ancient history that has become more intense, rapid, and pervasive in the contemporary era due to the impact of new communication technologies and the growing scope of specialized social systems, thus bringing about unprecedented (though unequally distributed) interconnectedness and social actors' more acute awareness of being part of a "global game."

The task of illustrating the trajectory of religion within globalization obviously begs the question of what religion is. While aware of postcolonial critiques of the concept of religion (e.g. Fitzgerald 2000), I contend that wariness of Western-centrism can be combined with the use of religion as a second-order concept providing a flexible framework for the study of a range of contemporary phenomena. With this in mind, in this chapter I will refer to religion as a social system that grants or denies access to a variety of this-worldly/other-worldly goods through the authority of a super-empirical agency (Dessì 2017: 29–34; see also Weber 1978 [1922]; Chaves 1994). This is, of course, just another definition of religion among many others. As will become clearer in the last section, however, it is also one consistent with the approach laid out above that distinguishes four main areas in the study of religion under globalization.

Against this background, this chapter will initially provide an overview of the state of the art for each of the abovementioned areas of enquiry and for their intersections, then suggest some possible new directions for research, including the integration of different levels of analysis and the exploration of the micro-dynamics of religious globalization.

GLOBALIZATION AND THE DIFFUSION OF RELIGION

The worldwide dissemination of a wide range of beliefs and practices is probably the most apparent aspect of the globalization of religion. As suggested above, there is nothing completely new in all this, given the role played by traditions such as Buddhism, Christianity, and Islam in the diffusion of culture since antiquity. Acknowledging this is certainly consistent with a *longue durée* perspective on globalization that precludes its identification with Western modernity and allows for a less Eurocentric approach to these dynamics. However, it is also apparent that the acceleration of the process of globalization has impacted dramatically on religion's worldwide diffusion. Following Thomas Csordas (2009a), we may distinguish four main means by which contemporary religions "traverse geographical and cultural space," that is, "missionization," "migration," "mobility," and "mediatization." While missionization and migration have played a crucial role already in past phases of globalization, today they also mark, in many respects, new modalities of religion's engagement with global society. With the dramatic development of the civil transportation sector also religious people, whether they are members of diasporic communities, pilgrims, migrant workers, or simply tourists, can travel more easily and more often than in the past, taking with them their beliefs and practices. And through the new communication media an unprecedented amount of religious ideas can be made available to people in other parts of the world. This is not to deny or minimize, of course, the reality of new and often unfair restrictions to human flows by nation-states, nor the manipulation of information flows by centers of economic power. Not everyone or everything has the same chances to participate in global flows.

The combined effect of the new opportunities offered by globalization to religions is exemplified by the success of Pentecostalism and Charismatic Christianity, which was one of the first topics that drew scholars' attention. Despite its internal diversification and multiple places of origin, Pentecostalism has been characterized as the prototype of a global community united by a common spiritual goal and reinforced by a wide network of international contacts, transnational groups, and reverse missionizing (e.g. Droogers 2001; Martin 2002; Ukah 2008; Jenkins 2011; Hefner 2013). Some scholars have highlighted continuities between aspects of Pentecostalism and local traditions, while others have emphasized discontinuities considering the strongly militant character of this strand of Christianity seeing itself in a global battle against demonic forces (Marshall-Fratani 2001; Robbins 2003). With reference to the largely overlapping Charismatic movement, it has been observed how various groups can present similarities with transnational corporations in terms of their organizational structure and use of the new communication technologies (Poewe 1994; Coleman 2000).

More generally, religious transnationalism has been studied for its implications for peace, conflict, and the formation of a transnational civil society (Rudolph and Piscatori 1997), with reference to migration and diaspora (Ebaugh and Chafetz 2002; Johnson 2007; Levitt 2007; Rocha and Vásquez 2013; Adogame 2014; Lau and Cao 2014), in terms of intersubjectivities transcending cultural borders (Csordas 2009b), at the intersection with spiritual tourism (Palmer and Siegler 2017), against the framework of multiple modernities (Michel et al. 2017), and in connection to specific traditions, such as the case of Yorùbá religious culture and its networks (Clarke 2004; Olupona and Rey 2008). A recent example of the ongoing interest in this aspect of religious globalization is the work of the Collaborative Research Center "Processes of Spatialisation under the Global Condition" at Leipzig University, which focuses on the dynamics underlying transnational space making with reference to Taiwanese religious organizations in South Africa, the United States, and East Asia (Broy et al. 2017; see also Clart and Jones 2020). Occasionally, the theme of religious transnationalism has provided the starting point for the conceptualization of religion. This is the case, for example, of Thomas Tweed's (2006) theory of crossing and dwelling, which interprets religions as "sacroscapes," that is, as the confluence of organic-cultural flows changing over time and moving across space. Writing from a materialist perspective on religion as the product of practices of individuals embedded in nature/culture and therefore deeply intertwined with non-religious processes, Manuel Vásquez (2011) has attempted to go beyond Tweed's "hydrodynamics of religion" by theorizing its fluidity with more attention to power asymmetries and the mechanisms of transnational biopower.

The worldwide dynamism of new religious movements emerging from different traditions is another example of transnational religion under conditions of globalization. New religious movements have been recognized as global cultures for their transnationalism and their search for new forms of spirituality (Hexam and Poewe 1997; Clarke 2006), and their interplay with globalization has been approached from various angles: with reference to the issue of globality and the new communication technologies (Beckford 2004), with attention to their organizational dimension, interactions, and historical development (Geertz and Warburg 2008), in terms of global communication and adaptation to local conditions (Chandler 2004; Arweck 2007), and as providers of religious social services through agencies and non-governmental organizations (Cherry and Ebaugh 2014). A partially overlapping case is represented by the New Age movement, which was acknowledged early on as a non-institutionalized example of the global quest for new forms of spirituality (Rothstein 2001). In this connection, much emphasis has been placed on the impact of Eastern spirituality in Europe and North America leading to a substantial "Easternization of the West" (Campbell 2007). However, others have observed how the undeniable presence of non-Western cultural elements in the New Age does not necessarily speak of an inversion of cultural flows. For Wouter Hanegraaff (2001), for example, the New Age is essentially a cultural criticism of Western dualism and materialist-reductionism mainly articulated from the standpoint of a secularized Western esotericism. What really matters to this movement, he suggests, is spreading such views to non-Western cultures while paying only "lip-service to local spiritualities," which ultimately qualifies it as being a form of "spiritual imperialism."

INTERACTIONS WITH GLOBAL SYSTEMS AND OTHER RELIGIONS

One of the implications of transnationalism is the interplay between religions and national societies and, by extension, between religion and the domain of politics. This dimension of religious globalization was prefigured in Robertson's theory, which included "national societies" among the reference points (together with "selves," "humankind," and the "world system of societies") for the analysis of the global-human circumstance (Robertson 1992). The much discussed and controversial thesis of the "clash of civilizations" originally presented by Samuel Huntington in 1993 also qualifies as an attempt to make sense of the political implications of religion in the post-Cold War global scenario (Huntington 1993). In those years, clear signs of religious resurgence in different parts of the world, such as the Islamic Revolution in Iran, the New Christian Right in the United States, and Hindu nationalism, were promptly captured as a global phenomenon of deprivatization (e.g. Beyer 1994; Haynes 1998; see also Haynes 2014). In particular, the political trajectories of Islam under globalizing conditions have attracted the interest of various scholars, with research focusing on topics as diverse as the reconceptualization of the *umma* as a gateway to a Muslim public sphere and new forms of translocal politics (Mandaville 2001, 2007); the deterritorialization brought about by globalization and migration flows and its nexus with the contemporary trend toward re-Islamization (Roy 2004); the construction of political identities among diasporic and post-diasporic Muslims in the West (Kinnvall and Nesbitt-Larking 2011); and the emergence of a new political Islam characterized by the communitarianism of its leaders and activists (Karagiannis 2018).

Often without any explicit reference to globalization theory, the changing relationships between religion and other secular spheres have come to be thematized, too. Interactions with the modern media (e.g. Hoover and Clark 2002; Stout 2012) and especially with the Internet have an obvious relevance here (e.g. Dawson and Cowan 2004; Grieve and Veidlinger 2015), not least for their implications for religious diffusion and transnationalism. A classic example of religious interactions with the market economy is illustrated by Mara Einstein's (2008) exploration of the phenomenon of religious branding in what she defines the "commercial age." Jeremy Carrette and Richard King (2005) have instead focused on religion's accommodation to the ideology of global capitalism, within which they distinguished four different modalities of interaction: revolutionary or anti-capitalist spiritualities (rejection of neoliberalism); business-ethics/reformist spiritualities (acceptance of a capitalism restrained through religious principles); individualist/consumerist spiritualities (interpretation of religious worldviews in terms of capitalism, consumerism and individualism); and capitalist spiritualities (subordination of religion to the logic of capitalism). From another perspective, Christian Karner and Alan Aldridge (2004) have argued that religion can function as a sort of antidote to the survival anxiety and sense of crisis caused by the forces of economic globalization, which explains the contemporary cases of religious revivalism and deprivatization, including the many attempts to repoliticize religion such as *Hindutva* nationalism (see also Karner 2006).

The pioneer in the study of this range of interactions intertwining the issue of global religion with that of (de)secularization was Peter Beyer, who first illustrated his systemic approach in *Religion and Globalization*, where he distinguished two main options available to religion under globalization. Through the conservative option, as exemplified by the New Christian Right and the Islamic Revolution in Iran, religion opposes functional differentiation (i.e.

secularization as the emergence of instrumental and technically oriented societal systems competing with religion) and strongly emphasizes sociocultural particularism; the liberal option, as in the case of Liberation Theology, implies instead the acceptance of functional differentiation, pluralism, and the core values of globalization. Here, Beyer also shed light on the mechanism through which religions engage with various global ("residual") problems created or left unsolved by the dominant global systems (Beyer 1994). In more recent contributions, Beyer elaborated in more detail on how religion as a global and internally diversified system emerges as a part of the overall process of functional differentiation (Beyer 2007). Among the few scholars who have attempted to operationalize Beyer's theory, Margit Warburg (1999) has noted that the Baha'i, while officially embracing pluralism, also manifests a tendency to dedifferentiate the political and religious systems.

The religious fundamentalism of the New Christian Right and the Islamic Revolution was a compelling example presented by Beyer of religion's attempt to dedifferentiate itself from politics and other systems while rejecting other religious traditions. Indeed, the search for fundamentals had already been acknowledged by Robertson (1992: 164–181) as one of the aspects of the globalization of culture, and the overlapping of dedifferentiation and exclusivism is apparent in studies of fundamentalism as a global phenomenon. One early example is Gabriel Almond and his colleagues' illustration of the general features of fundamentalism, among which one finds not only the reaction against secularization and a selective approach to modernity but also moral Manicheanism and an emphasis on the "chosen" (Almond et al. 1995; see also Turner and Khondker 2010: 82–101).

More generally, Beyer's exploration of religious attitudes toward functional differentiation and pluralism as a single theme is a useful reminder of the interconnectedness of such global dynamics, which also emerges in the work of other scholars. Tulasi Srinivas' (2013) analysis of the Sathya Sai movement, for example, is as much about the process of cultural translation and hybridization as it is about the underlying tendency toward religious inclusivism, which she understands in terms of multiple commitments and theological pluralism. Analogous dynamics have been observed in contexts such as Nigerian Pentecostalism by Ukah (2008: 281–292) and in Evangelical Christianity by George Van Pelt Campbell (2005), who, as I will illustrate below, mainly focuses on interactions between religious traditions but also touches upon the topics of religious hybridization and dedifferentiation. A similar overlapping has also emerged in my own research on Japanese religions (Dessì 2013, 2017).

It is interesting to note that the interplay between globalization and pluralism has also been acknowledged from a theological perspective. Marianne Moyaert, for example, has identified six factors contributing to the increasing relevance of inter-religious dialogue, the most important of which is the very phenomenon of globalization bringing about increased migration flows, mobility, interconnectedness through advances in communication technology, as well as an increased "awareness of a shared responsibility for this world" (Moyaert 2013).

INTERACTIONS WITH GLOBAL IDEAS

Still another area of interest within the broader field of religious globalization concerns the creative adoption of global ideas and practices by religious actors at the local level, which has been approached through conceptual tools such as glocalization, hybridization, and bricolage. Implicitly thematized by Robertson (1987) in an early contribution exploring the impact of aspects of Japan's religious culture (syncretism, polytheism, and purification) on the modality of its global involvement, the issue of religious glocalization was briefly discussed by David Lyon (1998) in an article on the Toronto Blessing religious revival in the late 1990s. Manuel Vásquez and Marie Marquardt (2000) were among the first scholars to employ this conceptual tool with their analysis of the Rainbow Madonna in Florida, in which they show how this new devotional tradition was used by the Vatican to "embody" itself in the local and implement its New Evangelization campaign. In their book *Globalizing the Sacred*, the two scholars explored similar dynamics at the border between Texas and Mexico, and illustrated how the success of the evangelization campaign Project Light undertaken in 1990 in Guatemala by the Christian Broadcasting Network was largely dependent on the tailoring of its messages to a local audience through the use of indigenous contents and familiar formats (Vásquez and Marquardt 2003: 197–222). The influence of Robertson's work can also be seen in Campbell's (2005) research, where some of the responses offered by tradition to relativization present analogies with glocalization: the "openness to rethinking the original traditions" (e.g. the modernist impulse in Protestantism) and three subtypes of "reinvention" responses, that is, "reinvention by selection" (e.g. American fundamentalism), "reinvention by deletion" (e.g. the prohibition of polygamy by the Mormons), and "reinvention by addition" (e.g. the adoption of Marxist ideas by Liberation Theology).

The most articulated use of the concept of glocalization within the study of Christianity was made by Victor Roudometof with his theory of "multiple glocalizations" applied to the Orthodox tradition. Roudometof distinguished four main modalities of interpenetration between (Christian) universalism and (local) particularism within this process: "vernacularization," through which religious universalism is blended with specific languages; "indigenization," through which religious universalism is blended with a particular ethnicity; "nationalization," in which the foundation for the religious claims to legitimacy is provided by the nation; and "transnationalization," which is a consequence of the global emergence of nation-states (Roudometof 2013, 2014). Among other things, Roudometof (2018) guest edited a special issue of the journal *Religions* on "Glocal Religions," including contributions on Hinduism, Japanese Buddhism, neo-Mayanity, religion in the Roman Empire, and Christianity.

In the field of Islam, one of the most thorough engagements with the theme of glocalization is offered by Emmanuel Karagiannis' (2018) work, in which he characterizes the new generation of Islamists as "glocalizers of universal ideas and norms" through the use of the master frames of human rights, democracy, and justice. To be sure, the emergence of hybrid forms in contemporary Islam had already been identified by other scholars such as Peter Mandaville (2001), with reference to the ongoing discussions of key doctrinal concepts such as *dar al-islam* ("the domain of Islam," i.e. wherever the principles of Islam are supported by Muslim rule) and *dar al-harb* ("the domain of war," i.e. not under Muslim rule) within sectors of the *umma*, and Olivier Roy (2004), with his reflections on the ongoing Westernization of diasporic communities.

The glocalization of Asian religions has been explored especially with reference to Japanese religions and Hinduism. As for the former, it is worth mentioning Rocha's analysis of the creolization/hybridization of Zen in Brazil, which shows how this Buddhist tradition has been decontextualized and reinvented to create a fashionable umbrella concept, and how this process has been facilitated by the presence in Brazil of Spiritism and Umbanda (Rocha 2006). In my own work, I have initially applied the concept of glocalization to the adoption of the discourse on human rights in Japanese Buddhism and the incorporation of the theme of "lost continents" by Kōfuku no Kagaku (Dessì 2013). In more recent contributions I have elaborated on the glocalization of religion as one modality of their global repositioning that relies on the creative adoption of global ideas and practices. In particular, I illustrated the process of glocalization with reference to the greening of religion in Japan, in which the resonance of the global idea of sustainability with traditional religious concepts plays a central role; and by focusing on how Hawaiian Shin Buddhist priests and followers have reshaped their own practice (which traditionally discards meditation) by adopting a variety of meditational techniques available in the global cultural network (Dessì 2017). The issue of glocalization in Japanese religions such as Risshō Kōseikai, Sōka Gakkai, and Shinnyōen has also been discussed by some of the contributions to the special issue "New Research on Japanese Religions under Globalization" of the *Journal of Religion in Japan*, guest edited by Galen Amstutz and myself (Amstutz and Dessì 2014).

As for the interplay of Hinduism with global and local cultures, one substantial contribution to this topic is offered by Srinivas with her analysis of the four stages of Sathya Sai's cultural translation overseas. The first two (cultural awareness and disembedding, codification and universalization) are related to the way cultural forms are made portable and exportable – e.g. by disembedding Sai Baba from local culture and connecting it to other religions – while the last two (latching and matching, contextualization and re-embedding) refer to the transmission of these cultural forms to host societies where they can be used to create new hybrids (Srinivas 2010). In a more recent research on neo-Hindu movements and the Kabbalah Centre in Europe and America, Véronique Altglas illustrated how leaders preliminarily detach imported religious forms from their ethnic aspects by reinterpreting core doctrines and altering specific practices. For her, the appropriation of these forms by local actors through the practice of bricolage (i.e. the creation of new religious identities by mixing a variety of elements from different religious traditions) is never free and unproblematic but rather intertwined with power issues, and depends on their domestication, through which such exotic cultural elements come to be seen as non-religious and universal forms of spirituality (Altglas 2014). The glocalization of Hinduism has also been discussed in other articles such as a study of the blending of Caribbean and Hindu elements in Indian funeral feasts in St. Lucia (Manian and Bullock 2016).

Within the context of Latin American spirituality, Raquel Romberg identified four main glocal layers in Puerto Rican *brujería* (witch-healing), starting from the early encounter between Spanish colonial rule with local culture to the addition of consumerist elements during the economic boom of the 1960s (Romberg 2005). In her account of the faith-healing practices of John of God in Brazil, Rocha instead used the concept of glocalization to explore the tension between processes of homogenization and heterogenization. Relevant to our discussion, she observed that these dynamics are at work in the activities of staffers and tour guides acting as cultural translators, who reframe and glocalize the leader's local discourse/ practices by relating them to elements of global culture already internalized by foreign visitors (Rocha 2017).

MAKING SENSE OF THE GLOBALIZATION OF RELIGION AS A COMPLEX/MULTILAYERED PHENOMENON

This overview shows how in the last two decades the globalization of religion has been researched from different and often complementary perspectives, and how such variety of methodological and conceptual approaches has contributed to enrich this field of studies. Many researches have focused on the diffusion of religion within the global context, even creating a certain unbalance within the field. Here, one of the potential risks is that an overemphasis on overseas transmission or transnationalism can reduce the globalization of religion to its geographical dimension. In other words, there is the need to cultivate the awareness that religions do not necessarily need to travel in order to be globalized. A fair amount of attention has also been paid to the interplay of religion with global ideas, probably because of the impact of more general studies on cultural hybridity. Far less attention has instead been devoted to interactions between religion and global systems and to those between religions, at least if one considers those approaches explicitly addressing these dynamics in dialogue with globalization theory. In this respect, it is rather surprising that so few scholars have attempted to elaborate on the pioneering work of Beyer on the systemic implications of religious globalization. It is also evident that some religions and areas (e.g. Christianity, America) have attracted more attention than others by scholars in the field, and that the historical dimension of religious globalization, despite progress made, still awaits to be fully acknowledged. In this connection, one wonders to what extent developments in this direction may be constrained by an enduring implicit understanding of globalization as Western modernization.

One of the thorny issues in the study of religious globalization is how to make sense of the complexity and interdependence of these dynamics through a comprehensive approach. As anticipated above, one possible solution has been suggested by Beyer with his focus on the worldwide appropriation of functional differentiation and the Western/Christian model by local religious traditions. For him, these are not simply religious responses to globalization, but more precisely historical processes of glocalization through which religion emerges as a plurality of traditions. In this sense, for Beyer "globalization is always also *glocalization*" (Beyer 2007). Another way of approaching the globalization of religion comprehensively is suggested by Campbell's analysis of religious responses to "relativization" (i.e. the sense of insecurity about one's own tradition caused by globalization and the confrontation with alien traditions). In his model, Campbell distinguishes between closed, open, reinvention, and exit responses. Closed responses imply the rejection of other traditions. Open responses can be of three types: the openness to rethinking the original tradition, the restoring of tradition, and the realization that "one cannot be secure in any tradition." Reinvention responses, too, present three options: reinvention by selection, implying the defense of a portion of the tradition; by deletion, when parts of the tradition are strategically rejected; and by addition, when new elements are incorporated to improve the tradition. And finally, Campbell distinguishes two types of exit responses, namely, defection to other traditions and abandonment of one's own tradition (Campbell 2005: 83–91). Relevant to our discussion, Campbell's religious responses to relativization, despite being primarily related to the confrontation with alien traditions, can account for other interactions under globalizing conditions. For example, his reinvention by addition is not only a "fine-tuning" of the tradition in the face of external pressure, but can imply a process of glocalization through the integration of external elements as well as an engagement with global problems (as in the case of Liberation Theology), the latter referring to religious interactions with secular systems.

In my own work, I have proposed another comprehensive perspective on religious globalization as a multilayered phenomenon by framing relativization as the process through which the increasing pressure exercised upon a religious system by other religious/social systems or external ideas calls into question its autonomy and the stability of its parts. This approach is based on my working definition of religion ("a social system that grants or denies access to a variety of this-worldly/other-worldly goods through the authority of a super-empirical agency") anticipated above, which distinguishes five main parts within religious systems: the this-worldly/other-worldly goods mediated by religion; the super-empirical agency through which access to these goods is granted/denied; the structure of legitimation encompassing the ways in which the super-empirical agency and these goods are related to one another through religious narratives, doctrines, and practices; religious professionals, who generally manage the structure of legitimation; and ordinary practitioners, who can achieve varying degrees of autonomy from them (Dessì 2017: 29–34).

My main argument is that under globalization religion's authority structure can be relativized in different ways by the augmented pressure exercised by other religions, other global systems, and specific global ideas and practices. In a nutshell, these three modalities of relativization can result in three different types of religion's global repositioning or adjustment to the global condition. The first is global repositioning at the inter-religious level, which presents four main options: exclusivism (rejection of the authority claims of other religions); inclusivism (conditional acknowledgment of these claims); pluralism (acknowledgment of these claims); and multiple commitment/conversion (simultaneous acceptance of the authority claims of two or more religions, or transition from one to another). The second is global repositioning at the inter-systemic level, which may result in anti-secularization (rejection of the authority claims of other social systems), conditional secularization (conditional acknowledgment of these claims), secularization (acknowledgment of these claims), and the stopgap function (attempt to remedy the shortcomings of other systems). Finally, the third type of global repositioning occurs at the discrete-elements level through the anti-homogenization (rejection of global ideas), chauvinistic glocalization (their creative adoption to promote religious chauvinism), glocalization (their creative adoption), and homogenization (their passive acceptance) options. As I have illustrated in my work on Japanese religions, such theoretical framework is flexible enough to take into account the role of religion as a carrier of globalization and a wide range of religious interactions under globalization, including those with other traditions, other social systems with a global reach, and ideas/practices circulating in the global cultural network. In my view, this allows a new and integrated perspective on current topics such as inter-religious dialogue, religious conflicts, bioethics, the marketing of religion, and religious ecologies. One example of the application of this conceptual model is the understanding of the greening of religion as an instance of the globalization of religion revealing various and simultaneous layers of interaction: between religion and powerful global ideas (i.e. sustainability), between religions (in that religious ecology often provides a framework for inter-religious dialogue), and between religions and global systems (e.g. a certain criticism of the market economy and the exploitation of the green solutions offered by the new technologies) (Dessì 2017: 162–186).

There is no doubt that the task of offering a comprehensive explanation of the different forms of religious globalization is open to a variety of perspectives that still largely wait to be explored. Among these, it is worth mentioning the potential interpretive strategy offered by a semiotic approach *à la* Lotman. From such perspective, religion can be framed as a "religio-sphere" with a dominant semiotic system at the core and a semiotic border acting as a bilingual mechanism, which, under globalizing conditions, is charged by the increasingly weighty task of translating communications coming from other semiospheres. Among other things, this semiotic approach could account for the instances of particularism typically intertwined with processes of religious globalization in terms of "specialization," that is, the cultivation of its own originality that any culture tends to emphasize once it enters a specific general culture (Lotman 2005).

Finally, there is abundant room for conceptual analyses aimed to clarify not only the general structure of the process of religious globalization but also its micro-dynamics. In this connection, it is revealing that to date there is still no monograph-length study focused on the incentives and constraints underlying the globalization of religion. Factors such as power differentials have been long acknowledged in this field of studies, not least because of the fundamental role played by the tension between the universal and the particular (to phrase it in Robertson's terms) in the general field of cultural globalization. However, there is still the need for systematic approaches that might be able not only to shed light on different typologies of power and power relations at different levels of analysis, but also to fully exploit the potential of concepts such as global consciousness and resonance for the study of religious globalization. And to this end, it is most likely that any in-depth exploration of such range of factors and their mutual interactions will require an increasing openness to both interdisciplinary and comparative approaches.

REFERENCES

Adogame, Afe (ed.) (2014), *The Public Face of African New Religious Movements in Diaspora: Imagining the Religious "Other"*, Farnham: Ashgate.
Almond, Gabriel A., Emmanuel Sivan, and R. Scott Appleby (1995), "Fundamentalism: Genus and species," in Martin E. Marty and R. Scott Appleby (eds), *Fundamentalisms Comprehended*, Chicago: University of Chicago Press, pp. 399–424.
Altglas, Véronique (2014), *From Yoga to Kabbalah: Religious Exoticism and the Logics of Bricolage*, Oxford: Oxford University Press.
Amstutz, Galen and Ugo Dessì (eds) (2014), *New Research on Japanese Religions under Globalization* (Special issue of *Journal of Religion in Japan*), Leiden: Brill.
Appadurai, Arjun (1996), *Modernity at Large: Cultural Dimensions of Globalization*, Minneapolis: University of Minnesota Press.
Arweck, Elisabeth (2007), "Globalization and new religious movements," in Peter Beyer and Lori Beaman (eds), *Religion, Globalization, and Culture*, Leiden: Brill, pp. 253–280.
Beckford, James A. (2004), "New religious movements and globalization," in Phillip Charles Lucas and Thomas Robbins (eds), *New Religious Movements in the 21st Century: Legal, Political, and Social Challenges in Global Perspective*, London: Routledge, pp. 253–264.
Beyer, Peter (1994), *Religion and Globalization*, London: Sage.
Beyer, Peter (2007), "Globalization and glocalisation," in James A. Beckford and N. Jay Demerath III (eds), *The Sage Handbook of the Sociology of Religion*, London: Sage, pp. 98–117.
Broy, Nikolas, Jens Reinke, and Philip Clart (2017), "Migrating Buddhas and global Confucianism: The transnational space making of Taiwanese religious organizations," *Working Paper Series des SFB 1199 an der Universität Leipzig*, 4, 1–36.
Campbell, Colin C. (2007), *The Easternization of the West: A Thematic Account of Cultural Change in the Modern Era*, London: Routledge.

Campbell, George Van Pelt (2005), *Everything You Think Seems Wrong: Globalization and the Relativizing of Tradition*, Lanham: University Press of America.

Carrette, Jeremy R. and Richard King (2005), *Selling Spirituality: The Silent Takeover of Religion*, London: Routledge.

Chandler, Stuart (2004), *Establishing a Pure Land on Earth: The Foguang Buddhist Perspective on Modernization and Globalization*, Honolulu: University of Hawai'i Press.

Chaves, Mark (1994), "Secularization as declining religious authority," *Social Forces*, 72 (3), 749–774.

Cherry, Stephen M. and Helen Rose Ebaugh (eds) (2014), *Global Religious Movements across Borders: Sacred Service*, Farnham: Ashgate.

Clarke, Kamari Maxine (2004), *Mapping Yorùbá Networks: Power and Agency in the Making of Transnational Communities*, Durham: Duke University Press.

Clarke, Peter B. (2006), *New Religions in Global Perspective: Religious Change in the Modern World*, London: Routledge.

Clart, Philip and Adam Jones (eds) (2020), *Transnational Religious Spaces: Religious Organizations and Interactions in Africa, East Asia, and Beyond*, Berlin: de Gruyter Oldenbourg.

Coleman, Simon (2000), *The Globalisation of Charismatic Christianity: Spreading the Gospel of Prosperity*, Cambridge: Cambridge University Press.

Csordas, Thomas J. (2009a), "Introduction: Modalities of transnational transcendence," in Thomas J. Csordas (ed.), *Transnational Transcendence: Essays on Religion and Globalization*, Berkeley: University of California Press, pp. 1–30.

Csordas, Thomas J. (ed.) (2009b), *Transnational Transcendence: Essays on Religion and Globalization*, Berkeley: University of California Press.

Dawson, Lorne L. and Douglas E. Cowan (eds) (2004), *Religion Online: Finding Faith on the Internet*, London: Routledge.

Dempster, Murray W., Byron D. Klaus, and Douglas Peterson (eds) (1999), *The Globalization of Pentecostalism: A Religion Made to Travel*, Oxford: Regnum Books.

Dessì, Ugo (2013), *Japanese Religions and Globalization*, London: Routledge.

Dessì, Ugo (2017), *The Global Repositioning of Japanese Religions: An Integrated Approach*, London: Routledge.

Droogers, André (2001), "Globalisation and Pentecostal success," in André Corten and Ruth Marshall-Fratani (eds), *Between Babel and Pentecost: Transnational Pentecostalism in Africa and Latin America*, London: C. Hurst & Co, pp. 41–61.

Ebaugh, Helen Rose and Janet Saltzman Chafetz (eds) (2002), *Religion across Borders: Transnational Immigrant Networks*, Walnut Creek: Altamira Press.

Einstein, Mara (2008), *Brands of Faith: Marketing Religion in a Commercial Age*, London: Routledge.

Fitzgerald, Timothy (2000), *The Ideology of Religious Studies*, Oxford: Oxford University Press.

Geertz, Armin W. and Margit Warburg (2008), *New Religions and Globalization: Empirical, Theoretical and Methodological Perspectives*, Aarhus: Aarhus University Press.

Grieve, Gregory Price and Daniel Veidlinger (eds) (2015), *Buddhism, the Internet, and Digital Media: The Pixel in the Lotus*, London: Routledge.

Hanegraaff, Wouter J. (2001), "Prospects for the globalization of New Age: Spiritual imperialism versus cultural diversity," in Mikael Rothstein (ed.), *New Age Religion and Globalization*, Aarhus: Aarhus University Press, pp. 15–30.

Hannerz, Ulf (1996), *Transnational Connections: Culture, People, Places*, London: Routledge.

Haynes, Jeff (1998), *Religion in Global Politics*, London: Longman.

Haynes, Jeff (2014), "Politics and religion in a global age," in Johann P. Arnason and Ireneusz Paweł Karolewski (eds), *Religion and Politics: European and Global Perspectives*, Edinburgh: Edinburgh University Press, pp. 37–58.

Hefner, Robert W. (ed.) (2013), *Global Pentecostalism in the 21st Century*, Bloomington: Indiana University Press.

Hexam, Irving and Karla Poewe (1997), *New Religions as Global Cultures: Making the Human Sacred*, Boulder: Westview Press.

Hoover, Stewart M. and Lynn Schofield Clark (eds) (2002), *Practicing Religion in the Age of the Media: Explorations in Media, Religion, and Culture*, New York: Columbia University Press.

Huntington, Samuel P. (1993), "The clash of civilizations?," *Foreign Affairs*, 72 (3), 22–49.

Jenkins, Philip (2011), *The Next Christendom: The Coming of Global Christianity*, New York: Oxford University Press.

Johnson, Paul C. (2007), *Diaspora Conversions: Black Carib Religion and the Recovery of Africa*, Berkeley: University of California Press.

Karagiannis, Emmanuel (2018), *The New Political Islam: Human Rights, Democracy, and Justice*, Philadelphia: University of Pennsylvania Press.

Karner, Christian (2006), *The Thought World of Hindu Nationalism: Analyzing a Political Ideology*, Lewistown: Edwin Mellen Press.

Karner, Christian and Alan Aldridge (2004), "Theorizing religion in a globalizing world," *International Journal of Politics, Culture and Society*, 18 (1), 5–32.

Kinnvall, Catarina and Paul Nesbitt-Larking (2011), *The Political Psychology of Globalization: Muslims in the West*, Oxford: Oxford University Press.

Lau, Sin Wen and Nanlai Cao (eds) (2014), *Religion and Mobility in a Globalising Asia: New Ethnographic Explorations*, London: Routledge.

Levitt, Peggy (2007), *God Needs no Passport: Immigrants and the Changing American Religious Landscape*, New York: New Press.

Lotman, Juri (2005), "On the semiosphere," *Sign Systems Studies*, 33 (1), 205–226.

Lyon, David (1998), "Wheels within wheels: Glocalization and contemporary religion," in Mark Hutchinson and Ogbu Uke Kalu (eds), *A Global Faith: Essays on Evangelicalism and Globalization*, Sydney: Centre for the Study of Australian Christianity, pp. 47–68.

Mandaville, Peter G. (2001), *Transnational Muslim Politics: Reimagining the Umma*, London: Routledge.

Mandaville, Peter G. (2007), *Global Political Islam*, London: Routledge.

Manian, Sabita and Brad Bullock (2016), "Sensing Hinduism: Lucian-Indian funeral 'feast' as glocalized ritual," *Religions*, 7, 8 (Special issue "Glocal Religions" guest edited by Victor Roudometof).

Marshall-Fratani, Ruth (2001), "Mediating the global and local in Nigerian Pentecostalism," in André Corten and Ruth Marshall-Fratani (eds), *Between Babel and Pentecost: Transnational Pentecostalism in Africa and Latin America*, London: C. Hurst & Co, pp. 80–105.

Martin, David (2002), *Pentecostalism: The World Their Parish*, Oxford: Wiley.

Michel, Patrick, Adam Possamai, and Bryan S. Turner (eds) (2017), *Religions, Nations, and Transnationalism in Multiple Modernities*, New York: Palgrave Macmillan.

Moyaert, Marianne (2013), "Interreligious dialogue," in David Cheetham, Douglas Pratt, and David Thomas (eds), *Understanding Interreligious Relations*, Oxford: Oxford University Press, pp. 193–217.

Nederveen Pieterse, Jan (2009), *Globalization and Culture: Global Mélange*, Lanham: Rowman and Littlefield.

Olupona, Jacob K. and Terry Rey (eds) (2008), *Òrìsà Devotion as World Religion: The Globalization of Yorùbá Religious Culture*, Madison: University of Wisconsin Press.

Palmer, David A. and Elijah Siegler (2017), *Dream Trippers: Global Daoism and the Predicament of Modern Spirituality*, Chicago: University of Chicago Press.

Poewe, Karla (ed.) (1994), *Charismatic Christianity as a Global Culture*, Columbia: University of South Carolina Press.

Robbins, Joel (2003), "On the paradoxes of global Pentecostalism and the perils of continuity thinking," *Religion*, 33 (3), 221–231.

Robertson, Roland (1987), "Globalization and societal modernization: A note on Japan and Japanese religion," *Sociological Analysis*, 47, 35–42.

Robertson, Roland (1992), *Globalization: Social Theory and Global Culture*, London: Sage.

Robertson, Roland (1995), "Glocalization: Time-space and homogeneity-heterogeneity," in Mike Featherstone, Scott Lash, and Roland Robertson (eds), *Global Modernities*, London: Sage, pp. 25–44.

Rocha, Cristina (2006), *Zen in Brazil: The Quest for Cosmopolitan Modernity*, Honolulu: University of Hawai'i Press.

Rocha, Cristina (2017), *John of God: The Globalization of Brazilian Faith Healing*, Oxford: Oxford University Press.

Rocha, Cristina and Manuel A. Vásquez (eds) (2013), *The Diaspora of Brazilian Religions*, Leiden: Brill.

Romberg, Racquel (2005), "Glocal spirituality: Consumerism and heritage in a Puerto Rico Afro-Latin-folk religion," in Franklin W. Knight and Teresita Martinez-Vergne (eds), *Contemporary*

Caribbean Cultures and Societies in a Global Context, Chapel Hill: University of North Carolina Press, pp. 131–155.

Rothstein, Mikael (ed.) (2001), *New Age Religion and Globalization*, Aarhus: Aarhus University Press.

Roudometof, Victor (2013), "The glocalisations of Eastern Orthodox Christianity," *European Journal of Social Theory*, 16 (2), 226–245.

Roudometof, Victor (2014), *Globalization and Orthodox Christianity: The Transformations of a Religious Tradition*, London: Routledge.

Roudometof, Victor (ed.) (2018), *Glocal Religions* (Special issue of *Religions*), Basel: MDPI.

Roy, Olivier (2004), *Globalised Islam: The Search for the New Ummah*, London: C. Hurst & Co.

Rudolph, Susanne H. and James P. Piscatori (eds) (1997), *Transnational Religion and Fading States*, Boulder: Westview Press.

Srinivas, Tulasi (2010), *Winged Faith: Rethinking Globalization and Religious Pluralism through the Sathya Sai Movement*, New York: Columbia University Press.

Srinivas, Tulasi (2013), "Towards cultural translation: Rethinking the dynamics of religious pluralism and globalisation through the Sathya Sai movement," in Robert W. Hefner, John Hutchinson, Sara Mels and Christiane Timmerman (eds), *Religions in Movement: The Local and the Global in Contemporary Faith Traditions*, London: Routledge, pp. 230–245.

Stout, Daniel A. (2012), *Media and Religion: Foundations of an Emerging Field*, London: Routledge.

Tomlinson, John (1999), *Globalization and Culture*, Chicago: University of Chicago Press.

Turner, Bryan S. and Habibul Haque Khondker (2010), *Globalization: East and West*, London: Sage.

Tweed, Thomas (2006), *Crossing and Dwelling: A Theory of Religion*, Cambridge: Harvard University Press.

Ukah, Asonzeh (2008), *A New Paradigm of Pentecostal Power: A Study of the Redeemed Christian Church of God in Nigeria*, Trenton: Africa World Press.

Vásquez, Manuel A. (2011), *More than Belief: A Materialist Theory of Religion*, New York: Oxford University Press.

Vásquez, Manuel A. and Marie F. Marquardt (2000), "Globalizing the Rainbow Madonna: Old time religion in the present age," *Theory, Culture & Society*, 17 (4), 119–143.

Vásquez, Manuel A. and Marie F. Marquardt (2003), *Globalizing the Sacred: Religion across the Americas*, New Brunswick: Rutgers University Press.

Warburg, Margit (1999), "Baha'i: A Religious Approach to Globalization," *Social Compass*, 46 (1), 47–56.

Weber, Max (1978 [1922]), *Economy and Society: An Outline of Interpretive Sociology*, Berkeley: University of California Press.

14. The gendered dynamics of migration deterrence and anti-trafficking interventions: the case of Nigerian sex workers in Kumasi, Ghana

Sam Okyere

INTRODUCTION AND CONTEXT

Human trafficking has become an issue of intense concern in international rights and migration circles. This construct which originated from the 1904 Suppression of the White Slave Trade legislation that was adopted in response to a moral panic that maliciously presented foreign men as being a danger to white women was renewed in 2000 by the adoption of the United Nations (UN) Protocol to Prevent, Suppress and Punish Trafficking in Persons, Especially Women and Children. European anxieties about citizenship and immigration pertaining to racial equality and rights of non-white subjects and bodies which were central to the 'white slave' rhetoric and have similarly evolved with the European Union (EU) anti-trafficking modalities. The EU's current anti-trafficking approaches largely treat the issue in terms of criminality and illegal border crossing and thus respond with repressive measures towards migration from Sub-Saharan Africa to Europe especially.

One of these measures is border externalisation or the outsourcing of border controls to African governments or actors (Boswell 2003; Andrijasevic 2009; Adepoju et al. 2010). A key aspect of this practice is that the EU requires cooperating governments to detain or frustrate the efforts of those trying to reach European shores via their territories, whether these are citizens of that African country or otherwise. For their cooperation, the African government or actor is given political support, aid, technical assistance and other rewards by the EU. In effect, using both coercion and bribery, the EU is able to compel African governments to act in ways that do not necessarily meet with the rights and interests of their citizens. In its European Agenda on Migration of 2015 the EU decided to intensify the use of this 'fight against criminal human trafficking networks', with Nigeria targeted as a site where such measures were to be ramped up (European Commission 2015: 2–9).

This objective has taken two main forms. First, the EU has increased its funding and technical support to the Nigerian government, non-governmental organisations and UN agencies such as the International Organization for Migration, UN Office on Drugs and Crime and UN Children's Fund for anti-trafficking, anti-smuggling and migration deterrence campaigns (European Union 2019: 2). In 2016, the EU awarded Nigeria's National Agency for the Prohibition of Trafficking in Persons (NAPTIP) approximately $11,217,550 for such activities. It has set aside a further $144,338,466 to strengthen Nigerian authorities' capacity to raise awareness about and prevent trafficking, smuggling and irregular migration by Nigerian nationals to the EU (European Commission n.d.). In 2018, the United Kingdom (UK) Department for International Development also committed over $50,000,000 to 'migration and modern slavery' initiatives in Nigeria. Numerous EU countries have also provided funding and technical support for the same mission.

The second arm of the revitalised EU border externalisation measures in Nigeria is the deployment of EU Immigration Liaison Officers (EU ILOs) to that country. At the time of writing, Nigeria is one of just 15 countries worldwide with more than 10 EU ILOs stationed in it (European Parliamentary Research Service 2018: 4). ILOs from at least 15 different EU member states (European Union 2018: 16) are currently stationed in that country. One of the key functions of these EU ILOs is to screen passengers seeking to fly from Nigeria to the EU and thereby prevent those with irregularities from doing so. EU ILOs are also charged with training immigration, anti-trafficking and anti-smuggling agents in Nigeria and facilitating the return and readmission of Nigerian nationals who have been deported from Europe (European Union 2015: 7; European Parliamentary Research Service 2018: 3–4).

These two aspects of the implementation of EU border externalisation measures in Nigeria coupled with the Nigerian government's own desire to address its 'image problem' in irregular migration discourses have resulted in a marked surge in anti-trafficking, anti-smuggling and other security screenings at the two international airports in Nigeria: Nnamdi Azikiwe in Abuja and Murtala Muhammed in Lagos. People travelling via these airports to the EU (and elsewhere) face extensive screening and detention if suspected of being involved in trafficking, smuggling and irregular migration. Such surveillance and control measures are portrayed in mainstream accounts as necessary for preventing the trafficking of vulnerable women and girls.

This chapter critically interrogates this idea and the construction of trafficking from Nigeria to Europe. Using the findings of research with a group of Nigerian women seeking to travel to Europe, the chapter argues that the ongoing anti-trafficking measures in Nigeria demonstrate how easily the construction of trafficking and anti-trafficking measures can be utilised for oppressive actions in the Global South by powerful actors in the Global North. In contrast to the discourse that presents these measures as a means of protecting vulnerable Nigerian women and girls from criminal gangs and traffickers in their own society, the chapter argues that these measures rather victimise the women and leave them susceptible to greater vulnerability.

RESEARCH DESIGN AND DATA COLLECTION

The main aim of this exploratory project which took place between May and June 2018 was to understand the drivers for a recent surge in the involvement of Nigerian women in prostitution in Ghana, as widely reported by the media and authorities in both countries over the last three years (Emmanuel 2017; Tenyah-Ayettey 2017; Ojoye 2018; *WuzupNigeria* 2018; Tijani n.d.). There is a historic and established trend of migration from Nigeria to Ghana for education and commerce primarily (Bosiakoh 2009). However, as observed in the media and public discussions the prostitution dimension is relatively new (*Daily Guide* 2017; *Punch* 2018; Busari 2018; *News Ghana* 2019; *Nigerian Voice* 2019) and therefore requires careful examination. This is the first known academic study of the drivers and dynamics of this phenomenon.

A total of 16 participants were involved in this study, all of whom were women. As discussed later, the participants' homogeneous gender reflects the way in which EU border externalisation measures disproportionately affect women and girls in Nigeria. The group comprised of two smugglers or travel facilitators, two 'fixers' who were in charge of lodgings and other logistics for the travellers and 12 others relying on the smugglers and fixers to facilitate their travels.

Data were collected on the women's life stories, journeys and lived experiences using a combination of unstructured interviews and interpretative phenomenological analysis (IPA). This methodological choice was firstly informed by the fact that the study wanted to gain vivid, in-depth stories about the women's participants' experiences on their own terms instead of those set by the researcher. These are some of the strengths of unstructured interviews and IPA, which situate meaning-making 'at the level of the person-in-context' and produce detailed personal narratives when used effectively (Smith 2004; Palmer et al. 2010: 99; Larkin and Thompson 2012: 102). IPA and unstructured interviews are also very well suited to the study of complex, evolving, ambiguous and emotionally laden topics such as that which formed the focus of this study (Smith and Osborn 2015: 41).

To gain access to participants, invitations were first sent out through a law firm which provides services to Nigerian migrants in the Kumasi where the study stook place. Notices were also posted at bars, food vendors and other businesses inviting interested persons to call the researcher. Those who responded to these invitations were offered one-on-one meetings during which they were given detailed information about the research and a chance to discuss any questions or concerns. Following these meetings, they were asked to reflect on the information and call the researcher once more if they wished to participate in the study.

In line with ethical standards all participants were informed of the voluntary nature of their participation and their right to withdraw from the study at any point without a reason for doing so. At the end of the interviews, the audio recordings were transcribed and analysed in line with the guidance by Smith et al. (2009) and Larkin and Thompson (2012: 106). First, I read all transcripts in detail, returning to the recordings where I felt the tone had not been adequately captured by the text. This was followed by first-line annotation (rapid coding) and a line-by-line coding to identify cumulative patterns and emergent idea families or categories. Finally, I syncretised cumulative ideas and patterns into major themes. Both processes of data collection and analysis were carried out with due regard for the hermeneutics of empathy with that of critique and questioning, as advocated by Smith et al. (2009).

FINDINGS AND DISCUSSION

'A State of Crises in Nigeria'

The primary aim of this study was to explore the factors driving a recent surge in the involvement of Nigerian women in prostitution in some Ghanaian cities. A dominant theme which emerged from the data analyses was that this phenomenon is in part driven by anti-trafficking and anti-smuggling operations that form part of the implementation of EU border externalisation measures in Nigeria. Per the research participants' accounts, women and girls (especially) faced heightened scrutiny and potential detention at international airports in their country. Those whose reasons for travel were deemed suspicious or whose documentation was deemed inauthentic faced detention and their travel plans being jeopardised. This 'crises' as the women described the situation had pushed them to pursue their travel ambitions via Ghana and other alternative routes.

The smugglers explained that they usually provide their clients with genuine or illicitly acquired passports, visas and other documents that would enable them to fly directly from Nigeria to Europe and other destinations and thereby avoid the precarious Sahara and Mediterranean passages. They work with informants in the Nigerian immigration, police and other services to help them avoid detection where possible. As Bella, one of the two smugglers, explained in the following interview extract their costs (and their clients in turn) have risen significantly because their contacts at the airports and elsewhere were now demanding exponentially more money, citing the heightened security: 'Naija airports don make too hot [Nigerian airports have become too hot]. Our guys inside there still help us, but they are always asking for more money, more money every day because of the situation. It's too much!'.

Even when the smugglers and their clients had paid the higher sums and had been given assurances that they could pass through the airports without detection, this was not guaranteed, as Pearl, the other smuggler, noted:

> Seven of our girls were stopped at Abuja just this January. We had already paid our people at Abuja and they said we should bring the girls to fly without any trouble, but they were still arrested. Their families and we had to pay a lot of money to get them out. Nigeria is too risky now.

The theme of crisis was also apparent in the narratives of the women who were using the smugglers' services, as exemplified by Mary's account of being prevented from travelling to Belgium in 2017:

> I was in the line when the two coppers came to remove me. They took me to a room and asked where I was travelling to. I told them. They now ask me where I got my passport and visa from and I told them. They said you're a liar, this is fake and you're going to do '*ashawo*' [prostitution].

Mary was detained for two weeks until her family paid a bribe to secure her release. She was very bitter about the situation not least because of her detention and the amount of money she and her family had lost as payment for her travel documents and the further amount as bribe for her release, but also because she felt she was stopped by the security personnel because she was a young woman. As she explained: 'Two boys that were with us were able to go through. Nobody said anything to them.' Here, we can see that the emphasis on women and girls (and children) as being at particular risk of trafficking produces a perverse scenario where their migratory opportunities are curtailed under the guise of 'rescuing' or 'saving' them from trafficking.

A third dimension of the crises theme that was linked to EU border externalisation measures was in relation to the hostility towards migrants in EU and European visa and immigration policies. Popular immigration rhetoric suggests that people should seek to travel via regular or legal channels. Yet, as Cindy, one of the women using the smugglers' services, explained, she had been driven towards that option after numerous unsuccessful attempts to obtain a UK visa to join her partner in Birmingham:

> The first [visa application] was for visit but they refused that one. He [boyfriend] sent new documents and we tried again, and they refused again. One of our friends advised us to try for a partner visa, but they refused again. They said his money [the minimum income threshold imposed on UK residents applying for partner or spousal visas] isn't enough.

Restricted Mobility: Enhanced Risks and Costs for Travellers

The issues discussed under the theme of crises surrounding the women's efforts to migrate show that the ongoing NAPTIP–EU operations in Nigeria are not only driving travellers towards the services of smugglers but are also shaping new migratory routes across West Africa. According to the women, they knew of others who were trying to migrate to Europe through other countries in the region. Their preference for Ghana was because of language and historical ties between the two countries as Chidinma, one of the travellers, explained:

> Ghana and Naija [Nigeria] are cousins as everyone says. We both speak English and many of our Nigerian people are here already. They know the 'big men' over here we can talk to. It is not the same in Togo or Benin. In Cameroon they always suspect Nigerians! Ghana is okay. You can even get back to Nigeria today, right now, if something happens.

Despite this account, the study found that the women's attempts to fly to Europe via Ghana and other West African countries and thereby overcome the limitations imposed on their mobility by the ongoing EU border externalisation measures in their own country came with heightened risks and costs. Their accounts and the data analysis showed that these extra risks and costs were the other critical factor behind the increasing number of Nigerian women involved in prostitution in Ghana.

Per the smugglers' accounts, it usually costs approximately $5,000 to secure passports, legitimately or illegitimately acquired visas, air tickets and bribes for police, immigration and airport staff to facilitate each client's entry into Europe via Nigeria. However, this cost had increased to approximately $10,000 in view of the new contacts they had been forced to establish in Togo, Benin and Ghana to facilitate their clients' travels across these West African countries. They typically charge $11,500 to $19,000 for their services depending on the client's circumstances, quality of the documents they are being offered, the relationship between the two parties and so on.

Not all travellers can afford all of this amount upfront. In fact, some of the women who were involved in this study were yet to pay the smugglers a penny at the time of the interviews. It is often the case therefore that the two parties enter into an agreement that the traveller will pay the smuggler for their services upon successfully arriving in Europe. The traveller usually agrees to pay interest on the travel costs once they arrive in Europe since the smuggler is going to bear all the financial costs for the journey and stands the risk of losing their money if the journey is curtailed or fails.

As such, instead of the original 'loan' amount of $11,500 to $19,000, the traveller could be required to pay as much as $50,000 once they arrive in Europe. Furthermore, owing to the fact that the traveller will be facing undocumented migrant status upon reaching Europe, there is often a tacit or unspoken acknowledgement between the two parties that paying back the colossal amount would necessitate participation in prostitution and other precarious labour forms. These arrangements have been similarly documented by Mai (2016: 1), who notes that 'contrary to the essentialist obliteration of consent introduced by abolitionist scholarship and policymaking, migrants can decide to endure bounded exploitative deals with people enabling their travel and work abroad in order to meet the economic and administrative (becoming documented) objectives they set for themselves'.

The study found that this migratory arrangement was being replicated on the Nigeria to Ghana route which smugglers and travellers were now using to facilitate their European travel plans. Per their accounts, the smugglers spent an average of $130 on transportation, lodging, meals and bribes to bring a client from Lagos in Nigeria to Kumasi or Accra in Ghana but asked for repayments of $1,300 or nearly tenfold the original cost. Most demand settlement of this amount before providing the required documents or arrangements for the European leg. As such, while women such as those involved in this study had envisaged participating in sex work and other precarious labour in Europe to pay off their debts, they were now having to do so in Ghana or much earlier than anticipated, with the attendant risks.

A Case of 'Victims' (Trafficked) and 'Perpetrators' (Traffickers)?

Mainstream accounts of trafficking, smuggling and 'modern slavery' may read as evidence of 'trafficking'. Such analysis tends to flatten such cases into a simplistic account of evil actors, consummate criminals or organised crime syndicates trafficking helpless and vulnerable women into prostitution and other precarious work in Europe (see Babatunde 2014; International Organization for Migration 2017; Kara 2017; Europol 2018; Nwaubani 2018). However, the participants painted a more complex picture of exploitation, benevolence and interdependencies which problematise portrayals of their relationship as a simple matter of criminals exploiting naïve or hapless victims.

In interviews with the travellers, they often indicated that they were grateful for the smugglers and their services. An instance of this is captured in the interview extract below featuring Vanessa's response to how she views herself vis-à-vis the smugglers and fixers:

> We didn't just rise up and say we were going to Ghana. Do you know anybody in Ghana or Germany? You don't know anybody there. So, someone must help you. For example, how could I have managed to get here if she [the smuggler] didn't help me … I would be back there [Nigeria] still suffering. I am still suffering now but at least I am seeing money also.

All of the travellers knew the smugglers prior to embarking on the journey. Two women worshipped at the same church as Bella, who was well known in their community as a reputable smuggler or travel facilitator. Negotiations of prices and other terms surrounding the trip involved each woman's family and Bella's instead of individual agreements. Owing to such social ties and a desire to maintain her reputation as a trustworthy smuggler, Bella also explained that she felt completely responsible for the safety of the two women. Their relationship was collaborative or reciprocal rather than antagonistic or purely exploitative, as also seen in Mary's account of how she ended up using the services of Pearl who happened to be her senior back in secondary school:

Mary: I didn't even know she had been taking people to abroad. One of the girls in our compound told me that we should go and meet her. When we got to her place and I saw it was Pearl, I now know that everything is OK because she was a good person at School.

S: What if she's changed since then?

Mary: I know her now and I also know her family. My Uncle and mother went with me to see her before we left. At first, she said she will charge $2,000 as deposit before we leave but because she knew me, she agreed that I will not pay until I begin to work. And now I am working, I also paying her back. I trust her and she also trust me.

Social or personal connections are therefore important to these arrangements. The involvement of family members in negotiations, for example, adds another layer of obligation on both parties to meet their part of the bargain: the smuggler to do their best to successfully get the traveller to their agreed destination and the traveller in turn to honour their commitment to paying the agreed amount. Thus, when asked about their knowledge of human trafficking and whether they saw themselves as trafficking victims, the travellers rejected that label, as seen in the following interview extract:

S: Another question which I want to ask – have you heard the term 'trafficking'?
P2:   Yes.
S: I have read from many places … the information I have is that young women such as you who are taken from Nigeria to do this work in Ghana or Italy and other places have been trafficked. Can I say this represents your situation?
P2:   I don't agree with that.
S: Why don't you agree with that?
P2:   Because nobody can force you.
S: Yeah?
P2:   Nobody can force you to do what you don't want to do; they can't just force you and bring you here to do this. It is you – if you wish to do it, you do it, if not you don't come with them. The money they want me to pay is too much, but that's the deal and I accepted.
S: Okay.
P2:   I don't think they are forcing somebody, but I don't know everybody's mind; I only know my own.

For sure, P2 and the other travellers took issue with the amount of money being demanded by their smugglers. The saw it as profiteering and exploitative, and it was the one issue most likely to damage the relationship between the two parties. Their displeasure notwithstanding, they completely rejected being presented as trafficking victims or naïve lambs to the slaughter as usually suggested in dominant anti-trafficking accounts. Most of them (including P2) in fact also rationalised the payments when we discussed the issue further.

S: I am quite amazed that you're paying this much to XXX. Have you discussed a reduction of the amount with her?
P2:   Yes, oo. But after we talked, I also now understand her. When we calculate the money, we do not add any of the kola nut [bribe] that she also has to give the coppers and other people for our safety. Right now, me, me sef [me, for instance], I didn't even give her a penny when we left Nigeria. She paid everything. All I did was to sit in the motor and come to Ghana because I want to go to Germany. It's all her money and I have only been working to pay her back so that we can continue. I understand her case. If it was me I think I will do the same thing. So, I am not happy about the money I am paying but I understand.

This account by P2 and other smugglers corroborated the smugglers' justifications for the exorbitant amounts they demanded after a successful trip. In the concluding section the chapter argues that if clandestine travel facilitation is primarily a business as suggested by some actors (Zhang 2007; Gammeltoft-Hansen and Sørensen 2013; Europol 2018), EU border externalisation measures and other migration deterrence efforts in West Africa unwittingly make the EU a major partner in this venture in this part of the world. The ongoing measures are 'manufacturing smugglers' (Brachet 2018) while efforts to repress their services tend to affect their clients as well (Sanchez 2014).

DISCUSSION AND CONCLUSION

Through the narratives of a group of women trying to travel to Europe via Ghana, this chapter has outlined some of the deleterious impacts of anti-trafficking and anti-smuggling initiatives being pursued in Nigeria as part of EU border externalisation measures and wider migration deterrence operations in West Africa. Notably, the chapter shows that the ongoing measures have led to the creation of a new smuggling route from Nigeria, Benin, Togo and eventually Ghana, where women become involved in sex work and other precarious labour in their attempts to pay off costs linked with their West African travel in order to secure passage for onward travel to Europe.

From the foregoing, while irregular migration facilitation via Nigerian airports may appear to have been minimised or defeated, success claims in relation to the wider EU migration deterrence objectives behind this measure are questionable and also show a lack of understanding of the history of similar interventions. Between 2007 and 2008, enforcement of similar EU border externalisation measures in Senegal saw a decline in the number of irregular migrants crossing from the Senegalese coast to Europe. However, this was accompanied by a concurrent rise in the number of people travelling across the Sahara Desert to try to make the crossing from Libya, Morocco and elsewhere along the North African coast into Europe (Collyer 2007; Maher 2018). In a similar vein, smugglers and travellers from Nigeria have simply found new routes in Ghana and elsewhere in West Africa in response to the efforts to supress their mobility and services.

The findings also show that people smuggling and irregular migration facilitation from West Africa to Europe is extremely diverse, with varying degrees of safety; from the most perilous such as journeys across the Sahara for boat crossings to Europe from the North African coast, to the safer option of using legitimate and illegitimately acquired documents for flights to Europe. The paradox is that even as smugglers are denounced for taking desperate migrants across perilous travel routes (Coonan and Thompson 2005; Europol 2016), the EU and collaborating West African governments are actively dismantling less perilous travel options. In this instance what would have been a seven-hour journey by direct flight from Nigeria takes at least two months, with greater risks and adverse repercussions for the women involved. The women's decisions to use the smugglers' services are also linked with their frustrations with European visa application processes and decisions coupled with wider hostile anti-migrant practices and rhetoric that now permeate many EU countries (Anderson 2013; Andersson 2014; Lemberg-Pedersen 2018). Several participants had entered into partnerships with the smugglers after persistent and unjust visa refusals by EU countries. While the smugglers' motivation may be financial the travellers' motivation is to arrive safely at their preferred destination.

Ultimately, therefore, the costs, risks and other issues surrounding the relationship between travellers and smugglers who participated in this study should also be understood in the larger context of how EU border externalisation measures are impacting on social lives within the affected communities in West Africa. The preoccupation with migration deterrence from Nigeria to Europe means that very limited attention has thus far been placed on how migratory practices within that country and across the region are also being impacted. There is an urgent need for further exploration of these changes to better understand their dynamics.

REFERENCES

Adepoju, A., Van Noorloos, F., and Zoomers, A. (2010) 'Europe's migration agreements with migrant-sending countries in the Global South: A critical review', *International Migration*, 48 (3): 42–75.

Anderson, B. (2013) *Us and Them? The Dangerous Politics of Immigration Controls*. Oxford: Oxford University Press.

Andersson, R. (2014) *Illegality, Inc*. Berkeley, CA: University of California Press.

Andrijasevic, R. (2009) 'Deported: The right to asylum at EU's external border of Italy and Libya', *International Migration*, 48 (1): 148–174.

Babatunde, A. (2014) 'Human trafficking and transnational organized crime: Implications for security in Nigeria', *Peace Research*, 46 (1): 61–84.

Bosiakohl, T.A. (2009) 'Understanding migration motivations in West Africa: The case of Nigerians in Accra, Ghana', *Legon Journal of Sociology*, 3 (2): 93–112.

Boswell, C. (2003) 'The "external dimension" of EU immigration and asylum policy', *International Affairs*, 79 (3): 619–638.

Brachet, J. (2018) 'Manufacturing smugglers: From irregular to clandestine mobility in the Sahara'. *ANNALS of the American Academy of Political and Social Science*, 676 (1): 16–35.

Busari, K. (2018) 'Special report: Inside the apprehensive world of Nigerian sex workers in Ghana', *Premium Times Nigeria*. www.premiumtimesng.com/news/headlines/295077-special-report-inside -the-apprehensive-world-of-nigerian-sex-workers-in-ghana.html

Collyer, M. (2007) 'In-between places: Trans-Saharan transit migrants in Morocco and the fragmented journey to Europe', *Antipode*, 39 (4): 668–690.

Coonan, T. and Thompson, R. (2005) 'Ancient evil, modern face: The fight against human trafficking', *Georgetown Journal of International Affairs*, 6 (1): 43–51.

Daily Guide (2017) 'Nigerian prostitutes flee Tamale' https://dailyguidenetwork.com/nigerian-prostitutes -flee-tamale/

Emmanuel, K. (2017) '32 Nigerian prostitutes arrested at Abeka Lapaz', *Pulse*, 14 November. www .pulse.com.gh/ece-frontpage/sex-workers-32-nigerian-prostitutes-arrested-at-abeka-lapaz/6tcbz72

European Commission (2015) 'European Commission agenda on migration'. https://eur-lex.europa.eu/ legal-content/EN/TXT/?uri=CELEX%3A52015AE4319, last accessed 14 June 2023.

European Commission (n.d.) 'EU emergency trust fund for Africa'. https://ec.europa.eu/trustfundforafrica/ region/sahel-lake-chad/nigeria_en

European Parliamentary Research Service (2018) 'Revision of the immigration liaison officers network'. www.europarl.europa.eu/RegData/etudes/BRIE/2018/621810/EPRS_BRI(2018)621810_EN.pdf

European Union (2015) 'Concept paper on the deployment of European Migration Liaison Officers'. www.statewatch.org/news/2015/nov/eu-council-euro-migration-liason-officers-1343-15.pdf

European Union (2018) 'Revision of the immigration liaison officers network Regulation (EC) 377/2004'. Briefing paper on immigration appraisal. www.europarl.europa.eu/RegData/etudes/BRIE/ 2018/621810/EPRS_BRI(2018)621810_EN.pdf

European Union (2019) 'Promoting better management of migration in Nigeria'. www.eeas.europa.eu/ node/56140_en

Europol (2016) *Migrant Smuggling in the EU*. The Hague: Europol.

Europol (2018) 'Trafficked by voodoo threats: One of the largest operations in Europe rescues 39 Nigerian women'. www.europol.europa.eu/newsroom/news/trafficked-voodoo-threats-one-of-largest -operations-in-europe-rescues-39-nigerian-women

Gammeltoft-Hansen and Sørensen, N., eds (2013) *The Migration Industry and the Commercialization of International Migration*. Oxford: Routledge.

International Organization for Migration (2017) 'UN Migration Agency issues report on arrivals of sexually exploited migrants, chiefly from Nigeria'. www.iom.int/news/un-migration-agency-issues -report-arrivals-sexually-exploited-migrants-chiefly-nigeria

Kara, S. (2017) *Sex Trafficking: Inside the Business of Modern Slavery* (2nd edition). La Vergne: Perseus Book LLC.

Larkin, M. and Thompson, A. (2012) 'Interpretative phenomenological analysis'. In A. Thompson and D. Harper (eds), *Qualitative Research Methods in Mental Health and Psychotherapy: A Guide for Students and Practitioners*. Chichester: John Wiley & Sons, pp. 99–116.

Lemberg-Pedersen, M. (2018) 'Making money from EU's migration policies in Libya EU's outsourced "migration control" to Libya has yielded a humanitarian disaster and billions in profit', *Al Jazeera*. www.aljazeera.com/indepth/opinion/making-money-eu-migration-policies-libya-180102100915057 .html

Maher, S. (2018) 'Out of West Africa: Human smuggling as a social enterprise', *Annals of the American Academy of Political and Social Science*, 676 (1): 36–56.

Mai, N. (2016) '"Too much suffering": Understanding the interplay between migration, bounded exploitation and trafficking through Nigerian sex workers' experiences'. *Sociological Research Online*, 21 (4): 1–14.

News Ghana (2019) 'Young Nigerian girls are engaging in prostitution'. www.newsghana.com.gh/ young-nigerian-girls-are-engaging-in-prostitution-eshun/

Nigerian Voice (2019) 'Prostitution: Ghanaian police arrest 41 Nigerian prostitutes'. www .thenigerianvoice.com/news/270076/prostitution-ghanaian-police-arrest-41-nigerian-prostitutes.html

Nwaubani, A.T. (2018) 'A Voodoo curse on human traffickers', *New York Times*, 24 April. www .nytimes.com/2018/03/24/opinion/sun day/voodoo-curse-human-traffickers.html

Ojoye, T. (2018) 'Ghanaian police arrest 41 Nigerian prostitutes', *Punch*, 1 September. https://punchng .com/ghanaian-police-arrest-41-nigerian-prostitutes/

Palmer, M., Larkin, M., De Visser, R. and Fadden, G. (2010) 'Developing an interpretative phenomeno- logical approach to focus group data', *Qualitative Research in Psychology*, 7: 99–121.

Punch (2018) 'Ghanaian police arrest 41 Nigerian prostitutes'. https://punchng.com/ghanaian-police -arrest-41-nigerian-prostitutes/

Sanchez, G. (2014) *Human Smuggling and Border Crossings*. New York: Routledge.

Smith, J.A. (2004) 'Reflecting on the development of interpretative phenomenological analysis and its contribution to qualitative research in psychology', *Qualitative Research in Psychology*, 1: 39–54.

Smith, J.A. and Osborn, M. (2015) 'Interpretative phenomenological analysis as a useful methodology for research on the lived experience of pain,' *British Journal of Pain*, 9 (1): 41–42.

Smith, J.A., Flowers, P. and Larkin, M. (2009) *Interpretative Phenomenological Analysis: Theory, Method and Research*. Los Angeles: SAGE.

Tenyah-Ayettey, L. (2017) '32 Nigerian prostitutes arrested at Abeka Lapaz', *DailyGuideNetwork*, 14 November. https://dailyguidenetwork.com/32-nigerian-prostitutes-arrested-abeka-lapaz/

Tijani, H. (n.d.) 'Young Nigerian prostitutes in Ghana … High Commissioner "weeps"', *Modern Ghana*. www.modernghana.com/news/809564/young-nigerian-prostitutes-in-ghanahigh-commissioner-wee .html

WuzupNigeria (2018) 'Illegal stay! Ghana to deport 72 Nigerian prostitutes', 23 September. https:// wuzupnigeria.ng/illegal-stay-ghana-to-deport-72-nigerian-prostitutes/

Zhang, S. (2007) *Smuggling and Trafficking in Human Beings: All Roads Lead to America*. Westport, CT: Praeger/Greenwood.

15. Glocalized subjectivities: Egyptian female identities

Amal Treacher Kabesh[1]

The phrase 'The Thing' is used by Toni Morrison (1998) to describe what cannot be grasped about postcolonial conditions. I remain haunted as 'The Thing' persists alongside a perpetual feeling that I cannot deliver because I cannot grasp whatever it is that eludes answering the impossible question – why do colonial socio-political-affective conditions endure and have to be endured? More specifically, what is the impact on female subjectivity of a history of colonization that persists in the present?

My attempt to think through and understand the vexed matter of female colonized subjectivities is troublesome and troubling and is frequently blocked as I am filled with anxieties, fantasies and unprocessed thoughts. I can be filled with pain as I think of women I know, some of whom I love, some I am fond of and others I like or indeed am indifferent to, but I cannot bear witnessing that which I perceive as the enduring impact caused by the persistence of perceptions and opinions that live on from the time of colonization. These perceptions and opinions undermine Egyptian women by rendering us as caricatures that are devoid of complexity, stripped of history and divested of thought.

These attitudes, alas, cannot just be located within the Western media as Western feminist theory tends to ignore feminist history, feminist activity and feminist theorizing that has existed since the middle of the nineteenth century in Egypt. As Abu-Lughod (2013) trenchantly points out, none of us who speak out against stereotyping are quiet on the issue of women's suffering but we are treated as if we are silent and our understanding is wiped out. These commonplace responses ignore the hard work that Middle Eastern feminists have been undertaking for a long time and the importance of these interventions. A robust engagement cannot take place. I hazard a guess that this is due to a profound reluctance to engage with an understanding that all of us exist within ideology, 'that we are all victims, down, to the very depths of our psyches of political and cultural domination' (Modleski 1991, p. 45) and interwoven with this psychic denial is an aversion to know about our own cruelties and aggressions – it is always the other.

In this chapter I draw on feminist postcolonial and psychoanalytic theory to explore Egyptian female subjectivity in relation to the domestic sphere. Feminist postcolonial theory has deepened analysis of many of the themes in Chandra Mohanty's essay *Under Western Eyes: Feminist Scholarship and Colonial Discourses* (1988). These pertinent themes include, but are not confined to, analysis of the differences between women due to class, religion, sexuality and thereby resisting the homogenizing category of 'women' who inhabit societies deemed as 'other'; tracing through the structures that oppress and dominate women; analysing the problematic structures of recognition and/or misrecognition that construct the relationship/s between women from the 'first' world and women from the 'third' world; and understanding the intricate complexes that structure women's resources and capacities to live a life of our own choosing.

This chapter is reliant on these understandings in order to explore agency, identification and patriarchy so that knowledge is extended and understandings are deepened of some aspects of the lived realities of Egyptian women's lives. Female subjectivities are complex, contradictory and dense, women are replete with emotions, fantasies and belief systems that push and pull in different directions. In this chapter I attempt to convey the complexities of Egyptian female subjectivities and the socio-politico-emotional structures that produce and restrict women's lives.

It is, needless to say, important to take an intersectional approach through which the chain of identities – class, religion, ethnicity, gender – are theorized as inextricably linked. While I have found an intersectional approach critical to my thinking, I have become increasingly wary about the use of an intersectional framework. This is for two main reasons that arise from my observations when the term 'intersectional' is used. First, there is a tendency to declare that an analysis is intersectional but there is little follow through on the intricate chain of aspects of subjectivities; second and interlinked with the previous point there is an inclination to prioritize gender as the main category of analysis.

My theoretical preference is to think through location as it is important to take full account of historical trajectories, specific contexts and psycho-political-social location. I assert that it is crucial to understand location, through its various aspects, in terms of history and temporality, place, class, religion and sexuality, as the basis for understanding female subjectivities, whether it be the women who are being thought about or the female reader/observer/scholar.

Thinking through locations does not entail rendering absent an analysis of global consciousness, to borrow a phrase from Roland Roberston (2011). Global consciousness, as I understand the concept, involves the imagination, interaction (whether through 'real' relations to those known or unknown), involvement and observation and engaging with social media. As Robertson argues, even though we tend to 'assume consciously that the local is, so to speak, the local and the global is distant, the "real" circumstance is that one cannot "imagine" a locality or a place in the absence of imagining a context in which the locality or the place is situated' (2011, p. 1340). Let me give an everyday example of food. Road 9 in Maadi (the central road in an area near where I live) is full of cafes and restaurants, some international and some specializing in Egyptian food. The international restaurants, along with cooking programmes on television, have changed the dietary habits of many middle-class Egyptians who now order sushi, hamburgers, caesar salad, pasta and pizza regularly. I used to think this was a middle-class phenomenon until I realized that poor children were asking for money to buy from McDonalds and/or Pizza Hut. These children are conscious of the trends in food, know the cost and want this international cuisine as they reject an Egyptian diet of ta'meya (falafel) and ful (fava beans) that is more healthy and certainly cheaper.

To draw on the phrase 'it's their culture' does not make sense as the boundaries between one culture and another are porous. As Helena Kaler suggests, there is the 'existence of a common imperial-colonial culture based on the networks of translation (or *mis*translations, as the case may be) that function to create a common body of meanings' (2006, p. 331). We cannot avoid the theoretical complexities by asserting that it is all so complex or 'it's their culture', so insisting that it is about culture paradoxically means that culture and socio-political conditions are not thought through as it becomes a closure of exploration. Many feminist scholars working on the Middle East – for example Nadje Al-Ali (2014) – refuse cultural explanations as they perceive the resort to 'it's their culture' not as a way through to understanding complex formations of culture but as a covert means of asserting innate differences and inferiority. While 'it's their culture' is resisted with good reason there remains the question of what do we obliterate or obfuscate by not thinking about culture differently? Suad Joseph puts this theoretical dilemma thus: 'How can the question of culture be addressed with more nuanced constructs to study Arab culture as operating on, between, among, by, for, against, and with Arab women as subjects without essentializing or dissolving culture, so that "Arab culture" informs rather than obstructs analysis of Arab women' (Joseph 2012, p. 13).

I want to be clear that I am in dialogue with the discourses embedded within Western and Egyptian feminisms. These discourses share similarities while simultaneously there are crucial differences and these focus, for example, on questions of religion and nationalism. I aim to engage with addressing the real material and psychic differences that divide us and, from that basis, I can then move, hopefully, towards constituting a somewhat different understanding of recognition. Recognition, I argue, is different if we allow the other to make a difference to the self. I am reliant on Elisabeth Young-Bruehl's exploration of empathy, and that entails allowing the other into the self (1998). It is certainly a different ethics if we attempt to trace through, and understand, the intricate spectrum of similarities and differences as opposed to using another human being (whatever their gender, class, religion or sexuality) to bolster the fragile self. This tendency has historical roots because in the nineteenth century British feminists 'used the image of the oppressed Third World woman and the discourse of universal feminism to further their own domestic political claims' (Kaler 2006, p. 332).

Like many feminist academics I turn to psychoanalysis because cultural and social theory does not deliver fully the answers that helped me understand subjectivities. I focus on psychoanalysis also with a sense of disappointment and dashed hopes but the persistent matter remains: what do those of us who turn towards psychoanalysis want? What is it we hope for and what are we lamenting? In short, to echo Freud's question, what do we want? We search for answers as to why our political and personal lives are not otherwise, as no matter our attempts at liberation our socio-political-affective conditions continue to provoke anger and disappoint.

Fantasy is a critical aspect of human beings and within a psychoanalytic paradigm it accompanies thought, emotions, beliefs and perceptions. Fantasy is one route through which we tie ourselves to one another and enter the social world. Fantasy is not a private matter but rather, as Jacqueline Rose writes, 'like blood, fantasy is thicker than water, all too solid – contra another of fantasy's more family glosses as ungrounded supposition, lacking in foundation, not solid enough' (1998, p. 5). In short, fantasy is shot through all socio-political discourses, narratives and representations that render the socio-political sphere as freighted with that which is biased, partial and limited.

In addition, academic knowledge is laden with emotion, fantasy and ideological beliefs. Personally, the powerful emotions of anxiety, disappointment, loss and regret have been stirred up while I have been attempting to think. Robyn Wiegman urges us not to pretend that what we want from our theoretical frameworks is straightforward and, perhaps more problematically, that theory can help us to grasp the world we inhabit. For Wiegman the issue at stake is 'more simple, if confounding: What am I without them?' (2012, p. 8). There was (is) at work the nuances of 'mood' (Pedwell 2014) and a state of mind that is full of longing and a wishful insistence that 'life' was different and that the consequences of colonization would disappear into the ether. Jackie Stacey, in her article 'Wishing away ambivalence' (2014), explores investments in repair and I have modified her questions as follows: What exactly is the nature of the desired repair? What damage does it indicate? What do we imagine will heal the socio-political wounds that continue to bleed? By wounds I am referring to always being placed as inferior and this representation is internalized profoundly and the *khwagga* (foreigner as superior) complex is taken as fact and perpetuated by both women from the West and Egypt. This ideological viewpoint is internalized from an early age. For example, a young girl (aged about eight) complemented a piece of jewellery that I was wearing and was convinced that I had bought it in London but was profoundly taken aback when I told her that I had purchased it in a shop in Cairo.

A strong theme running through postcolonial and psychoanalytic theory is the viewpoint that the past persists in the present inexorably. There is nothing inevitable about the persistence of the effects of a colonized history and I want to be clear that this is not a natural situation because Egypt as a society and Egyptian people are backward and locked in tradition but rather that for a complex of reasons it has been difficult for Egyptian society to overcome the consequences of its vexed history.

The fantasy that the past is behind us, I argue, works to hold us together and to provide the illusion that investments in the present and future will ensure that the wounds and scars of the past have been overcome. The difficulty is that the past persists in the present and cannot be wished away despite the urgent wish that the past along with the consequent injuries will disappear into thin air. These difficulties are compounded by the socio-political injunctions in Egypt to deny the damage that has taken place alongside the anxieties about who we are, what we have become and what we may be perpetuating. This is unconscious but that does not mean that denial as a state of mind does not have powerful effects on inter and intra relationships.

Hope can be a state of mind that overcomes thinking and can function as 'cruel optimism', to draw on a phrase of Lauren Berlant (2011). Silences can function within and through human beings to conceal and disavow the damage done to, and perpetuated by, the socio-political orders and in turn the destruction inflicted on human beings by other human beings. We are on the whole silenced by our loyalty and visceral need that life is different, better and more optimistic than it actually is, and we are too deeply embedded in the psycho-social mindset of disavowing the damage caused by our colonial inheritance. De Alwis' phrase 'absent presences' offers an important understanding of the way that events, histories, memories, narratives and subjectivities are replete with traces that are inescapable and simultaneously enigmatic as the trace is undecipherable, neither fully present nor fully absent (2009, p. 238). These absent presences, I argue, are silent but these omnipresent shards persist unbidden and unwanted, in beleaguered psyches and in socio-political formations.

Emotions and fantasies unsettle any imagined boundary between self and other, psyche and body, private and public, past and present as emotions and fantasies leak and are porous as they perturb narratives that may be imagined as settled. Boundaries do not exist in any society and I take this as a universal given. In any case, people in Egypt gain their selfhood from their relationships with others and people's sense of self is formed through relationality, obligation and responsibility. In short, identity is claimed through what can be described as a 'we-self' and is based on 'I am, because we are'.

It is a different selfhood that is built from dependency, reliance and bonds. Autonomy and self-sufficiency are not given valency but rather bonds and affiliations are perceived as central to integrity. Western judgements of independent selfhood cannot, should not, be taken as the litmus paper of proper femininity. These judgements are in any case problematic for all women whichever place they inhabit as they are based on a model 'of the rational, deliberative, unified self' and a self that is 'overly rational and overly unified … with no space for fantasy, desire or unconscious investments, or splits or contradictions' (Gill 2007, p. 76). Žarkov (2016) argues stringently that within Western thought women who are deemed as other are reduced to the same ontological category and positioned resolutely as passive, without any real capacity to think and above all are confined to the domestic sphere.

We are all bound to socio-political conditions for our very existence, as subjectivity is always embedded within socio-political and affective structures. The formation of gendered subjectivity does not take place prior to its imbrication in socio-political structures but, rather, is formed within these structures. All human beings are constituted through the subjectivities of others. We internalize and inhabit other people (primarily the family) so that it becomes difficult, if not impossible, to recognize the boundary between self and other. Identification, as Diane Fuss points out (1995), cuts across and through the interior and exterior as identifications take place through various others – parents, grandparents, aunts and uncles, siblings, cousins and friends – and all are significant. We inherit socio-political histories and the values and beliefs embedded in these histories. Most of us are born into families and inhabit their values, beliefs and ways of being, as 'we all find ourselves in particular social worlds. We are placed in certain social classes and communities in specific countries at distinct historical moments. Our desires are forged in these conditions and our choices limited by them' (Abu-Lughod 2013, p. 18). In short, we need to reflect on our experiences, limitations and challenges to being-in-the-world, no matter our geo-politico-temporal location.

The family is perceived by nearly all Egyptians as the foundation of a good society and this ideological belief is shared by the majority of people no matter what gender, class or religion. There is much family pressure on people who are single to marry and to marry young. Marriage and the family are perceived as the foundation for living a satisfying and fulfilling life. Personal networks (university, work, friends) are the way that most people meet and marry. Intermarriage (marrying a cousin) is now less common than previously. Having said that, tradition still counts, as approximately one third of young Egyptians under 30 'mainly poor, young, rural, less educated, and from the more conservative south of the country' marry a relative (El Feki 2013, p. 32). The practice of marrying a relative is based on a profound belief that members of the family will look after one another more than those who are outside of the family network.

Inheritance is a crucial aspect of all subjectivities in Egypt. Women retain the family name even on marriage and this is taken for granted and without question. Moreover, the second name is the father's first name, whatever the gender. For example, my name is Amal Ahmed and on official papers the names of my grandfather and great-grandfather are included. Every time I use my identity card (in Egypt this is frequent) I am reminded of my inheritance that goes back generations. People are proud of their inheritance and are delighted when a person comments that they are like their mother, father, aunt, uncle. The pull into similarity is commonplace and is a source of pride and satisfaction. The identification to be like an important member of the family is embraced and not shunned, as being different and separate from the family evokes distress and anguish.

Looking after other members of the family, especially one's parents, is a responsibility that is taken on without question, and this responsibility is borne mainly by women. It is positive as bonds, affiliations and responsibility are the marks of maturity and central to having an honourable self. Feeling obligated is not uniformly expected across members of the family as the first obligation is to parents and grandparents, then siblings, then aunts and uncles followed by cousins and nephews/nieces. It is women who are expected to undertake any care that is required.

The dominant discourse in relation to marriage is that husbands and wives are equal but different and, from this belief, a leap is made into a value that men and women have different responsibilities, duties and obligations. Women are responsible for the domestic sphere and it is seen as their 'kingdom', where they have power and control. My father was fond of quoting a commonplace Egyptian idiom that 'men are the head of the household and women the shoulders that move it'.

Both my families – birth and marital – are full of women who are well educated (many in my birth family are professors) and carry immense responsibilities for the family – emotional and material. Before any assumptions are made about women and work, working-class women do work – domestic labour or the service industry more generally. At the end of the street where I live two women and their daughters sit day after day apparently patiently selling a few produce from the farm, tolerating some individuals from the middle class arguing with them about the price of the produce they sell and bargaining over the price of their goods. It is impossible to get accurate statistics of the earning power of women because women conceal the amount they earn. They do this so as not to humiliate their husbands (note, protecting men), to save in case their husbands divorce them and to give money to their children. We cannot assume that it is only men that contribute to material conditions (though according to the Qur'an and social custom it is men's responsibility). As always, these injunctions are negotiated. I know women who are the sole providers for their family; for example, one of my sisters-in-law provided all the money for food, housing, clothing and education for her five daughters as their father refused to take any financial responsibility (she is formidable!).

The raising of children falls on the mother, and the children's behaviour, values and moral integrity are her concern and responsibility. Women as wives, mothers and daughters are held responsible for guaranteeing the social order. It is women, this is possibly a universal truth, who have to ensure the good behaviour of their family, that their family members are moral human beings full of socially acceptable thoughts and feelings. Women are held responsible for upholding the honour of the family (honour is the litmus paper by which people are judged) and the question 'does s/he come from a good family' is commonplace. Mothers are idealized and cannot be openly criticized or judged, and any criticism from a child is dismissed as only God can judge a mother. The injunction goes as follows – love God, love your mother, love your mother, love your mother and then love your father.

No account of family life is complete without discussing sexual activity. Sexual intimacy is only acceptable if the couple is married and religiously sanctioned through matrimony; anything else is ''*ayb* (shameful), *ilit adab* (impolite), *haram* (forbidden) – a seemingly endless lexicon of reproof' (El Feki 2013, p. 4). While sex before marriage is forbidden it does of course take place. It is difficult to get official statistics but it is well known that the sewing up of the hymen is a commonplace operation before marriage. Following the first marital night, sheets are checked for blood. This is especially the case in rural Upper Egypt that is more 'traditional' than cities such as Alexandria or Cairo. When I was growing up in a suburb of Cairo, Heliopolis (from the Greek 'City of the Sun'), it was common for sheets to be hung out for neighbours to witness that the bride had been a virgin. Women are held responsible for sexual abstinence before marriage. This is based on a profound contradiction because when it comes to sexual desire women are perceived as rational and as capable of controlling their sexual impulses, unlike men who are understood as irrational and as prone to being easily led by their sexual desires.

The expectation is that husbands should satisfy their wives. Foreplay is encouraged by Prophet Mohammed, who advised that 'kissing is the messenger'. Whether this actually takes place is difficult, if not impossible, to know as people are reluctant to discuss such an intimate matter and sex is perceived as an activity that is not a matter for discussion. We cannot, however, underestimate the role of the media as information is easily accessible. Heba Kotb (a popular sex therapist) had her own TV show called Big Talk and is often on TV programmes discussing sexual matters from masturbation to pornography. Women are now more knowledgeable and perhaps more demanding in relation to sexual satisfaction. In any case, women talk to one another and the accessibility of information must impact on women's desires and fantasies.

Homosexuality is illegal in Egypt and the police can be brutal – raiding clubs and practising anal testing to 'discover' if any anal deformity is a sign of sodomy. Egyptians are alert to, and condemning of, any sign of effeminacy. Homosociality, however, is taken for granted in Egypt – when greeting one another it is common for men to hug, it is normal to see men sitting together in *ahwas* [traditional coffee shops] smoking shishas and drinking tea or coffee and men walk down the street holding hands. Homosociality is taken for granted and perhaps can be a safe cover for homosexual desire. It is perhaps easier for women who identify as lesbian to desire their own gender. For example, it is commonplace for women to masturbate one another; this is seen as 'play' and not intimate desire as 'intercourse' does not take place.

There are non-governmental organizations (NGOs) who struggle for the rights of the LGBT community alongside NGOs who are fighting against the Personal Status Law. It is the Personal Status Law that most fuels much feminist anger in Egypt. The Personal Status Law (legislation that covers marriage, divorce, child custody) is regarded as profoundly restrictive and as a barrier against women gaining full citizenship. The Personal Status Law has a complex history. Under Sadat's rule (President of Egypt from 1970 until 1981 when he was assassinated) many commitments to gender equality were abandoned and yet paradoxically the Personal Status Laws were reformed in favour of women's rights. Known as 'Jehan's Law' (Jehan was Sadat's wife), the Personal Status Law of 1979 accorded women legal rights in marriage, divorce and child custody that granted a woman the right to divorce, the right to travel without her husband's permission and raised the legal age of marriage to 18.

Under the presidency of Hosni Mubarak and the increasing pressures of the ever growing Islamic movement, the Personal Status Law was amended and many of the rights that women had attained were revised. However, soon after these amendments were instituted the law was changed yet again which restored some of the benefits. Feminist organizations and NGOs have become more prevalent since the mid-1980s and alongside this proliferation there is increasing state control (who can sit on the board of these organizations, the insistence by government officials to see minutes and reports).

The Personal Status Law remains controversial and contentious for those on the left of the political divide but not for those deeply involved in the Islamic Revival, and that includes women. Within Islamic movements there is a strong belief that women's spiritual equality to men should be honoured. Alongside this belief in spiritual equality there exist other values: that women should be given their rights according to Islam, that all women should be supported, valued and cared for in marriage emotionally and materially and that if divorce occurs then women and children should be properly supported financially. Women can want a divorce but the resources available limit, if not constrain, getting a divorce. To give three different possibilities: first, a woman wants a divorce and is supported by her family (emotional, social, financial) and her ex-husband is willing to support her and their children financially. This 'support' facilitates a divorce. Second, a woman has the financial resources, albeit limited, to gain a divorce as she and her children can live with her birth family and she is employed. Third, a woman is exceptionally poor and gaining a divorce is impossible due to gross poverty. Gaining a divorce is not just class based in Egypt as religion is key: Copts are not allowed to divorce no matter how miserable and/or aggressive is the marital situation (this is not the case for Catholics or Protestants – only Copts but as Copts constitute 90–95 per cent of the Christian population this affects many unhappy couples).

To state the necessary but obvious we (Western and secular feminists) have to accept that some women might want different things from what Western and/or secular feminists want for them. The differences are products of 'different histories, expressions of different circumstances, and manifestations of differently structured desires' (Mahmood 2005). For example, living in a family, servicing others is perceived as of value and honour is the litmus paper of living a good life. Many Muslim women are shocked that anyone could believe that religion is oppressive, as being a Muslim is deeply meaningful and faith in God is integral to a sense of self and community. There are different values in relation to justice, equality, liberation and what makes for a good life. In any case, we cannot assume that believing in God and being pious is passive as it takes much willpower to accept one's fate and to believe that reward will be delivered in paradise.

The insistence that Middle Eastern women should be agentic and possess autonomy and power is problematic because these responses remain locked within neo-liberal values of subjectivity. The ideology of neo-liberalism is that of freedom, untrammelled choice and autonomy. The independent self is valued; and this is a self that is free of history and the demands of the other and is able to live a life without constraint. Thinking through, and being bound by, discourses of freedom and choice can entail wiping out the intricacies involved in any analysis of female subjectivity so that we (that is, feminists, whether from the West or the Middle East) only perceive agency as that which is 'against custom, tradition, transcendental will, or other obstacles – whether individual or collective' (Mahmood 2005, p. 8). We need to be vigilant in ensuring that feminism is not complicit with neo-liberal notions and values of freedom, autonomy and choice. As I am arguing that all subjectivities are formed within, even if in part, the discourses of neo-liberalism, then there is an inexorable inevitability to this complicity. Our identity itself, along with the values and belief systems through which we make judgements, must always be questioned no matter the risk to the fantasies of ontological security and certainty.

In the novels *The Open Door* (Al-Zayyat 2005) and *Butterfly Wings* (Salmawy 2014), the central female protagonists – Layla and Doha, respectively – are depicted as autonomous individuals free of dependencies, possessing the capacities required to transform their lives. In this way, the representations of these female characters coincide with the neo-liberal discourse that individuals should be autonomous entities, separate from relationships and independent of social strictures. These novels also illustrate that Egyptian women negotiate the normative socio-cultural narratives that are not absorbed without thought.

The Open Door explores the complex dynamics of family life through one central protagonist – Layla. The novel begins with her adolescence and ends in her early to mid-adulthood and tackles issues of sexuality, love and the social expectations that are brought to bear on young women. It explores the internal and external conflicts of this young protagonist in her quest for freedom and to break free from socio-cultural-emotional constraints. It also depicts the pressures on parents to sustain a particular social order through what Layla describes as the 'fundamentals'. The 'fundamentals' relate to marriage, maintaining an outward persona, security, material possessions and, above all, status. The book explores the conflicts within the family and within Layla, together with the political conflicts that are rife (the novel starts in 1946 and ends at some point in the 1950s).

The Open Door is an influential book and the novel *Butterfly Wings* (Salmawy 2014) reverberates with many of the same themes: freedom, sexuality and marriage interwoven through imagined political upheaval. While *The Open Door* is intent on being 'modern' and describing Layla as wanting to leave the 'imprisoning' past behind her, *Butterfly Wings* is more intent on reclaiming the past – which is represented as authentic and, importantly, as a point of difference from the West.

These two novels illustrate that some Egyptian women negotiate socio-emotional conditions and are intent on making a life of their own choosing. This is in contradiction to a tendency from many Western feminists to position women from the Middle East, Sub-Saharan Africa and South Asia as victims of patriarchal and familial structures that are firmly embedded within oppressive socio-political configurations. From this vantage point of superiority, 'brown' women are perceived and represented as in need of rescuing from 'dangerous brown men' (Bhattacharyya 2008) and are securely positioned within a myth of rescue. More problematically, Middle Eastern women are perceived as lacking the 'enlightened consciousness of their "Western sisters", and hence doomed to lives of servile submission to men' (Mahmood 2005, p. 15).

In an attempt to counteract this dominant narrative, some feminist theorists working on the Middle East think through the pressures for women of living in patriarchal societies, taking full account of the nuanced pressures on women (a classic example is Deniz Kandiyoti's 1988 essay 'Bargaining with patriarchy'), while other feminists working on the Middle East and within postcolonial theory (Abu-Lughod, for example) tend to assert the opposite – that women from the Middle East have agency, control and the capacity to resist the oppressive conditions in their lives. Making heroines of women and of the oppressed, however, can obscure the web of local relations which provide the context for and often the limits of resistance.

Freedom is frequently conceived as freedom from constraint and control, especially the demands from other human beings. The demand for freedom and autonomy are problematic in my view for at least two different reasons. First, autonomy is frequently conceived as freedom from relationships with others, as if sovereignty of the self is achievable or even desirable. The complexities and dynamics involved in communicating and being in relationships with others are impediments to be avoided, if not shunned. The yearning to be free from the demands of other human beings is a longing that can be in contradiction with the pleasures and securities that others provide.

Deniz Kandiyoti's article (1988) provides a broad-brush yet textured approach to understanding women's strategies towards patriarchy. Kandiyoti argues that some women in certain patriarchal conditions can optimize their life options 'with varying potential for active or passive resistance in the face of oppression' (1988, p. 274). Women's strategies, she argues, are always played out in the context of 'patriarchal bargains' and these arrangements (conscious and unconscious) act as implicit scripts that define, limit and inflect options (1988, p. 275). It is important to point out that defining patriarchy is not straightforward and cannot be wrapped up as if we all know what patriarchy means and how it functions, as it is not trouble-free 'to put one's finger on how power works' (Abu-Lughod 2013, p. 6). There is always acceptance, accommodation, adaptation and collision of interests alongside conflicts over resources, rights and responsibilities (Kandiyoti 1988, p. 285).

Men are embedded within patriarchal structures and are the main beneficiaries of, and profoundly invested in, these psycho-political structures. Men, however, do not always support other men unquestioningly and I give an example from fiction. I could provide many similar instances from my personal experience but the people involved could be easily identified. In the novel *Butterfly Wings* Doha, after many years in a very unhappy marriage, is thinking through whether or not to divorce her husband. When she is talking with her brother about her dilemma he responds with unconditional support and says 'I'm your brother. I can't abandon you or let you down', and then he continues:

> We only live once, so we have to enjoy it. There's no reason to put up with unhappiness as long as we can still change it. This might seem strange, but in all honesty I tell you that you must ask for a divorce. I promise you I'll back you up all the way. (Salmawy 2014, p. 115)

Patriarchy is subtle and changes over time as it adapts to fluctuating socio-economic conditions. Currently, due to the dire economic conditions in Egypt, more women are working and, simultaneously, more men are forced to stay at home. Many men are now required to undertake childcare while the women go out to work. This changing landscape in the domains of men and women effects the experiences and perceptions of young people as they witness the shifts in economic power. While this, at one level, can be seen as positive, it can, of course, lead to an entrenchment of patriarchy, as men fear the possible loss of status, power and control. We need to be vigilant in ensuring that we do not circumvent an understanding that men are also positioned within and caught up in patriarchal structures due to their age, class or profession. Nor should we bypass the knowledge that it can be men who protect women by providing them with an education, prevent female circumcision, step in to refuse a marriage arrangement that is in the process of being organized or support their daughters in gaining a divorce. Who holds power in a family is always complex and not always easily discerned and understood. For example, my youngest stepdaughter, despite being the youngest by far of the four adult children, is the 'patriarch' of the family and all of her immediate family (including her father) leap to do her bidding.

Women frankly can also perpetuate damage and harm. Part of the politics of recognition must consist of perceiving and understanding when it is women who oppress other women through the quest for power and status. Spivak (1999) is clear that it is important to be attentive to the particular balances of power and power between women. This is never unidirectional – from the privileged to the marginal – but circulates within and across all self–other relations (Hemmings & Treacher Kabesh 2013). Thinking through political identities throws us up against our unconscious and conscious investments in power, which is frequently gained through a subordination of 'the other'.

Older women can control and exert authority over younger women (sisters, daughters, daughters-in-law) and, in this way, the internalization of power circulates inexorably. Everyday behaviour may take the form of creating or perpetuating the continued subjugation of other women, for example, the exploitation of those who provide domestic services such as porters, women who clean and young children who shop for small items. Exploitation takes various forms such as underpayment, rudeness, that can, on occasion, verge on verbal abuse, and the persistent suspicion of theft.

Women hold power albeit within the domestic sphere but let us not imagine that Egyptian men hold power in the public sphere. Men humiliated and shamed throughout colonial times and in the present have been diminished and lessened. This humiliation persists – recently, near where I live, there was a car accident between an American who works at the Embassy and an Egyptian. By all accounts it was the American at fault but it was the Egyptian who was held responsible and held to account. Due to colonization and postcolonial conditions, I do think that women have been less damaged – psychically, socially, politically; I know this is contentious, and in any case how can it be evidenced, but I want to explore this as a possibility. As granddaughters, daughters, sisters, wives of men who have been colonized we protect them, we pretend they have power, we collude in their sense of themselves as having authority. We are all implicated in this intricate fabrication.

Being haunted is a socio-political-emotional necessity as it confronts all of us (no matter our heritage) with knowing how we have internalized socio-political-personal histories (Butler 2005). In addition and perhaps more important is how we are complicit in, and perpetuate, inexorable structures of domination and oppression, and that means being aware of when women of colour are silenced and unable to speak and when white women take up space by claiming victimhood and thereby denying that all of us are wounded but with different effects and consequences. Being haunted involves the awareness of the ways that even feminism as theory, as activism and as ideology can constrain and paralyse women of colour. The question posed by Gail Lewis and Clare Hemmings, 'Where might we go if we dare'? (2019), is the most pertinent question and involves letting go of assumptions, moving into a different relationship of recognition, knowing that being white involves privilege, power and status. I have attempted in this chapter to convey that Egyptian female subjectivities are intricate as we are full of pushes and pulls, conflicts, loyalties, we live complex lives and do so sometimes with acceptance, resignation, humour, resentment, complicity and resistance. We live within and through a palimpsest of histories and inheritances while simultaneously we move towards forging our lives with commitment and energy. Recognizing the complexities of female subjectivities is one way through to living otherwise.

NOTE

1.   Tragically, our dear friend and colleague, Amal Treacher Kabesh, passed away very suddenly only two months after completing this chapter. Amal will be missed terribly, both professionally and personally, by so many of us. We are heart-broken and also feel honoured to be able to include one of her last – of her many – contributions to scholarly debate in this handbook.

REFERENCES

Abu-Lughod, L. 2013, *Do Muslim Women Need Saving?*, Harvard University Press, Cambridge, MA.
Al-Ali, N. 2014, 'Reflections on (counter) revolutionary processes in Egypt', *Feminist Review*, 106 (1): 122–128.
Al-Zayyat, L. 2005, *The Open Door* (transl. M. Booth), American University in Cairo Press, Cairo.
Berlant, L. 2011, *Cruel Optimism*, Duke University Press, Durham, NC.

Bhattacharyya, G. 2008, *Dangerous Brown Men: Exploiting Sex, Violence and Feminism in the War on Terror*, Zed Books, London.

Butler, J. 2005, *Giving an Account of Oneself*, Fordham University Press, New York.

De Alwis, M. 2009, '"Disappearance" and "displacement" in Sri Lanka', *Journal of Refugee Studies*, 22 (3): 378–391.

El Feki, S. 2013, *Sex and the Citadel: Intimate Life in a Changing Arab World*, Chatto & Windus, London.

Fuss, D. 1995, *Identification Papers: Readings on Psychoanalysis, Sexuality, and Culture*, Routledge, New York.

Gill, R. C. 2007, 'Critical respect: The difficulties and dilemmas of agency and "choice for feminism"', *European Journal of Women's Studies*, 14 (1): 69–80.

Hemmings, C. & Treacher Kabesh, A. 2013, 'The feminist subject of agency: Recognition and affect in encounters with "the Other"', in S. Madhok, A. Phillips, K. Wilson & C. Hemmings (eds), *Gender, Agency and Coercion*, Palgrave Macmillan, Basingstoke, pp. 29–46.

Joseph, S. 2012, 'Thinking intentionality: Arab women's subjectivity and its discontents', *Journal of Middle East Women's Studies*, 8 (2): 1–25.

Kaler, H. 2006, 'Inscribing gender in the imperial context: The "woman question" in nineteenth century Egypt', *HAWWA*, 4 (2–3): 328–355.

Kandiyoti, D. 1988, 'Bargaining with patriarchy', *Gender and Society*, 2 (3): 274–290.

Lewis, G. & Hemmings, C. 2019, 'Where might we go if we dare: Moving beyond the "thick, suffocating fog of whiteness" in feminism', *Feminist Theory*, 20 (4): 405–421.

Mahmood, S. 2005, *Politics of Piety*, Princeton University Press, Princeton, NJ.

Modleski, T. 1991, *Feminism without Women*, Routledge, New York.

Mohanty, C. 1988, 'Under Western eyes: Feminist scholarship and colonial discourses', *Feminist Review*, 30 (Autumn): 61–88.

Morrison, T. 1998, *Playing in the Dark: Whiteness and the Literary Imagination*, Harvard University Press: Cambridge, MA.

Pedwell, C. 2014, 'Cultural theory as mood work', *New Formations*, 82: 47–63.

Robertson, R. 2011, 'Global connectivity and global consciousness', *American Behavioral Scientist*, 55 (10): 1336–1345.

Rose, R. 1998, *States of Fantasy*, Clarendon Press, Oxford.

Salmawy, M. 2014, *Butterfly Wings* (transl. R. Cohen), American University in Cairo Press, Cairo.

Spivak, G. 1999, *Critique of Postcolonial Reason: Towards a History of the Vanishing Present*, Harvard University Press: Cambridge, MA.

Stacey, J. 2014, 'Wishing away ambivalence', *Feminist Theory*, 1: 39–45.

Wiegman, R. 2012, *Object Lessons*, Duke University Press: Durham, NC.

Young-Bruehl, E. 1998, *Subject to Biography: Psychoanalysis, Feminism, and Writing Women's Lives*, Harvard University Press, Cambridge, MA.

Žarkov, D. 2016, 'Co-option, complicity, co-production: Feminist politics on war rapes', *European Journal of Women's Studies*, 23 (2): 119–123.

16. The American guitar in the global market: worldwide flows of people, commodities and symbols

Frédéric Moulène

Since the early twentieth century, American popular music has consistently produced impressive, original forms enjoying great international success: jazz, blues, country, rhythm and blues, rock and roll, soul and funk are some of the most prominent cases in point. This is all the more striking considering that such a young nation might have been expected to harbour a kind of cultural inferiority complex in comparison with the longer, (classical) music histories of the great European states (Demierre, 1986). This remarkable artistic vitality has significantly contributed to the power of the United States (US) and fascinated people all around the world, at least since the end of the Second World War in 1945. The development of the mass media and the US military presence in the Western Bloc boosted the global spread of new forms of musical expression. While the Parisian jazz clubs of Saint-Germain-des-Près are a famous example, the 'invasion' – or movement in the opposite direction – of the US by young British musicians, in the 1960s, who played a brand of rock and roll that directly derived from Black blues, is an even more telling development in (multi-directional) musical 'diffusion'.

This chapter aims to shed light on the contribution of the musical instruments industry to cultural globalization. Many studies have shown that the American melting pot has given risen to new artistic forms (Davis, 2003; Thompson, 2010) but very few so far have addressed the key role of instruments such as the guitar in the cultural diffusion process. Beyond the mere flow of goods that characterizes globalization, the role of US instrument makers in this process, by renewing techniques and designs and by drawing on skills developed by various communities who made the US their home, is particularly interesting to consider. The perspective adopted here lies at the conceptual and thematic 'crossroads' of international trade, human encounters and cross-cultural exchanges with a symbolic dimension. It should also be noted that many European influences informed the making of string instruments. In a supreme irony, string instruments originally designed in Italy, Germany or Spain were refashioned in places like New York or Chicago and went on to travel back to the old continent in their newer incarnations, thus promoting the prestige of the US everywhere and serving as models for European instrument makers. Since the 1960s, many Japanese companies have filled gaps in the guitar market, first by releasing good – if not excellent – copies of American models, while at the same time, Epiphone and other famous brands started to relocate to reduce production costs. These are yet other instances of *circulation*, involving a wide range of phenomena: the mixing of people, cultures and goods, the transformation of a musical style (i.e., Black blues was morphed into white rock and roll, which in turn led a wide audience to rediscover blues) and of music instruments. This chapter is aimed at exploring all these facets of globalization, at the intersection of popular culture, migrations, mixing and the industrial process. The guitar (and related string instruments) has a particularly significant standing in that it brings together all of these facets, symbolizing the richness of American popular music: the acoustic guitar evokes the vast wilderness spaces celebrated in the country's folklore, and the electric guitar brought us the energy of rock by taking advantage of a superpower's technological breakthroughs. Today, the guitar is an entirely globalized symbol of America (even if it is now widely produced in Asian factories), associated with dreams, freedom, peace and protest, and even sometimes authenticity and sustainability. In the following, the birth of the American guitar in the context of American traditional music is first recounted; second, the acceleration of musical circulation in parallel to the backdrop of the country's rise to global power is analysed, with a focus on the guitar's key role in that process; and lastly, the impact of globalization on the production and representation of the instrument and its symbolic implications are discussed.

THE BIRTH OF THE AMERICAN GUITAR AND ITS SOCIAL BACKGROUND

The original context in which American traditional music emerged was characterized by a melting pot shaped by a number of circulations: the sale of commodities, monetary flows and social relationships whose principle is not economic, even if they allow the market to operate (Steiner, 2011: 109). In this regard, the first exchanges between the people who contributed to the foundation of the US, especially in the context of the triangular trade, deserve mention. In 1865, at the time of their emancipation, 4 million Black people were living in the country, having been deported and enslaved between 1620 and 1810 (Behrendt & Rawley, 2005). Beyond their demographic weight and their economic contribution as labourers, they brought their singing and dancing styles to the 'new' continent. This 'African source' gave America some of its leading musical cultures. The first musical expressions of the African American people were entirely or almost entirely vocal – worksongs and spirituals, followed by gospel – since they lived in deprivation and had likely not been allowed to cross the Atlantic with their own possessions, let alone musical instruments. As the Black Codes (from 1830) prohibited percussions (Ferris, 2009) so as to prevent the scattered slaves not only from playing music but also from communicating, some built koras (West African stringed instruments resembling banjos) from memory (Carlin, 2016: 11–28). Black people were so closely identified with these instruments that they were a subject of stereotypes and jeers, particularly in minstrel shows. This is why the guitar became an instrument of choice for many African American musicians (Herzhaft, 2011: 146–148), as banjos were redesigned by instrument makers to fit the new musical styles of the early twentieth century, such as jazz with the tenor model and bluegrass or country with the five-string one. For its part, the guitar travelled to Mexico and other areas under Spanish influence. It offered several advantages, being cheap, easily transportable and versatile for accompanying vocalists. The guitar was thus favoured by many bluesmen: it could be used in a percussive manner, as in the flamenco tradition, but also using a fingerpicking style in order to highlight the bass strings in a way that suited rhythm-oriented African music. The blues, which appeared between 1885 and the very early twentieth century (Gates, 1965), was rooted in African music (Kubik, 1999)[1] and, more accurately, African spirituality, which could give listeners strength to endure hard physical labour, oppression, loneliness and separation from their communities and families (Herzhaft, 2005: 236).

The guitar also played a key role in intercultural mixing by providing many opportunities for dialogue between black and white cultures: many musical elements from different origins *circulated* in this way and were amalgamated, such as Delta blues, Hillbilly country, Celtic tunes, Neapolitan Tarantella and Slavic polkas. Sometimes, as happened with rock and roll, the fusion led to the birth of a new genre. Black and Native Americans were also in contact, linked by the common experience of extreme discrimination. There are many reasons today to think that the pentatonic scale of blues came from Asia rather than Africa (Herzhaft, 1981: 8). Native artists would later play guitar blues (Cain, 2006), and sometimes influenced white rockers.[2] Overall, the intercultural entanglements are so complex that it is often very difficult to pinpoint singular sources.

The country's economic dynamic contributed to the circulation process as the music market expanded along with the rise of the phonograph and of the recording industry. One of the first landmark blues records was *Guitar Blues* by Sylvester Weaver, released in 1923 (Oakley, 1997: 146). After 1918, the northward migration of Black workers intensified, fuelled by the urge to escape deep-seated racism in the South and by the labour demand in industrialized areas. Unfortunately, this often turned out to be a trap: many Black people did not escape violence and were confined to ghettos in the North, working draining jobs on assembly lines. However, the big cities were home to a more diverse melting pot, and Black musicians discovered such instruments as the Irish fiddle and the Italian mandolin.[3] In addition, large urban and industrialized areas (mainly New York and its region, Boston, Chicago and Los Angeles) were sources of innovation and emulation, including in instrument making. Gibson, which was founded in Michigan in 1902, created a mandolin that followed the violin design (a carved single block of wood with a flat bottom), a technique that many European music makers adopted in the following years (Carter, 2017). Many successful companies were launched by immigrants such as the Germans Christian F. Martins, Oscar Schmidt and Friedrich Gretsch,[4] the Czech Dopyera brothers and the Greek Epaminondas Stathopoulos, who established Epiphone in 1928, but also the Italian John D'Angelico and the Swiss Adolph Rickenbacker in the early 1930s. The great challenge was to give the guitar a more powerful sound, especially to be heard in a band setting (banjos, pianos, woodwinds and brass instruments were louder). Martin was among those that made the most significant effort to raise the instrument's acoustic volume, in particular by increasing its size – the dreadnought model appeared in 1916 (Dudley, 2014: 91) and, 11 years later, National String Instrument released the resonator guitar (Bacon, 2012: 40), with a full metal body and a set of aluminium cones which substantially amplified the sound. Above all, Rickenbacker was a pioneer in the field of electric instruments with its 1931 lap-steel model (Hatschek & Wells, 2018: 110) before Gibson's 1936 ES-150. While the music market was not immune to the consequences of the Great Depression, it demonstrated a remarkable ability to adapt: in addition to steady productivity gains since the dawn of the century, manufacturers catered to low-income customers with a wide array of cheap instruments made with modest materials, especially birch wood. Robert Johnson and many other bluesmen probably started playing with such guitars; a number of companies such as Stella, Kay and Kalamazoo prospered in this way (Carter, 2018: 143, 174).

In parallel, the rise of mass communication stimulated flows of individuals, goods and cultures: ambitious musicians now went on country-wide tours, mail-ordered their guitars[5] and were exposed to an ever growing number of local influences – i.e., blues was strongly jazz-tinged in New Orleans, blended with French/Acadian and Caribbean features in Louisiana and Spanish/Mexican accents in Texas (Herzhaft, 1981: 35–41).

These factors all contributed to the rise and renewal of the guitar in America, particularly for country and blues music. The concept of transnational circulation is highly relevant to account for the dynamics of popular American music, in which the guitar played a crucial role. However, until 1945, only jazz music was en vogue in Paris and London and the guitar, even in such luxurious incarnations as the Gibson Super-400 or the Martin D-28, was far from the limelight yet.

THE GUITAR IN THE POST-WAR BOOM: A SIGNIFICANT INSTRUMENT OF AMERICAN HEGEMONY

By 1945, the US had reached an outstanding position of international hegemony, after its crucial contribution to winning the Second World War, the Marshall Plan and the installation of military bases as the Cold War ramped up. Alongside its financial, technological and geo-political resources, Americans were well prepared to mobilize soft power to persuade other countries to stand with and behind the US (Nye, 2004). Exporting popular music also served this purpose. Every economic condition was met for this to be effective: Europe and Japan had to recover ahead of the Eastern Bloc, people were starved for entertainment after the long years of war and deprivation and consumer demand was a major preoccupation for both Keynesian economists and trade unions. During the post-war boom, people used newly discretionary income to buy transistors, turntables, records and television sets.

At the same time, the guitar – increasingly electric – spread quickly across popular genres: jazz with Wes Montgomery and Charlie Christian, country with Chet Atkins, blues with B. B. King and John Lee Hooker. Rhythm and blues appeared in the 1950s with Little Richard and Fats Domino, who paved the way to rock and roll: even though piano and brass were still front and centre, the guitar had what it took to sublimate the rhythmic dimension of this new sound, especially considering it was still being improved technically. New models were so well designed – like the 'solid-bodies' Fender Telecaster (1949) Stratocaster (1954) and Gibson Les Paul (1952) – that they remain popular even today[6] (Gruhn & Carter, 2010). Likewise, the electric bass (in particular Fender's 1951 Precision Bass) emerged at the expense of the upright bass and major improvements were made in the domain of amplification. The new sound would soon be showcased in stunning ways in such works as Ike Turner's *Rocket 88* (1951), Bill Haley's *Rock around the Clock* (1952), Chuck Berry's *Maybellene* (1955) and Eddie Cochran's *C'mon Everybody* (1958) (Pirenne, 2011: 26).

In the US itself, however, the charts were also segregated (with Black musicians confined to the 'Race records/Rhythm and blues' category and their white counterparts listed under 'Popular'), and racial prejudice was still a strong barrier to the development of a mixed audience and of a single market (Herzhaft, 2005: 243–244). But the problem was not insurmountable: in 1955, Fats Domino's *Ain't That a Shame* was a hit in both chart categories, which would at last be merged in 1963. Other factors came into play. First, American popular music was boosted by cultural go-betweens, who were able to adapt music to the taste of the masses – especially white audiences. Some charismatic white singers gave it a wider reach by covering songs by Black musicians (Herzhaft, 1981: 88)[7] and by playing with Black artists.[8] The producer Sam Phillips, from Sun Records in Memphis, showed great artistic vision when he bet on Elvis Presley in 1954, recording his *That's Alright Mama* based on a blues song by the Black musician Arthur Crudup. Europe had been far more open to Black artists since the Virginia Minstrels had arrived in 1843 (Cugny, 2014: 68); in Paris and London, many were fond of 1920s jazz, and a number of instrument makers adopted the American banjo. The

British skiffle was a remarkable mix of country, blues and jazz (Brocken, 2003) that primed United Kingdom listeners to appreciate American music. Many young Britons, like their American contemporaries, had a revelation when they heard 'Elvis' for the first time on the radio and then saw him on television. The 'British invasion' of the US started in 1964–1965 – with the first Beatles tours and the Rolling Stones recording at Chess, the famous blues label, in Chicago – and continued with The Who, The Animals and others.[9] These journeys offered opportunities for musicians on both sides of the Atlantic to meet. Strikingly, the European enthusiasm for American popular music boosted the US's positive image, despite the country's racial problems (Everett & Riley, 2019: 95; Selvin, 2016) and the intervention in Vietnam. Jimi Hendrix made a career in England and John Lee Hooker, who was ignored in the 1950s by a US Black audience that preferred soul music, reaped the rewards of the up-and-coming British musicians' fascination with the blues.

The guitar played a key role in this musical revolution. In the 1950s and 1960s, American instruments were difficult to find and unaffordable for most European musicians. But a myriad of European companies emerged or expanded, selling cheap instruments, like Burns in England (the maker of Vox and Marshall amps), Höfner in Germany, Eko in Italy and Hagström in Sweden (Bacon, 2006). Many rising rockstars had played their first chords in their teens and purchased American models during their travels. Even the Soviet Bloc was not left out of this phenomenon. As propaganda denounced the 'bourgeois decadent music' broadcasted on Radio Free Europe, records from the West were secretly peddled and the Eastern regimes resigned themselves to regulating the movement instead of repressing it (Bayou, 2006). In 1967, the Rolling Stones were allowed to play in Warsaw, and B. B. King performed in the Soviet Union in 1979. Starting in the 1960s, Jolana (Czechoslovakia), Musima (German Democratic Republic) and Tonika (Soviet Union), among others, sold electric guitars which were seen as symbols of freedom (Ramet, 2019), like Woody Guthrie, Pete Seeger, Joan Baez or John Lennon were in the West. Still, the guitar-manufacturing sector played 'the game of capitalism' early on, partaking in an endless race for innovation and pursuing mergers, acquisitions and concentration strategies; in 1957, Gibson bought its old rival Epiphone and in 1969 was itself acquired by a non-musical investment group at the risk of sacrificing quality (Carter, 1995).

GLOBALIZATION AND THE GUITAR: CIRCULATION COMES FULL CIRCLE AND EXPERIENCES A RENEWAL

The recent era has seen the guitar's circulation take on a global scale. As rock music has travelled the world over, with its gigantic concerts in overcrowded stadiums, the music instrument industry faces worldwide competition.

In the early 1970s, Led Zeppelin and Deep Purple successfully toured in Japan. The best local companies were already able to offer some excellent copies of American models at low prices, driving Gibson to prosecute Ibanez in 1977 for unfair trade (Bacon, 2006: 201–214). As in the car production sector, American instrument makers found it increasingly difficult to compete with Japan. Epiphone, which morphed in a kind of subsidiary of Gibson, moved its production plants to Japan to reduce costs and take advantage of the local workforce (1970). However, Japan in turn became expensive and executives decided to relocate most of the production to South Korea in the late 1980s, then to China and other parts of Asia at the turn of the twenty-first century. The other rivals pursued similar strategies. Fender continued to make its premium products in the US, the mid-range ones in Japan and the entry-level ones in Mexico, while its own 'budget brand' Squier relocated production entirely to China and Indonesia. Most European and Japanese companies fell in line with such market tricks (i.e., Höfner and Yamaha make their best instruments domestically and the others in China). This has become a truly global market: as the guitar is an object of mass consumption, companies need labour-intensive capacities, low wage costs and flexibility in a context of continuous competition, as well as access to the large and dynamic Asian market. There is a startling price gap between a very limited edition of the (American-made) Epiphone Texan, which retails at around 2500€, and the Chinese high-end model DR 100 NT (under 150€).[10] This can be read positively in terms of a democratization of music practice, although a critical view would denounce such marketization of music (Adorno, 2020). There is, still, a case to be made for the vitality of the guitar in the digital age. There are continuing reasons to believe that the guitar makes people dream in a way no other instrument does. Traditional instrument making still exists and tries to escape the confines from a 'niche market' by offering a rare level of quality to as wide an audience as possible. Many companies appear to refuse to 'downsize', like the most Spanish and East European brands, Godin in Canada and Deering Banjos in California, drawing on high levels of skill, experience and wood resources. The prestige attached to brand names of the past is coveted and often appropriated; for some 20 years, the vintage market has been breaking records. In China, the Loar company uses the name of Lloyd Loar, who was one of the designers of Gibson's mandolin in the 1920s. Choosing an American brand name was already the strategy of countless Japanese companies in the 1960s, with Coral, Winston or Lafayette (Meyers, 2015). After the South Korean Cort which started business in 1973, Eastman, from Beijing, offered hand-made mandolins from 1992. Moreover, many old and iconic brands founded in the 1920 or 1930s have been relaunched: Regal, Paramount, Silvertone or Recording King designed in the US all now produce in Asia. In 2018, the Singaporean company BandLab Technology resurrected Harmony, a venerable brand started in Chicago in 1892 and ceased in 1975, while the Japanese competition was getting tough. Thus, music makers, even Asian, spotlight their 'American genuineness' and fight for the (iconic) symbols in question. The American companies Kentucky, Alabama, Tennessee and Appalachian expressly refer to the mythical wilderness, even if the instruments they produce are imported from the Far East. Such 'fights' for symbols are striking: the Chinese/Taiwanese Walden guitars are named after the poet Henry David Thoreau (1817–1862), who is often seen as a standard bearer for environmentalists and pacifists, at a time when global warming casts doubt over the sustainability of the wood used in the industry, even for the leading company Gibson, which has been prosecuted for illegal wood traffic.[11] Some might call this 'greenwashing', which is further proof that the guitar industry is a good representative of wider, economic dynamics.

Other manufacturers prefer a different strategy, such as Yamaha and K. Yairi in Japan. In 2011, Takamine offered the remarkable 'Yozakura' guitar celebrating the colours of the Japanese springtime.[12] For its part, Ibanez, founded in Nagoya, takes its brand name from its Spanish supplier Salvador Ibáñez from which Japan imported acoustic guitars in its early years (1929–1939). The reputation of the Spanish guitar was probably a strong argument in favour of such a choice and Epiphone, too, followed a similar logic with its Caballero model in the 1960s. In Europe, Central and Eastern European countries have also carved out a place of their own as instrument makers. Even if the names of the Czech Furch and the Polish Maruszczyk do not sound Anglo-Saxon, they are broadly based on the American models, respectively Fender and Martin.

Japan and Korea are still fascinated by the guitar and the musical genres in which it has played a key role. The jazz festivals of Mont-Fuji and Seoul foreground some local stars, and large audiences of local fans continue to listen to Charlie Patton playing on vintage American guitars as well as on the traditional shamisen. Great British and American guitarists like Buddy Guy, John Mayall, Taj Mahal and Keb Mo played at the Mahindra Blues Festival (Mumbai, India) in the 2010s.

By comparison, Africa seems to stay outside the guitar industry and is still highly dependent on imported instruments. The festivals of Saint-Louis (Senegal) and Cape Town (South Africa) offer some important opportunities for local musicians who adapt blues or rock to their own taste, mixing guitar with ngoni (a kora-like). Mali is a breeding ground for many talented blues musicians. Thus, Ali Farka Toure played with the American Taj Mahal or Ry Cooder and earned a Grammy Award in 1994; Boubacar Traoré performed with Corey Harris and Leyla McCalla and Habib Koité with Eric Bibb. But the most striking symbol of circulation between America and the lands where its former slaves came from is offered by the Senegalese Guelel Kumba and Eric Deaton with their project *Afrissippi*. The 'Tuaregs bluesmen' emerged in the 1980s, played on electric Fender and often claimed in their songs that there was a parallel between the history of America and their own – one of political exclusion and non-recognition.

CONCLUSION

The guitar has played a major role in the circulation of American popular music. After a long history as a craft item, the six-strings instrument found worldwide success when blues and jazz artists picked it up in the early twentieth century. Arguably, no other instrument has circulated this extensively and been so well suited to popular music once it had been adapted to stereophony and mass broadcasting. Some blues tunes that were originally played in obscure juke joints are today played by the Rolling Stones in huge stadiums during shows that are sometimes streamed worldwide. Above all, the guitar is the star instrument of rock and roll, the music that has encapsulated youth, its emancipation and its dreams of freedom. The guitar as a symbol appears on a huge number of records and films, in the company of many artists – Elvis Presley's *Guitar Man* (1967), Nicholas Ray's *Johnny Guitar* (1954), the *Zorro* series also released in 1957 and even in Japanese manga with Goldorak's Actarus (1978). In the 1960s, the pop boom both led to the mass production of recordings and gave the guitar a mass audience. The great French luthier Jacobacci once admitted that everyone had started wanting an American guitar (Grenet, 2007). Today, guitars, flat mandolins, bluegrass banjos and Hawaiian ukuleles fuel a prosperous business widely influenced by US mythology. But only the guitar may be seen as the perfect globalized instrument symbolizing America as an object of dreams, purported freedom,[13] as a symbol of both peace and protests[14] and even sometimes authenticity and sustainability.

NOTES

1. See also the documentary *Feel Like Going Home* by Martin Scorsese (2003).
2. See Catherine Bainbridge's film *Rumble: The Indians Who Rocked the World* (2017).
3. Many Black bluesmen were great violin players, like Big Bill Broonzy (1903–1958), or mandolinists, like Yank Rachell (1903–1997).
4. They respectively started their businesses in 1833, 1871 and 1883.
5. The most famous company of this kind was probably Sears & Roebuck, established in 1892 in Illinois.
6. Thus, many recent innovations did not add a lot to the basic concept: neither the 'robotization' of the guitar, with a self-tuning system (Gibson, 2007), nor its 'digitalization' (Line 6 Variax, 2010) were really successful.
7. In 1943, the white singer Peggy Lee had a hit in the Popular Charts with *Why Don't You Do Right*, which had first been sung by the Black artist Lil Green two years before.
8. In 1938, the white guitarist George Benson toured his with Black colleague Big Bill.
9. See the film *Red, White and Blues* by Mike Figgis (2003).
10. We report the prices from the website of Thomann, the largest online specialized shop in Europe. See www.thomann.de.
11. See www.reuters.com/article/us-usa-gibsonguitar-madagascar-idUSBRE8751FQ20120806.
12. See https://fr.audiofanzine.com/guitare-folk-western-electro-acoustique/takamine/yozakura/.
13. See the lyrics of *Guitar Man* by Jerry Reed Hubbard (1957) that became a great hit with Elvis Presley's version.
14. The guitar plays a crucial part in protest songs (e.g., Joan Baez, the 'first' Bob Dylan) and Woody Guthrie used to write 'this instrument kills fascists' on his Martin bodies.

REFERENCES

Adorno, T. (2020). *The Culture Industry: Selected Essays on Mass Culture*. Taylor & Francis.
Bacon, Tony (Ed.) (2006). *The Electric Guitars: The Illustrated Encyclopedia*. Quantum.
Bacon, Tony (2012). *History of the American Guitar: 1833 to Present Day*. Backbeat Books.
Bayou, Céline (2006). Le rock russe. Conquérir une liberté intérieure. *Le Courrier des pays de l'Est*, 1058, 6.
Behrendt, S. D. & Rawley, J. A. (2005). *Transatlantic Slave Trade: A History*. University of Nebraska Press.
Brocken, M. (2003). *The British Folk Revival, 1944–2002*. Ashgate.
Cain, C. M. (2006). Red, Black and Blues: Race, Nation and Recognition for the Bluez. *MUSICultures*, 33, 1–14.
Carlin, B. (2016). *Banjo: An Illustrated History*. Backbeat Books.
Carter, W. (1995). *Epiphone: The Complete History*. Hal Leonard.
Carter, W. (2017). *Mandolin in America: The Full Story from Orchestras to Bluegrass to the Modern Revival*. Backbeat Books.
Carter, W. (Eds) (2018). *The Acoustic Guitars: The Illustrated Encyclopedia*. Chartwell Books.
Cugny, L. (2014). *Une histoire du jazz en France. Tome 1: Du milieu du XIXe siècle à 1929*. Outre-Mesure.
Davis, F. (2003). *History of the Blues: The Roots, the Music, the People*. Da Capo Press.
Demierre, J. (1986). Avant-propos. *Contrechamps*, 6, 7–10.
Dudley, K. M. (2014). *Guitar Makers: The Endurance of Artisanal Values in North America*. University of Chicago Press.
Everett, W. & Riley, T. (2019). *What Goes On: The Beatles, Their Music and Their Time*. Oxford University Press.
Ferris, W. (2009). *Give My Poor Heart Ease: Voices of the Mississippi Blues*. University of North Carolina Press.

Gates, T. (1965). South Texas Negro Works Songs: Collected and Uncollected Songs Secured 1987–1905. In J. F. Dobie (Eds), *Rainbow in the Morning.* Folklore Associates.

Grenet, S. (Ed.) (2007). *Guitares Jacobacci. Un atelier de lutherie à Paris, 1924–1994.* Somogy.

Gruhn, G. & Carter, W. (2010). *Electric Guitars and Basses: A Photographic History.* Backbeat Books.

Hatschek, K. & Wells, V. A. (2018). *Historical Dictionary of the American Music Industry.* Rowman & Littlefield.

Herzhaft, G. (1981). *Le Blues.* Presses Universitaires de France.

Herzhaft, G. (2005). *Americana. Histoire des musiques de l'Amérique du Nord.* Paris: Fayard.

Herzhaft, G. (2011). *La grande encyclopédie du blues.* Fayard.

Kubik, G. (1999). *Africa and the Blues.* University Press of Mississippi.

Meyers, F. (2015). *History of Japanese Electric Guitars.* Centerstream.

Nye, J. S. (2004). *Soft Power: The Means to Success in World Politics.* Public Affairs.

Oakley, G. (1997). *The Devil's Music: A History of the Blues.* Da Capo Press.

Pirenne, C. (2011). *Une histoire musicale du rock.* Fayard.

Ramet, S. P. (2019). *Rocking the State: Rock Music and Politics in Eastern Europe.* Taylor & Francis.

Selvin, J. (2016). *Altamont: The Rolling Stones, the Hells Angels and the Inside Story of Rock's Darkest Story.* Dey Street Books.

Steiner, P. (2011). *La sociologie économique.* La Découverte.

Thompson, D. (2010). *Bayou Underground: Tracing the Mythical Roots of American Popular Music.* ECW Press.

PART IV

POLITICS

17. Globalization: opportunity or threat to the European Union?

Robert Kissack

This chapter examines European integration in the wider context of accelerated political, social and economic globalization since the end of the Cold War. It analyses the European Union (EU) as an actor in world politics and as a supranational political system, as well as exploring how it shapes, and is shaped by, globalization. The chapter contributes to the interdisciplinarity of this volume by drawing on International Relations (IR) and political science studies of the EU, following the preference of both to take the state and its institutions as the primary (but not exclusive) unit of analysis. Since globalization remains a contested concept within the social sciences, the definition used here likely differs from other authors. The centrality of transnationalism emphasized by Beck (see also Roudometof 2005: 118; Mazlish 2005) was first considered in IR nearly 50 years ago (Keohane & Nye 1972, 1977) to challenge the state-centricity and primary concern for security emphasized by realism, the dominant IR theory of the time. Although the division between liberalism and realism is considerably less constitutive of the discipline today than in the past, the way in which globalization (or indeed the recognition of the EU as an actor in international politics) is theorized still bears the hallmarks of the cleavage, with regard to the importance of non-state actors, the immutability of state sovereignty and territorial integrity or the possibility of international authority (Zürn 2019). Sceptics of globalization's potential to upend the state-centricity of international politics point to national governments' utilization of the digital technologies responsible for 'transworld simultaneity' and 'transworld instantaneity' (Scholte 2002: 18) for surveillance, propaganda and the manipulation of foreign states, globalization's redistribution of wealth as a facilitator of multipolarity in the international system and the importance of state institutions in the face of crisis, evidenced by the COVID-19 pandemic.

In this chapter, globalization is considered as 'both a process and a[n emerging] structure' (Lemert 2015: 95). Treated as a process, it argues that the EU (or at times actors within the EU) has sought to use its agency to exert influence over the direction and social purpose of globalization. Conversely, when considering the structural ramifications of globalization, the EU has encountered serious challenges to its internal cohesion and external projection. The EU is considered both as (1) an actor in its own right in global politics pursuing objectives that are *European* by virtue of EU institutions having explicitly formulated them and (2) a multilevel governance structure in which European and national political systems simultaneously experience the disruptions of a globalizing world (Hill & Smith 2011: 8). The chapter is structured in four sections, systematically considering the relationship between, on the one hand, globalization as a process and a structure, and on the other hand, the EU from the 'top down' and from the 'bottom up'. A summary of the main points, as well as a reflection on new avenues of study, is provided in the conclusion.

'EXPERTS IN INTERCONNECTEDNESS': THE EU AS AN ACTOR AND THE PROCESS OF GLOBALIZATION

The acceleration of 'transworld simultaneity' and 'transworld instantaneity' noted above and characterizing the unique attributes of contemporary globalization were made possible by the third (Internet) and fourth (social media-driven content) disruptive digital technologies (Swan 2015), and coincided with deepening European integration initiated by the ratification of the Maastricht Treaty in 1993. In order to consolidate the Single Market, more policy areas became Community competencies and among them, a number entailed an external policy dimension necessitating greater EU engagement with global governance institutions. Examples include the preparations for the Kyoto Protocol of the United Nations (UN) Framework Convention on Climate Change in 1997 and working with the International Labour Organization on the 'Social Dimension of Globalisation'. Likewise, in the field of foreign policy, the creation in 1993 of the Common Foreign and Security Policy as the institutionalization of two decades of cooperation (Smith 2004), and the establishment of the High Representative for the Common Foreign and Security Policy in the Amsterdam Treaty of 1997, demonstrated the EU's ambitions as a political actor in the post-Cold War world. Such ambitions resonated with the resurgence of liberal values following the fall of the Soviet Union and the UN's increased human rights orientation evidenced by the 1993 World Conference on Human Rights that established the UN High Commissioner for Human Rights and Kofi Annan's tenure as Secretary General from 1997. Taken in sum, the advancements during the decade amounted to the consolidation of a 'Liberal Leviathan' (Ikenberry 2011) which the EU aspired to lead by virtue of its supranational legal order, proven success at transnational market integration and regulation and normative commitment to the promotion of the rule of law, human rights and development. However, some states in the Global South remained convinced the EU's real goal was to use the multilateral system to serve its own interests (Kissack 2010), behaviour they expected from *all* states in the international system, coupled with first-hand experience of Europe's colonial history. Yet the EU was argued to be different, a 'sui generis' international actor unambiguously committed to peaceful cooperation and coexistence without the history of war-making or colonialism of its member states, captured in Ole Weaver's argument that the EU's identity-other was its own history, although the 1957 EEC treaties include provisions for French Algeria and implicate the EU in colonialism as well (Fisher Onar & Nicolaïdis 2013). 'Normative Power Europe' (Manners 2002) was a widely accepted thesis explaining the EU's role in world politics that noted how the end of the Cold War demonstrated the importance of ideas in changing state behaviour, and also the decreasing utility of coercive means, be they military or economic. Europe's 'power' was through exemplary behaviour that established the norms other states chose to comply with, echoing Rosecrance's (1997) observation that the EU had a power of attraction unlike other consolidating blocs in history, which instead fuelled distrust and insecurity. Diez (Diez & Manners 2007) and Aggestam (2008) both question the direction of causation in Manners' argument, proposing that the EU was swimming *with* the tide of liberalization led by the United States (US) rather than generating its own wave of enlightened liberal order through the example it set.

Despite rifts between member states over support for the US-led invasion of Iraq in 2003, the EU entered a 'golden period' of self-proclaimed leadership of the multilateral system from which the unilateralist US had disengaged under President G. W. Bush. The 2003 European Security Strategy (Council of the European Union 2003) mapped out a world of complex threats and challenges, from terrorism, the proliferation of weapons of mass destruction and climate change through to the need to promote human rights, sustainable development and energy security. 'Effective Multilateralism' became the leitmotif of EU foreign policy (Kissack 2010), seeking to regulate and steer the process of globalization through governance institutions and serve as a benign and enlightened actor. Its efforts to helm the ship during a hiatus of American disinterest in the multilateral system built after 1945 under its hegemony (Ruggie 1992) floundered with the collapse of Lehman Brothers' bank on 14 September 2008. The subsequent global financial crisis set in motion structural changes that redefined Europe's experience of, and attitude towards, globalization. The Irish banking crises caused by exposure to US sub-prime assets (Breen 2013), followed by recession and the eurozone liquidity crisis of 2010 in Southern European states (Hodson 2014), made the impact of austerity measures clear to whole populations, beyond the former industrial areas hurt by competition wrought by globalisation. More broadly across the multilateral system, emerging economies from the Global South began demonstrating their unwillingness to follow European leadership, most conspicuously in the 2008 Geneva Ministerial of the World Trade Organization seeking to complete the Doha Development Round and the 2009 COP 15 negotiations in Denmark, where two years of preparations for a post-2012 legally binding emissions system failed to convince emerging powers or the US (Falkner et al. 2010).

GEOPOLITICS AND MULTIPOLARITY: EUROPEAN UNION RESPONSES TO STRUCTURAL CHANGE

IR's top-down perspective on the structural changes wrought by globalization inevitably leads to a focus on the international system: the distribution of power within it, the economic production supporting it; the identification of threats and challenges emanating from it; and the normative constitution of its order. During the decade after the 2008 financial crisis, the global order underwent a rapid reconfiguration away from Western centricity (Acharya 2017) that characterized the liberal international order established with the first wave of globalization after 1870 and its institutionalization since 1945 (Ikenberry 2018). The often mentioned emerging powers of Brazil, China, India and South Africa, coupled with Russia's economic revival through energy production, as well as the growth of Mexico, Turkey, Indonesia, South Korea and Australia, concretize the redistribution of global wealth previously concentrated in North America, Europe and Japan more widely across Asia-Pacific and into Central and South America. The three 'glorious decades' of European integration in which labour and capital were able to share welfare gains from increased productivity (Varghese 2018) are a distant memory, as returns on capital have exceeded those on labour in the Global North, causing long-term wage stagnation for middle classes and exacerbating income inequality through the relocation of production outside Europe (Milanovic 2016). Domestic political accountability for the demise of manufacturing has historically been sidestepped, as tariffs protecting such sectors were reduced as part of global trade agreements that yielded aggregate gains elsewhere in the European economy and justified as the price to secure large liberalization deals. Zürn (2004) identifies this as 'executive multilateral' without parliamentary scrutiny and suggests it is one reason for the populist backlash against globalization (Zürn 2019). Jahn (2018) offers a long-term analysis of liberal internationalism, arguing that since its beginning in seventeenth-century England, the liberal domestic order has required an external (colonial) 'other' to import profit and export problems. As marketization expands globally it applies competitive pressure on the liberal centre as well as leaving ever less 'other' to dominate, resulting in today's opposite interaction whereby profit is exported and problems are imported. In 2017, Commission President Juncker used his State of the Union address to promote the New Industrial Policy Strategy. The war in Ukraine heightened awareness of global supply chain vulnerabilities and the need to repatriate critical industries.

The normative constitution of the international order has also altered as a result of structural changes from globalization. The EU Global Strategy paints Europe's position starkly, saying 'we live in times of existential crisis, within and beyond the European Union. Our Union is under threat. Our European project, which has brought unprecedented peace, prosperity and democracy, is being questioned' (European Union 2016b: 3). The Franco-German initiative in the UN to form an *Alliance of Multilateralists* spearheads a post-Brexit EU presence in the UN, acknowledging that sovereign states need to be conspicuous, a pragmatic turn away from earlier efforts to realize the Treaty of Lisbon's elevation of the EU to the international inter-locutor of its member states, signifying that EU supranational multilateralism yields to UN intergovernmental multilateralism (Laatikaienen & Smith 2006). The alliance gathers middle powers with common interests in response to the flagrant violation of human rights by China with regard to the Uyghur minority, to Russian disregard for sovereign integrity evidenced by the 2014 annexation of Crimea and since 2022 in its military invasion of Ukraine, as well as the former Trump administration's disdain for all international organizations in general. There are now many other actors, 'either acting alone or joining ranks with longstanding contesters' (Johansson-Nogués et al. 2019: 2), challenging rules, norms and values the EU supports. Yet, contestation over norms and values taken by Europeans to be self-evident is not necessarily a reason for concern. Wiener's (2014) 'theory of contestation' centres on the legitimacy gap between the creation of norms at an international level and the rules that implement them at the local level. She posits that contestation, when conducted within structured parameters, serves as a legitimization process, giving voice to those politically excluded and potentially strength-ening global governance in the long term. The EU, by contrast, has traditionally placed greater stock on agreeing norms in multilateral forums and subsequently establishing rules of com-pliance through hard and soft legal mechanisms. Wiener and other scholars, who emphasize the need to give greater prominence to the deliberate nature of international norms throughout their entire lifespan (Krook & True 2010; Deitelhoff & Zimmerman 2018), acknowledge the redistribution of power and influence towards the Global South, and as a readjustment of the Western-centric bias in IR theory more generally. Both corrective steps challenge the com-fortable narrative of the EU as a leader of a globalizing world and instead stress the need for a greater diversity of voices and perspectives consequent of the underlying changes brought about by globalization.

GLOBALIZATION, DENATIONALIZATION, POLITICIZATION: NEW CLEAVAGES IN EUROPEAN SOCIETY

How has the process of globalization impacted upon the political, economic and social devel-opment of the EU from within? As the Cold War ended, the EU finalized a major step toward the goal of ever closer union with the realization of the Single Market in 1992. It posited four fundamental freedoms across the member states: the movement of persons, goods, capital and the provision of services, promoting both 'negative integration' (the removal of barriers to trade) and 'positive integration' (the creation of supranational regulation) (Scharpf 1999: 45). Successive enlargements in 1995, 2004, 2007 and 2013 sought to carry these freedoms, firstly to northern, then to Central and Eastern Europe. The advancements in the field of information technology that permitted reimagining economic networks of production and social networks of communication on a European level were epitomized with Garton Ash's 'generation EasyJet' experiencing mobility of life and work across national borders, thus realizing a European network society (Castells 2002). As a process, agency to shape, if not determine, the direction taken is assumed possible, although when viewed from the bottom up within Europe, many actors have sought to shape the process in different ways and with different goals in mind.

The integration of markets and the complexity of economic interdependence catalysed the development of a new analytical lens to study European governance structures that rejected the liberal intergovernmental claim that national preferences are the key explanatory variable determining EU outcomes, and the neofunctionalist claim that supranational integration begot elite support for more supranational integration (Börzel & Risse 2008: 218). Instead, multilevel governance (Marks et al. 1996) was developed to explain how, why and with what effect policy making was divided between sub-national, national and supranational authorities. It reasoned that the EU, while undoubtedly a unique political structure, was similar to many other political systems that *in their own way* were also unique. It permitted concentration on policies and their effectiveness rather than the polity and transformed the position of the EU in research from being a dependent to an independent variable (Jachtenfuchs 2006). Multilevel governance draws attention to the redistribution of political and legal authority across national boundaries implied in both European integration and globalization, a process that 'open[s] up and unbundle[s] the boundaries of nation-states' (Kriesi 2008: 222) labelled 'denationaliza-tion' by Zürn. Thus, the decisions taken by elites in the name of European integration became 'politicized' in the 1990s, meaning that formerly technical and bureaucratic matters became 'a subject of public discussion' (Zürn 2014: 48) by citizens, civil society groups, political parties and governments. An alternative to the left/right cleavage emerged as a result of politi-cization, referred to as 'integration versus demarcation' (Kriesi et al. 2008) or 'traditionalism/ authoritarianism/nationalism' and 'green/alternative/libertarian' (Hooghe & Marks 2008: 16), which has been utilized by European political parties to redefine their purpose and goals. With this shift, identity, rather than economic wellbeing and redistributive policies, has become the primary indicator of how and where citizens stand in relation to their support for European integration and openness to globalization. Hooghe and Marks characterize this change as one from a functionalist to a postfunctionalist theorizing of European politics, and with the demotion of economic justifications for integration, European publics no longer have to accept a 'permissive consensus' toward an ever closer union, but instead represent a 'constraining dissensus' (Hooghe & Marks 2008). There is no doubt that the 2010s have accelerated both the politicization of EU integration with, *inter alia*, the eurozone financial crises, the Transatlantic Trade and Investment Partnership and Comprehensive Economic Trade Agreement negotia-tions, the 2015 'migration crisis', the 2016 Brexit decision, some member states' closeness to China and Russia and a lack of solidarity in responding to the COVID-19 pandemic. Across Europe, right-wing nationalist-populist parties are attracting more support and entering gov-erning coalitions, with their frequently anti-elite rhetoric that targets globalists, Europeanists and liberals (widely spanning support for trade openness to human and minority rights support) becoming accepted language in political discourse.[1]

'FORTRESS EUROPE'

The final section considers globalization as an emerging structure impacting upon the inside of the EU. Europe is being pulled in multiple directions by seemingly contradictory forces. On the one hand, it is the destination sought by a growing number of international migrants, the flows of which are recognized as 'a source of prosperity, innovation and sustainable development in our globalized world' (UN 2018: §8). Those arriving choose Europe for the opportunities – including employment – that are attainable, as well as those refugees seeking protection from persecution. Yet European publics, as well as their politicians, are increasingly divided on whether migrants can and should be accepted. In Austria, for example, the city of Vienna has developed highly elaborate integration and housing schemes to prevent ghettoization and isolation, while the federal government has shifted to the right and stands starkly opposed (Rheindorf & Wodak 2017). The division is repeated across many cities vis-à-vis their national governments (Mayors of EU Capital Cities 2015) and is representative of a larger tension in politics globally between the emergence of cities as international actors participating in networked cooperation to deliver policies providing global public goods (such as emissions reductions), and sovereign states reluctant to commit to action without assurances that others will not renege on agreements (Curtis & Acuto 2018). Migration into Europe has also highlighted a tension between the EU's normative commitment to the global promotion of human rights and its treatment of migrants, scrutinizing the increased use of military-type technologies and surveillance on its land and sea borders (Huysmann 2000; Neal 2009; Little & Vaughan-Williams 2016). The EU has turned to biopolitics to justify its stance, presenting its border force Frontex as protecting both the European demos and the migrant attempting to enter from a common enemy: human traffickers (Vaughan-Williams 2015). Efforts to disrupt people-smuggling networks, confiscate assets and destroy boats are presented as humanitarian actions protecting future victims and serving European publics, seemingly reconciling EU border management practice and international humanitarian law obligations. What is overlooked is that a proportion of smuggled individuals have willingly undertaken the cost and the risk in order to arrive in Europe. Indeed, Carling (2017) argues that some asylum seekers and refugees with legitimate claims to seek refuge in Europe are forced to use trafficking because no other methods of entry exist.

Yet on the other hand, while many outsiders see Europe as a place of opportunity, the future of work in the EU is a source of uncertainty given the relative expense of European labour in manufacturing compared to countries in the Global South and in the services sector compared to automation and artificial intelligence (AI). 'The Industrial Revolution changed the world, and all it did was replace human muscle … But the digital revolution will replace the human brain' (Drum 2018: 43). Klaus Schwab refers to the advent of 'Industrialisation 4.0' as an era in which manufacturing in Europe can only continue by incorporating the highest levels of technology and productivity, as well as the individualization of production (contrary to earlier industrialization through mass production). The EU has recognized it is behind the US and China and is seeking to address this shortcoming, evidenced in the Declaration of Cooperation in AI of April 2018 (for a full overview see Stix 2019). These consequences of global restructuring resulted in a pivot taking place from the early years of enthusiastically embracing globalization as an opportunity to advance the EU's influence in the world to one where consequences are framed as threats and challenges that will test European resilience (Wagner & Anholt 2016).

As noted above, the EU Global Strategy repositions the EU in the rapidly altering geopolitical reality of declining Western influence and the growth of the emerging powers. It identifies 'terrorism, hybrid threats, economic volatility, climate change and energy insecurity' (European Union 2016a: 9) as the three most pressing dangers faced, as well as reducing the scale and ambition of EU influence from one with global aspirations in 2003 to one concerned overwhelmingly with its Southern and Eastern neighbourhood. The focus on regional order, societal resilience and a 'comprehensive approach to conflicts and crisis' (European Union 2016a: 9) not only seeks to enhance regional peace but also addresses some of the underlying causes of Islamic extremist terrorism, dating back to the attacks in Madrid in 2003 and London in 2005, and more recently in Paris, Berlin and other European cities. While Europe has known terrorism since the 1970s, its re-emergence has brought into sharp relief the link between foreign policy and Europe's perceived stance towards placing freedom of expression over and above the protection of religious beliefs and practices. European cities, like cities globally, are becoming increasingly integrated through the flows of people and information, through the opportunities they offer migrants, the value they create and their vulnerability as terrorist targets (Coaffee & Murakami Wood 2006). European cities are expected to become more resilient (Brassett et al. 2013; Dunn Cavetly et al. 2015) and better able to cope with these changes. In this way, while not equating globalization to neoliberalism (Scholte 2002), we nevertheless find the expectation of resilient cities to be consistent with structural changes consequent of globalization. As a political union of sovereign states, we could expect to see growing trans-European cleavages between cosmopolitan metropolitan areas that find ever more in common with each other than with the peripheral suburbs and rural areas of their national hinterlands.

CONCLUSION

This chapter draws on the research from IR and European studies to assess the impact of globalization on the EU, both as a process and in its crystallizing structural form. The former was understood to be (in principle) open to agentic guidance, and the EU saw itself as being uniquely capable of steering the direction globalization took in the decade after the end of the Cold War. The latter was understood as the constraints and limitations imposed by globalization on all actors, the EU included. Moreover, the chapter distinguished between the politics within the EU and the EU seeking to act in the world, highlighting tensions between globalization's impact domestically and its implications for the EU's foreign policy goals. Europe's initial hopes of directing globalization filled with ambition and optimism have been replaced by wariness toward globalization as an economic force and as a catalyst for geopolitical change. It seems unlikely that Europe can raise the drawbridge to secure itself from the structural changes brought about by globalization, given its prosperity and geographic location. Furthermore, the deeply engrained commitment (at least rhetorically) to a liberal respect for human rights, international law and market openness is diametrically opposed to the mindset calling for closure, meaning that the EU's self-identity and perceived place in the world is being questioned in the face of globalization.

NOTE

1. Examples include the Front National in France, Alternative for Deutschland in Germany, Vox in Spain, Five-Star Alliance in Italy, Shining Path in Greece, as well as those in power in Hungary, Poland and in minority governments in Belgium and the Netherlands. This is not a new phenomenon, if one recalls Heider's position in the Austrian coalition government of 1999.

REFERENCES

Acharya, A. (2017). 'After Liberal Hegemony: The Advent of a Multiplex World Order'. *Ethics and International Affairs*, 31(3), 271–285.

Aggestam, L. (2008). 'Introduction: Ethical Power Europe?' *International Affairs*, 84(1), 1–11.

Börzel, T. A. & Risse, T. (2008). 'Revisiting the Nature of the Beast – Politicization, European Identity, and Postfunctionalism: A Comment on Hooghe and Marks'. *British Journal of Political Science*, 39(1), 217–220.

Brassett, J., Croft, S. & Vaughan-Williams, N. (2013). 'Introduction: An Agenda for Resilience Research in Politics and International Relations'. *Politics*, 33(4), 221–228.

Breen, M. (2013). *The Politics of IMF Lending*. Palgrave.

Carling, J. (2017). 'Expert Panellist Statement on the Smuggling of Migrants'. Fifth Thematic Consultation Session, UN Global Compact for Migration, Vienna, 4–5 September. http://refugeesmigrants.un.org/sites/default/files/ts5/Jorgen_carling.pdf

Castells, M. (2002). 'Local and Global: Cities in the Network Society'. *Tijdschrift voor Economische en Sociale Geographie*, 93(5), 548–558.

Coaffee J. & Murakami Wood, D. (2006). 'Security Is Coming Home: Rethinking Scale and Constructing Resilience in the Global Urban Response to Terrorist Risk'. *International Relations*, 20(4), 503–517.

Council of the European Union (2003). *A Secure Europe in a Better World: European Security Strategy*. Brussels, 12 December.

Curtis, S. & Acuto, M. (2018). The Foreign Policy of Cities'. *THE RUSI Journal*, 163(6).

Deitelhoff, N. & Zimmerman, L. (2018). '"Things We Lost in the Fire": How Different Types of Contestation Affect the Robustness of International Norms'. *International Studies Review*. doi: 10.1093/isr/viy080

Diez, T. & Manners, I. (2007). 'Reflecting on Normative Power Europe. In F. Berenskoetter & M. J. Williams (Eds), *Power in World Politics* (pp. 173–188). Routledge.

Drum, K. (2018). Tech World'. *Foreign Affairs*, July/August, 43–48.

Dunn Cavelty, M., Kaufmann, M. & Soby Kristensen, K. (2015). 'Resilience and (In)security: Practices, Subjects, Temporalities'. *Security Dialogue*, 46(1), 3–14.

European Commission (2014). 'For a European Industrial Renaissance'. Communication COM/2014/014 Final, Brussels.

European Commission (2017). 'Investing in a Smart, Innovative and Sustainable Industry'. COM/2017/0479 Final, Brussels.

European Union (2016a). *European Union Global Strategy*. Brussels: European Commission. www.eugs_review_web_0.pdf

European Union (2016b). 'Shared Vision, Common Action – a Stronger Europe: A Global Strategy for the European Union's Foreign and Security Policy'. European External Action Service.

Falkner, R., Stephan, H. & Volger, J. (2010). 'International Climate Policy after Copenhagen: Towards a Building Blocks Approach'. *Global Polity*, 1(3), 252–262.

Fisher Onar, N. & Nicolaïdis, K. (2013). 'The Decentring Agenda: Europe as a Post-Colonial Power'. *Cooperation and Conflict*, 48(2), 283–303.

Hill, C. & Smith, M. (Eds) (2011). *International Relations and the European Union.* Oxford University Press.

Hodson, D. (2014). 'The IMF as a De Facto Institution of the EU: A Multiple Supervisor Approach'. www.bbk.ac.uk/politics/IMFasdefactoinstitutionRIPE2014.pdf

Hooghe, L. & Marks, G. (2008). 'A Postfunctional Theory of European Integration: From Permissive Consensus to Constraining Dissensus'. *British Journal of Political Science*, 39(1), 1–23.

Huysmans, J. (2000). 'The European Union and the Securitization of Migration'. *Journal of Common Market Studies*, 38(5), 751–777.

Ikenberry, G. J. (2011). *Liberal Leviathan: The Origins, Crisis, and Transformation of the American World Order.* Princeton University Press.

Ikenberry, J. (2018). 'The End of Liberal Order'. *International Affairs*, 94(1), 7–23.

Jachtenfuchs, M. (2006). 'The European Union as a Polity (II)'. In K. E. Jørgensen, M. A. Pollack & B. Rosamond (Eds), *Handbook of European Union Politics* (pp. 159–173). SAGE.

Jahn, B. (2018). 'Liberal Internationalism: Historical Trajectory and Current Prospects'. *International Affairs*, 94(1), 43–61.

Johansson-Nogués, E., Vlaskamp, M. C. & Barbé, E. (Eds) (2019). *European Union Contested: Foreign Policy in a New Global Context.* Springer.

Keohane, R. O. & Nye, J. S. (1972). *Transnational Relations and World Politics.* Harvard University Press.

Keohane, R. O. & Nye, J. S. (1977). *Power and Interdependence: World Politics in Transition.* Little, Brown.

Kissack, R. (2010). *Pursuing Effective Multilateralism: The European Union, International Organisations and the Politics of Decision Making.* Palgrave.

Kriesi, H. (2008). 'Rejoinder to Liesbet Hooghe and Gary Marks, A Postfunctional Theory of European Integration: From Permissive Consensus to Constraining Dissensus'. *British Journal of Political Science*, 39(1), 221–224.

Krook, M. L. & True, J. (2010). 'Rethinking the Life Cycles of International Norms: The United Nations and the Global Promotion of Gender Equality'. *European Journal of International Relations*, 18(1), 103–127.

Laatikainen, K. V & Smith, K. E. (Eds) (2006). *The European Union at the United Nations: Intersecting Multilateralisms.* Palgrave.

Lemert, C. (2015). *Globalization: An Introduction to the End of the Known World.* Routledge.

Little, A. & Vaughan-Williams, N. (2016). 'Stopping Boats, Saving Lives, Securing Subjects: Humanitarian Borders in Europe and Australia'. *European Journal of International Relations*, 23(3), 533–556.

Manners, I. (2002). 'Normative Power Europe: A Contradiction in Terms?' *Journal of Common Market Studies*, 40(2), 235–258.

Marks, G., Hooghe, L. & Blank, K. (1996). 'European Integration since the 1980s: State-centric v. Multi-level Governance'. *Journal of Common Market Studies*, 34(3), 341–378.

Mayors of EU Capital Cities (2015). 'A Strong Voice in Europe'. 21 April, Vienna.

Mazlish, B. (2005). 'The Global and the Local'. *Current Sociology*, 53(1).

Milanovic, B. (2016). *Global Inequality: A New Approach for the Age of Globalization.* Belknap Press of Harvard University Press.

Neal, A. (2009). 'Securitization and Risk at the EU Border: The Origins of Frontex.' *Journal of Common Market Studies*, 47(2), 333–356.

Rheindorf, M. & Wodak, R. (2017). 'Borders, Fences, and Limits – Protecting Austria from Refugees: Metadiscursive Negotiation of Meaning in the Current Refugee Crisis'. *Journal of Immigrant & Refugee Studies*, 16(1–2), 15–38.

Rosecrance, R. N. (1997). 'The European Union: A New Type of International Actor'. In J. Zielonka (Ed.), *Paradoxes of European Foreign Policy.* European University Institute.

Roudometof, V. (2005). 'Transnationalism, Cosmopolitanism and Glocalization'. *Current Sociology*, 53(1), 113–135.

Ruggie, J. G. (1992). 'Multilateralism: The Anatomy of an Institution'. *International Organization*, 46(3), 561–598.

Scharpf, F. W. (1999). *Governing in Europe: Effective and Democratic?* Oxford University Press.

Scholte, J. A. (2002). 'What Is Globalization? The Definitional Issue – Again'. CSGR Working Paper No. 109/02. https://warwick.ac.uk/fac/soc/pais/research/researchcentres/csgr/research/abstracts/abwp10902/

Smith, M. E. (2004). *Europe's Foreign and Security Policy: The Institutionalization of Cooperation.* Cambridge University Press.

Stix, C. (2019). *A Survey of the European Union's Artificial Intelligence Ecosystem.* Leverhulme Centre for the Future of Intelligence, University of Cambridge.

Swan, M. (2015). *Blockchain: Blueprint for a New Economy.* O'Reilly Media.

UN (2018). 'Global Compact for Safe, Orderly and Regular Migration'. A/73/L.66.

Varghese, R. (2018). 'Marxist World: What Did You Expect from Capitalism?' *Foreign Affairs*, 97(4), 34–42.

Vaughan-Williams, N. (2015). *Europe's Border Crisis: Biopolitical Security and Beyond.* Oxford University Press.

Wagner, W. & Anholt, R. (2016). 'Resilience as the EU Global Strategy's New Leifmotif: Pragmatic, Problematic or Promising?' *Contemporary Security Policy*, 37(3), 414–430.

Wiener, A. (2014). *A Theory of Contestation.* Springer.

Zürn, M. (2004). 'Global Governance and Legitimacy Problems'. *Government and Opposition*, 39(2), 260–287.

Zürn, M. (2014). 'The Politicization of World Politics and Its Effects: Eight Propositions'. *European Political Science Review*, 6, 47–71.

Zürn, M. (2019). *A Theory of Global Governance: Authority, Legitimacy and Constitution.* Oxford University Press.

18. Cosmopolitans versus communitarians? Or something altogether more nuanced?

Christian Karner

INTRODUCTION

In his influential account of *supermodernity*, Marc Augé distinguishes between two different kinds of locales. Augé (2008: viii; x) terms the first 'non-places', which he defines as 'spaces of circulation, consumption and communication' (as well as of 'solitary individuality') and which he links to aspects of globalization that pertain to the worldwide 'extension … of the so-called free market, the technological networks of communication … and a planetary consciousness'. Such 'shrinking of the planet', Augé argues, becomes apparent in the anonymity of non-places that include commercial centres (e.g. supermarkets, service stations, big stores dominated by universally recognized company logos and brand names), places and modes of transport (e.g. high-speed roads, railways, interchanges and airports), as well as today's 'temporary abodes' of both luxurious (i.e. hotel chains, holiday clubs) and inhumane (i.e. refugee camps and 'shanty towns threatened with demolition') varieties (Augé 2008: 25–79). The second type of locality, less typical of supermodernity, is continuous with the types of places humans have inhabited for millennia. Those are 'anthropological places', they are places with historical depth, where individual and collective identities are formed 'through complicities in language, local references, [and] the unformulated rules of living know-how' (Augé 2008: 81).

The impact of our era's multiple global flows on non-places is obvious, for it is often primarily or in the first instance there that transnationally circulating goods, signs, capital, information and people 'touch down'. In what follows, I examine an arguably less immediately obvious dimension arising from Augé's typology of places in our supermodern times. I do so by examining how one particular global flow – or what Arjan Appadurai (1990) has famously described as the transnationally mobile 'ethnoscapes' of people – is responded to by some of the locals inhabiting anthropological places. On one level, this echoes a classical sociological question, namely how social formations respond to 'the stranger' – according to Georg Simmel (1992 [1908]), a person who 'comes today and stays tomorrow' – in their midst. According to some of the twentieth century's most influential social scientists, political responses to cultural 'otherness' fall into the two contrasting, albeit often co-existing, strategies of expulsion (*anthropoemic*) and forced assimilation (*anthrophagic*) (Bauman 1993; Lévi-Strauss 2011 [1955]). Notably, this binary of expulsion versus assimilation leaves no conceptual space for a third response, one that respects and enables enduring cultural diversification through inward migration.

In what follows, I reflect on some recent examinations of select, local responses to migration and ethnic pluralism through the interpretive prism furnished by another conceptual dyad commonly employed in the associated literature: namely, the juxtaposition of cosmopolitanism(s) to communitarianism(s). The fundamental question addressed thereby is whether today's local responses to global migratory flows can be meaningfully classified and analysed through these contrasting responses to ethnic diversity: a cosmopolitan embrace of formerly geographically, now merely culturally, distant 'others'; and a communitarian entrenchment of narrow boundaries and exclusions. The analytical trajectory of my argument proceeds from definitional remarks and a brief history of ideas to a meta-discussion of empirical studies that reference, push beyond and in important ways complicate the cosmopolitanism-versus-communitarianism binary. As it turns out, a sociologically more compelling understanding of local responses to global flows of people demands careful structural contextualization and an appreciation of some notable ideological ambivalences and nuances.

A BRIEF HISTORY AND DEFINITIONAL OVERVIEW OF A CONCEPTUAL(/POLITICAL) DICHOTOMY

Working definitions of cosmopolitanism abound in the scholarly literature. Their shared conceptual core revolves around 'an essentially moral view of the individual as having allegiances to the wider world' (Delanty 2006: 26) beyond their ascribed or otherwise taken-for-granted 'communities', and a sense of 'belongingness to different geographical entities, including the "world as a whole"' (Szerszynski & Urry 2002: 461). To Ulf Hannerz, cosmopolitanism constitutes a perspective, or 'mode of managing meaning', that is defined by a 'willingness to engage with a … plurality of cultures'; to those of a cosmopolitan orientation, there is 'value in diversity', which acts as a condition for a(n emerging) 'world culture' premised on a particular 'organization of diversity rather than by a replication of uniformity' (Hannerz 1990: 237–239, 250). Similarly, Michael Skey (2012: 472, original in italics) ties 'the idea of the cosmopolitan' to 'processes of interaction and imagination that extend beyond local or national contexts' and create 'novel forms of sociability and community that are both *meaningful* and *durable*'. While 'openness' to culturally and/or geographically distant 'others' thus constitutes a feature frequently attributed to the cosmopolitan, it has also long been acknowledged (Szerszynski & Urry 2002: 469) that there is 'no one form of cosmopolitanism', and that the term tends to 'function as an "empty signifier"' that gets filled, across different contexts, 'with specific … often different content'. Szerszynski and Urry's more extensive model regards the following 'predispositions and practices' as cosmopolitanism's constitutive building blocks: mobility and the associated 'capacity to consume' different places; an openness, curiosity and 'willingness' to 'encounter the "other"'; a reflexive ability to 'map one's own society' comparatively, historically and geographically; and the 'semiotic skill' required to 'interpret images of various others' (Szerszynski & Urry 2002: 470). In anticipation of a later theme in this discussion, one may consider already at this stage how such dispositions and practices implicate, either directly or more implicitly, the possession of particular economic, social and cultural capital.

  On this definitional basis, overlaps between cosmopolitanism and another, relatively closely aligned concept are worth noting. The proximate phenomenon in question is what Paul Gilroy calls *conviviality* and defines as the 'process of cohabitation and interaction that have made multiculture an ordinary feature of social life'; conviviality connotes a 'radical openness that … makes a nonsense of closed, fixed and reified identity' (Gilroy 2004: xi). This conceptual bridge to Gilroy's influential work enables us to ask what cosmopolitanism and conviviality are commonly contrasted to. Gilroy (2004: 6) pits conviviality against 'ethnic absolutism', or those divisive definitions of 'identity and belonging that are overly fixed or too easily naturalized' as purportedly 'exclusively national[/ethnic] phenomena'. Similarly relevant are

Solomos and Back's observations (1994: 156) of contemporary racisms as being articulated through various 'coded signifiers', whose common denominator lies in their 'attempt to fix human social groups in terms of [allegedly] natural properties of belonging'. For the purposes of this discussion, I here employ the term *communitarianism* as a higher-order category denoting political discourses, practices and self-understandings that draw narrower, exclusive, more or less rigidly guarded boundaries around a community of purported belonging thus constructed.

The cosmopolitanism-versus-communitarianism binary builds on a formidable genealogy within the social sciences and on a yet much longer history of ideas in political-philosophical discourse. In terms of the latter, the ideational roots of cosmopolitanism can be located as far back as antiquity (e.g. Delanty 2006: 25; Appiah 2007), namely in stoicism. Yet, its major philosophical impetus was provided in the eighteenth century by Immanuel Kant's normative understanding of the values to be held by 'citizens of the world' (Skey 2012: 472). Classical social science narratives, meanwhile, were quick to recognize cosmopolitanism as one of two mutually opposed political forces that were shaping modernity. Writing in 1908, Georg Simmel thus traced two competing ideological configurations: one highly individualistic rooted in the French Revolution, premised on universal human rights and hence on the 'largest possible social circle' (i.e. the cosmopolitan) imaginable; and an alternative, romantic blueprint with its ontology of collective particularisms, which saw people as members of 'historical groups' that were in turn defined in ethno-national(ist) terms (Simmel 1992 [1908]: 812–814). In anthropological and historical circles, the opposition of cosmopolitanism to communitarianism came to occupy a prominent heuristic position used to shed light on defining aspects of the late nineteenth and early twentieth centuries, such as the rise of nationalism across Europe (e.g. Gellner 1998). In sociological circles, it was Robert Merton's study of a town on the Eastern Coast of the United States during the Second World War that helped establish the opposition of cosmopolitan to localist self-understandings and social networks as part of the discipline's conceptual 'vocabulary' (Hannerz 1990: 237).

Subsequent and more recent social scientific engagement with cosmopolitanism and its ideological opponents has, as we shall discover, tended to discover greater nuance and variation *within* the phenomena in question. An early example of this emerged from Ulf Hannerz's delineation of seven distinctive, ideal typical subject positions (i.e. locals, tourists, exiles, 'metropolitan locals', expatriates, cosmopolitans, labour migrants), each of which exemplifies distinctive experiences of mobility or encounters with 'the other' (Hannerz 1990: 241–247). Importantly, such a typology is not exhaustive. Clearly, there are other structural experiences that also involve encounters with, and in some cases openness towards, 'the other'. Suffice it to remember today's many types of migration: from high-powered, executive business travellers on one end of the spectrum; to the experience of 'forced [im]mobility' (Stock 2019) endured by many (would-be) asylum seekers on the other. Concurrently, we shall discover that considerable research attention has been paid to the many and diverse contexts in which locals' life-worlds intersect with different migratory flows. Importantly, it should not be assumed that occupants of any of the subject positions in question inevitably display a cosmopolitan openness or an endorsement of an automatic solidarity with 'the other', whom dominant communitarian discourses and existing institutional structures (continue to) construct as lying outside their purported communities of (ascribed) membership. Within cosmopolitanism more narrowly, we should bear in mind that there have been 'manifold genealogies', which in turn have resulted in various forms of cosmopolitanism that are underpinned by different traditions and motivations (Delanty 2006: 28). Michael Skey alerts us to such diversity through two key questions that the cosmopolitan question inevitably raises: 'What is "openness"? Which "others"?' (Skey 2012: 472). As we shall see, the answers to these questions are not always uniform or straightforward.

Even this briefest possible definitional overview thus begins to reveal a plurality of cosmopolitanisms and to underscore the importance of the specific contexts in which encounters with pluralism take place and social, political and ethical questions for all involved arise. It is in the direction of some such encounters and the ensuing political contests and choices that we turn next.

FROM DIVIDED POPULATIONS TO THE 'COSMOPOLITAN IMAGINATION'

If cosmopolitanism and communitarianism, as outlined in the previous section, capture competing ideological dispositions and blueprints, how do they manifest in the life-worlds of particular localities? How are we to think about the relationships, or negotiations, between individuals, groups and the philosophical-political stances in question?

Recent work by Magdalena Nowicka, Łukasz Krzyżowski and Dennis Ohm provides some empirical traction in this regard. On the basis of survey data provided by a sample of 2,500 Polish migrants residing in Germany, Nowicka et al. document a diversity of positions with regard to their research participants' perceived boundaries of belonging and associated 'obligation of solidarity'. At first sight, the ideological choices seem self-evident, with cosmopolitanism expected to offer a 'universal' morality that 'encompasses all humans without exception', as opposed to particularistic (i.e. national) ideologies that limit their adherents' obligation of solidarity to an exclusive, narrowly defined in-group (Nowicka et al. 2019: 383–387). Once again, it bears analytical dividends to map such rival positions with contrastingly porous or rigid external boundaries of inclusion/exclusion onto Paul Gilroy's work. According to Gilroy, today's politics of race unfold around an 'ethnically absolutist' *postmodern nationalism*, which in some European versions appears to be psychodynamically motivated by a loss of geopolitical importance (or 'postimperial melancholia', in Gilroy's formulation); and, conversely, around the *convivial*, 'ordinary hybridity' and 'multiculture of the postcolonial metropolis' (Gilroy 2004: 132–136). Future research will indeed need to do more to examine how these competing vectors of contemporary politics manifest in particular settings. Where Nowicka et al. (2019: 386) push the debate already in fruitful new directions is by documenting that the cosmopolitan-versus-localism/nationalism binary may not exhaust all ideological options, that people's '"we" is not necessarily fixed, but open with regard to various contexts'. On one hand, Nowicka et al. show that certain characteristics such as education and length of residence abroad correlate positively with more cosmopolitan inclinations among their sample of Polish migrants in Germany. At the same time, however, Nowicka and her colleagues also reveal an important temporal dimension and significant, perceived differences within the category of 'the other' that impact people's feelings of solidarity: in other words, research participants endorsed short-term humanitarian support for (would-be) asylum seekers much more readily than the long-term inclusion into their 'community of belonging' of especially Muslim refugees (Nowicka et al. 2019: 393). Translated into the terms of our wider discussion, we here encounter evidence that context matters. Rather than being an absolute, permanent property of social actors' political dispositions, cosmopolitanism here emerges as a context-bound inclination that people apply in certain circumstances and that reflects both the time-frame and the cultural characteristics of 'the other' involved.

At this point in the discussion mention should be made of a tendency in parts of the literature to conceive of relatively polarized populations. Ulrich Beck, to name but one prominent exemplar of such perceptions, mentions two forms of such bifurcations: first, a generational divide pitting 'old Neandertals' against younger cohorts who, allegedly, exemplify 'homo cosmopoliticus'; and a regional division between 'cosmopolitan world cities and rural, conservative areas' (Beck 2017: 223, 243). In partial corroboration of Beck's postulate, we may cite voting patterns documented around much of the world in recent years, particularly in cases where neonationalist swings to the right have been significantly aided by rural dwellers and older generations. Not dissimilarly, there is evidence of cities and their administrations becoming major political players in the (cosmopolitan) fight for migrants' rights and inclusion. For example, Janina Stürner and Petra Bendel have shown how a number of European and North American cities have come to take decisive initiative in the struggle to 'localize human rights' in two ways: through the local safeguarding of (forced) migrants' political, social, cultural and economic rights (e.g. in the areas of housing, health, education, employment, social cohesion); and, in the absence of pertinent national legislation, through 'soft governance' and 'transnational municipal networks' that advocate for integration and migrants' rights (Stürner & Bendel 2019: 220–223). While such insights appear to lend some empirical weight to Beck's observations, later parts of this discussion will also provide reason to be cautious with absolutist attributions of cosmopolitan or communitarian dispositions to either specific regional populations or to generational cohorts.

Other empirical studies of how the competing blueprints of cosmopolitanism and communitarianism are enacted in specific localities include Ralph Grillo's (2005) study of Saltdean, a largely white-collar suburb of Brighton, on England's southern coast. The context to Grillo's study was provided by the United Kingdom's then new Asylum and Immigration Act in 2002 and its plans for new, geographically dispersed 'induction centres' for asylum seekers' 'preliminary processing and health checks'. Against this backdrop, one of Saltdean's local hotels was rumoured to become one such induction centre, which led to local debate and growing political polarization among the residents of Saltdean. Grillo documents the two competing discourses (i.e. one localist, the other cosmopolitan), their argumentative strategies, as well as their emerging and rivalling organizational vehicles (i.e. local civil society groups that came to be known as 'Saltdean Residents Action Group' and 'Saltdean for Tolerance and Respect'). At first sight, then, Grillo appears to provide empirical reasons to adhere to a relatively clear-cut analytical distinction between (inclusively) cosmopolitan and (exclusively) communitarian local responses to potential inward migration that are akin to two 'relatively coherent … sub-cultures' (Grillo 2005: 250). At closer inspection, however, Grillo also points us in the direction of somewhat greater complexity: he addresses the question as to whether the defensive localism qualifies – its advocates' disclaimers notwithstanding – as a form of middle-class racism and xenophobic populism, by comparing it with the language of the extreme right. And while Grillo confirms that the two discourses (i.e. Saltdean's localism and the British National Party's xenophobia) 'intersect', they do not seem to be identical, for Saltdean residents 'lack the BNP's language of culture, race, and "our people"' (Grillo 2005: 253). The wider implication of this argument is that there may indeed be 'layers and layers' (Grillo 2005: 256) to how, in specific localities, exclusions are variously imposed and endured and potential inclusion gets negotiated.

A slightly different analytical avenue emerges from Gerard Delanty's concept of the 'cosmopolitan imagination', which 'occurs when and wherever new relations between self, other and world develop in moments of openness'; such 'world openness' is 'not reducible' to the demographic fact of pluralism, instead it requires a critical, reflexive attitude capable of 'self-problematization' and hence able to aid societal transformations. (Delanty 2006: 27, 35) Thus, instead of regarding cosmopolitanism as the hard kernel of particular political positions, or as the defining feature of a certain personality structure – akin, so to speak, to a cosmopolitan counterpart to what Adorno et al. (2019 [1950]) long ago and famously described as an 'authoritarian personality' – the notion of the *cosmopolitan imagination* offers a more flexible analytical tool. As such, it is arguably better suited for making sense of the many moments and settings in which openness to (global) others becomes possible. In some of my own research I have documented examples of such a 'cosmopolitan imagination' in a monthly street magazine published in the (southern) Austrian region of Styria. The magazine's regular journalistic features include a column in which a local writer or the magazine's editor records the biographical story of a migrant, often an asylum seeker, currently living in Styria. The ensuing insights into difficult migrations, and sometimes similarly challenging arrivals in Austria, are thus co-produced by locals and asylum seekers; theirs are clearly encounters that require 'world openness' and involve dialogical transformation; the results of such a cosmopolitan imagination are addressed at a local readership that is interested in how its life-world intersects with migratory flows and critical of existing configurations of power and inequality (see Karner 2021).

By way of an analytical bridge to the next section in this discussion, mention should be made of a slightly more dated, though enduringly significant, contribution to the literature. In his ethnography of Southall in London, anthropologist Gerd Baumann documented some 25 years ago that the fault line between cosmopolitanism and communitarianism does not necessarily run through populations but, instead, at times through individuals. Baumann demonstrated this through his notion of 'dual discursive competence'. Residents in this multi-ethnic suburb of London were thereby shown to skilfully manoeuvre and switch between two very different models of self-understanding and wider social relationships. Baumann termed these conflicting models 'dominant' and 'demotic' discourses: the dominant discourse assumes that individuals' ethnic (and hence ascribed) 'communities' constitutes a person's primary source of (reified) identity and social network; the demotic discourse, by contrast, centres on 'newly forged communities' that cut across ethno-religious boundaries and create alternative notions of solidarity and belonging (Baumann 1996: 188–191). Importantly, the same groups and individuals are here shown to employ either and both of these discursive (and political) frames, depending on the circumstances. With this acknowledgement of greater complexity in mind, we turn the final analytical corner in this discussion.

CONDITIONS OF POSSIBILITY, NUANCE AND AMBIVALENCE

Once again returning to Ulrich Beck, we may note a further conceptual distinction in Beck's final book that offers a way of side-stepping an overly simplified attribution of specific political positions to individuals or demographic groups. Instead, Beck here reminds us that professed political opinions need careful analytical disentanglement from people's social practices. Put differently, Beck distinguishes people's beliefs (*Glaubenssätze*) from their 'frames of action' (*Handlungsräume*). Applied to our topic at hand, Beck points out that while the former can, and for many people are, centred on particularisms (i.e. that may in turn be communitarian ideas, be it in anti-European, nationalist, religiously fundamentalist or other exclusivist fashions), today's frames of action are irrevocably cosmopolitan insofar as social and economic practices implicate geographically distant 'others' and transnational interdependencies (Beck 2017: 21–23). Retranslated into the terms of the present discussion, Beck's distinction enables us to notice more nuanced empirical possibilities. For example, we may thus examine how self-confessed nationalists may still (need to) be open to transnational connections and networks in their lived, political practices. Or conversely, we may interrogate how committed cosmopolitans also (inadvertently) play their part in the ongoing reproduction of exclusionary and discriminatory institutional structures. We may indeed wonder what the various shades and combinations of political beliefs and lived social practices in-between absolutist positions may be.

Recent and influential contributions to the literature have gone a long way towards a more thorough contextualization that can facilitate understanding of the structural conditions of possibility underpinning any and all societal responses to inward migratory flows. German sociologist Andreas Reckwitz, for example, offers a careful discussion of the new class divisions of our post-Fordist age, their spatial manifestations and global interconnections. Late modern social structures, Reckwitz argues, have come to involve three distinct classes in many parts of the world: a well-educated, new middle class that resides particularly in metropolitan regions and often displays a cultural-cum-political inclination we may broadly describe as cosmopolitan; an old middle class that is now clustered into infrastructurally disadvantaged (semi-)rural areas and feels itself, at times, to be on the 'cultural defensive'; and finally, a precarious class that supplies our post-industrial, service economy with vital labour, yet faces chronic economic uncertainty and structural marginalization (Reckwitz 2020: 98–109). Philip Manow (2019: 10), meanwhile, goes yet another step further in arguing that there is a 'dearth of theorizing and excess in moralizing' when it comes to scholarly responses to today's populisms both on the left and on the right of the political spectrum. Instead, Manow advocates a political economy approach that shows different populisms to constitute contrasting symptoms of how different social formations are exposed in different ways to globalization. Populisms, Manow argues (2019: 14–15), cannot be adequately explained in culturalist fashion, as the purported protest of nostalgic communitarians against the supposed universalism of a cosmopolitan, global elite. Instead, Manow argues that what is needed is a contextualizing understanding of how different types of exposure to global capitalism (or 'different capitalisms') trigger different 'populist counter-reactions'. Manow illustrates this through the contrasting conditions and ideological trajectories of populisms in Northern and Southern Europe. Export-oriented, Northern European economies by and large experience global trade as an asset rather than a threat; concurrently, however, Northern European welfare states tend to be 'generous and accessible', as a consequence of which migratory flows are relatively commonly seen to constitute a problem (i.e. with inward migration being constructed as a threat to generous welfare provisions) and populist protest veers to the right. In Southern Europe, by contrast, the situation tends to be the inverse: economies are less focused on export and more on meeting domestic demand, while the welfare state is less accessible to migrants; consequently, in Southern Europe it is less migration than the 'neoliberal', free circulation of goods and capital that is seen as a threat, leading local populisms to more typically lean to the left (Manow 2019: 11, 18–30).

In addition to such important structural contextualization enabled by the likes of Reckwitz and Manow, other recent literature illuminates some perhaps surprising ideological nuances that an overly simplistic – as well as often morally connoted – dichotomization of cosmopolitanism versus communitarianism is likely to miss. Danielle Every and Martha Augoustinos, for example, have employed critical discourse analysis to Australian parliamentary speeches to reveal some such generally unanticipated ambivalences. By paying attention to the rhetorical functions to which various nation-centred political positions are put in parliamentary discussions, Every and Augoustinos (2008: 562–576) demonstrate that 'refugee advocates' as well as those seeking stricter asylum and immigration laws engage in talk that centres on, and variously constructs, Australia's past, present and future; consequently, nationalist discourse is shown to display a degree of 'flexibility', which enables both 'exclusive and inclusive' uses, some of which are more accurately captured by more graded notions such as 'liberal nationalism' or 'rooted cosmopolitanism' (see Appiah 2007) than by understandings of cosmopolitanism and nationalism as absolute, mutually exclusive categories. If *some* nation-centred discourses may thus incorporate cosmopolitan angles and thereby represent an unsuspected ideological configuration, how about the possibility of an anti-globalization stance that takes on cosmopolitan features? Elisabeth Kirtsoglou and Dimitrios Theodossopoulos capture such other, perhaps also unanticipated, political entanglements as articulated by some of the world's subaltern rather than the relatively privileged. In such settings, the question arises as to how 'disenchantment' with 'the neoliberal world economy' (Theodossopoulos 2010: 12) gets expressed. For instance, Kirtsoglou and Theodossopoulos capture an 'ethnographic paradox' among working- and middle-class residents of the middle-sized Greek cities of Patras and Volos: there, an (at times conspiratorial) 'anti-globalism' opposes what its advocates view as 'just another imperium' (i.e. the global economy and its political conditions of possibility) today. Concurrently, such anti-globalization attitudes, often of distinctly nationalist bent, also combine with 'strong empathy with people and nations that are imagined to [also] be deprived of power'; in other words, anti-globalization rhetoric here derives some of its discursive energy from a 'global awareness of an imagined community of discontent' that constructs a quasi-cosmopolitan 'allegiance … to disparate groups such as the Serbs, the Palestinians, the Iraqis and the Afghans' on the basis of shared histories of disempowerment compared to the West (Kirtsoglou & Theodossopoulos 2010: 83–98). At the very least, empirical findings such as these call for further analytical disentanglement of experiences of the global economy from political self-understandings that may include, and indeed combine, cosmopolitan and nationalist strands.

Long-established typologies have done much to deconstruct singular and hence simplistic understandings of cosmopolitanism. This is clearly illustrated, for instance, by distinctions concerning the different motivations underpinning forms of 'instrumental' and 'normative' cosmopolitanisms on one hand, and by differences in the degree of consciousness involved (i.e. *reflexive* as opposed to *banal* cosmopolitanisms) on the other (Skey 2012: 484). As early as 2002, Bronislaw Szerszynski and John Urry (2002: 465–467) confirmed the existence – on the level of media production and circulation – of a 'banal globalism … publicly screened within various broadcast genres, including advertisements', which includes global images, universal perspectives and 'deictic pointing' at distant places or global celebrity outside more narrowly defined 'communities'. Growing acknowledgement of such *banal globalism*, itself grounded in Michael Billig's (1995) seminal work on *banal nationalism*, further aids us in decoupling cosmopolitanism from particular individuals (let alone from specific personality types) or indeed from moralizing judgements. Instead, in locating both nationalism and cosmopolitanism on spectra that stretch from reflexive or 'hot' to instrumentalist, widely taken-for-granted or banal endpoints, we are able to start interrogating the processes (and their conditions) (e.g. Karner 2020) that transform one type of (communitarian) nationalism *or* cosmopolitanism into another. Concurrently, the existence of a banal globalism or indeed of a banal nationalism in the media domain does not by itself tell us much about their appropriations and uses, to which social and political actors put such interpretative stances. Rather than seeing either of these ideological specimens as anyone's possession or enduring trait, we are able to conceive of nuances within them; and we are able to see communitarianisms as well as cosmopolitanisms as contrasting, as well as internally heterogeneous, vectors of social and political action that always need to be located and understood in their generative contexts.

All of this points towards greater complexity than a straightforward juxtaposition of cosmopolitanism to its various ideological 'others' (i.e. whether communitarian, localist, nationalist, populist or a combination thereof) would suggest. Michael Skey's (2012: 471) contribution to such an acknowledgement consists of a 'move beyond labelling people and practices as cosmopolitan' and a recognition of how contradictory, conditional and indeed 'fragile' political stances can be. Skey illustrates this through focus group data that show participants engaged in 'dilemmatic thinking', whereby ideological contradictions are 'puzzled over' and negotiated in interaction. The particular 'ideological dilemma' in question concerns the wider political-cum-cultural tension between Enlightenment universalism, parochial particularisms as well as Skey's research participants' appreciation of socially desirable positions and associated strategies of impression management. In other words, Skey's data show – not unlike Gerd Baumann's aforementioned work on *dual discursive competence* – that 'individuals are more than able to shift between discourses, and this may involve them adopting contradictory [i.e. cosmopolitan as well as parochial] positions as they struggle to make sense of particular issues' (Skey 2012: 482).

CONCLUDING REMARKS

This contribution has attempted to respond to Victor Roudometof's recent plea (2019: 812, original italics) to 'take the local seriously' and his insistence that '*place* should have a place in analysing globalization's impact upon our lives'. My conceptual starting point for such an undertaking was Marc Augé's distinction of *supermodern* 'non-places' from 'anthropological places', which poses the arguably less immediately obvious but certainly no less significant question as to how global flows in general, and global migratory flows in particular, are responded to within particular local settings (or anthropological places). The cosmopolitanism-versus-communitarianism binary then provided a heuristic lens, through which associated literature was discussed but which the latter in turn clearly pushes beyond. Put another way: this chapter has posed the question as to how helpful the distinction between (various) cosmopolitanisms and (various) communitarianisms is for a political sociology focused on local constructions of, and responses to, Georg Simmel's category of 'the stranger'.

The ensuing discussion has led us from working definitions through a brief history of ideas towards growing acknowledgement of greater complexity and nuance than the cosmopolitan-versus-communitarian binary offers at least at first sight. Increasingly, the idea that populations or individuals can be classified according to their political inclinations in a cosmopolitan or communitarian direction has come to be questioned. The backdrop to this was arguably best captured in Ulrich Beck and Edgar Grande's observations that today's 'cosmopolitan modernity differs significantly from a Kantian world of "perpetual peace"'; instead, our globalizing world is defined by 'conflicting processes' involving 'centripetal, [or] unifying' as well as 'centrifugal, [or] diversifying' forces (Beck & Grande 2010: 418–419). In such a context, cosmopolitanisms and communitarianisms play important roles as some of the conflictual forces, centripetal and centrifugal, that are shaping our present. However, and as this discussion has demonstrated, it is important to consider this observation to be the start, rather than the conclusion, to some important debates. Whether the notion of a merely momentary 'cosmopolitan imagination' (Delanty 2006), empirical evidence of social actors' 'dual discursive competence' (Baumann 1996) or 'dilemmatic thinking' (Skey 2012), or indeed an emerging political economy of today's defining ideological forces (e.g. Manow 2019; Reckwitz 2020), much suggests that simplistic classifications of individuals or groups by their purported political leanings will not do. Instead, and to capture how global forces impact localities and how locals variously respond, a more finely woven analytical net is needed: one grounded in thorough contextualization, structural and historical, and sensitive to both the multiplicity and the fragility of the various political and ethical positions at all our disposal.

REFERENCES

Adorno, T., Frenkel-Brunswik, E., Levinson, D. & Sanford, N. (2019 [1950]). *The Authoritarian Personality*. Verso.

Appadurai, A. (1990). Disjuncture and difference in the global cultural economy. In M. Featherstone (Ed.), *Global Culture* (pp. 295–310). Sage.

Appiah, K. A. (2007). *Cosmopolitanism: Ethics in a World of Strangers*. Penguin.

Augé, M. (2008). *Non-Places: An Introduction to Supermodernity*. Verso.

Bauman, Z. (1993). *Postmodern Ethics*. Blackwell.

Baumann, G. (1996). *Contesting Culture: Discourses of Identity in Multi-Ethnic London*. Cambridge University Press.

Beck, U. (2017). *Die Metamorphose der Welt*. Suhrkamp.

Beck, U. & Grande, E. (2010). Varieties of second modernity: The cosmopolitan turn in social and political theory and research. *British Journal of Sociology*, 61 (3), 409–443.

Billig, M. (1995). *Banal Nationalism*. Sage.

Delanty, G. (2006). The cosmopolitan imagination: critical cosmopolitanism and social theory. *British Journal of Sociology*, 57 (1), 25–47.

Every, D. & Augoustinos, M. (2008). Constructions of Australia in pro- and anti-asylum seeker political discourse. *Nations and Nationalism*, 14 (3), 562–580.

Gellner, E. (1998). *Language and Solitude: Wittgenstein, Malinowski and the Habsburg Dilemma*. Cambridge University Press.

Gilroy, P. (2004). *After Empire: Melancholia or Convivial Culture?* Routledge.

Grillo, R. (2005). 'Saltdean can't cope': Protests against asylum-seekers in an English seaside suburb. *Ethnic and Racial Studies*, 28 (2), 235–260.

Hannerz, U. (1990). Cosmopolitans and locals in world culture. In M. Featherstone (Ed.), *Global Culture* (pp. 237–251). Sage.

Karner, C. (2020). *Nationalism Revisited: Austrian Social Closure from Romanticism to the Digital Age*. Berghahn.

Karner, C. (2021). The Styrian Megaphon: Bridging representations and uneasy 'conviviality' in a regional counter-public. *Journal of Austrian Studies*, 54 (1), 103–124.

Kirtsoglou, E. & Theodossopoulos, D. (2010). Intimacies of anti-globalization: Imagining unhappy others as oneself in Greece. In D. Theodossopoulos & E. Kirtsoglou (Eds), *United in Discontent: Local Responses to Cosmopolitanism and Globalization* (pp. 83–102). Berghahn.

Lévi-Strauss, C. (2011 [1955]). *Tristes Tropiques*. Penguin Classics.

Manow, P. (2019). *Die Politische Ökonomie des Populismus*. Suhrkamp.

Nowicka, M., Krzyżowski, Ł. & Ohm, D. (2019). Transnational solidarity, the refugees and open societies in Europe. *Current Sociology*, 67 (3), 383–400.

Reckwitz, A. (2020). *Das Ende der Illusionen: Politik, Ökonomie und Kultur in der Spätmoderne*. Suhrkamp.

Roudometof, V. (2019). Recovering the local: From glocalization to localization. *Current Sociology*, 67 (6), 801–817.

Simmel, G. (1992 [1908]). *Soziologie: Untersuchungen über die Formen der Vergesellschaftung*. Suhrkamp.

Skey, M. (2012). We need to talk about cosmopolitanism: The challenge of studying openness towards other people. *Cultural Sociology*, 6 (4), 471–487.

Solomos, J. and Back, L. (1994). Conceptualizing racisms: Social theory, politics and Research. *Sociology*, 28 (1), 143–161.

Stock, I. (2019). *Time, Migration and Forced Immobility: Sub-Saharan African Migrants in Morocco*. Bristol University Press.

Stürner, J. & Bendel, P. (2019). The two-way 'glocalization' of human rights, or: how cities become international agents in migration governance. *Peace Human Rights Governance*, 3 (2), 215–240.

Szerszynski, B. & Urry, J. (2002). Cultures of cosmopolitanism. *The Sociological Review*, 50 (4), 461–481.

Theodossopoulos, D. (2010). Introduction: United in discontent. In D. Theodossopoulos & E. Kirtsoglou (Eds), *United in Discontent: Local Responses to Cosmopolitanism and Globalization* (pp. 1–19). Berghahn.

19. Alternative globalization

Luke Martell

In the 1970s and 1980s globalization meant, for many, the spread of neoliberalism. An anti-globalization movement grew geared around global justice and inequality, most visible in large confrontational protests at meetings of world economic and political leaders, bottom up and outside mainstream politics. It was comprised of strands from socialist, union and labour, to radical green and anarchist and many other positions, with formally organized and informal parts. The movement was not against globalization completely but neoliberal globalization and its form in imperialist corporate projects, free trade deals, international organizations and capital mobility. The anti-globalization movement criticized the depoliticization of decisions when neoliberalism is inscribed in treaties and shifted beyond the control of governments and electors. It drew attention to the exploitation of labour as corporations moved to areas where workers had the worst pay and conditions and countries the weakest environmental and labour regulations. Anti-globalization highlighted concerns previously more marginal in politics, such as health concerns about food, water and pharmaceuticals, environmental issues, the rights of indigenous peoples and the extension of western media and consumerism in a homogenizing fashion.

FROM ANTI-GLOBALIZATION TO ALTER-GLOBALIZATION

Being against neoliberal globalization rather than all globalization meant it was possible to be for alternative globalization. Alter-globalization became a better description. One approach more oriented to political power than social movements and civil society was espoused by liberal and social democratically inclined proponents (see Held 2004).

Global Governance

Political alternative globalization is in part a response to the view that nation-states have to compete to attract globally mobile capital. Political liberalization and technological change from the 1970s made it easier for capital to move across borders and invest where it can get the best deal. This leads to a race to the bottom by governments, stripping back regulations and protections for labour and the environment and reducing tax and public spending to attract capital for whom these are burdens. This undermines social democratic policies. Consequently, regulation must be pursued across nation-states, so capital has nowhere to flee. This calls for common norms and standards at a global level implemented through institutions such as the World Trade Organisation, International Monetary Fund and United Nations, beefed up in power and enforcement, with social as well as economic goals, more democratic and inclusive. This can be supplemented with new global institutions for pursuing social goals, focused on issues such as labour rights, the environment and global equality.

To be truly global and democratic all states have to be equally involved in agreeing common regulations. But this requires common ground ideologically and in material interests that is not likely. Ideologically there is too much dissimilarity and states in the world have such clashing interests it is difficult to see how global governance with equal input can achieve agreements, let alone ones that are sufficient and effective. Outside global institutions the participants are unequal in power and economically and this translates into unequal sway in those institutions and different interests and conflicts. Powerful states often use global institutions to impose their aims as much as pursue global goals.

Opportunities for social democratic global governance have not been taken up. The financial crisis could have led to greater global regulation with public support. But governments bailed out finance nationally rather than reconstructing it. It seems it was an ideological commitment to deregulation that led to this. If the financial crisis did not provide a basis for the global regulation of capitalism it is not easy to see what could. Globalization to tackle development often leads poor countries into investment and trade agreements that have many parts to their disadvantage, because of the power of actors from the North they are engaging with. There have been numerous attempts at global agreements to tackle climate change, but they have been around abstract targets, such as degrees of warming, rather than concrete means. They have been undermined by the conflicting interests of those involved, weak in ambition and lacking the teeth to ensure conformity. There are annual international meetings to tackle nuclear proliferation, but they have failed to make serious inroads into making the world safer and to disarmament.

National and bilateral approaches, international but below global, pursuing concrete measures rather than abstract targets, have been more successful. Below-global and bottom-up work has worked better than global and top down. National governments took responsibility for tackling Covid-19, with barely a nod to global approaches to a global disease, which was perhaps a rational response to where possibility and effectiveness lie. Global agreements can be made in areas like development, humanitarian aid, peacekeeping, international law and human rights. There have been important achievements in such fields through international institutions like the United Nations. But in terms of an alternative that departs from and changes the neoliberal content of globalization there are limits in ideology and interests to pursuing such a project through inclusive action at global political levels.

Global cosmopolitan goals do not have the global cosmopolitan politics that will work for them. A more feasible approach is for cosmopolitanism to be pursued at lower-down supra-national or sub-global international levels where state actors can find selected others with related material interests, likeminded ideologies or compatible geopolitical aims. This could be regionally, for instance via the European Union, although what was supposed to be a social Europe became one of negative integration, involving the reduction as much as enhancement of regulations. Developing countries formed the G77 sub-global international alliance to pursue their shared interests. President Chavez of Venezuela tried to build an internationalism below global level with actors with similar ideological aims or geopolitical interests. With conflict rather than consensus politics at global level the left may be better off looking for a collaboration of the global left rather than a global government. This involves a sub-global selective internationalism.

Furthermore, while I do not underestimate the power of exit, evidence does not support the simple subordination of social democracy to global capital. States can pursue a regulatory and social democratic approach without capital fleeing and this has been possible in countries pursuing higher tax and spending programmes (Mosley 2005). They may have skilled workers, an infrastructure of science, transport, education, technology and health services, positive industrial relations involving strong unions, fair employment practices, social and industrial investment and public spending policies that boost the economy. These rather than a race to the bottom can be attractive to capital. For some businesses the cost of relocating if a social democratic government comes to power are too great so staying put ends up as the best decision.

National and Local Alternatives

One turn that alternative globalization can take, then, is a retreat from globalization, from anti- and political globalization to below-global strategies, yet still a response to global processes such as neoliberalism or climate change: globally oriented and to globalization if not global in means. This approach has ensued from the failure of global solutions to global issues like climate change. Actors pursue bottom-up concrete measures, like carbon reduction, non-neoliberal economics, labour and social goals; on-the-ground practical strategies rather than top-down abstract targets. These are national, intra-nationally regional or local, for instance via local government, community or economic innovations.

At national level there can be measures such as bans on diesel or petrol car sales, support for renewable energy, financial transaction taxes raising funds for environmental projects, ethical banking and green new deal policies. A more democratic economy with extensions of public ownership and co-ops can ensure that collective concerns are taken more into account over private profit in company decision-making, and green new deal measures realign the economy to greater sustainability and carbon neutrality. Some local governments keep wealth circulating in the community economy rather than siphoning it out to big corporations by encouraging local anchor institutions to purchase services and goods from community businesses, especially those co-operatively owned and with ethical and social objectives: this is 'community wealth building', a localist alternative to global neoliberalism (see Guinan & O'Neill 2020). These approaches are at local and national more than global levels. The idea of supra-national co-ordination and regulation is not central to them, if not ruled out.

There are local civil society approaches for alter-globalization. Anti-globalization has transitioned, not losing its origins, but reforming, to alter-globalization; from what it is against to alternatives to that, not just proposing but also creating them. These respond to global neoliberalism but construct alternatives locally. The positivity extends to reaching out to the local community, for instance migrants and the economically excluded, more than building a political force more with the like-minded and in conflict with the enemy. The approach is less conflictual and more about outreach. Examples include sustainable economic activities, co-ops, sharing economies, alternative food production and distribution, eco-communities, attempts to save public spaces for the local community, alternative social centres, alternative education, squats and occupations. Many of these are oriented around social rather than neoliberal or profit objectives and have green aims. They try to build decommodified economies where exchange is done without markets or money but in kind and for free. They are co-operative or collectively run, often with horizontal rather than hierarchical decision-making. So, they are non-market and non-capitalist, with green and anti-waste values to the fore and in an autonomous sphere separate from the state even if necessarily interacting with it. This is anti- and alter-neoliberal globalization but at local as much as global sites, while with a global consciousness and linked to global networks of similar initiatives.

The model of change is less state-oriented, whether revolutionary or reformist, or protest; more building local alternatives as a basis for change. Alternatives are: experimental, seeing by trial and error whether the alternative can work; demonstrative, showing how it works; and prefigurative, laying a basis for wider possible change. They are materialist as much as about ideological persuasion, change coming from practice as much as argument. The means can be an end, too, practised for their own sake and benefits. The approach differs from large-scale utopianism in the future, but is still utopian by micro-utopianism now. Holloway (2010) calls these alternatives 'cracks', where non-capitalist forms are built and can be expanded to undermine capitalism.

Holloway rejects using power to achieve change, but I believe social alternatives need to accompany and be intertwined with political institutional change. The approaches can be related: negatively through dichotomy or absorption of one by the other; but also complementary, overlapping, mutually supportive, cross-fertilizing and combining (Pleyers 2010). Alter-globalization can be connected with state politics and be a type of protest via constructive alternatives. Local alter-globalizations can focus on their communities and neglect opponents, power and change and the possibilities of state and politics. They can become separate from wider society and about alternative lifestyle and identity rather than political change. They can become multiplicities with a lack of overall coherence. But none of these are necessary. Material extra-political change creates contradictions with dominant forms and can be linked in a multilevel way with political institutions. This allows wider universality, engagement with political and social change rather than detachment from society, and politics can create bridges and coherence across experiments and alternatives.

OPEN BORDERS

I have expressed doubts about alter-globalization at a global level. However, there is an alternative globalization that can be pursued globally: open borders.

Philosophical and Principled Arguments

What is the case for open borders in their own right? One argument is on the basis of freedom and rights. Liberals are for freedom of speech, belief and assembly. It is inconsistent then to not be in favour of other freedoms that allow autonomy and self-determination, such as freedom of movement. Similarly, if you believe people should be free to emigrate to pursue liberty or a better life it is contradictory to not support immigration for the same things. Restrictions on free movement are related to other transgressions of liberty and rights such as the right to family life, trial before detention, freedom of association and from undue surveillance. Denial of entry may lead to immigrants' loss of freedoms in their home countries to the extent of torture and death.

Other principled arguments for immigration are on the basis of obligations to others, especially the less well off. A communitarian approach is that obligations are primarily to those from our community, defined in this case in terms of national borders. A cosmopolitan perspective puts the emphasis not on common membership of community, unless the community is the whole globe, and extends obligations to all regardless of where they are from. This includes welcoming people beyond our national borders to the benefits and freedoms we have where those are lacking in their country. Some may say that to have access to resources of our state immigrants should have made a contribution. But exclusion prevents them from doing this. The answer is to allow migrants in so they can contribute.

This links to arguments on the basis of equality. One is about the equal worth of all humans. Some have greater opportunities and life chances because of the luck of the country they were born in. Others are restricted from improving their chances through moving to where opportunities are better. So, people do not have equal chances because of an arbitrary fact out of their control. Allowing free movement would enable more similar chances globally; not allowing it prevents this. This is an injustice on the basis of the moral equality of all. Another case on the basis of equality concerns economic equality. Many who migrate do so from a position of material inequality to where they can better their economic circumstances. Migration does not itself eliminate structures of economic inequality but helps some to move from a poorer position to a better-off one and in that position to send money to their home country that helps that country become better off too. So, while it may not overturn basic structures of economic inequality it may be a factor that mitigates them.

A narrative on open borders and immigration can focus on freedom, obligation and equality. However, some argue that whatever the justice of it, free movement should be restricted because of the negative economic and social consequences for destination countries.

Economic and Social Arguments

Immigration, the story goes, leads in rich receiving countries to lower wages, the loss of jobs to migrant workers, a burden on welfare and social services and a decline of community and trust. Immigration may be connected sometimes to lower wages at the bottom of the ladder. However, this is not caused by immigration but by employers taking on migrants on lower wages and so reducing pay at the bottom. The cause is employers operating on the labour market rather than immigration. The solutions, therefore, are stronger trade unions and labour market regulations to ensure good wages, rather than cutting immigration. Average wages do not seem to come down in times of high immigration.

The argument that migrants take domestic workers' jobs assumes a fixed number of posts. With a higher birth rate or immigration new workers take existing jobs. However, a supply of new workers can lead to more employment. Areas of the economy where it is difficult to find employees, perhaps low-paid work, farm labouring, construction or health services, for example, find labour, are boosted and can grow. The workers spend money, boosting demand, leading to more production and jobs in manufacturing, services and retail. New employees pay tax so increasing government revenue that can fund public services. Migrant workers may sometimes take jobs that domestic workers have applied for but the supply of jobs in the economy increases. So, the effect is an increase in employment and employment chances for home workers.

Overall, studies of immigration suggest it leads to economic growth because migrants move from being unproductive to being productive and businesses can better match supply of labour to demand. The evidence is almost universal on the positive effects of international migration economically (Dustmann and Preston 2019).

A problem affecting sending countries is the 'brain drain' of skilled labour. It is a serious issue but is offset by remittances workers send home. Migrants benefit and get experience and training they can take back. There are ways of responding to brain drain other than immigration restrictions, such as brain circulation where rich country workers go abroad, compensation and requirements for skilled workers to work at home for a limited period in return for training. Root causes for people leaving can be addressed.

The argument that immigrants put an undue burden on welfare and public services is off the mark. Most migrants work. They are often net contributors to welfare and public services, paying more in than they get out, while home citizens are sometimes net beneficiaries. By entering employment and stimulating economic growth migrant workers facilitate greater tax revenue to fund public services (OECD 2013; Vargas-Silva 2015). They do jobs in public services that home workers are less keen to do. Immigration control is costly so more open borders would reduce public spending.

Some studies suggest that community and trust decline with immigration and diversity (e.g. Putnam 2007). But this is as much to do with the hostility of the host population as the arriving one. Developing community and trust takes time and snapshot pictures should be resisted. Where people live side by side with limited contact, diversity is associated with less cohesion, although not at apocalyptic levels. But in contexts like work or education with more contact and integration, there is greater trust and cohesion. Mixing reduces negative attitudes to immigrants and can be facilitated by policies for integration and tolerance. Diversity is also associated with greater trust amongst the young, more likely to be accustomed to it from an early age. So, if contact increases over time and as the young age and migrants become a larger proportion of the population trust in diverse areas will grow (Dinesen et al. 2020; Green et al. 2020).

Are Open Borders Possible?

Popular perceptions of massive migration from poor to rich countries are inaccurate (Duffy & Frere-Smith 2014; Gorodzeisky & Semyonov 2020). Furthermore, historical evidence from open borders does not support that they lead to huge and unsustainable population movements. Economists hypothesize that people will cross open borders for more money. But this assumes we are individual economic maximizers. In fact, humans are social animals and our decisions are affected by social, emotional, psychological and not simply economic factors. Given the opportunity to migrate internationally many will stay because of attachments to community and family and considerations like expense and language.

In rich immigration countries there is negativity towards immigrants and immigration. But some types are less unpopular. Temporary, student, skilled, legal migration and reunification with close family are more positively looked on as maybe are refugees (Heath & Richards 2019; De Coninck 2020). More unpopular types are illegal and permanent immigration. Young, educated and metropolitan groups see immigration as bringing benefits and are less anti-migrant. They will make up more of the population as the young get older and the proportion educated to degree level grows. Those in high immigration areas are more pro-immigration and, as we have seen, contact is associated with higher levels of trust between diverse groups suggesting that immigration leads to more positive attitudes to immigration (ESS 2016; Heath & Richards 2019).

Attitudes are the product, in part, of narratives and explanations. Sections of the media encourage anti-immigration sentiment and racism. Politicians are so fearful of the electoral consequences of a pro-immigration stance that they will not challenge anti-immigration attitudes. If they do, they can help change those attitudes. They can explain, for instance, that low wage levels are caused by employers setting low wages, not immigrants, and that housing shortages are due to a lack of housing, especially state housing, and not immigration. They can tell a story of compassion and the benefits of migration. So, amidst high levels of anti-immigration sentiment there are bases for support for open borders in growing groups.

CONCLUSIONS

Anti- and alter-globalization movements have opposed neoliberal globalization and fought for alternatives, through protest and constructing them, often locally. Global regulation for a more social democratic globalization is limited by ideological and material differences. Political international change is more viable at the level of sub-global selective international co-ordination where interests and ideology coincide. Local alter-globalization and sub-global internationalism can be supplemented by alternatives at a national level, democratizing the economy to more collective forms. While cosmopolitan goals and alternatives to neoliberal globalization are best followed politically below global level, cosmopolitanism can be pursued more globally through open borders. A narrative of compassion and common humanity can supplement evidence on the benefits of global migration. This can build on positive attitudes to immigration among growing strata and on the community fostered with contact between diverse groups.

REFERENCES

De Coninck, D. (2020). 'Migrant categorizations and European public opinion: Diverging attitudes towards immigrants and refugees'. *Journal of Ethnic and Migration Studies*, 46 (9), 1667–1686.

Dinesen, P.T., Schaeffer, M. & Sonderskøv, K.M. (2020). 'Ethnic diversity and social trust: A narrative and meta-analytical review'. *Annual Review of Political Science*, 23, 24.1–24.25.

Duffy, B. & Frere-Smith, T. (2014). *Perceptions and Reality: Public Attitudes to Immigration*. Ipsos MORI.

Dustmann, C. & Preston I.P. (2019). 'Free movement, open borders and the global gains from labor mobility'. *Annual Review of Economics*, 11, 783–808.

ESS (European Social Survey) (2016). *Attitudes towards Immigration and Their Antecedents: Topline Results from Round 7 of the European Social Survey*. European Research Infrastructure Consortium.

Gorodzeisky, A. & Semyonov, M. (2020). 'Perceptions and misperceptions: Actual size, perceived size and opposition to immigration in European societies'. *Journal of Ethnic and Migration Studies*, 46 (3), 612–630.

Green E.G.T., Visintin, E.P., Sarrasin, O. & Hewstone, M. (2020). 'When integration policies shape the impact of intergroup contact on threat perceptions: A multilevel study across 20 European countries'. *Journal of Ethnic and Migration Studies*, 46 (3), 631–648.

Guinan, J. & O'Neill, M. (2020). *The Case for Community Wealth Building*. Polity Press.

Heath, A. & Richards, L. (2019). *How Do Europeans Differ in their Attitudes to Immigration: Findings from the European Social Survey, 2002/3 – 2016/17*. OECD.

Held, D. (2004). *Global Covenant: The Social Democratic Alternative to the Washington Consensus*. Polity Press.

Holloway, J. (2010). *Crack Capitalism*. Pluto Press.

Mosley, L. (2005). 'Globalization and the state: Still room to move?'. *New Political Economy*, 10 (3), 355–362.

OECD (Organisation for Economic Co-operation and Development) (2013). *International Migration Outlook 2013*. OECD.

Pleyers, G. (2010). *Alter-Globalization: Becoming Actors in the Global Age*. Polity Press.

Putnam, R.D. (2007). 'E pluribus unum: Diversity and community in the twenty-first century'. The 2006 Johan Skytte Prize Lecture. *Scandinavian Political Studies*, 30, 137–74.
Vargas-Silva, C. (2015). *The Fiscal Impact of Immigration in the UK*. Migration Observatory.

20. The rise of racism and antisemitism in the age of globalization

Gerald J. Steinacher

INTRODUCTION

In August 2017, hundreds of white supremacists gathered in Charlottesville, Virginia. They marched through the streets giving Nazi salutes, waving swastika flags, and shouting, "White lives matter!"; "Sieg Heil"; and "Jews will not replace us." As is now common, the violent imagery from the racist march in Charlottesville spread quickly online thanks to smartphones and easy internet access. This was a wake-up call for many who thought that racism and anti-semitism were in decline. The opposite, in fact, is true. A range of research data shows a strong rise in racism and antisemitism across the globe recently, particularly in Europe and the United States (US). According to the Federal Bureau of Investigations, in 2018 violent hate crimes in the US reached their highest peak in 16 years. The previous year, antisemitic incidents in the US surged by an eye-popping 57 percent (Anti-Defamation League, 2018; Astor, 2018; Levin, 2019). A 2018 German study showed that about 25 percent of interviewed citizens were xenophobic, and that negative sentiments about Jews and Muslims were high (Schulte v. Drach, 2018). Racist and antisemitic ideas are booming worldwide, and extreme right-wing conspiracy theories are enjoying a renaissance. In recent years in the US and Europe we see openly racist ideas moving into parliaments and presidential residences. These developments are happening against the background of an increasingly globalizing world. This chapter seeks to make sense of this surge in racism and antisemitism and to place it within the broader context of globalization's rise.

UNDERSTANDING RACISM

At the core of racism is the belief that one group of people is inherently different and inferior to another. The idea of "us versus them" has existed since ancient times, as the antithesis "Greek versus Barbarian" shows (Hund, 2018, p. 45ff.). The idea that those different from us are to be treated with suspicion, fear, or disdain—what can be broadly characterized as xenophobia—was initially not based on biological markers, but rather on language and culture. Racism, however, is more than just xenophobia: it is instead a system of discrimination and suppression.

The idea of modern racism has its roots in the Enlightenment. Scholars of that era obses-sively worked to categorize the world and all its creatures. External visual characteristics of the body, such as skin color, were used to organize humanity in four groups or "races" (white/ Caucasian, Mongoloid/Asian, Negroid/Black, and Australoid). These races were then attrib-uted intrinsic inner qualities that led to a hierarchy of human value. White Europeans were allegedly more civilized, intelligent, industrious, more suitable for Christian morality, and better able to control their passions (sexuality). German philosopher Immanuel Kant stated that humanity at its best comes as the race of the whites (Hund, 2011, pp. 69–98). Other races were, therefore, viewed as inherently less civilized, and showing more vices than virtues. Zygmunt Bauman's (1989, p. 60) short definition of racism illustrates the problem: "Man *is* before he *acts*; nothing he does may change what he is. This is, roughly, the philosophical essence of racism."

The reality, however, is that modern research has convincingly shown that biological racism is built on nothing more than fiction—there is no meaningful distinction of traits based on race. New genetic findings reveal that there are more differences among individuals inside a race than between one race and another: "We as a species have been estimated to share 99.9% of our DNA with each other. The few differences that do exist reflect differences in environments and external factors, not core biology" (Chou, 2017). In terms of biology, individual humans are uniquely diverse, not human groups.

But many nineteenth-century intellectuals painted a very different picture. Charles Darwin's "survival of the fittest" theory was applied to human society and history. The ensuing social Darwinism gained traction. Comte Joseph Arthur de Gobineau preached racial inequality and believed that every pure race would degenerate when mixed with others—ideas that are still very much alive. Because Enlightenment ideals aimed to organize the world and society in a rational way, it appeared logical to imagine communities as people with similar ancestry and language, and to consider these ethnic "nations" as natural entities (Anderson, 1991). The European political scientist Florian Bieber (2020, p. 188) states:

> After all, nations and nationalism are relatively recent phenomena and thus might be replaced as they displaced earlier types of collective identity. Yet, it is a deeply ingrained feature of societies and the international system and offers a strong category responding to the human need to belong to an identifiable group.

The merging of ethnic nationalism, racism, and social Darwinism has proved particularly toxic and impactful on political right-wing ideologies from the nineteenth century to the present (Mosse, 1985).

While this history is critical to understanding racism's origins, racism cannot be fully grasped without acknowledging the element of power in its hierarchy. As argued by the Anti-Defamation League (2020), a Jewish non-governmental organization, racism is "The marginalization and/or oppression of people of color based on a socially constructed racial hierarchy that privileges white people." White-skinned Europeans established the idea of the intrinsic inferiority of others and their own superiority for political and economic gains.

Racism has undergone various transformations that reflect societal changes. Its evolution in the US illustrates this point well. Beginning with the genocidal treatment of indigenous Native Americans, it was followed by slavery, Jim Crow, and modern racism. In the 1960s, against the backdrop of the Cold War and decolonization, the US Congress finally outlawed legal racism and enforced voting rights for African Americans. Even with these steps forward, African Americans were bullied and beaten at the ballot box and it took until 1967 to strike down the prohibition of intermarriage (Fredrickson, 2002). In the post-Civil Rights era racism changed its form and was less overt. We know that racism is a social construct, but still remnants of biological thinking about race persist. Racism in various forms continues to impact the present age of globalization. George Mosse (1985, p. xxvii) articulated what was (and remains) seemingly attractive about these concepts: "Racism gave everyone a designated place in the world, defining him as a person and, through a clear distinction between 'good' and 'evil' races, explaining the puzzling modern world in which he lived. Who could ask for more."

UNDERSTANDING ANTISEMITISM

Antisemitism, the negative stereotyping and hatred of Jews, has overshadowed Western history for over 2,000 years. In the twentieth century, antisemitism led to the Shoah, the systematic state-sponsored murder of 6 million Jews by Nazi Germany and its allies. After the horrors of the Holocaust and Second World War, antisemitism as a state ideology was discredited in most Western societies (Kendi, 2017). In recent decades, antisemitism significantly diminished in popularity in the Western world, and there was hope that this ideology could soon be consigned to the past. On the contrary, the last few years have witnessed a drastic increase of antisemitism in Western societies, often paired with far right-wing activism, racism, and xenophobia (Steinacher, 2020).

Modern antisemitism originated in Christian antisemitism. Christians accused Jews of murdering their Messiah and hated them for rejecting his teachings. Jews were discriminated against, separated in ghettos, and kept in misery. Jews should not be killed, Christian leaders reasoned, because there was hope for their ultimate conversion. During the European Middle Ages, Jews remained the only tolerated religious minority (if only barely) in the Christian world. The Middle Ages saw the creation of vicious allegations against Jews, the predecessors of modern-day conspiracy theories. Many accused Jews of constantly plotting against Christians, bringing about plagues, and murdering Christian children. Many of these fabricated allegations remain with us.

In Western Europe from the Middle Ages to the nineteenth century, Jews constituted only about 1 to 2 percent of the total population—a tiny religious minority. In the US today, Jews still make up less than 2 percent of the population. With the Enlightenment, rulers gave Jews citizenship rights and allowed them to leave their ghettos (though not until 1917 in Russia). However, the first strain of antisemitism (religious antisemitism) did not disappear but was instead flanked by a secular version of antisemitism. Against the background of pseudo-scientific theories about race in the late nineteenth century, Jews were not seen simply as adherents of a different religion or culture but as a separate "race" (Steinacher, 2020). In this case visible biological markers objectively did not exist, but they were claimed anyway (like an alleged typical Jewish form of the nose) (Mosse, 1985, p. xxix).[1] For the racial antisemite, conversion or assimilation was not an option that would solve "the Jewish question" (Judaken, 2017). Antisemitism has proved to be extremely adaptable and like a shapeshifter appeared in many political movements (MacShane, 2008).

When studying antisemitism, we learn very little, if anything, about Jews, but we learn a lot about the hate fantasies and negative stereotypes that gentiles have about Jews. Antisemitism operates by using fictional allegations, often centered around quite complicated conspiracy theories. For these reasons, fighting antisemitism with factual arguments is difficult. Doris Bergen (2016, p. 3) notes that "Prejudices are habits of thought, they are not reasoned responses to objective realities."

Antisemitism also acts as a vehicle for scapegoating, which is perhaps the cause of its persistence through the centuries. Allegations against the "other" don't need to be factual as long as they satisfy fear and hate. In recent years, we have seen a dramatic rise in antisemitic language, vandalism, violence, and even mass murder. Now in the age of increased globalization it serves again to explain all ills of our time.

THE RISE OF GLOBALIZATION

Globalization refers to the exchange of goods, technologies, labor, capital, and ideas among different parts of the world. Human civilizations have communicated and connected with each other in various ways since ancient times, but within that long history, different stages of globalization (often categorized by intensity and speed) can be identified. International trade, for example, increased swiftly among Western countries in the 1970s and then expanded across developing countries in the 1980s. Rapid technological progress, including the creation of the internet, has swept much of the world since the 2000s. Each of these forces has steadily integrated the world.

One might assume that integration and exchange would reduce racism and antisemitism. It is, therefore, somewhat surprising that racism and antisemitism are on the rise. While globalization brings the world together in some ways, it furthers divisions and insecurity in other ways. As the Polish-British sociologist Zygmunt Bauman (1998, p. 2) aptly put it: "Globalization divides as much as it unites; it divides as it unites—the causes of division being identical with those which promote the uniformity of the globe." Growing globalization over the last few decades has coincided with a worsening standard of living for blue-collar workers in the US and Europe, as well as an increase in income inequality. There is some evidence, albeit no consensus, that this is not merely a coincidence. Some have argued that globalization results in less-skilled workers losing their jobs as companies move their operations to low-cost countries and/or replace these workers with immigrants willing to work for lower wages (Slaughter & Swagel, 1997). It is, therefore, not surprising that less-skilled workers blame globalization and immigrants for their hardships. Globalization seems ripe with contradictions.

The widening income gap between college graduates and high school graduates also inflames less-skilled workers' resentment. Although higher unemployment among the less skilled and income inequality seem to coincide with globalization, it is unclear if globalization is the sole cause of these developments. Globalization might be less to blame than the technological changes that have created opportunities for skilled workers to the detriment of less-skilled ones and/or replaced less-skilled workers with robots (Slaughter & Swagel, 1997). Whatever the exact causes of these inequalities, the recent recession made them worse. In 2008, the global economic crisis hit many middle-class people in the US particularly hard. Difficulties at Wall Street spiraled into a banking crisis and burst the US housing bubble. From the resultant global recession, millions of people (especially in the US) lost their houses, savings, and jobs. The Great Recession of 2008–2009 was arguably the worst economic crisis since the Great Depression of the 1930s.

Inequality appears to be a driving force for the rise of populist anti-globalization movements in Western countries. Researchers found that income inequality has grown in rich countries. The poor are getting poorer and the rich are getting richer. Populist politicians rage against "elites," "the establishment," "immigrants," or other scapegoats—exploiting fears and deep-seated divisions. Political scientist Bieber (2020, p. 192) states: "nationalist leaders often target those co-nationals who are 'unreliable' members of the nation, scapegoat other nations or minorities or they direct their grievances against some global elite. These are structural features of nationalist movements going back to the late eighteenth century and are by no means novel."

Campaigning against "globalization," they address the people's frustration about increasing inequality. And as a result, in democratic societies voters express their dissatisfaction by voting for populist parties. The 2016 British vote to leave the European Union (EU) as well as Donald Trump's victory in the US election are expressions of that phenomenon. It is somewhat surprising that the rise of populism in Western countries occurred when the economy was doing very well and the unemployment rate was low. Lubos Pastor and Pietro Veronesi (2020, p. 36) state that the model used "also predicts the backlash is more likely when the economy is strong because that is when inequality is particularly large." There can be little doubt that the rise of populism is one form of pushback against globalization.

In sum, whether or not the sole reason for social changes taking place, globalization has encouraged an increase in resentment, division, and polarization at the global, continental, national, regional, and local level. These feelings and dynamics have expressed themselves in a myriad of ways—the resurgence of racism and antisemitism being chief among them.

RACIALIZED IMMIGRATION

Increased globalization has also contributed to increased mobility, not just in terms of tourism and business, but also in immigration. Military conflicts around the world have also added to the number of people on the move, as refugees leave their homes in search of safety. These trends have triggered strong, often racialized, anti-immigration movements in the US and Europe.

Europe in the 1980s and 1990s saw a rise of far right-wing political forces that all too often used xenophobia and racism as part of their platform (Eco, 1995, 2020). In 1994 Italy, where the traditional postwar party system collapsed, the media tycoon-turned-politician Silvio Berlusconi became prime minister. In many ways, Italy was a forerunner of the current wave of national populism (Gallmetzer, 2019). In France, the right-wing Front National party gained momentum and won local elections. In Austria, the far right-wing, antisemitic, and xenophobic Freedom Party became part of a national government coalition in 2000, causing an international outcry (Black, 2000; Gstettner, 2006, pp. 184–191). What was unusual in Europe had become the norm 20 years later. In 2018, nationalist and xenophobic parties ran the governments of eight EU countries (Traverso, 2019, p. 1).[2]

What fuels these movements is often a reaction to globalization, particularly to immigration and the opening of markets and borders. In the past three decades we have seen an influx of refugees and immigrants from Africa and the Middle East, for which most European nations were not prepared. Some Europeans feared the loss of the familiar in the face of cultural change. Populist politicians, making scapegoats of immigrants and refugees, answered people's anxieties about identity, jobs, and security. The immigrant has become the outsider, depicted as criminal, threatening the community. Politicians have played the "tough on crime" card most recently evidenced in the US 2016 presidential election (Bauman, 2006, pp. 36–40). Inside the EU, citizens enjoy freedom of travel and movement, but the EU's outside borders have become increasingly more impenetrable.

While immigration restrictions are not necessarily racist, they are often racialized. Ireland provides a case in point. Most Irish thought that given their own history as a discriminated people they were immune to xenophobia and racism. Reactions to increased immigration (including people from Africa and Asia) to Ireland in the last 20 years has shown otherwise. Irish citizenship law privileges applicants with Irish ancestry, while children of newcomers born in Ireland can be denied the right to citizenship (Lentin & McVeigh, 2006)·This has a minimal impact on non-Irish EU citizens, because they have the right to live and work in Ireland. But for immigrants from Kabul, Istanbul, or Mombasa the negative consequences are real. The *Irish Times* called this a law "with a dangerous edge of racism" (O'Toole, 2003).

In 2015 over 1.3 million refugees came to the EU, particularly Germany, and fueled hostility and right-wing populist energies. Most of these refugees had fled war-torn countries or climate extremes in the Middle East (e.g. Syria) or Africa. Faced with death because of war or starvation, they made a desperate choice in the hope of a better future. They did not always receive a warm welcome in Europe. On the contrary, most recently in 2019 there were more than 1,600 attacks on refugees and asylum-seekers in Germany (*Deutsche Welle*, 2020). In February 2020 a shooter killed nine people in the German town of Hanau near Frankfurt am Main. The victims of his attack had migration backgrounds and the shooter was motivated by ant-immigrant and racist hate ideology, as the police later concluded. After the murder he drove home and shot his 72-year-old mother before he killed himself. Before the attack he had posted a manifesto on the internet, which revealed his antisemitic, racist, and anti-Muslim world view mixed with conspiracy theories and paranoia.

The xenophobic and anti-Islam right-wing party Alternative für Deutschland (AfD) won almost 13 percent of the vote in 2017. Accusations of xenophobia and racism against the AfD are made repeatedly: in 2020 a local AfD branch distributed children's coloring books with denigrating caricatures of Muslims and Black people. Other groups in Germany openly challenge the country's democratic constitution. An estimated 24,000 potentially violent neo-Nazis live in Germany, who discriminate against immigrants, Muslims, and Jews alike (Bendersky, 2021, introduction). In other Western countries as well as Germany, racialized immigration goes far back. Social scientist Steve Garner cites the anti-Chinese and anti-Japanese US migration laws of the 1880s, or the 1901 laws that banned non-Europeans from coming to Australia in order to "keep" the new nation white (Garner, 2017). Traditional rules like citizenship laws in Ireland and Italy (and traditionally also in Germany) based on ancestry and "blood lines" (*jus sanguinis*) have been in the books for generations. But these fantasies around "the mystique of blood," are no longer suitable for today's increasingly diverse Europe, or indeed, world (Traverso, 2019, p. 45). And things are indeed slowly changing in some countries. German citizenship laws have been reformed in recent years with a trend towards *ius solis*, that is, granting rights to people born in Germany no matter their ethnic or racial background. In other words, the law is now more in line with the diverse realities on the ground. An ethnically homogenous nation is (and always was) a fiction; the reality is much more complex. The US has struggled with this fiction, too.

RACISM AND ANTI-RACISM

The US's history with racism is long. Recently, injustices as old as the country's founding have come again to national attention. As an answer to rampant systemic racism, the Black Lives Matter movement started around 2013 and, while already prevalent, gained mass support after the 2020 murder of George Floyd, a 46-year-old Black American man. Black Lives Matter has become a modern global movement against racism and the legacies of slavery and colonialism, with demonstrations across Canada, Australia, Japan, and elsewhere (Buchanan et al., 2020). In some ways today's movement echoes the 1960s civil rights movement and shows that many issues of racism have been left unaddressed. Disparity is one of them. Black people make up 13.2 percent of the US population but own only 2.7 percent of the nation's wealth (Kendi, 2017, p. 2). Residential segregation is also a reality in US cities. Anti-racist movements challenge the founding myths of the US, for example that white men alone created the nation with no help from others. This whitewashed official narrative has left Native Americans, African Americans, Asian Americans, and others mostly out of the picture.

In Europe, too, the legacy of colonialism and racial stereotypes have come under scrutiny. Cultural traditions like Black Pete in the Netherlands (the figure of an African servant to Saint Niklaus, normally involving blackface and racial stereotyping) are being challenged. One of the heated debates includes monuments, which often have connections to racist and colonial history. Statues of Confederate officials continue to be toppled in the US. In Belgium statues of the colonial era King Leopold II, who oversaw genocide in Congo, spurred great controversy. The Black Lives Matter movement shed light on the fact that racial harassment and discrimination against Africans (and people of African ancestry) is still very widespread in Europe, as well as in the US.

After September 11, 2001, the US government launched the global war on terror and radical Islam. As so often occurs in a time of "us versus them," distinctions and cautious language were pushed aside. The "enemy" was dehumanized. Not just the radical violent Islamist was targeted, but soon ordinary Muslims faced discrimination, xenophobia, and racism (Said, 2006, pp. 41–44).[3] Many US politicians argued for a tough stance on immigration, targeting Muslims. And on top of such a tense situation, a struggling economy made everything worse.

The French-Italian historian Enzo Traverso put it well when he wrote: "With the election of Donald Trump as the president of the United States, the rise of a new nationalist, populist, racist, and xenophobic right has become a global phenomenon" (Traverso, 2019, p. 1). Donald Trump is a part of a long line—and indeed is the culmination—of increasing populist conservatism in the US since the 1960s. US historian Richard Hofstadter (2008) in the mid-1960s commented that American right-wing extremism has a long tradition and from time to time moves from the fringes of society into mainstream politics.

However, Trump's explicit biological racism stands out in modern US presidential history. His immigration policies illustrate the point: Trump objected to immigration from places like Haiti or African nations, which he called "shithole countries," while at the same time called for more immigrants from Norway (Kirby, 2018). Trump's rhetoric also highlights racism's adaptable nature (Braune, 2020, pp. 207–222). He and his supporters have verbally attacked and discriminated against different groups at different times: from Mexicans, African Americans, Asian Americans, and Muslims, to people with disabilities or "foreign" accents (Hund, 2018, p. 7). This racism in the US is arguably also a fear of the loss of power by European Americans (white Americans) as the country closes in on a demographic shift. According to census predictions, by 2044 white Americans will no longer be a majority. For the first time since the founding of the US, European Americans will be in the minority (United States Census Bureau, 2015).

White supremacists in Europe and the US are peddling the conspiracy theory of an alleged "great replacement" of white Europeans by Africans and Jews, a "masterplan" in which Jews pull the strings. In this "white genocide" Western civilization is being destroyed by anti-racist protesters, non-white immigrants, and open borders (Guerrero, 2020). Xenophobic voices warn that globalization and foreign influences will destroy their perceived national identity; newcomers from the "Third World" will corrupt the roots of a society through "blood mixing." In the words of replacement guru Renaud Camus: "the brutal change of population which has been taking place in France (and in Europe) since the beginning of the last quarter of the last century" is destroying the essence of Western culture (2018, p. 19). Troublingly, this hateful rhetoric can turn into physical violence. In August 2019 a shooter in the US city of El Paso, Texas, who killed 21 people with an AK-47-style rifle, explicitly targeted Mexicans and Latinos in a shopping mall close to the Mexican border. The manifesto he posted online just before the massacre was full of vile language against immigrants, referring to their presence as an "invasion" (Baker, 2019). Antisemitism expert Robert Wistrich, when writing about the British case, points out that ethnic nationalism targets everyone considered "foreign," including Jews:

> For the moment it is Asians and blacks who are more usually portrayed by nationalists as representing everything that is alien to ... society and culture, but it is in the logic of exclusivist nationalism and of those who advocate a monolithic conception of [Western] culture to regard all minorities with suspicion. Jews were traditionally the favorite targets of this kind of hostility. (Wistrich, 1991, pp. 112–113)

THE RISE OF ANTISEMITISM

This replacement conspiracy theory provides ideological support for a significant amount of the white supremacist and racist activism we have seen in recent years. Additionally, it is closely linked to antisemitic conspiracy theories dating back to the nineteenth century that allege a Jewish plot to bring down white Christian societies. The most impactful actor spreading this conspiracy theory was Édouard Drumont and his 1886 *La France juive*. Most recently, this theory found a second life in Renaud Camus' *Le Grand Remplacement*, in which the Muslim (and non-white) immigrants of today stand in for the Jews of Drumont's France (Kohen & Steinacher, 2021, introduction).

A number of recent attacks by domestic terrorists can be linked to this theory. In October 2018 an antisemite attacked the Tree of Life synagogue in Pittsburgh, Pennsylvania, murdering 11 people. This was the bloodiest antisemitically motivated attack and worst mass murder of Jews in the history of the US. The killer accused Jewish organizations of helping "migrant caravans" from Latin America enter the country and destroy "white America." It would appear that the 46-year-old shooter was a believer in the white supremacist "great replacement" theory. In April 2019, a man with an assault-style rifle killed one worshipper and wounded three others in the Chabad of Poway synagogue in California. The attacker, a declared white supremacist, wrote in an open letter that he was fighting back against the Jews because they were plotting a genocide of the white European race. On Yom Kippur in 2019, a heavily armed gunman attacked the synagogue in the German town of Halle, stating later that he was fighting an "invasion" of Arabs and Jews. In today's antisemitic fantasies, Jews are no longer conspiring with Satan, rather they want to harm gentiles and bring evil to the world.

Other antisemitic lies and conspiracy theories have also experienced a strong comeback in recent years. Among them is the "Protocols of the Elders of Zion" hoax. The Protocols are an antisemitic forgery put together by the Russian secret police and first printed in 1903 through

1905. The document recounts alleged meetings of anonymous Jewish leaders plotting to bring Christians under their worldwide rule. Despite being repeatedly exposed as a complete fabrication, it was quickly translated into all major languages and became a classic of antisemitic propaganda around the world (Lipstadt, 1993, p. 41). Millions worldwide still believe Jews are puppet masters pulling the strings of global power. Arab governments have promoted antisemitic propaganda for decades as well, receiving an enormous boost from the internet and social media. In these propaganda materials, prominent community leaders of Jewish background are demonized and presented as evidence for the Jewish world conspiracy.

The well-known Hungarian American billionaire and philanthropist for liberal causes George Soros, for example, has been cast as the all-powerful Jewish bogeyman for anti-globalization right wingers. The current right-wing government in Hungary under prime minister Viktor Orbán uses "international Jew" Soros repeatedly as a hated scapegoat for all kinds of problems (especially regarding issues of immigration). The demonization of Soros "shows the enduring power of the myth of the omnipresent, omnipotent Jew on the far-right of European politics," the Israeli newspaper *Haaretz* put it (Hoare, 2019; Porat, 2013, p. 471). Protester signs in Hungary show Soros' image with devil horns and billboards in Budapest reading "Stop Soros." For antisemites "globalist" is often a code word for "Jew." One of the latest iterations of the "Protocols" is QAnon, a group that is spreading the theory of a cabal purportedly focused on a satanic pedophile ring in the US led by Democratic politicians and Jews conspiring against Trump. The internet and social media enable conspiracy theorists and bigots to propagate and reinforce biases, as well as to spin conspiracy theories in dark corners of the world wide web.

Protectionism and nativism played huge roles in Donald Trump's 2016 presidential campaign. Once president, his continued rhetoric left little doubt about his position. In a September 2018 speech to the assembly of the United Nations he said: "We will never surrender America's sovereignty to an unelected, unaccountable, global bureaucracy. America is governed by Americans. We reject the ideology of globalism, and we embrace the doctrine of patriotism" (Bieber, 2020, p. 190ff.). Trump praised nationalism as the only true ideology, while rejecting socialism and liberalism. Steve Bannon, Trump's early advisor and ambitious ideologue of the new far right, made no secret that he was firmly against globalization and supported isolation. For antisemites and the far right, the term "globalist" is a common code word for Jew, often used in the context of conspiracy theories revolving around "globalists" and "capitalists." Anti-globalization forces on the political left and the political right use antisemitic tropes in their critiques. But antisemitic-motivated violence remains in the far right's domain.

Antisemitic speech and violence have significantly increased in the US, Europe, and Australia since 2016 (Lipstadt, 2019; Rosenfeld, 2015; Steinacher, 2020; Weiss, 2019). Anti-globalization forces on both the political left and the political right use antisemitic tropes in their critiques. But antisemitic-motivated violence resides more firmly within the domain of the far right and its racism. What complicates the situation further is antisemitism hidden as a critique of Israel, both from the political right and left. Every government can and should be criticized if democratic standards are transgressed or if human rights violations occur. However, some attacks from all sides of the political spectrum go far beyond that criticism by calling into question the very existence of Israel. At the same time in recent years we have seen far right-wing activists and antisemites very publicly supporting Israel. The self-serving nature of these statements are revealed in antisemitic circles calling for Jews to go "home, where they belong" and evangelical Christians hoping for a second coming of Jesus when Jews return to Israel and eventually convert. These examples again illustrate the adaptable nature of antisemitism to every generation. As British politician Denis Macshane (2008, p. 12) puts it: "Today, [antisemitism] is the world's most pernicious ideology and practice, international in its reach and capable of taking different forms from the University campus to the upper-class dinner party."

There is now a tendency among right wingers and white nationalists to distance themselves from Hitler and the Holocaust (also through Holocaust denial in various forms) so as to make far-right ideologies more acceptable to mainstream society. The conservative student organization Turning Point USA (TPUSA) demonstrates this trend. Founded in 2012, TPUSA's stated goal is to appeal to young conservatives, especially on college campuses, to push back on liberal views. In December 2017, the *New Yorker* (Mayer, 2017) reported that this conservative non-profit was accused of "racial bias and illegal campaign activity." In February 2019, a video became public showing the organization's communications director, Candace Owens, talking about Hitler and nationalism: "If Hitler just wanted to make Germany great and have things run well—okay, fine. The problem is that he … had dreams outside of Germany [and] wanted to globalize." Owens' statement from a December 2018 event in London also drew attention and criticism. In a congressional hearing about the rise of white nationalism, Owens, who is African American, defended and clarified her statement by saying she tried to separate the term *nationalist* from its associations with Hitler and the Nazis, adding, "He wasn't a nationalist … He was a homicidal, psychotic maniac" (Amatulli, 2019; Anti-Defamation League, n.d.). However, Owens got the facts wrong. The Nazis established the first concentration camps in Germany in 1933, only weeks after they took power. So, the "problem" with the Nazis was not "globalization," but their inherent racism and genocidal violence (Steinacher, 2020).

CONCLUSION

The last 50 years have delivered the globe enormous changes. The bipolar world of the Cold War years was replaced by an increasingly globalized one, characterized by many economic, technological, and cultural changes. While it is not easy to pinpoint a single cause for the rise of racism and antisemitism, globalization and technological changes have certainly had an impact. But so have armed conflicts and massive displacements of refugees. For many, this fast-moving globalized reality feels increasingly out of their control, which produces anxiety and fear—an ideal breeding ground for racism and antisemitism. In 2017, the prominent US historian Ibram X. Kendi (2017, p. xi) stated: "If Barack Obama came to embody America's history of racial progress, then Donald Trump should come to embody America's history of racist progress. And racist progress has consistently followed racial progress." Globalization appears to be a catalyst for both racial progress and racist progress. Many Western societies are deeply divided between two opposing impulses: integrate or isolate. The 2020 US presidential election underscores this trend; the country seemed to be almost evenly divided between those who wanted to live in a more integrated and diverse world, and those who wanted to literally wall themselves and their country off from outsiders. The COVID-19 pandemic of 2020–2021 has further contributed to the growing anxieties of the lower middle class. The resulting economic crash of the pandemic has engendered a fertile climate in which racism, ethnic nationalism, xenophobia, and antisemitism thrive. Anti-Asian racism skyrocketed in the US in 2020–2021 also because of the pandemic. And antisemitism, too, is out in the open. On January 6, 2021, a mob of Trump supporters packed with racists and antisemites stormed the US Capitol building. From their signs, shirts, and statements, Rev. Bryan N. Massingale (2021) wrote the same evening: "What we saw today is a clear declaration that many white people would rather live in a white dictatorship than in a multiracial democracy." An open question remains: was this attack just another wave of (old and new) racism and antisemitism that will eventually subside, or are we at a point where the most basic principles of Western democracies, like human rights and mutual respect, are at risk? One thing is certain: the age of globalization, with all its technological advancements but antiquated prejudices, has left many of our worst instincts fundamentally unchanged.

ACKNOWLEDGMENTS

I want to thank Anne Johnson, Stas Nikolova, Steven Wees, Timothy Turnquist, Michael Miller, and Christian Karner for their valuable feedback and suggestions. Patrick Jones and Prag Katta provided much input on the history and presence of racism in the US. Given the challenges addressing such a sensitive and very present topic I am particularly thankful to all of them and others who helped with this piece.

NOTES

1. In early modern Spain people of Jewish ancestry, even if long converted and Christian (the so-called *Conversos*), were still seen as foreign, and their blood considered "not pure" (Mosse, 1985, p. xxix).
2. Austria, Belgium, Denmark, Finland, Hungary, Italy, Poland, and Slovakia.
3. This is not to say that radical Islam is not a threat also in Western societies: in early November 2020 a domestic terrorist killed 4 people and injured 23 more in the Austrian capital of Vienna. The perpetrator, a 20-year-old sympathizer of the radical-Islamicist terror organization ISIS, was heavily armed when he started his shooting spree in the traditional Jewish quarter of Vienna. He held dual citizenship (Austrian and Northern Macedonian) and already had a criminal record. In 2019 he was sentenced to 22 months in prison, because he was caught in Turkey while trying to join the Islamic State in Syria.

REFERENCES

Amatulli, J. (2019). Rep. Ted Lieu plays Candace Owens' Hitler remarks during white nationalism hearing. *HuffPost*. www.huffpost.com/entry/ted-lieu-candace-owens-white-nationalism-hitler_n_5cacede9e4b0e833aa3210dc (Accessed: January 20, 2021).

Anderson, B. (1991). *Imagined Communities: Reflections on the Origin and Spread of Nationalism*. Verso.

Anti-Defamation League (2018). Murder and extremism in the United States in 2018. www.adl.org/murder-and-extremism-2018 (Accessed: January 17, 2021).

Anti-Defamation League (2020). Racism. www.adl.org/racism (Accessed: February 9, 2021).

Anti-Defamation League (n.d.). Turning point USA. www.adl.org/resources/backgrounders/turning-point-usa (Accessed: June 12, 2019).

Astor M. (2018). Anti-Semitic incidents surged 57 percent in 2017, report finds. *New York Times*. www.nytimes.com/2018/02/27/us/anti-semitism-adl-report.html (Accessed: January 15, 2021).

Baker, S. (2019). The gunman at a California garlic festival reportedly referenced a white supremacist manifesto on Instagram before the shooting. *Insider*. www.insider.com/gilroy-garlic-festival-shooter -shared-neo-nazi-ideas-instagram-reports-2019-7 (Accessed: January 13, 2020).

Bauman, Z. (1989). *Modernity and the Holocaust*. Cornell University Press.

Bauman, Z. (1998). *Globalization: The Human Consequences*. Columbia University Press.

Bauman, Z. (2006). The crisis of the human waste disposal industry. In D. Macedo and P. Gounari (Eds), *The Globalization of Racism* (pp. 36–40). Paradigm Publishers.

Bendersky, J. (2021). *A Concise History of Nazi Germany*. 5th edn. Rowman and Littlefield.

Bergen, D. (2016). *War and Genocide: A Concise History of the Holocaust*. Rowman and Littlefield.

Bieber, F. (2020). *Debating Nationalism: The Global Spread of Nations*. Bloomsbury Academic.

Black, I. (2000). Europe rallies against Haider coalition. *The Guardian*. www.theguardian.com/world/ 2000/feb/04/austria.ianblack (Accessed: December 15, 2020).

Braune, J. (2020). The outsider as insider: Steve Bannon, fourth turnings, and the neofascist threat. In S. Gandesha (Ed.), *Spectres of Fascism: Historical, Theoretical and International Perspectives* (pp. 207–222). Pluto.

Buchanan, L., Bui, Q., Patel, J.K. (2020). Black Lives Matter may be the largest movement in US history. *New York Times*. www.nytimes.com/interactive/2020/07/03/us/george-floyd-protests-crowd -size.html (Accessed: October 13, 2020).

Camus, R. (2018). *You Will Not Replace Us!* Chez l'auteur.

Chou, V. (2017). How science and genetics are reshaping the race debate of the 21st century. http:// sitn.hms.harvard.edu/flash/2017/science-genetics-reshaping-race-debate-21st-century/   (Accessed: February 11, 2021).

Deutsche Welle (2020). Germany: More than 1,600 crimes targeted refugees and asylum-seekers. March 27.   www.dw.com/en/germany-more-than-1600-crimes-targeted-refugees-and-asylum-seekers/a -52935715 (Accessed: December 15, 2020).

Eco, U. (1995). Ur-fascism. *New York Review*. www.nybooks.com/articles/1995/06/22/ur-fascism/ (Accessed: December 15, 2020).

Eco, U. (2020). *Der ewige Faschismus: Mit einem Vorwort von Roberto Saviano*. Carl Hanser Verlag.

Fredrickson, G.M. (2002). *Racism: A Short History*. Princeton University Press.

Gallmetzer, L. (2019). *Von Mussolini zu Salvini, Italien als Vorreiter des modernen Nationalpopulismus*. Kremayr and Scheriau.

Garner, S. (2017). *Racisms: An Introduction*. Sage.

Gstettner, P. (2006). Austria: Right-wing populism plus racism at a governmental level. In D. Macedo and P. Gounari (Eds), *The Globalization of Racism* (pp. 184–191). Paradigm Publishers.

Guerrero, J. (2020). Stephen Miller's dystopian America. *New York Times*. www.nytimes.com/2020/08/ 28/opinion/stephen-millers-dystopian-america.html (Accessed: January 17, 2021).

Hoare, L. (2019). Move over Soros: Meet the anti-Semites' new "dirty," "all-powerful" Jewish bogey-man. *Haaretz*. www.haaretz.com/world-news/.premium-move-over-soros-meet-the-anti-semites-new -all-powerful-jewish-bogeyman-1.7286028 (Accessed: December 13, 2020).

Hofstadter, R. (2008). *The Paranoid Style in American Politics and Other Essays*. Vintage Books.

Hund, W. (2011). It must come from Europe: The racisms of Immanuel Kant. In W. Hund, C. Koller and M. Zimmerman (Eds), *Racisms Made in Germany* (pp. 69–98). Lit Verlag.

Hund, W. (2018). *Rassismus und Antirassismus*. Papyrossa Verlag.

Judaken, J. (2017). Antisemitism and the Jewish question. In M.B. Hart and T. Michels (Eds), *The Cambridge History of Judaism* (pp. 529–558). Cambridge University Press.

Kendi, I.X. (2017). *Stamped from the Beginning: The Definitive History of Racist Ideas in America*. Bold Type Books.

Kirby, J. (2018). Trump wants fewer immigrants from "shithole countries" and more from places like Norway. *Vox*. www.vox.com/2018/1/11/16880750/trump-immigrants-shithole-countries-norway (Accessed: December 15, 2020).

Kohen, A. and Steinacher G.J. (Eds) (2021). Antisemitism: *The 1930s and Today*. University of Nebraska Press.

Lentin, R. and McVeigh, R. (2006). *After Optimism? Ireland, Racism and Globalisation*. Metro Éireann.

Levin, S. (2019). Violent hate crimes in US reach highest levels in 16 years, FBI reports. *The Guardian*. www.theguardian.com/society/2019/nov/12/hate-crimes-2018-latinos-transgender-fbi (Accessed: February 17, 2021).

Lipstadt, D. (1993). *Denying the Holocaust: The Growing Assault on Truth and Memory*. Free Press.

Lipstadt, D. (2019). *Antisemitism: Here and Now*. Scribe.

MacShane, D. (2008). *Globalising Hatred: The New Antisemitism*. Weidenfeld & Nicolson.

Massingale, B. (2021). The racist attack on our nation's capitol. *America: The Jesuit Review*. www.americamagazine.org/politics-society/2021/01/06/us-capitol-trump-riot-racist-239662 (Accessed: February 9, 2021).

Mayer, J. (2017). A conservative nonprofit that seeks to transform college campuses faces allegations of racial bias and illegal campaign activity. *The New Yorker*, December 21. www.newyorker.com/news/news-desk/a-conservative-nonprofit-that-seeks-to-transform-college-campuses-faces-allegations-of-racial-bias-and-illegal-campaign-activity (Accessed: December 20, 2019).

Mosse, G.L. (1985). *Toward the Final Solution: A History of European Racism*. University of Wisconsin Press.

O'Toole, F. (2003). Law with a dangerous edge of racism. *Irish Times*. www.irishtimes.com/news/law-with-a-dangerous-edge-of-racism-1.346648 (Accessed: January 13, 2021).

Pastor, L. and Veronesi, P. (2020). Inequality aversion, populism, and the backlash against globalization. *Chicago Booth Research Paper*, no. 20–11, Fama-Miller Working Paper. https://papers.ssrn.com/sol3/papers.cfm?abstract_id=3224232 (Accessed: February 11, 2021).

Porat, D. (2013). Holocaust denial and the image of the Jew, or: "They boycott Auschwitz as an Israeli product." In A. Rosenfeld (Ed.), *Resurgent Antisemitism: Global Perspectives* (pp. 468–481). Indiana University Press.

Rosenfeld, A.H. (Ed.) (2015). *Deciphering the New Antisemitism*. Indiana University Press.

Said, E. (2006). Racism and Middle East politics. In D. Macedo and P. Gounari (Eds), *The Globalization of Racism* (pp. 41–44). Paradigm Publishers.

Schulte v. Drach, M. (2018). Leipziger Studie: die Deutschen werden immer intoleranter. *Süddeutsche Zeitung*. www.sueddeutsche.de/politik/auslaenderfeindlichkeit-muslime-studierechtsextremismus-1.4199261 (Accessed: February 9, 2021).

Slaughter, M.J. and Swagel, P. (1997). Does globalization lower wages and export jobs? *Economic Issues*, International Monetary Fund, no. 11. www.imf.org/external/pubs/ft/issues11/ (Accessed September 2, 2021).

Steinacher, G.J. (2020). The oldest post-truth? The rise of antisemitism in America and beyond. In M. Gudonis and B.T. Jones (Eds), *What Happens to History in a Post-Truth World?* (pp. 121–141). Routledge.

Traverso, E. (2019). *The New Faces of Fascism: Populism and the Far Right*. Verso.

United States Census Bureau (2015). New Census Bureau report analyzes US population projections. www.census.gov/newsroom/press-releases/2015/cb15-tps16.html (Accessed: February 20, 2021).

Weiss, B. (2019). *How to Fight Anti-Semitism*. Crown.

Wistrich, R. (1991). *Antisemitism: The Longest Hatred*. Pantheon Books.

21. The globalization of extremism: an odd paradox

Joshua Skoczylis and Matthew Leavesley

> A global economy is characterized not only by the free movement of goods and services but, more
> important, by the free movement of ideas and of capital.
>
> George Soros (1998)

This chapter explores the relationship between globalization and extremism. The gains of glo-balization have not been equal and even in the Western world, globalization has left millions behind. The deterioration of the low-skilled labour market, pessimism about the future, low levels of education and few opportunities to escape the carousel of bad jobs, low benefits and unemployment increase the attractiveness of extremist ideologies across the political spec-trum. As globalization has gained momentum, the world has become more interconnected, surpassing social spheres including economics, culture and politics. Despite varying levels of collaboration between societies, globalization has helped fuel socio-economic and political dislocation, that in many places has led to a loss of identity. To counter this perceived threat, extremism and nationalism have increasingly taken hold in an attempt to remove *the other* and return to the *golden age* of the past. Globalization and neoliberalism have brought many bene-fits, but at the same time, they have created the perfect setting for extremism to flourish and go global. The paradox is that those seeking to wind back the clock of globalization and neolib-eralism are using its tools and an interconnected world to spread their message of discontent.

UNDERSTANDING EXTREMISM

Many argue that they know what extremism is when they see it. Others argue that it relates to *the centre* or *norms* of any given society (Kruglanski et al., 2017). Although definitions from the political centre exclude historical political movements including racial slavery, the Holocaust and aspects of British Imperialism, hindsight allows such perceptions to change. Therefore, a more precise definition is required. Berger argues:

> extremism refers to the belief that an in-group's success or survival can never be separated from the need for hostile action against an out-group. The hostile action must be part of the in-group's definition of success. Hostile acts can range from verbal attacks and diminishment to discriminatory behaviour, violence, and even genocide ... The need for harmful activity must be unconditional and inseparable from the in-group's understanding of success in order to qualify as extremist. (2018: 74–75)

History is littered with examples of extremism, from the Viking raids across Britain in the eighth century to the Khmer Rouge murdering educated Cambodians in the 1970s. Popular discourse, however, continually shapes and reshapes *the other* (Skoczylis, 2017). Extremism is an insidious phenomenon that can lead to the complicity of people adopting its beliefs and values without them having to commit any acts of violence and/or aggression (Berger, 2018). Extremists see the world through a Manichaean lens, a world that is polarized and divided into two factions (Skoczylis, 2015), 'one responsible, the other as irresponsible, which require some kind of initiative on part of the former to [preempt] dangers that issue from the latter' (Asad, 2010: 3). This situation can be exploited by groups, legitimizing their worldview and any resulting actions. 'The enemy … represents absolute evil … it follow[s] that any past or future agreement with him [is] impossible' (Orwell, 2000: 31).

Propaganda, a powerful tool, is used by extremist groups to achieve their aims and control the narrative about the *other*. The Nazi regime, for example, with their total control over the print, radio, film and education, was able to successfully change the narrative casting Jews as the *other* who posed a threat to German existence (Bachrach & Luckert, 2009). Once the *other* is identified as a threat, it becomes easier to tacitly support and even legitimize and engage in violence against the enemy (Moghaddam, 2005), though this process is not necessarily linear (Lygre et al., 2011). The *other* is not just someone with whom one has a dispute. Rather, the process of othering leads to an intense separation of *us* versus *them* (Schmitt, 2006). Such conflicts, according to Schelling, must end in the extermination of one or the other (Schelling, 1960). According to von Clausewitz, war is merely the continuation of policy by other means. 'War, therefore, is an act of violence intended to compel our opponent to fulfil our will' (von Clausewitz, 1982, p. 101). Applying this concept to extremism, one can easily see how extremist ideologies move from *othering* to violence. Violence becomes an extension of the *policies* of extremism; where one strives to compel others to submit to their will using physical violence if necessary.

Extremism is about ideology, whereas radicalization is about individuals or groups adopting a new ideological position, though this does not necessarily need to be extreme. Individual radicalization is usually precipitated by group radicalization. Berger argues that groups must go through the following four steps beforehand:

- define the in-group;
- define an out-group;
- define the existence of the out-group as an acute crisis for the in-group; and
- define hostile actions (solutions) that must be applied to the out-group (Berger, 2018).

It is extremely rare for individuals to become radicalized without reference to existing extremist movements or ideologies. Rather, individual radicalization is similar to political mobilization, emphasizing identity and crisis solutions, tapping into pre-existing extremist movements and ideologies (Berger, 2016; González-Bailón et al., 2011). Interest in extremist ideologies can stem from socio-economic, environmental factors or exposure to extremist ideologies, which are later reinforced by members of their communities (Mills et al., 2019). Even *lone wolves*, such as Anders Breivik and Thomas Mair (Cobain & Taylor, 2016; Melle, 2013), interacted with extremist movements on and offline (Holt et al., 2019). Extremist ideologies act like contagions and radicalization requires multiple exposures to the ideology before being adopted (Youngblood, 2020).

The example of Nazi Germany demonstrates how pervasive extremism can become, especially if one has absolute control over education and has mastered the art of propaganda. Within a few years, the Nazi regime successful shifted cultural attitudes towards Jews, casting them as the *other* who posed a threat to German identity, culture, and way of life. Such shifts in attitudes allowed for a Clausewitzian war against the Jews (Voth & Voigtländer,

2015). Education was the most effective at conditioning and fostering extremist attitudes and behaviours, as it tapped into pre-existing prejudices that helped to indoctrinate its young people. Education combined with propaganda become very powerful tools to shape attitudes and behaviour towards the *other*. What has changed since the 1930s, though, is the speed at which people can communicate. The internet has accelerated the spread of extremist beliefs and values, maximizing exposure. This can be seen as a byproduct of globalization (Khiabany, 2003). Worryingly, nationalism no longer remains at the fringes as politicians tap into nationalist rhetoric to appeal to voters. Right-wing governments, encouraged by the right-wing media and fellow politicians (Bland & Elgot, 2020; O'Brien, 2020; Owen & Carlin, 2020), are combining their access to the levers of education and propaganda to challenge *woke* ideas and promote nationalism. In Poland, recent reforms have removed teaching about the Holocaust and are actively portraying homosexuals as paedophiles (*Deutsche Welle*, 2017; Savage, 2020). Whist in the United States (US), President Trump has indicated he will pull funds from schools that challenge the historical narrative surrounding slavery (Gerstmann, 2020). And in the United Kingdom (UK), teaching British values has become part of the national curriculum, with anti-capitalism being banned from the curriculum (Luff, 2020; Skoczylis & Andrews, 2020).

GLOBALIZATION AND EXTREMISM

Humans have always interacted, traded, and communicated with each other (Chanda, 2008). The *big bang* of globalization, however, did not occur until the late 1820s. 'Globalisation became economically meaningful only with the dawn of the nineteenth century, and it came on in a rush' (O'Rouke and Williamson, 2004: 109). Since the 1980s there has been an ambitious agenda of economic liberalization and deep integration; also known as *hyper globalization* (Rodrik, 2011). Hyper globalization has been accompanied by a revolution in communication technology enabled by the internet. Globalization has morphed into a *hegemonic* process that continues to impose *Western culture* upon most of the world, led by the US and other rich Western nations (Kroupkamp, 2011; Marsella, 2005). The internet and changes in communication are at the core of a new digital economy which is developing. Improvements in communication are significant drivers of globalization. The internet has made it faster and cheaper, allowing for growth, innovation, and higher productivity as well as forcing decisions to be taken more rapidly, though not all benefits are advantages (Aronson, 2004; MacNamara, 2009; Mikail & Aytekin, 2016). Gordon Brown, former UK prime minister, sums up the general feeling towards globalization, highlighting that: 'wave after crushing wave of globalisation appears not as an opportunity but as a threat: less as the opening up of a world awash with fresh chances for them and their children but more akin to a runaway train that seems out of control and uncontrollable' (Brown, 2016).

Therefore, in a world of instant connections via the internet and social media, the growing popularity of more extremist ideas should not come as a surprise or be underestimated. Indeed, social media algorithms have knowingly promoted extremist content to increase traffic to their platforms to maximize profits (Dearden, 2019; Reed et al., 2019). Social media and the internet have allowed extremist ideologies to go global. It is worth highlighting that although social media has relaxed geographic constraints on communication, online social networks still exhibit spatial clustering and online *echo chambers* that can map onto particular locations

(Bailey et al., 2018; Bastos et al., 2018; Liu et al., 2018). 'The probability of information diffusion on social media decays with increasing distance' (Youngblood, 2020). Ideas and ideologies spread between these clusters. Each cluster will react differently to the information shared and will challenge and weaken narratives or encourage their spread.

As globalization gains pace, the social spheres (economy, culture, and politics) that once were completely separate, compared with their tribal ancestors, are increasingly merging. Information flows become permanent and become a *common good* that determines and defines social life and interactions (Castells, 2010). Multinationals and global brands permeate urban, suburban, and even rural landscapes (Holt et al., 2004; Klein, 2001). And to no surprise, they also dominate the digital space. These trends are exemplified across *clone* towns and cities which have become common and can be found across six of the seven continents. McDonaldization of our on and offline worlds has brought efficiency, calculability, standardization, and control. Such processes have reduced diversity in towns and cities across the globe, replacing local culture, traditions, and economies with hyper-global brands and multinational companies (Michael, 2014; Ritzer & Miles, 2019). McDonaldization in the virtual world is even starker. Amazon, Microsoft, Apple, Google, and Facebook have a disproportionate impact on how we access and use the virtual world, manipulating users to change their habits (Frick, 2016; Meyer, 2014; Ritzer & Miles, 2019). The products, services, and shops of Amazon, Coca-Cola, Nike, McDonald's, Starbucks, L'Oréal, and Disney, to name but a few, can now be accessed from virtually anywhere and their advertising is ever present. They have become permanent features of our day-to-day lives. It is no surprise that these global brands have become a lightning rod for anti-globalization movements:

> Identikit commercial culture has a darker side too. The death of diversity undermines democracy, attacks our sense of place and belonging and therefore well-being. It hands power to an unaccountable corporate elite; ultimately pulling apart the rich weave of natural systems upon which our livelihoods and the economy depend. (Simms et al., 2005: 5)

Such processes undermine a sense of unique identity which can lead to social problems such as isolation, alienation, crime, and more (Twohig, 2014). The socio-economic, cultural, political changes, and social dislocation that have occurred over the last 20 years or so could collectively be described as revolutionary.

Although globalization has brought many benefits and increased the wealth of the global elite, social dislocation and the impact of the homogenizing of our cultures and identities is keenly felt amongst the left-behind groups. A higher national gross domestic product does not translate to a better quality of life for most (Heffernan, 2014). 'While hegemonic globalization claims to be driven by the pan-human values of liberty, democracy, human rights, and justice, these appeals often become passing entry points for cultural penetration and control by Western political and economic forces' (Marsella, 2005: 17).

There are serious concerns about the hegemonic imposition of the *American Dream* and there is legitimate angst about the impact of globalization on local traditions, cultures, and identity. Associated values, including individualism, materialism, competition, hedonism, rapid change, profit, greed, consumerism, commodification, reductionism, celebrification, privatization, and English-language preference, carry with them a way of life that is alien and offensive to many people, even residents in Western cultures (Kiernan, 2005; Nye, 2019).

These values and the associated way of life is seen by many Muslim communities as a threat to their way of life, creating a culture of fear. Together with decades of colonization, social injustice, and defeat, such fear has triggered hatred and anger, motivating a rise in extremism and terrorism (Baytiyeh, 2018). Similar trends can be observed in other societies where globalization is active. Collective family and community ties have been eroded, leaving many isolated (Marsella, 2011). This coupled with the deterioration of the low-skilled labour market, pessimism about the future, lack of education, and few opportunities to escape the carousel of bad jobs, low benefits, and unemployment increases the attractiveness of extremist ideologies across the political spectrum (Briggs & Goodwin, 2012). Diamond (2010) notes, however, that these outcomes are not inevitable and are policy choices. The polity's pursuit of globalization combined with neoliberal socio-economic policies seeks to bring about utopia when in reality it is a ruse that reflects the *tragedy of capitalism* and its endless war of plunders, leaving millions behind (Le Billion, 2012; Springer, 2016):

> The peace operations and humanitarian interventions of the late twentieth and twenty-first centuries may be seen as a revival [of imperialism], albeit in less violent form, of yesterday's savage wars of peace. The ultimate goal was similar: fling open markets to the global economy, bring government to the hitherto ungovernable, end tribal conflict and ethnic cleansing, and recruit converts for the Western way of life. (Porch, 2001: 16)

Resistance against globalization and neoliberalism are spreading faster and, ironically due to the forces of globalization, drawing in larger and larger constituencies who are deeply entrenched and resistant to change. Brexit is one example of large sections of society blaming the *other* for a lost utopia of the past (Goodwin, 2019). Although extremism has been around for as long as humans have, globalization and neoliberalism create the perfect conditions to foster and spread extremist ideologies across the globe on an unprecedented scale (Yuval-Davis et al., 2006).

GLOBALIZING EXTREMISM

The backlash against neoliberal globalization is accompanied by a switch from the left to far-right issues (Horner et al., 2018). Fuelled by economic stagnation and McDonaldization of their identities and communities, far-right ideologies are taking hold in many white working-class communities across the globe, blaming migrants and the radical left (DeCook, 2020). Brexit and Make America Great Again are two examples where mainstream politicians have tapped into the resentment of white working-class communities, putting fuel on the fire and encouraging extremism (BBC News, 2016; Timberg & Dwoskin, 2020). The case of a far-right Australian who shot 51 people at a mosque in Christchurch New Zealand demonstrates the paradox of globalization and extremism. The 28-year-old terrorist was actively engaged in online message boards in Europe that enabled his views to be expressed and lauded without challenge. He was radicalized within months, demonstrating the power of the internet in sharing extremist ideas and beliefs (Ebner, 2019).

The far right has indeed become global. The tools of globalization are used to their fullest, whether this is using the internet to promote its ideology, the ability to easily move money, or to provide training globally. It is worth noting that the far right is not structurally unified; rather, its members and networks have embraced a *divide we stand* approach. The far right is linked transnationally through shared ideologies based on the *Great Replacement*, *White Genocide*, and *QAnon* (CEP, 2020). America's Christian right, for example, has spent millions of dark money on supporting far-right groups across Europe (Fitzgerald & Provost, 2019). The recent COVID-19 pandemic has been widely used by the far right to spread conspiracy theories highlighting its usual fear and anxieties around globalization, multiculturalism, and government cover-ups. Anti-lockdown protests in Germany and anti-5G protests in the UK have boosted the popularity of far-right groups (Jasser, 2020).

Jihadist movements have also emerged in the late twentieth century and are at odds with the merging socio-political and economic spheres of globalization that are taking place across the Muslim world (Barber, 2003). As globalization has gained momentum in recent years, so too has global jihadism; although the two are not necessarily mutually exclusive (Lutz & Lutz, 2015; Zimmerman, 2011). Social dislocation has increased the appeal of jihadi extremism amongst Muslim communities around the world. Just as the far right, Jihadi groups such as ISIS and Al Qaeda have also taken advantage of the freedoms that go hand in hand with a globalized world (Cronin, 2002). Interestingly, these groups also appeal to a global audience by highlighting the impact of imperialism and globalization on Muslims worldwide (Low, 2016).

Jihadi extremism and terrorism have been transnational for some time now, however, the social dislocation brought about by neoliberalism and globalization has accelerated jihadi extremism and terrorism adding *legitimacy* to their cause, but also the ability to become a global network (Nesser, 2018). People have experienced the unravelling of traditional identities as the world has become more globalized (Castells, 2010). Jihadi propaganda, therefore, looks to exploit those disaffected by these cultural and societal changes to become part of a collective identity that brings a sense of brotherhood and kinship (Torres et al., 2006). The war in Iraq and its aftermath have been a catalyst in creating ISIS, fuelling conflict in the Middle East and Syria (Gerges, 2016). This conflict was highly successful in attracting Muslim men and women to their cause using social media (Blanchard & Humud, 2018). By using digital communication, ISIS was able to utilize a global platform to manipulate 'Islamic cultural narratives to influence the perceptions of Muslims, exploiting their grievances and appealing to their opposition to American foreign policy' (Mahood & Rane, 2017: 33). Ironically, jihadi extremists have benefited from globalization as much as it has claimed to fight against it. Globalization has given Islamic extremism a new lease of life (Waters, 2001).

CONCLUSION

Neoliberalism and globalization have stripped away many socio-economic protections, eroding local cultures, traditions, and identities. This has led to a backlash from many of the *left-behind* communities creating space for resistance. Extremist ideologies tap into this anger placing the blame on *the other* while providing utopian solutions. Although extremism has always existed, globalization has supercharged it by fostering an environment in which it can thrive. Providing them with a plethora of new enemies and the tools to spread their ideologies has enabled them to go global. Polities have attempted to present neoliberal globalization as the only alternative, but in doing so have created the perfect conditions for extremism to flourish. Angst about loss of identity and culture coupled with being left behind in an uncertain world will continue to feed extremism. The sad thing is that the malaise that accompanies neoliberalism and globalization is not inevitable as these are the result of continued policy choices by the polity to enrich a small section of society, rather than acting for the benefit of all. While there is hope for a different future, extremism will continue to proliferate and challenge the status quo.

REFERENCES

Aronson, J. (2004). 'The causes and consequences of the global communication revolution', in: J. Baylis & S. Smith (eds), *The Globalization of World Politics*, 3rd ed. Oxford: Oxford University Press, pp. 621–643.

Asad, T. (2010). 'Thinking about terrorism and just war'. *Cambridge Review of International Affairs* 23(1): 3–24.

Bachrach, S. & Luckert, S. (2009). *State of Deception: The Power of Nazi Propaganda*. United States Holocaust Memorial Museum.

Bailey, M., Cao, R., Kuchler T., Stroebel, J. & Wong, A. (2018). 'Social connectedness: Measurement, determinants, and effects'. *Journal of Economic Perspectives* 32(3): 259–280.

Barber, B. (2003). *Jihad vs. McWorld*. Corgi.

Bastos, M., Mercea, D. & Baronchelli, A. (2018). 'The geographic embedding of online echo chambers: Evidence from the Brexit campaign'. *PLOS ONE* 13(11).

Baytiyeh, H. (2018). 'Have globalisation's influences on education contributed to the recent rise of Islamic extremism?'. *Globalisation, Societies and Education* 16(4): 422–434.

BBC News (2016). 'Migration anger "could lead to violence"'. Available at: www.bbc.co.uk/news/av/uk-politics-eu-referendum-36317915 (accessed 22 December 2020).

Berger, J. M. (2016). *Making CVE Work: A Focused Approach Based on Process Disruption*. ICCT. Available at: http://icct.nl/app/uploads/2016/05/J.-M.-Berger-Making-CVE-Work-A-Focused-Approach-Based-on-Process-Disruption-.pdf (accessed 17 December 2020).

Berger, J. M. (2018). *Extremism*. MIT Press.

Blanchard, C. M. & Humud, C. E. (2018). *The Islamic State and US Policy*. Congressional Research Service. Available at: https://fas.org/sgp/crs/mideast/R43612.pdf (accessed 17 December 2020).

Bland, A. & Elgot, J. (2020). 'Dissatisfied Tory MPs flock to ERG-inspired pressure groups'. Available at: www.theguardian.com/politics/2020/nov/11/dissatisfied-tory-mps-flock-to-erg-inspired-pressure-groups (accessed 12 December 2020).

Briggs, R. & Goodwin, M. (2012). 'We need a better understanding of what drives right-wing extremist violence'. *LSE Blog*. Available at: http://eprints.lse.ac.uk/48364/1/blogs.lse.ac.uk-We_need_a_better_understanding_of_what_drives_rightwing_extremist_violence.pdf (accessed 21 December 2020).

Brown, G. (2016). 'Leaders must make the case for globalisation'. Available at: www.ft.com/content/a0849e08-4921-11e6-8d68-72e9211e86ab#axzz4EkYFtI2T (accessed 17 December 2020).

Castells, M. (2010). *The Rise of the Network Society: The Information Age, Economy, Society, and Culture*, 2nd ed. Wiley-Blackwell.

CEP (2020). *Violent Right-Wing Extremism and Terrorism: Transnational Connectivity, Definitions, Incidents, Structures and Countermeasures*. Counter Extremism Project. Available at: www.counterextremism.com/sites/default/files/CEP%20Study_Violent%20Right-Wing%20Extremism%20and%20Terrorism_Nov%202020.pdf (accessed 22 December 2020).

Chanda, N. (2008). *Bound Together: How Traders, Preachers, Adventurers, and Warriors Shaped Globalization*. Yale University Press.

Cobain, I. & Taylor, M. (2016). 'The slow-burning hatred that led Thomas Mair to murder Jo Cox'. Available at: www.theguardian.com/uk-news/2016/nov/23/thomas-mair-slow-burning-hatred-led-to-jo-cox-murder (accessed 17 December 2020).

Cronin, A. K. (2002). 'Behind the curve: Globalization and international terrorism'. *International Security* 27(3): 30–58.

DeCook, J. (2020). 'Coronavirus and the radical right: Conspiracy, disinformation, and xenophobia'. Available at: www.opendemocracy.net/en/countering-radical-right/coronavirus-and-radical-right-conspiracy-disinformation-and-xenophobia/ (accessed 22 December 2020).

Dearden, L. (2019). 'Social media companies "actively" serve up extremist material to users, MPs say'. Available at: www.independent.co.uk/news/uk/home-news/youtube-facebook-twitter-extremist-content-profit-home-affairs-a8884881.html (accessed 17 December 2020).

DeCook, J. (2020). 'Coronavirus and the radical right: conspiracy, disinformation, and xenophobia'. Available at: www.opendemocracy.net/en/countering-radical-right/coronavirus-and-radical-right-conspiracy-disinformation-and-xenophobia/ (accessed 22 December 2020).

Deutsche Welle (2017). 'Poland education reform to slash thousands of teachers' jobs'. Available at: www.dw.com/en/poland-education-reform-to-slash-thousands-of-teachers-jobs/a-40333721 (accessed 17 December 2020).

Diamond, P. (2010). 'How globalisation is changing patterns of marginalisation and inclusion in the UK'. JRF Programme Paper: Globalisation. York: Joseph Rowntree Foundation. Available at: www.jrf.org .uk/sites/files/jrf/globalisation-marginalisation-inclusion-full.pdf (accessed 21 December 2020).

Ebner, J. (2019). 'Christchurch shooting: What terror looks like in the social media age'. Available at: www.thetimes.co.uk/article/christchurch-shooting-what-terror-looks-like-in-the-social-media-age -knglzwqxl (accessed 18 December 2020).

Fitzgerald, M. & Provost, C. (2019). 'The American dark money behind Europe's far right'. Available at: www.opendemocracy.net/en/5050/the-american-dark-money-behind-europes-far-right/ (accessed 22 December 2020).

Frick, W. (2016). 'Who controls the internet?'. *Harvard Business Review*. Available at: https://hbr.org/ 2016/06/who-controls-the-internet (accessed 7 December 2020).

Gerges, F. (2016). *ISIS: A History*. Princeton University Press.

Gerstmann, E. (2020). 'Trump says he will punish schools that teach the *New York Times*' "1619" project by withholding federal funds'. Available at: www.forbes.com/sites/evangerstmann/2020/09/06/trump -says-he-will-punish-schools-that-teach-the-new-york-times-1619-project-by-withholding-federal -funds/ (accessed 17 December 2020).

González-Bailón, S., Borge-Holthoefer, J., Rivero, A. & Moreno, Y. (2011). 'The dynamics of protest recruitment through an online network'. *Scientific Reports* 1(1): 1.

Goodwin, M. (2019). 'Extreme politics: The four waves of national populism in the West', in: D. Needham & J. Weitzdörfer (eds), *Extremes*. Cambridge University Press, pp. 104–123.

Heffernan, M. (2014). *A Bigger Prize: Why No One Wins Unless Everyone Wins*. London: Simon & Schuster.

Holt, D., Quelch, J. & Taylor, E. (2004). 'How global brands compete'. *Harvard Business Review*. Available at: https://hbr.org/2004/09/how-global-brands-compete (accessed 17 December 2020).

Holt, T., Freilich, J., Chermak, S., Mills, C. & Silva, J. (2019). 'Loners, colleagues, or peers? Assessing the social organization of radicalization'. *American Journal of Criminal Justice* 44(1): 83–105.

Horner, R., Schindler, S., Haberly, D. & Aoyama, Y. (2018). 'Globalisation, uneven development and the North–South "Big Switch"'. *Cambridge Journal of Regions, Economy and Society* 11(1): 17–33.

Jasser, G. (2020). 'The social media platform that welcomes QAnon with open arms'. Available at: www .opendemocracy.net/en/countering-radical-right/social-media-platform-welcomes-qanon-open-arms/ (accessed 22 December 2020).

Khiabany, G. (2003). 'Globalization and the internet: Myths and realities'. *Trends in Communication* 11(2): 137–153.

Kiernan, V. (2005). *America, the New Imperialism: From White Settlement to World Hegemony*. Verso.

Klein, N. (2001). *No Logo: No Space, No Choice, No Jobs*. HarperCollins.

Kroupkamp, H. (2011). 'South Africa's response to the global financial crisis: Implications for public administration'. *Journal of Public Administration Research and Theory* 46(1): 801–811.

Kruglanski, A., Jasko, K., Chernikova, M., Dugas, M. & Webber, D. (2017). 'To the fringe and back: Violent extremism and the psychology of deviance'. *American Psychologist* 72(3): 217–230.

Le Billion, P. (2012). *Wars of Plunder: Conflicts, Profits and the Politics of Resources*. Hurst.

Liu, L., Chen, B., Ai, C., He, L., Wang, Y., Qiu, X. & Lu, X. (2018). 'The influence of geographic factors on information dissemination in mobile social networks in China: Evidence from WeChat'. *ISPRS International Journal of Geo-Information* 7(5): 189.

Low, R. (2016). 'Making up the Ummah: The rhetoric of ISIS as public pedagogy'. *Review of Education, Pedagogy, and Cultural Studies* 38(4): 297–316.

Luff, J. (2020). 'Anticapitalism wasn't banned in English classrooms during the Cold War – why is it now?'. Available at: http://theconversation.com/anticapitalism-wasnt-banned-in-english-classrooms -during-the-cold-war-why-is-it-now-147121 (accessed 22 December 2020).

Lutz, B. & Lutz, J. (2015). 'Globalisation and terrorism in the Middle East'. *Perspectives on Terrorism* 9(5): 27–46.

Lygre, R., Eid, J., Larsson, G. & Ranstorp, M. (2011). 'Terrorism as a process: A critical review of Moghaddam's "Staircase to Terrorism"'. *Scandinavian Journal of Psychology* 52(6): 609–616.

MacNamara, J. (2009). *The 21st Century Media (R)Evolution: Emergent Communication Practices.* Peter Lang Publishing.

Mahood, S. & Rane, H. (2017). 'Islamist narratives in ISIS recruitment propaganda'. *Journal of International Communication* 23(1): 15–35.

Marsella, A. (2005). '"Hegemonic" globalization and cultural diversity: The risks of global monoculturalism'. *Australian Mosaic* 11(13): 15–19.

Marsella, A. (2011). 'The challenges of ethno-cultural diversity in an era of asymmetric globalization'. *Dynamics of Asymmetric Conflict* 4(1): 52–58.

Melle, I. (2013). 'The Breivik case and what psychiatrists can learn from it'. *World Psychiatry* 12(1): 16–21.

Meyer, R. (2014). 'Everything we know about Facebook's secret mood manipulation experiment'. Available at: www.theatlantic.com/technology/archive/2014/06/everything-we-know-about-facebooks-secret-mood-manipulation-experiment/373648/ (accessed 7 December 2020).

Michael, C. (2014). 'Clone wars: City replicas around the world – in pictures'. *The Guardian.* Available at: www.theguardian.com/cities/gallery/2014/jun/03/clone-wars-city-replicas-in-pictures (accessed 7 December 2020).

Mikail, E. & Aytekin, C. (2016). 'The communications and internet revolution in international relations'. *Open Journal of Political Science* 6: 345–350.

Mills, C., Freillich, J., LaFree, G. et al. (2019). 'Social learning and social control in the off-and online pathways to hate crime and terrorist violence'. *Studies in Conflict & Terrorism* 1: 1–29.

Moghaddam, F. (2005). 'The staircase to terrorism'. *American Psychologist* 60(2): 161–169.

Nesser, P. (2018). *Islamist Terrorism in Europe.* Hurst.

Nye, Jr., J. S. (2019). 'The rise and fall of American hegemony from Wilson to Trump'. *International Affairs* 95(1): 63–80.

O'Brien, N. (2020). Neil O'Brien: Johnson should instruct a team of Ministers to wage war on woke. Available at: www.conservativehome.com/thecolumnists/2020/09/neil-obrien-johnson-should-empower-a-ministet-to-wage-war-on-woke.html (accessed 21 December 2020).

O'Rouke, K. & Williamson, J. (2004). 'Once more: When did globalisation begin?'. *European Review of Economic History* 8(1): 109–117.

Orwell, G. (2000). *Nineteen Eighty-Four.* Penguin.

Owen, G. & Carlin, B. (2020). 'Tory MPs urge Boris to go to war on BBC and National Trust wokery'. Available at: www.dailymail.co.uk/news/article-8973679/Tory-MPs-urge-Boris-Johnson-war-BBC-National-Trust-wokery.html (accessed 21 December 2020).

Porch, D. (2001). *Wars of Empire.* Cassell.

Reed, A., Whittaker, J., Votta, F. & Looney, S. (2019). *Radical Filter Bubbles: Social Media, Personalisation Algorithms and Extremist Content.* Global Research Network on Terrorism and Technology 8. Available at: https://rusi.org/sites/default/files/20190726_grntt_paper_08_0.pdf (accessed 17 December 2020).

Ritzer, G. & Miles, S. (2019). 'The changing nature of consumption and the intensification of McDonaldization in the digital age'. *Journal of Consumer Culture* 19(1): 3–20.

Rodrik, D. (2011). *The Globalization Paradox: Democracy and the Future of the World Economy.* Norton and Company.

Savage, R. (2020). Poland mulls law denouncing sex educators as paedophiles and gay activists. Available at: https://uk.reuters.com/article/us-poland-lgbt-education-trfn-idUSKCN21X2ZA (accessed 22 December 2020).

Schelling, T. (1960). *The Strategy of Conflict.* Harvard University Press.

Schmitt, C. (2006). *Political Theology: Four Chapters on the Concept of Sovereignty* (trans. G. Schwab). University Of Chicago Press.

Simms, A., Kjell, P. & Potts, R. (2005). *Clone Town Britain: The Survey Results on the Bland State of the Nation.* New Economics Foundation.

Skoczylis, J. (2015). *Local Prevention of Terrorism: Strategy and Practice in the Fight against Terror.* Palgrave.

Skoczylis, J. (2017). 'Counterterrorism and society: The contradiction of the surveillance state – understanding the relationship among communities, state authorities, and society', in: S. Romaniuk, D. Irrera, S. Webb et al. (eds), *Palgrave Handbook of Global Counterterrorism.* Palgrave, pp. 117–134.

Skoczylis, J. & Andrews, S. (2020). 'Can Prevent be saved? No, but …'. *Critical Social Policy* 40(3): 350–369.

Soros, G. (1998). 'Toward a global open society'. *The Atlantic*. Available at: www.theatlantic.com/magazine/archive/1998/01/toward-a-global-open-society/307878/ (accessed 10 October 2022).

Springer, S. (2016). 'Fuck neoliberalism'. *ACME: An International Journal for Critical Geographies* 15(2): 285–292.

Timberg, C. & Dwoskin, E. (2020). 'Trump's debate comments give an online boost to a group social media companies have long struggled against'. Available at: www.washingtonpost.com/technology/2020/09/30/trump-debate-rightwing-celebration/ (accessed 22 December 2020).

Torres, M. R., Jordán, J. & Horsburgh, N. (2006). 'Analysis and evolution of the global jihadist movement propaganda'. *Terrorism and Political Violence* 18(3): 399–421.

Twohig, D. (2014). *Living in Wonderland: Urban Development and Placemaking*. Harriman House Publishing.

von Clausewitz, C. (1982). *On War* (trans. J. J. Graham). Penguin.

Voth, H.-J. & Voigtländer, N. (2015). 'Nazi indoctrination and anti-Semitic beliefs in Germany'. *Proceedings of the National Academy of Sciences* 112(26): 7931–7936.

Waters, M. (2001). *Globalization*, 2nd ed. Routledge.

Youngblood, M. (2020). 'Extremist ideology as a complex contagion: The spread of far-right radicalization in the United States between 2005 and 2017'. *Humanities and Social Sciences Communications* 7(1): 1–10.

Yuval-Davis, N., Kannabiran, K. & Vieten, U. (2006). 'Situating contemporary politics of belonging', in: N. Yuval, K. Kannabiran & U. Vieten (eds), *Situating Contemporary Politics of Belonging*. Sage, pp. 1–14.

Zimmerman, E. (2011). 'Globalization and terrorism'. *European Journal of Political Economy* 27(1): 152–161.

22. From multiculturalism to superdiversity and (in)hospitality? Shifting policy responses to global migratory flows in the UK

Sureyya Sonmez Efe

INTRODUCTION

International migration has been an integral part of globalization processes throughout history. In the past, migratory movements included those from the centres of colonizing empires to the colonized parts of the world. In contrast, today, there are reverse migrations from former colonies and economically less developed countries to the developed Western or non-Western countries. Such a shift in migratory movements is multifaceted, which illustrates the growing interconnectedness of states through the global economy, politics, communities, technology and knowledge. International mobility is described within the 'processes of global integration' (De Haas et al., 2020, p. 3) which incorporates all these facets for improving human mobility with more effective global cultural interchange. However, what we see at the national level is more complex than explaining migratory movements through global integration or global cultural interchange. The concept of 'integration', at the national level, can have different meanings as in the contemporary world integration of migrants has become a growing and contested issue within migration policies of the migrant-receiving countries. For host countries, migration has increasingly been perceived as something to be managed and prevented for the assumptions of migration as a security issue and its links to global terrorism; increasing migrant populations and (super)diversity are widely constructed as a threat to host communities' values with their purportedly *alien cultures*, and migrants are widely seen as potential competitors within the labour market who 'steal' citizens' jobs. In line with these assumptions, the declared key challenge for policymakers concerns the integration of migrants with diverse cultural identities. Over recent decades, we have witnessed shifts from multicultural policy approaches to the increasingly protectionist approaches witnessed across Europe.

Despite the growing far-right sentiments within migration policies in many host countries, the current global political culture resonates cosmopolitan principles. For instance, the *cosmopolitan right to hospitality* advocates a peaceful coexistence of individuals and states in the global order. When world communities decided to end the Second World War, they also agreed to create a global political culture that consists of new international norms of rights. Freedom of movement of individuals is one of these norms that is an essential component of the globalization process. In this context, contemporary hospitality (Sonmez Efe, 2021) is considered a *universal right* that ought to be incorporated into states' domestic jurisdiction that gives migrants' access to membership or citizenship rights in the host countries. The universal right to hospitality also 'prohibits states from denaturalizing individuals by denying them citizenship rights and state protection' (Arendt, 1979, pp. 296–299). Hence, this right not only plays a crucial role in human mobility and enables freedom of movement to prevail, but it also mediates between international law and domestic policies.

The impact of migratory movements on most host countries' domestic law is felt rapidly, particularly after the Second World War. As a result, new migrant identities were constructed as well as new legal statuses defined in international law, such as *refugees, asylum seekers, stateless persons* and *migrant workers*. States recognize and accommodate these new legal identities within their domestic policies through adopting policy approaches such as *multiculturalism, interculturalism, community cohesion* and *social cohesion*. However, this chapter will argue that the integration of migrant communities in the host countries has not been a straightforward process and has its challenges, particularly in the communities that are hostile and unwelcoming to new migrants. The concept of integration creates a paradox between global political culture of rights and political culture of nation-states where legal identities of migrants are negotiated and legally recognized under the jurisdiction of migrant-sending or receiving states. Even the common global use of 'sending–receiving' and 'host–home' terminology uncover the shared perception of the state's role of organizing and deciding on who can come and leave (De Haas et al., 2020, p. 29). Hence, states are primary actors in the international system of law that participate in the policy debate on designing and making decisions on the legal status of migrants.

These migrant identities are constructed within migration policies that are fluid concepts, in constant transformation and based on various internal and external factors such as shifts in global economic and political structures and states' political culture. Benhabib interprets the process of construction of new identities for migrants as part of the 'political reflexivity of liberal democracies', which envisages the identity formation of the sovereign nation within 'the process of fluid, open and contentious public debate: the lines separating we and you, us and them, more often than not rest on unexamined prejudices, ancient battles' (2004, p. 178). This type of public debate enables communities to form, negotiate and reinvent legal identities for foreigners, aliens, non-members and migrants that is a dynamic and continuous process of iterations and reiterations of statuses. This process has become an integral part of policy-making procedures where political citizenship is revisited and shaped based on the new social landscapes created due to migratory movements such as (super)diversity, multiculturalism and diaspora communities. This process is described with *democratic iterations*, which means:

> complex processes of public engagement, deliberation, and exchange through which universalist rights claims and principles are contested and contextualised, invoked and revoked, posited and positioned, through legal and political institutions, as well as in the associations of civil society. These can take place in the 'strong' public bodies of legislatives, the judiciary, and the executive as well as informal and 'weak' publics of civil society association and media … every act of iteration involves making sense of an authoritative original in a new and different context … Meaning is enhanced and transformed … Iteration is the appropriation of the origin … its dissolution … preservation through its continuous deployment. (Benhabib, 2004, p. 179)

Each time we debate and revisit a political issue such as migration and integration policies, we do not merely replicate the *original* within the international or national law statements, but we go beyond and transform it with the inclusion of new contexts and actors in the deliberation process. We revisit the existing identities, through either reimagining or preserving them with the values that we agree upon collectively. Through this process, we can make sense of the policies that reflect and/or transform the public's perceptions about migration, migrant communities and their rights and presence in the host communities.

In this chapter, I will focus on integration policies in the United Kingdom (UK) within the framework of *contemporary hospitality* (Sonmez Efe, 2021) and *democratic iterations* (Benhabib, 2004) to illustrate the continuities and transformations of migrant identities. The chapter attempts to clarify the evolution of migrant identities within integration policies in the UK and elucidate the impact of different policy approaches on forming new identities and values. For example, it will explore how integration policies have shifted from multiculturalism to interculturalism and what this shift means for migrants' identities and their rights in the *superdiverse* Britain. The chapter argues that recent transformations in integration policies reinforce the change from the global political culture of rights to security culture where there are tradeoffs between state interests and migrants' rights.

(SUPER)DIVERSE AND/OR MULTICULTURAL BRITAIN

British society has a long history and experience with migratory movements within its national territories. The majority of migration to Britain between 1800 and 1945 was from Europe, such as Irish, Jewish, Italian, French and German migrants. Migration to Britain from European countries continued after 1945 and extended from Western Europe to Eastern Europe; later, it included non-Western countries such as the West Indies, South Asian countries (India, Pakistan, Bangladesh), Iran, China, several African countries and Syria. These migratory movements indicate that we can talk about the continuity of the *Europeanization of migration* in Britain and a shift to the *internationalization of migration*, particularly after the 1960s. The latter has changed Britain's social landscape to a multicultural community, and since 2000 the country has been described as a superdiverse (Vertovec, 2007).

Migrant identities were constructed in Britain under the shadow of the world wars during the nation-building process at the beginning of the twentieth century, when foreigners were described as 'aliens' and perceived as 'possible suspects' (Cantle, 2005, p. 29). This approach was entrenched in the 'Aliens Act 1919' which proposed an acute solution to international conflicts to protect British citizens from the *enemies* (1919). The 1919 Act was a continuation of the 1914 Act with stricter entry regulations against 'aliens', particularly 'undesirable ones'. It is argued that both Acts (1914, 1919) had an additional purpose beyond taking a mere security approach to border control, which also meant a 'regulation of unwanted aliens'. After the Aliens Restriction (Amendment) Act 1919, the Special Restriction (Coloured Alien Seaman) was passed by Parliament in 1925 initially aimed at regulating the entry and stay of Black seamen in some cities, which was extended throughout the country in 1926. The Restriction was enacted after the 1911 race riots in Cardiff, Liverpool, London and Newport, where there was 'violent racial upheaval with white crowds attacking black localities' (Cantle, 2005, p. 31). These legislations came into force to respond to the riots and only offered acute solutions to the social unrest. They did not address the root causes of the disturbances which concealed a growing intolerance towards the 'other' based on strong ethnocentric values. In this era, in addition to the Black population, 'anti-Irish' and 'anti-Catholic' sentiment prevailed as they were not considered part of 'British national identity' (Parekh, 2000, p. 21). Thus, immigration policies' priority was to preserve the superiority status of the 'indigenous population' within the community where 'migrant identities and rights' were not in Britain's policy agenda.

The conundrum that policymakers faced in 1960s Britain (and Europe) was a shortage of labour migration after the Second World War and the prevailing structural racism and discrimination against migrants of non-white communities from (including former) Commonwealth countries. Immigration from these countries increased between 1961 and 1966 (Rose, 1969, p. 82), which was addressed at the Conservative Party Conference under the banner of 'immigration control' (Foot, 1969, p. 34). The Labour Party also supported this demand in the House of Commons, and the British media illustrated the attitude with racially intolerant headlines such as 'calling for the tremendous influx of coloured people' (MacMaster, 2001, p. 179). The political confusion, coupled with negative sentiment within the public perception of non-white immigrants in Britain, led to riots in the country after the arrival of Black people from a Caribbean background. In response to the 'abusive' and 'violent' reaction to these migrants, so-called 'race riots' broke out in 1948 (in London and Deptford), 1949 (London) and 1958 (Nottingham and London) (Cantle, 2004). The general attitude of the policymakers focused on 'immigration control' (Foot, 1969) rather than examining the root causes of the riots. Thus, the political debate in Britain between 1948 and the 1960s (1948 Nationality Act and 1962 Commonwealth Immigrants Act) arguably mirrors the discriminatory public reactions and 'non-tolerance' towards migrants from racially and ethnically diverse backgrounds. The social and political sentiment in this era depicts a process of ethnocentric construction of a 'white identity' based on 'supremacy of the dominant race' that is defined with its 'other' who is the 'non-white and alien migrant'. Despite the need for labour migrants for the country's economic recovery in the aftermath of two devastating wars and consequently a need for the growth of the non-white migrant population, such ethnocentric sentiment prevailed in Britain throughout the 1960s. For example, according to data from a survey conducted in Britain in 1969, 'only 22 per cent of British people believ[ed] that they were [at the] same level or inferior to the people in Africa ... and only 23 per cent took the same view for the people from Asia, 56 per cent in respect to the European[s], and 69 per cent in respect to American people' (Rose, 1969, p. 567). White supremacist language was also a part of the Conservative candidate Peter Griffith's electoral campaign, with his anti-immigrant and racist slogan: 'if you want a ****** for a neighbour, vote Labour'[1] (cited in Cantle, 2004; Jeffries, 2014; Stanley, 2013).

In response to the discriminatory approach by the Conservatives, the new Labour Government formally recognized the 'race problem' in Britain and introduced the 1965 Race Relations Act and the Race Relations Board (1965). This Act was the first legislation in the UK to address overcoming discrimination in the public sphere on the grounds of colour, race, ethnicity and nationality. However, the 1965 Act fell short in focusing on the central issues within which racial discrimination was most prevalent, such as employment and fair housing. Thus, the government expanded the scope of the 1965 legislation with the 1968 Race Relations Act, which recognized housing and employment issues among migrant communities. In the context of 'cohesion', the 1965 and 1968 Acts are vital in terms of *recognition* of Britain as *multicultural*; with policies that promote 'integration of immigrants' and 'good relations between immigrants and native population' through neighbourhood-based committees (Rose, 1969). However, Enoch Powell made his infamous 'Rivers of Blood Speech' in the same year, which located 'race' at the heart of the immigration debate. Thus, despite Labour's anti-discrimination policies that advocated equality of opportunities for migrants, there was still a long way to go to transform social norms and perceptions from being unfavourable towards migrant identities with those that were positive and inclusive.

By the same token, the international mobility of people and capital as part of the globalization process entailed a policy debate in Britain that incorporated multiculturalist concepts. The 1976 Race Relations Act was enacted to provide a clear definition of *discrimination*, mandating to fight against racial discrimination of migrants and promoting the integration of migrants through the 'good relations' of communities. This Act was a turning point for curbing the worst discrimination cases in employment and access to services, which also positively impacted 'the general climate of public opinion' (Parekh, 2000, p. 264). However, race relations and equal opportunities of migrants were tested again with riots in Brixton, Liverpool, Bristol and London in 1980 and 1981. Soon after the riots, Lord Scarman's report was published in 1981, which analysed the root causes of the unrest and offered recommendations. The report made connections between youth unemployment and the police's relationship with the Black and minority ethnic (BME) communities where 'institutional racism' was under the spotlight (Cantle, 2004). The report also claimed that the root cause of the unrest was intertwined with BME communities' social conditions and proposed that the government improve police training about community matters and minority communities.

The wave of migration in postwar Britain was different and mainly about 'race', 'ethnicity', 'culture' and 'religion'. The growth of the migrant population from non-European ethnic backgrounds after the 1960s transformed the policy debate in Britain, where concepts of race, equality, integration and community came under scrutiny within the framework of new concepts such as multiculturalism. Britain formally became a 'multicultural community', particularly after the 1960s, and a 'superdiverse[2] community' after the 2000s. The shifts in policy debate led to the emergence of 'race relation policies', 'integration measures', 'equalities programmes' and 'community cohesion programmes' in Britain (Cantle, 2005). The sociological debate has increasingly been about the 'diversity' of British society, and the political debate has been about the management and/or accommodation of culturally diverse minority populations. Most importantly, both disciplines stress the notion of 'identity' within the framework of 'multiculturalism'. The former addresses it through the concept of 'plural identities' and 'identity classifications' and the latter through the concepts of 'citizenship', 'civic identity' and 'rights'. Both perspectives have been central in policy debates and incorporated in integration policies in Britain.

POLICY INTERVENTION AND THE INTEGRATION OF MIGRANT COMMUNITIES IN BRITAIN

The concept of 'integration' is realized in various policy intervention models in democratic and modern societies. Diverse policy models may impede European countries to reach consensus on the definition of integration due to a lack of clarity. Two factors influence this: (1) economic protectionism, which restricts or expands migrant admittance; and (2) nation-states' political agendas such as security approaches to global trends including migration.

The term integration had connotations to assimilation, which is an expectation of migrants culturally becoming like the host community (Brubaker, 2001). Until recently, 'integration' was conveniently buried within the 'cohesion agenda' (Spencer, 2011, p. 201), which was inherently reminiscent of the previous failures of policy interventions. For instance, the more recent reports and policy approach continued to connect migrant communities to the issues of 'riots', 'disturbances'[3] and describe them as a 'problem' to be formally resolved. The most needed investigation about these riots was their root cause, which remained the same as 'race', 'ethnicity', 'inequality' and 'discrimination' of the migrant communities. We can identify multiple causes that prompted the 'disturbances' in 2001 such as 'the frustration of young Pakistani and Bangladeshi men with deprivation and social marginalisation, their vilification in local media, the visible activities and incursions of BNP and insensitive and inappropriate local policing' (Amin, 2002, p. 1413). This time, the communities involved in these riots were white and Asian communities, rather than Black communities. These communities were second-generation migrants who had benefited from the equality and anti-discrimination legislation (Cantle, 2004, p. 46). The official reports coupled with the media representation of the disturbances as an 'Asian problem' went in line with the demonization of young immigrant communities as 'criminals, disloyal subjects, ungrateful immigrants, cultural separatists … Islamic militants' (Amin, 2002, p. 964). Despite the multiple causes of the disturbances, the official reports emphasized 'the very worrying drift towards self-segregation' and the importance of 'arresting and reversing this process' (Robinson, 2005, p. 1413). Cantle carried out the initial inquiry and reviewed the disturbances. The report suggests that the review committee was not surprised by the 'physical segregation' of communities in inner-city areas; however, the central issue was the depth of polarization of the towns and cities which is described with the concept of 'parallel lives' (Community Cohesion Independent Review Team, 2001, p. 9): migrant communities living parallel lives and 'not well integrated' into the dominant community. In this policy debate, the concept of 'integration' remains unclear.

After the Cantle Report the problem was identified, and the most needed policy intervention was introduced, namely a 'community cohesion agenda (CCA)'. The definition of community cohesion promotes some kind of integration of minorities into the dominant community through a shared vision, that is 'about helping micro-communities to gel or mesh into an integrated whole. These divided communities would need to develop common goals and a shared vision … such groups should occupy a common sense of place as well' (Lynch, 2001, p. 70) through building 'understanding between different groups, and to build mutual trust and respect by breaking down stereotypes and misconceptions about the "other"' (Cantle, 2020). This agenda's key aspects are common values and civic culture, social order and social control, social solidarity and reductions in wealth disparities, social networks and social capital and place attachment and identity (Forest & Kearns, in Community Cohesion Independent Review Team, 2001, p. 13). All these dimensions for creating a cohesive community are akin to key aspects of 'integration processes' that have structural, social, cultural, civic, political and identity dynamics (Spencer, 2011, p. 203). In this context, it is not clear what distinguishes community cohesion programmes from the integration policy agenda in Britain. Perhaps, only the wording is different between the two approaches; but both approaches incorporate all these five dimensions that need to be communicated and met at local and national levels with the inclusion of migrants, individuals and representatives of the institutions that facilitate this debate and interaction.

The key factors that are argued to be facilitating or impeding integration processes can be summarized in three key domains: relating to migrants, relating to the society and policy interventions (Spencer, 2011, p. 204). The factors that hinder integration are related to migrants' lack of employment skills, language proficiency, problems with legal status, lack of knowledge of the labour market, length of stay, health, discrimination and hostility. Language proficiency, in particular, plays a key role for migrants to participate in economic and social life in the host country which is central for the creation of a sense of attachment and belonging to the neighbourhood and society. Although CCA promotes contact between communities, there is too much emphasis on minorities living in segregation which leads to a lack of scrutiny on the host communities' commitment to participate in this process. Integration is not a 'migrant problem'; on the contrary, it requires communication of both migrant and dominant communities. Hence, policy intervention becomes paramount in facilitating contact and resolving the issue of conflict between communities. According to Kundnani (2001, p. 2), one of the main culprits of 'residential segregation was the result of racist policies pursued by some of the local authorities in question', such as Oldham Local Authority found guilty of operating a segregationist housing policy. Although CCA aims to create social inclusion of migrant communities by increasing contact and promoting equality, it fails to address the issues of 'white privilege' and 'ethnic and cultural superiority' within the public policy debate. According to de Haas et al. (2020), the home–host dichotomy creates further cleavages as it explains the notion of 'home' through ideas or ideologies that are fixed. This form of essentialist approach to the concept of community is fundamentally against the inclusive integration policies that intend to create contact between communities.

Recently, community cohesion programmes have been combined with the Prevent Strategy (2019), with the aim of integrating ex-combatants and people with terror charges into the community, bringing a security dimension into the policy debate. The cities that the Cantle Report (2001) focuses on and the communities the Centre for Social Cohesion (CSC) pinpoints are new or existing Muslim communities in Britain and their lack of integration into the community. The CSC suggests that the main threat to social cohesion comes from 'the tensions between newly arrived immigrants and British citizens for public sector jobs and the radicalisation of disaffected British-born Muslims' (Conway, 2009, p. 127). This assessment puts migrants and ethnic minorities from Muslim backgrounds under scrutiny. These groups are deemed 'problematic' and 'of alien values' and are considered to have difficulty integrating into British communities. Thus, the CSC agenda adopts an exclusionist approach towards the Muslim mainstream which reduces the meaning of the CCA to a 'civilisational struggle between Western and non-Western, liberal and oppressive values (Conway, 2009, p. 127). This approach is a clear indication of the generation of moral panic by government policymakers, described by Valier (2002) as a 'gothic' nature of most contemporary risks in advanced Western societies, such as inner terrorists. Security is usually associated with borders and boundaries; thus, in this perspective, the government needs to eliminate the risks to protect the community. Order discourses feed law and order strategies that generate populist laws to agree on the justification of long-term consequences (Valier, 2002). This type of strategy arguably creates social divisions and social exclusion of minority groups and has become a globalized phenomenon with a rise in far-right movements in many Western countries, including Britain, particularly after Brexit.

Community cohesion programmes as a policy model seem to be aimed at tackling the integration processes of long-term immigrants and minority citizens; however, it overlooks the superdiversity and greater mobility of migrants in recent years (Vertovec, 2007). This policy model also envisages a blinkered view on migration, which overlooks the internationalization of migration as part of global processes. In other words, this model adopts an essentialist view of migration with connecting fixed and static features to migrant communities, which dismisses the reality where 'people's characteristics like knowledge, ideas, skills as well as identities, perceptions and aspirations typically change over time' (De Haas et al., 2020, p. 28). Moreover, migrants can have multilayered identities and 'often foster multiple, transnational belonging that defies the idea of singular belonging to one nation or state' (De Haas et al., 2020, p. 28). Policymakers need to acknowledge these complexities of human mobility and accept migration as a social process in the contemporary world. Hence, the cohesion discourse and most recently interculturalism (Cantle, 2015) need to transcend the old ways of acute problem-solving policy strategies of 'social control' and defy the home–host binary approach. This will only be possible when migration is acknowledged as a dynamic and integral part of the globalization process, which generates multiple social processes within territorially bound communities. The recognition of contemporary communities as multicultural and superdiverse can enable policymakers to debate migration processes with the inclusion of international legal concepts such as freedom of movement.

COMMUNICATING 'MIGRANT IDENTITIES' THROUGH 'CONTEMPORARY COSMOPOLITANISM'

Migrants' (and individuals') identities and their sense of belonging and feeling of home are socially constructed and tend to transform over the life course (De Bree et al., 2010; Ghorashi, 2005). In this context, identity is a fluid concept and migrants can possess transnational identities and multilayered belongings. Vertovec uses the term 'superdiversity' to explain and underline a level and kind of complexity the condition of 'a dynamic interplay of variables among an increased number of new, small and scattered, multiple-origin, transnationally con-nected, socio-economically differentiated and legally stratified immigrants who have arrived over the last decade' (2007). Some European states adopt a multicultural approach when designing their policies which values diverse and cultural traditions of migrant communities, recognizing their identities and giving this recognition an institutional form (Vertovec & Wessendorf, 2010, p. 3). The recognition of 'diversity' at policy level disputes the percep-tions of natural links between individuals, culture and territory (De Bree, 2007; Pedersen, 2003). Valuing migrants' cultural heritage creates a positive identity which means a formal recognition of community support for individuals making their way to the hostile environment (Spencer, 2011, p. 207). The formal recognition of migrants' membership and their rights can create a sense of belonging and attachment to the host community and strengthen a civic engagement on the same civic goals as a community. As Spencer and Rudiger (2003, p. 208) put it, 'multicultural integration policies support neither the crossing of boundaries from one culture to another, as do assimilation policies, nor the preservation of these boundaries, as segregation, but aim to foster therein permeability'. Hence, this type of integration policy can be successful by adopting 'porous values' such as 'dignity' and 'worth' (Sonmez Efe, 2021) which are flexible enough to create a sense of coexistence of individuals from diverse backgrounds within the same public sphere. The concept of porous values enables individuals to make sense of their identity and membership status within the community. As mentioned above, migrants have multiple identities based on multilayered belonging to more than one community, which creates both 'sameness' and 'difference' in the country of residence that is considered 'home'. Integration policies focus on 'sameness' and recognize 'difference' to an extent, both of which are negotiated collectively as part of a public debate.

As Madood (2015) suggests, multiculturalists are not against integration, or even assimi-lation of migrant communities into the dominant culture, as long as this process is voluntary and non-coercive. The key issue in this process is the perceptions of migrant minorities as 'problematic' and 'alien', which creates segregation in the wider society. When some groups are identified as 'problem', their values will be in question concerning the values of the dominant nation, which creates 'non-acceptance' and 'misrecognition' of their identities. Migrants ought to be recognized through civic membership rather than as outsiders who 'need' to be integrated into the dominant community.

CCA still offers a platform for 'intercultural dialogue' among communities in Britain with more power given to local authorities to create their own cohesion strategies and central principles. This dialogue provides room for the public to debate, repackage and rebrand the meaning of 'the British people' to create unity out of diversity (Mcghee, 2003, p. 377). The 2002 White Paper emphasizes the re-creation of common sense of citizenship between host and migrant communities which has been the core strategy of community cohesion programmes (McGhee, 2005, p. 71). This new approach stresses citizenship based on shared values and identities with the renewal of communities' 'social fabric'. This approach was evident in the Labour Government's commitment for creating commonality through shared principles (McGhee, 2003, p. 382) which is described as 'a commonplace for diverse cultures and beliefs, consistent with the core values we uphold' (Blunkett, 2001, p. 2). Nationwide democratic debates are required to enable 'dialogue' among particularly young populations in order to achieve this goal (Community Cohesion Independent Review Team, 2001, p. 11). Democratic public debates create cross-cultural 'contact' between different communities that aim to eradicate 'ignorance' and 'myths' and foster ' an understanding and respect' at local and national community levels (Community Cohesion Independent Review Team). This is a type of citizenship based on civic virtues where difference and diversity are incorporated into the civic identity of 'sameness'.

The Commission on Integration and Community Cohesion (CICC) report suggests that 'people with complex and multiple sources of identity are more positive about other groups, more integrated and less prejudiced' (2007, p. 35). The notion of identity in the CICC fosters fluid and transnationally globalized forms of identity that are multilayered. This paper argues that migrant communities possess multiple identities, are resilient to challenges and when/if the host community welcomes them, they enrich the culture of the community. Cosmopolitan model integration advocates this approach with the inclusion of cosmopolitan principles that enable peaceful coexistence of communities with diverse identities in a shared public space. However, the CICC takes a 'problem-solving' practical approach where multiple identities under the umbrella of common citizenship are undermined because the notion of mutual respect fades away (Dobbernack & Madood, 2013, p. 158). The CICC report remained important for the Coalition Government after the 2010 elections. Since the defeat of the Labour Government, the political debate has steadily continued to move away from multiculturalism towards diversity within the context of community cohesion.

Despite the efforts of the policy analysis on the new forms of 'ethno-religious' diversity in Britain, there are also criticisms; for instance, Communities Minister Ruth Kelly's speech on multiculturalism encouraged separateness (Dobbernack & Madood, 2013, p. 156). There is a consensus on multiculturalism as a failed political concept for not answering contemporary social struggles and leading to a society where communities live parallel lives (Robinson & McGuinness, 2015, p. 7). However, these criticisms are considered ambiguous on the ideas and political practices these critics are with (Lentin & Titley, 2011; Meer & Madood, 2009; Vertovec & Wessendorf, 2010). I argue that multiculturalism is still relevant as a social and political concept, and CCA has been presented as an alternative model to show the failure of multicultural model integration in Britain after the 2001 riots. The core meaning and features of the CCA, such as 'recognition of difference', 'realization of multiple identities' and 'diversity', show that CCA and multiculturalism are not distinct concepts. CCA is arguably an extension or rearticulation of multiculturalism which offers practical solutions to overcome contemporary social challenges and create a cohesive community. It transcends Kymlicka's (2000, 2011) notion of multiculturalism that focuses on multinationalism and rights of indigenous peoples, and includes Madood's (2013, p. 57) notion of post-migration polyethnicity.

On the other hand, CCA is influenced by the security discourse with the recent global conflicts and terror events that resulted in an increasing focus on Muslim communities (Flint & Robinson, 2008, p. 3). The states' role is shifting away from being 'neutral to difference' towards 'intervention' and a 'law and order' approach, particularly after 9/11 in the United States and 7/7 in London. The UK's Counter-Terrorism Strategy (CONTEST) and the Prevent strategy aim to stop people from becoming terrorists (Home Office, 2011, p. 6) and use some of the principles of the CCA in terms of addressing the root causes of radicalization of some groups in Britain. The Prevent official paper suggests that lack of trust between ethnic and faith groups and dominant groups, lack of civic integration, active participation and segregation create more vulnerable individuals for radicalization (p. 27). Similar to CCA, Prevent also promotes a stronger sense of belonging and citizenship, integration, democratic participation and interfaith dialogue. However, new and old migrant communities are under the scrutiny of the security agenda based on their 'difference' from the mainstream culture and incompatibility with the British democratic system, as CONTEST (2015) blamed some communities for segregation and suggested practical solutions to these challenges through keeping the existing programmes and introducing new ones such as National Citizenship Service and English-language training (Home Office, 2015, p. 37). Muslim communities are under scrutiny within new programmes as, according to the Casey Review on integration, they are stereotyped and singled out for lack of integration and language skills (2016). This evaluation creates more divisions in the British community by delivering a rounded view of one minority as 'difficult' to integrate. The UK Race and Europe Network also highlights this problem, which suggests that disproportionate focus is placed on migrant communities' capabilities to integrate leading to stereotyping of migrant communities as being a 'real problem' (Public Policy Exchange, 2019). According to the survey conducted by Opinium (Multicultural Britain in 21st Century), there are differing perceptions of the communities in Britain, where white Britons blame minorities for not making enough effort to integrate into the wider community whereas BME communities think otherwise (2017). In fact, these opposing views implicitly suggest that 'integration' is a two-way process that requires 'mutual will' for participation from multiple communities.

Young suggests three forms of exclusion that reinforce a lack of integration in some communities: 'economic exclusion from labour markets; social exclusion between people in civil society and the ever-expanding exclusionary activities of the criminal justice system and private security' (Young, 1999, p. vi). Rather than inclusion of the security discourse in integration policies, an analysis of the root causes of exclusion of migrant communities will arguably increase awareness about Britain's social polarizations. Madood describes the current situation as a 'totalistic dichotomization of West-Islam/Muslims' (2013, p. 60). He further suggests that the dichotomizing obscures the variety of views in the West, such as Western geopolitical domination of the Muslim world undercutting ongoing efforts for building trust and contact, alliances, synthesis and so on that are necessary elements for multicultural model citizenship. I argue that an individual can possess a multilayered identity that is fluid and transformative, and active participation in a civic nation will enable him/her to share common aspirations.

The analysis illustrates that the CCA has some elements of cosmopolitanism, multiculturalism and security. The discourse does not offer a brand new concept for political debate of migrant integration; it instead fosters a rearticulation of 'multiculturalism' and 'anti-discrimination' laws. It offers a new perspective on the meaning of 'British nation'. In this democratic iteration process, there has been an opportunity to rearticulate the original laws and new agendas, echoing Beck's model of 'dialogism of cosmopolitanization' that incorporates a perspective for 'an imagination of alternative ways of life and rationalities, which includes the otherness of the other' (2002, p. 18) through 'the coexistence of rival ways of life in the individual experience, which makes it a matter of fate to compare, reflect, criticize, understand and combine contradictory certainties' (McGhee, 2005, p. 171). Thus, the multicultural project as a cosmopolitan model incorporates three stages for peaceful coexistence:

> (a) promoting respect in society for diverse cultures; at the same time as (b) attempting to de-essentialize encoded and racialized identities; while rising the challenge of (c) questioning the ways in which national cultures privilege certain identities over others, thus beginning to process whereby dominant groups' unlearn their own privilege. (Stevenson, 2003, p. 53)

Cosmopolitan citizenship does not reject individuals' loyalty and emotional attachment to their local and national communities; it offers a legal platform for the construction of identities with the inclusion of these commitments and with the adoption of common moral values such as 'respect' and 'dignity'. 'Cosmopolitan Patriots' can create such a balance between loyalties and commitments to particular cultures and traditions and identities and encourage the fostering of wider 'civic and political allegiances' (McGhee, 2005, p. 172). The difference of 'civic patriotism' from 'nationalist patriotism' is that the former does not consider the notion of nation in an ethnic sense (Benhabib, 2008, p. 152). De-ethnicization of national identity enables individuals to imagine their commonality through 'cosmopolitan humanity'. According to cosmopolitanism, common national ancestry leads to patriotism; however, it also suggests that 'all humans come from the same ancestors who have the duty of love for one's co-nationals and duty of general love of humans' (p. 152). A transparent dialogue between diverse cultures sits at the core of cosmopolitan citizenship, which is also an essential element of civic participation and active citizenship.

In contemporary policies, cosmopolitan norms are embedded in the legal and political culture where an individual can have rights by virtue of residency rather than cultural identity (Benhabib, 2004, p. 177) as long as he has a legal membership status. Moreover, most nation-states allow migrants (who are legal residents and not yet citizens) to exercise some degree of civic participation and create social inclusion to an extent. Therefore, this chapter's argument on 'integration of migrant communities' is also relevant to the migrant communities of non-citizen status in Britain as cosmopolitan values include these groups based on their 'contemporary right to hospitality' principle (Sonmez Efe, 2021). All three policy approaches – multiculturalism, community cohesion and interculturalism – incorporate some elements of the contemporary right to hospitality that foster an 'acceptance' and 'inclusion' of new and old migrant communities.

CONCLUSION

The discussions in this chapter reaffirm that national communities have entered into a system of world communities that are interconnected and multicultural. Cross-border movements are an integral part of the globalization process which shapes contemporary societies. The chapter discussed how (super)diverse Britain responded to this process by analysing migrant identities and integration policies. The integration policies in Britain thus far have emerged as a political reaction to social unrest or riots within the community where the concept of integration has turned into crisis-management programmes to deal with 'problematic' migrant communities that are 'difficult' to integrate into the wider community. When the central focus is on the concept of 'segregation' of migrants, the root cause of social issues are overlooked, such as social inequalities and growing far-right ethnocentric sentiments towards migrant communities in Britain.

The chapter illustrates a process of democratic iterations in Britain where migration policies are in constant transformation with the inclusion of new conditions and actors in the policy debate. The chapter concludes that the multicultural policy approach is still relevant to integration policies; the security agenda impacts the perceptions of migrant integration and identities; and integration policies need to transform from offering acute policy solutions to reinforcing civic integration in Britain. This chapter claimed that adoption of the cosmopolitan model integration (Madood, 2013) at policy level arguably could foster an inclusive community that recognizes 'migrant communities' as part of 'we' in multicultural Britain. In other words, with this model, the 'act of migration' as one of the fundamental freedoms has been normalized as part of globalization processes. Thus, there is a need to evaluate past policy triumphs and mistakes and take a holistic approach to integration policies in Britain that acknowledge multicultural societies' future in the globalized world community.

NOTES

1. The offensive historical racist language, reflecting the brutality of racist political rhetoric at the time, has been removed from this quotation. The reader can check the source for the original quotation wording.
2. Superdiversity is a concept developed by Vertovec (2007) which describes 'a notion intended to underline a *level and kind of complexity* surpassing anything the country has previously experienced. Such a condition is distinguished by a *dynamic interplay of variables* among an increased number of new, small and scattered, multiple-origin, transnationally connected, socio-economically differentiated and legally stratified *immigrants* who have arrived over the last decade' (emphasis added).
3. Migrant minorities in Britain were again the focus of public debate when riots broke out in 2001 in northern towns such as Burnley, Bradford and Oldham. These riots were officially classed as 'disturbances' by the police (Cantle, 2004, p. 45), which shows the shift of focus in terminology from 'race' to 'disturbances'.

REFERENCES

Aliens Act (1914). Aliens Restriction Act [4 & 5 GEO. 5, Ch. 12]. Available at www.legislation.gov.uk/ukpga/1914/12/pdfs/ukpga_19140012_en.pdf. Accessed on 15 May 2019.
Aliens Act (1919). Aliens Restriction (Amendment) Act, [9 & 10 GEO. 5, Ch. 92]. Available at www.legislation.gov.uk/ukpga/1919/92/pdfs/ukpga_19190092_en.pdf. Accessed on 15 May 2019.
Amin, A. (2002). 'Ethnicity and the multicultural city: Living with diversity'. *Urban Studies*, 42 (8), 1411–1428.
Arendt, H. (1979). *The Origin of Totalitarianism*. Harcourt Brace Jovanovich.
Beck, U. (2002). 'The Cosmopolitan society and its enemies'. *Theory, Culture and Society*, 19 (1–2), 17–44.
Benhabib, S. (2004). *The Rights of Others: Aliens, Residents and Citizens*. Cambridge University Press.
Benhabib, S. (2008). *Another Cosmopolitanism: The Berkeley Tanner Lectures*. Oxford University Press.
Blunkett, D. (2001). 'Blunkett calls for honest and open debate on citizenship and community', in D. McGhee (Ed.), *Moving to 'Our' Common Ground: A Critical Examination of Community Cohesion Discourse in Twenty-First Century Britain*. Blackwell Publishing.
British Nationality Act (1948). [11&12 GEO. 6, CH. 56]. Available at www.legislation.gov.uk/ukpga/1948/56/pdfs/ukpga_19480056_en.pdf. Accessed on 30 April 2019.
Brubaker, R. (2001). 'The return of assimilation? Changing perspectives on immigration and its sequels in France, Germany and the United States'. *Journal of Ethnic and Racial Studies* 24 (4), 531–548.
Cantle, T. (2004). 'The end of parallel lives? The report of the Community Cohesion Panel'. Available at https://tedcantle.co.uk/pdf/TheEndofParallelLives.pdf. Accessed on 16 December 2020.
Cantle, T. (2005). *Community Cohesion: A New Framework for Race and Diversity*. Palgrave Macmillan.
Cantle, T. (2015). 'Interculturalism: "Learning to live in diversity"'. *Ethnicities* 16 (3), 1–24.
Cantle, T. (2020). 'About community cohesion'. Available at http://tedcantle.co.uk/about-community-cohesion/. Accessed on 16 December 2020.
Casey, L. (2016). Casey Review: A Review into Opportunity and Integration. Department for Communities and Local Government.
Commission on Integration and Community Cohesion (CICC) (2007). Report. Available at www.equallyours.org.uk/commission-on-integration-and-cohesion-final-report/. Accessed on 16 December 2020.
Commonwealth Immigration Act (1962). [10 & 11 Eliz. 2, CH. 21]. Available at www.freemovement.org.uk/wp-content/uploads/2018/04/CIA1962.pdf Accessed on 30 April 2019.
Community Cohesion Independent Review Team (2001). Community cohesion: A report of the Independent Review Team, chaired by Ted Cantle (Cantle Report). Home Office.
CONTEST (2015). UK strategy for countering terrorism: Annual report for 2015. Available at www.gov.uk/government/collections/contest. Accessed on 16 December 2020.
Conway, D. (2009). 'Disunited kingdom: How the government's community cohesion agenda undermines British identity and nationhood', in J. Dobbernack & T. Madood (Eds), *Tolerance, Intolerance and Respect: Hard to Accept*. Palgrave.
De Bree, J. (2007). *Belonging, Transnationalism and Embedding: Dutch Moroccan Return Migrants in Northeast Morocco*, MA thesis, Redbound University, Nijmegen.
De Bree, J., Davids, T. & de Haas, H. (2010). 'Pot-return experiences ad transnational belonging of return migrants: A Dutch-Moroccan case study'. *Global Networks*, 10, 489–509.
De Haas, H., Castles, S. & Miller, M.J. (2020). *The Age of Migration: International Population Movements in the Modern World*. Palgrave.
Dobbernack, J. & Madood, T. (2013). *Tolerance, Intolerance and Respect: Hard to Accept*. Palgrave.
Flint, J., & Robinson, D. (2008). *Community Cohesion in Crisis: New Dimensions of Diversity and Difference*. Polity Press.
Foot, P. (1969). *The Rise of Enoch Powell*. Penguin.
Ghorashi, H. (2005). 'Layered meanings of community experiences of Iranian women exiles in "Irangeles"', in T. Davis & F. V. Driel (Eds), *The Gender Question in Globalisation*. Ashgate.
Home Office (2011). Prevent Strategy. June, Cm 8092. Home Office.
Home Office (2015). Counter-Extremism Strategy. October, Cm9148. Home Office.

Jeffries, S. (2014). Britain's most racist election: The story of Smethwick, 50 years on. Available at www .theguardian.com/world/2014/oct/15/britains-most-racist-election-smethwick-50-years-on. Accessed on 30 April 2019.

Kundnani, A. (2001). *From Oldham to Bradford: The Violence of the Violated in the Three Faces of British Racism*. Institute of Race Relations.

Kymlicka, W. (2000). 'Politics of multiculturalism', in W. Kymlicka (Ed.), *Multicultural Citizenship*. Oxford University Press.

Kymlicka, W. (2011). 'Multicultural citizenship within multination states'. *Ethnicities*, 11 (3), 281–302.

Lentin, A. & Titley, G. (2011). *The Crisis of Multiculturalism: Racism in a Neoliberal Age*. Zed Books.

Lord Scarman Report (1981). The Brixton disorders 10–12 April 1981 report of an Inquiry by the Right Honourable the Lord Scarman, OBE, presented to parliament by the Secretary of State for the Home Department by command of Her Majesty. Great Britain Home Office.

Lynch, R. (2001). 'An analysis of the concept of community cohesion', Appendix C in Community Cohesion: A report of the Independent Review. Home Office.

MacMaster, N. (2001). *Racism in Europe: 1870–2000*. Palgrave Macmillan.

Madood, T. (2013). *Multiculturalism*. Polity Press.

Madood, T. (2015). 'What is multiculturalism and what can it learn from interculturalism?', *Ethnicities*, 16 (3), 1–24.

McGhee, D. (2003). Moving to 'our' common ground: A critical examination of community cohesion discourse in twenty-first century Britain. *Sociological Review*.

McGhee, D. (2005). *Intolerant Britain? Hate, Citizenship and Difference*. Open University.

Meer, N. & Madood, T. (2009). 'The multicultural state we're in: Muslims, "multiculture" and the "civic re-balancing" of British multiculturalism'. *Political Studies* 57 (3), 473–497.

Opinium (2017). *Multicultural Britain in the 21st century*. Available at www.opinium.co.uk/wp-content/ uploads/2017/07/Multicultural-Britain-2017-v6.pdf. Accessed on 22 May 2019.

Parekh, B. (2000). *The Future of Multi-Ethnic Britain*. Profile Books.

Pedersen, M.H. (2003). 'Between homes: Post-war return, emplacement and the negotiation of belonging in Lebanon', New Issues in Refugee Research: Working Paper no. 79. Denmark: United Nations High Commissioner for Refugees.

Public Policy Exchange (2019). 'A two-way street: Improving integration, social cohesion and toler- ance in the UK – a public policy exchange symposium: overview'. Available at www.publicpoli cyexchange.co.uk/events.php. Accessed on 4 April 2023.

Race Relations Act (1965). Parliamentary Archives. Available at www.parliament.uk/about/living -heritage/transformingsociety/private-lives/relationships/collections1/race-relations-act-1965/race -relations-act-1965/. Accessed on 30 April 2019.

Race Relations Act (1976). Chapter 74. Available at www.legislation.gov.uk/ukpga/1976/74/pdfs/ukpga _19760074_en.pdf. Accessed on 1 May 2019.

Robinson, D. (2005). 'The search for community cohesion: Key themes and dominant concepts of the public policy agenda'. *Urban Studies*, 42 (8), 1411–1428.

Robinson, D. & McGuinness, M. (2015). *Racial Equality Strategy 2015–2015*. Available at www .executiveoffice-ni.gov.uk/publications/racial-equality-strategy-2015-2025. Accessed on 19 May 2019.

Rose, E.J.B. (1969). *Colour and Citizenship: Report on British Race Relations*. Oxford University Press.

Sonmez Efe, S. (2021). *Rights of Migrant Workers: An Analysis of Migration Policies in Contemporary Turkey*. Transnational Press.

Spencer, S. (2011). *The Migration Debate*. Policy Press.

Spencer, S. & Rudiger, A. (2003). 'Social integration of immigrants and ethnic minorities, policies to combat discrimination'. Paper presented to the Economic and Social Aspects of Migration Conference.

Stanley, T. (2013). 'Peter Griffiths and the ugly Tory racism of the 1960s killed rational debate about immigration'. Available at https://web.archive.org/web/20131201001553/http://blogs.telegraph.co .uk/news/timstanley/100248091/peter-griffiths-and-the-tory-racism-of-the-1960s-killed-rational -debate-about-immigration/. Accessed on 30 April 2019.

Stevenson, N. (2003). *Cultural Citizenship: Cosmopolitan Questions*. Open University Press.

Valier, C. (2002). 'Punishment, border crossings and the powers of horror'. Available at https://journals .sagepub.com/doi/10.1177/136248060200600305. Accessed on 16 December 2020.

Vertovec, S. (2007). 'Super-diversity and its implications'. *Journal of Ethnic and Racial*, 30 (6), 1024–1054.

Vertovec, S. & Wessendorf, S. (2010). *The Multiculturalism Backlash: European Discourses, Policies, and Practices*. Routledge.

Young, J. (1999). *The Exclusive Society: Social Exclusion, Crime and Difference in Late Modernity*. Sage.

PART V

GLOBALIZATION AND THE LIFE COURSE

23. Globalization, uncertainty and changing life courses in modern societies

Hans-Peter Blossfeld and Gwendolin Josephine Blossfeld

INTRODUCTION

Since the early 1990s, globalization has increased the pace of social and economic change in modern societies. Globalization is an inherently complex concept (Guillén, 2001). It has become a central reference point for the media, politicians, academics, and policy-makers to understand the accelerating social and economic changes in modern societies. The theoretical approach to globalization proposed in this chapter can be summarized under four interrelated structural shifts (see Figure 23.1): (1) the rapid internationalization of markets after the fall of the Iron Curtain and the collapse of the East–West divide (economic globalization); (2) the rapid intensification of competition among nation-states based on policies of deregulation, privatization, and liberalization (political globalization); (3) the accelerated diffusion of knowledge and the proliferation of global networks linking all kinds of actors on the globe through the transformation of information and communication technologies (ICTs) (informational globalization); and (4) the increasing importance of markets and their dependence on random shocks occurring anywhere on the globe (network globalization). Together, these four global forces have generated unprecedented levels of structural uncertainty in modern societies in recent decades. They are filtered through domestic institutions such as education systems, labor market structures, welfare regimes and family traditions and channeled to particular social groups.

This chapter focuses on the role of nation-specific institutions in the process of globalization and describes how these institutions influence individual life courses in 17 different countries. Based on selected theoretical and empirical findings from the international comparative *Globalife*[1] project (Blossfeld & Hofmeister, 2008; Blossfeld et al., 2005, 2006a, 2006b), this chapter describes the interaction of global forces and country-specific institutions and shows how these changes generate path dependencies on domestic institutions and affect the life-course outcomes of individuals in different countries. The *Globalife* project involved about 70 researchers from different types of educational systems (stratified versus unstratified, occupation-specific versus general vocational training), labor market structures (open versus closed labor markets), welfare regimes (liberal, conservative, social-democratic, familistic and post-socialistic) and family traditions (strong versus weak family support).

The following 17 countries were studied in the *Globalife* project: Canada, Czech Republic, Denmark, Estonia, France, Germany, Hungary, Ireland, Italy, Mexico, the Netherlands, Norway, Poland, Spain, Sweden, United Kingdom and United States.

The empirical analyses of the *Globalife* project covered the historical period from the 1980s to the mid-2000s. The cross-national comparison of structurally different countries makes it possible to gain an empirically grounded theoretical understanding of how globalization, and the apparent uncertainty that it generates at the individual level, leads to changes for young people entering the labor market, for men and women in mid-life and for late-career transitions.

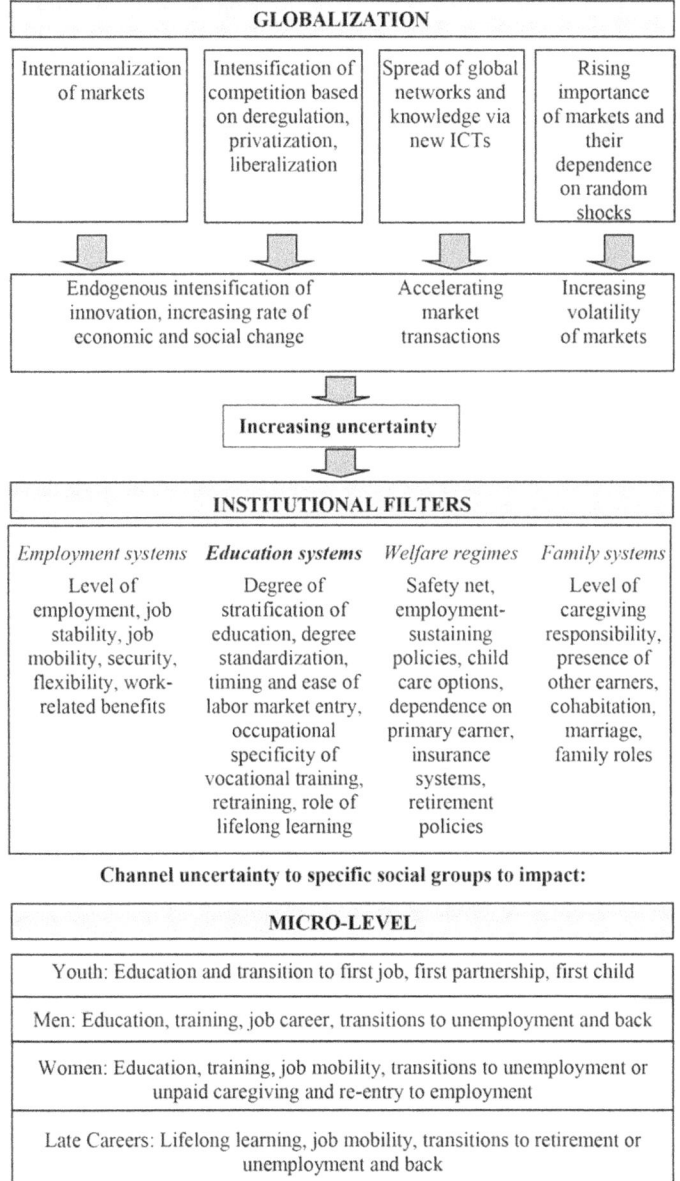

Figure 23.1   *How globalization creates increasing uncertainty and impacts life-course transitions*

THE PROCESS OF GLOBALIZATION SINCE THE EARLY 1990S

Four Structural Shifts of Globalization

Since the early 1990s, four interrelated globalization shifts have been observed in modern societies. The first structural shift of globalization refers to the internationalization of markets and the subsequent decline of national borders (see Figure 23.1). It is associated with policy changes in laws, institutions or practices which make various transactions (in terms of commodities, labor, services and capital) across national borders easier or less costly. Internationalization of markets also means the integration of previously "isolated" nations into the global economy. For example, several countries in the *Globalife* study previously experienced isolation from the outside world, such as former communist East Germany, the Czech Republic, Poland, Estonia and Hungary. After the fall of the Iron Curtain, these countries quickly integrated into global competition.

The second structural shift of globalization refers to the intensification of exchange and competition between nation-states (see Figure 23.1), i.e., the idea that capital and labor are increasingly mobile, forcing national economies to continuously adjust. For nation-states, this implies an increased importance for governments to make their economies internationally competitive. These policies include improving the functioning of markets by removing or relaxing government regulation of economic activities (deregulation). It also indicates a shift to rely more on the price mechanism to coordinate economic activities (liberalization), and a transfer of assets or businesses that were previously publicly owned to private owners and control (privatization). This neoliberal shift often means pressures to adjust prices, products, technologies and human resources more rapidly and comprehensively (Montanari, 2001; Regini, 2000a, 2000b).

A third feature of globalization is the spread of global networks of people and companies connected by ICTs such as computers, smartphones and the Internet (see Figure 23.1) (Castells, 2000). These ICTs, along with modern social media, transmit messages and images instantaneously and permit a faster dissemination of information and knowledge over long distances and across countries. They increasingly allow to create instantaneous common global benchmarks. Thus, ICTs have fundamentally altered the scope (expanding the reach of networks of social activity and power), intensity (regulated connections) and speed (accelerating interactions and social processes) of societal transformations (Held et al., 1999).

The fourth structural shift of globalization is inherently linked to the increasing interconnectedness of people and markets around the globe (see Figure 23.1). It increases the relevance of distant events to local decision makers in all modern societies. These developments inherently increase the global interdependence of decision making.

The development of worldwide globalization between 1970 and 2018 can be described by the *KOF (Konjunkturforschungsstelle) Globalisation Index* (Gygli et al., 2019). This measure is based on the same conceptual framework of globalization that has been used in the *Globalife* project and utilizes 42 yearly indicators (covering the economic, social, political and ICT dimensions of globalization) from 185 nations. Missing values of indicators within some country-specific time series are imputed using linear interpolation. Although globalization is not a new phenomenon, the KOF Globalisation Index clearly shows that the slope of change of the globalization process rose steeply after the early 1990s and levelled off at a much higher

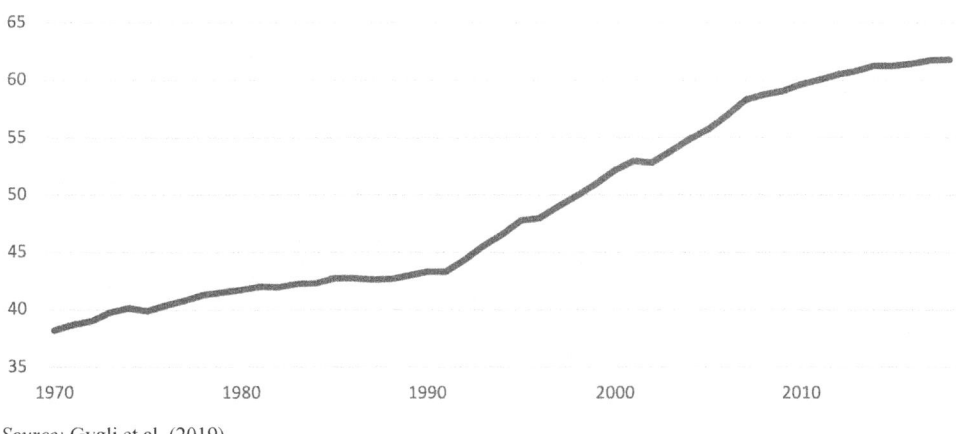

Source: Gygli et al. (2019).

Figure 23.2   *Description of the globalization process based on the KOF Globalisation Index, 1970–2018*

degree of globalization at around 2010 (see Figure 23.2). Thus, there was an enormous acceleration of globalization after the end of the Cold War.

Globalization and Increasing Life-Course Uncertainty

Globalization does not just mean that actors are increasingly in the hands of anonymous global markets. What is equally important is that the changes on these markets are becoming more dynamic and less predictable. Thus, globalization is a catalyst of uncertainty in modern societies. First, the globalization of markets endogenously intensifies competition between firms, forcing them to be more flexible and innovative, to use the latest technologies or to invent new products. This in turn increases the volatility of markets (Streeck, 1987). Second, modern ICTs as well as deregulation, privatization and liberalization policies allow individuals, firms and governments to respond faster to observed market changes and accelerated market transactions (Castells, 2000). Subsequentially, this makes long-term developments of globalizing societies inherently more difficult to predict. Third, global prices tend to become more vulnerable to exogenous fluctuations because world supply, world demand or both are increasingly dependent on random shocks triggered somewhere on the globe (e.g., by major scientific discoveries, technical inventions, new consumer fashions, major political upheavals such as wars and revolutions). Accelerated market dynamics and the increasing dependence of prices on random events occurring somewhere on the globe lead to a higher frequency of surprises in market development and market prices that differ significantly from what people could have reasonably expected given the limited information available to them. In other words, the increasing dynamics and volatility of the outcomes of globalized markets make it more difficult for individuals, firms and governments to predict the future of the market and to make decisions between different alternatives and strategies. Increasing uncertainty about economic and social developments is therefore a defining feature of globalization in advanced economies. At the individual level, increasing uncertainty has several consequences for actors:

(1) rational decision making becomes increasingly difficult because the future outcomes of decisions are harder to predict; (2) alternative decision-making mechanisms (traditions, local social norms, local framing, habits, rules of thumb) gain importance to compensate for declining rational decision making; (3) there is a shift toward short-term time horizons and decision making; (4) long-term self-binding life-course decisions (in education, training, career, family and children) become more problematic; and (5) contexts of social reciprocity and trust (in partnerships, family, welfare state, etc.) are undermined by increasing uncertainty. In the *Globalife* project, uncertainty was operationalized by the precariousness of employment (e.g., type of job, occupational standing), by the quality of employment contracts (e.g., fixed-term contracts, part-time work) and by returns to education in terms of benefits as well as earnings over the life course.

GLOBALIZATION, UNCERTAINTY AND CHANGES IN LIFE COURSES

Based on these empirical indicators, all countries of the *Globalife* project showed an increase in social and economic uncertainty as globalization accelerated. The *Globalife* project studied these rising uncertainties at four key life stages: (1) the transition from youth to adulthood; (2) men's mid-career trajectories; (3) women's mid-life pathways between employment and family responsibilities; and (4) late careers and transitions to retirement.

Changes in the Transition from Youth to Adulthood

First, the *Globalife* project examined the extent to which the globalization process has influenced young people's ability to establish themselves as independent adults in the workforce, to form partnerships and to become parents (Blossfeld et al., 2005). It was found that the young generation faced a particularly high degree of uncertainty when entering the labor market. This manifested itself in increasingly precarious and low-quality employment relationships, such as fixed-term contracts, part-time work or irregular working hours as well as a lower occupational standing when entering the labor market. This, in turn, left recent labor market entrants with a more uncertain future. Young people who have less labor market experience and are not yet shielded by internal labor markets are more exposed to the forces of globalization, making them the "losers" of globalization.

The *Globalife* project also provided empirical evidence that the country-specific institutions do not converge worldwide in the course of globalization. Rather, the national institutions have a strong inertial tendency and interact with global forces. As the globalization process leads to different problems in different institutional settings, nation-states and individual actors respond to global changes in different ways. This leads to path dependencies in country-specific institutions that have been quite persistent, directing uncertainty in unique ways and toward particular qualification groups. For example, the youngest age cohorts in Italy (Bernardi & Nazio, 2005) and Spain (Simó Noguera et al., 2005) took increasingly longer to find their first job and were less likely to convert the growing number of temporary contracts into permanent ones. Thus, in these two countries, younger cohorts faced rising youth unemployment and, as a result, decided to participate longer in education. In other words, young adults from Spain and Italy opted increasingly for the role of student rather than leaving the education system and becoming unemployed. To some extent, the education system has become a "parking lot" for otherwise unemployed youth. In Spain, where the share of college graduates has risen particularly sharply, this expansion of educational participation has also been associated with a trend toward overqualification. In Italy and Spain, highly educated young people must find a job matching their educational qualifications when they enter the labor market. Because of the importance of a good job match in these closed employment systems, higher-educated youth are very selective and therefore have a longer search time. If they got a job below their skill level, it was much harder for them to resume a normal career. In these two countries, it is the highly skilled young people who have been particularly affected by globalization.

In Germany, in contrast, there was a clear and significant stratification of the type of youth that experienced unemployment due to the dual vocational training system and certification-oriented system of higher education. The dual system, which combines theoretical learning with practical experience in the workplace, clearly served as a kind of bridge between the general education system and the labor market, so the unemployment rate among young people with vocational training was particularly low. The unemployment rate was also very low among German graduates of higher education, since in the German qualification space job opportunities are strongly linked to the requirements of diplomas and certificates. In Germany, therefore, it is mostly the unskilled who experienced particularly high youth unemployment and it is very hard for them to move out of secondary labor market positions.

This German pattern of transition from the education system to the labor market stands in stark contrast to the "stop-gap" pattern generated by the system of in-company, on-the-job training combined with the open employment labor market in the United States. There, for many young (highly) qualified entrants, lower entry-level jobs have comparatively less harmful consequences for their later careers. This means that even if the first job is precarious, they can easily transition to a normal career sooner or later because job careers are based on the logic of on-the-job training in the organizational space.

Thus, certain groups of youth are disproportionately affected by globalization, but the risks of globalization clearly accumulate at the bottom. The "insider–outsider" split was even more pronounced in societies with a closed employment system where uncertainty was clearly channeled to the unskilled. Particularly in the closed employment systems (as in Germany, Italy or Spain), uncertainty took the form of employment relationship or temporal uncertainty (the reduced attractiveness of long-term contracts). In these countries, qualified insiders were particularly protected. For employers, the only way to introduce flexibility into companies was by shifting market uncertainty to outsiders. The least qualified labor market entrants were increasingly in precarious, fixed-term contracts in Germany, Spain and Italy. The use of fixed-term contracts has skyrocketed in many countries. In the Netherlands (Liefbroer, 2005), for instance, the number of young people on permanent contracts has fallen significantly and the number of temporary, part-time or training contracts has risen. The results of the *Globalife* project regarding open employment systems (as in the United States (Berkowitz King, 2005), United Kingdom (Francesconi & Golsch, 2006) and Canada (Mills, 2005)) were also confirmed. Here, the relative shielding of qualified workers was much less pronounced, with globalization risks spread over a broader base, leaving youth to rely much more on their own human capital. Although uncertainty was more pervasive, inequality still accumulated disproportionately in groups with low human capital (Blossfeld et al., 2011b). The employment situation of young people had clear implications for their family formation processes. Economic, temporal and employment relationship uncertainties translated into a higher likelihood of postponing or forgoing partnership and parenthood (Blossfeld et al., 2011c). In other words, young people developed rational responses to growing uncertainties, which the *Globalife* project identified in terms of four different behavioral strategies: (1) postponement of labor market entry (in particular in Southern Europe); (2) multiple roles and messy transitions from the education to the employment system; (3) flexible partnerships (e.g., cohabitation); and (4) postponed transitions into parenthood.

Changes in Men's Mid-Career Trajectories

The *Globalife* project has also shown that there are indeed some groups, such as mid-career men, who generally emerge as "winners" of the globalization process (Blossfeld et al., 2006b). With respect to mid-career experiences, a key finding was that there was generally employment stability for qualified men in periods of accelerated globalization in social-democratic (Denmark, Norway and Sweden), familistic (Italy, Spain, Mexico and Ireland) and, to a lesser extent, conservative welfare regimes (Germany, the Netherlands and France). Employment patterns remained relatively constant particularly for qualified men in countries such as Denmark and Sweden, where welfare regimes largely shielded them from globalization. In the familistic regimes of Italy and Spain, mid-career men were the clear "insiders". As insiders, qualified mid-career men in "insider–outsider" countries are largely shielded by labor force experience, internal labor markets and work council power structures. The forces of globalization are therefore shifted strongly to the labor market outsiders such as young adults, the unemployed or women who have interrupted their careers for family reasons. However, there were also a few examples of increased employment instability among men. For example, Mexico's (Parrado, 2006) focus on economic integration, exports and privatization reduced upward mobility for qualified men and increased their representation in the informal sector. Men in the highly flexible, deregulated labor markets of the United Kingdom and United States were more likely to experience increased employment instability. Finally, the collapse of socialism opened the gates to globalization in post-socialistic countries (Czech Republic, Estonia, Poland and Hungary), accompanied by rapid and profound political and economic changes. This led to a significant increase in employment instability even for established qualified men in post-socialist countries. In general, educational investments increased the chances of career success and lowered the risk of mid-career employment failure for (mostly male) employees.

Changes in Women's Mid-Life Pathways

Country-specific institutions also have a strong impact on women's careers, mediating specific aspects of their employment trajectories such as employment stability, duration of caregiving and re-entry after unemployment or caregiving. The *Globalife* project found that globalization appears to pass uncertainty to women who have interrupted their careers for family reasons (e.g., rearing children or caring for the elderly) in countries (Blossfeld & Hofmeister, 2008) such as Germany, Italy, Spain and Ireland. Due to their family role, they have become "outsiders" in the globalized labor market. The ways in which qualified women responded to this increasing uncertainty varied. Some of them responded by voluntarily decreasing their attachment to the labor market and, turning to caregiving options, while others committed themselves more firmly to any kind of paid work to support their families financially. There were exceptions where qualified women received strong state support in the form of further education (as in the Netherlands, Sweden and Denmark). In general, education increased the chances of career success and reduced the risk of employment failure for qualified mid-life women, but there were notable exceptions, including Germany and the post-socialist countries, where high education did not protect women from labor market vulnerability (in terms of unemployment or downward mobility) after family-related employment interruptions.

Changes in Late Careers and Transitions to Retirement

In a globalizing world, the higher job security and wage levels of late-career employees are often at odds with the faster obsolescence of their skills and competencies, the lower returns of their retraining investments and their reduced competitiveness against the often better qualified (and less expensive) younger generation for newly created jobs. As a result, companies view late-career employees as an increasingly expensive and inflexible burden. In an era of accelerating globalization, employers can either (1) retrain late-career workers and adapt their skills to the new demands of the workplace (employment maintenance), which is comparatively costly, or (2) lay them off, which threatens mid-career employees' motivation and trust in the company, or (3) cut their wages, which is often difficult and de-motivating, or (4) try to send them into early retirement (employment exit) – if this option structurally exists in their country (Blöndal & Scarpetta, 1998). In general, the *Globalife* project showed that higher qualifications increase the chance of remaining in the labor market and lower the risks of experiencing unemployment or adverse late-career mobility (e.g., downward mobility).

Older workers in all modern societies have experienced increased early exclusion from the labor market since the late 1970s. Beginning in the 1990s, the *Globalife* project's country studies showed that the extent to which globalization forced the employment exit of older workers increased (Blossfeld et al., 2006a, 2011a; Hofäcker, 2010). However, this trend varied considerably across countries, and these differences essentially confirm the "employment maintenance" and "employment exit" strategies.

In conservative (e.g., Germany) and Southern European countries (e.g., Italy or Spain), older workers were most affected by exclusion from the labor force. In these countries, early retirement schemes were used on a massive scale to cope with increased global competition and needs for economic restructuring. For example, Germany (Buchholz, 2006) used early retirement and the Netherlands (Henkens & Kalmijn, 2006) introduced complementary welfare programs (e.g., disability insurance) to facilitate the early labor force exits of older workers (Guillemard, 1991). In contrast, Southern European countries implemented targeted, group-specific early retirement schemes that allowed workers in declining industries to leave the labor market under financially acceptable conditions. These early retirement programs provided a solution to the serious labor market problems of redundant older workers in highly regulated, closed employment systems. At the same time, in these "employment exit" regimes, mobility within the labor market remained low in times of accelerated globalization. On the one hand, when older workers became unemployed, they were not given further training opportunities, which limited their chances of re-entry into the rigid "insider–outsider" labor markets. On the other hand, they were offered generous early retirement benefits, which reduced their demand to re-enter the labor market. In Central and Southern European countries, older workers are either in continuous and secure employment or in a permanent state of inactivity, but do not participate widely in lifelong learning or job-related further education programs (Blossfeld et al., 2014).

In comparison, late careers in liberal countries showed a very low trend toward early exclusion, but were instead characterized by high levels of on-the-job training, job mobility, lifelong learning and labor force participation. The *Globalife* country studies from the United States (Warner & Hofmeister, 2006) and United Kingdom (Golsch et al., 2006) demonstrated that in market-induced maintenance regimes, labor market flexibility and extensive on-the-job training enabled older workers to adapt to globalization by increasing their labor market mobility. At the same time, the virtual lack of public early retirement programs in these liberal welfare regimes pushed these older workers to remain in employment until personal savings made permanent retirement possible.

In Northern European countries (such as Sweden, Denmark or Norway), late careers were stable and the stratification of late career risks was low in times of accelerated globalization. These countries maintained the public-induced maintenance pattern through public support of the social-democratic welfare state. They placed a strong emphasis on continuous education and retraining of older workers and the state had a protective role as a large employer.

Finally, in the period of rapid globalization after the fall of the Iron Curtain, the post-socialist countries (such as Hungary, Estonia, Poland and the Czech Republic) formed a very special case within the dichotomy of "employment exit" versus "employment maintenance." Under communism, old age employment was high and stable, but the exposure to a competitive, globalized market and the transition from a planned to a market economy placed high restructuring and rationalization demands on firms and the economy as a whole. These post-socialist country studies impressively demonstrate that under these combined pressures, most post-socialist countries opted for a strategy of early retirement. Thus, for many years, lifelong learning for older qualified workers has not been a characteristic of these countries to respond to global pressures (Blossfeld et al., 2014).

SUMMARY

The *Globalife* project departed from previous globalization research in several crucial ways. First, it took an empirical approach by constructing testable hypotheses and conducting comparative empirical research. Second, it examined in detail how the overarching global changes affect life courses in modern societies. Third, the *Globalife* project focused on the individual and used longitudinal micro data that covered longer historical periods. This allows to link macro- and meso-level changes to individual behavior at the micro level. Fourth, the empirical analyses of the *Globalife* project have not heralded the demise of the nation-state, but rather have shown that nation-state institutions are not largely losing their importance, but are subject to a more general path-dependent change. Finally, the *Globalife* project empirically studied whether globalization is leading to new social and economic inequalities within modern societies.

The most vulnerable group with regard to increasing social and economic uncertainties are the low qualified and unskilled in all countries. In other words, qualifications and skills protect individuals against the risks and uncertainties of globalization. However, there are remarkable differences in how workers are affected by globalization over their life span. In most countries, the uncertainties are channeled to the younger generation leaving the education system and entering the labor market. Depending on the nation-specific institutional framework, young people face higher unemployment rates, lower wages, precarious employment or worse employment contracts (e.g., fixed-term contracts, part-time work). In particular in "insider–outsider" labor markets, it takes much longer until young adults establish themselves in the labor market and pursue a stable job career. Thus, while youth can be described as the "losers" of globalization, established mid-career men are clearly the "winners" of globalization. They enjoy both lower prices for all goods on a globalized market, which lead to higher living standards in times of globalization, and high employment protection through the institutions of internal labor markets. Particularly in conservative and familistic welfare regimes, where mainly women are interrupting their employment careers (e.g., for family-related care work) and thus become "outsiders," mid-life women are exposed to rising global uncertainties and have difficulties re-entering the labor market in positions that fit their educational attainment. Finally, there are large country differences in the extent to which globalization affects older workers. In "employment exit" regimes, older workers are either in continuous and secure employment or in a permanent state of inactivity, but are not participating widely in lifelong learning or job-related further education programs. The post-socialist transition countries, that were suddenly exposed to a competitive, globalized market in the 1990s, have also opted for the early retirement strategy. In the "employment maintenance" regimes of the liberal and social-democratic welfare states, older workers show a very low trend toward early exclusion from the labor market but instead experience high levels of on-the-job training, job mobility, lifelong learning and labor force participation.

NOTE

1. The Project, *Globalife – Life Courses in the Globalization Process*, was funded by the Volkswagen Foundation (Hannover, Germany) from 1999 to 2005.

REFERENCES

Berkowitz King, R. (2005). The case of American women: Globalization and the transition to adulthood in an individualistic regime. In H.-P. Blossfeld, E. Klijzing, M. Mills, & K. Kurz (eds), *Globalization, Uncertainty and Youth in Society* (pp. 305–326). Routledge.

Bernardi, F., & Nazio, T. (2005). Globalization and the transition to adulthood in Italy. In H.-P. Blossfeld, E. Klijzing, M. Mills, & K. Kurz (eds), *Globalization, Uncertainty and Youth in Society* (pp. 349–374). Routledge.

Blöndal, S., & Scarpetta, S. (1998). *The Retirement Decision in OECD Countries*. OECD Working Paper No. 202, OECD Economics Department. https://dx.doi.org/10.1787/565174210530

Blossfeld, H.-P., & Hofmeister, H. (eds) (2008). *Globalization, Uncertainty and Women's Careers: An International Comparison*. Edward Elgar Publishing.

Blossfeld, H.-P., Klijzing, E., Mills, M., & Kurz, K. (eds) (2005). *Globalization, Uncertainty and Youth in Society: The Losers in a Globalizing World*. Routledge.

Blossfeld, H.-P., Buchholz, S., & Hofäcker, D. (eds) (2006a). *Globalization, Uncertainty and Late Careers in Society: The Losers in a Globalizing World*. Routledge.

Blossfeld, H.-P., Mills, M., & Bernardi, F. (eds) (2006b). *Globalization, Uncertainty and Men's Careers: An International Comparison*. Edward Elgar Publishing.

Blossfeld, H.-P., Buchholz, S., & Kurz, K. (eds) (2011a). *Aging Populations, Globalization and the Labor Market: Comparing Late Working Life and Retirement in Modern Societies*. Edward Elgar Publishing.

Blossfeld, H.-P., Buchholz, S., Hofäcker, D., & Kolb, K. (eds) (2011b). *Globalized Labour Markets and Social Inequality in Europe*. Palgrave Macmillan.

Blossfeld, H.-P., Hofäcker, D., & Bertolini, S. (eds) (2011c). *Youth on Globalized Labour Markets. Rising Uncertainty and Its Effects on Early Employment and Family Lives in Europe*. Barbara Budrich Publishers.

Blossfeld, H.-P., Kilpi-Jakonen, E., Vono de Vilhena, D., & Buchholz, S. (eds) (2014). *Adult Learning in Modern Societies: An International Comparison from a Life-Course Perspective*. Edward Elgar Publishing.

Buchholz, S. (2006). Men's careers and career exits in West Germany. In H.-P. Blossfeld, S. Buchholz, & D. Hofäcker (eds), *Globalization Uncertainty and Late Careers in Society* (pp. 55–78). Routledge.

Castells, M. (2000). *The Rise of the Network Society, The Information Age: Economy, Society and Culture* (Volume 1). Blackwell Publishers.

Francesconi, M., & Golsch, K. (2006). The process of globalization and transitions to adulthood in Britain. In H.-P. Blossfeld, E. Klijzing, M. Mills, & K. Kurz (eds), *Globalization, Uncertainty and Youth in Society* (pp. 249–276). Routledge.

Golsch, K., Haardt, D., & Jenkins, S. P. (2006). Late careers and career exits in Britain. In H.-P. Blossfeld, S. Buchholz, & D. Hofäcker (eds), *Globalization Uncertainty and Late Careers in Society* (pp. 183–210). Routledge.

Guillemard, A.-M. (1991). Die Destandardisierung des Lebenslaufs in den europäischen Wohlfahrtsstaaten. *Zeitschrift für Sozialreform*, 37(2), 620–639.

Guillén, M. (2001). Is globalization civilizing, destructive or feeble? A critique of five key debates in the social science literature. *American Review of Sociology*, 27, 235–260.

Gygli, S., Haelg, F., Potrafke, N., & Sturm, J.-E. (2019). The KOF Globalisation Index – revisited. *Review of International Organizations*, 14(3), 543–574.

Held, D., McGrew, A., Goldblatt, D., & Perraton, J. (1999). *Global Transformations: Politics, Economics and Culture*. Polity Press.

Henkens, K., & Kalmijn, M. (2006). Labor market exits of older men in the Netherlands: An analysis of survey data 1979–99. In H.-P. Blossfeld, S. Buchholz, & D. Hofäcker (eds), *Globalization Uncertainty and Late Careers in Society* (pp. 79–100). Routledge.

Hofäcker, D. (2010). *Older Workers in a Globalizing World: An International Comparison of Retirement and Late-Career Patterns in Western Industrialized Countries*. Edward Elgar Publishing.

Liefbroer, A. (2005). Transition from youth to adulthood in the Netherlands. In H.-P. Blossfeld, E. Klijzing, M. Mills, & K. Kurz (eds), *Globalization, Uncertainty and Youth in Society* (pp. 83–104). Routledge.

Mills, M. (2005). The transition to adulthood in Canada: The impact of irregular work shifts in a 24-hour economy. In H.-P. Blossfeld, E. Klijzing, M. Mills, & K. Kurz (eds), *Globalization, Uncertainty and Youth in Society* (pp. 277–304). Routledge.

Montanari, I. (2001). Modernization, globalization and the welfare state: A comparative analysis of old and new convergence of social insurance since 1930. *British Journal of Sociology*, 52(3), 469–494.

Parrado, E. A. (2006). Globalization and labour market mobility over the life course of men: The case of Mexico. In H.-P. Blossfeld, M. Mills, & F. Bernardi (eds), *Globalization, Uncertainty and Men's Careers. An International Comparison* (pp. 365–392). Edward Elgar Publishing.

Regini, M. (2000a). Between deregulation and social pacts: The responses of European economies to globalization. *Politics and Society*, 28(1), 5–33.

Regini, M. (2000b). The dilemmas of labor market regulation. In G. Esping-Andersen & M. Regini (eds), *Why Deregulate Labor Markets?* Oxford University Press.

Simó Noguera, C., Casto Martín, T., & Soro Bonmat, A. (2005). The Spanish case: The effects of the globalization process on the transition to adulthood. In H.-P. Blossfeld, E. Klijzing, M. Mills, & K. Kurz (eds), *Globalization, Uncertainty and Youth in Society* (pp. 375–402). Routledge.

Streeck, A. (1987). The uncertainties of management in the management of uncertainties: Employees, labor relations and industrial adjustment in the 1980s. *Work, Employment and Society*, 1, 281–308.

Warner, D., & Hofmeister, H. (2006). Late career transitions among men and women in the United States. In H.-P. Blossfeld, S. Buchholz, & D. Hofäcker (eds), *Globalization Uncertainty and Late Careers in Society* (pp. 141–182). Routledge.

24. Does a higher minimum salary protect youth from in-work poverty? Cross-national evidence from the EU

Kadri Täht, Marge Unt and Thomas Biegert

INTRODUCTION

Successful integration of youth in the labour market is an essential part of leaving the parental home and becoming a financially independent adult. It is not only about getting a foothold in the labour market per se, but transitioning into a quality job that provides sufficient income to avoid the risk of poverty. The inclusion of youth in the labour market and the consequences of labour market vulnerability has received a lot of attention as it affects other life domains such as health and well-being, and labour market insecurity may leave lasting scars (O'Reilly et al., 2019; Unt et al., 2021). However, in a time when employment is viewed as the best and safest route out of poverty, it is striking that one tenth of young people experienced in-work poverty (IWP) in 2019 (Eurostat, 2022a). Successful labour market integration of young adults is also important from a macro-economic perspective as Western societies are ageing and welfare states are under heavy pressure to uphold and increase the social citizenship of all groups while buffering the increasing volatility of labour markets.

We live today in a hegemonic model of free market globalisation which fosters labour market flexibility and precarity (Kalleberg, 2008). New labour market entrants are particularly affected by the changes induced by globalisation due to labour market flexibilisation at the margins, including new forms of work in a gig economy disproportionally held by youth and characterised by an accelerated erosion of labour rights due to unclear labour status. Still, it is important to note there is no clear linear increase of temporary work rate among the European labour force over the last decades (see Latner, 2022). But youth is more strongly affected by business cycle fluctuations (Dietrich, 2013). Clearly, precarious work constitutes a global challenge and may have detrimental effects on the future of young people (Unt et al., 2021). Therefore, effective public policies should seek to help people deal with the uncertainty and unpredictability of their work (Kalleberg, 2008). In the European Union (EU), the European Commission has actively promoted measures to counterbalance labour market flexibilities threatening the living conditions of employees. One of these initiatives was a proposal for a Directive of the European Parliament and of the Council on an adequate minimum wage in the EU in 2020. This initiative aims at improving working conditions by ensuring that workers in the EU have access to an adequate statutory minimum wage allowing for a decent living wherever they work (European Commission, 2020). However, if youth IWP is mainly driven by unemployment spells, a higher minimum salary might not contribute or could be even counterproductive for lowering the youth IWP risk.

This chapter aims to add to our knowledge of youth quality of jobs and the ability of institutions to mitigate the global influences of precariousness. We define work quality as the ability to pursue a minimum standard of living in a given country. Therefore, we adopt the in-work at-risk-of-poverty concept which encompasses those who work but still live in households facing poverty risks which hinders their possibility of being a full member of society and able to make longer life plans. For this we first examine cross-national differences and developments of youth IWP risks over time from both an objective (measured) and subjective (perceived) perspective. Second, we look at youth early-career trajectories and how they relate to IWP risks. Third, we assess the moderator effect of labour market policy measures on youth IWP risks. More precisely, we assess minimum wage levels as a potential institutional solution to the aforementioned problem.

THEORY AND RESEARCH QUESTIONS

Labour market regulations and structural factors might be classified as contributing either to greater labour market flexibility or to stability. The neoliberal revolution spread globally, emphasising the centrality of markets and market-driven solutions, privatisation of government resources and removal of government protection. These macro-level changes led employers to seek greater flexibility in their relations with workers (Kalleberg, 2008). The forces that led to the growth of precarious work are not likely to abate any time soon under the present hegemonic model of free market globalisation (Kalleberg, 2008). Like uncertainty, also complexity and interconnectedness are among important changes introduced by the processes of globalisation. This highlights the fact that people's lives have become closely related to the actions and decisions of others, who often originate in places far from their physical location (Colombo & Reburghini, 2019). This process means that while studying social processes, we need even more than before to account for the subjectivity of agents.

Crettaz and Bonoli (2011) identify three main 'mechanisms' that lead to IWP: low pay, low labour force attachment and large family size. Halleröd and colleagues (2015) point out that a high degree of IWP among the core labour force indicates that IWP is a low wage problem. At the same time, a high prevalence of IWP among the peripheral labour force would indicate that IWP is an unemployment problem. Their study on 22 European countries finds that for the adult population IWP is mainly an unemployment problem, not a low-wage problem. However, we lack empirical evidence if this assertion holds also for youth, who often experience a more vulnerable labour market situation and due to their early careers also lower salaries. Thus, the aim of this chapter is to examine more closely the labour market trajectories of youth to detect whether *IWP is foremost a low-wage or an unemployment problem*. Given the gendered nature of labour markets, we pay special attention to *gender differences*. As poverty is a multidimensional concept, next to relative poverty risk, we aim to consider the subjective poverty risk of youth to account for perceived deprivation. Previous studies (Easterlin & Plagnol, 2008; Hagerty et al., 2001) have shown that in order to capture the nature of quality of life, both objective and subjective dimensions of well-being are important' (Stiglitz et al., 2009, p. 15).

Frazer and Marlier (2010) highlight next to individual characteristics also institutional factors such as minimum wage and social protection. In our chapter, we aim to assess the current role of minimum wages for youth labour market trajectories.

However, do higher levels of minimum wage indeed contribute to lower IWP risks of youth drawing from differences across the EU? Or does the buffering effect of minimum wage vary by different pathways?

DATA AND METHODOLOGY

Data and Variables

In order to assess young people's labour market situation and its relationship to poverty risk, we use panel data from the EU Survey of Income and Living Conditions (EU-SILC). To compile the panels, we use a modified and extended version of the 'ado eusilcpanel' (Borst, 2018). We constrain our data to the years 2005–2019 and differentiate between three periods: (1) 2005–2008, before the economic crisis; (2) 2009–2011, during the economic crisis; and (3) 2014–2019, after the economic crisis. We choose the latter period as 2014–2019 because by 2014, European economies had by and large recovered from the economic and financial crisis while the COVID-19 pandemic and related labour market disruptions had not yet started in 2019. After excluding some countries due to a lack of data for some of the years observed in the study (Croatia, Switzerland, Serbia) or because lack of retrospective data (Germany), our data set contains information from 28 European countries. For the analysis of IWP and the (moderator) effect of policy measures (here the minimum income scheme), the sample size of countries is reduced to 18, i.e. we can include in the analysis only countries that have an existing minimum income scheme.

We define youth as being 18 years or older at the start of our observation period. We only consider persons who are not older than 30 years of age at the end of our observation period. As we are interested in young people who have entered the labour market already, we exclude individuals who indicate more than three months of education in a calendar year. We adopt the standard indicator of IWP which has been included in EU social reporting since 2005 (Bardone & Guio, 2005). For this, the sample was reduced to those who were actively particthe ipating in the labour market, but excluding self-employed. As income is available only as an annual indicator, the common definition requires that an individual must have worked more than six months in a year to count as working (Lohmann & Marx, 2019) and thus to qualify as potentially working poor. These restrictions result in an effective sample of 130,929 individual cases.

We use two poverty measures. First, we use the standard measure of relative poverty, according to which a household with a lower income than 60 per cent of the national median income is considered as 'at risk of poverty'. The measure we use is adjusted for household composition, using the Organisation for Economic Co-operation and Development (OECD) equivalence scale. This assigns a weight of 1.0 to the first person aged 14 or more, a weight of 0.5 to other persons aged 14 or more and a weight of 0.3 to persons aged 0–13 (Eurostat, 2022b). We refer to this also as the 'objective' poverty measure. Second, what we call a 'subjective' poverty measure is the respondent's judgement of ability to make ends meet. Answer options in the survey are making ends meet (1) with great difficulty; (2) with difficulty; (3) with some difficulty; (4) fairly easily; and (5) easily. We turn this scale into a binary indicator for which agreement with the statement 'I have great difficulty making ends meet' was used as a proxy of subjective poverty. In case of each measure, to count as in-work poor, an individual has to be working but fall into the category of being objectively or subjectively poor.

For measuring the institutional effect of minimum wage, we use the Kaitz Index. Given that the standard of living across the countries varies considerably, comparing just the minimum wage levels (numeric size) would not be a reasonable option here. Instead, we opt for the Kaitz Index, which represents the ratio of the minimum wage to the median wage in a given country. The data for the indicator were derived from the OECD statistics website (2022) and presents yearly data.

Methods

In the descriptive part of the analysis, we look at youth IWP levels, i.e. the share of poverty (using both subjective and objective poverty measures) among young adults who were employed more than six months in the respective calendar year across European countries. The analysis is carried out for different time periods separately.

In order to study the early employment trajectories, we used longitudinal information based on the last two-year (24 months, starting in January) information of monthly employment status,[1] which is coded as full-time employment (3), part-time employment (2), unemployment (1) and inactivity (0) information. Part-time employment is considered as 30 or fewer hours of work a week and follows the EU-SILC standard definition. Based on monthly employment status information, we identify the most typical labour market trajectories for young adults using group-based trajectory modelling (Nagin, 2005). The conceptual aim of this method is to identify clusters of individuals with similar trajectories (here: employment trajectories); a trajectory is 'the evolution of an outcome over age or time' (Nagin, 2005). Group-based trajectory modelling is an application of finite mixture models. The estimated parameters are not the result of a cluster analysis, they are rather a product of maximum likelihood estimation. The aim is to identify rather than assume groups of distinctive developmental trajectories.

In order to assess the effect of employment trajectories on poverty risk, i.e. IWP, we use a multilevel modelling approach (Hox, 2017), where individuals are nested in countries. We use fixed-effect models, with the dependent variable being in-work poverty and main independent variable the employment trajectory type based on the labour market behaviour in the last two years from the data collection. In order to test for the moderator effect of minimum salary in the country, the interaction effect between individual-level trajectories and country-level measure (Kaitz Index) are included. In the models, we control for gender, age, education and household composition measures (number of children, presence of other adults in the household, employment situation of other members).

CROSS-NATIONAL DIFFERENCES IN IN-WORK POVERTY

We present first the descriptive evidence of how youth objective and subjective IWP rates have differed across Europe during the last decades. Results from our analysis show that IWP levels vary across countries and time. Moreover, they vary considerably across the poverty measures used. Figure 24.1 displays the presence of IWP among young adults in European countries using the relative poverty or what we denote here as objective measure. As the poverty risk tends to be affected by the general economic situation, the data are grouped into three time periods. According to our data, from young adults who worked at least six months out of 12 months in the respective reference year, about 7 per cent lived in a household that can be characterised as living in relative poverty during the pre-crisis (2005–2008) period. The lowest IWP share (2.5 per cent) could be found in the Czech Republic (CZ) and the highest (18.6 per cent) in Romania (RO). Youth IWP appeared to be surprisingly high among rather wealthy countries such as Luxemburg (LU) and Norway (NO), which may indicate the limitations of a relative poverty measure in rather prosperous country cases. When looking at the crisis (2009–2011) and post-crisis (2014–2019) periods, in both country cases the relative poverty level was considerably lower than during the pre-crisis period, leaving behind countries such as Spain (ES), Portugal (PT), Greece (EL), Poland (PL), Estonia (EE) and Bulgaria (BG), of which many were hit hard by the economic crisis. On average, the IWP rate among households of young working adults increased to almost 8 per cent during the crisis period and reduced only slightly in the post-crisis period.

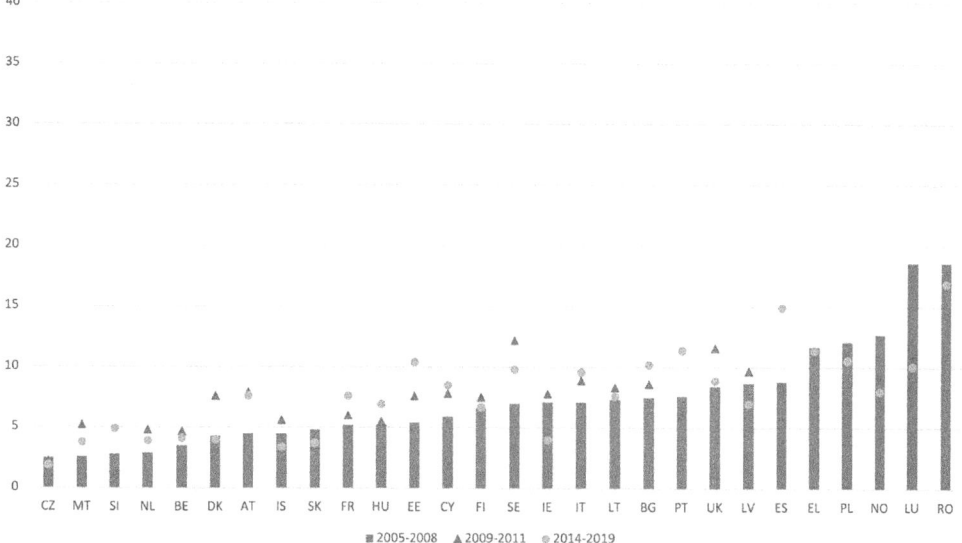

Source: EU-SILC; authors' calculations.

Figure 24.1   *Relative poverty of young adults in EU countries, 2005–2019*

When looking at the IWP via our subjective poverty measure, i.e. the perceived difficulty in making ends meet (Figure 24.2), the picture changes somewhat. According to this measure, on average 8.4 per cent of young adults working most of the time during the pre-crisis period (2005–2008) felt that their household had great difficulty making ends meet. The level of poverty varied here from 1 per cent in Estonia to 34 per cent in Bulgaria. During the economic crisis period, the average subjectively perceived level of poverty increased (reaching 9.8 per cent) and declined again after the crisis, yet remained higher than before the economic crisis (at the mean level of 9.2 per cent). The countries in which young adults suffered the most economic insecurity and hardship during the economic crisis in terms of the subjective measure were Bulgaria, Portugal, Hungary (HU), Greece and Cyprus (CY) – countries where the IWP risk (subjectively perceived) among young adults was rather high already before the economic crisis and remained high or even increased after the period of economic crisis.

For countries like Luxemburg or Norway that showed high poverty risk in terms of the objective measure, the perceived poverty level among young adults was and has remained very low throughout the observed period. This is a trend characteristic also with some more affluent countries. For less affluent countries the picture is often the opposite – even when the relative poverty level is low on average, young adults often feel that they have difficulty making ends meet.

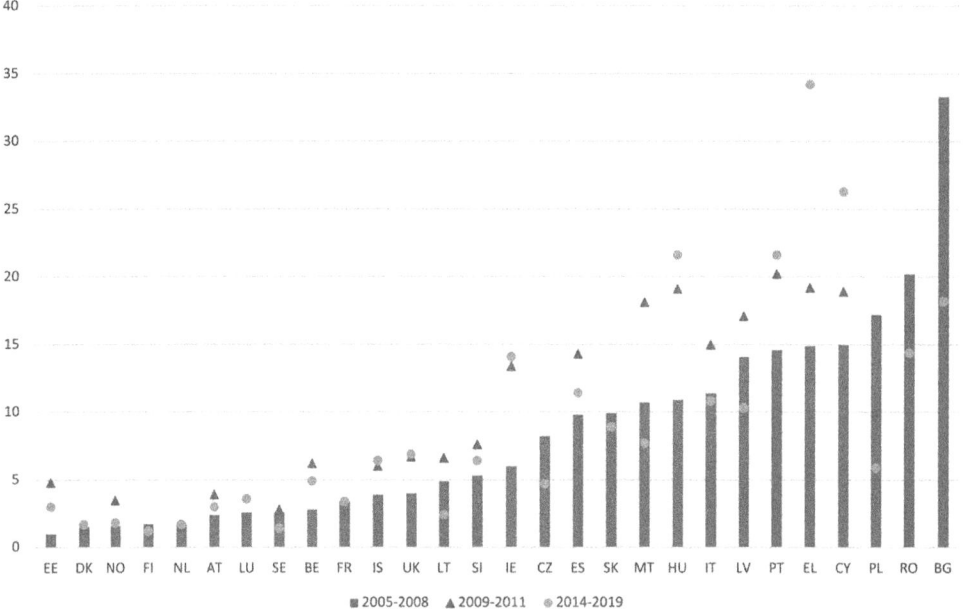

Source: EU-SILC; authors' calculations.

Figure 24.2   *Subjectively perceived poverty of young adults in EU countries, 2005–2019*

Although the objective and subjective measures give somewhat different results (regarding the prevalence of IWP in the country), both measures display similar trends over time. On average, the IWP poverty level has increased over the observed time period, indicating that on average almost every tenth young adult who is working the majority of the year is living in severe poverty, but in some countries this is every third young adult. During the economic crisis the situation of young adults worsened even more and remained higher than during the pre-crisis period.

YOUTH EMPLOYMENT TRAJECTORIES AND IN-WORK POVERTY IN EUROPE

Before we scrutinise which employment trajectories of working youth are the most prone to IWP risk and if a higher minimum wage buffers the IWP risk, we will give an overall picture of all working youths' typical employment trajectories, including both those whose households are in poverty risk and those whose are not. Based on group-based trajectory modelling and monthly employment status data, the most common trajectory (Figure 24.3, trajectory 6) of young adults in Europe was 'full-time employment'. The work intensity of young adults in this group remained throughout the observed two-year period on the highest attachment, i.e. they were full-time employed most of the time. In this category there were 68.9 per cent of young adults. The next most common trajectory (11.2 per cent of cases) was 'part-time' (trajectory group 1), where young adults remained throughout mostly in part-time employment. The third largest trajectory group can be characterised by a transition from unemployment to full-time employment or short 'unemployment – full time'. This group comprised 7.7 per cent of the observed cases. The fifth largest trajectory (6.1 per cent of the cases) indicates a transition from full-time employment to part-time employment. Then we have two small but distinctive groups in the analysis, one characterised by a transition from 'unemployment to full-time employment' (5 per cent) and the second 'inactivity to full-time employment' (1 per cent).

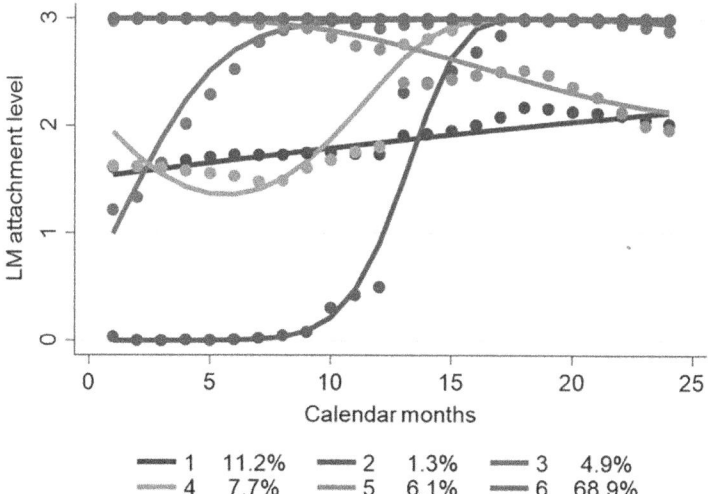

Source: EU-SILC; authors' calculations.

Figure 24.3   Employment trajectories of young adults in Europe

In short, we are interested in youth who are most of the time over 12 months in the labour market, i.e. those considered working youth. Two thirds are mostly employed full time over two years. One-third has more dynamic employment trajectories.

Next, we will show which individual-level characteristics are related to higher IWP risk, especially with regard to previous employment history. The empty model of the multilevel regression model (Model O0 and S0 in Table 24.1) shows that there is a considerable amount of variability between the countries in terms of IWP levels. Considering the objective measure, about 9 per cent of the variability can be attributed to the country level, whereas in the case of the subjective measure, about 19 per cent of variability is on the country level.

When comparing the trajectory groups that include some type of employment insecurity or weaker labour market attachment with the 'full-time' trajectory group (Model 0.1 and Model S.1 in Table 24.1), we see a significantly higher risk for IWP for the latter group of trajectories measured by both the objective and subjective indicators. The 'objective' IWP risk is highest for the 'part-time' trajectory.

The main effects of the trajectory groups weaken somewhat when additionally including socio-demographic controls to the model (Models O2 and S2 in Table 24.1), but in general the patterns remain the same. The effects are in the expected direction and by and large consistent across both measures. As shown by several previous studies for total working-age population (Lohnmann & Marx, 2019), the risk for IWP is significantly lower for females (other characteristics kept constant) in the case of objective poverty measures, which is likely due to the buffering effect of income of other household members. At the same time, females have significantly higher IWP for subjective measures than males. This supports the very important criticism in feminist research that measuring only objective poverty at the household level tends to underestimate poverty among women (Berthonnet, 2021). The household is not necessarily a homogeneous unit in which all members have equal access to resources regardless of resource origin.

In the final models (Models O3 and S3), we additionally include macro-level indicators: the official minimum wage levels (relative to median income) and the interaction effects of employment trajectories with the macro-level minimum wage policy indicator that varies over the observed time (i.e. yearly data and not aggregated over the observed period) within countries. The findings show a statistically significant relationship between IWP level and minimum wage policy for the case of the *subjective measure* – the closer the minimum wage is to the median wage level within a country, the less likely are young adults in these countries to be working poor. For the *objective measure*, the direction of the effect is the same, however, the observed relationship is statistically not significant. The interaction effect of the country policy measure and typical employment trajectory on the IWP risk showed no significant moderating effects, except for the trajectory group of 'inactive – full time' in the case of the objective measure.

These findings suggest that in the country context where minimum wages are closer to or above the median wage, the otherwise significantly higher IWP risk of the 'inactive – full time' employment group becomes significantly reduced. The latter suggests that in more regulated and protected labour market (in terms of minimum wage), young adults (mostly women) returning to employment from inactivity face fewer risks of ending up being IWP. The interaction effects were statistically (on $p < .10$) significant also for the 'part-time' and 'full-time – part-time' trajectory groups, but the effect was reduced once country wealth level control (gross domestic product (GDP) per capita) was introduced to the model.[2] Probably in wealthier countries, the effective wage level of part-time work is more likely to allow an escape from poverty risk, but not in countries with lower GDP.

Table 24.1   Multilevel regression model for in-work poverty

	In-work poverty: objective				In-work poverty: subjective			
	Model O0 Empty model	**Model O1** Main effects	**Model O2** + controls	**Model O3** + cross-level interactions	**Model S0** Empty model	**Model S1** Main effects	**Model S2** + controls	**Model S3** + cross-level interactions
Intercept	-2.702**	-3.168**	-1.263**	-1.198**	-2.546**	-2.823**	2.170**	2.199**
Individual level								
Trajectories (ref: full time)								
– Part time		1.528***	1.350**	0.837**		0.856**	0.577**	0.642*
– Inactive – full time		0.915***	0.733**	3.278**		0.756**	0.508**	-0.265
– Unemployment – full time		0.638***	0.508**	0.980		0.516**	0.424**	0.111
– Part time – full time		0.809***	0.599**	0.679		0.818**	0.621**	0.827*
– Full time – part time		0.836**	0.689**	-0.075		0.478**	0.358**	-0.297
Female			-0.134**	-0.137**		0.088**	0.088**	0.089**
Age			-0.034**	-0.034**		-0.043**	-0.043**	-0.043**
Education (ref: low)			0.000	0.000		0.000	0.000	0.000
– Medium			-0.642**	-0.639**		-0.570**	-0.571**	-0.570**
– High			-1.563**	-1.557**		-1.327**	-1.327**	-1.327**
Number of children			0.480**	0.480**		0.240**	0.239**	0.240**
Adults of working age in household			0.057**	0.057**		0.160**	0.160**	0.160**
Other household members employed			-1.379**	-1.380**		-0.922**	-0.922**	-0.922**
Time period (ref: 2005–2008)			0.000	0.000		0.000	0.000	0.000
– 2009–2011			-0.127**	-0.128**		0.160**	0.160**	0.160**
– 2014–2019			0.097	0.102		0.303**	0.303**	0.302**
Country level								
– Minimum relative to median wage			-0.344	-0.477		-1.397*	-1.397*	-1.483*
– GDP per capita			0.000	0.000		-0.000**	-0.000**	-0.000**
Interactions: minimum relative to median wage x								
– Part time				1.066				-0.137
– Inactive – full time				-5.444**				1.630
– Unemployment – full time				-0.998				0.659
– Part time – full time				-0.182				-0.444

	In-work poverty: objective				In-work poverty: subjective			
	Model O0	Model O1	Model O2	Model O3	Model S0	Model S1	Model S2	Model S3
	Empty model	Main effects + controls	+ controls	+ cross-level interactions	Empty model	Main effects + controls	+ controls	+ cross-level interactions
– Full time – part time				1.608				1.390
ICC	0.097				0.198			
N	65,442	65,442	55,013	55,013	65,392	65,392	54,971	54,971
Countries	18	18	18	18	18	18	18	18

Note: * p < 0.05, ** p < 0.01.
Source: EU-SILC; authors' calculations.

CONCLUSIONS

In this chapter, we examined the cross-national differences and developments of IWP using both objective and subjective dimensions of poverty measures. The findings indicate and confirm in line with previous similar studies that for estimating the poverty level, both objective (relative poverty) and subjective (great difficulty making ends meet) should be considered. As shown also by our findings, depending on the measure we get a somewhat different picture about poverty risk, indicating the multidimensionality of the phenomenon in youths' lives. In general, in more affluent countries, when the objective measure shows on average higher levels of IWP among young adults, subjectively perceived levels of difficulty making ends meet remain rather low. For less affluent countries it is often the opposite – even when the relative poverty level is on average low, these young adults often feel that they have difficulty making ends meet in subjective terms.

The analysis also provided new insights about how objective and subjective dimensions of job quality and IWP relates to the employment trajectories of young adults and to different labour market regulations such as minimum salary levels. The risk for IWP is highest for the 'part-time' trajectory group compared to the 'full-time' trajectory group (which has the lowest IWP risk anyway). Thus, low attachment to the labour market seems to trigger higher IWP risk. The risk for IWP is significantly lower for females (other characteristics kept constant) in the case of the objective poverty measure, which confirms several earlier findings (Halleröd et al., 2015; Lohmann & Marx, 2019; Maitre et al., 2012) concerning the adult population. It is mostly explained by the fact that female IWP risk is shielded by the second earner in the household. However, we also investigated a subjective measure of IWP risk and, alarmingly, females have a significantly higher risk here. This reflects the multidimensionality of poverty and questions the assumption behind the equally shared household income, which should be reconsidered and studied further.

For the time-period effect, the economic crisis (compared to the pre-crisis) period increased significantly the subjectively measured IWP risk, while the objectively measured IWP risk showed just the opposite effect. However, the decrease of objective IWP risk was not related to the increase in youth resources but declining inequality, i.e. due to a decline of overall median income, which was dramatic in some EU countries.

The structural changes that contribute to precarious work and employment relations are not fixed; neither are they irreversible, inevitable consequences of economic forces (Kalleberg, 2008). The degree of precarity varies among youth inside the EU and we scrutinised the effect of minimum wages. Interestingly, the findings showed that a buffer effect of minimum wage policy on IWP was especially visible for the case of the subjective measure – the closer the minimum wage is to the median wage level in a country, the less likely do working young adults in these countries have difficulty making ends meet. For the objective measure, the direction of the effect is the same, however, the observed relationship was statistically not significant.

Thus, we found that higher levels of minimum wages do contribute to lower subjective IWP risks, endorsing the initiative of the European Commission to counterbalance labour market insecurity with adequate minimum wages across Europe. However, the effect of the minimum wage level on the objective IWP risk is marginal, with one important exception: higher minimum salaries buffer the more female-dominated pathway from inactivity to full-time employment, guaranteeing a lower IWP risk for this (vulnerable) pathway to the labour market.

In short, higher minimum wage policies have the capacity to buffer an objective IWP risk of the female-dominated pathway from inactivity to full-time employment. Especially effective are higher minimum wages to buffer youth against subjective IWP in times of globalisation.

NOTES

1. A two-year time period was used to reduce problems due to attrition.
2. This additional model is available upon request from the authors.

REFERENCES

Bardone, L. & Guio, A. C. (2005). *In-Work Poverty: New Commonly Agreed Indicators at the EU Level.* Eurostat.

Berthonnet, I. (2021). Where exactly does the sexist bias in the official measurement of monetary poverty in Europe come from? *Review of Radical Political Economics.*

Borst, M. (2018). EU-SILC tools: Eusilcpanel – first computational steps towards a cumulative sample based on the EU-SILC longitudinal datasets. GESIS Papers, 2018/11. Köln: GESIS - Leibniz-Institut für Sozialwissenschaften. https://doi.org/10.21241/ssoar.57347

Colombo, E. & Reburghini, P. (2019). A complex uncertainty: Young people in the riddle of the present, in E. Colombo & P. Rebughini (Eds), *Youth and the Politics of the Present.* Routledge, 1–16.

Crettaz, E. & Bonoli, G. (2011). Worlds of working poverty: National variations in mechanisms, in N. Fraser, R. Gutiérrez & R. Peña-Casaan (Eds), *Working Poverty in Europe: A Comparative Approach.* Palgrave Macmillan, 46–72.

Dietrich, H. (2013). Youth unemployment in the period 2001–2010 and the European crises: Looking at the empirical evidence. *Transfer: European Review of Labour and Research,* 19 (3), 305–324.

Easterlin, R. A. & Plagnol, A. C. (2008). Life satisfaction and economic conditions in East and West Germany pre- and post-unification. *Journal of Economic Behavior & Organization,* 68(3–4), 433–444.

European Commission (2020). Commission staff document. Impact assessment. Accompanying the document Proposal for a Directive of the European Parliament and of the Council on adequate minimum wages in the European Union, COM(2020) 682 final – SEC(2020) 362 final – SWD(2020) 246 final.

Eurostat (2022a). In-work at-risk-of-poverty rate by age and sex. EU-SILC, Ilc_iw01.

Eurostat (2022b). Income and living conditions: Metadata. https://ec.europa.eu/eurostat/cache/metadata/en/ilc_esms.htm

Frazer, H. & Marlier, E. (2010). In-work poverty and labour market segmentation in the EU. European Network of Independent Experts on Social Inclusion, No. 2010–02. CEPS/INSTEAD.

Hagerty, M. R., Cummins, R. A., Ferriss, A. L., Land, K., Michalos, A. C., Peterson, M. et al. (2001). Quality of life indexes for national policy: Review and agenda for research. *Social Indicators Research,* 55 (1), 1–96.

Halleröd, B., Ekbrand, H. & Bengtsson, M. (2015). In-work poverty and labour market trajectories: Poverty risks among the working population in 22 European countries. *Journal of European Social Policy,* 25 (5), 473–488.

Hox, J. J. (2017). *Multilevel Analysis. Techniques and Applications,* 2nd edition. Routledge.

Kalleberg, A. (2008). Precarious work, insecure workers: Employment relations in transition. *American Sociological Review,* 74 (1), 1–22.

Latner, J. P. (2022). Temporary employment in Europe: Stagnating rates and rising risks. *European Societies,* 1–26.

Lohmann, H. & Marx, I. (2019). *Handbook of In-Work-Poverty.* Edward Elgar Publishing.

Maitre, B., Nolan, B. & Whelan, C. (2012). *Low Pay, In-Work Poverty and Economic Vulnerability: A Comparative Analysis Using EU-SILC.* The Manchester School.

Nagin, D. S. (2005). *Group-Based Modeling of Development*. Harvard: University Press.

O'Reilly, J., Leschke, J., Ortlieb, R., Seeleib-Kaiser, M. & Villa, P. (Eds) (2019). *Youth Labor in Transition: Inequalities, Mobility, and Policies in Europe*. Oxford University Press.

OECD (2022). Minimum relative to average wages of full-time workers. https://stats.oecd.org/Index .aspx?DataSetCode=MIN2AVE

Stiglitz, J. E., Sen, A. & Fitoussi, J.-P. (2009). Paris: Commission on the measurement of economic performance and social progress. https://ec.europa.eu/eurostat/documents/118025/118123/Fitoussi+ Commission+report

Unt, M., Gebel, M., Bertolini, S., Deliyanni-Kouimtzi, V. & Hofäcker, D. (2021). *Social Exclusion of Youth in Europe: The Multifaceted Consequences of Labour Market Insecurity*. Policy Press.

25. Globalization and the transition from education to employment in the MENA region
Michael Gebel

INTRODUCTION

It is often argued that the school-to-work transition has been affected by globalization (Blossfeld et al. 2008). While much research on the school-to-work transition has been produced on Western countries (Blossfeld et al. 2008; Kogan et al. 2011; Shavit and Müller 1998), our knowledge on non-Western countries is limited. This Western-centrism is worrisome given that the great majority of young people live in non-Western countries, which are most affected by globalization.

This chapter fills this research gap by synthesizing the existing research on the school-to-work transition in the Middle East and Northern African (MENA) region in the context of globalization. The review of the empirical literature is focused on quantitative-empirical studies. Seminal empirical studies have been published in the last two decades, focusing on countries with appropriate survey data, such as Egypt, Iran, Jordan, Syria and Tunisia. For other countries, particularly the Gulf countries, there is no or only very limited research available that meets these criteria.

This chapter is structured as follows. The next section describes MENA countries in the context of globalization. Against this background, the subsequent section summarizes key findings from the empirical literature on school-to-work transition in MENA. The final section identifies research gaps and outlines avenues for future research.

MENA COUNTRIES IN THE CONTEXT OF GLOBALIZATION

Until the mid-twentieth century the MENA region was characterized by low economic development (Adams and Page 2003; Yousef 2004). The "traditional life course" dominated in this pre-industrial period, which was characterized by direct moves from childhood into adulthood due to short or even no education enrollment and early marriage (Dhillon and Yousef 2009).

This dramatically changed with the onset of the oil boom that became possible due to the increasing internationalization of trade as one aspect of globalization and the increasing dependence of the globalized world economy on oil. Not only the oil-rich Arab countries and Iran generated strong growth in gross domestic product (GDP) from oil revenues, but also oil-poor MENA countries, such as Egypt and Jordan. Such economic spillover effects occurred via processes of international labor market migration to oil-rich Gulf countries and remittances (Naufal and Genc 2015). This reflects another aspect of globalization in terms of the internationalization of labor markets. Further growth stimuli were generated by intraregional investments and development assistance flows from oil-producing countries (Assaad 2005). The oil-boom period was characterized by state-directed interventionist economic development with a large subsidized public sector, the obligation of the state to provide work to its citizens and redistributive policies that offered free education, housing, health care and generous subsidies for food (Amin et al. 2012). While the oil-exporting MENA economies benefitted from international trade, many governments adopted import-substitution and protectionist policies as barriers against global competition (Yousef 2004). The nationalist orientation could be seen as a strategy of nation-building in the post-colonist era (Yousef 2004). The high oil-related revenues were also used by governments to establish authoritarian rule protected by strong security and military apparatuses. Assaad (2014) argues that public-sector jobs were used by authoritarian regimes to appease politically salient groups. Dhillon and Yousef (2009) named the predominant life-course pattern of this period the "welfare life course," which was characterized by increased education attainment, low unemployment risks and stable employment in public-sector jobs. Next to the family, the state gained importance in structuring youths' life courses and there was a clearer separation of familial, educational and work spheres (Grant and Furstenberg 2007).

This period came to an end starting with the oil price drop in 1979 (Amin et al. 2012). The oil price crisis reduced labor exports to oil-producing countries and remittances and resulted in the repatriation of millions of MENA migrant workers from the Gulf countries. After prosperous growth rates of 4–6 percent in the 1960s and 1970s, annual GDP growth rates stagnated below 1 percent in the 1980s and 1990s (Yousef 2004). With the dry-out of capital inflow through labor remittances and bilateral aid, particularly the oil-poor MENA countries experienced declining state revenues and increasing levels of public debt. Foreign debts increased as governments had to finance persistently high levels of state expenditures in an environment of declining state revenues. In reaction, several indebted countries, such as Egypt, Jordan, Morocco, Syria and Tunisia, introduced economic stabilization and austerity measures, cutting subsidies and reducing public spending (Yousef 2004). Moreover, supported and pressed by international organizations such as the World Bank and the International Monetary Fund, neoliberal market-oriented economic reforms were enacted that aimed at privatization, trade liberalization and market deregulation. Privatization efforts aimed at stimulating private sector-led growth and scaling back the oversized and inefficient public sector. However, this state-controlled liberalization and privatization process maintained the strong role of the state and tried to socially buffer the consequences for the population (Gebel 2012). Reforms were restricted to the economic sector aiming at politically stabilizing the authoritarian regimes.

However, reforms were not fully implemented or successful. With the exception of oil-rich Gulf countries, the downsizing of public-sector jobs was not compensated by a growth of jobs in the formal private sector (Amin et al. 2012). New jobs were mainly created in the informal job division. Job creation was in general not sufficient such that high unemployment rates hit many MENA countries. Imbalances in the labor market were further increased by continued education expansion (Dimova et al. 2016). Education expansion was driven by young people's prevailing preferences for public-sector jobs that require educational credentials for access (Assaad 2014; Assaad and Krafft 2021). Moreover, expanding the human capital stock of a society was a common growth-oriented policy strategy of governments and also promoted by international organizations such as the World Bank and International Monetary Fund. However, given the lack of high-skilled jobs in the private sector and declining job opportunities in the public sector, there has been a growing skill mismatch in many MENA labor markets.

Dhillon and Yousef (2009) named the predominant life-course pattern of this enduring period the "post-welfare life course," which is characterized by increased informal-sector employment and periods of "waithood" and uncertainty when queuing for the diminished opportunities of public-sector jobs. In the literature on globalization and youth labor markets, the increased uncertainty is seen as a defining feature of globalization (Blossfeld et al. 2008).

Another problem is that rigid labor markets and unsupportive business environments have prevailed despite liberalization and privatization efforts (Dhillon and Yousef 2009). Only the oil-rich Gulf countries stand out as being successful in creating a business-friendly environment. Entrepreneurship has remained discouraged due to complicated business registration processes, weak enforcement of property rights and laws, corruption and inconsistent and unpredictable policy implementations (Kabbani and Kothari 2005; Salehi-Isfahani and Dhillon 2008). In combination with the prevailing protective trade regimes this has also caused low levels of foreign direct investment, making the MENA region one of the least integrated regions in the global economy (Amin et al. 2012). Excluding oil trade, there has been a decline in international trade and even in trade within the MENA region (Yousef 2004). Matallah and Ghazi (2015) therefore classified the MENA region as a latecomer in globalization.

Labor market regulations in MENA are among the most rigid in the developing world (Forteza and Ramab 2006). Some countries, such as Egypt, Morocco and Iran, implemented partial deregulation-enabling firms to use temporary contracts more easily. However, these reforms intensified labor market segmentation and many firms operate in the informal sector to circumvent the persistent rigidities (Kabbani and Kothari 2005; Salehi-Isfahani and Dhillon 2008). As labor legislation is widely evaded in the informal economy, most workers in MENA countries remain unprotected in terms of labor standards.

While the scenario of increasing uncertainty for youth due to globalization has also been described for Western countries, youths in MENA countries have additionally suffered from demographic and political crises. First, a high population growth produced the so-called "youth bulge," which resulted in larger cohorts of youths competing in the education system and the labor market (Assaad and Barsoum 2009; Kabbani and Kothari 2005). Second, political instability in the MENA region further contributed to increased uncertainty, such as the Arab-Israeli wars, the Gulf wars and various uprisings and revolutions (Matallah and Ghazi 2015). Youth protests against unemployment, precarious work and uncertainty on the future were a supporting pillar of the "Arab Spring" revolutions, uprisings and civil wars (Amin et al. 2012). This induced migration crises in various MENA countries due to the massive inflow of refugees from neighboring countries.

SYNTHESIS OF EMPIRICAL LITERATURE

Against this background, this section reviews the empirical literature on school-to-work transition in MENA countries. There are only very few empirical studies that directly measure the influence of globalization on youth labor markets, and these are restricted to Western countries (Gebel and Giesecke 2016; Lange et al. 2014). Hence, this section follows the alternative approach of theoretically contextualizing the findings with regard to globalization as was done, for example, by Blossfeld et al. (2008). The focus is on findings on time trends in school-to-work transition, which capture the joint effects of the contextual developments described before. The review is structured along three important aspects of the dynamic process of school-to-work transition: the transition from education to labor market activity; the duration of the transition from education to first job; and the quality of the first job.

Transition from Education to Labor Market Activity

After leaving education the first crucial decision is whether someone actively participates in the labor market or not (Gebel 2019). Labor market inactivity is defined as being neither (self-)employed nor unemployed. In Western-centered research, this group is often ignored because it is a rather small group. However, in MENA, the share of inactive persons is quite large as many women fully devote their time to housework and/or care work after leaving education. A specific MENA puzzle is the prevalence of low female labor force participation despite strong female educational expansion and fertility decline (Assaad 2014; Spierings 2015). Women's employment came under pressure in previous periods when increased wealth related to oil-based revenues led to labor reallocation towards male-dominated industries and reduced incentives for women to become second earners due to income effects (Ross 2008). In recent decades, women's employment opportunities also declined due to the shrinking of the public sector and traditional employment in family businesses. Heyne (2017) concluded in her worldwide comparative study that structural factors, such as oil and economic development, explain the low female labor force participation in MENA only to a small extent and that cultural factors, such as religion, gender norms and attitudes, are more relevant. Regarding attitudes towards gender and work, Gebel and Heyne (2017: 67) find based on 2012–2014 Arab Barometer data that more than 80 percent of young women in MENA agree that married women should be allowed to work outside home. However, 74 percent also say that children suffer when a mother works for pay and 65 percent say that men should have more right to a job than women when jobs are scarce (Gebel and Heyne 2017: 69, 73).

Against this background of low female labor force participation and prevailing labor market barriers for women, recent studies extended the standard framework of "school-to-work transition" research by investigating the specific pattern of the "school-to-home transition" (Gebel and Heyne 2014). Gebel and Heyne (2014: 107) find that the share of women making a school-to-home transition was highest in Iran (66 percent), followed by Jordan (63 percent), Egypt (57 percent) and Syria (37 percent). In multivariate analyses, there is little influence of parental socio-economic backgrounds on the probability of a school-to-home transition, once controlling for individual education. Instead, having a working mother is a key driver of becoming active in the labor market, which underlines the role of norms and exemplified behavior in young women's socialization processes. Demand for housework and care work within the family also matters as the probability of inactivity increases in case of early marriage. The most influential factor is the respondent's education: the higher the education level the lower is the probability of women being inactive after leaving education in all four countries. This strong education effect is also found for Iran (Egel and Salehi-Isfahani 2010) and Jordan (Amer 2014).

There are almost no studies on time trends in women's transition from education to inactivity. One exception is Assaad and Krafft (2021), who find for Egypt that female inactivity rates after leaving education were higher in the 2000s compared to previous cohorts. While there were almost no changes for lower-educated women, the increase in inactivity was most pronounced among the secondary-educated women and higher-educated women from higher parental socio-economic status (SES) backgrounds. This matches the expectation that high-educated women were hit by the decline in preferred public-sector employment in the course of liberalization and privatization.

Duration of Transition from Education to First Job

Youth unemployment rates in MENA are twice as high as the global average (Dimova et al. 2016). The youth unemployment rate offers a snapshot perspective on the youth labor market. Overcoming the static nature of the unemployment rate, several studies on MENA countries performed longitudinal analyses on the duration of joblessness after leaving education. For example, Amer (2014) finds that young men make a faster transition from education to a first job than women in Jordan. Heyne and Gebel (2016) show for Egyptian young men that transition rates to the first job decline with the level of education, whereas for women there is a U-shaped relationship between education and transition rates to first job. This U-shaped pattern for women is also found by Gebel and Heyne (2014) for Egypt, Iran, Jordan and Syria, where women from the lowest-level education group stand out by making the fastest transition into the labor market. The fast transition to the first job among the low educated is related to the high share of informal jobs in family businesses or the private sector that are directly available. Slower transition rates for high-educated women can be explained by their longer waiting time for the preferred public-sector jobs. When analyzing transitions to public-sector jobs separately, Gebel and Heyne (2014) find that higher education increases women's transition rate to public-sector jobs. Similarly, Dimova et al. (2016) find for men and women in Egypt, Jordan, the Occupied Palestinian Territory, Lebanon and Tunisia that higher education shortens the duration of finding a first stable job, which is primarily in the public sector.

There are also studies on time trends. Assaad et al. (2010) find for Egyptian men that the youngest birth cohort (1986–1990) makes a speedier transition to the first job compared to older birth cohorts (1976–1985). They explain this result with the decreasing share of formal jobs and the increasing share of informal jobs in the course of privatization and liberalization. Similarly, when comparing school leaver cohorts of the 1970s to 2000s in Egypt, Heyne and Gebel (2016) find faster school-to-work transitions for later male cohorts, specifically for those with upper-secondary education or less. In contrast, there is a downward trend in the transition rates to first job for women with secondary or tertiary education, which can be related to their preference for increasingly scarce public-sector jobs. Thus, in terms of the speed of finding a first job, men profit and higher-educated women are disadvantaged in periods of privatization and liberalization in the course of globalization.

Some trend studies directed their specific attention to the impact of recent crises. Selwaness and Roushdy (2019) find that the probability of finding a first job is higher in the aftermath of the financial crisis (2008–2009) and the 2011 uprisings (2011–2012) in Egypt, especially for men. The impact of the crises is different in Jordan. Alhawarin and Alawad (2021) show that Jordanian young people who left education during the period of the financial crisis (2007–2010) made slower transitions to first jobs than the education leaver cohorts of 2000–2006. This also applies to exit cohorts 2011–2016, who were affected by the regional instability of the Arab Spring, which affected Jordan particularly with the influx of huge numbers of Syrian refugees. Similarly, Amer (2019) finds an increase in the time to first job for both Jordanian men and women and all education groups when comparing school exit cohorts 2006–2016 to school exit cohorts 1995–2005. Among men, the prolongation of the transition to first job was especially pronounced among those with post-secondary education. Finding a first formal job was also delayed for all female education groups and lower-educated men, whereas the chances did not deteriorate for men with at least secondary education. Overall, the consequences of specific crises had more mixed consequences for the speed of labor market entry than the longer-term trends of liberalization and privatization.

Quality of the First Job

In MENA, the quality of the first job is usually assessed in terms of having a formal or informal job. Compared to formal jobs, informal jobs lack a written work contract and they usually lack social security, have longer working hours and lower occupational and skill levels (Barsoum 2015; Gebel and Heyne 2014). The lower quality of informal jobs is also reflected in lower satisfaction with informal jobs, which is mainly due to lower satisfaction with job security and wages, followed by type of work, working hours, working conditions and education–job match (Barsoum 2015). Formal jobs are predominately found in the public sector, whereas only a small proportion of private-sector jobs are formal. Dimova and Stephan (2020) show that a great majority of students in Egypt, Jordan and Tunisia aim at entering public-sector jobs. Barsoum (2015) finds that applying for public-sector jobs is a key search strategy among unemployed Egyptian youth. They would even accept lower pay in exchange for accessing public-sector jobs, which shows that non-monetary job-quality aspects of public-sector jobs matter.

The sectors also differ in terms of the methods of finding a job. Informal job-search methods via family and friends in general play an important role in MENA. This applies especially to the private (informal) sector, where jobs are often obtained via contacts of family and friends, as was found in studies on Egypt, Iran, Jordan and Syria (Barsoum 2015; Gebel 2012; Gebel and Heyne 2014). While social connections and nepotism (so-called *wasta*) also play a role in the public sector, a substantial share of youth entered public-sector jobs via formal competition.

Studies on youths' job mobility reveal a strong labor market segmentation, i.e. low mobility between the sectors. For example, Amer and Atallah (2019) find very high persistency rates of more than 90 percent among female and male labor market entrants in public, private formal and private informal jobs even four years after leaving education in Egypt. Amer (2019) also finds a very high persistency rate among Jordanian men who entered the labor market via a formal job. Although the mobility rate out of first jobs in the informal sector is slightly higher, just one quarter of Jordanian men are able to leave the informal sector within the first four years of their early labor market career. Similarly, Gebel (2012) finds a high degree of employment stability among labor market entrants in Syria. The only exception is the study of Egel and Salehi-Isfahani (2010), who find strong mobility between the informal and formal sectors among Iranian youth.

Given the low mobility, the initial job placement is of central importance. There are only few comparative studies on the incidence and determinants of formal and informal jobs among labor market entrants in MENA. Dimova et al. (2016) find for Egypt, Jordan, the Occupied Palestinian Territory, Lebanon and Tunisia that, on average, just around 44 percent of working youth have a written work contract compared to 56 percent relying on oral agreements. They also report that more than 75 percent of young workers are informally employed. Kovacheva et al. (2018) show for Morocco, Algeria, Tunisia, Egypt and Lebanon that only 14 percent of young people hold public-sector jobs. A key finding is that higher education and being a woman increases the probability of getting a formal job among active young people (Dimova et al. 2016; Heyne and Gebel 2016; Kovacheva et al. 2018). Assaad et al. (2018) show that the type of higher education does not matter in Egypt and Jordan. This is an interesting finding from the perspective of globalization research because neither attending a private higher education institution nor studying in the field of information technology creates any labor market (dis)advantages.

There are only a few trend studies. Assaad and Barsoum (2009) document a decline in public-sector jobs and an increase in formal and informal private-sector employment for entrant cohorts of the period 1975–2005. Comparing school leaver cohorts of the 1970s to 2000s in Egypt, Heyne and Gebel (2016) find a strong decline in public-sector first jobs for men from 25 percent in the 1970s to 12 percent in the 2000s, whereas the share was rather stable above 40 percent for women. The share of private formal employment doubled for men and tripled for women but reached only 10 percent for the 2000s cohorts. There was an increase in private informal-sector jobs for men from 47 to 57 percent and from 13 to 27 percent for women. Self-employment and working as a family helper strongly declined for women, whereas the shares did not change much for men. There was a decline in the probability of getting a public-sector job for both sexes. The decline is most pronounced among men and women with upper-secondary education and women with post-secondary vocational education. Assaad and Krafft (2021) further distinguish between higher-education groups from different parental SES backgrounds. They show that the decline in public-sector employment is also very pronounced among higher educated from lower SES backgrounds. Also higher-educated women from higher SES backgrounds experienced a decline in the probability of public-sector employment, whereas there is no significant change across cohorts for higher-educated men from higher SES backgrounds.

There is one comparative trend study on the initial labor market placement of 1980s–2000s school exit cohorts in Egypt, Jordan and Tunisia by Assad et al. (2019). For Egypt, the findings are similar to the results of Assaad and Krafft (2021) that were reported above. In Tunisia, the probability of formal private-sector and public-sector employment also declined for higher-educated men and women. This was accompanied by an increase in private-sector employment for women and an increase in informal private-sector employment for men. Thus, for Egypt and Tunisia the expectations on the consequences of globalization are met: privatization and liberalization decreased the chances of obtaining preferred public-sector jobs.

However, for Jordan there were opposing trends (Assaad and Krafft 2021). There was an increase in public-sector employment for the high educated and a U-shaped trend for other education groups. Private formal employment increased, particularly for the high educated. In contrast, there was no clear time trend in informal private employment. Jordanian women increasingly found first jobs in the private sector, whereas public-sector employment remained stable at low levels. In view of the mixed findings on time trends in just three MENA countries one can conclude that there was no universal impact of privatization and liberalization on young people's first job quality in the course of globalization in the MENA region.

RESEARCH GAPS AND AVENUES FOR FUTURE RESEARCH

The literature review highlighted that there is an impressive amount of quantitative-empirical research on school-to-work transition in MENA. Many of the empirical papers go beyond descriptive analyses and provide advanced multivariate analyses on the dynamics of school-to-work transition. The studies rely on various high-quality, large-scale, nationally representative surveys: the Labor Market Panel Surveys for Egypt, Jordan and Tunisia (e.g. Assaad et al. 2019), the school-to-work transition surveys for Egypt, Iran, Jordan, the Occupied Palestinian Territory, Lebanon and Tunisia by the International Labour Office (Dimova et al. 2016; Gebel and Heyne 2014) and for Syria by the European Training Foundation (Gebel 2012) as well as the youth surveys of the SAHWA project (Kovacheva et al. 2018). These data sources are an impressive source for research as they go beyond typical cross-sectional data offering retrospective/prospective longitudinal information on the school-to-work transition dynamics. However, the coverage of MENA countries is limited, particularly with regard to the Gulf countries. To reach a full understanding of the school-to-work transition across the whole MENA region, one important avenue for future research is to collect appropriate data on the missing countries.

The limited data coverage of MENA countries also constrains opportunities for quantitative comparative research. The literature review highlighted a few articles that performed qualitative comparative analysis of quantitative micro data for very few countries. If data cover more MENA countries and more periods, new opportunities for quantitative multilevel research may emerge. This includes repeated cross-section data such as harmonized labor force surveys. This may allow to better quantify the impact of globalization on youth labor markets by using quantitative macro indicators on globalization in multilevel analyses as was done in European research (Gebel and Giesecke 2016; Lange et al. 2014).

Another promising avenue of comparative research would be to compare school-to-work transitions in MENA to neighboring regions and other world regions. This would allow detecting similarities and differences across regions and a better contextualization of findings of countries with different globalization experiences.

REFERENCES

Adams, R.H. and J. Page (2003), "Poverty, inequality and growth in selected Middle East and North Africa countries, 1980–2000," *World Development*, 31(12), 2027–2048.

Alhawarin, I. and A. Alawad (2021), "Transition to a first job with reference to the role of macroeconomic crises: The case of Jordanian youth," *Al-Hussein Bin Talal Journal of Research*, 7(2), 1–12.

Amer, M. (2014), "The school-to-work transition of Jordanian youth," in R. Assaad (ed.), *The Jordanian labor market in the new millennium*, Oxford University Press, pp. 64–104.

Amer, M. (2019), "School-to-work transition in Jordan, 2010–2016," in C. Krafft and R. Assaad (eds), *The Jordanian labor market between fragility and resilience*, Oxford University Press, pp. 225–58.

Amer, M. and M. Atallah (2019), *The school to work transition and youth economic vulnerability in Egypt: ERF Working Paper No. 1353*, Cairo: Economic Research Forum.

Amin, M., R. Assaad, N. al-Baharna, K. Dervis, R.M. Desai, N.S. Dhillon, A. Galal, H. Ghanem, C. Graham and D. Kaufmann (eds) (2012), *After the spring: Economic transitions in the Arab world*, Oxford University Press.

Assaad, R. (2005), "Informalization and defeminization: Explaining the unusual pattern in Egypt," in N. Kudva and L. Benería (eds), *Rethinking informalization: Poverty, precarious jobs and social protection*, Cornell University Open Access Repository, pp. 86–102.

Assaad, R. (2014), "Making sense of Arab labor markets: The enduring legacy of dualism," *IZA Journal of Labor & Development*, 3(1), 1–25.

Assaad, R. and G. Barsoum (2009), "Rising expectations and diminishing opportunities for Egypt's young," in N. Dhillon and T. Yousef (eds), *Generation in waiting: The unfulfilled promise of young people in the Middle East*, Brookings Institution Press, pp. 67–94.

Assaad, R. and C. Krafft (2021), "Excluded generation: The growing challenges of labor market insertion for Egyptian youth," *Journal of Youth Studies*, 24(2), 186–212.

Assaad, R., C. Binzel and M. Gadallah (2010), "Transitions to employment and marriage among young men in Egypt," *Middle East Development Journal*, 2(1), 39–88.

Assaad, R., C. Krafft and D. Salehi-Isfahani (2018), "Does the type of higher education affect labor market outcomes? Evidence from Egypt and Jordan," *Higher Education*, 75(6), 945–995.

Assaad, R., C. Krafft and C. Salemi (2019), *Socioeconomic status and the changing nature of school-to-work transitions in Egypt, Jordan and Tunisia*, ERF Working Paper No. 1287, Economic Research Forum.

Barsoum, G. (2015), "Young people's job aspirations in Egypt and the continued preference for a government job," in R. Assaad and C. Krafft (eds), *The Egyptian labor market in an era of revolution*, Oxford Univ. Press, pp. 108–126.

Blossfeld, H.P., S. Buchholz, E. Bukodi and K. Kurz (eds) (2008), *Young workers, globalization, and the labor market*, Edward Elgar Publishing.

Dhillon, N. and T. Yousef (eds) (2009), *Generation in waiting: The unfulfilled promise of young people in the Middle East*, Brookings Institution Press.

Dimova, R. and K. Stephan (2020), "Inequality of opportunity and (unequal) opportunities in the youth labour market: How is the Arab world different?," *International Labour Review*, 159(2), 217–242.

Dimova, R., S. Elder and K. Stephan (2016), *Labour market transitions of young women and men in the Middle East and North Africa*, Work4Youth Publication Series No. 44, ILO.

Egel, D. and D. Salehi-Isfahani (2010), "Youth transitions to employment and marriage in Iran: Evidence from the school to work transition survey," *Middle East Development Journal*, 2(1), 89–120.

Forteza, A. and M. Ramab (2006), "Labor market 'rigidity' and the success of economic reforms across more than 100 countries," *Journal of Policy Reform*, 9(1), 75–105.

Gebel, M. (2012), *The transition from education to work in Syria: Results of the Youth Transition Survey 2009*, European Training Foundation.

Gebel, M. (2019), *The transition from education to work: Theoretical framework and state-of-the-art*, TEW-CCA Working Paper No. 1, TEW-CCA Project, University of Bamberg.

Gebel, M. and J. Giesecke (2016), "Does deregulation help? The impact of employment protection reforms on youths' unemployment and temporary employment risks in Europe," *European Sociological Review*, 32(4), 486–500.

Gebel, M. and S. Heyne (2014), *Transitions to adulthood in the Middle East and North Africa: Young women's rising?*, Palgrave Macmillan.

Gebel, M. and S. Heyne (2017), *Familienverständnis in Nordafrika und dem Nahen Osten: Analysen zu familiären Rollen und zur Abgrenzung vom Staat*, University of Bamberg Press.

Grant, M.J. and F.F. Furstenberg (2007), "Changes in the transition to adulthood in less developed countries," *European Journal of Population*, 23(3–4), 415–428.

Heyne, S. (2017), *Culture and female labor force participation in international comparison*, University of Mannheim.

Heyne, S. and M. Gebel (2016), "Education effects on the school-to-work transition in Egypt: A cohort comparison of labor market entrants 1970–2012," *Research in Social Stratification and Mobility*, 46, 37–49.

Kabbani, N. and E. Kothari (2005), "Youth employment in the MENA region," Social Protection Discussion Paper No.0534, World Bank.

Kogan, I., C. Noelke and M. Gebel (eds) (2011), *Making the transition: Education and labor market entry in Central and Eastern Europe*, Stanford University Press.

Kovacheva, S., K. Roberts and S. Kabaivanov (2018), "Education to employment transitions in South and East Mediterranean countries," *International Journal of Social Science and Economic Research*, 3(2), 532–559.

Lange, M.d., M. Gesthuizen and M.H.J. Wolbers (2014), "Youth labour market integration across Europe: The impact of cyclical, structural, and institutional characteristics," *European Societies*, 16(2), 194–212.

Matallah, S. and N. Ghazi (2015), "Globalization, FDI and the links with economic growth: An empirical investigation for MENA countries," *British Journal of Economics, Management & Trade*, 8(3), 215–229.

Naufal, G.S. and I.H. Genc (2015), "Structural change in MENA remittance flows," *Emerging Markets Finance and Trade*, 51(6), 1175–1178.

Ross, M.L. (2008), "Oil, Islam, and women," *American Political Science Review*, 102(1), 107–123.

Salehi-Isfahani, D. and N. Dhillon (2008), "Stalled youth transitions in the Middle East: A framework for policy reform," Middle East Youth Initiative Working Paper, Wolfensohn Center for Development.

Selwaness, I. and R. Roushdy (2019), "Young people school-to-work transition in the aftermath of the Arab Spring," *International Journal of Manpower*, 40(3), 398–432.

Shavit, Y. and W. Müller (eds) (1998), *From school to work: A comparative study of educational qualifications and occupational destinations*, Clarendon Press.

Spierings, N. (2015), *Women's employment in Muslim countries: Patterns of diversity*, Palgrave Macmillan.

Yousef, T.M. (2004), "Development, growth and policy reform in the Middle East and North Africa since 1950," *Journal of Economic Perspectives*, 18(3), 91–116.

26. Reimagining globalization through a gender lens

Esuna Dugarova

INTRODUCTION

Today humanity is going through multidimensional crises. The COVID-19 pandemic, a deepening climate emergency, intensifying geopolitical tensions and conflicts, and rising living costs in various countries have disrupted development progress (UNDP 2022). These crises have exposed intrinsic power imbalances, exacerbated pre-existing inequalities, and exposed unequal distributions of resources, with deep-rooted patriarchy and misogyny that generate and reproduce yawning gender gaps (UN 2022). Yet, policy responses to these challenges tend to overlook the needs of women who often bear the brunt of the economic and social fallout of the crises. Notably, the COVID-19 Global Gender Response Tracker shows that the global policy response to the pandemic has largely been blind to gender equality, as only 19 per cent of labour market and social protection measures enacted during the pandemic supported women's economic security and unpaid care work. This can be partly attributed to the underrepresentation of women in political decision-making during the COVID-19 response, which reflects pre-existing power gaps, patriarchal structures, discriminatory laws, and deeply embedded social norms biased against women in politics (Dugarova 2021, 2022). Women and girls, especially those with intersectional identities, are particularly disadvantaged during the crises due to unequal structures and social norms that prevent them from accessing basic services, including healthcare and education, and participating in decision-making processes that affect their lives.

The shifts associated with the multifaceted crises are shaping the global development landscape and have the potential to either enhance the development gains or further derail the prospects of progress. This points to the pressing need for a holistic policy action with renewed commitment, rebuilding solidarity within and between countries, and gender-responsive strategies and innovative solutions to address complex interlinked challenges. While the ongoing challenges are threatening to reverse improvements on gender equality achieved over the past decades, it is also a once-in-a-generation opportunity to rethink our approach and reinvigorate action to remove all barriers to the empowerment of women and girls as a fundamental prerequisite for people-centred development. Such a gendered pathway approach is not only a development imperative but is also a prerequisite for an ethical world order (Dugarova 2020).

Against this backdrop, the current chapter offers a gender perspective on globalization trends, highlighting the failures of the existing economic model to deliver on the promise of inclusive growth, democratic backsliding, digital transformation, migration and displacement, climate change, and the state of multilateralism and financing for gender equality. Based on an analytical review through a gender lens, it suggests a way forward for a gender-responsive policy choice that can build more egalitarian, resilient, and sustainable societies.

THE FAILING ECONOMIC MODEL

Even prior to the COVID-19 crisis, the world was already in a state of disarray characterized by heightened global uncertainty and increasing popular discontent with the existing political and economic order. Mass demonstrations and protests had been escalating in different parts of the world, with a common perception of a weakening social contract and accumulation of overlapping deprivations and long-standing inequalities. As global gross domestic product had grown, the economic disparities between countries and regions and within individual societies had increased (World Bank 2016). At the root of this global unrest have been power asymmetries underpinned by the failure of the neoliberal model – manifested in lowering taxes on the rich, deregulation of labour and product markets, and financialization – to share growth benefits equitably across different segments of society. In many situations, this resulted in the erosion of social protection systems, exacerbated poverty and deteriorated the quality of work, profoundly affecting the lives of countless people and leaving them excluded and unheard.

Such a dominant development model has perpetuated gender inequality, and in this volatile context, the rights of women have come under fire, aggravating gender-based discrimination, violence, and abuse. While economic growth created employment opportunities for women across various settings, many of these reproduced discrimination and segregation that are embedded in labour markets. As such, many women, particularly in low-income countries, continue to undertake work that is seen to be an extension of their traditional gender roles: in low-end retail jobs, domestic service, and labour-intensive agricultural work. Such jobs, many of which are informal, tend to be characterized by low wages, poor working conditions, instability, and insecurity. This reinforces the status of women as secondary earners within their households and they may remain invisible within the economic system (Braunstein and Houston 2015).

Perhaps even more significantly, capitalist markets and production continue to function as they do because they rely on unpaid labour. The lion's share of unpaid work is done by women across the board (ILO 2018). The nature of this work often essentializes women as caregivers, necessitating them to fulfil these socially prescribed roles, which not only puts stress on them but also limits their opportunities, capabilities, and choices to participate in paid employment and public life. Austerity measures, including cuts in family and child allowances, old age benefits, and care services across regions, have negative effects on gender equality. Poor labour market outcomes and the disproportionate burden of unpaid care work are in fact among the key reasons for gender poverty gaps, with women and girls 4 per cent more likely than men and boys to live in extreme poverty (UN 2019a). Despite growing attention, unpaid care work continues to be undervalued or 'externalized' in capitalist economic models. Yet, by overexploiting human capital and eroding the values of care and social security, the existing economic model risks becoming socially unsustainable.

The effects of the ongoing crises have aggravated this state of affairs. For example, the closure of national borders and lockdown measures during the COVID-19 pandemic paralysed economic activities across the world, laying off millions of workers worldwide. Unlike previous economic crises, the COVID-19 economic downturn affected economic activity featuring a large share of female employment. An estimated 510 million globally work in the hard-hit sectors that include retail, hospitality, food service, and manufacturing, especially the garment industry (ILO 2020). These effects were particularly devastating for workers and their livelihoods in the informal sector, where women are overrepresented worldwide, accounting for around 90 per cent in South Asia and Sub-Saharan Africa (UN Women 2015). The cascading global crises have led to a resurgence of poverty and its further feminization. By the end of 2022, 383 million women and girls globally are projected to live in extreme poverty compared to 368 million men and boys (UN 2022).

Moving forward, global economic growth is predicted to slow down in the coming years (IMF 2022), leaving lasting scars on gender equality due to declining investments, disrupted supply chains, unemployment, and unattained learning outcomes. Against this background, it is likely to become more challenging to sustain development gains and yet even more pressing to reinvigorate collective forces to fight for gender equality. While there is no magic bullet that can cure the economic and political malaise, there may be a viable alternative to create a comprehensive economic agenda that prioritizes quality education, decent employment, and climate policy with an active role of the state and enables social organization that allows people to work together for the common good. Integrating a gender lens into such agenda entails a gender-inclusive approach that ensures equal rights, opportunities, and outcomes for all.

DEMOCRATIC BACKSLIDING

The past few years have witnessed a mounting wave of backsliding democracies across the globe, from Eastern Europe to Latin America, led by populist and nationalist forces from both right and left wings of the political spectrum. A greater number of countries are seeing a deterioration in the quality of their democracies, with almost one third of the world's population living in countries undergoing democratic reversals (V-Dem Institute 2019). In 2021, the world saw a record number of 33 countries autocratizing in the last 50 years, which are home to 36 per cent of the global population or 2.8 billion people (V-Dem Institute 2022). Along with this, polarization is increasing to toxic levels in many countries, leading to electoral victories of anti-pluralist leaders. Processes of democratic backsliding seem to be related to a wider discontent with liberal democracy, declining levels of political participation and trust, and an erosion of traditional party systems (Waldner and Lust 2018). The Democracy Index saw continuous decline in global democracy, with diminishing political rights and a further crackdown on civil liberties such as freedom of expression (Economist 2022).

In such context of backsliding and de-democratization, there is a growing backlash against gender equality and women's rights both in national and international fora. While women have incrementally entered public life, the glass ceiling remains low. According to the Inter-Parliamentary Union, in 2021, only 21 countries had a female head of state or government. Political will to change power relations in accordance with international commitments on gender equality is lacking. If this continues at the current pace, by 2030 nearly 2 billion women and girls will still face discrimination in opportunities for public leadership, and balance at the pinnacle of power will not be reached for another 130 years (UN 2020).

In fact, women's rights are particularly vulnerable in fragile and nascent democracies, where such rights have been established more recently and where the space of civil society is often limited (Baker et al. 2017). While gender equality has always been contested, in the past years opposition to gender equality and women's rights activism has become more vocal, with a variety of long-established actors and newly emerging anti-gender ideology movements (Roggeband 2019; Verloo 2018). Their agendas are imbued with discriminatory and patriarchal tendencies, with a focus on sexual and reproductive health and rights, but the impact has extended to questioning violence against women, work and family reconciliation policies, and the content of public education. These developments pose renewed challenges to women's rights and limit the scope for action to institutionalize non-discrimination and gender equality through laws and policies.

Along with democratic backsliding, civic space is diminishing across countries. Civil society organizations and in particular those defending human rights are facing increasing political restraints all over the world. The closure of civic space is a gendered phenomenon, as it not only obstructs women's rights activists in exercising their rights, but also limits their role in safeguarding existing gender equality policies and arrangements (Krizsán and Roggeband 2021). In some cases, instead of directly eroding existing laws and policies on gender equality, the core dimensions challenged by backsliding processes are dismantling implementation and disrupting accountability, which may reflect a more general trend to sideline democratic processes and can undermine the democratic functioning and legitimacy of states (Batory et al. 2017).

Yet, in the absence of effective policy processes, civil society and women's rights groups in several countries are turning to mobilizing grassroots capacities in an unprecedented manner. More disruptive and participatory strategies of mobilization are used, partly relying on social media and generating new alliances with pro-democracy actors. In this process, there is a generational and intersectional diversification within women's groups which creates new tensions and debates about possible strategies but also sparks mobilization with new repertoires of action (Roggeband and Krizsan 2020). Such wide-ranging coalition work is not only a strategy widening the constituency for women's rights claims but can also have the potential to mainstream gender equality to a wider political agenda.

DIGITAL TRANSFORMATION

The world is seeing an era of unprecedented technological revolution, with digitalization transforming economies, governments, and societies (Schwab 2016). This revolution is characterized by advances ranging from smart phones, the Internet of Things, and artificial intelligence (AI) to big data, cloud computing, and robotics. These span public and private industries, including healthcare, education, governance, manufacturing and finance.

At the same time, digitalization brings disruption, exacerbates inequality, and widens gender gaps, as critical disparities prevail across income, location, gender, and other dimensions (Sey and Hafkin 2019). According to Organisation for Economic Co-operation and Development (OECD) estimates, 14 per cent of jobs in developed countries are at high risk of automation (OECD 2019), and an estimated 180 million female jobs globally could be displaced by technology within the next two decades (IMF 2018). While jobs in science and technology are some of the fastest growing worldwide, women are underrepresented in these sectors, which is the result of gender stereotypes and discriminatory institutional barriers.

New risks and challenges are also emerging in relation to fairness and inclusion, privacy and autonomy, accountability and transparency. While the internet was initially viewed as a democratizing platform through, for example, information sharing and civic engagement, major online platforms are now found complicit in the spread of hate speech and cyber harassment (Wajcman et al. 2019). There are also concerns about unprecedented levels of data mining, algorithms, and predictive risk models that entrench existing inequalities and power dynamics, threaten rights, and enable new forms of surveillance (Zuboff 2019).

Rapidly evolving digitalization and AI highlight the need for gender equity in AI. Women represent a meagre 22 per cent of the world's AI practitioners, resulting in (sub) conscious biases in AI systems (WEF 2016). Combating these inequities in the future of work will become more critical, requiring tech-savvy skills, flexibility, and technology access. Mitigating gendered risks of digital transformation entails going beyond 'getting more women and girls in tech' and focusing on addressing unequal power structures and gender practices that mediate the Fourth Industrial Revolution.

In this dynamic environment and constant change, governments will need to be more responsive to citizens' needs and experiences and be more integrated, as breaking down silos and connecting data and process flows are instrumental to finding new solutions and enhancing security (Deloitte 2019). At the same time, in mitigating these risks, digital technologies should be seen as part of a wider structural context that shapes power structures and gender relations, often in connection with other forms of identity such as race and class. For example, gendered norms and (sub)conscious biases govern participation in science, technology, engineering and medicine and information and communication technology education, which in turn reinforces gendered divisions of labour around technology and magnifies women's exclusion from technological pursuits in the workplace (Gurumurthy et al. 2018). Within the broader trends and institutional changes, it is necessary to go beyond 'getting more women and girls in tech' and rather address the root causes of unequal power structures and gender practices that mediate the digital revolution and influence the process of technological change.

MIGRATION AND DISPLACEMENT

We live in a time of greatest human mobility, in which international migration has reached exceptionally high levels. According to the latest available estimates, there were 280.6 million international migrants in 2020, of whom nearly half were women (Migration Policy Institute 2022). As migration is increasing, the factors that drive migration are becoming more complex, as many people move involuntarily due to ineffective governance, entrenched poverty and inequalities, climate change and environmental degradation, and violent conflict.

Along with international migration, internal migration taking place within countries had also been growing, driving much of the rise of megacities and a rapid increase in urbanization, with the share of the world's population projected to reach 60 per cent (or 5.1 billion) by 2030 (UN 2015). Triggered by demographic shifts, slow and uneven economic growth, and environmental degradation, urbanization on the one hand fosters productivity and creates opportunities for a better quality of life, but on the other hand it aggravates gender inequality, multidimensional poverty, and environmental risks (Dugarova and Gulasan 2017).

Ongoing conflicts around the world continue to cause forced displacement. According to early estimates, in May 2022 over 100 million individuals were forcibly displaced worldwide as a result of persecution, conflict, violence, or human rights violations, among whom are refugees, asylum seekers, and internally displaced persons (UNHCR 2022). Refugees and displaced persons tend to be more vulnerable to abuse and exploitation, and women and girls face a higher risk of sexual and gender-based violence, as well as trafficking and exploitation (UN Women 2017). The international response to migration and displacement has been unbalanced, and in some cases, nationalism and xenophobia have flourished, resulting in negative public attitudes and punitive measures towards migrants and displaced persons that deny their rights and withhold basic needs.

Conflicts, increasing militarization, and social and economic deterioration have had detrimental impacts on women's security, mobility, and participation in the economy and public life. The unsustainable patterns of development that tend to prioritize large-scale investments in infrastructure, extractive industries, and commercial agriculture not only bypass women who remain confined to small-scale and local initiatives (UN 2018), but also risk pushing them further behind through processes of displacement and eviction (Elson 2018).

At the same time, women's representation and meaningful participation in formal peace processes remain limited due to deeply entrenched barriers, including institutionalized gender bias and discrimination, low levels of political participation, and lack of economic and social rights (UN 2018). From food insecurity and limited access to health and education, to increasing maternal mortality and intensified poverty, women and girls bear the brunt of violence (Tabbara 2019). Women's exclusion from peace processes and multiple deprivations they experience are linked to wider political and social exclusion and inequalities that are embedded and reproduced in societal attitudes and practices, legal norms, national and international institutions, as well as within humanitarian systems (Goetz and Jenkins 2016).

Moving forward, it is important to revisit gender divisions in societies that reinforce structural inequalities, enabling militarized masculinities and exacerbating violence (True 2019). Promoting the accountability of states and external actors to ensure the social and economic rights of women is a critical step in this path. These rights, including the right to access and control resources, to work and participate in decision-making processes, provide the precondition for structural changes. Such an approach requires the development of Women, Peace and Security frameworks that establish physical and social infrastructures as an integral part of securing peace, rebuilding economies, and achieving gender equality.

CLIMATE CHANGE AND ENVIRONMENTAL DEGRADATION

The world is witnessing the escalating impacts of climate change as seen, for example, in rising temperatures and more frequent extreme weather events, and intensifying environmental stresses such as loss of natural capital and biodiversity. For example, in just the past 50 years, we have lost nearly 60 per cent of the populations of more than 16,000 species and half of all tropical forests worldwide (IUCN 2017). Key recent environmental assessments point to a growing crisis in natural and human environments, and many may already be past sustainability tipping points (IPBES 2019; IPCC 2014, 2022; UNEP 2019).

The climate crisis is aggravated by the fact that countries suffering the worst are those least responsible for global warming. Inequalities play a large role in determining who is most impacted by climate change. While climate change disrupts livelihoods across the board, women and girls tend to be disproportionately affected due to their unequal socioeconomic status and lack of rights and resources. For example, in Myanmar, women accounted for 61 per cent of fatalities caused by Cyclone Nargis (Reliefweb 2008). All societies contain deeply rooted gender inequalities, but when gender intersects with other forms of identity such as class, ethnicity, or race, the challenges are greater yet, particularly in the context of natural disasters.

Addressing the structural barriers of gender inequality is key to gender-responsive climate action. A growing body of evidence shows that gender equality is crucial to addressing the impacts of climate change and protecting planetary ecosystems. Women around the world have been critical in mitigating and adapting to climate change, reducing disaster risks, and managing natural resources. The contributions of women are attributed to their participation and leadership at the community and political levels, and to their local knowledge, skills, and experiences regarding the environment and management of food, water, and other natural resources. Yet, women's roles and contributions are still overlooked as a climate change solution. Around a quarter of revised Nationally Determined Contributions – countries' climate actions to reduce national emissions and adapt to climate impacts – are gender-blind, with no mention of gendered experiences or women's roles (IUCN 2021). These limitations not only undermine women's agency and their rights, but also can result in the failure to meet the 1.5°C global target.

While women's critical roles are increasingly featured in national and global debates, such narratives are often partial and incomplete. In some cases, such as in climate change adaptation, policymakers adopt a narrow, technocentric approach to gender, assuming that women will supply unpaid work – sustaining people and environment – without granting this due recognition, support, or consideration of redistribution with men and others. These narratives tend to ignore gender relations and women's rights, voice, and power, and overlook vital intersections that shape their interests, knowledge, and capabilities, resulting in the 'instrumentalization' of women and worsening gender inequalities (Leach 2016).

Yet, the reverse is possible. Solutions to climate change exist and if countries find the political will to act, honour pledges to cut emissions, and mobilize funding for gender-responsive climate action, catastrophe can be averted.

THE STATE OF MULTILATERALISM AND FINANCING FOR DEVELOPMENT

Discontent with globalization and governments' policy responses to the crises have intensified populist and nationalist sentiments in many countries, challenging the virtue of international cooperation and questioning the power, legitimacy, and relevance of multilateralism (Gowan and Dworkin 2019; UN 2019b). A recent tendency towards a 'variable geometry' that replaces universal institutions with small 'coalitions of the willing', groups of countries that act together and independently of formal multilateral deliberation, has aggravated the risk (UN 2019b). In this context, the ability and effectiveness of the UN system to deliver on its mandate has been severely constrained.

Yet, to address intricate transnational challenges – from climate change, poverty eradication, and migration to gender inequality, violent extremism, and digital transformation – we need stronger and more inclusive multilateralism that links local actions with global priorities and gives voice to a diverse range of countries and stakeholders, including civil society and women's grassroots organizations. In our interdependent world, no country acting alone will be able to manage the gamut of threats that exist today.

Strong international cooperation is also needed to transform the global financial architecture and increase funding for sustainable development. Official development assistance (ODA) remains a critical source of public finance for development. ODA provided by members of the

OECD's Development Assistance Committee (DAC) members totalled USD 178.9 billion in 2021, representing 0.3 per cent of their combined gross national income (GNI) (OECD 2022a). While reaching an all-time high level, it is falling short of actual commitments to reach 0.7 per cent of combined GNI. ODA allocated by OECD DAC members constitutes an important contribution to financing gender equality and women's empowerment. Progress in this area has been slow, as gender equality remains vastly underfunded. According to the latest available data, 44.5 per cent of ODA, or USD 53 billion, was allocated to gender equality and women's empowerment in 2018–2019, which is higher than ever before (OECD 2022b). However, of these funds, only 5 per cent, or USD 5.6 billion, goes to programming with gender equality as a principal objective. The rest of development aid remains gender-blind.

To achieve gender equality and sustainable development, drawing on all sources of finance – public and private, domestic and international – in all countries is essential. This requires enhancing the impact of available resources, while catalysing additional sources of financing into investments in gender equality. Innovative financing mechanisms and new partners are needed. As part of this effort, in 2018–2019, private philanthropic foundations provided USD 1.9 billion to gender equality and women's empowerment (OECD 2022b). While this is a promising sign, concerted efforts are required to mobilize resources to transform gender equality commitments into reality.

As we move forward, multilateral engagement that is based on the rule of law and respect for fundamental freedoms provides critical opportunities to tackle these challenges. Seizing these opportunities in turn depends on the widely shared 'global commons' of international governance that embed universal aspirations for peace, dignity, and gender equality, while establishing a foundation for designing and implementing global collective action (Dugarova and Gulasan 2017). The ongoing challenges serve as a springboard for global action to mobilize efforts and reinvigorate the social contract with gender equality at its heart. This will require political will, gender-responsive institutions, and greater financing for gender equality.

While there is no magic bullet that can make it happen overnight, a bold approach is needed to promote a new generation of policies that prioritize shifting social norms, discriminatory practices, and unequal power relations. After all, gender equality and sustainability reinforce each other and offer powerful tools for reimagining the future in a way that embraces social, economic, and environmental justice.

REFERENCES

Baker, A., Boulding, C., Mullenax, S., Murton, G., Todd, M., Velasco-Guacahlla, X. and Zackary, D. (2017). Maintaining civic space in backsliding regimes, USAID/DCHA/DRG Working Papers Series. Boulder: University of Colorado.

Batory, A., Krizsan, A., Sitter, N. and Zentai, V. (2017). Backsliding in area of constitutional safeguards and independent institutions, corruption control, and general equality and minorities, CPS Working Papers 7/2017. Budapest: CEU Center for Policy Studies.

Braunstein, E. and Houston, M. (2015). 'Pathways towards sustainability in the context of globalization: A gendered perspective on growth, macro policy and employment'. In M. Leach (Ed.), *Gender Equality and Sustainable Development*. Abingdon: Routledge.

Deloitte (2019). Government trends 2020: What are the most transformational trends in government today? www2.deloitte.com/content/dam/Deloitte/ec/Documents/public-sector/DI_Government -Trends-2020.pdf

Dugarova, E. (2020). *Progress towards gender equality and women's empowerment.* New York: United Nations.

Dugarova, E. (2021). *A springboard for change? Opportunities for a sustainable and inclusive care system post-COVID.* London: Global Institute for Women's Leadership, King's College London. www.kcl.ac.uk/giwl/assets/essays-on-equality-december-2021.pdf

Dugarova, E. (2022). Global policy response and decision-making in times of crisis. *Companion Blog to the Social Policy and Society Journal.* https://socialpolicyblog.com/2022/07/21/global-policy-response-and-decision-making-in-times-of-crisis/

Dugarova, E. and Gulasan, N. (2017). *Global trends: Challenges and opportunities in the implementation of the Sustainable Development Goals.* New York: UNDP and Geneva: UNRISD.

Economist (2022). A new low for global democracy. www.economist.com/graphic-detail/2022/02/09/a-new-low-for-global-democracy

Elson, D. (2018). Push no one behind, CDP Background Paper No. 43. New York: United Nations Department of Economic and Social Affairs.

Goetz, A.-M. and Jenkins, R. (2016). Agency and accountability: Promoting women's participation in peacebuilding. *Feminist Economics,* 22 (1), 211–236.

Gowan, R. and Dworkin, A. (2019). *Three crises and an opportunity: Europe's stake in multilateralism.* Policy brief. London: European Council on Foreign Relations.

Gurumurthy, A., Chami, N. and Billorou, C.A. (2018). Gender equality in the digital economy: Emerging issues, DJP Issue Paper 1/2018. https://itforchange.net/digital-justice-project/issue-paper-1/

ILO (2018). *Care work and care jobs for the future of decent work.* Geneva: ILO.

ILO (2020). *ILO monitor: COVID-19 and the world of work,* Fifth edition. Geneva: ILO.

IMF (2018). *Gender, technology, and the future of work.* Washington, DC: IMF.

IMF (2022). *World economic outlook, October 2022,* Washington, DC: IMF.

IPBES (2019). *Global assessment report on biodiversity and ecosystem services of the Intergovernmental Science–Policy Platform on Biodiversity and Ecosystem Services.* Bonn: IPBES Secretariat.

IPCC (2014). *Climate change 2014: Impacts, adaptation, and vulnerability, Part A: Global and sectoral aspects.* Contribution of Working Group II to the Fifth Assessment Report of the Intergovernmental Panel on Climate Change. Cambridge: Cambridge University Press.

IPCC (2022). *Climate change 2022: Impacts, adaptation and vulnerability.* Contribution of Working Group II to the Sixth Assessment Report of the Intergovernmental Panel on Climate Change. Cambridge: Cambridge University Press.

IUCN (2017). *Deforestation and forest degradation.* www.iucn.org/resources/issues-briefs/deforestation-and-forest-degradation

IUCN (2021). *Gender and national climate planning: Gender integration in the revised nationally determined contributions.* Gland: IUCN.

Krizsán, A. and Roggeband, C. (2021). *Politicizing gender and democracy in the context of the Istanbul Convention.* Basingstoke: Palgrave Pivot.

Leach, M. (Ed.) (2016). *Gender equality and sustainable development.* Abingdon: Routledge.

Migration Policy Institute (2022). Top statistics on global migration and migrants. www.migrationpolicy.org/article/top-statistics-global-migration-migrants

OECD (2019). *Embracing innovation in government: Global trends 2019.* Paris: OECD. https://trends.oecd-opsi.org/embracing-innovation-in-government-global-trends-2019.pdf

OECD (2022a). *COVID-19 assistance to developing countries lifts foreign aid in 2021.* Paris: OECD. www.oecd.org/dac/covid-19-assistance-to-developing-countries-lifts-foreign-aid-in-2021-oecd.htm

OECD (2022b). *Development finance for gender equality and women's empowerment: A 2021 snapshot.* Paris: OECD. www.oecd.org/development/gender-development/Development-finance-for-gender-equality-2021.pdf

Reliefweb (2008). *Myanmar: Females hit worst by Cyclone Nargis.* https://reliefweb.int/report/myanmar/myanmar-females-hit-worst-cyclone-nargis

Roggeband, C. (2019). International women's rights: Progress under attack, KFG Working Paper Series No. 26. Berlin: Berlin Potsdam Research Group.

Roggeband, C. and Krizsan, A. (2020). Democratic backsliding and backlash against women's rights: Understanding the current challenges for feminist politics. Discussion paper. New York: UN Women.

Schwab, K. (2016). The Fourth Industrial Revolution: What it means, how to respond. www.weforum
.org/agenda/2016/01/the-fourth-industrial-revolution-what-it-means-and-how-to-respond/

Sey, A. and Hafkin, N. (2019). Taking stock: Data and evidence on gender equality in digital access,
skills and leadership. Macau: United Nations University Institute on Computing and Society/
International Telecommunications Union.

Tabbara, H. (2019). What invisibility reveals: Reflections on women's participation in peace, security,
and humanitarian action in West Asia. Expert paper. New York: UN Women.

True, J. (2019). The Women, Peace and Security Agenda 25 years after Beijing: What difference could
a feminist political economy perspective make? Expert paper. New York: UN Women.

UN (2015). *Population 2030: Demographic challenges and opportunities for sustainable development
planning*. New York.

UN (2018). *Report of the Secretary-General on women and peace and security*, S/2018/900. New York.

UN (2019a). *The gender snapshot 2019: Progress on the Sustainable Development Goals*. New York.

UN (2019b). *World economic situation and prospects 2019*. New York.

UN (2020). *Women's full and effective participation and decision-making in public life, as well as the
elimination of violence, for achieving gender equality and the empowerment of all women and girls*.
New York.

UN (2022). *Progress on the Sustainable Development Goals: The gender snapshot 2022*. New York.

UN Women (2015). *Progress of the world's women 2015–2016: Transforming
economies, realizing rights*. New York.

UN Women (2017). *Making gender-responsive migration laws*. New York.

UNDP (2022). *Human development report 2021/22: Uncertain times, unsettled lives: shaping our future
in a transforming world*. New York.

UNEP (2019). *Global environment outlook 6*. New York.

UNHCR (2022). Refugee statistics. www.unrefugees.org/refugee-facts/statistics/

V-Dem Institute (2019). *Democracy facing global challenges: V-Dem annual democracy report 2019*.
Gothenburg: V-Dem Institute.

V-Dem Institute (2022). *Autocratization changing nature? Democracy report 2022*. Gothenburg:
V-Dem Institute.

Verloo, M. (Ed.) (2018). *Varieties in opposition to gender equality in Europe*. Abingdon: Routledge.

Wajcman, J., Young, E. and Fitzmaurice, E. (2019). *The digital revolution: Implications for gender
equality and women's rights 25 years after Beijing*. New York: UN Women.

Waldner, D. and Lust, E. (2018). Unwelcome change: Coming to terms with democratic backsliding.
Annual Review of Political Science, 21, 93–113.

WEF (2016). *Global gender gap report 2018*. Geneva: World Economic Forum.

World Bank (2016). *Poverty and shared prosperity 2016: Taking on inequality*. Washington, DC.

Zuboff, S. (2019). *The age of surveillance capitalism: The fight for a human future at the new frontier of
power*. New York: Public Affairs.

27. Pension governance in a globalizing world

Bernhard Ebbinghaus

INTRODUCTION

Demographic ageing is seen as challenging the sustainability of pensions across advanced economies. Until recent reforms, people tended to exit from work ever earlier, and while their life expectancy and thus time in retirement augmented, both trends put additional financial burden on welfare states. Advanced economies spend about a tenth of their annual economic output on old age, survivor, and disability pensions or about half of overall social spending in the European Union and less so overseas (see Table 27.1). These rapidly ageing societies face considerable financial sustainability problems, particularly in respect to public pay-as-you-go pensions that use yearly contributions to pay for current pensioners (World Bank, 1994). Public pension expenditure is still large across most European welfare states, though private pension pay-outs have increased and pension fund assets vastly accumulated in some multi-pillar systems such as in Anglophone countries, the Netherlands, and Switzerland. However, flexibilization of labour markets and ongoing retrenchment of benefits can lead to increased old age poverty and inequality. While the Global South has still young societies, life expectancy increases and fertility will further decline, thus population ageing is the future prospect.

Given these challenges, pension reforms have been on the political agenda for over three decades across Organisation for Economic Co-operation and Development (OECD) countries, though systemic changes were less frequent than gradual and phased-in adjustments (Myles and Pierson, 2001). The main reforms aimed at privatization, marketization, and financialization of retirement income responsibility: a shift from state to private responsibility, an emphasis on contribution-linked benefits, and a rise of pension fund capitalism across the world. Since the global financial crisis of 2008, there is more awareness that financialization generates its own problems and requires better regulation (Ebbinghaus and Wiß, 2011). The reform and governance of pension systems in ageing societies in a globalizing world is thus a major policy issue for national states and international organizations (Holzmann and Stiglitz, 2001).

While sociological research has contributed to policy debate and evaluation, the field of pension studies is multidisciplinary, including also welfare economics, political economy, policy science, and comparative politics. The comparative study of welfare state regimes (Esping-Andersen, 1990) has led to comparative studies of pension systems and their effects (Hinrichs and Lynch, 2010). The 'new politics' approach (Pierson, 2001) studied why reforms towards multi-pillar pensions were rather gradual and path dependent. Sociological approaches have added a life-course perspective (Kohli, 2007; Mayer, 2009) in studying late careers, retirement patterns, and old age income and living situations across different societies (Blossfeld et al., 2006, 2011).

This chapter will outline the main challenges due to demographic ageing, the main differences in analysing pension systems, the major pension reform trends towards multi-pillarization, the role of international organizations, and global governance issues. While mainly

Table 27.1   Social expenditure and assets for public and private pensions, OECD, 2017/2018

	Old age, survivor, and disability pensions						Pension fund assets		
	SOC % GDP	OSD % GDP	OSD % SOC	Public % GDP	Private % GDP	Private % OSD	% Global	Rank	% GDP
Core EU	**30.1**	**15.5**	**51.7**	**13.9**	**1.6**	**10.2**	**1.7**	–	–
Austria	29.5	17.1	57.9	15.6	1.5	8.7	0.1	32	6.6
Belgium	30.6	15.7	51.5	14.5	1.3	8.0	0.4	18	37.5
France	35.1	17.1	48.8	15.7	1.3	7.9	0.6	12	11.2
Germany	29.0	14.8	51.2	12.5	2.4	15.9	0.6	11	8.1
Luxembourg	22.6	11.9	52.6	11.0	0.9	7.2	0.0	56	2.9
Southern EU	**26.7**	**16.5**	**61.6**	**15.7**	**0.8**	**4.6**	**0.9**	–	–
Greece	25.6	17.4	67.8	17.2	0.2	1.0	0.0	57	1.0
Italy	29.5	18.8	63.5	17.5	1.3	6.9	0.5	14	12.7
Portugal	25.2	15.5	61.4	14.5	1.0	6.3	0.1	33	11.4
Spain	25.2	14.3	56.7	13.8	0.4	3.1	0.4	19	14.4
Eastern EU	**19.2**	**10.5**	**55.1**	**10.4**	**0.1**	**1.1**	**0.2**	–	–
Czech Republic	19.4	10.1	51.9	9.6	0.4	4.3	0.0	34	9.6
Hungary	20.0	10.1	53.1	10.1	0.0	0.1	0.0	45	5.6
Estonia	17.3	8.9	51.1	8.9	0.0	0.0	0.0	47	21.5
Latvia	16.0	9.3	58.4	9.3	0.0	0.0	0.0	48	19.5
Lithuania	15.8	8.6	54.3	8.5	0.1	1.4	0.0	49	9.5
Slovak Republic	18.5	10.1	54.5	9.5	0.5	5.4	0.0	40	14.4
Slovenia	22.8	12.3	54.1	12.3	0.0	0.0	0.0	53	7.9
Poland	21.3	12.8	60.2	12.8	0.0	0.0	0.1	31	6.5
Nordic Union	**28.8**	**16.0**	**55.5**	**12.8**	**3.2**	**21.7**	**5.9**	–	–
Denmark	33.0	17.2	52.3	14.5	2.7	15.7	1.8	8	238.9
Finland	31.0	17.3	55.8	16.5	0.7	4.3	0.3	21	56.1
Iceland	22.5	12.4	55.1	6.1	6.3	51.2	0.1	29	205.6
Norway	27.8	16.1	58.1	13.6	2.6	15.8	0.1	27	12.5
Sweden	29.8	16.8	56.4	13.2	3.6	21.5	1.1	9	95.0
Multipillar	–	**15.4**	–	**9.3**	**6.1**	**39.9**	**6.3**	–	–
Netherlands	30.1	15.0	50.0	8.9	6.2	41.0	4.0	4	210.3
Switzerland	–	15.8	–	9.7	6.1	38.8	2.3	7	149.1
Anglophone	**25.6**	**11.7**	**45.2**	**7.3**	**4.4**	**34.8**	**82.4**	–	–

	Old age, survivor, and disability pensions						Pension fund assets		
	SOC % GDP	OSD % GDP	OSD % SOC	Public % GDP	Private % GDP	Private % OSD	% Global	Rank	% GDP
Australia	23.3	12.2	52.6	7.2	5.0	41.1	3.5	5	131.8
Canada	25.1	11.1	43.9	5.6	5.5	49.5	5.6	3	174.1
Ireland	16.3	6.4	39.4	5.5	0.9	14.8	0.3	22	34.4
New Zealand	19.3	7.3	37.6	7.3	0.0	0.0	0.2	25	33.9
UK	26.9	13.6	50.6	7.8	5.8	42.4	6.3	2	118.5
US	30.9	13.6	44.1	8.1	5.6	40.9	66.6	1	164.8
Latin America	**12.8**	**5.0**	**38.6**	**4.3**	**0.7**	**12.5**	**1.1**	–	–
Chile	15.1	5.4	35.7	3.5	1.9	34.5	0.4	17	75.8
Colombia	15.7	6.6	42.2	5.9	0.7	10.9	0.2	23	29.8
Costa Rica	12.4	5.5	42.2	5.2	0.2	4.5	0.0	37	37.0
Mexico	7.9	2.6	34.4	2.6	0.0	0.0	0.5	15	20.4
East Asia	**19.0**	**9.8**	**46.5**	**8.1**	**1.7**	**17.6**	**3.4**	–	–
Japan	25.2	14.9	59.0	12.4	2.5	17.0	3.0	6	29.5
Korea	12.8	4.6	34.0	3.8	0.8	18.2	0.5	16	13.3

Note: Own calculations based on OECD social expenditure 2017/2018, OECD Global Pension Statistics (2020); underlined countries were double weighted in regional average; except single sum of pension fund assets global percentage; OSD = old age, survivor, and disability, SOC = social expenditure.
Source: Data from 2018 (or 2017) pension fund (and DC plan) assets: 2020 (ranked among 69 countries).

focusing on ageing and pensions in advanced economies, the contribution will also discuss implications for the Global South.

GLOBAL CHALLENGES

Demographic ageing has become a global mega-trend (Rowland, 2009): advances in life expectancy were made initially among the newly born and subsequently among adults throughout the twentieth century across the more developed world. Prolonged life expectancy and declining birth rates both contributed to rapid demographic ageing, with a shift toward ageing societies across the Global North. While at the beginning of the millennium, about one older person (65+) in five people lived in advanced economies (but only 7 per cent worldwide), the share of this group (and thus the 'grey voter' block) is forecast to double by 2050 (albeit 16 per cent worldwide) with considerable economic consequences. Demographic ageing in the Global South is slower as life expectancy increases with a delay and societies are still very young due to higher birth rates. Although older people are still a smaller group, they are tripling from 5 per cent in 2000 to 14 per cent in 2050, thus ever more also need income support.

From an economic perspective, old age dependency (older people 65+ in percentage of the working population 16–64) is crucial for burden sharing: it doubled from 22 per cent in 2000 to 47 per cent in 2050 for developed countries (Rowland, 2009). While more than two people in working age supported one elderly person in the past, this will be one to one within a few decades. Thanks to life expectancy increases, the period in retirement will augment if retirement age is not increased at the same pace (Ebbinghaus and Hofäcker, 2013). Although migration influx might alleviate the demographic pressure concurrently, it will not alleviate this in the long run since young migrants grow old and will draw on pensions in their host countries. Advocates of funded pensions instead call for investment in still demographically growing societies to achieve higher returns, albeit at higher investment risks.

A further link between globalization and welfare state retrenchment is much debated (Heimberger, 2021; Rieger and Leibfried, 2003). Advanced economies are exposed to increased competition through economic globalization, they thus have limited possibilities to finance demographic ageing through higher contributions or taxes, particularly given fierce labour cost competition from younger societies. In contrast, some argue that advanced welfare states, particularly in open economies, tend to compensate for the volatility of world markets through automatic stabilizers during economic downturns (Garrett, 2000). While this compensation thesis explains some generous welfare states that remain competitive, overall economic pressures and fiscal constraints have increased over time.

Following rising public debt during the twentieth century and the Great Recession of 2008, there are also considerable constraints on public borrowing as a strategy to finance pension liabilities. The European Monetary Union has set strict 'Maastricht' criteria for public debt (less than 60 per cent of gross domestic product (GDP)) and borrowing limits (3 per cent), putting fiscal limits on member states (in addition to national 'debt breaks' such as in Germany). The International Monetary Fund (IMF) and European Union (EU) exercised additional reform pressures during the Euro sovereign debt crisis of 2010, and rating agencies downgrade countries with unsustainable liabilities with similar effect.

Demographic ageing, international competition, and fiscal limits are seen as major challenges to welfare states, particularly public pay-as-you-go pensions relying on workers financing retirees. The call for funded pensions, in line with overall financialization (van der Zwan, 2014), also entails risks, most evident in the financial market crisis. Following the 2008 crash, returns were negative or below expectations, leading to increased liabilities of defined benefit (DB) schemes or immediate losses in defined contribution (DC) schemes for those relying on savings for their retirement (Ebbinghaus, 2015). Where home ownership is important in retirement, the financial crisis led many to run into difficulties to pay their mortgage. Moreover, in search for higher returns, pension fund investment in housing feeds rising housing prizes for working people and increases rents for pensioners.

PENSION SYSTEM TYPOLOGIES, PILLARS, AND TIERS

In industrializing societies, age-related disability and old age were seen as a 'social risk' in need of public provision, institutionalizing retirement through income support via pensions (Atchley, 1982). Welfare states mandated social insurances or tax-financed public pensions to reduce poverty due to incapacity or old age. The introduction of old age and disability pensions as social insurance or basic benefits were spread by diffusion (Hu and Manning, 2010) across industrializing countries and later more globally. From the first old age social insurance in Germany and a people's pension in Denmark in the 1890s, most European countries introduced retirement income support during the early twentieth century (Kuhnle and Sander, 2010). Beyond Europe, the United States (US) introduced social security for the old with the New Deal in 1935 in order to alleviate the Great Depression. Since the 1950s, many advanced economies expanded the scope and generosity of pensions, providing poverty reduction through means-tested or universal public pensions, while also adding contributory supplementary pensions of a mixed variety of public and private providers. While pension provision was introduced across Latin America in the formal economy relatively early, non-contributory social pensions have emerged since the 1970s across emerging economies and post-colonial societies in the Global South (Böger and Leisering, 2020).

The main purpose of pensions is to secure income throughout retirement, allowing people to partially if not fully withdraw from work. Two major goals of public pension policy, weighted differently across countries (Hinrichs and Lynch, 2010), are the reduction of poverty risks in old age (independent of prior contributions) and the maintenance of living standards previously achieved during working life (in line with contributions). Poverty reduction is achieved either by providing a universal basic pension to all residents or means-tested social assistance for those in need; both are usually tax-financed. Income maintenance is the result of public earnings-related contributory (pay-as-you-go) schemes and/or private supplementary schemes with DB or DC plans that are usually prefunded. There might also be social pension provisions in contributory public schemes, guaranteeing a social pension for those who have contributed for a minimum period or meet an income test.

In comparative pension system analysis (Immergut et al., 2007; Ebbinghaus, 2011), it is common to distinguish between two models (Bonoli, 2003): (1) Bismarckian social insurance which aims at status maintenance beyond work through earnings-related contributory pensions with pay-as-you-go financing; and (2) Beveridgean basic pension, providing universal (tax-financed) flat-rate benefits to all citizens/residents, aimed at poverty reduction. While there are further variations in respect to more or less redistributive elements (such as minimum pension, care-giving credits, etc.) in Bismarckian systems, the Beveridge basic pension model gives rise to additional pillars filling the income gap for those above the poverty line.

In respect to governance of pensions, i.e. the question who is responsible, it is common to distinguish three pillars (Leimgruber, 2012): the first (public), the second (occupational), and third (personal) pillars. In addition, we can distinguish several layers in the income function of retirement income provision (Ebbinghaus, 2011): first-tier minimum income provision (basic pension or means-tested social assistance) to combat poverty among older people, a second tier of (usually mandatory) contributory pension for most working people, and additional topping up (often voluntary) saving schemes for the higher-income groups.

During the last century, reducing poverty in old age was the pressing aim, though with some variations according to the pension system (Ebbinghaus, 2021; van Vliet et al., 2019). Inequality in retirement income reproduced some of the market-income differences during working age, partly due to labour market attachment but also uneven pension coverage. Today's pension systems provide low poverty and inequality rates in Nordic and some Central Eastern European countries, while Bismarckian Germany and Beveridge-model Britain are only in a middle position, though some European countries in the periphery are worse off (also Switzerland). In North America and other Anglophone countries, poverty rates tend to be high. In the Global South (where such data are available), poverty and inequality rates are also high due to a lack of adequate pensions. By and large, only employees in the formal economy are insured and therefore minimum income support is crucial to fight poverty (Böger and Leisering, 2020).

PENSION REFORMS ACROSS THE GLOBE

In advanced economies, pension systems were well established and extended during the golden age of welfare expansion by the 1970s (Ferrera, 2008). The two oil shocks of the 1970s, leading to mass unemployment and slower growth, led to a debate about the 'growth to limits' of welfare states (Flora, 1986). With ever earlier retirement despite increased life expectancy, the sustainability of pensions was questioned, not least by international organizations and economic experts. The Greenspan Commission on Social Security Reform advanced a major readjustment of US pensions through a gradual increase in retirement age and other measures. Similarly, under the Conservative Thatcher government, retrenchment was under discussion but led to fewer grand reforms than planned. Pierson's study of US and United Kingdom reform efforts argued that retrenchment was politically difficult given the popularity of acquired rights and the blame avoidance of politicians (Pierson, 1994).

The 'New Politics' (Pierson, 2001) approach claimed that policy feedback led to path-dependent, gradual adaptation. Systematic change is difficult in public pay-as-you-go pension systems, in which the working population pays for the current pensions of retired people who had contributed in the past. A systemic change to funded pensions was only possible through a long transition, given the 'double-payer' problem (Myles and Pierson, 2001) for the current working generation: honouring the acquired rights of pensioners while asking them to also save for their own future.

Since the 1990s, the economic policy community pushed towards a multi-pillar pension system, while politicians, public opinion and organized labour were more reluctant to embrace far-reaching reforms. Nevertheless, reform efforts were multiple (Ebbinghaus, 2015; van der Zwan, 2014):

- *Privatization* involves a shift in responsibility from the state to private actors. This could involve an occupational pension promised by employers via trusts for their employees, collectively negotiated pension schemes jointly held by employers and unions, or individuals' responsibility to save for a personal pension provided by the financial service sector.
- *Marketization* would strength the link between contribution and benefits through actuarial calculations and demographic formula in DB or returns on capital in DC schemes.
- *Financialization* is the reliance on prefunded savings, the importance of seeking higher returns in investments in global financial markets.

These reforms towards a multi-pillar system show considerable variations, depending on the pension system legacy and political economy. Beveridge-type pension systems with a basic pension and top-up earnings-related pensions tended to have already more private occupational and personal pension pillars with funded pensions at a time when a Bismarckian social insurance system with earnings-related generous pensions started to develop supplementary funded pensions (Ebbinghaus, 2011).

In Bismarckian pension systems, parametric changes such as increasing contributions, altering benefit formulas, and gradually increasing the retirement age were the first cautious steps; later steps introduced some forms of funded pensions as 'institutional layering' without changing the core provision (Palier, 2010; Ebbinghaus, 2011). In Beveridgean systems with multi-pillar systems, reforms led to an increased reliance on funded options, while the minimum income function of public pensions gained more attention. For example, in Britain, 'nudging' strategies that relied on behavioural economics to boost voluntary savings led to an increase in coverage for workplace-related pensions, while the basic pension was improved (Hills, 2006). Across the globe, the funded multi-pillarization policies were advanced by international organizations even in systems which lacked sufficient public pension pillars (Brooks, 2007; Holzmann, 2013).

TRANSNATIONAL POLICY ADVOCACY

International organizations have played a role in the diffusion of pension policies ever since the foundation of the International Labour Organization in 1919. The International Labour Organization (ILO) is a global tripartite forum of governments, trade unions, and employer organizations, adopting labour and social rights conventions. The OECD publishes regular reports on demographic ageing, the need for pension reform, and active ageing. The EU, particularly since its Lisbon strategy, developed the 'open method of coordination' (Eckardt, 2005) to facilitate transnational learning on pension and other social policy reforms, calling, for instance, on increasing retirement age and old age employment across Europe.

The Washington Consensus propagated by the IMF and World Bank has propagated the multi-pillar pension model since the 1990s (Holzmann, 2000): adding to the public basic provision which also funded occupational and private pillars. As Latin America faced financial crises from the 1980s and Eastern Europe transformed into market economies in the 1990s, the World Bank advocated a shift toward mandatory funded pensions, though it led to a partial reversal following the 2008 financial market crash (Orenstein, 2011). More recently, there has been a paradigm shift in the World Bank and ILO due to political and staff changes (Heneghan and Orenstein, 2019) towards a reassessment of welfare provision as an automatic stabilizer during crises.

Financialization as a global trend affected also pension financing, while the multi-pillar shift further intensified financialization across advanced economies (Dore, 2008; van der Zwan, 2014; Natali, 2018). With the rise of 'pension fund capitalism' (Ebbinghaus, 2015), large pension schemes and sovereign funds became global investors. The US and other Anglophone economies hold four fifths of global pension fund assets, the US alone two-thirds (see Table 27.1). US pension funds held assets of 20 trillion US dollars (or 95 per cent of US GDP) and other retirement vehicles of 14 trillion (or 28 per cent of US GDP); in total these US investments are two-thirds of all OECD pension-related assets (OECD, 2021). US pension funds hold a third of their assets in equities, another quarter in collective investments, and another in bonds. A further 10 trillion US dollars in assets are held by British, Australian, Canadian, Japanese, and Swiss funds. Large continental European economies, such as Germany or Italy, however, play only a minor role globally, though some Nordic and Dutch funds are relatively large in respect to their economies.

Pension financialization has a global impact, particularly concentrated in institutional investors in some advanced economies that rely on funded pension pillars. Shareholder interests are concentrated in some state-controlled funds, while they are more scattered in private sectors, dominated by some multinationals, many large to small company trust funds but also collectively negotiated schemes (Netherlands, Nordic countries, US). The top 300 pension and sovereign funds combine 20 trillion US dollars (Pensions & Investment, 2020), about two-thirds of all global pension fund assets. Among the largest are state-run 'silver' funds (a third of global pension fund assets) and public-sector pensions (another third) from East Asia (Japan, South Korea, Singapore, China), the Netherlands, and Nordic countries. While international accounting standards of multinationals have put pressure on these private companies to shift from DB to DC schemes, thereby giving up responsibility for covering any shortfalls during a crisis, 60 per cent of the top 300 assets are still DB schemes.

The United Nations' 'Transforming our World: The 2030 Agenda for Sustainable Development' (2015) set a number of global goals for future policy. There is a growing awareness that stakeholders in pension funds, such as employee or union representatives but also consumer activists, might be able to seek social, ethic, and green investment strategies. Pension funds investing in green and ethical agribusiness, health, technology, or energy have been found to yield higher than market returns (Martí-Ballester, 2020). Trade unions have also campaigned for advancing labour standards and social rights via union-controlled, collectively negotiated, or stakeholder-influenced funds. The EU developed the Institute of Occupational Retirement Provision for pension funds across the EU single market in lieu of national regulation (Autenne, 2017). Pension fund governance is discussed also at the international level (particularly OECD and IMF), while the social aspects remain the concern of the ILO and World Bank.

GLOBAL GOVERNANCE ISSUES: AN OUTLOOK

Pensions have become a major institution in modern societies, spreading among advanced economies to provide relatively elaborate public and private provisions. With some delay we see also a spread of some public pension provision and reliance on private pensions in the emerging economies of the Global South. Given demographic ageing and international competition, financial sustainability of public pay-as-you-go pensions has come under scrutiny, leading to a multitude of adaptation and a shift towards multi-pillar pensions. While the Great Recession and the recent pandemic have shown that public pensions are an automatic stabilizer, pension fund assets often faced negative or low returns. Thus, the last decade has led to a rethinking of pension reforms by international organizations but also national governments, though any change in the pension policy area tends to be more gradual than systemic. The demographic challenges will remain an issue in advanced economies, requesting adaptions of retirement age, demographic adjustment to benefit provision, and measures to reduce poverty and inequalities produced by market processes.

From a global perspective, the rise of pension fund capitalism has led to a considerable concentration of assets in just a few large funds under state or collective control and many privately funded schemes in some of the richest economies, seen as institutional investors for good long-term returns. There are, however, many economies in the Global North as well as most countries in the Global South that have relied much less on funded capitalism, though shifts towards funded pensions might change this in the future. Informed public policy reform as well as well-designed governance and regulation will be needed to balance the different interests across generations and stakeholders. Beyond the financial sustainability concern, social science expertise on the politics of pension reforms and their social consequences will be crucial to address these pressing societal problems to develop social protection for the old while taking into consideration intergenerational equity.

REFERENCES

Atchley, R.C. (1982) Retirement as a social institution. *Annual Review of Sociology* 8: 263–287.
Autenne, A. (2017) Occupational pension funds: Governance issues at the international and European levels. *European Journal of Social Security* 19(2): 158–171.
Blossfeld, H.-P., Buchholz, S. and Hofäcker, D. (2006) *Globalization, Uncertainty and Late Careers in Society*. London: Routledge.
Blossfeld, H.-P., Buchholz, S. and Kurz, K. (2011) *Aging Populations, Globalization and the Labor Market: Comparing Late Working Life and Retirement in Modern Societies*. Cheltenham, UK and Northampton, MA, USA: Edward Elgar Publishing.
Böger, T. and Leisering, L. (2020) A new pathway to universalism? Explaining the spread of 'social' pensions in the global South, 1967–2011. *Journal of International Relations and Development* 23: 308–338.
Bonoli, G. (2003) Two worlds of pension reform in Western Europe. *Comparative Politics* 35: 399–416.
Brooks, S.M. (2007) When does diffusion matter? Explaining the spread of structural pension reforms across nations. *Journal of Politics* 69: 701–715.
Dore, R. (2008) Financialization of the global economy. *Industrial and Corporate Change* 17(6): 1097–1112.
Ebbinghaus, B. (2011) *The Varieties of Pension Governance: Pension Privatization in Europe*. Oxford: Oxford University Press.
Ebbinghaus, B. (2015) The privatization and marketization of pensions in Europe: A double transformation facing the crisis. *European Policy Analysis* 1(1): 56–73.
Ebbinghaus, B. (2021) Inequalities and poverty risks in old age across Europe: The double-edged income effect of pension systems. *Social Policy & Administration* 55(3): 440–455.
Ebbinghaus, B. and Hofäcker, D. (2013) Reversing early retirement in advanced welfare economies: A paradigm shift to overcome push and pull factors. *Comparative Population Studies* 38(4): 807–840.

Ebbinghaus, B. and Wiß, T. (2011) Taming pension fund capitalism in Europe: Collective and state regulation in times of crisis. *Transfer* 17(1): 15–28.

Eckardt, M. (2005) The open method of coordination on pensions: An economic analysis of its effects on pension reforms. *Journal of European Social Policy* 15(3): 247–267.

Esping-Andersen, G. (1990) *Three Worlds of Welfare Capitalism.* Princeton, NJ: Princeton University Press.

Ferrera, M. (2008) The European welfare state: Golden achievements, silver prospects. *West European Politics* 31(1–2): 82–107.

Flora, P. (1986) Introduction. In: Flora, P. (ed.) *Growth to Limits: The Western European Welfare States since World War II.* Berlin: de Gruyter, pp. xii–xxxvi.

Garrett, G. (2000) The causes of globalization. *Comparative Political Studies* 33(6): 941–991.

Heimberger, P. (2021) Does economic globalization affect government spending? A meta-analysis. *Public Choice* 187: 349–374.

Heneghan, M. and Orenstein, M.A. (2019) Organizing for impact: International organizations and global pension policy. *Global Social Policy* 19(1–2): 65–86.

Hills, J. (2006) From Beveridge to Turner: Demography, distribution and the future of pensions in the UK. *Journal of the Royal Statistical Society* A169(4): 663–679.

Hinrichs, K. and Lynch, J.F. (2010) Old-age pensions. In: Castles, F.G., Leibfried, S., Lewis, J., Obinger, H. and Pierson, C. (eds) *The Oxford Handbook of the Welfare State.* Oxford: Oxford University Press, pp. 353–367.

Holzmann, R. (2000) The World Bank approach to pension reform. *International Social Security Review* 53(1): 11–24.

Holzmann, R. (2013) Global pension systems and their reform: Worldwide drivers, trends and challenges. *International Social Security Review* 66(2): 1–29.

Holzmann, R. and Stiglitz, J.E. (2001) *New Ideas about Old Age Security.* Washington, DC: World Bank.

Hu, A. and Manning, P. (2010) The global social insurance movement since the 1880s. *Journal of Global History* 5(1): 125–148.

Immergut, E., Anderson, K. and Schulze, I. (2007) *The Handbook of West European Pension Politics.* Oxford: Oxford University Press.

Kohli, M. (2007) The institutionalization of the life course: Looking back to look ahead. *Research in Human Development* 4(3–4): 253–271.

Kuhnle, S. and Sander, A. (2010) The emergence of the welfare state. In: Castles, F.G., Leibfried, S., Lewis, J., Obinger, H. and Pierson, C. (eds) *The Oxford Handbook of the Welfare State.* Oxford: Oxford University Press, pp. 61–80.

Leimgruber, M. (2012) The historical roots of a diffusion process: The three-pillar doctrine and European pension debates (1972–1994). *Global Social Policy* 12(1): 24–44.

Martí-Ballester, C.P. (2020) Examining the financial performance of pension funds focused on sectors related to sustainable development goals. *International Journal of Sustainable Development & World Ecology* 27(2): 179–191.

Mayer, K.U. (2009) New directions in life course research. *American Sociological Review* 35: 413–433.

Myles, J. and Pierson, P. (2001) The comparative political economy of pension reform. In: Pierson, P. (ed.) *The New Politics of the Welfare State.* New York: Oxford University Press, pp. 305–333.

Natali, D. (2018) Occupational pensions in Europe: Trojan horse of financialization? *Social Policy & Administration* 52(2): 449–462.

OECD (2021) *Pension Funds in Figures.* Paris: OECD.

Orenstein, M.A. (2011) Pension privatization in crisis: Death or rebirth of a global policy trend? *International Social Security Review* 64(3): 65–80.

Palier, B. (2010) *A Goodbye to Bismarck? The Politics of Welfare Reforms in Continental Europe.* Amsterdam: Amsterdam University Press.

Pensions & Investment (2020) *Global Top 300 Pension Funds.* London: Thinking Ahead Institute. www .thinkingaheadinstitute.org/content/uploads/2020/11/TAI_PI300_2020.pdf

Pierson, P. (1994) *Dismantling the Welfare State? Reagan, Thatcher, and the Politics of Retrenchment.* New York: Cambridge University Press.

Pierson, P. (2001) *The New Politics of the Welfare State.* New York: Oxford University Press.

Rieger, E. and Leibfried, S. (2003) *Limits to Globalization: Welfare States and the World Economy.* Cambridge: Polity.

Rowland, D.T. (2009) Global population aging: History and prospect. In: Uhlenberg, P. (ed.) *International Handbook of Population Aging.* New York: Springer, pp. 37–65.

United Nations (2015) *Transforming Our World: The 2030 Agenda for Sustainable Development.* New York: United Nations.

van der Zwan, N. (2014) Making sense of financialization. *Socio-Economic Review* 12(1): 99–129.

van Vliet, O., Caminada, K., Goudswaard, K. and Wang, J. (2019) Poverty reduction among older people through pensions: A comparative analysis. In: Greve, B. (ed.) *Routledge International Handbook of Poverty.* London: Routledge, pp. 363–375.

World Bank (1994) *Averting the Old Age Crisis: Policies to Protect the Old and Promote Growth.* Oxford: Oxford University Press.

28. Globalization and the transition from work to retirement

Dirk Hofäcker, Stefanie König and Moritz Heß

INTRODUCTION

Over the last decades, the age structure of societies has undergone substantial changes. In many cases, the interplay of declining fertility and improvements in health, which led to an increase in life expectancy, have resulted in a gradual ageing of societies (Harper 2015). Low fertility is particularly common in Western industrialized countries, where it will lead to an overall decrease in population numbers if it is not counteracted by migration. Yet, the aforementioned changes have not only led to dwindling populations as a whole, but also to changes in the working population. The share of people in working age is lowered by extended education while the share of older people is increasing due to better health and longevity. If retirement ages are not increasing at the same time, this will result in a decline in the working-age population.

Yet, while the process of population ageing is particularly pronounced in Western industrialized countries, it represents a 'Global phenomenon' (United Nations 2019). While in Europe and North America the percentage of those aged 65 and above (as of the total population) is projected to rise from 18.7 in 2022 to 26.9 in 2050, similar figures are expected for Eastern and South East Asian countries (6.4 in 2022, 25.7 in 2050). Figures for Sub-Saharan Africa (expected to rise from 3.3 to. 4.7) and North Africa and West Asia (from 5.5 to 12.5) start from a significantly lower point of departure, yet, they nonetheless point towards gradual future population ageing also in these countries (data from United Nations 2022: 8).

Increasingly, concerns are being raised that the ageing of societies is putting pressure on the financial sustainability of social security systems, particularly in so-called public pay-as-you-go pension systems (see also Ebbinghaus, this volume). The main reason behind these worries is that an increasing number of beneficiaries from public transfer payments – in this case particularly pensioners – is faced with a decreasing number of social security contributors – in this case particularly those in employment. In addition, the increasing cost of health and long-term care is also a financial challenge that societies will have to address (Bech et al. 2011). Particularly in countries where population and workforce ageing are most widespread, policy makers and other stakeholders have reacted to these challenges by implementing different types of pension system and labour market reforms aimed at delaying retirement and, hence, extending working live (König et al. 2016). Examples are the increase of the statutory retirement age, the closing of early retirement pathways and the investment in older workers' employability. The rationale of the reforms was that longer working lives should counterbalance current trends in the ratio of pension beneficiaries and contributors.

The chapter at hand will explore how exactly these reforms were implemented and how they have impacted on older workers and their labour market engagement. It will first describe the general policy shift from early retirement to extending working lives. It then explores how late-career employment and retirement transitions have developed against the background of this policy shift with a particular focus on social inequalities in late career and retirement. In the description of trends, we will largely focus on developments in modern industrialized countries, given data constraints; yet our findings will outline some general developmental alternatives relevant for setting the political course in other countries as well. The chapter ends with a summary of results and some recommendations for future policies.

POLICY SHIFT FROM EARLY RETIREMENT TO EXTENDING WORKING LIVES

Early Retirement

Looking historically at the development of older workers' employment throughout the last decades, there was an emphasis on early retirement, especially in times of crisis. Early retirement policies were a popular measure to adjust to economic shocks. Already during the oil crisis in the 1970s, a wave of early retirement occurred as a consequence of mass unemployment and favourable options for older workers to retire. Previous studies described these phases of predominantly early retirement as being the result of the interaction of so-called *push* and *pull* factors (e.g. Ebbinghaus 2006; Hofäcker and Radl 2016; Kohli et al. 1991). Pull factors referred to financial incentives, provided by either the state or employers, which offered individuals an attractive and socially acceptable opportunity to leave the labour market early. In contrast, push factors referred to conditions that – metaphorically speaking – pushed individuals out of the labour market involuntarily, i.e. when older workers were made redundant for operational reasons.

Previous literature has explicitly linked the expansion of early retirement policies to the acceleration of globalization processes since the 1970s (Blossfeld et al. 2006; Buchholz et al. 2009; see also Blossfeld and Blossfeld, this volume). Early retirement offers and early exit pathways via other social security benefits were used as a socially acceptable way to 'make space' for younger cohorts pushing into the labour market. Older workers were more commonly employed in more traditional labour market segments in the production sector, which became less and less important during the shift from an industrial to a knowledge-based society. At the same time, rapidly accelerating market transactions as well as increasing competition from Asia – especially Japan – made it necessary for labour market actors at the national as well as the enterprise level to adapt more swiftly to changing market conditions. Such flexibility demands often stood in contrast to the employment situation of older workers. In contrast to younger workers, they often earned higher 'seniority wages' and benefited from higher levels of employment protection. At the same time, their education and occupational qualifications, often acquired early in their careers and not consistently updated thereafter, were considered to become increasingly outdated in times of rapid technological change. Early retirement policies thus provided a welcome opportunity to solve the perceived contradiction between high employment costs and outdated qualification profiles by sending older employees into a socially accepted state of retirement.

Such early exit measures were extensively used in conservative Central European welfare states (Hess 2016). Through offering early retirement programmes, national policy makers could fight unemployment in a socially compatible way. Early exit incentives were offered via different 'early retirement pathways': for example, early pensions for those who had contributed to the pension system for a certain amount of time. Unemployment insurance and disability pensions were also used as early retirement pathways. Trade unions frequently supported these programmes as they provided their members with a 'comfortable' labour market exit before the statutory retirement with low or even no pension reductions (Ebbinghaus and Hofäcker 2013). Firms could top up these benefits through additional payments – so-called 'golden handshakes' – and thereby increase their flexibility in allocating their staff. Such combined financial incentives for retirement well before the statutory retirement age were at the core of the early retirement policy in European countries during the 1980s and 1990s. In some countries, the policy of early retirement was accompanied by an emerging 'culture of early retirement' in which a labour exit well before the statutory retirement was the social rule rather than the exception.

Extending Working Lives

After the financial crisis in the 1990s, a paradigmatic shift from early retirement to extended working lives could be observed (e.g. Ebbinghaus and Hofäcker 2013). One main driver of this shift was rapid population ageing and the resulting financial pressure on the pension systems as described above. In some countries, this was accompanied by a lack of skilled labour, which is assumed to become even more pronounced with the large Baby Boomer cohorts leaving the labour market. Delaying retirement and extending working lives were considered to be a possible solution to these challenges, as they would provide the labour market and companies with skilled and experienced workers while at the same time balancing the ratio of pension beneficiaries and contributors.

Many countries implemented reforms of their pension systems, including stricter requirements for access to early retirement routes such as disability pensions (Naumann 2014) and restrictions for other early exit. Other reforms included raising statutory retirement ages or increasing the contribution years for early retirement. Several countries have linked retirement ages or pension benefit calculations to average life expectancies (e.g. United Kingdom, Sweden, Finland, Denmark, Portugal, Italy and the Netherlands; De Tavernier and Boulhol 2021). The idea behind linking pension ages and life expectancy is that for every year of increased life expectancy the statutory retirement increases automatically by a certain number of months. In addition, pension contribution rates have been increased and occupational and private pensions were strengthened so that shortcomings in pension income from public pensions could be better compensated (Ebbinghaus 2011). In some countries, changes in pension calculation were implemented, such as the switch from defined benefit to defined contribution systems and partial replacement from pay-as-you-go to fully funded pension systems (Börsch-Supan and Courney 2018). These described changes and reforms occurred in many countries across the globe. Between 1995 and 2021, retirement ages increased in 63 countries, contribution rates increased in 79 countries and benefit calculations were adjusted in order to decrease pension benefits in 62 countries (FIAP 2021).

Multiple political actors have urged to complement such purely pension-oriented measures with so-called policies of 'active ageing' (Jepsen et al. 2002) that not only increase the economic incentives of working longer, but also improve the 'employability' of older workers, i.e. their ability to remain employed. Such measures included active labour market policies specifically targeted at older workers, the improvement of working conditions as well as education and training policies to reduce possible qualification deficits of the older workforce (e.g. Council of the European Union 2012; Eurofound 2017; OECD 2006). Existing research shows that such measures have been introduced in different welfare regimes. Yet, the degree to which this has taken place clearly varies and often the extent of such reforms falls behind that of the pension reforms described above (Hofäcker et al. 2016; OECD 2019). Despite active ageing reforms, older workers' participation in continued education and training, for example, is still significantly below that of their younger counterparts (OECD 2020).

The shift from early to late retirement was described in academic contributions as complementing push and pull factors with two additional institutional mechanisms. While push and pull factors mainly promoted either voluntary or involuntary early retirement, the two new categories referred to the voluntary and involuntary prolongation of working life. Factors that promoted the postponement of retirement transitions through investments in older workers' employability were described as *maintain* factors. These include facilitation of continued work, e.g. through supported jobs or continued education and training. On the other hand, factors that increased the pressure to continue working out of financial necessity were referred to as so-called *need* factors (Hofäcker and Radl 2016).

RETIREMENT TRANSITIONS IN THE CHANGING POLICY CONTEXT

Developments in Older Workers' Aggregate Employment

Following the extensive set of reforms aiming at prolonged working lives, a clear increase in older workers' employment rates could be observed (OECD 2019). This increase was partly due to improvements in overall health (Laun and Palme 2018), higher educational levels (Qi 2016) and a better integration of women into the labour market (Eurofound and European Commission Joint Research Centre 2021). However, changes in policies played an important role as well (Boissoneault et al. 2019; Gruber and Wise 1999).

Figure 28.1 displays the development in employment rates between the 1980s and 2019, i.e. from the 'heyday' of early retirement policies up to the period with an increasing focus on active ageing. For an overview, figures are given for both the European Union as well as the Organisation for Economic Co-operation and Development (OECD) and are divided by gender.

Despite considerable variation in employment rates cross-nationally, there generally is a clear trend towards higher employment among the age group 60 to 64 years across both OECD and European countries. For women, we observe a continuous increase due to their persistently rising integration into the labour market. However, even among women, there is a more rapid increase since the 2000s, i.e. the onset of active ageing policies. Nevertheless, female old age labour participation remains still below male employment rates. Among men, a drop around the 1990s can be observed, yet employment rates of 60–64-year-old men have recovered since the early 2000s. For men and women in Europe, employment rates among this age group increased more rapidly compared to the OECD average, thereby leading to a gradual convergence between the two groups of countries.

Focusing more specifically on male employment rates and national trends, the most drastic changes took place in Germany and the Netherlands, but also in Eastern European countries

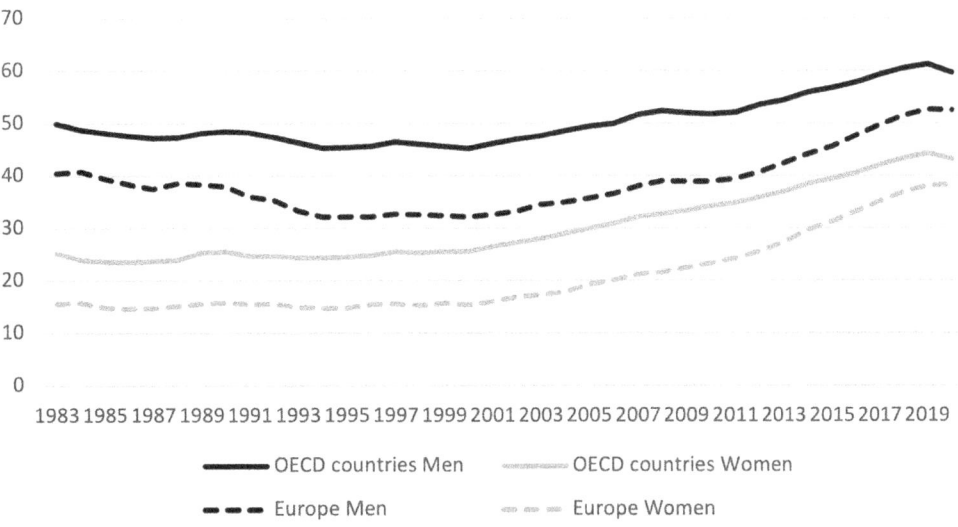

Source: Labour Force Survey for European Union (2020); OECD (2022).

Figure 28.1   *Employment rate age 60–64*

such as the Czech Republic, where employment rates increased from below 30 per cent to over 60 per cent between the early 1990s and 2020 (OECD 2022). With employment rates above 60 per cent, these countries approximated other historically late exit countries, such as the United States, Canada, Israel and Sweden. Other European examples also reveal clear increases in employment but remain on much lower levels, such as Austria, France and Slovak Republic (between 34 and 42 per cent).

These trends can be perceived positively from a macro-economic perspective, given that longer working lives lead to reduced pressures on pension systems through longer periods of contributions and overall less time in retirement. In addition, longer working lives result in higher tax revenues and provide the labour market with skilled and experienced employees; they thus can mitigate labour shortages in some countries and sectors so that also employers benefit. Older workers build up higher pension claims, which is also positive. However, it can be problematic from an individual's perspective when delayed retirement is not desired but necessary to secure a sufficient pension.

Inequalities in Extending Working Life

Even though there is a general trend towards better health and longer working lives, there are variations between different societal groups in the degree to which they can navigate their late careers and retirement transitions.

Those in a high socio-economic position are often in a relatively advantageous situation. Data on retirement preferences show that they are best able to adapt their retirement plans to the active ageing paradigm (Hess 2017; Hofäcker 2014). They more often are employed under comparatively favourable working conditions and have a high intrinsic motivation to work. They are often able and willing to continue their employment and are fostered in this endeavour by their employers. Hence, they more often retire late and primarily do so for voluntary reasons, stating primarily non-financial reasons for working longer (Hess 2018; Hofäcker et al. 2019). At the same time, their higher retirement age implies higher pension claims, often not only from public pensions but also from occupational and private pensions to which they have better access. They hence have more agency over their retirement timing as they can better 'afford' pension cuts in the case of early retirement.

In contrast, those in lower socio-economic positions are more often found in precarious occupational positions with low earnings. Their lower income correlates with low pension capital, which in turn frequently forces them to delay their labour market exit due to financial pressure. At the same time, they are maintained less by their employers due to their lower human capital and often show also lower motivation to continue working (Hofäcker et al. 2019). Often, they are working in occupations that are threatened by automatization and technological change. Such workers thus often face the contradiction between the need to work longer and few opportunities or personal willingness to do so. They are either pushed out of the labour market early (with negative consequences for their pension) or work longer involuntarily (Hofäcker et al. 2019).

These trends raised the concern that there are rising social inequalities in retirement decisions (Hess et al. 2016) and a risk for increasing economic inequalities among older people (ISF 2020). Social inequalities between educational or occupational groups are further amplified by differential patterns in life expectancy. Existing research shows that life expectancy is not increasing equally across different social groups. Women have a higher life expectancy than men, but there are not many gender differences for healthy life expectancy, which means remaining years in good health. Lower-educated individuals have a lower life expectancy than higher-educated individuals (Mäki et al. 2013) and the same applies for certain occupational groups, mainly those with lower qualifications (Deeg et al. 2021). Thus, in general, a lower socio-economic position is associated with a lower life expectancy. While individuals from this group are expected to (and in some cases also tend to) work longer, their remaining time that would be spent in retirement is shorter than for those in a higher socio-economic position. Lower-qualified individuals thus not only are disadvantaged in the disposal about their retirement decision; they also disproportionately spend shorter time in (healthy) retirement.

CONCLUSION

The shift from early retirement in the 1990s to longer working lives today occurred due to improvements in health and working conditions, but also due to political efforts to increase old age employment. Pension and labour market reforms were implemented to reduce the financial repercussions of ageing societies for social security systems, which increased the financial incentives for older employees to work longer. The main components of these reforms were increases in pension age, cuts in pension benefits and restrictions of early retirement pathways. At the same time, though not always to the same degree, policies were implemented to simultaneously improve the employability of older workers through active labour market policies and continued education and training.

The juxtaposition of these changes in the political landscape with actual employment patterns among older workers showed that, while older workers' employment generally has increased, social inequalities between older workers in the ability to work longer have equally risen. While older workers, particularly the higher qualified, have the possibility to adjust to these changes by continuing to work under favourable working conditions and in good health, there are other workers who are unable to do so. Particularly lower-educated older workers with strenuous working conditions risk getting low pensions when they leave the labour market early or risk compromising their health if they involuntarily choose to continue working due to financial reasons. Confronting older workers with the challenges of a flexible, globalized labour market without sufficiently investing in their employability and/or pension security may thus come at the expense of increasing social inequalities among the older population.

The most recent political debates recognize this concern. Particularly international organizations have renewed and intensified their call for more comprehensive active ageing policies, as outlined earlier (e.g. Business Europe et al. 2017; OECD 2020, 2019). Yet, not all groups of older workers may be able to actively profit from such measures, e.g. due to qualification or health restrictions. Thus, several countries are discussing ways to either allow older workers to retire earlier or to increase their pension. A recent report described these efforts and different reforms aiming to facilitate early retirement for certain groups (ISF 2021). Some of these programmes include the newly implemented Arne-pension in Denmark (Government – Denmark 2020), the years-of-service pension in Finland (ETK 2022), the financial bonus for early workers (*Frühstarterbonus*) in Austria (Federal Ministry of Social Affairs, Health, Care and Consumer Protection – Austria 2022), specific rules for early workers (*Lavoratori precoci*) in Italy (INPS 2022), lower requirements for disability pensions for individuals approaching retirement age in Sweden (Government – Sweden 2021) and early retirement options for certain occupations with physically demanding work in the Czech Republic (Senate Parliament of the Czech Republic 2021).

All these schemes have either been recently implemented or are about to be implemented. Even though they are partly directed to different groups, they all aim at compensating for new social inequalities in older age. Some schemes increase pension benefits for certain groups, while others allow for early exits without severely reduced pensions. All have in common that they are directed to either individuals with strenuous work, those who started working early and thereby have lower educational levels and/or individuals with compromised health and lower work ability (Bengtsson et al. 2022; ISF 2021).

While active ageing reforms may open new opportunities for those individuals with potential future employability, the reforms outlined above may create exit options for those individuals who will find it structurally hard to accommodate active ageing demands. The parallel implementation of both types of programmes may help to reduce inequalities, not only in the voluntariness of retirement transitions, but also in the duration of the remaining (healthy) years in retirement.

REFERENCES

Bech, M., Christiansen, T., Khoman, E., Lauridsen, J., and Weale, M. (2011). Ageing and health care expenditure in EU-15. *European Journal of Health Economics*, 12(5), 469–478.
Bengtsson, M., König, S., Schönbeck, S., and Wadensjö, E. (2022). Leaving the labor market early in Sweden: Learning from international experience. IZA Discussion Paper No. 15327.
Blossfeld, H.-P., Buchholz, S., and Hofäcker, D. (eds) (2006). *Globalization, uncertainty and late careers in society*. London: Routledge.

Boissoneault, M., Mulders, J.O., Turek, K., and Carriere, Y. (2019). A systematic review of causes of recent increases in ages of labor market exit in OECD countries. *PLoS ONE*, 15(4).

Börsch-Supan, A.H., and Courney, C. (2018). Social security programs and retirement around the world: Reforms and retirement incentives – introduction and summary. NBER working papers 25280.

Buchholz, S., Hofäcker, D., Mills, M., Blossfeld, H.-P., Kurz, K., and Hofmeister, H. (2009). Life courses in the globalization process: The development of social inequalities in modern societies. *European Sociological Re*view, 25(1), 53–71.

Business Europe, SGI Europe, SMEUNited and European Trade Union Confederation (2017). *European Social Partners Autonomous Framework Agreement on Active Ageing and an Intergenerational Approach*. Brussels.

Council of the European Union (2012). *Council Declaration on the European Year for Active Ageing and Solidarity between Generations: The Way Forward*. Brussels.

De Tavernier, W., and Boulhol, H. (2021). Automatic adjustment mechanisms in pension systems. In OECD (ed.), *Pensions at a glance 2021*. Paris: OECD Publishing.

Deeg, D., De Tavernier, W., and de Breij, S. (2021). Occupation-based life expectancy: Actuarial fairness in determining statutory retirement age. *Frontiers of Sociology*, 6, 675618.

Ebbinghaus, B. (2006). *Reforming early retirement in Europe, Japan and the USA*. Oxford: Oxford University Press.

Ebbinghaus, B. (2011). *The varieties of pension governance: Pension privatization in Europe*. Oxford: Oxford University Press.

Ebbinghaus, B., and Hofäcker, D. (2013). Overcoming early retirement in Europe. *Comparative Population Studies*, 38(4), 807–840.

ETK (2022). *Years-of-service pension*. Available at: www.etk.fi/en/finnish-pension-system/pension -security/earnings-related-pension-benefits/years-of-service-pension/

Eurofound (2017). W*orking conditions of workers of different ages: European Working Conditions Survey 2015*. Luxembourg: Publications Office of the European Union.

Eurofound and European Commission Joint Research Centre (2021). *European Jobs Monitor 2021: Gender gaps and the employment structure*. Luxembourg: European Jobs Monitor series, Publications Office of the European Union.

Federal Ministry of Social Affairs, Health, Care and Consumer Protection – Austria (2022). Compensatory allowance and pension bonus. Available at: www.sozialministerium.at/Themen/ Soziales/Sozialversicherung/Pensionsversicherung/Ausgleichszulage-und-Pensionsbonus.html

FIAP (2021). Parametric reforms in the public PAYGO pension programs 1995 – June 2021. Available at: www.fiapinternacional.org/en/parametric-reforms-in-the-public-paygo-pension-programs-1995 -june-2021/

Government – Denmark (2020). New right to early retirement. Available at: www.regeringen.dk/media/ 9875/tidlig_pension.pdf

Government – Sweden (2021). Disability pensions for older people of working age. Available at: www .regeringen.se/rattsliga-dokument/proposition/2022/04/prop.-202122220/

Gruber, J., and Wise, D.A. (1999). *Social security and retirement around the world*. Chicago: University of Chicago Press.

Harper, S. (2015). The challenges of the twenty-first-century demography. In C. Torp (ed.), *Challenges of aging: Retirement, pensions, and intergenerational justice*. Houndmills: Palgrave Macmillan, pp. 17–30.

Hess, M. (2016). Germany: A successful reversal of early retirement? In D. Hofäcker, M. Hess and S. König (eds), *Delaying retirement: Progress and challenges of active ageing in Europe, the United States and Japan*. Houndmills: Palgrave Macmillan, pp. 147–169.

Hess, M. (2017). Rising preferred retirement age in Europe: Are Europe's future pensioners adapting to pension system reforms? *Journal of Aging & Social Policy*, 29(3), 245–261.

Hess, M. (2018). Expected and preferred retirement age in Germany. *Zeitschrift für Gerontologie und Geriatrie*, 51(1), 98–104.

Hess, M., König, S., and Hofäcker, D. (2016). Retirement transitions under changing institutional conditions: Towards increasing inequalities? Comparing evidence from 13 countries. In D. Hofäcker, M. Hess and S. König (eds), *Delaying retirement: Progress and challenges of active ageing in Europe, the United States and Japan*. Houndmills: Palgrave Macmillan, pp. 363–378.

Hofäcker, D. (2014). In line or at odds with active ageing policies? Exploring patterns of retirement preferences in Europe. *Ageing & Society*, 35(7), 1529–1556.

Hofäcker, D., and Radl, J. (2016). Retirement transitions in times of institutional change: Theoretical concept. In D. Hofäcker, M. Hess and S. König (eds), *Delaying retirement: Progress and challenges of active ageing in Europe, the United States and Japan*. Houndmills: Palgrave Macmillan, pp. 1–21.

Hofäcker, D., Hess, M., and König, S. (eds) (2016). *Delaying retirement: Progress and challenges of active ageing in Europe, the United States and Japan*. Houndmills: Palgrave Macmillan.

Hofäcker, D., Hess, M., and König, S. (2019). Wandel von Ruhestandsübergängen im politischen Paradigmenwechsel Europas. *Zeitschrift für Gerontologie und Geriatrie*, 52(Supplement 1), 40–51.

INPS (2022). Pension for early workers. Available at: https://www.inps.it/en/en.information-english .pensions.types-of-pension.pension-for-early-workers.html

ISF (Swedish Social Insurance Inspectorate) (2020). Tidig och sen pensionering. Report 2020:7.

ISF (Swedish Social Insurance Inspectorate) (2021). Options for early retirement. Report 2021:7.

Jepsen, M., Foden, D., and Hutsebaut, M. (eds) (2002). *Active strategies for older workers*. Brussels: European Trade Union Institute.

Kohli, M., Rein, M., Guillemard, A.-M., and van Gunsteren, H. (eds) (1991). *Time for retirement: Comparative studies of early exit from the labour force*. Cambridge: Cambridge University Press.

König, S., Hess, M., and Hofäcker, D. (2016). Trends and determinants of retirement transition in Europe, the United States and Japan: A comparative overview. In D. Hofäcker, M. Hess and S. König (eds), *Delaying retirement: Progress and challenges of active ageing in Europe, the United States and Japan*. Houndmills: Palgrave Macmillan, pp. 23–51.

Labour Force Survey (2020). Employment rates in Europe. Available at: https://ec.europa.eu/eurostat/ statistics-explained/index.php?title=EU_labour_force_survey_%E2%80%93_data_and_publication

Laun, L., and Palme, M. (2018). Kan seniorer arbeta längre? Delegationen för senior arbetskraft. Report 1, S 2018:10.

Mäki, N., Martikainen, P., Eikemo, T., Menvielle, G., Lundberg, O., Ostergren, O., Jasilionis, D., and Mackenbach, J. (2013). Educational differences in disability-free life expectancy: A comparative study of long-standing activity limitation in eight European countries. *Social Science & Medicine*, 94, 1–8.

Naumann, E. (2014). Raising the retirement age: Retrenchment, feedback and attitudes. In S. Kumlin and I. Stadelmann-Steffen (eds), *How welfare states shape the democratic public: Policy feedback, participation, voting, and attitudes*. London: Edward Elgar Publishing, pp. 223–243.

OECD (2006). *Ageing and employment policies: Live longer, work longer*. Paris: OECD.

OECD (2019). *Working better with age, ageing and employment policies*. Paris: OECD.

OECD (2020). *Promoting an age-inclusive workforce: Living, learning and earning longer*. Paris: OECD.

OECD (2022). Employment database. Available at: www.oecd.org/employment/emp/onlineoe cdemploymentdatabase.htm

Qi, H. (2016). *Live longer, work longer? Evidence from Sweden's ageing population*. Lund: Department of Economic History, Lund University.

Senate Parliament of the Czech Republic (2021). Draft law amending Act No. 155/1995. Available at: www.senat.cz/xqw/xervlet/pssenat/htmlhled?action=doc&value=100729

United Nations (2019). *World population ageing 2019: Highlights*. New York.

United Nations (2022). *World population prospects 2022: Summary of results*. New York.

PART VI

METHODOLOGICAL AND CONCEPTUAL LESSONS, EMERGING QUESTIONS

29. Global – and local – commodity circuits

Dawn Lyon

INTRODUCTION

Global supply chains have attracted growing interest in social science and popular literatures in recent years, including accounts that focus on global social justice, through stories of trainers, shirts, tea and fish. They also gained an unlikely prominence in public debate in the United Kingdom (UK) from early 2020 in the context of the ongoing impact of Brexit (the exit of the UK from the European Union) and the global COVID-19 pandemic. New forms of governance and regulation in imports and exports as a result of Brexit and changes in consumption practices and increases in production costs arising from the global COVID-19 pandemic led to a lack of HGV drivers and a shortage of fuel, interruptions in energy supply, empty shelves in supermarkets and news stories of queues of container ships at global ports. A lack of basic (and luxury) goods for importing countries for some populations (largely in the global north) also meant impoverished livelihoods in producing countries (largely in the global south) (Palpacuer & Smith, 2021).

Interruptions in the supply of both goods and services and shortages of commodities and/or components or the labour required to finalise them for sale highlight the complexities of global 'chains' or commodity circuits that easily go unnoticed when operating smoothly. They reveal complex configurations of politics and power across time and space and the inherent vulnerabilities of dominant just-in-time systems of provisioning – not least in access to personal protective equipment in the UK at the start of the COVID-19 pandemic when low stock levels and a surge in demand worldwide led to heightened risks for individual health-care workers (Bailey & Pierides, 2021). Recent problems in supply in the UK and elsewhere are part and parcel of the issue of the coordination of socio-economic life. The literature into global commodity or global value chains or circuits seeks to explore and explain the social organisation and operation of the global economy. The study of the trajectories of specific commodities – from cocoa to care – and the processes that bring them into being or transform them into goods and services for distribution, exchange and consumption in different parts of the world contribute to an understanding of the phenomenon of globalisation itself.

Research into the circulation of commodities is a multidisciplinary effort including from sociology, economics, anthropology, geography, political economy, international relations, management studies and more. This chapter – from a sociological starting point – takes fish and seafood as a 'sounding' to examine how commodity circuits operate. It offers an analysis which decentres the economy (Knowles, 2014, 2015; Pettinger, 2019) and seeks to recognise the varied embodied, mobile, material and interactional practices that make for the movement and manipulation of fish. Ahead of this discussion, I consider some of the key terminology and perspectives through which the movement of commodities, associated labour and social relations are cast. The chapter then discusses key studies and areas of research which illuminate the social relations of globalisation and the perspectives which social sciences bring to them, drawing on examples of flip-flops (Knowles, 2014) and tomatoes (Barndt, 2007; Harvey et al., 2002; Heuts & Mol, 2013). The final part focuses on fish and seafood (Lyon, 2016, 2020) through a discussion of communication, mobility, temporality, materiality, vitality and the production of value in local and global circuits.

TERMINOLOGY: CHAINS, NETWORKS AND CIRCUITS

Global commodity circuits account for a large share of world trade in the twenty-first century in which firms and regions across different parts of the world are linked in transnational geographies of production. However, this flexible production is a 'factory without walls' (Tsing, 2009, in Pettinger, 2019: 42), where distance and complex subcontracting mean that low pay and poor working conditions, including modern slavery, in some parts of the chain, network or circuit are not visible elsewhere – and enable lead firms to deny responsibility of knowledge of the suffering of workers and communities (Pettinger, 2019: 43). These same workers are vulnerable to the vagaries of consumption practices and the preferences of lead firms who can easily excise subcontractors from their trading networks.

Variously formulated as global supply chains, global value chains, global commodity chains and global production networks, these conceptualisations vary according to their focus on interfirm relations, politics, power relations between firms, workers, governments and activists and/or embeddedness in social, institutional and regulatory contexts. World Systems Theory in the 1970s sought to show the geography and politics of interconnectedness across nation states and corporations and the new international divisions of labour that came about through huge technological and organisational changes and the liberalisation of trade and finance at a global scale in the 1970s and 1980s (see Kano et al., 2020; Ponte et al., 2019). Development scholars in the 1990s further highlighted vast disparities in political and economic power and the unequal distribution of surplus between 'core', 'semi-periphery' and 'periphery' (terms used in the literature at the time) (Gereffi & Korzeniewicz, 1994; Hopkins & Wallerstein, 1986; Lee, 2010).

The new literature on global commodity and value chains then became a 'popular and powerful means of more precisely interrogating the specific organizational and logistical frameworks and relationships by which globalizing processes in different industry sectors occurred over time and space' (Argent, 2016: 806). However, there are problems with the conceptualisation of these forms of interconnectedness in terms of supply, value or commodity chains as they depict the circulation of commodities along stable pathways established by 'lead firms', flowing smoothly and seamlessly in space – or in a 'more-or-less flat ontological plane' in which political, environmental and social consequences are neglected (Argent, 2016: 806). Whilst the notion of circuits is an explicit attempt to depart from this assumed linearity, it cannot easily shake off all its implications. The early global commodity chain approach was criticised for emphasis on organisational linkages at the expense of attention to the human actors involved in the production and movement of commodities (Lee, 2010), and the social relationships and trajectories that constitute them. The current crises in supply reveal faltering, hold-ups, disruptions and the ongoing live and practical creation of 'routes' to move materials around the world. In this section, I draw attention to some key perspectives and associated terminology from new economic sociology, cultural economy, valuation studies and feminist global value chain analysis (including for services) to better grasp the contested understandings of global commodity chains or circuits.

The so-called new economic sociology that emerged in the Anglo-American academy in the 1980s recognised the economy as infused with social relationships, arguing that key economic processes should be subject to sociological analysis. Karl Polanyi's concept of 'embedded-ness' is central here, emphasising the economic as enmeshed in social contexts, and networks, trust, interactions, information and cultural practices have become key aspects of sociological research into economic processes (Granovetter, 1985). However, they risk contextualising the economic rather than analysing central economic processes. Polanyi's (1957) 'instituted economic processes' suggest that there are historically different ways of instituting the economic and that the boundary between economic, social, legal, political and cultural processes varies in time and space (Harvey et al., 2002: 11). For Harvey et al., this leads to a recognition of interdependencies across four interrelated processes: production, distribution, exchange and, crucially, consumption. This approach sidesteps the danger of losing sight of specifically economic processes and recognises how work activities at different points in the process are interconnected, mutually shaping one another, especially production and consumption (Glucksmann, 2009). This approach has been developed in research on recycling, call centres, ready-made food, the cultivation of tomatoes, mobile phone technologies and much more.

The emergence of 'cultural economy' perspectives has further challenged the separation of production and consumption and the economic from the socio-cultural and material as part of a 'pragmatic turn' in the study of markets and economic processes more generally (Muniesa et al., 2007). Associated with the work of Michel Callon and colleagues, cultural economy draws on Actor Network Theory, science and technology studies and the notion of 'assemblage' and contributes to a sociology of valuation. The 'performativity' of markets, including the role of economic theory and expertise as scripts for how markets happen, flips assumptions about the determinism of the economic. Instead, attention is given to the role of 'market devices' – pricing models, merchandising tools, signs and displays – which make economic calculation possible. Practices of calculation and valuation – the processes through which people differentiate between goods and assign value – include 'qualification' and 'singularisation' in which 'the gradual definition of the properties of the product' emerges, 'shaped in such a way that it can enter the consumer's world', or become 'entangled' within it. This is a 'living world' of 'commodities in motion' (Bridge and Smith, 2003: 266). If commodity chains or circuits are articulations through which value is produced, value does not reside in the commodity itself but in the relationships between commodities, producers, sellers and consumers and the social practices through which these relationships take shape. This implies attention to the specific valuation practices and processes through which commodities are produced and rendered as valuable – as in the case of Heuts and Mol's (2013) 'good tomato' which I discuss in the following section. Following Arjun Appadurai, grasping value involves tracing the 'social life of things' and 'the conditions under which economic objects circulate in different *regimes of value* in space and time' (1986: 4, emphasis in original).

A further critique of existing global commodity chains literature is its inadequate attention to relations of gender and ethnicity, including the impact of consumption practices in the Global North on different forms of work and income generation for women in particular in the Global South. Wilma Dunaway's edited collection, *Gendered Commodity Chains* (2014), highlights the role of households in global production processes. The rise of global retail in particular has transformed relations of production, distribution and sale, drawing more women into global value chains both as workers and consumers. Stephanie Barrientos' *Gender and Work in Global Value Chains* (2019) shows how women in low-income countries have been involved as workers producing goods they previously made in the home, resulting in the commercialisation of their activity. Drawing on feminist political economy and labour studies, Barrientos proposes what she calls 'Global (re)Production Networks' to grasp the impact of global retail value chains on the feminisation of labour, recognising the articulation between commercial production and social reproduction and the gendered identities that are constituted through these processes. In addition, McCarthy et al. (2021) explicitly argue that the significance of masculinity in global value chains has not been well understood with implications for governance. And Campling and Quentin (2021) propose the 'global inequality chain' to draw attention the private accumulation of wealth for firms in these chains such that workers are deprived of value and states lose their redistributive capacity.

The current supply chain crisis is as much about labour as goods and about services as well as manufacturing, as shortages of HGV drivers and workers in health and social care expose. Arlie Hochschild's concept of 'Global Care Chains' has been used to analyse the interconnectedness of cross-national care work, and to recognise 'a series of personal links between people across the globe based on the paid or unpaid work of caring' (Hochschild, 2000: 131). This involves predominantly women in the Global South leaving their own households – often including their children – to deliver care to homes in the Global North, with implications for the delivery of care in the migrants' countries of origin and for the lived experience of transnational families. The title of Rhacel Salazar Parreñas' book (2015) about Filipina women who care for members of middle-class families in Europe and the United States and who send remittances to their own parents to care for their children captures the international division of reproductive labour this rests on – they are in effect *Servants of Globalization*.

KEY STUDIES: FROM FLIP-FLOPS TO TOMATOES

Specific commodities in motion have often been the starting point for research into global and local commodity circuits, including bananas, cocoa, coffee, shirts and trainers. In this section, I select two 'objects' or 'probes' – flip-flops and tomatoes – and consider the different intellectual approaches they use to explore the complexities of the global circulation of commodities.

The subtitle of Caroline Knowles' (2014) book, *Flip-Flop: A Journey through Globalisation's Backroads*, brilliantly captures both the quiet and conspicuous ways in which global commodity production and globalisation itself take shape and place. Through her focus on a single object – the flip-flop – she tells a tale of movement and connection across geography and social and material worlds. Her mobile ethnography is both theoretically and empirically rich, offering a ground-up account of the challenges of navigation and the instability of connections, contra the idealised notion of 'flow' in the globalisation and mobilities literatures (Knowles, 2014: 7). Knowles critiques global commodity chain analysis for being blind to place, the variety of ways in which disparate places are connected and the relationship between production, distribution and landscape (Knowles, 2014: 6). She takes issue with how the lives of those involved in production are presented either as abstract labourers or solely as workers, disconnected from the broader contexts and relations in which they live. Instead, from oil extracted in Kuwait converted to petrochemicals in South Korea, she follows the small, white pellets that are transformed into flip-flops in rural-turned-industrial villages in China. They move through the port a second time as the flip-flops head onto world markets (Knowles, 2014: 62), landing in Djibouti then to Ethiopia when official and unofficial routes are entwined. She traces three trails here – to exchange at the huge outdoor Mercato; through the journeys of local people, always walking; and as discarded flip-flops make their way to a huge landfill site. Her study is a 'micro-macro patchwork' (Knowles, 2014: 6) which shows how thinking in terms of 'trails' and 'journeys' makes it possible to recognise the multiplicity of routes involved in the production, use and disposal of flip-flops and how 'they are animated by the topographies they cross, by the feet, flesh and lives, living in particular, local, connected worlds' (Knowles, 2014: 6).

My second set of examples is concerned with the global trails and interconnections of another good: the tomato. In *Exploring the Tomato* (2002), Harvey et al. consider the tomato as both an object – tracked from seed to supermarket shelf – and a probe – to offer new perspectives on change and variation in contemporary capitalism. They are critical of object biographies which are too narrowly focused, failing to capture the linkages and contexts that exceed them. Instead, 'it is necessary to step outside single and linear analysis': for instance, to appreciate the tomato and its production into ketchup, it is essential to consider the hamburger in the United States diet especially (Harvey et al., 2002: 10–11). The ketchup bottle is understood as a socio-economic institution, crucial to the tomato's existence in its current forms. They develop Polanyi's concept of 'instituted economic processes' and take issue with the production and consumption of tomatoes as a purely economic process (of technology, transport, firm market share, profit, etc.) 'as if the economic tomato was *autonomous* from the social, cultural, biological or legal tomato' without regard to law, custom, national cuisine, biology or ecology (Harvey, 2007: 168).

Barndt's (2007) *Tangled Routes: Women, Work and Globalization on the Tomato Trail* traces the journey of the tomato from its cultivation in Mexico to its purchase at the supermarket check-out and consumption in fast-food restaurants in Canada. Combining scholarship and activism, the book takes stock of the current 'moment' of globalisation and other critical moments that gave rise to it, notably colonialism, to consider the impact of the liberalisation of trade on workers in agriculture, transport and supermarkets. It is a story of a border-crossing commodity which is a vehicle to explore the economic, ecological, gendered, political and cultural process of globalisation, again going beyond a narrow focus on linear and vertical supply chains.

Heuts and Mol (2013) offer a different take, using the tomato to explore the activity of valuing tomatoes. They analyse tensions between and within registers of money, handling, time, nature and sensual appeal which 'push and pull' in different directions, especially between monetary and sensory valuing. The 'good enough' tomato emerges as the commodity which can tolerate handling, refrigeration and transport and survive well enough to be exchanged. They show how valuing tomatoes is neither wholly about judgement nor formal classification schemes but relies on knowledge and practices of care and attention (pruning, watering, protection) which just might enhance the qualities of the tomato for their inevitable destruction/consumption.

THE COMMODITY CIRCUIT FOR FISH: VIEWS FROM A WHOLESALE MARKET

I now turn to a consideration of fish and seafood as a 'sounding' to explore the circulation of these 'intimate commodities' on a global and local scale (Winson, 1994). The global fish trade is in trouble. The industry is dominated by huge trawlers with access, via quotas, to the largest share of the world's fish. The resultant diminishing stocks have made life harder for poor coastal communities at the extractive end of commodity chains (Fabinyi et al., 2018: 89). Governance to promote traceability and environmental sustainability, such as the Marine Stewardship Council, focuses on ecological and financial value (Wijen & Chiroleu-Assouline, 2019). Whilst there are interventions to foster socially responsible seafood, for instance, Seafish's Responsible Fishing Vessel Standard in the United Kingdom, which challenge poor and exploitative working conditions to capture and process fish for sale, notably in the Global South, these are often hampered in practice by weak legislative contexts and voluntary certification.

Analysis of seafood commodity chains has often focused on financial value, assuming linear, vertical connections from fishers to consumers (Fabinyi et al., 2018). In this section, I focus on the interconnections between supply and exchange in a more restricted span. This allows me to take a 'node' along/across the supply chain and delve into the ordinary transactions and market work which generate and sustain the commodity circuit, and reveals it as fragile and contingent (Neyland et al., 2018). To do this, I revisit my research on Billingsgate (Lyon, 2016, 2020), London's long-established wholesale fish market, and ask: What does the circulation of commodities look like from the perspective of the fish merchant – and the fish?

Billingsgate is an interesting site to study, not because it accounts for a large volume of current trade, most of which passes through supermarkets and their direct suppliers, but because it exposes some of the articulations in the circulation of commodities and the social relationships and forms of coordination they rest on. The market operates in a single 'hall' where samples of fish are on display for those who buy in person, with orders coming in by telephone to the stands or their associated office spaces. The fish merchants who operate at the market occupy a pivotal position in the fish trade. They have a direct relationship with (some) fishers and agents buying on their behalf at markets where fish are landed or seafood sold – and they have close connections to buyers in the catering and retail trades. This gives them a view upstream and downstream and insights into the relationships between consumer practices, taste, loyalty and trust, conditions at sea, value and the shape and movement of the fish itself.

The case of a specialist merchant in pelagic fish – oily fish such as herring and mackerel – both fresh and smoked, illuminates trading customs and cultures. As soon as we start discussing his purchasing decisions, David talks about being 'in the hands of what happens retail wise'. Whilst Tuesday, the first day of the trading week – his temporal reference point – is always busy, Wednesday is 'tricky', a 'difficult day to assess': 'I'm ordering fish for the next day,' he explains, 'before they've [fishmongers] even opened their shop on the Tuesday.' He bases his decisions on judgements about availability and price – and what customers will accept – as well as quality, and intuition arising from his long experience in the game: 'What we're ordering for the next day depends on how we feel the demand is going to be', a 'feel' accrued through talk – to customers, suppliers and others involved in the business. Sales are not isolated events on single days: preparation 'culminates' in one sale as anticipation generates the next. What happens if the weather turns and people don't come out to buy? He has a tactic for this – on Wednesdays, he encourages regular customers 'from further afield' to come to the market with the offer of more attention and the possibility of a discount – and some other tricks up his sleeve as a practised salesman. Nevertheless, the challenge of spatio-temporal coordination is considerable (see Bestor, 2001).

There is no stable and certain supply chain in the fish business. Indeed, as Knowles (2014) discusses, the depiction of smooth flows in theorizations of globalization lacks empirical grounding. The reputation of David's business, established by his father decades earlier, is for the 'best available at that time', where neither quality nor price are consistent. If the 'weather is wild', remarks David, and there's a fraction of the anticipated supply, there is a different kind of work to do. This becomes clear when we talk about 'substitution' or 'worthwhile alternatives', as he puts it: 'It's up to us to get our salesmen's coat on and say, but we have got such and such, which are superb quality and are a sensible alternative.' He animates the buyer such that a new 'attachment' can be formed, and the buyer can 'take on' the good into their own world. I listen to his account of how he works as I try to understand the relevance of the specific properties or qualities of fish.

A fish is not just a fish. It is measured, judged and categorised. There are criteria for quality and categories based on size (see Appadurai, 1986: 14). Some properties matter more than others (see Appadurai's distinction between the 'singular' and 'homogenous'; 1986: 16). If calculation at the market 'is distributed among human actors and material devices' (Callon & Muniesa, 2005: 1245), the fish itself operates as part of a 'collective calculative device', indicating quality (freshness, flavour and texture) and value. Fresh or not-long-dead fish is a 'lively commodity' of sorts (Collard & Dempsey, 2013, in Gillespie, 2021). As David comments, 'the fresh sprats come in and they're almost still jumping'. The speed at which its vitality dissipates varies by species, size, grade and type, determining the duration of its 'afterlife' and potential for value (Gillespie, 2021). The rhythm of the market itself also shapes value as the attraction of fish that have already been on the market one, two or three days diminishes next to their newly arrived gleaming counterparts. This 'liveliness' is both sustained by the fish merchants' labour and the infrastructure of the market – icing, chilling and packing – and supported by a narrative performance. Indeed, the fish merchants have a deep grasp of their situation in the market and recognise the active work they must do to accomplish their place in it. They do not simply occupy positions in a network or social structure but 'negotiate, contest, and enact the roles they think they are playing' (Wherry, 2012: 205). They make and remake the market through their actions – deals, explanations, normative positions about how to treat suppliers and buyers, long-term relationships and emotional connections.

At Billingsgate, trade happens 'pairwise', directly between fish merchant and customer. David's customers are 'highly skilled retailers' in their own right, buying prime fish for catering (hotels, restaurants and pubs) and retail (fishmongers). His business is built on long-term relationships, in which trust, loyalty and fairness are key and quality is his trading edge. Some customers also ask for lower-quality produce, and he explains that he cannot supply this but 'if they want to go and buy something really cheap elsewhere, I've no objection'. I hear the explicit permission he gives in this remark so the customers' actions do not threaten their established trading relations. Economic sociologists have been criticised for paying insufficient attention to *how* social ties matter in trade. Zelizer (2012) argues that in all economic action people do 'relational work' as they 'engage in the process of differentiating meaningful social relations' through boundary-making and marking, and the distinctive understandings that operate in connection to those boundaries. David is clear about which sorts of economic transactions are appropriate or not. If a customer asks for something that he does not ordinarily supply but is of equivalent quality to the fish he does, he will source it for them. He is 'pally' with a salmon supplier – they have a reciprocal arrangement for just this occurrence. This is a widespread arrangement; there is even a period of internal market trading for 15 minutes before the market officially opens.

The 'performance' of fish on the market also shapes the process of its commodification upstream. David works with processors but mostly uses an 'agent' to buy for him at wholesale markets in Aberdeen, Peterhead, Grimsby or Brixham. Between them, 'we've taught the suppliers exactly what is required', he comments, 'educated' them about cuts, presentation and colouring (in the case of smoked fish) for over 20 years or more. The work of keeping the commodity chain in good shape is an ongoing practical accomplishment, based on human bonds and human–fish entanglements.

CONCLUSIONS

There are big challenges facing both the operation and understanding of global commodity circuits, including the destructive social and environmental impacts of the current organisation of supply chains globally. The study of these circuits is not straightforward given the complexity of connections and the variation in formal and informal practices and trajectories – as Knowles' (2014, 2015) research makes clear. And social relationships and consequences continue to be concealed in the language of circuits, chains and commodities. They can, however, be made visible through approaches which critique, challenge and expose both practices and conceptualisations that disregard the fragility and instability of the circuits themselves and the lives and labour that bring them about. This kind of work requires intricate and innovative mobile and multisite ethnographies whilst not getting altogether lost in ethnographic specificity (Callon & Muniesa, 2005). Goldstein and Newell (2019) propose the combination of *in situ* (interviews, surveys and observation) and *ex situ* (trade data, documentary analysis and mapping) research and call for a research agenda which focuses on the operation of corporations and the development of a 'political-industrial ecology of supply chains' which can recognise environmental consequences in conjunction with their implications for justice, equity and welfare work. They also highlight the importance of collaborations between academics and non-governmental organisations to identify 'hotspots' and promote social responsibility. Similarly, with insights from activists and academics, Palpacuer and Smith (2021) carve a path towards 'responsible global value chains' and document the achievements and promise of collective community organisation and transnational alliances to transform global commodity circuits in more sustainable and equitable ways.

REFERENCES

Appadurai, A. (ed.) (1986) *The Social Life of Things, Commodities in Cultural Perspective*. Cambridge University Press.
Argent, N. (2016) 'Rural geography I: Resource peripheries and the creation of new global commodity chains'. *Progress in Human Geography* 41 (6), 803–812.
Bailey, S. & Pierides, D. (2021) 'Just in time pandemic management'. Paper presented to the Decent Work and Productivity Research Group, March.
Barndt, D. (2007) *Tangled Routes: Women, Work and Globalization on the Tomato Trail*, second edition. Rowman & Littlefield.
Barrientos, S. (2019) *Gender and Work in Global Value Chains, Capturing the Gains?* Cambridge University Press.

Bestor, T.C. (2001) 'Supply-side sushi: Commodity, market and the global city'. *American Anthropologist* 103 (1), 76–95.

Bridge, G. & Smith, A. (2003) 'Intimate encounters: Culture – economy – commodity'. *Environment and Planning D* 21, 257–268.

Callon, M. & Muniesa, F. (2005) 'Economic markets as calculative collective devices'. *Organization Studies* 26 (8), 1229–1250.

Campling, L. & Quentin, C. (2021) 'Global inequality chains: How global value chains and wealth chains (re)produce inequalities of wealth', in F. Palpacuer & A. Smith (eds) *Rethinking Value Chains, Tackling the Challenges of Global Capitalism*. Policy Press.

Dunaway, W. (ed.) (2014) *Gendered Commodity Chains, Seeing Women's Work and Households in Global Production*. Stanford University Press.

Fabinyi, M., Dressler, W.H. & Pido, M.D. (2018) 'Moving beyond financial value in seafood commodity chains'. *Marine Policy*, 94, 89–92.

Gereffi, G. & Korzeniewicz, M. (eds) (1994) *Commodity Chains and Global Capitalism*. Greenwood Press.

Gillespie, K. (2021) 'The afterlives of the lively commodity: Life-worlds, death-worlds, rotting worlds'. *EPA: Economy and Space*, 53 (2), 280–295.

Glucksmann, M. (2009) 'Formations, connections and divisions of labour'. *Sociology* 43 (5), 878–895.

Goldstein, B. & Newell, J.P. (2019) 'Why academics should study the supply chains of individual corporations'. *Journal of Industrial Ecology* 23, 1316–1327.

Granovetter, M. (1985) 'Economic action and social structure: The problem of embeddedness'. *American Journal of Sociology* 91 (3), 481–510.

Harvey, M. (2007) 'Instituting economic processes in society', in M. Harvey, R. Ramlogan & S. Randles (eds), *Karl Polanyi: New Perspectives on the Place of the Economy in Society*. Manchester University Press.

Harvey, M., Quilley, S. & Benyon, H. (2002) *Exploring the Tomato, Transformations of Nature, Society and Economy*. Edward Elgar Publishing.

Heuts, F. & Mol, A. (2013) 'What is a good tomato? A case of valuing in practice'. *Valuation Studies* 1 (2), 125–146.

Hochschild, A.R. (2000) 'Global care chains and emotional surplus value', in W. Hutton & A. Giddens (eds), *On the Edge: Living with Global Capitalism*. Jonathan Cape.

Hopkins, T.K. & Wallerstein, I. (1986) 'Commodity chains in the world-economy prior to 1800'. *Review* 10 (1), 157–170.

Kano, L., Tsang, E.W.K. & Wai-chung Yeung, H. (2020) 'Global value chains: A review of the multi-disciplinary literature'. *Journal of International Business Studies* 51, 577–622.

Knowles, C. (2014) *Flip-Flop: A Journey through Globalisation's Backroads*. Pluto Press.

Knowles, C. (2015) 'The flip-flop trail and fragile globalization'. *Theory, Culture and Society* 32(7–8), 231–244.

Lee, J. (2010) 'Global commodity chains and global value chains'. In *Oxford Research Encyclopedia of International Studies*. International Studies Association and Oxford University Press.

Lyon, D. (2016) 'Doing audio-visual montage to explore time and space: The everyday rhythms of Billingsgate Fish Market'. Sociological Research Online 21 (3), 57–68.

Lyon, D. (2020) 'The role of rhythm in the production of "thick" places', in T. Edensor, A. Kalandides & U. Kothari (eds), *The Routledge Handbook of Place*. Routledge.

McCarthy, L., Soundararajan, V. & Taylor, S. (2021) 'The hegemony of men in global value chains: Why it matters for labour governance'. *Human Relations* 74 (12), 2051–2074.

Muniesa, F., Millo, Y. & Callon, M. (2007) 'An introduction to market devices'. *Sociological Review* 55 (2), 1–12.

Neyland, D., Ehrenstien, V. & Milyaeva, S. (2018) 'Mundane market matters: From ordinary to profound and back again'. *Journal of Cultural Economy* 11 (5), 377–385.

Palpacuer, F. & Smith, A. (eds) (2021) *Rethinking Value Chains, Tackling the Challenges of Global Capitalism*. Policy Press.

Parreñas, R.S. (2015) *Servants of Globalization Women, Migration and Domestic Work*, second edition. University of Stanford Press.

Pettinger, L. (2019) *What's Wrong with Work?* Policy Press.

Polanyi, K. (1957) 'The economy as instituted process', in K. Polanyi, C.M. Arensberg and H.W. Pearson (eds), *Trade and Market in the Early Empires, Economies in History and Theory*. Free Press.

Ponte, S., Gereffi, G. & Raj-Reichert, G. (eds) (2019) *Handbook on Global Value Chains*. Edward Elgar Publishing.

Wherry, F.F. (2012) 'Performance circuits in the marketplace'. *Politics & Society* 40 (2), 203–221.

Wijen, F. & Chiroleu-Assouline, M. (2019) 'Controversy over voluntary environmental standards: A socioeconomic analysis of the Marine Stewardship Council'. *Organization & Environment* 32 (2), 98–124.

Winson, A. (1994) *The Intimate Commodity: Food and the Development of the Agro-Industrial Complex in Canada*. Garamond Press.

Zelizer, V. (2012) 'How I became a relational economic sociologist and what does that mean?' *Politics & Society* 40 (2), 145–174.

30. Travelling methods

Caroline Knowles

This chapter reflects on the *travelling research work* entailed in studying a tiny fragment of globalization as it is being generated. I understand globalization as produced in innumerable translocal movements of objects, people, materials, social, economic and political processes, algorithms and the rest, across dispersed territories of different scales – cities, towns, neighbourhoods, streets – spanning nation state borders. This chapter focuses on the travels of an object and its constituent materials, although I have also studied movements of people, migrant constituents of globalization (Knowles & Harper 2010). Distinguishing object and people movements is a matter of emphasis: in practice they move together. Instead of conceiving globalization as a monolithic abstraction driven by relentless imperatives and logics (Held & McGrew 2003; Sassen 2007), I take a more fragmented and empirical approach, piecing globalization together from small sequences of movement – travel. Travel describes one of globalization's key logics – its engine. Travel also offers a way of conceiving of globalization empirically, placing movement in the research frame for exploration and analysis.

Studying life on the move demands methods adapted to these purposes: travelling research methods. In social sciences, methods are heavily freighted by templates, pedagogies, lessons learned and transmitted: a *rough guide* to research, to reuse the title of a popular travel guide series. My intentions here are rather more modest. On the one hand, there are methods commonly used for gathering data in all manner of situations, and on the other are the challenges of deploying these methods on the move, in studies of movement. Travelling methods transport researchers along with their objects of investigation, as they unpack their social, material and environmental constituents. Travelling methods are familiar research techniques, repurposed by the exigencies of investigation on the move. I think of them as open experiments in researching on the go, improvised and revised along the way, afterwards subjected to critical reflection, always retrospective.

The methods I describe here are ethnographic, biographical and spatial. They are focused on the making and mapping of translocal spaces through movements within and between them. My reflections are grounded in my travels with an everyday object across the scenes of its production and consumption. My intention was to explore some of the social and environmental substance created in making, transporting and consuming this object, from inside the logics of travel: the travels of a researcher-and-object-on-the-move across the multiple, emerging uncertainties of the unfamiliar.

The everyday object is a pair of plastic flip-flops; the world's cheapest (highest-selling) shoe, often a first step into the world of footwear, particularly in the global south, where a billion people still walk barefoot. Between 2006 and 2013 I followed the shoe, an elemental tool in human mobility, piecing together its biography, the production of its objectness, the feet it transported around the neighbourhoods of its biggest markets and, finally, its disposal.[1] The shoe's travels began beneath the sands of Kuwait as oil, shipped to be made into plastic pellets in Korean petrochemical plants, made into flip-flops in small Chinese factories and then transported to one of the biggest markets for Chinese plastics, Ethiopia, where I followed them on the feet of an elderly woman, until they reached the Addis Ababa landfill site. The shoe led, and I followed, sometimes unsure where it was heading, often losing it altogether.

The shoe's story was published as *Flip-Flop: A Journey through Globalisation's Backroads* (Knowles 2014).[2] I think of it as a long trudge through a small, insignificant strand of *globalization*, along with zillions of other object-and-people movements. Because, as I suggested earlier, different kinds of travel are globalization's constituents, it is important to explore travel in order to understand globalization's logics and mechanics – by which I mean how it works, which is a way of thinking about what it is. From the vantage point of the trail cocreated by flip-flops, globalization turned out to be a whole lot messier, more fragile, shifting, improvised and rigged together, than high theorists of globalization suggest in asserting its robust inevitability.[3]

In this kind of project, the researcher cedes control of the travel routes or trails – these are created along the way and must be discovered – as well as key dimensions and scenes of the research. These are shaped by the routes and the social, geographical and environmental contexts they pass through and cocreate. The shoe led, I followed; always behind, a bit disoriented, hopeful that things would somehow work out, anxious that they might not. Looking back at my field notebooks, I am struck by my uncertainties and anxieties, as well as my willingness to persevere, to somehow make it all add up to something, to an analysis of globalization on the ground via some of its less travelled routes. 'A bit daunted by the research assignment I have set myself', my Addis Ababa diary entry read. A panicked understatement: my uncertainties grew along the trail.

Global trails are long, so I divided this one into manageable sections, conceiving each as a separate journey that would lead to others, returning to London in between as my professional life – teaching students – and personal circumstances – raising three children – demanded. This sacrificed the continuous arc of the trail I imagined following. But it had the virtue of providing time between travels for reflection, refining my approach, and reviewing how things were working out empirically and conceptually, as messy, on-the-ground, rigged-together configurations of how this bit of globalization actually worked, began to surface.

Travelling methods depend on advanced preparation. Assembling a travel kit of ideas, potential research sites, contacts and contingencies proved crucial in supporting the flexibility and experimentation which followed. Trips were packed with action, with movement, with mapping, remapping, observations and interviews, as well as problem solving along the way. Survival and rerouting when things did not work out as anticipated took priority over reflection time. Before leaving London, I read anthropological studies, as well as popular accounts of travellers and journalists. I estimated the route – which I often got wrong – and I tried to identify potential research sites and make contacts at crucial points along the way. I anticipated my need for interpreters, advisors, research assistants, a whole world of interlocutors. I contacted local universities and offered casual employment to early-career academics and post-graduate students. Local contacts and on-the-ground knowledge provided lifelines in a sea of uncertainty.

A tool kit of others' ideas, some quite abstract, guided me through the messy realities of research. Jane Jacobs's (1961: 52) insistence on the significance of everyday choreographies of the streets and spatial behaviour shaped my observations and mappings. Norman Denzin (1989), who suggests the social and collective importance of biography and everyday doings, framed my interviews and observations. Conceptions of landscape and movement provided flexible underpinning guides. The understanding that unfamiliar landscapes can be known through tracing the journeys people make and the stories they tell opened routes into what I did not know. Arnason et al. (2012) suggest, with Heidegger's help, that the routes, paths and possibilities of landscape, as well as social encounters along the way, are ways of living and forging social ties in motion. The notion that landscapes coproduce social textures and the people who live them on the move suggested perspectives onto the trail. The conception that objects, as well as people and their lives, can be understood through where and how they move (Tilley 2012) framed my observations, questions and mappings. That lives are not lived along pre-set pathways, but through meandering, improvised, open-ended and fluid travel routes, as people feel their way through everyday landscapes (Edensor 2007; Hallam & Ingold 2007; Ingold 2011; McFarlane 2012) provoked my exploration of flip-flop movements and the human agents propelling them. Improvisation and navigation – finding a way – are key strategies underpinning the travelling methods toolkit (Amit & Knowles 2017).

Like travel, travelling methods are shaped by logistics. Shifting combinations of coordination moved flip-flops and the materials from which they were fabricated. While oil, petrochemicals and flip-flops travelled in tankers, pipes and shipping containers, I travelled along international air routes to main cities, on parallel journeys. Flights were followed by further journeys on foot, by scooter, bus, taxi and train. Uncertain outcomes complicated logistic calculations. How long would it take to get the data I needed? Trips were one-offs on cost and time grounds, making it imperative to get the material I needed, leaving no gaps I could not later fill. Time felt like my taskmaster and, sometimes, like my enemy. It drove me relentlessly, as I discovered short bursts of manic energy.

I learned to travel light. Frequent moves made repacking a time-consuming chore. I prioritized equipment over clothes and shoes, which must be serviceable, comfortable, washable. Simple, robust equipment – two tape recorders (just in case), mobile phone, batteries, laptop for downloading sound files, a small camera, a tripod, maps, notebooks, pens and pencils, a head torch for reading and navigating unfamiliar spaces after dark – formed my world on the move. My baggage contained a portable field office, from which I worked along the road. My diary entry in Kuwait City admits: 'I struggle to keep up with all the fieldnotes, download sound files from interviews, label and back them up, change batteries each day, recharge my camera and i-phone'. Each night I would fall into bed exhausted and wake early to work on the challenges of the day: making appointments with potential interlocutors, finding more interlocutors with different perspectives, how to get where I needed to be.

Travelling methods involve places to rest along the road. At the end of long international flights, which rarely landed in exactly the right place, were simple hotels and guesthouses, like the Sea-and-Tell Guest House near Daesan in Korea. This is memorable because the airline lost my baggage, and so I lived there without it for several days. I learned not to check in baggage, and new habits of minimalist living and working. Hotels on the road are office and home: places to live, meet interlocutors, places to return to as I travelled back and forth along sections of the trail, drawing and photographing and making notes, writing-up notes, charging batteries and sampling local life. Travel logistics dominate and shape the research methods of itinerant researchers. Where to stay? How to get there? Is there a bus? Car or taxi? Is it too far to walk?

My travelling research began from a misconception. I thought I would be *following* flip-flop trails, which I imprecisely identified and mapped from desk research in London. Perhaps all travel begins this way: at home, with anticipation, webs of expectation, suitcases loaded with preconceptions. But on the road, most of my time was spent *searching* for trails. By trails

I mean key sites of the research and the routes connecting them. Sometimes these sites were obvious. But often they were not. And sometimes they had to be created. When the sites and the routes connecting them were settled – and they never were – I had to navigate access routes *into* these sites as well as find my way between them. What follows are vignettes describing how this worked in practice at different moments along the road, from inside the logics of travel.

Petrochemical plants were the most obvious and visible scenes of this research: they sprawl across the South Korean landscape. No trouble finding them. But how to get inside, as they are guarded by impenetrable security systems. Kuwaiti oil-drilling sites are equally visible and securitized. I navigated access to these through government ministries with the help of local interlocutors. Emails and phone calls in English and Korean drew a blank on petrochemical access. I considered giving up. Then I booked a flight to Seoul, took a bus to Daesan and stood outside one of the largest plants, along with a Korean sociologist studying at Berkeley, who agreed to help me. Sitting in a café opposite the main gate, we watched men in blue uniforms inhale steaming bowls of noodles at lunchtime. When a senior-looking man in the group went outside for a cigarette, Berkeley joined him. Half an hour later we drove through the main gate. Later, this led us to workers' homes and dinners with them in restaurants: to access to their landscape, their world, and their ways of being in it. My diary entry after I arrived back in Seoul:

> a bit depleted from the work and happy to be back in the city with my thoughts about petrochemical life. Tired from a lack of sleep and that research attentiveness you need to gather all the material needed in such a short time, and turn every encounter, every moment, into research.

The routes oil and chemicals travel from these sites are opaque. Tankers, pipelines and trucks transport them to ports. Ports are off bounds on security grounds, except in Kuwait City, where a union contact let me operate the container-unloading simulator. Joy! Ships and containers travel sea routes. With no way to get aboard, these parts of the trail relied on the documented stories of seamen. Sometimes I might see the cargo off, and hope to meet it again later. At breakpoints like these I lost the trail. Between Daesan (Korea) and Fuzhou (China) I lost it completely.

I knew (from internet research) that there were thousands of small flip-flop factories around Fuzhou in southeast China, but I could not find them. I walked miles through the port industrial zone, to find only large factories making global brands like Nike. I had to navigate this part of the trail with the help of a single contact, an exporter who commissioned flip-flops from several factories. No factory boss would allow me to observe production and speak with workers. In the run-up to the 2008 Beijing Olympics, international journalists were keen to expose labour conditions in Chinese factories. They made my route more difficult, as factory bosses feared exposure and the trouble this might cause with state authorities. Complete disclosure: I was travelling on a tourist visa. Requesting permission risked refusal. And even if granted, state minders would inhibit conversations with workers.

My contact drove me round factories and introduced me to bosses. We talked Chinese politics in the privacy of his car on the way. He was surprisingly critical. His stories on the road helped me understand how his export business lived alongside the authoritarian politics of the regime and globalization with Chinese characteristics. By the time my Chinese-speaking co-researcher and photographer, Michael Tan, arrived from Singapore, I had identified a factory in which we could observe and interview workers, slotting our conversations into the rhythms of work. My contact found us a good hotel and negotiated the rate; he introduced us to his wife and daughter. We often ate together, and when I left for London, he made sure I had 10 kilos of lychees for the journey. Such is the kindness and generosity of strangers. And such was the tenuousness of the entire project, which could have collapsed at any moment.

Flip-flop trails splinter into thousands of directions and I had to decide which to follow and imagine the places and research scenes each might lead to. From Chinese factories, for example, flip-flops move all over the world. Earlier along the trail I invented rules of the road for myself. I would follow the biggest volumes of plastic, oil, flip-flop producers and the biggest markets. These rules brought some consistency to my fragile project. Travelling methods are full of unexpected discoveries, contingencies, losses and rerouting, but it need not be random.

Ethiopia, the biggest market for Chinese plastics, took me to Addis Ababa. Between Fuzhou and Addis I lost the trail again. I thought flip-flops left the port of Fuzhou and landed in Djibouti, to be transported on trucks to the giant inland port of Dire Dawa on the Somaliland/Ethiopia border and then on to Addis. Indeed some do, as truck drivers confirmed. But standing on this border – which my university prohibited me from crossing on security grounds – an official (as opposed to freelance) border policeman told Michael and I that the biggest volumes of flip-flops took another route entirely. Landing unofficially on the coast of Somaliland, traded on markets in Hargeisa, and driven along backroads into Ethiopia illegally, flip-flops evade customs duties. This makes them cheaper for customers and more profitable for traders. Surprised by this fork in the road we rapidly adapted our route and focus.

This route was plied by smugglers, who were difficult to find and reluctant to speak. A student at Addis University, a former smuggler himself, led me to them. Smugglers were understandably reluctant to describe the shifting matrix of routes they travelled. While I spoke with them, their armed escorts sat nearby. The location of our meetings was changed several times at the last moment. Trust was an issue – smuggling carries heavy penalties in imprisonment – and the student had to reassure them that they would not be identified.

I suggested earlier that some scenes of the research were invented, rather than discovered. When the trail passed through a city like Fuzhou or Addis Ababa, I would find junction points that worked as proxies for the many trails that would make the research unwieldy if I tried to follow them all. Because it is impossible to study an entire city, I constructed viable flip-flop routes through them. By this I mean routes that stayed true to the logics of the trail rather than fictionalizing it, and articulated its broader context at the same time. This was like choosing a location for a documentary film. While the research revealed some of the lived realities of the city, and the traces flip-flops left in people's lives and the landscapes in which they lived and worked, I needed to find microcosms that could articulate specific stories in their bigger context: life in the city for poor flip-flop wearers. Trails from flip-flop wholesalers in Addis's Mercato, for example, ran through low-income settlements all over the city: which to choose?

Walking along the main road from the Mercato one day I discovered a capsule of roadside commerce set on rough ground. Here was a kiosk selling flip-flops and groceries, a trader selling pots and pans, a vehicle repair man and welder, a number of small boys playing football with a tin can and people just passing the time of day. This pocket of informal commerce served passing traffic, and the poor, informal community living in corrugated iron dwellings tucked behind it. This microcosm of low-income Addis life allowed me to explore the social textures of everyday life around buying and wearing flip-flops. I focused on the kiosk trader, who turned out to have a good grasp of global commerce as well as how it moved through his neighbourhood. He understood his customers' lives, too. I spoke with many of his customers. But identifying a single flip-flop wearer to follow over many days was fraught with ethical difficulties. An uncomfortable auction in Amharic I did not understand determined which households would work with the 'ferenji'. An elderly woman who wore flip-flops repaired with a nail agreed I could follow her daily routes and activities. I spent many hours with her, her family and friends, developing a picture of their lives and concerns. I assuaged the guilt the differences between their lifestyle and mine created, with gifts of shoes, footballs, small sums of money, coffee and colourful wraps. As contrived and fraught as this is, it allowed me to explore one of the many trails that passed through this city, through the stories people told about the travels composing their daily lives.

Sometimes, key research scenes were not what they seemed. This complicated my navigating them, and compounded my uncertainties. The Addis landfill site, where the flip-flop trail ends, is open to the main road that passes it. In a taxi with a colleague and Amharic speaker from the university, we reviewed this vast site from the road. The taxi driver was anxious to leave. My colleague was nervous, and so was I. We crossed the road via a footbridge guarded by three ragged young men. They openly surveyed my camera and money bag as they let us pass. As we stepped onto the landfill the supervisor swooped and demanded our permission documents. This surprising formality guarded what looked open and informal, and sent us to the ministry. Following complicated negotiations that revealed the operation of municipal bureaucracy, we were allowed back on site, under the supervisor's protection. Over the coming days, I learned that the supervisor managed the invisible (to me) violent and sometimes illegal activities that ran through the site, where mafias operated as informal (shadow) authorities. How naïve was I to think it was just a garbage site.

There was more. The landfill routed another set of global routes from villages in the countryside to the capital city and on to the Middle East, for young Ethiopian women seeking work as maids. Who knew that a garbage site routed transnational mobilities and new lifestyle-enhancing beginnings? Significant deficits in my knowledge and the need for constant detective work describe this research. Travelling methods cover so much surface, they sacrifice depth, and, I was often out of my depth. Literally. Hardest to bear was my disgust and fear at sinking up to my knees in garbage surrounded by birds of prey, marauding dogs and the brown-grey filthy figures of 'scratchers' who scavenged for recyclables. 'So sad I cried. Also very scared. Looking into the angry eyes of a young woman scratcher, I didn't know where to look or what to do,' read my notebook.

Travel is about the rhythms of movement and stopping. Stopping is crucial in slowing things down and watching the mobile elements of the landscape pass by. In the industrial villages making flip-flops in China I would often sit on a stoop and watch what passed. What kinds of errands were people embarked upon? What kinds of machines, from diggers, to cycles and (infrequent) cars. Stopping, I could appreciate an entire village on the move, on the journeys of everyday life. I discovered this by accident. When we were thrown out of one of the factories as the owner worried about what we might be doing – were we setting up our own factory? – we sat dejectedly outside. As they came off shift, the migrant workers took us home, adding new, unexpected scenes to the research.

The road is not just a means of keeping up with a travelling object, but a crucial part of the research scene. Routes between trail points offered valuable information about life on the move. Where distances are too far to walk, buses, which are packed with local life and concerns, provided valuable data, and Michael would photograph them loading, unloading and just passing by. As revealing as my investigations on the Ethiopia and Somaliland border proved in locating the flip-flop trail and its unseen variations, the road between Addis and the border was just as helpful in unpacking the textures of everyday life. The road trip is indispensable in the travelling methods toolkit. Car hire in Ethiopia is difficult and expensive. A colleague at the university suggested we rent his friend's car. Already attuned to these informalities, I was renting a sim card from the maid at the guest house, rather than apply for one from the government, even though this meant taking her messages. We collected the car and parked it at the guest house for an early start. The guest house owner reviewed it and declared it unfit for the long journey to the border. She was right. But it only broke down once when it sprung an oil leak; a roadside mechanic fixed it with a bar of soap, and we made it back to Addis.

We set off for the Ethiopia/Somaliland border with Michael at the wheel and me taking notes. Who is on the road and how are they travelling? What are the activities, materials and objects on the road? I leaned out of the window to take photos – notes for later reference – and scribbled in my notebook. As we left the city, people were beginning work or walking with crops or grass carried on their heads. People were walking along the railway tracks of the country's only rail line linking Addis with Djibouti. As we drove along a tarmacked road, with single-file traffic in each direction, we saw trucks, rickshaw scooters, minibuses, 'Jesus is the only way to heaven' and other slogans on the back, and occasional state-run blue and white buses. But most people walk. And they walk in flip-flops and other plastic, Chinese-manufactured shoes, or they walk barefoot. We passed crops in the fields – *teff* – circular houses with mud walls and goat herders with sticks across their shoulders and their hand dangling over them. One had an automatic weapon instead of a stick. Constant army and police checkpoints counteract smuggling. Travelling methods attend to the technologies and routes of movement and the social fabrics of the road.

As we neared the town of Kalubi and the pilgrimage spot at Gebriel Church we passed crowds of pilgrims walking along narrow roads among traffic. Our road trip coincided with a major date in the pilgrim calendar. It was dark and Michael had been driving all day when we got to Dire Dawa. Every hotel was full of pilgrims. We drove back along the same road, branching off to Harar, where we guessed there might be hotel rooms. This time I was at the wheel. There was no street lighting, and round each bend crowds of pilgrims emerged out of the darkness. I drove slowly and nervously, terrified of hitting someone. Michael took photographs, experimenting with headlights coming towards us, producing some stunning images of traces of light. Unlike my photo notes, his photographs were to display and document the research. We arrived in Harar to find hotels were full here, too. We contemplated sleeping in the car and asked advice from local people. A man jumped in the car and directed us to a small hotel with one free room we would never have found for ourselves. The next day we made our way to Dire Dawa and the border and discovered the smuggling. The excitement of this discovery revived us, despite having to sit for three hours in the pilgrimage traffic jam on the way back to Addis. My diary reminds me:

> We drove fast, non-stop trying to get back to Addis before dark, when the roads are particularly stressful and full of the hazards of darkness. It was hard to know where we were. Few of the town display their names. They know who they are and few people visit them. We got into Addis at 10.30pm. We got lost and had to pay a taxi driver to lead us back to the guest house. The taxi got lost too. We arrived at 11.30pm. The gate is locked, but the night watchman remembers us, and lets us in.

The road trip had taken several unexpected turns, and the route was full of the textures of local devotional life.

Travelling methods are constantly adapted and rerouted through new landscapes and stories. They are voyages of discovery navigated by the usual qualitative methods of mapping, tracking, biographical interviews and observations, all applied on the move. They share common challenges of navigating access with all research projects, but research on the move presents more of them, in more languages, on unfamiliar landscapes than more stationary research, where researchers generally have better place-based expertise. Travelling research is semi-skilled labour. Anthropologists spend a professional lifetime gaining detailed knowledge of just one of the points along my trail. My research was different. I did not need deep knowledge, I needed to understand how these points were connected. This meant taking short-cuts through secondary data. It meant getting lost and navigating uncertainties along the road. My mission was also limited. Flip-flop travels were the lens I used in understanding places and their translocal connections; partial knowledge in the service of understanding the movements of a travelling object, and the traces it leaves in places and the lives lived in them, all on the move.

NOTES

1. Kopytoff (1986) pioneers the concept if not the practice of the object biography.
2. See also Knowles (2015, 2017) and www.fliploptrail.com.
3. This argument is set out in detail in the conclusion to Knowles (2014).

REFERENCES

Amit, V. & Knowles, C. (2017). 'Improvising and Navigating Mobilities: Tacking in Everyday Life'. *Theory, Culture and Society*, 34 (7–8), 165–179.
Arnason, A., Ellison, N., Vergunst, J. & Whitehouse, A. (2012). 'Introduction', in A. Arnason, N. Ellison, J. Vergunst & A. Whitehouse (Eds), *Landscapes beyond Land: Routes, Aesthetics, Narratives* (pp. 3–5). Berghahn Books.
Denzin, N. (1989). *Interpretive Biography*. Sage.
Edensor, T. (2007). 'Mundane Mobilities, Performances and Spaces of Tourism'. *Social and Cultural Geography*, 8 (2), 199.
Hallam, E. & Ingold, T. (2007). 'Creativity and Cultural Improvisation: An Introduction', in E. Hallam & T. Ingold (Eds), *Creativity and Cultural Improvisation* (pp. 1–24). Routledge.
Held, D. & McGrew, A. (Eds) (2003). *The Global Transformation Reader*. Polity.
Ingold, T. (2011). *The Perception of the Environment: Essays on Livelihood, Dwelling and Skill*. Routledge.
Jacobs, J. (1961). *The Death and Life of Great American Cities*. Bodley Head.
Knowles, C. (2014). *Flip-Flop: A Journey through Globalisation's Backroads*. Pluto.
Knowles, C. (2015). 'The Flip-Flop Trail and Fragile Globalisation'. *Theory, Culture and Society*, 32 (7–8), 231–244.
Knowles, C. (2017). 'Untangling the Translocal Urban Textures of Trash: Plastics and Plasticity in Addis Ababa'. *Social Anthropology/Anthropology Sociale*, 25 (3), 288–300.
Knowles, C. & Harper, D. (2010). *Hong Kong: Migrant Lives, Landscapes and Journeys*. University of Chicago Press.
Kopytoff, I. (1986) 'The Cultural Biography of Things: Commoditization as Process', in A. Appadurai (Ed.), *The Social Life of Things* (pp. 64–91). Cambridge: Cambridge University Press.
McFarlane, C. (2012). *Learning the City: Knowledge and Translocal Assemblage*. Wiley-Blackwell.

Sassen, S. (2007). *A Sociology of Globalization*. W.W. Norton.

Tilley, C. (2012). 'Walking the Past in the Present', in A. Arnason, N. Ellison, J. Vergunst & A. Whitehouse (Eds), *Landscapes beyond Land: Routes, Aesthetics, Narratives* (pp. 15–31). Berghahn Books.

Epilogue

Christian Karner and Dirk Hofäcker

A handbook as thematically complex and broad as ours demands some concluding thoughts. The purpose of those should be to take stock, to map what has been offered here onto what came before and to provide further suggestions for future work in the sociology of globalization. While we see no need to restate specific content covered by our expert contributors, we wish to bring this project to a productive conclusion by reflecting on a number of conceptual, definitional, political and methodological strands that have meandered, in a manner of speaking, through different sections and chapters in this book. These strands can themselves be thought of as falling into a number of interrelated, thematic clusters.

I

More than 20 years after Ulrich Beck (2000) dedicated a book to addressing the question as to *what globalization is*, the term continues to be shrouded, at least in the domains of public and everyday discourse, in definitional vagueness. Already then, Beck was acutely conscious of how talk about globalization had all too often conflated different phenomena and social spheres. To counteract such confusion, Beck introduced some much-needed nuance by distinguishing the following: *globalism*, *globalization* and *globality*.

Globalism, Beck argued, was tantamount to the "view that the world market eliminates or supplants political action – that is, the ideology of rule by the world market, the ideology of neoliberalism." Implicit in globalism thus defined is a reduction of the "multidimensionality of globalization to a single, economic dimension"; consequently, if other dimensions of globalization – be they those of "ecology, culture, politics, civil society" – are acknowledged at all, they are unhelpfully "plac[ed] under the sway of the world-market system" (Beck 2000: 9) By some contrast, *globalization* proper, so to speak, describes much more numerous and diverse "processes through which sovereign national states are criss-crossed and undermined by transnational actors with varying prospects of power, orientations, identities and networks" (Beck 2000: 11). Finally, the concept of *globality* reminds us that "we have been living for a long time in a world society, in the sense that the notion of closed spaces has become illusory"; globality thus "denotes the totality of social relationships which are not integrated into or determined (or determinable) by national-state politics" (Beck 2000: 10).

Beck's more fine-grained typology therefore distinguishes the economic-cum-ideological from the political and the social. Globalism approximates and helps legitimize (neoliberal) ideas about (the claimed desirability of) the transnational "marketization" (e.g. see Fraser 2014) or "commodification" (Polanyi 2001 [1944]) of formerly extra-economic domains. Globalization, in Beck's terminology, captures much more varied phenomena that all transcend and thereby challenge, whether explicitly or indirectly, the institutions of the (nation-) state, which in turn claim or exercise a territorially bounded "monopoly over the legitimate use of force" (Weber 1972 [1921]: 822). Globality, finally, (re)turns our attention to the historical dimension by alerting us to how social life has long reflected extraterritorial influences and has been (co-)shaped by connections to, and interdependencies with, a distant elsewhere.

By way of some concluding reflections on this research handbook on globalization, two observations that relate back to Beck's influential argument of two decades ago are worth making. First, between them, our authors' contributions address and cut across each conceptual node of Beck's three-fold typology. While some of our chapters subject (neoliberal) globalism to further and much-needed critical scrutiny, other contributions have examined the multiple political and cultural *flows* (Appadurai 1990) that routinely (criss-)cross national borders and connect geographically distant locales and actors. Yet other contributions have helped deepen our appreciation of the *longue durée* histories of such global connections and have sharpened our understanding of the methodological innovations that such connections and flows demand of social scientists. Translated into Beck's terminology, we may therefore reflect back on this handbook's foci as subsuming the sociology of globalism, globalization and globality.

The second observation to make here relates to, and helps explain, the fact that the very term "globalization," often particularly in its least carefully defined invocations, has invited controversy, misunderstanding and sometimes political or outright polemical point scoring. This is shown, to name but one set of examples, by the way in which the far right across much of the world now presents itself in outright opposition to "the globalists"; the latter – whoever "they" are assumed to be in any one example of such far-right discourse – are constructed as an increasingly prominent trope used by nationalists the world over to identify what, or who, they blame for the major ills purportedly afflicting their life-worlds. Concurrently, however, there is also ample evidence of very prominent voices at or near the opposite end of the traditional ideological spectrum finding grave fault with globalization, particularly in its economic manifestations. Some recent examples of such critical counter-narratives focus on the risks and consequences of global supply lines (e.g. Dohmen 2021; Fischer et al. 2021), on our profound environmental crises (e.g. Mattmann-Allamand 2021) or they purport to explain our era's widening inequalities and juxtapose (neoliberal) "globalism" to democracy (Streeck 2021; also see Brown 2015). As we have made clear throughout, there are very good reasons indeed to be critical of many of the facets, and particularly the injustices, of the contemporary world. What is more, many of our contributors have shown that such a critical angle must be part and parcel of a sociology of globalization (globalism and globality). At the same time, a puzzle remains, namely how we might account for why ideological opponents – i.e. many on the far right and others on or much closer to the far left of the spectrum – both claim to identify the roots of some of today's deepest crises in select features of what they associate with globalization.

It is in this respect that Ulrich Beck's more nuanced typology can help and has retained its relevance. By distinguishing *globalism* from *globalization*, Beck enables us to analytically disentangle the economic from the political manifestations of some of the many global flows and interdependencies shaping the world at present. And in so doing, Beck's typology also aids our understanding of why ill-defined tropes of globalization – as opposed to the social scientific conceptualizations this handbook hopes to help foreground – serve important rhetorical functions on both ends of the political spectrum. More simply put: since globalism advocates neoliberal, free market ideology, the opposition by much of the traditional left to this particular facet of "globalization" is hardly surprising. At the same time, the far right's opposition to political globalization – i.e. to the undermining of nation states by transnational forces and actors, as defined by Beck – is fully consistent with nationalism's world view and political blueprint. Put differently, since nationalism is characterized by the will to ensure a

"congruence" of political and cultural "units" (Gellner 1983), the apparent offence nationalists feel at influences, forces and flows that emanate from elsewhere but cut across national
boundaries, thereby indirectly underscoring just how "imagined" (Anderson 1983) or socially
constructed national units are, is also ideologically consistent. In other words, the left and
the far right oppose very different dimensions of our globalizing world, which only a more
fine-grained conceptualization of social changes (long) under way helps us name and comprehend. Additional complexities and contestations arise on the back of Beck's third concept.
Globality challenges, if only inadvertently, some of the very methodological premises that
have underpinned the social sciences for much of their histories. More accurately, if, as Beck
claims (2000: 10), "we have been living for a long time in a world society," then sociology's
and other social scientific disciplines' long-dominant "methodological nationalism" (Wimmer
and Glick-Schiller 2002) needs to be complemented by perspectives that shift the focus
beyond the traditional understanding on "nation states." Recent decades have already seen
much progress across the social sciences towards methodological and conceptual innovations
demanded for an adequate understanding of, and engagement with, the many facets of today's
"world society" (e.g. see Holmwood 2007; Beck and Grande 2010; Knowles 2014).

Taking stock, then, of what we think the present handbook accomplishes, we are confident
that our contributors enable us to reflect anew on the multidimensionality as well as on the
ambivalences of how (economic-cum-ideological) *globalism*, (political) *globalization* and
lived *globality* are each (re)shaping life-worlds across the globe today. We are equally confident that this does not exhaust the full relevance and spread of our contributions. By way
of further concluding reflections, we thus offer a number of additional thoughts on how this
handbook builds on existing sociologies of globalization and sketches important terrain for
future work.

II

As has been made clear throughout this handbook, a sociology of globalization worthy of its
name and tradition must be informed by a critical engagement with much that has come to
feature prominently in our shared world of interconnections in the early twenty-first century.
After all, there is indeed much to be critical about: from ever widening inequalities of wealth
and life chances to the most profound environmental crises to have ever threatened humanity;
from the politics of exclusion and discrimination in their many contemporary forms to societal
polarizations that see ever fewer spaces of discursive engagement where others with diverging
experiences and positions are listened to, let alone truly recognized. It is stating the blatantly
obvious to point out that this briefest of listings of today's ills could be added to at will. In fact,
our contributors have provided plenty of evidence of the many domains, in which a critical
sociology is urgently needed. So endemic, so widespread are today's crises that anything other
than a social science that is critical of what it records would be a betrayal, making it part of the
problem it purports to shed light on rather than of any attempt to reshape the world in more
inclusive, less violent, more sustainable ways.

It has long been recognized (e.g. Bauman 1991) that the sociologist's craft differs from
more laboratory-based sciences in two important respects: first, as sociologists we are *both*
participants in, and researchers of, the social; second, sociologists cannot claim a monopoly
over the act of interpreting the social world, as this is an activity shared with other academic

disciplines and, arguably, with anyone seeking to make sense of their worlds. In other words, sociologists occupy two subject positions simultaneously, that of social actor and that of social analyst. Concurrently, our professional commentaries on the social world sit alongside, and in many cases compete with, countless other accounts on offer. Implicit in these characteristics are two forms of blurring: in the first case, a blurring of our different roles (i.e. professional sociologist, social actor-cum-citizen); in the second case, sociologists face the challenge of not only making sense of the social world but of also demonstrating what makes their accounts social scientific, and hence distinctive from politically motivated or everyday social commentaries in circulation. For us and the present research handbook, both these observations relate back to the case for a critical sociology. Sociologists' dual subject positions as both social scientists and (engaged) citizens make the idea that our professional work can – or indeed should – be hermetically sealed from our normative orientations and political concerns at the very least contestable. Concurrently, the fact that sociological discussions share at least some discursive spaces with a much wider range of diverse accounts of social life means that sociological work is, by definition, public and engaged (see Burawoy 2005). The implication for sociologists of globalization is that our work cannot help but be drawn into wider public discussions that, given our subject matter, are likely to unfold across geographical scales, from the local to the transnational; and that critical engagement with the world we experience, encounter and record is not only desirable but indeed necessary. Such engagement may imply to question the ways in which current policies at the national or other levels have mediated the impact of globalization on the individual, and to call for a revision of political approaches in various fields.

The case for a critical, politically engaged sociology of globalization should not, however, be misread as implying that easy, ideologically clear-cut answers will follow. In fact, there are parts of our handbook that have shown or implied that accounts – typically encountered in discussions around what Beck terms globalism – that reduce all global interconnections and flows to the specter of neoliberalism can themselves be problematic and distortive. Philip Manow (2019: 9, our translation) argues this yet more forcefully in observing that a sometimes "unspecific lament about 'neoliberalism'" may purport to "explain everything but ends up explaining nothing." Where contextualization falls short, where moralizing becomes "excessive" and theory is lacking (Manow 2019: 19), ideology indeed risks displacing sociological analysis. The more productive alternatives sketched by our contributors, by contrast, regard critical engagement as the outcome of reflexively conducted research processes and the empirical insights they generate. Time and again, the discussions collected in this handbook have shown how thorough definitional and conceptual work, sound methodological choices and carefully contextualized research findings based on solid empirical data and the application of methodological scrutiny of any kind (be it quantitative or qualitative) can lead us towards understandings and insights that avoid ideological, a priori absolutes; instead, it is here only on the basis of the empirical nuances revealed by sociological research that a critical stance vis-à-vis carefully delineated facets of our globally interconnected world becomes possible. We believe that this approach underpinning our contributions is in keeping with some of the most convincing analyses of the widespread "backlash" against globalization: there, too, careful contextualization combines with necessary criticism of structural inequalities, whilst avoiding the political oversimplifications that were mentioned earlier and that are typically encountered on both ends of the classic left–right spectrum (Crouch 2019).

Since we have repeatedly seen how critical engagement with our subject matter is only made possible by sound methodologies and theoretically informed analyses of empirical data, it is worth reflecting further on some of the methodological and conceptual work also accomplished by our contributors. This leads us to another cluster of thematic strands that have run through this handbook and that also interface with existing work in the sociology of globalization.

III

Beck had begun to see cosmopolitanization as a structural fact, one frequently maligned or ignored by its political opponents and detractors. Yet, regardless of one's ideological orientation and normative positions, the "world's 'others' are right among us, while we ourselves find ourselves elsewhere" (Beck 2017: 102, our translation). In light of our epoch's ubiquitous and diverse entanglements of "here" with many distant elsewheres, Beck's conclusion that "nationally and geographically separate locations" have to be subsumed under a new, higher-order category leads him to call for a "methodological cosmopolitanism" (Beck 2017: 126). Along with his general call for a "historical sociology of the present," Beck (2017: 242) thereby issues precisely the kind of conceptual and methodological invitation that parts of our handbook have also attempted to respond to constructively.

The first way in which some of our contributors have provided us with a sense of what a *methodological cosmopolitanism* – as opposed to a methodological nationalism – entails has been through the very specifics of their empirical expertise. More accurately, we have deliberately encouraged (some of) our contributors to draw on their expertise on particular contexts and to view "the global" from such very particular vantage points. Attentive readers may indeed have registered with a degree of surprise that a significant number of chapters in this research handbook on the sociology of globalization has therefore been grounded in very particular local, regional or national settings. Crucially, however, each of those context-bound discussions has extended its analytical gaze far beyond the particular localities in question; the purpose and intention, of course, was to illustrate precisely how the particular settings and lives in question are being (re)shaped by distant forces, transnational flows and global interconnections. Instead of thinking of the local (or national) and the global as separate or alternative social domains, the contributions in question thereby make considerable headway towards a refinement and broadening of our units of research and analysis. Whether local experiences of identity construction, national frameworks for the governance of highly pluralistic societies, particular genres of music, religious traditions or discursive fields being contested by competing political blueprints, in each of these – and many other similar cases – the local and specific can now in fact only be made sense of by factoring in global flows, purportedly distant, yet in actual fact co-present "others" and "our" deep and deepening entanglements with "them." "We" and "they," "here" and "there" are – certainly from the perspective of a methodological cosmopolitanism – categories of very limited utility. The sociology of globalization sketched here, by contrast, insists on interrogating such categories, on exploring the conditions of their making, as well as the crucial connections and interdependencies *between* the people and locales those categories purport to describe.

At first sight, some of our endeavors may thus appear to approximate Roland Robertson's seminal concept of *glocalization*: "the reconstruction" of "home, community and locality" under new conditions, through which "the local" is recognized as "an aspect of globalization," namely through the "simultaneity and [mutual] interpenetration" of the two geographical scales, the distant and the close-by (Robertson 1995: 30). At the same time, however, parts of our handbook have pushed considerably beyond the conceptual and into the methodological. Caroline Knowles's further reflections on her highly innovative "travelling methods" (also see Knowles 2014) as well as Magali Peyrefitte's considerations of how contemporary globalization impacts, methodologically, C. Wright Mills's (2000 [1959]) understanding of *the sociological imagination* have been the most obvious cases in point.

Yet, while there is good reason to go beyond the notion of the nation state when discussing and investigating globalization, we should be careful not to discard its role prematurely. The contributions in this handbook in no uncertain manner have shown that nation-specific policies in various fields – such as education, welfare or the labor market – continue to exert an influence on how globalization changes the lives of individuals in contemporary societies. Despite the progressive importance of levels beyond or below the nation state, it is still the path-dependent nature of national institutions that has a significant bearing on how gains and losses incurred through globalization are being distributed among individuals. Results in this volume suggest that, unlike often assumed, the unifying influences of globalization do not reduce social inequalities within or between societies, but rather tend to amplify them. Risks and insecurities arising from globalization still tend to affect those most seriously that are not sufficiently protected through nation-specific welfare or labor market policies. A sociology of globalization today thus needs to endure the ostensible discrepancy between the need to go beyond the nation state while at the same time acknowledging its persistent importance.

Concurrently, the methodological strand running through parts of our book also intertwines with the historical. Long-standing questions pertaining to the *longue durée* of globalization have therefore here been revisited, in particular by Zinovia Lialiouti (this volume). More general questions concerning the various shapes that global interconnections assume at this precise historical moment have of course featured in, and underpinned, our project in its entirety. In elaboration of John Holmwood's call (2007) for the development of "new connections" that globalization requires social scientists to draw, we have sought to sketch new avenues for future research that will need to cut across not only geographical distances but also across historical time as well as across disciplinary boundaries. Our interest in how globalization thus "sits" in the disciplinary interface between history and sociology also has important echoes in the wider literature. For instance, Gurminder Bhambra's critical rethinking of long-established, sociological accounts of modernity should be remembered here. With reference to historian Sanjay Subrahmanyam, Bhambra argues for a widening of the standpoints being considered, and for a re-reading of sources and existing accounts "against the grain": the results, as she demonstrates, can include the discovery of "connected histories" that cross boundaries and distances and, consequently, a "rescuing [of] history from the nation" (Bhambra 2007: 30–32). In spirit and substance, this handbook has attempted to continue along those very methodological and conceptual trajectories.

There is an additional thread connecting our historical-cum-sociological lens onto globalization with seminal parts of the existing literature. We ought to therefore also here remember Norbert Elias's important account of a series of transformations across different parts of Europe that occurred during the late Middle Ages and early modernity: from a knightly, feudal society of relatively small, relatively autarkic regional units towards larger, more centralized, in due course increasingly absolutist political units. As Elias demonstrates, the money economy, larger, supra-regional markets, "longer production chains" and more wide-reaching entanglements in traffic and trade played crucial roles in these incremental processes of historical transformation (Elias 2017 [1939]: 42–43, 69–70, 100). As Elias (2017 [1939]: 127) himself also anticipated, it is indeed possible and arguably necessary to think of these earlier structural shifts as constituting pre-history to globalization. Put differently, the processes that Elias captured for earlier centuries – the closer structural integration of production, trade and traffic across and between different regions – have been replicated and deepened on yet larger geographical scales in the course of globalization. We are confident that it is precisely such processes of transnational integration that our contributors have here helped illuminate through their work on our era's cultural, human, economic and material flows, on our (infra-) structural interdependencies and their social consequences, as well as on the political and ideological responses generated in response.

IV

A further cluster of themes emerging from this handbook pertains to what has been described as a "postmodern planetary consciousness": a "reimagining" that recognizes the world as "a small, fragile and finite place … with strictly limited resources that are allocated unequally"; and an ensuing recognition that our many crises "do not stop at national boundaries and a feeling that the sustainability of our species is itself in question" (Gilroy 2004: 83). In a closely related vein, Étienne Balibar favors the term *planetarity* to capture the "idea of a community of interests of human groups and individuals (and perhaps, beyond them, living individuals) that should prevail over ruthless competition – in order to avoid mutual destruction – and create a 'civilization' … in which 'communities' overlap everywhere" (Balibar 2011: 20). Different types of ideas converge in such accounts: first, the structural fact of our contemporary interdependency across the globe; second, a descriptive-empirical recording of today's profound and growing inequalities and of our profound and deepening crises; third, a normative wish for a different, more inclusive and sustainable politics; and fourth, the accounts above resonate with a growing awareness of humans' truly global and detrimental, environmental impact during our current age, i.e. the Anthropocene (e.g. see Lövbrand et al. 2015). It is, we believe, not overstating the facts to argue that different parts of our handbook contain elements of each of these types of ideas. By way of further conclusions, some additional thoughts about the wider disciplinary significance of these ideational strands are called for.

To return to an argument already mentioned in the Introduction, Anna Amelina, Manuela Boatcă, Gregor Bongaerts and Anja Weiß (2021: 311) argued that the processes of "globalization, transnationalization and postcoloniality" raise the very question as to "how we want to do sociology" today. This provides an apt way of summarizing parts of the motivation behind the present handbook, although we would prefer an ever firmer formulation. Recent decades have seen shifts and changes across geographical scales, from the local to the global, that make this a question not about options but about imperatives. The question, for us, is less about how "we want to do sociology" but how *we have to do sociology* in the face of far-reaching transformations and prominent political responses to them. We are, of course, far from the first to call for (and to observe an already underway) disciplinary reorientation in light of historical, era-defining shifts witnessed across the globe. To name but one precedent, already at the turn of the new millennium John Urry (2000: 1) argued that contemporary mobilities, "networks and flows" were in the process of "transform[ing] the historic subject-matter of sociology" and that this would demand new categories and "new rules" for sociological analysis. More than two decades on, we consider our work here to continue in a similar vein. The intervening period has seen further social and political changes in urgent need of sociologists' attention, who are undeniably having to recalibrate some of their long-established conceptual categories and to refine their tried and tested methodologies in order to meet the challenges at hand. Our handbook testifies to both the successes thus far and to the continuing challenges of this disciplinary reorientation.

Sylvia Walby has highlighted some necessary dimensions to be included in such a rethinking of sociological priorities and approaches: required for a meaningful grasp of globalization is an ability to address, in parallel, how neither our highly "differentiated institutional domains" (e.g. economy, polity, civil society) nor our "multiple regimes of inequality" (e.g. class, ethnicity, gender) are now "contained in a nation-state." Walby also demonstrates, though, that this does not automatically mean that any of these dimensions have therefore necessarily become "fully global." Instead, the challenge is to recognize, theorize and capture institutional domains and structural inequalities that are "partially but not completely overlapping, non-nested, non-congruent, with different spatial and temporal reach," and complexly interconnected (Walby 2021: 317–326). When mapped onto sociology's longer intellectual history, it becomes apparent that such a dual focus – on institutional domains *and* inequalities – also cuts across and thereby partly synthesizes theoretical traditions often thought of as mutually exclusive, namely those of functionalism and conflict theorizing, respectively. This, in turn, strengthens the case yet further that our globalizing age indeed requires sociology to move with the times and to make some necessary adjustments to its conceptual vocabulary and methodological arsenals alike.

Read in their entirety, our chapters have contributed to each of the strands summarized in this section: there have been glimpses of a "planetary consciousness" sitting alongside assessments of how sociology already has adjusted to the wider scales and transnational interconnections of the present; there have been important sketches of what remains to be done, conceptually and methodologically; there have been sustained attempts to capture and analyze the complexities of our national and transnational institutional domains and relations of inequality; further, our collective focus has also included accounts that capture some of the political and ideological responses to globalization on offer. All this having been said, there is much that remains to be done and we most certainly do not claim to have offered a fully comprehensive account of globalization in all its facets. In our final set of reflections, we thus turn to some of the many remaining and emerging issues.

V

As has been made clear throughout this handbook, we have considered the delineation of emerging questions that call for further research to be part of our challenge. The sociology of globalization outlined here is, in other words, a(n inter)disciplinary field in flux and continually responding to further developments as they unfold as well as to questions that remain as yet unanswered. We therefore think that the most meaningful way in which to bring our project to a conclusion is by highlighting a number of such emerging and remaining questions, in the hope that future research will address them with the urgency they demand.

Each of our empirically focused and contextually grounded chapters offers an obvious invitation for similar issues to be addressed in other settings, be they questions – to name just some of those addressed by our contributors – about sex trafficking, about postcolonial subjectivities, about tourism or about care work. Concurrently, other contributions – such as one of the editors' examinations of some ambivalences surrounding cosmopolitan and communitarian discourses – call for further, methodologically very specific research: in the particular case in question, there is an obvious need for future quantitative research to test the causal relationships between various demographic and socio-economic variables and advocacy of the competing political blueprints in question. Among others, this requires further and better data, both to empirically capture the many facets of globalization as well as to link it to various societal as well as to individual-level outcomes. At the same time, such relationships will have to be read in the context of their local and national histories; for as we have made clear, it is always in specific settings that global influences are experienced and politically negotiated. Adequate data and methodologies to research globalization will need to consider this processual character of globalization and its embeddedness in various contexts, ideally by providing both longitudinal as well as multilevel information on relevant factors. The methodologically focused and innovative contributions to our handbook, meanwhile, raise additional questions: namely, how the new avenues for research they offer articulate with other, recent attempts (e.g. see Lyon and Back 2012; Rhys-Taylor 2013; Karner 2022) to enlarge social scientists' methodological toolkits for our globalizing times.

Thematically, there is, as has already been conceded, much that remains to be explored. Some such themes warrant specific mention. For instance, we had hoped to include additional, thematically focused contributions (e.g. on the globalization of food) that would have further expanded our overview of the many social and cultural domains that have long been shaped by global flows. Some such planned contributions have fallen through, in all cases because of the particular institutional and personal pressures the prospective contributors in question have had to face during the pandemic. These partial setbacks and resulting absences reflect, yet again, the particular historical circumstances in which we currently find ourselves; and such absences clearly point towards further areas of discussion that still await the kind of sustained attention that our existing contributions pay to a range of other themes.

The particular thematic clusters that are "digitalization" and "postcoloniality" have received important attention in the chapters by Kristian Kloeckl and the late Amal Treacher Kabesh, respectively. Through his work on digital networked technologies and (global) cities, Kristian Kloeckl helps us relate globalization to the digital revolution in ways that have often escaped sociologists' attention. Amal Treacher Kabesh, meanwhile, relates both the global to the local, and the historical to the present, in order to demonstrate how a history of colonization is shaping female, Egyptian subjectivities today. We are very confident that Kloeckl and Treacher Kabesh thereby also make significant strides towards a closer integration of the sociology of globalization with research on digitalization and postcolonial theorizing, respectively. Similarly, Zsuzsa Gille's chapter on global waste provides crucial momentum for further explorations of the interface between the sociology of globalization and environmental sociology.

In other cases, all we can offer here is an anticipation of further foci that will also require more or renewed attention: the interface of the sociology of globalization with the sociology of financial markets (see Preda 2007) provides one such example. Perhaps yet more clearly, the Covid pandemic will of course have an enduring impact on the world's sociologists; discussions about how exactly the discipline is being impacted, in some respects perhaps partly reshaped, by the epidemiological crisis that commenced in early 2020 will inevitably continue for years to come. Alongside this, there are other thematic strands that parts of this handbook have touched upon and that will warrant considerably more research attention in the future. One such strand relates to the domain of cultural representations and their transnational diffusion. To name but one example, what might a sociological analysis of the current, new and near global popularity of South Korean cinema include? Parts of it would of course need to locate South Korean cinema in its regional, historical context. Other parts would need to document the political economy of Korean cinema and investments made in it over recent decades. In addition, the technological side – particularly the role played by digital streaming platforms – is certainly also crucial. On a conceptual level, one may conclude that this is but one example of how Western, cinematic (and hence cultural?) hegemony has at long last been broken. In fact, the current popularity of South Korean cinema may be seen as merely one recent and particularly prominent example of a much wider phenomenon that Stuart Hall observed and named 25 years ago. Hall (1997: 183) spoke of "the most profound cultural revolution" of the late twentieth century as "a consequence of the margins coming into representation – in art, in painting, in film, in music, in literature, in the modern arts everywhere, in politics and in social life generally." Seen in these terms, South Korean cinema is thus but a particularly successful example – if measured in terms of its transnational audiences and reception – of historically "silenced or marginalized" communities "find[ing] their own … voice" and cultural channels (Cohen 1992: 85), in this particular case notably on a global stage and far beyond the Korean diasporic community.

All of this, and much more, also falls under the purview of a sociology of globalization. Examples like that of Korean cinema could be multiplied at will. There is, thus, an enormous amount of work to be done for sociologists of globalization. This applies even more to those who conceive of their endeavors, as we have done here, in interdisciplinary terms, whereby social scientists of different disciplines and methodological orientations learn from each other and collaborate. At the same time, the wide and continually expanding applications for the sociology of globalization should not be mistaken for an excuse for thinking in terms of historical inevitabilities. We should know better than to imagine humanity as walking a supposedly straight(forward) path in any one particular direction. For us, this means that the future may but will not necessarily entail "more globalization" in its economic and political dimensions. Among the most consequential political developments of recent years, Brexit has demonstrated that transnational, structural integration can be undone and reverted, albeit to enormous costs and huge risks. The forces of neonationalism are indeed ubiquitous today, many of them portraying themselves unapologetically as "anti-globalist"; others are unapologetically European Union-phobic, while purporting to combine this with a "global outlook." All of them find grave fault with, and stubbornly oppose, at least some of the transnational flows and interconnections that this handbook has analyzed. Yet, such and other political counter-reactions also have to be part of the many foci for a sociology of globalization, as notably our chapters on communitarianism, extremism and contemporary racism and anti-Semitism have shown.

What we can say with certainty about our collective future is that the broader phenomenon that is *globality* will continue to play crucial, albeit not uncontested, roles in all our lives. This handbook, then, is perhaps best read as an attempt to sketch what we already know about such globality, and what remains to be explored. Between them, our contributors have unearthed much that should speak to us all: as sociologists, and more generally as social scientists; and yet more widely, as well as perhaps most importantly, as human beings.

REFERENCES

Amelina, Anna, Boatcă, Manuela, Bongaerts, Gregor and Weiß, Anna (2021) "Theorizing societalization across borders: Globality, transnationality, postcoloniality," *Current Sociology* 69 (3), 303–314.
Anderson, Benedict (1983) *Imagined Communities*, London: Verso.
Appadurai, Arjun (1990) "Disjuncture and difference in the global cultural economy," in Mike Featherstone (ed.), *Global Culture: Nationalism, Globalization and Modernity*, London: Sage, pp. 295–310.
Balibar, Étienne (2011) "Cosmopolitanism and secularism: Controversial legacies and prospective inter-rogations," *Grey Room* 44, 7–25.
Bauman, Zygmunt (1991) *Intimations of Postmodernity*, London: Routledge.
Beck, Ulrich (2000) *What Is Globalization?* Cambridge: Polity.
Beck, Ulrich (2017) *Die Metamorphose der Welt*, Berlin: Suhrkamp.
Beck, Ulrich and Grande, Edgar (2010) "Varieties of second modernity: The cosmopolitan turn in social and political theory and research," *British Journal of Sociology* 61 (3), 409–443.
Bhambra, Gurminder K. (2007) *Rethinking Modernity: Postcolonialism and the Sociological Imagination*, Basingstoke: Palgrave Macmillan.
Brown, Wendy (2015) *Die schleichende Revolution: Wie der Neoliberalismus die Demokratie zerstört*, Berlin: Suhrkamp.
Burawoy, Michael (2005) "For public sociology," *American Sociological Review* 70 (1), 4–28.
Cohen, Philip (1992) "'It's racism what dunnit': Hidden narratives in theories of racism," in James Donald and Ali Rattansi (eds), *"Race," Culture and Difference*, London: Sage, pp. 62–103.
Crouch, Colin (2019) *The Globalization Backlash*, Cambridge: Polity.
Dohmen, Caspar (2021) *Lieferketten: Risiken globaler Arbeitsteilung für Mensch und Natur*, Berlin: Wagenbach.
Elias, Norbert (2017 [1939]) *Über den Prozeß der Zivilisation: Soziogenetische und psychogenetische Untersuchungen (Zweiter Band)*, Frankfurt a.M.: Suhrkamp.
Fischer, Karin, Reiner, Christian and Staritz, Cornelia (eds) (2021) *Globale Warenketten und ungleiche Entwicklung*, Wien: Mandelbaum.
Fraser, Nancy (2014) "Can societies be commodities all the way down? Post-Polanyian reflections on capitalist crisis," *Economy and Society* 43 (4), 541–558.
Gellner, Ernest (1983) *Nations and Nationalism*, Oxford: Blackwell.
Gilroy, Paul (2004) *After Empire: Melancholia or Convivial Culture?* London: Routledge.
Hall, Stuart (1997) "The local and the global: Globalization and ethnicity," in Anne McClintock, Aamir Mufti and Ella Shohat (eds), *Dangerous Liaisons: Gender, Nation and Postcolonial Perspectives*, Minneapolis: University of Minnesota Press, pp. 173–187.
Holmwood, John (2007) "'Only connect': The challenge of globalization for the social sciences," *Twenty-First Century Society* 2 (1), 79–94.
Karner, Christian (2022) *Sociology in Times of Glocalization*, London: Anthem.
Knowles, Caroline (2014) *Flip-Flop: A Journey through Globalisation's Backroads*, London: Pluto Press.
Lövbrand, Eva, Beck, Silke, Chilvers, Jason, Forsyth, Tim, Hedrén, Johan, Hulme, Mike, Lidskog, Rolf and Vasileiadou, Eleftheria (2015) "Who speaks for the future of Earth? How critical social science can extend the conversation on the Anthropocene," *Global Environmental Change* 32, 211–218.
Lyon, Dawn and Back, Les (2012) "Fishmongers in a global economy: Craft and social relations on a London market," *Sociological Research Online* 17 (2).
Manow, Philip (2019) *Die Politische Ökonomie des Populismus*, Berlin: Suhrkamp.
Mattmann-Allamand, Peter (2021) *Deglobalisierung: Ein ökologisch-demokratischer Ausweg aus der Krise*, Wien: Promedia.

Mills, C. Wright (2000 [1959]) *The Sociological Imagination*, Oxford: Oxford University Press.

Polanyi, Karl (2001 [1944]) *The Great Transformation: The Political and Economic Origins of Our Time*, Boston: Beacon Press.

Preda, Alex (2007) "The sociological approach to financial markets," *Journal of Economic Surveys* 21 (3), 506–533.

Rhys-Taylor, Alex (2013) "The essence of multiculture: A sensory exploration of an inner-city street market," *Identities: Global Studies in Culture and Power* 20 (4), 393–406.

Robertson, Roland (1995) "Glocalization: Time-space and homogeneity-heterogeneity," in Mike Featherstone, Scott Lash and Roland Robertson (eds), *Global Modernities*, London: Sage, pp. 25–44.

Streeck, Wolfgang (2021) *Zwischen Globalismus und Demokratie: Politische Ökonomie im ausgehenden Neoliberalismus*, Berlin: Suhrkamp.

Urry, John (2000) *Sociology beyond Societies: Mobilities for the Twenty-First Century*, London: Routledge.

Walby, Sylvia (2021) "Developing the concept of society: Institutional domains, regimes of inequalities and complex systems in a global era," *Current Sociology* 69 (3), 315–332.

Weber, Max (1972 [1921]) *Wirtschaft und Gesellschaft: Grundriss der verstehenden Soziologie*, Tübingen: J.C.B. Mohr.

Wimmer, Andreas and Glick-Schiller, Nina (2002) "Methodological nationalism and beyond," *Global Networks* 2 (4), 301–334.

Index

'absent presences' 177
absorption 73, 181, 220
Abu-Lughod, Janet 17–18, 174
'active ageing' policies 321, 322–3
activism, emergence of 131
actor network theory 48–9, 331
Adorno, Theodor W. 146–7, 211
'advocacy networks' 131–2
Africa
    EU border control 164
    music industry 192
African American culture 187
agency 21, 30, 37–8, 40, 181
Aggestam, L. 197
AI *see* artificial intelligence
Akama, J. 111
Al-Rodhan, N.R.F. 16
Alamgir, F. 39
Alawad, A. 292
Aldridge, Alan 154
Alexander, Jeffrey 147–8
Alhawarin, I. 292
Allen, Bruce 46
Almond, Gabriel 155
alter-globalization 217–24
Altglas, Véronique 157
'ambivalences of globalization' 120, 211–14
Amelina, Anna 11, 354
Amer, M. 292–3
American popular music 186–94
Amnesty International 130–131
Amstutz, Galen 157
'ancient' globalization 16–18
Anderson, Benedict 130
Annan, Kofi 197
Anthropocene 78–80, 354
'anthropological places' 206
anthropology 25
anti-globalization 213, 217–24, 228, 233, 241
anti-racism 230–232
anti-trafficking 164–73
antisemitism 225–37
Appadurai, Arjun 6, 9–10, 25, 110, 206, 331
Arab Spring 31, 290
Arnason, A. 341
artefacts in storytelling 28–30
artificial intelligence (AI) 301–2
Ash, Garton 200
Assaad, R. 289, 291–2, 294

Assmann, Aleida 147
asylum seekers 100, 101, 103, 201, 209–11, 230
Atallah, M. 293
Augé, Marc 206, 214
Augoustinos, Martha 213
austerity 34, 198, 289, 299
authoritarian regimes 130–131, 289
autonomy as freedom 182

Back, L. 208
Bair, Jennifer 48
Balibar, Étienne 354
banal cosmopolitanism 213–14
Bannerjee, S.B. 39
Bannon, Steve 233
Baram, Michael 86
Barndt, D., *Tangled Routes* 333
Barrett, Hazel R. 48
Barrientos, Stephanie, *Gender and Work in Global Value Chains* 331–2
Barsoum, G. 293, 294
Basel Convention 89
Bauman, Zygmunt 27, 226, 228
Baumann, Gerd 211, 214
Baxi, Upendra 133
Bayly, Christian 19, 21
Beck, Ulrich 6–7, 11, 72, 196, 210–212, 215, 258, 348–52
    The Metamorphosis of the World 7
Becker, K. 122
Behrsin, Ingrid 90
Bell, Duncan, *Memory Trauma and World Politics* 148
Bendel, Petra 210
Benhabib, S. 249
Benjamin, Walter 142
Bergen, Doris 227
Berger, J.M. 238
Berlant, Lauren 177
Berlusconi, Silvio 229
Beveridgean basic pension 312–14
Beyer, Peter 151, 155, 158
    Religion and Globalization 154
Bhambra, Gurminder 353
Bieber, Florian 226, 228
big data 63
bilateral approaches 218
Billig, Michael 214
biodiversity loss 79

biopolitics 201
Bismarckian social insurance 312–14
Black and minority ethnic (BME) communities 252, 257
Black Lives Matter 31, 230–231
Blofield, M. 122
Blossfeld, Hans-Peter 10, 290
blues music 187–8, 193
BME communities *see* Black and minority ethnic communities
Bonoli, G. 276
border control mechanisms 98
border externalisation 104, 164–5, 166–8, 171, 229
borders 52–3, 220–223
Borges, Jorge Luis, *On Exactitude in Science* 65
Bott, Esther 10
Brah, Avtar 28–9
Breivik, Anders 239
Brexit 34, 199, 200, 242, 329, 357
bricolage 157
Brown, Gordon 240
Burawoy, Michael 11, 25
Burton, Sarah 26
Bush, G.W. 197
Butterfly Wings (Salmawy) 181–3
Buurtzorg organization 123

Callon, Michel 331
Campbell, Colin C. 156, 158
Camus, Renaud 232
Cantle Report 253–4
capital
    EU structural change 198
    global governance 217–19
    neoliberalization of 36
capitalism 21–2, 47–8, 76, 84, 154, 212, 242
Capitalocene 90
care work 117–41, 299, 332
Carling, J. 201
Carrette, Jeremy 154
Carrigan, A. 112
Carroll, Lewis 148
Cassin, Réné 131
Castells, Manuel 17, 61
CCA *see* community cohesion agenda
'chain' concept 46, 48, 330–332
Charismatic Christianty 152
Chavez, President Hugo 218
"cheap nature" 85
child care 179
Christian antisemitism 227, 233–4
Christianity 152, 156
Chua, Charmaine 50
Chun, J.J. 122

'circuits' approach 48–9, 330–332
circulation 47–8, 49–54, 186, 188–92, 329
cities 67, 202
    mapping 62–4
    as networks 60–61
citizen participation 65–6, 68
citizenship 129, 256, 258
civic space 301
civil society 89–90, 219, 301
class divisions 212
climate change 198, 202, 218–19, 303–4
clone towns 241
closed employment systems 269, 271
Clover, Joshua 54
Coe, N. 35
Cold War 130–131, 197
collective memory 142–4, 146–7
colonialism 22, 111–12, 231, 248
colonized subjectivities 174, 176–7, 184
commodification 112–13, 118–19, 122–3, 186–94, 348
commodities, value of 110
commodity chains/circuits 35–6, 45–59, 329–88
communitarianism 154, 206–16, 220
community cohesion agenda (CCA) 253–4, 256–8
'community wealth building' 219
complex systems 74
complexity 72–3, 77, 79–80
'compression' 129
Condorcet, Nicolas de 144
Confino, Alon 143
connected devices 61–2
consciousness 128–33, 175
conspiracy theories 231–3, 243
consumer revolution 19–20
consumption 22, 84, 86
contemporary cosmopolitanism 255–8
contemporary globalization 16–18
contemporary hospitality 248–50
contestation theory 199
contracts 55
"converging divergences" 7
conviviality 207–8, 209
corporate globalisation 112
'cosmopolitan imagination' 209–11
cosmopolitanism 73, 206–16, 218, 352
    hospitality 248
    human rights 129
    migrant identities 255–8
    tourism 109–10
counterlogics of looting 53–4
country-specific institutions 264, 268, 270
coupling 73–4, 77, 79–80
COVID-19 pandemic 1–2, 45–6, 53, 218, 357

conspiracy theories 243
EU responses 200
existential risks 78–9
inequalities 31, 40, 298
localism 55
racism and 234–5
supply chains 329
systemic risks 76–8
tourism and 108
work during 34
Cowen, Deborah 49–51
Cox, Amanda 64
Crang, Philip 48
Cresswell, Tim 45
Crettaz, E. 276
crises 77, 166–8, 292, 298–9, 304
    see also COVID-19 pandemic
critical sociology 351–2
cross-border flows 97
Crossley, É 110
Crudup, Arthur 189
Csordas, Thomas 152
cultural economy 331
cultural trauma thesis 147
cultural values 110
'culture' subjectivities 175–6
Cuppini, Niccolò 51
Czaika, M. 101

Darwin, Charles 226
data exchange 63
data visualization 64, 65
De Alwis, M. 177
de Haas, H. 101, 254
De Rosa, Salvatore Paulo 90
Dejung, Christof 21–2
Delanty, Gerard 211
Deleuze, Jacques 62
democratic backsliding 300–301
democratic governance 217–19
democratic iterations 249–50
demographic ageing 308–18
'demotic' discourses 211
denationalization 199–201
Denzin, Norman 340
development policy 112–13, 298–9, 304–5
Dhillon, N. 289–90
Diamond, P. 242
diaspora 28
Dicken, Peter 47
Diez, T. 197
differential mobilities 52–3
digital connectivity 31
digital maps 64–5
digital networks 60, 62–3, 64–6, 356

digital revolution 201
digital storytelling (DS) 28–9
'digitalised risks' 80
digitalization 301–2, 356
Dimova, R. 292–3
disability pensions 312, 321
discrimination, definition 252
displaced persons 302–3
    see also forced migration
disruption mechanisms 53
domestic workers 122, 221
'dominant' discourses 211
Douzinas, Costas 129
Drumont, Édouard 232
DS *see* digital storytelling
dual discursive competence 211, 214
Dugarova, Esuna 10
Dunant, Henry, *A Memory of Solferino* 144
Dunaway, Wilma, *Gendered Commodity Chains*
    331

e-commerce 56
e-waste 91
early retirement policies 320–322
Easterling, Keller 51
Ebbinghaus, Bernhard 10
Echtner, C.M. 111
ecology 113
'ecomodernist' discourse 80
economic crises 228, 277, 279–80, 299–300
    see also financial crises
economic globalization 264, 266, 350
economic migration *see* migrant workers
economic spillover effects 288
education 240, 269, 271, 288–97
efficiency 50
Egypt 174–86, 291, 293, 294
Einstein, Mara 154
Elias, J. 122
Elias, Norbert 353–4
elite tourism 108–9
emancipation 117–41
'embeddedness' 331
empathy 144, 147
employment 34–44
    care migration 121
    domestic workers 122, 221
    from education to 288–97
    of older workers 322–3
"employment exit" strategies 271–2
employment instability 270
"employment maintenance" strategies 271–2
employment regulation 35, 37
environmental degradation 303–4
environmental justice movement 83

Erdoðan, Recep Tayyip 145
Ericson, Matthew 64
Eriksen, Thomas Hylland 6
Erll, Astrid 143
'error-avoiding' systems 74
'error-prone' systems 74, 78
esthetics of memory 147–8
ethics 127–41, 146–7
ethnic absolutism 207
ethnic nationalism 226
ethnic pluralism 206–7
ethnographical studies 25–6
ethnographies 25–6
ethnoscapes 9, 206
European Union (EU) 9, 196–205
    anti-trafficking interventions 164–5
    border externalisation 166–8, 171, 229
    commodity circuits 45
    cosmopolitan goals 218
    in-work poverty 275–87
    integration measures 200, 202
    pension governance 311, 315
    refugee movements 104
    retirement transitions 322–3
Europeanization of migration 250
Every, Danielle 213
everyday life, materiality of 28–9
exclusion 52, 104, 192, 209, 221, 257, 271–2, 303
existential risks 72, 78–80
exploitative labour practices 37, 39–40
exploitative subjectivities 169–70, 183–4
extremism 238–47

'failing states' 100–101
Faist, T. 101
fantasy 176, 177
feedback loops
    complex interactions 74
    digital networks 64–6
female identities 174–86
feminist theory 174, 175–6
Fickling, David 53
fictitious commodities 118, 120
financial crises 31, 34, 76–7, 198, 218, 292, 308,
    314, 321
    see also economic crises
financialization 308, 312, 314–15
Finkelstein, Norman, *The Holocaust Industry* 147
fish markets 329, 333–6
Fisher, Dana 89
'fit' 51
flags of convenience 52, 55
flip-flops 332–3, 339–46
flows
    counter-reactions to 2

intensity of 77
"flows and scapes" 9, 110
food production 87
food safety standards 88
food security 47
food waste 87–8
forced migration 97–107, 302
Fraser, Nancy 8, 117–20, 123
    Scales of Justice 119
Frazer, H. 276
Fredericks, Rosalind 84
free trade agreements 37
freedom, autonomy as 182
freedom of movement 45, 220–221, 248–9
French Revolution 18, 20, 208
Freudenburg, William 89
Fukuyama, Francis 145
functional differentiation 154–5, 158
fundamentalism 155
Fuss, Diane 178

Garner, Steve 230
GCCs *see* global commodity chains/circuits
Gebel, M. 291, 293, 294
gender 298–307
    emancipation movements 120–121
    global commodity circuits 331–2
    in-work poverty 276, 282
    life-course uncertainty 270–271
    migration deterrence 164–73
    retirement transitions 322
    subjectivities 174–86
    waste labour 89
gender inequality 291–4, 298–9, 303–4
generational divide 210
geopolitics 45, 53–4, 78, 198–9, 218
Gereffi, Gary 48
Ghana 164–73
Ghazi, N. 290
Gilroy, Paul 207, 209
global cities 17, 31
global commodity chains/circuits (GCCs) 35–6,
    45–59, 329–88
global community 128–30, 132–3, 152
global consciousness 130, 175
global flows 6, 31, 79, 206–7, 352
global governance 217–19
global inequality chains 332
"global memory" 145, 147
Global North
    anti-trafficking 165
    asylum seekers 103
    food safety standards 88
    gender relations 331–2
    migratory flows 104

production systems 47
unfree labour 39
waste 86–7
global production networks (GPNs) 35–41
global risks 72–82
global sociology, levels of 11
Global South
    anti-trafficking 165
    demographic ageing 308
    EU and 197, 199
    fish markets 334
    gender relations 331–2
    migration 101, 102, 104
    pension systems 312
    production systems 47
    tourism 111, 112–13
    unfree labour 39
    waste 84, 86–7, 89
global supply chains (GSCs) 35–8, 40–41
global value chains (GVCs) 35–6, 39–40, 76–7
global warming 79, 303
Globalife project 264–87
globalism 348–9, 351
globalists 233, 349
globality 348, 350, 357–8
globalization
    contextual conditions 5–7
    definitions 4–5, 348
    early 1990s 266–8
    origins of 16–24
    triple movement 117–41
    use of term 1, 348–9
glocalization 6, 25, 123, 156–9, 174–86, 352–3
Gobineau, Comte Joseph Arthur de 226
Goldstein, B. 336
Goodale, Mark 133
Gordon, A. 27, 29
Gottfried, H. 122
Gourlay, Ken A. 85
governance
    EU structures 200
    labour 40–41
    migration 97–8, 102–4
    nation-states 97–8, 217–19
GPNs *see* global production networks
Grande, Edgar 215
greening 84–5, 157, 159
'greenwashing' 191
Griffith, Peter 251
Grillo, Ralph 210
group-based trajectory modelling 278, 281
GSCs *see* global supply chains
Guattari, Félix 62
Guillén, M. 77–8
guitar market 186–94

Gutberlet, Jutta 84
GVCs *see* global value chains

Halbwachs, Maurice 144
Halévy, Daniel 143
Hall, Stuart 12, 357
Halleröd, B. 276
Hanafi, Sari 11
Hanegraaff, Wouter 153
Hannerz, Ulf 207–8
Hardt, Michael 142
Harvey, M. 331
    Exploring the Tomato 333
hazardous waste 83, 84, 86
hegemonic processes 240–241
Heidegger, Martin 341
Hemmings, Clare 184
Henderson, J. 35
Hendrix, Jimi 190
heterogenization 157, 199
Hetherington, Kevin 90
Heuts, F. 331, 333
Heyne, S. 291, 294
high-risk systems 73–4, 77
historical contexts 4–5, 10, 16–24, 143,
    353–4
Hobsbawn, Eric 18–19
Hochschild, Arlie 332
Hofäcker, Dirk 10
Hofstadter, Richard 231
Holloway, J. 220
Holmes, H. 30, 145
Holmwood, John 353
Holocaust 146–7, 234, 240
home-making 29
homogenization 6, 157, 159
homosexuality 180
homosociality 180
Hooghe, L. 200
Hooker, John Lee 190
Hopkins, Terence K. 48
hospitality 248–62
household waste 84, 86
Hughes, Alex 48–9
human rights 98, 104, 127–41, 156–7, 197, 201,
    210
human trafficking 164–73, 201
humanitarianism 144–5, 148
Hunt, Lynn 129–30
Huntington, Samuel 154
Huyssen, Andreas 146, 148
hybrid cities 60–71
hybrid governance 76
hybridity 155, 157–8, 209
hyper globalization 240

ICT *see* information and communication
    technology
identity 12, 28, 29, 174–86, 252
identity politics 6
ideological dilemmas 214
ideoscapes 9
Ignatieff, Michael 129
ILO *see* International Labour Organization
ILOs *see* Immigration Liaison Officers
IMF *see* International Monetary Fund
immigration 220–221, 223, 228–31, 251
    see also migration
Immigration Liaison Officers (ILOs) 165
immobility 52, 104
improvisation 341
in-work poverty (IWP) 275–87
income maintenance 312–13
"indigenization" 156
Industrial Revolution 18–19
industrialization 21
inequalities 34, 77
    institutions and 355
    pension income 313
    power relations 39
    racism and 228–9
    retirement preferences 323–4
    see also gender inequalities; social
        inequalities
informal work 84, 89–90, 109, 289, 294, 343
information age 6, 17
information and communication technology (ICT)
    75, 266
information networks 60–61
information technology systems 66
informational globalization 264
infrastructure risks 75
inheritance 178
insecurity 47, 158, 202, 275, 299
institutions
    creation of 21
    inequalities and 355
'integration' concept 248–9, 252, 257
integration policies 200, 250, 252–5, 257–8
interactions 3, 73–4, 76–7, 111, 151, 155–7
interdisciplinarity 2–3, 8–12, 355–6
'international', use of term 21
International Labour Organization (ILO) 122, 314
International Monetary Fund (IMF) 311
International Relations (IR) 196, 198–9
internationalism 4, 198, 218
internationalization of migration 250, 254
internet
    evolution of 301–2
    extremism and 240–241
    infrastructure 80

interpretative phenomenological analysis (IPA)
    166
intersectionality 27, 175, 301
intersubjectivity 28–9
IPA *see* interpretative phenomenological analysis
IR *see* International Relations
Islam 154, 156, 180, 231, 235, 243
IWP *see* in-work poverty

Jackson, Peter 48
Jacob, Jane 340
Jahn, B. 198
Japan 156–7, 159, 190–192
Jevons Paradox 87
"Jewish question" 227
    see also antisemitism
jihadism 243
JIT systems *see* just-in-time systems
job quality 285, 293–4
Jokela, M. 122
Joseph, Suad 176
Juncker, Jean-Claude 199
just-in-time (JIT) systems 50, 53, 55
justice 119, 129

Kabesh, Amal Treacher 10, 11, 184, 356
Kaczyński, Jarosław 145
Kaitz Index 278
Kaler, Helena 175
Kandiyoti, Deniz 182
Kant, Immanuel 148, 208, 225–6
Karagiannis, Emmanuel 156
Karner, Christian 154
Kendi, Ibram X. 234
Keynes, John Maynard 22
King, Richard 154
Klein, Lee 143
Kloeckl, Kristian 356
Knowles, Caroline 11, 27, 90, 335–6
    Flip-Flop 332, 340
Kocka, Jürgen 21
KOF Globalisation Index 266–7
Kōfuku no Kagaku 157
Kolokotronis, Theodoros 20
Korzeniewicz, Miguel 48
Koselleck, Reinhart 20
Kotb, Heba 180
Kovacheva, S. 293
Krafft, C. 291, 294
Krastev, I. 145
Krzyżowski, Łukasz 209
Kumasi, Ghana 164–73
Kundnani, A. 254
Kurasawa, Fuyuki 133
Kymlicka, W. 257

labour
    commodification of 118
    EU structural change 198
    marketization of 118
labour agency 37–8, 40
labour disputes 121–2
labour governance 40–41
labour market deregulation 34, 36
labour migration *see* migrant workers
labour networks 37
Lanzmann, Claude 146
large technical systems (LTS) 72–5, 77–9
Larkin, M. 166
Larsen, J.A. 121
Lauren, Paul 130
'law naïveté' 134
Le Coze, Jean-Christophe 11
Le Grande, Manuel 11
legal instruments, human rights 128, 132
legal settlement of migrants 103
Lemert, Charles 5, 8
Lemkin, Raphael 131
Lepawsky, Joshua 91
Levy, Daniel 147–8
Lewis, Gail 184
LGBT rights 180
Lialiouti, Zinovia 4, 10, 353
liberal internationalism 198–9
liberalism–realism connection 196
liberalization 75, 87, 266, 292
Liboiron, Max 87
life-course uncertainty 10, 264–87, 290
life expectancy 311, 321, 324
linear systems 74
Little, Peter 86
"local–global nexus" 6–7
local/global perspectives 117, 120–123, 155–6,
        329–88
localism 55, 210
localities 6, 133, 209–11, 352
localizing strategies 6
locations 175
logistical rationality 55
logistics 46, 49–52, 54, 55, 341
logistics hubs 55
loosely coupled systems 73–4
looting 53–4, 55–6
López, José 10
"losers" of globalization 268, 273
Lotman, Juri 160
LTS *see* large technical systems
Lucier, Cristina 86
Luhmann, Niklas 151
Lyon, David 156
Lyon, Dawn 10

MacBride, Samantha 87, 91
Macshane, Denis 234
McCarthy, L. 332
McDonaldization 6, 241, 242
McLuhan, Marshall 147
McMichael, Phillip 108–9
Madood, T. 255, 257
Maerdi, G. 40–41
Mai, N. 168
Maier, Charles 148
'maintain' factors 322
Mair, Thomas 239
Mandaville, Peter 156
Manichaean views 239
Manow, Philip 212–13, 351
maps 62–5
Marginson, P. 40–41
market devices 331
market volatility 267
marketization 8, 117–19, 199, 348
    of care work 120
    of labour 118
    local/global perspective 121
    pension reform 314
    popular music 186–94
markets–migration relationship 99–100, 102–4
Marks, G. 200
Marlier, E. 276
Marquardt, Marie 156
marriage 178–81
Martell, Luke 10
Martin, Christian F. 188
Marx, Karl 21
mass media 147
mass tourism 108–9
Massingale, Rev. Bryan N. 235
Matallah, S. 290
materiality 28–9, 85
May, T. 27
Mazower, Mark 132
MDGs *see* Millennium Development Goals
Medina, Martin 84
memory 29, 142–50
MENA region *see* Middle East and Northern
        African region
men's career trajectories 270
Merry, Engle 133
Merton, Robert 208
methodological cosmopolitanism 352
methodological nationalism 85, 350
Mezzadra, Sandro 52
middle classes 21–2, 212
Middle East and Northern African (MENA)
        region 288–97
Middle Eastern subjectivities 174–86

Miele, Mara 48
migrant communities 252–5, 257–8
migrant identities 249–50, 255–8
migrant workers 38–9, 100, 103, 121–2, 221–2, 249, 251, 289
migration 97–107, 121, 208, 210–211, 221–3
   demographic ageing and 311
   deterrence of 164–73
   dynamics 100–102
   European responses 201–2
   gender and 302–3
   hospitality 248–62
   local responses 206–7
   religion and 152
   storytelling 28–30
   welfare states and 212
   see also immigration
'migration–asylum nexus' 99
migration governance 97–8, 102–4
Millar, Kathleen 84
Millennium Development Goals (MDGs) 112
Mills, C. Wright 9, 26–7, 30, 353
Mills, Melinda 7, 27
minimum wage initiatives 275–87
Miraftab, Faranak 84
missionization 152
Mitchell, William 63–4
Mitropoulos, Angela 45, 53
mobilities 27, 355
   commodities 48–9, 52–3
   forced migration 98–100, 102
   objects 339–47
   supply chains 53–4
   tourism 109–10
   travel risks/costs 168–9
   voluntary migration 99
mobility flows 45
modern slavery 165, 169
modernist movement 68
modernity 17, 18–23, 73, 353
Mohanty, Chandra, *Under Western Eyes* 174
Mol, A. 331, 333
Moore, Jason 85, 90
moral community 128–30
moral horizon 127–41
moral imperative 146
Morrison, Toni 174
Mosse, George 226–7
Moyaert, Marianne 155
Moyn, Samuel 131
Mubarak, Hosni 180
multiculturalism 248–62
multilateralism 199, 304–5
multilevel governance 200
multilevel modelling 278, 281–4

multi-pillar pensions 313 14
multipolarity 198–9
municipal waste 84
Munir, K. 41
Murdoch, Jonathan 48
musical instruments market 186–94

nationalism 213–14, 303, 349–50
   extremism and 238, 240
   memory 145–7
   racism and 226, 229, 233
   waste 85
"nationalization" of religion 156
Nationally Determined Contributions 304
nations/nation-states 11, 353
   governance 217–19
   as imagined communities 130
   justice 119
   memory 143–4, 146–8
   migration governance 97–8, 103
   religion 154
'need' factors 322
negative externalities 73–5, 79, 169–70, 209
negotiation 25, 28, 119
Negri, Antonio 142
Neilson, Brett 52
neocolonialism 111–12
neoliberal globalization 217, 266
neoliberal policies 34, 299
neoliberalism 34–5, 52, 181, 213, 238, 242, 351
neonationalism 357
network economy 61
network globalization 264
network society 17, 23
networked technologies 68
networks 35, 60–71, 77, 330–332
   cities as 60–61
   commodity circuits 48–9
   ICT connections 266
   labour 40–41
new economic sociology 331
'New Politics' approach 313
Newell, J.P. 336
NGOs *see* non-governmental organizations
Nigeria 164–73
Nolli Map 63
non-governmental organizations (NGOs), LGBT rights 180
'non-places' 206
Nora, Pierre 143–4
'normal accident' thesis 74
norms
   extremism relationship 238
   human rights 128, 132, 133
   multilateral forums 199

Nowicka, Magdalena 209

objective poverty 277, 278, 280, 282
objects
    in storytelling 28–30
    travelling methods 339–47
O'Brien, Martin 90
official development assistance (ODA) 304–5
Ohm, Dennis 209
oil boom 288–9
Okyere, Sam 10
old age dependency 311
Olick, Jeffrey 144
open borders 220–223
The Open Door (Al-Zayyat) 181–2
'openness' to 'others' 207–9, 211
Orbán, Viktor 233
organisations analysis 74
Osterhammel, Jürgen 19, 23
Osterweil, Vicky 54
'other'
    expulsion/assimilation 206, 238
    'openness' to 207–9, 211
    propaganda 239
    self and 176, 178
    tourism 110
    women as 174
Owens, Candace 234

Palpacuer, F. 336
Paris Treaties 20
Parreñas, Rhacel Salazar, *Servants of
        Globalization* 332
part-time work 281–2
particularism 155–6, 160, 209, 212
past-oriented moral imperative 146
Pastor, Lubos 229
patriarchy 182–3
patriotism 258
pension funds 308, 312, 315–16
pension governance 308–18, 319, 321
pension reform 308, 313–14, 316, 322
Pentecostalism 152, 155
people trafficking 164–73
Perrow, C. 73–8
personal protective equipment (PPE) 45, 47, 329
Personal Status Law, Egypt 180
Peterson, Niels P. 19
Peyrefitte, Magali 9, 10, 353
Phillips, Sam 189
Picard, D. 110
planetarity 354, 355
plastic wastes 88
pluralism 155, 159, 206–7, 209
Polanyi, Karl 117–19, 123, 331, 333

The Great Transformation 117
policy shifts
    retirement transitions 320–322
    UK migratory flows 248–62
political approaches 9, 154, 207–9
political globalization 264, 349–51
political imaginary 119, 127, 134–5
politicization 199–201
pollution 79
popular culture 148
popular music 186–94
populism 212, 228–9, 231
porous values 255
Posner, Eric 134
postcolonialism 111–12, 177, 182, 356
postconsumer e-waste 91
postharvest loss 87–8
postmodern nationalism 209
poverty 34, 52, 109–10, 112, 277–8, 312–13
poverty risk 278–80
Powell, Enoch 251
power relations 39, 183–4
PPE *see* personal protective equipment
Prasad, P. 111
precarious work 38–9, 89, 212, 275–6
Presley, Elvis 189–90, 193
private pensions 309–10, 316, 321
privatization 266, 289, 292, 314
processes 5, 196
production globalization 35–6
production systems 47
production waste 84
propaganda 239–40
prostitution 165
protest movements 31, 142, 146, 290, 299
protest songs 193
"Protocols of the Elders of Zion" hoax 232–3
psychoanalytic theory 174, 176–7
public pensions 308–10, 312, 314–16, 319
public sociologies 8–12
pull factors 320, 322
push factors 320, 322
Putin, Vladimir 145

race relations 251–2
race riots 250–251, 259
racialized immigration 229–31
racism 188, 208, 210, 225–37
radicalization 231, 235, 239, 257
real-time cities 62, 64–5
realism–liberalism connection 196
Reckwitz, Andreas 212–13
recognition 176, 183
recycling 84, 87
reflexive cosmopolitanism 213

refugees 97–8, 100–104, 201, 209, 230, 302
regional divisions 210
Reimer, Suzanne 48–9
relative poverty 277, 278–9
"relativization" 158–9
religion 151–63, 181
Reno, Alexander and Joshua 87
retail power 88
retirement transitions 271–2, 319–27
"retrotopias" 145, 148
revolutionary processes 18–21, 241
rhizomes 62
Rickenbacker, Adolph 188
Rieff, David 148
riots 250–251, 253, 259
risk 72–82, 168–9, 278–80
'risk society' 72–3
Rittel, Horst 68–9
Ritzer, George, *The McDonaldization of Society* 6
Robertson, Roland 6, 16, 19, 22–3, 127–9, 154–6, 175, 352
Rocha, Cristina 156
Romberg, Raquel 157
Roosevelt, Eleanor 131
Rosa, Hartmut 4
Rose, Jacqueline 176
Rosecrance, R.N. 197
Roudometof, Victor 156, 214
Roy, Olivier 156
Rudiger, A. 255
Russell, Bertrand 146

Sack, Robert 47
"sacroscapes" 153
Sadat, Anwar 180
Salazar, N.B. 111
Salehi-Isfahani, D. 293
Santos, Boaventura de Sousa 133
Sartre, Jean-Paul 146
Sassen, Saskia 17, 31, 61, 91
scalar hierarchy 91
scapegoating 227–8
'scapes' 25, 110
Schelling, T. 239
Schnaiberg, Allan 84
school-to-home transition 291
school-to-work transition 288–97
Schuerkens, U. 26
Second World War 130, 208
secularization 155, 159
security discourse 254, 257
segregationist policies 254, 256–7
self
    identities 177
    neoliberalism 181

other and 176, 178
Selwaness, I. 292
semiotic systems 160
sex trafficking 164–73
sexual activities 179–80
SEZs *see* Special Economic Zones
Simmel, Georg 4, 8, 206, 208, 214
    Soziologie 3
Single Market, EU 199–200
Skey, Michael 209, 214
slavery 187, 192, 231, 240
Slobodian, Quinn 52
slum tours 109
Smart, Carol 27, 29
smart cities 63, 66–9
smart materials 66
smart technologies 66–7
smartphones 65–6, 68
Smil, V. 78
Smith, Anthony 145, 166, 336
social circles 3
social Darwinism 226
social democracy 217–19
social inequalities 7, 31, 40, 324, 353
social media 240–241
social protectionisms 8, 35, 117, 119, 121, 122
social ties 335
'society' 11
sociological imagination 25–32, 353
sociologists' roles 350–351
sociology
    definition of approaches 2
    disciplinary coherence 3
    history of 4
sociotechnological risks 73–5
soft power 147
Solomos, J. 208
Soros, George 233
Soundrarajan, V. 41
spatial logic 61
'spatial products' 54
spatio-temporalities 47–9
Special Economic Zones (SEZs) 51, 52, 55
"specialization" 160
Spencer, S. 255
Spivak, G.C. 111, 183
Srinivas, Tulasi 155, 157
standardization 51, 52, 55
Star, Susan Leigh 51
states 52, 99–100, 102–4, 249
    see also nations/nation-states
Stephan, K. 293
Stiglitz, J. 34
stockpiling 45–6, 50, 53–4
storytelling 26–30

Stoudmann, G. 16
the stranger 3, 206
structural change 198–9, 266–7
structural drivers waste 90
structures 5, 196
Stürner, Janina 210
subjective poverty 277–80, 282
subjectivities 169–70, 174–86
Subrahmanyam, Sanjay 353
suburbanization 28
superdiversity 102, 248–62
supermodernity 206
supply chain management 46, 50
supply chains 35–6, 39, 50, 52–5, 329
supranational institutions 52
supranational integration 200
sustainable development 112, 304–5
systemic risks 75–8
'systems approaches' 50
Szerszynski, Bronislaw 207, 213
Sznaider, Natan 147–8

technological risks 72
technoscapes 9
technoscience 72, 78, 80
terrorism 202, 231–2, 242
Thomas, H. 41
Thompson, A. 166
Thoreau, Henry David 191
Thorne, Lorraine 49
tightly coupled systems 73–4
Tolia-Kelly, D.P. 29
tomatoes 332–3
total cost analysis 50
tourism 108–16
trade unions 40, 122, 315, 321
trafficking activities 164–73, 201
trails 340, 341–3, 344
transhumanist ideology 78
transnational circulation 188–9
transnational corporations 46–7
transnational flows 7, 9
transnational waste 86–9
transnationalism 17, 153–4, 156, 158,
        314–15
travel 109–10, 165, 166–9, 339–47
Traverso, Enzo 231
triangular trade 187
'trickle-down' effect 112
Tronto, Joan 124
Trump, Donald 34, 199, 229, 231, 233, 240
Tsing, Anna 50
Tucker, H. 111
Turnbull, P. 41
Tweed, Thomas 153

UDHR *see* United Nations Universal Declaration
        of Human Rights
UK *see* United Kingdom
Ukah, Asonzeh 155
UN *see* United Nations
uncertainty 73, 264–87, 290
unemployment 269, 276, 281, 292
unemployment insurance 321
unfree labour 39
United Kingdom (UK)
        Covid-19 pandemic 329
        migratory flows 248–62
United Nations (UN) 132
United Nations Universal Declaration of Human
        Rights (UDHR) 128, 130, 132
United States (US)
        consumption patterns 22
        COVID-19 pandemic 45
        pension system 312, 315
        popular music 186–94
        racism 231–2
'universal' morality 209
universal rights 248–9
universalism 147, 156
urban dashboards 65
urban data 63, 65
urban informatics 60
Urry, John 27, 47, 207, 213, 355
US *see* United States

Valier, C. 254
value chains 35
value regimes 110–111, 331
Van Pelt Campbell, George 155
Vásquez, Manuel 153, 156
'vernacularization' 133, 156
Veronesi, Pietro 229
Vertovec, S. 102, 255
Vicol, M. 39
"victimhood nationalism" 146–7
victimization 169–71
violence 239
voluntary migration 97–8, 99–100, 102
von Clausewitz, C. 239

Walby, Sylvia 355
Wallerstein, Immanuel 21, 47–8
Walzer, Michael 145
Warburg, Margit 155
waste 83–95
waste collection 84, 89
waste distribution 88–90
waste treatment 88–9
Weaver, Ole 197
Wechselwirkungen 3–4, 8

welfare states 212, 308, 311–12
Whatmore, Sarah 49
white supremacy 225–6, 231–2
wholesale markets 333–6
wicked problems 68–9
Wiegman, Robyn 176
Wiener, A. 199
Wiesel, Elie 146
"winners" of globalization 270, 273
wish-cycling 87
Wistrich, Robert 232
women
    in-work poverty 282
    labour market activities 291–2
    mid-life pathways 270–271
    see also gender
women's rights groups 300–301
Wood, A.J. 118
Woodiwiss, Anthony 134
work 34–44
work intensity 281

work quality 275–6
work–retirement transitions 319–27
'world-economy' 18
world-systems theory 17, 47, 330

xenophobia 225, 229–30, 232, 303

Yeung, H.W. 35
Young, J. 257
Young-Bruehl, Elisabeth 176
Yousef, T. 289–90
youth–adulthood transition 268–70
youth employment 275–87, 290,
    293–4

Žarkov, D. 178
Zelizer, Barbie 143, 335
Zinkina, Julia 17
Žižek, Slavoj 20
Zürn, M. 198, 200